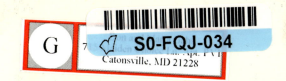
12/1/07 — 1/19/08

Baltimore:

A LIVING RENAISSANCE

Washington Monument   A. Aubrey Bodine

Baltimore

A LIVING RENAISSANCE

EDITED BY

Lenora Heilig Nast

Laurence N. Krause

R. C. Monk

HISTORIC BALTIMORE SOCIETY, INC.

1982

Copyright © 1982 by Historic Baltimore Society, Inc.
Library of Congress Catalog Card Number 82-80490
ISBN 0-942460-00-6
Printed by Waverly Press, Baltimore, Maryland

Library of Congress Cataloging in Publication Data

Main entry under title:

Baltimore, a living renaissance.
   Includes index.
   1. Baltimore (Md.)—History—Addresses, essays, lectures. I. Nast, Lenora Heilig.
II. Krause, Laurence. III. Monk, R. C. (Richard C.) IV. Historic Baltimore Society.
F189.B157B34 1982   975.2′604   82-80490

Cover photo: Joanne Rijmes

Acknowledgments

Baltimore: A Living Renaissance represents the work of many contributors. It is a Baltimore product from conception to printing. The editors are indebted to all who helped.

We wish to thank the members of the board of the Historic Baltimore Society for their continued interest and advice in seeing this project to its completion. We also thank the writers and photographers who have shared our enthusiasm in their respective areas of expertise. Historians who read the manuscript for accuracy were Joseph Arnold, Gary Browne, Richard Cox, and Morgan Pritchett—all knowledgeable about Baltimore's history. We are indebted to Edward Lyell Gunts and H. Clifton Osborn who read the entire manuscript and made many valuable suggestions.

Sherie Brook Libber and Devorah Leibtag deserve special thanks for their conscientious assistance in researching, editing, proofing, and indexing. Ms. Libber also shared her knowledge about many issues pertinent to the book. Richard P. Davis was particularly cooperative, always available to answer questions about the rebuilding of the city as well as suggesting articles. Larry Reich gave special assistance and our deepest thanks go to him.

Alice Cherbonnier gave needed editorial assistance. Others who helped with editing were Joseph Arnold, Gary Browne, Anne Gafos, Frederick Kelly, and Jacques Kelly. Those who further researched facts to make the book accurate were Claire Pula and Patty Watts. Francis X. Heaphy lent us his many years experience as a proofreader.

Thomas L. Benson, Mary Camerer (secretary of the Johns Hopkins University Writing Seminars), Dean Esslinger, Walter Fisher, Rose Spain Goodman, Richard Hart, Theodore E. Klitzke, Sidney Kobre, Richard A. Macksey, Margaret Masson, Bennard Perlman, and John Walton each contributed in areas of his/her special expertise, such as education, black history, art, journalism, literature, and women's history. The Enoch Pratt Library Reference Service and Maryland Room were invaluable.

Beverly Carrington, Marge Jones, Nancy McLaughlin, Teri Marecki, Phyllis Mooring, Valerie Ringgold, and Sylvia Williams have our appreciation for typing pages and pages of manuscript. Without them the book would not have been finished.

John Brain, Sandy Eisenberg, Reva Kobre, Walter Orlinsky, Jake Slagle, Jr., and Ronald Stiff contributed to the work of making this book and we appreciate their assistance.

We want to thank George McManus, Jr. and John Ruth for legal assistance, the accounting firm of Fried and Beares, Municipal Art Society and O'Connor Communications for financial contributions.

Waverly Press and its personnel who were involved must be thanked. We are grateful especially to Patricia Chalfant, Phyllis Ecker and Robert Bounds for their kindness and patient concern with the book's publication.

Sue Bishop, the designer of the book, has our special appreciation for her contribution and cooperation. Thanks go, also, to Jim Mulligan for his work on the cover, and, of course, Joanne Rijmes for allowing us to use her photograph for our cover.

We appreciate the use of Aaron Sopher's work contributed by Mary Weinman and Mr. and Mrs. Mose I. Speert, who also own the Clements painting. Peter Handakas photographed these works for the book. B/L Labs, Inc. printed the photos. Mrs. A. Aubrey Bodine kindly contributed her husband's photo and Dennis K. McDaniel the Bennard Perlman painting. Thanks to Cathy Burroughs for photo suggestions.

Much material for a contemporary history comes from personal interviews that form primary sources. *Baltimore: A Living Renaisance* is typical then as it involved this method. We are grateful to all contributors for their generosity with their time devoted to conversations with the authors. Some interviews were taped, and some merely personal interviews.

In sum, like the fabled travelers who stopped to throw pebbles into a stone soup (the broth of which turns out delicious), we thank our many supporters and contributors. If it had not been for their patient prodding and encouragement, as well as careful reading, many more errors would have gone undetected in this anthology. The editors assume all responsibility for errors remaining and any resulting indigestion.

Publication of *Baltimore: A Living Renaissance* was aided by the efforts of Historic Baltimore Society's board member, Gregory Barnhill of Alex Brown & Sons.

Preface

Aristotle argued 2,300 years ago that the goal of the city is to make man happy and safe. During the Middle Ages, a mere five hundred years ago, if a serf could remain inside the walls of a city for a year and a day, he was considered free.

Nowadays it is peculiar to view the cities as making people happy, safe, or free. In fact, dissatisfaction with urban life has grown so strong that a 1972 Gallup Poll found that 80 percent of all respondents would prefer to live somewhere other than in a city. Yet, in 1980, approximately 75 percent of all Americans lived in urban areas. Homo Sapiens' "greatest achievement and most horrible creation, its cities," remain contradictory and problematic.

It is our contention that of all American cities, Baltimore in many ways comes closest to making its citizens "happy, safe, and free." This was not always so. Until recently in its history, Baltimore experienced all the strains and deterioration that characterize the decline of most urban areas. Then, roughly 25 years ago, changes began. So pervasive are these changes that we argue they are not simply "redevelopment" or "urban renewal." Instead, recent Baltimore is a "living renaissance," a period of vigor and creativity.

This anthology is for those who share with us a feeling of exhilaration at what is happening in Baltimore and a sense of curiosity as to how and why this urban renaissance came about and the direction in which it might be going. The articles are also for the people who are living the city's renaissance and those city dwellers elsewhere who might be able to benefit from knowledge of Baltimore's experience.

How did the book come about? In 1978 coeditor Larry Krause realized that Baltimore's well–known changes were going far beyond the ritualistic renewal programs of other cities. Larry has lived in Baltimore since grade school. In the early 1970s, he founded the *Baltimore Chronicle* (formerly the *City Dweller*) as well as other community newspapers.

His initial intention was to do a series of articles, along with friend and coeditor, Alice Cherbonnier, on changing Baltimore. Very quickly, though, they realized that there was more, much more, that needed to be said and by many more people than they originally envisioned.

Within a month Larry contacted Dr. Lenora Nast, a historian, who has been a Baltimorean for over 30 years and is actively involved in research and teaching the humanities. Lenora, after discussing the project with her husband, Richard, immediately began preparation with Larry of an outline for Baltimore's "living history." She drew upon impressive resources that include extensive contacts throughout the Baltimore community, acquaintance with many Baltimore scholars, and expert knowledge of local archives and other data sources.

Soon afterward, I agreed to participate in collecting and editing papers. As a sociologist and former reporter, it was assumed that I could be a balance between a journalist and historian.

In January, 1979, the Historic Baltimore Society was founded for the purpose of publishing *Baltimore: A Living Renaissance*. An initial publication deadline of September, 1980, was made. However, as the project grew it became clear that even with the aid of three editors and many assistants, *Baltimore: A Living Renaissance* would take longer than 18 months to record adequately. (see Joseph Arnold's "How to Research History" in the Appendix for a discussion of some of the problems and strategies of doing history). Thus the project extended over three years and we, frankly, still have a deep sense of a lack of closure or completeness. But we already run the risk of having several articles "dated." In addition, our very subject matter, Baltimore's renaissance, is by nature ongoing and open–ended. Even in the throes of a conservative political climate and national government, it shows no signs of losing its vitality. Moreover, our aim was never to be a definitive history. Instead, it is the much more modest objective of selectively presenting the "spirit" or attitudes of the times and of the people creating them. Another volume is needed for anything else.

Whatever insight into the city's renaissance

has been achieved is due to our writers who, along with other Baltimoreans, gave form to the project.

In selecting writers, we used three criteria. First, knowledge and expertise in substantive areas was required. However, we were delighted to find many young, fairly inexperienced writers as well as several more well–known scholars meeting this qualification. Thus we were able to achieve something close to a balance between new writers and more mature ones with the late Gerald Johnson's article (as far as we can determine, the last one he wrote) personifying the latter.

The second requirement was interest in and enthusiasm for the subject matter. This turned out to be frequently a "propinquity" factor. Since the book is a collection of essays on a living history of a city, many of the writers were close to or even a part of the events they describe. In order to control partially possible biases introduced by this tactic, we sometimes selected two or more authors to cover the same areas to achieve a balance of perspective. To us, the encouraging of several authors to spell out the inherent ironies and contradictions of urban processes and their respective interpretations is methodologically more adequate than purporting to let the facts "speak for themselves" through the voice of a single author. However, this strategy, which we feel is a good one, sometimes results in, along with the usual overlap of subject areas, necessary redundancies in some sections. This appears to be a worthwhile penalty to pay in doing a living history in which both the facts and their assessments have not yet been successfully sorted out.

The third criterion for selection was freshness of approach. Often this meant leaving out some of the familiar. Thus, in searching for both freshness and importance in writers and subject areas, many things of value were passed over. This is yet another penalty to pay when undertaking an inherently unwieldy project such as mapping the renaissance of a city. Nonetheless, for these omissions an apology is due, even in a work that is avowedly selective and nondefinitive in scope.

We view Baltimore's renaissance as extending roughly from 1956 through the present. Since 1956 was the inception of Charles Center, we use that year as a benchmark. However, as in the case of all historical periods, there is often overlap in dates and times. Definitions and theoretic distinctions sometimes blur in reality. But if this anthology captures important elements of Baltimore's renaissance, and makes others aware of the achievement and at least some of the people who made it possible, then we will immodestly claim success.

R. C. Monk

Contents

III
THE ARTS

IV
WHAT MAKES BALTIMORE BALTIMORE

APPENDIX

Introduction

Baltimore's transformation during the past generation has been astonishing. National, even international, attention has been riveted upon the city's ever more visible achievements. Uniquely combining the old with the new, the city today epitomizes dynamic urban America.

How did these changes occur, and why? That you will discover in the essays that make up this volume. Written by Baltimoreans from many different walks of life, these essays cover the spectrum of artistic, economic, political, religious, and social life in Baltimore. Indeed, their breadth and range constitute one of the strengths of this book. And that they do so in ways that convey the unique character of the city is itself a tribute to the genius of the editors, for they thereby reveal how well they understand Baltimore.

The substance of *Baltimore* is divided into four parts. Part I, entitled "Baltimore Builds," appropriately begins with the foundation of the community. The bedrock of Baltimore is its neighborhoods; and several essays discuss the revival of this important, grass–roots structure. They also discuss various programs, organizations, and movements that have contributed to neighborhood revitalization. Other essays focus upon the dramatic and highly visible changes in the city's downtown area, and upon important developments in science and health, two areas that have had long and important associations with the city.

Part II, "Social Perspective," deals with Baltimore's most important asset—its people. Here, the reader encounters a series of essays, each one dealing with a new aspect of the life of the city. Baltimore's rich ethnic heritage and its revival begins the series. Religion, the black community, the women's movement, education, politics, the media, and senior citizens constitute the themes of those that follow. In subject, structure, and tone, these vibrant essays reveal the ways in which Baltimoreans met life's challenges during the past generation.

"The Arts" is the focus of Part III. Here, we find discussions of the theatre, music, the visual arts, dance, film, architecture, and poetry and literature. I venture to predict that everyone will learn something new about Baltimore in this section. The rich array of its "Arts" is incredible, and the sense of "something for everyone" suggests the cosmopolitan and sophisticated character of Baltimore's society. Indeed, when we reflect upon "The Arts" information in conjunction with Baltimore's "Social Perspective," we gain even deeper insight into the ethnic, media, and educational dimensions of "The Arts" in addition to their aesthetic and entertainment values.

"What Makes Baltimore Baltimore" constitutes Part IV, the final section of the book. Several essays discuss business and economic developments as well as organizations whose purpose is to promote the city's economy. Another group discuss the political aspects of the city. Appropriately, they focus upon the personalities and offices of the mayor and city council, as well as political issues. A unique concluding group addresses a variety of themes in their Baltimore context.

Thankfully, the editors have structured this book to make it eminently usable. Besides this introduction, we have a preface, and then a brief "Editors' Introduction" introduces each of the four parts by way of establishing the general themes for each part. At the end, in an appendix, we have an excellent guide in "How to Research History" by Professor Joseph Arnold, a well–known local historian; a basic chronology of Baltimore's renaissance; identification of the authors; and an index. Altogether, this adds up to a very attractive, interesting, and useful package.

But don't be fooled by looks alone. *Baltimore: A Living Renaissance* represents far more than passing interest as commentary about the city's recent past. Baltimore is one of the few major metropolitan centers in America whose roots extend far back into our colonial heritage. Long in tradition and experience, the city's history has been punctuated by periods of adjustment to new forces of change such as those that occurred during the 1960s and 1970s. The resiliency of the urban community and the appearance of dynamic, forceful leaders on these occasions has been consistently remarkable. Baltimoreans are justifiably proud of their heritage. But what has happened to their city during the past generation has been enormously different from previous occasions. The forces of change have been far more complex and difficult to deal with. That is why Baltimore's contemporary renaissance is all the more remarkable. And let us remember: we are not outsiders to that process. We are part of the renaissance whether we know it or not. And that is not a small part of our lives.

Gary L. Browne

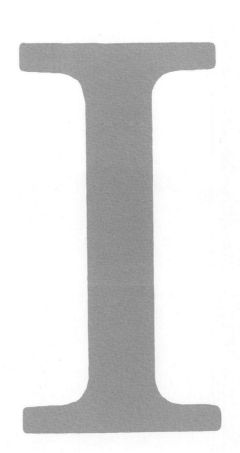

BALTIMORE

Since Homo Sapiens began to crawl out of the original muck and built cities some 10,000 years ago, the earth's landscape as well as men and women's relations with each other and the environment were permanently altered.

America's cities are noted for their rapid expansions and, until recently, continuous solid building. First were all those foreigners coming to these shores, primarily from northern Europe. They took the land from the Indians, then established mudhole settlements that became mudhole cities. However, two centuries later at the end of the 1800s, the cities and their building had reached magnificence. Tides of immigrants, now coming from Eastern and Southern Europe, were increasing. The cities then were proud achievements which like America symbolized for the masses hope and opportunity.

Shortly before and during World War I and later during World War II, blacks and poor whites left the farms, swamps, and hills, making their way to the bowels of America's cities. After World War II Hispanics repeated the process, followed in the 1970s and 1980s by Orientals, though in smaller numbers. However, for the past two generations the shape and meaning of the city in America have deteriorated significantly.

Many no longer were finding the city either to be a place of hope or a place to call home. Instead, the city had become a temporary resting spot, to be retreated from as soon as possible and exchanged for what seemed to some an antiseptic existence of a plastic suburban mausoleum, barely within commuting distance of some downtown and to others a move to the quiet of a cottage in the country, the fulfillment of the American dream.

Clearly, by the 1940s and 1950s, the splendid architectural and engineering achievements of the late 1800s and early 1900s through the 1920s

were eclipsed by blight. With a few glaring exceptions, cities appeared capable of now producing only destructive freeways, parking lots, and monstrous government housing. In the heart of the cities retail establishments, small businesses, public recreational areas, and waterways declined and disappeared.

Obituaries for most American cities, including Baltimore, began to appear routinely 30 years ago and funeral notices were sent out.

The first section of this anthology, "Baltimore Builds," shows that reports of Baltimore's death, unlike that of other cities, were greatly exaggerated.

The 15 selected articles examine representative aspects of a rapidly building city often beginning at its very roots. The articles, all of which, like contributions in the rest of the anthology, appear here in print for the first time, are frequently as rich and diverse as parts of Baltimore itself. The articles range in scope, subject matter, and detail in their treatment of neighborhoods, the City Fair, and urban homesteading. The authors dealt with relevant government agencies and science and medicine as examples of a Baltimore undergoing rebirth.

Virtually no block, street, or square has not undergone some building, some change, some improvement during Baltimore's renaissance. Extensive physical alterations and sheer architectural feats, such as Charles Center and the Inner Harbor, are discussed. However, many far more subtle aspects of the city's recent evolution are also identified. A neighborhood group decides to clean up a street, pioneers reclaim abandoned homes to rebuild the splendor of a Baltimore block of 80 years ago. Baltimoreans go to the Salvage Depot to buy objects saved from the wrecker's ball. After being cleaned and refurbished, these artifacts such as doorknobs, bannisters, chandeliers, and yard ornaments, find their way into some city neighborhood where they once more complement even the most elegant surroundings. The artifacts also preserve another thread from the city's past connecting the present and emerging future. All of this as

The World Trade Center and Harborplace Seen Through *"Red Buoyant,"* the Sculpture by Mary Ann Mears in Front of the IBM Building on Pratt Street. Photo by Jan Sutherland Starr

BUILDS

well as the solid medical, scientific, and technological achievements of a progressive, urban population are introduced in this section.

In discussing Baltimore builds, what could be more important than its neighborhoods, and who could do a better job of recording grass-roots efforts to revitalize and preserve neighborhoods than Jacques Kelly? In "Neighborhood Revitalization" Kelly traces the efforts of many local groups and documents the importance of working at the grass-roots level.

Rawley M. Grau's "City Fair" provides us with an account of one innovation that since its inception in 1970 proves that an entire city can work together to create an important annual event.

"Black East Baltimore Rebuilds" combines with several other articles in this and other sections to distinguish this anthology from almost all others dealing with Baltimore, or, for that matter, most other American cities. First, Richard P. Davis, as in his two earlier articles in this section, emphasizes the role of neighborhoods in contributing to urban success. However, in addition, Davis pays needed attention to the black contribution and helps integrate it with the rest of the city's renaissance.

"Urban Homesteading" argues that a variant of American pioneerism has established a mood for the city. In this article and his "Public Housing," Richard P. Davis documents the contributions to different aspects of Baltimore housing by both the middle and lower classes in the city to their mutual benefits.

Frances Morton Froelicher shows in "CPHA's Impact 1941–1969: A Personal Appraisal" a single association's influence on a building city and her own modestly presented accomplishments on behalf of her city. Leslie Rehbein Marqua and Patty Watts continue the story in their "CPHA Since 1970."

Marie Lehnert adds to this in "The Magic of Preservation" by tracing recent history of preservation, legislation, and legal work of CHAP.

Laren E. Stover shows in "The Salvage Depot" how since 1975 an immanently rational idea has prevented many Baltimore treasures from being destroyed.

Elliot Lieberman's "A Changing Downtown" captures the interplay between commercial and political interests in building Baltimore's downtown, with progress resulting from the significant role given to planning and "pure luck" that things went the way they did for the city.

Morgan Pritchett's "Charles Center" is a case study of how one pivotal city plan stimulated renewal on several fronts, resulting in Baltimore's catching up with other cities and eventually surpassing them in important areas that had been allowed to lag.

"Inner Harbor: A New View for Baltimore" by Jake Slagle, Jr. is immensely helpful in pinpointing several important steps beginning in the 1940s that resulted in what is rapidly becoming Baltimore's most famous renaissance achievement. Slagle, like Lieberman, weaves into his account several fortuitous events, such as the arrival of the tall ships that represented good luck being combined with planning and hard work to help create the renaissance.

R. C. Monk's "Science and Medicine" is an introduction to one specific area of achievement that has helped make many other contributions possible. Sherie Brook Libber's "Baltimore Hospitals" is a detailed, factual account of the medical institutions that have made the city famous throughout the world and have made important gains during the renaissance.

Lisa L. Adams in "Maryland Science Center" traces the transformation of a very unusual institution into a science center.

The Neighborhoods

NEIGHBORHOOD REVITALIZATION

If Baltimore's neighborhoods could be thought of as antiques, the year 1956 was just about the time contemporary urban thinking dictated that older residential areas were hopelessly outdated. Baltimore's neighborhoods were consigned to the trash heap. In the fifties through the sixties, $5,000 to $10,000 would have purchased any rowhouse in Baltimore. Guilford mansions took months to sell for $28,000—the same figure for which they were built years before.

Baltimore's predicament was little different from that of other American cities. The post-World War II generation rejected city living. GI benefits and easy FHA mortgages underwrote the great American middle-class exodus to the suburbs. Added to this, the suburbs were being tied together by new highways. Baltimore, Anne Arundel, Harford, and Howard counties dominated the new construction market, all at the expense of Baltimore city. The migration of these years seemed inevitable.

Baltimore's neighborhoods did not fall apart overnight, but changes did come alarmingly fast. The 1950s were a time of fear in Baltimore. Racial change frightened whole portions of East and West Baltimore. By the 1960s, crime statistics became a grim fact of life. The city school system was said to be slipping. In short, the city was getting to be the repository for the elderly, who did not want to move away, or for those who simply could not afford another location.

The Trend Reverses. During this period, two neighborhoods did serve to give a glimpse of what would eventually signal the saving of the city. In the late 1940s, a group of persons purchased tiny, but architecturally interesting, rowhouses on Tyson Street. They painted the facades bright colors—a bohemian approach to what we would now call renovation. At the time, Tyson Street was considered an acceptable oddity—one of those quirky things that will happen in a city but nothing to take too seriously.

Just a few blocks away, however, a more far-reaching development was taking place. In 1955, some "garden–club ladies," as one source tells it, named a spot called Bolton Hill. Difficult as it is to believe today, prior to 1955, there was no name Bolton Hill. Of course, there was the Mount Royal Improvement Association, but no Bolton Hill. The Mount Royal name failed to identify the neighborhood with the permanence that Bolton Hill has, and probably for good reason. Baltimoreans seem to enjoy identifying streets, or individual blocks, rather than whole neighborhoods. When neighborhoods were identified, the label tended to be geographic—West Baltimore, South Baltimore (not Union Square or Federal Hill).

Tyson Street Open House Day—Beginning Its Fourth Decade

That christening of Bolton Hill was a considerable start. It identified a specific section, the area of residences behind the Maryland Institute and between Eutaw Place and Mount Royal Avenue. Renovation did not sweep through the neighborhood overnight. For more than a decade, houses hovered below the $10,000 bracket. Bolton Hill was viewed somewhat skeptically by Baltimoreans, but it did attract some out-of-towners and those who had been keeping an eye on Georgetown, Washington, D.C., and Society Hill, Philadelphia. The very name Bolton Hill, in fact, seemed to have the same ring as its cousin neighborhoods in Washington and Philadelphia.

Urban renewal was the city's method of dealing with the problems of the decade. On the one hand, a place such as Bolton Hill was making a modest comeback, attracting middle-class families, while the city was actively tearing down other sections of town. This wholesale clearance had a collective way of saying the city was dead, cancerous, unreclaimable. Bolton Hill and scores of other neighborhoods that resisted change, at least admitted to being alive, fairly healthy, and worth the investment.

It was not until the mid-1960s that Baltimore began to recognize that its neighborhoods were not the disposable commodities that some urban renewal planners were leading people to believe.

Why did this change take place? The 1960s were a time of unrest. The golden suburbs were beginning to tarnish, especially in the eyes of the captive generation raised there. The sons and daughters of Levittown saw the sameness of suburbia and expressed contempt. Even in those early days, energy predictions were forecasting that city housing was more economical and fuel efficient than suburban. New construction, bloated by inflation, became expensive, especially for first-time home buyers. Various subdivisions were enacting restrictive growth plans. In short, the bloom was off the suburban rose.

But once again, all this did not signal an immediate turnaround for Baltimore. People change slowly. But the 1960s, as a time of experiment, saw a few individuals try city living, with pockets of rehabilitation in Seton Hill, Fell's Point, Charles Village, and Federal Hill. It was all new and chancy, something that newspapers and magazines regularly featured, but a pattern of living hardly taken seriously by bankers, insurance companies, and real estate agents.

With every brightly colored shutter and newly planted tree, however, there was that much more hope in the city. Something positive was happening—far more encouraging than demolition making way for warehouselike federal projects. Call it preservation, restoration, discovering Baltimore, or the city renaissance movement, its effects suddenly began showing. All over Baltimore were the signs.

Return from Suburbia. Families came back to Baltimore, mortgaging their futures on its past. Buying bankrupt houses in insolvent neighborhoods, they had as collateral their hope, mixed with sweat and determination. And the equity they built shows in the stock of restored blocks of houses now paying dividends to the entire city.

You can see it in Fell's Point's eighteenth-century waterfront homes, where cleaning has returned old exteriors to their softly suntanned brick patina; or in Union Square, an emerald of a Victorian city park faceted by high, wide, and handsome rowhouses; and especially on Stirling Street, where time and neglect had tarnished a twin-sided block of 1830-vintage residences beyond recognition. Now the street is shining again, the proud trophy of dedicated homesteaders.

People are actively searching out the housing heirlooms available over the city's length and breadth. The bargains sit cobwebbed by neglect, peeling paint, and drab neighborhood surroundings. But the selling record of the past few years indicates that sooner than you might think, the good word can't be kept secret any longer.

More recently, the city government has recognized the value of this self-proclaimed renewal and helped stimulate it. Renovation of old rowhouses is being encouraged rather than burial by bulldozers. Special preservation districts now have their distinctive architectural character protected by municipal law. And woodwork, doors, iron work, and fixtures are being saved from demolition projects and sold by the city government to in-town renovators.

It all marks a new confidence in Baltimore, a

House Stripper. Photo by Documentary Photographic Project

sturdy but smoke-stained city that is being recycled through this concerted effort. People are learning quickly how to inhabit its old quarters, renewing on their own what time has proved will survive indefinitely. And they are realizing what it is to live graciously, with real wood floors, solid plaster walls, and broad windows, in homes sized to people and human relationships rather than to economics.

Considering the costs and complexities of building today, who again will ever construct homes with 14-foot parlor ceilings festooned with classical-style plaster details? Where could you get marble fireplaces, parquet floors, and wainscoting, all in a home so close to the downtown that a car isn't a necessity?

In many ways the renewers and preservers of this kind of urban past admit to being opportunists, living off the legacy their ancestors bequeathed. Baltimore is rich in her old-house inheritance. Values depreciated markedly during the years of the evacuation to the suburbs

but more recently have made a dramatic upswing.

And the good vibrations of neighborhood revival move in other directions. Bolton Hill, the city's stately Victorian professional enclave, has lent some of its success to neighboring Reservoir Hill, now undergoing reemergence through similar processes of urban rehabilitation.

Mayor William Donald Schaefer and former Housing Commissioner Robert C. Embry, Jr. noted the advantage the city enjoys with its solid housing stock when they toured several blocks in Reservoir Hill. These substantially built and generously sized 1890s homes are now the basis of large cooperative apartment units, the type of housing that under old urban renewal methods would have been ruled unworthy and promptly demolished.

Similar methods proved the salvation of Washington Hill, the neighborhood to the south of the Hopkins medical institution in East Baltimore. Here the city has converted the interiors of Victorian row homes into two cooperative apartment units, while sprucing up their exteriors with colorful paint schemes.

Community Leadership. It's not just a case of throwing a coat of paint over the neglect of the past 30 years. Old house renovation and neighborhood revival can be a trial of patience and endurance. There are the built-in ills of crime, a school system that doesn't compare favorably with those in the suburbs, air and street pollution, and the advance of highways and traffic around every corner. Old houses are plagued with bad wiring and plumbing, flaking plaster walls, and rooms that drink up gallons of paint. But many neighborhoods have demonstrated that these problems aren't insurmountable, once an active community association is formed that demands the respect of City Hall.

A case in point is Union Square. Its first symptom of life and concern surfaced in 1967, when about 60 people met to form an association. They acknowledged that the happy days of H.L. Mencken, Union Square's most famous resident, were gone. What had been the square's distinctive garden centerpiece of greenery had gone to dreary seed. Its cast-iron fountain had been scrapped, trees had died, and the pavements were cracked and broken. Just as sick were the houses that lined the square on three sides. Though older residents hung on, their hopes sank as one house after another fell vacant or was carved into a transients' rooming house.

Self-assurance was characteristic of the Union Square Association, largely the creation of Robert and JoeAnne Whitely, a young couple determined to nurse their neighborhood back to good health. Mrs. Whitely, who has lived in West Baltimore all her life, found a ready acceptance for her ideas about how Union Square should pull itself up and not wait for a handout from city government. Her first project called for replacing the cast-iron fountain that once gushed water into a circular basin in the square. To raise funds, the group set aside a day in June for an annual Union Square Festival, the proceeds from which went toward casting a new fountain.

At the same time she began digging into the annals of city history to locate every fact surrounding this early park, given to the city by the Donnell family in 1847. As her investigation progressed, many forgotten facets were uncovered and helped the association convince the city's Department of Recreation and Parks that it was worth spending some $260,000 for Union Square improvements. The goal was to restore it to its nineteenth-century appearance, all the way down to rose-tinted concrete walks, scored in diamond-shaped patterns, and including reproduction gas lamps in an authentic design used in city parks, herringbone pattern sidewalks around the perimeter of the square, and trees and shrubs that were popular during the mid-1800s.

"Preservation spreads instead of blight. I cleaned the bricks on my house and soon other people were doing it, even some absentee landlords," Mrs. Whitely said. "But to me, a neighborhood is not just facades and buildings, but is total living environment. There's nothing demeaning about having to call the sanitation department or the rodent control people. Urban living problems are all part of Union Square," she continued.

The same year, 1967, signaled the turnaround for the north-central Baltimore neighborhood of Charles Village. Rich in stained-glass windows, big front porches, and golden oak wood-

work, it was poor in fresh paint and in homeowners who appreciated the fine interiors these roomy, turn-of-the-century houses afforded. It was a neighborhood lacking an identity, save as the spillover district for Hopkins University students and their fraternities.

To the rescue came Grace Darin, an East Twenty-sixth Street resident, who parlayed a hunch into a success story. Correctly diagnosing the area's chronic identity crisis (only the older residents could recall its original name of Peabody Heights), she christened as Charles Village the area to the east and south around Johns Hopkins University. Miss Darin saw to it that Charles Village got noticed in the press, so the name soon became a household word.

Originally, the rowhouse renaissance of Charles Village was clustered around the pastel row on Twenty-sixth Street, but the good news of the highly pleasing renovations sent branches of renewal out in all directions. The annual spring house tour drew hundreds of visitors as the once anonymous streets assumed the collective identity imparted by characteristic rooftop architecture, turrets, and brick and tile dunce caps, the last laugh of late Victorian whimsy that the utilitarian modern era didn't find the least bit funny.

Homeowners United. Despite the rather fast good fortunes of Charles Village, homeowners had to put up good arguments before the banks or the FHA would grant mortgages in the area. Added to this, it took a united fight on the part of the Charles Village Civic Association to keep the city from widening one of its main thoroughfares, Calvert Street, and dumping more traffic into a neighborhood designed for the horse and wagon era.

The fight against governmental bureaucracy continues today despite the homeowners' good example of preserving and restoring the old homes. The state announced that it considered the neighborhood's 1896, Romanesque-style school outdated, and demolished it for a modern building, even though a substantial majority of the village residents voted against the school's demolition.

The jury was long out on the fate of two of Baltimore's oldest neighborhoods, Fell's Point and Federal Hill. Both these early harborside sections (which face the Patapsco from opposite sides of the river) were under threat of disfiguration by eight-lane legs of an expressway system Baltimoreans had been saying for 25 years they didn't want. Highway planners took what they thought would be the path of least resistance by carving a route for their concrete spillway along the harbor's edge, obliterating portions of the older historic communities of Federal Hill, Fell's Point, and Canton. In the latter section, the roadbuilders were successful in demolishing 200 early houses (several with fine cast-iron balcony porches left from the days when Baltimore was a leading manufacturer of decorative iron work). Most of the properties were solid housing, well-maintained by Polish families who took pride in their homes.

But in Federal Hill and Fell's Point, road proponents met major resistance. Here is where the city had really begun, with small, meandering streets that end along bulkheads where ocean-going vessels still tie up. This working waterfront provides a dramatic cityscape for the steep hip-roofed houses, with their protruding dormers and centuries-old chimney pots. For more than 10 years, people have been discovering Fell's Point and Federal Hill, some doing careful restorations that return old woodwork to former glory; others remodeling the interiors of their homes into studios, apartments, and comfortable contemporary quarters.

Preserving Old Baltimore. With little government money being spent to help them (except for the negative aspects of costly expressway planning studies), the two communities have been reborn at the considerable expense of their residents who appreciate a living history and some of the best views of the waterfront to be had in any East Coast American city.

Federal Hill's two main thoroughfares, Warren Avenue and Montgomery Street, are lined with houses that range from the enormous to the miniature, some painted soft pastel shades, others cleaned down to warm, natural brick facades. Long considered the "Park Row" of South Baltimore, Warren Avenue's matronly residences are doubly blessed with views of both the

harbor and downtown skyline; and of Federal Hill Park, a large grass plateau that takes its name from the huge festival staged there in 1788 to celebrate the ratification of the Federal Constitution.

Fell's Point remains true to its origins. A settlement distinct from Baltimore Town, this colonial-era neighbor harbored the larger sailing vessels that called here, because of its deeper channel. As a result, its square-rigged past flavors the present renewal efforts with seafaring reminders. Artists rent its lofts and warehouses for studios. Tavern keepers do a busy trade in bars whose former clientele of sailors has given way to singles in a new style of ship's café society. One-time mariners' and ship-chandlers' residences are being restored along Bond, Thames, Shakespeare, Lancaster, Aliceanna, Anne, and Wolfe streets.

Fell's Point is an outdoor museum where indigenous ethnic groups mix with newcomers who have discovered the pleasures of restoration, a sense of making a substantial contribution to their city, and a neatly scaled neighborhood where friendships can still be formed over the backyard fence and on front steps.

A force behind the harborside renewal is the Society for the Preservation of Federal Hill and Fell's Point. In cooperation with established community groups, it has spearheaded the attack against the expressway system planned to encircle its precincts like a concrete octopus. The question is whether a road planned by engineers who shrug at old neighborhoods has any validity. Will the addition of autos and trucks, with their noise and fumes, improve the existing vista of church steeples, gulls, freighters, and tugboats? The city claims it needs more roads; Fell's Point residents respond that it needs better neighborhoods.

The high-budget federal grants of the fifties and sixties designed to "improve" cities have been questioned when their accomplishments are weighed against their promise. The expressways they funded only sent the middle class fleeing to the suburbs, while unresolved highway plans continue to menace old city neighborhoods that have managed to stall the roads' construction. A similar problem has hampered the big urban renewal plans of the era. The promised

Masonic Temple F&AM, Formerly the Eutaw Place Temple (Oheb Shalom). Photo by Eleanor Merryman Roszel

reuse by Center Stage of the old Loyola High School and College complex just to the north. Ten years ago, he points out, few people would have considered using an old white elephant structure like that; today it seems more than logical. Fortunately, it seems to be the nature of Baltimoreans to "let live" anything they consider of value. Only their government, enamored of federal funds, seems demolition–prone.

Happily, urban renewal planners, once dictatorial and single–minded in laying out their expressways and dramatic vistas, interspaced with densely packed housing towers, are changing, too, so that rehabilitation of existing housing is called for, rather than demolition and total rebuilding.

Never have plans been so accommodating as along Stirling Street, a gently winding block that climbs from just north of the Belair Market to Monument Street. Planners of the Oldtown urban renewal project saw it as urban debris, worn out housing that could never be reclaimed. A parking lot and new housing were scheduled to be built on the street's grave.

Homesteading: The Panacea. Then came homesteading, the concept wherein a new owner buys a city–owned home for a dollar, but inherits the liability of bringing the property up to code standards set by the city. That liability, in the case of the Stirling Street homes, averaged $26,000. There, 25 homesteaders converted 42 houses (some small properties were joined to make one large one) into an outstanding example of creative recycling. Key to this success was the Stirling Street Neighbors Group, led by chairman Ian Jewitt. Patience, persistence, and levelheadedness have proved the soundness of their idea.

Ian Jewitt has recalled the early negotiations: "At first, the city housing representatives began saying, 'You'll do it our way.' It was only through our prodding questions and eventual mutual agreements that their defenses dropped. The city was waiting for us to back off, but the longer we hung in, our confidence was raised. I don't know that things ever got into a confrontation with the city, but we're certainly not a retiring group."

There is something about homesteading that makes it popular with a broad spectrum of Bal-

funds turned out to be mirages; homes were demolished, but never replaced.

In the Mount Vernon neighborhood, ugly urban renewal scar tissue takes the form of a parking lot. In the late 1960s, after a fight failed to save historic Waterloo Row on Calvert Street, the block of homes, designed by the distinguished architect Robert Mills, was demolished. Today, after almost a decade of life as a parking lot, the block is to be rebuilt as Chesapeake Center, a mix of offices, shops, and apartments.

Robert Klepper, past president of the Mount Vernon–Belvedere Improvement Association, has said, "Waterloo Row was a casualty of its times. Five years ago, conservation of older buildings wasn't taken seriously. Certainly Waterloo Row would have been retained if programs such as homesteading had been available." While the 600 blocks of North Calvert and St. Paul streets were total losses, he believes the community has made an appreciable gain with timore's population. When plans were announced to sell as dollar–house properties the unit block of South Durham Street (east of Broadway and south of the Johns Hopkins complex), the homes sold out quickly. An open-house tour of the Otterbein area in Inner Harbor West drew over 3,000 visitors and yielded 700 actual applications for approximately 100 homes. Even though rehabilitation costs for an average Otterbein house are upwards of $50,000, there was spirited bidding for them.

The Otterbein homes fit Baltimore's classic mold as properties once scheduled to be demolished for an urban renewal project. Today, the area promises to be a centerpiece of lived-in history and charm for Baltimore's major downtown rebuilding project; a relic of former elegance blooming in a field of rubble, the only houses left in a gargantuan hole created for a new city heart. It represents the last piece of the past in a district scheduled for the future.

The pulse of popularity connected with preservation can be felt each Saturday at the Salvage Depot, the city government's highly successful attempt to recycle architectural hardware back into private hands. Mayor Schaefer was nearly swept off his feet the day he opened it and 500 persons poured in for a "bargain sale" of old doors, flooring, staircases, and cast-iron pieces rescued by the city from demolition and rebuilding projects. The depot continues to do a brisk business in recycled architectural plunder made available to qualified restorers.

Aaron Sopher, *"Green Street Near Barre"* Courtesy of Mr. and Mrs. Mose I. Speert. Photo by Peter Handakas

Yet renewal contradictions persist around every corner. While the city government has become increasingly sympathetic to preservation, it continues to map the expressway. The expressway's gouges have disfigured large portions of West Baltimore, especially along the Franklin-Mulberry corridor and Fremont Avenue. Canton, in the southeast section of the city, saw 200 homes go down to the highwaymen. It is trying to salvage what remains by having its area placed on the National Register of Historic Places to discourage further losses. Only gradually is Baltimore learning that its future may actually lie in its past.

The Fruits of Neighborhood Pride. About the same time that the Federal Hills, Charles Villages, and Union Squares of Baltimore were being discovered by the middle class returning to Baltimore, there was also a resurgence of confidence in such well-established communities as Hampden, Highlandtown, Canton, Monument Street, Remington, and whole sections of South Baltimore and Southwest Baltimore. Small community groups—often representing a block or two—began to petition City Hall and, more often than not, be heard. Neighborhood self-respect blossomed. It was never more obvious than at the first City Fair, that annual exposition of neighborhood pride each September.

Along with the movement to renovate older homes—and escalating real estate values—came a commercial revitalization. Neighborhood shopping districts—places such as the Cross Street Market area of South Baltimore, Monument Street east of Hopkins Hospital (with the Northeast Market), Waverly (Thirty-third and Greenmount), Thirty-sixth Street in Hampden, Corned Beef Row on East Lombard Street, West Baltimore Street off Union Square, and, of course, the Old Town Mall*—became a focus of residents who had turned to the suburban shopping centers. Just as old homes were proving popular, old, established stores are now gaining new customers.

In the last years of the 1970s, several issues faced neighborhoods the way highways and urban renewal did 10 years earlier. Displacement—the uprooting and removal of one group of per-

* Old Town Mall and Oldtown for the neighborhood.

Waverly Terrace. Photo by Documentary Photographic Project

sons by another who is usually wealthier—is affecting many neighborhoods. Grass-roots groups are demanding that existing residents be given the chance to remain in their old homes. At the same time, many older homeowners fear higher taxes as renovation sweeps through their neighborhood.

As in the past, the city's housing department has addressed these issues by offering a number of programs to the economically disadvantaged. Whether the poor will actually benefit from the city's best intentions remains to be seen.

Jacques Kelly

CITY FAIR

In September, 1970, the great old city of Baltimore, still licking its wounds from the 1968 riots and the violence of the May 1970 Flower Mart, received a gift from the people of Balti-

more, a little something to cheer it up. It was the City Fair.

Robert C. Embry, Jr., then the city's housing commissioner, and Hope D. Quackenbush, the assistant director of information services at the Department of Housing and Community Development, wanted to do something to prove to everyone that Baltimore was a good place to live. They wanted to show off the city's most vital resources, it neighborhoods. Their original idea was to have a number of simultaneous neighborhood festivals with shuttle buses running from one to the other. When that proved unfeasible, they sought to show their exhibits of urban renewal at the annual arts festival. The arts festival refused them. Finally, someone said (nobody wants to take full credit for the idea), "Let's have a city fair!" They conceived an urbanized country fair with neighborhood exhibits replacing goats, cows, and squash, and ethnic foods replacing (or alongside of) apple cider and corn on the cob.

City officials, including Mayor Thomas J. D'Alesandro III, were naturally nervous about the idea of bringing several thousand people of all races, creeds, and tax brackets together downtown. Finally a supporter was found in William Donald Schaefer, then City Council president,

City Fair in the Inner Harbor, 1978. Photo by M. E. Warren

who saw the positive impact the fair could have on the way people thought about the city.

Next Hope Quackenbush and Sandy Hillman, Housing and Community Development, went about convincing local business leaders that an urban festival was just what the city needed. After much disappointment, they convinced the Greater Baltimore Committee and the Retail Merchants Association to finance a dinner at the Bolton Hill Dinner Theatre, where Hope Quackenbush presented the idea to about 50 representatives from 20 neighborhoods. She recalls, "Some black lady, an elderly lady, stood up and said, 'This is a wonderful idea. What we've got to do is show our love for one another.' She had us all nearly in tears. But that did it. From then on, the idea was sold."

Neighborhoods began organizing themselves, and the City Fair was given office space at Charles and Franklin streets by the archdiocese of Baltimore. A local architect, W. Boulton Kelly, was enlisted as president of the fair corporation. Robert Embry contributed the full support of the Department of Housing and Community Development and even loaned Hope Quackenbush to serve as the executive director of the fair.

Sandy Hillman had the idea of gaining the support of businesses by selling them huge blocks of tickets to the fair at a cut-rate. Many were skeptical, but a few businesses, such as the National Brewing Company, gave enough financial support to pull the thing off.

Thousands of details had to be worked out. No one in the whole country had ever put on a city fair, and no one really knew what to do. So they winged it. Charles Center was chosen as the site, because the organizers wanted to prove that it could be a "people place."

The city fair office was opened July 1, and a big sign in its window began to attract the curious. A mammoth publicity campaign, led by Hope Quackenbush and Sandy Hillman, was initiated with evangelistic fervor. Local newspapers, radio, and television were extremely helpful, telling the public about all the fair's attractions in an exciting manner. And people got involved, hundreds of people, from the street, from the housing office, but most of all from the neighborhoods. They were what the fair was about—and everyone knew it.

Christopher C. Hartman, then with the *News American* and chairman of the first three fairs, and Kenneth Webster, then a Housing and Community Development employee and a leader in the black community, went around to the neighborhoods, telling them what the fair would do for Baltimore. They explained that the city was rich because of its diversity, and the fair would prove it. In a time of extreme tensions between black and white, rich and poor, the fair would display Baltimoreans who were proud of their heritage and their neighborhoods: they were able to work together and learn from each other to overcome the problems city dwellers face.

And people responded. Neighborhoods got together some first-rate exhibits, such as the Govans slide show, the Hollins Park history display, and the Greek community's pastries. More than 20 community groups participated from all sectors of the city. Besides the three already mentioned, there were the American Indian Studies Center, Bolton Hill, Charles Village, Druid Lake,

Mayor William Donald Schaefer at a Neighborhood Festival—Fell's Point, 1979. Photo by John Clark Mayden

East Baltimore–Gay Street, Echo House, Ednor Gardens–Lakeside, Fell's Point, For–Win–Ash Garden Club, Hampden–Woodberry, Greater Homewood, the Model Neighborhood Council Corporation, Mount Holly, Greater Northwood, SAGA, Seton Hill, Southeast (SECO), South Baltimore, Union Square, and Windsor Hills. Educational, cultural, and medical institutions also set up booths and displays. There were 37 of these at the first fair.

The fair was to demonstrate that (in Mrs. Quackenbush's words) Baltimore is not a melting pot, but a stew with many different ingredients. To this end, white neighborhood groups found themselves next to black neighborhood groups, poor next to middle class. Different cultures met and began to talk to each other for the first time, and friendships were formed.

There were logistical problems. A couple of weeks before the fair, the organizers discovered that nothing had been arranged about electricity for vendors. Contractors were hired to do a six-week wiring job in two weeks. More sanitation maintenance was needed than had been expected, but the Department of Sanitation handled the situation beautifully with extra crews and trash pickups. Everyone seemed determined to make the fair a success, from the Public Works Department to the city police.

Finally, after a gargantuan amount of work by hundreds of volunteers (and everyone was a volunteer), the First Annual Baltimore City Fair opened on September 25, 1970, with a launching of 2,000 balloons and a Parade of Neighborhoods. Although primarily located under circus tents in Center, Charles, and Hopkins Plazas, some exhibits such as a German beer garden were on Pier One at the Inner Harbor. An open air trolley connected the disparate parts.

Right up to the opening day, a question was haunting everybody's mind: "Is anyone really going to come?" That was soon answered as thousands poured into Charles Center. Another question was answered, too. They came in peace, intending to have some good, clean, and corny fun. Over 300,000 people descended on a few acres of the city during the course of the weekend: no riots, no major vandalism, no unnecessary roughness. Baltimore simply and purely enjoyed itself.

Friday and Saturday the weather was perfect.

Then, early on Sunday morning, a violent rainstorm blew down several neighborhood pavilions. The spirit of cooperation and friendship was never more evident, however, than when everyone pitched in to restore the displays. Union Square lent a hand to Gay Street, Mount Holly helped rescue Charles Village. Even early visitors helped clean up the mess.

The fair offered the usual attractions of music, food, and amusement rides and ended with fireworks on Sunday. Acclaimed singer Ethel Ennis gave a concert for her hometown. But the stars of the fair were the people—those who organized it, those who manned the booths, those who attended. In spite of losses, the event was judged as a success. The money that the neighborhoods earned by selling pretzels, pastries, crafts, or whatever else, was donated to neighborhood improvements such as home repairs, building funds for community centers, and the planting of shrubs and flowers. Everyone was eagerly awaiting the next year's fair.

The second and third fairs, Richard Davis says, proved that the success of the first fair was not a fluke. Mr. Davis is director of information services at the Department of Housing and Community Development and has been involved with the fair since its beginning, serving as president of the fair corporation for the fourth and fifth fairs. During these years the fair was expanded to the Inner Harbor. New attractions were added, such as the All–Nations Festival, which became part of the fair in 1972 and later evolved into the International Village, spotlighting the city's ethnic diversity. A Living–Space exhibit of home crafts was also begun that year, set up in Hopkins Plaza. It was successful and developed in later years as the crafts exhibit.

Each year, different people have organized the fair. The original leaders—Robert Embry, Hope Quackenbush, Christopher Hartman, and Sandy Hillman—gradually gave way to a "second generation" of leaders: Ed Kane, Robert Hillman, James Smith, Richard Davis, and JoAnn Copes. And these stalwarts are now relinquishing the direction to others, such as Dale Jefferson and Dave Gillece. People grow up from within the fair to assume increasing responsibilities in other endeavors.

The fourth year the fair was located totally at the harbor, with Light and Calvert Streets closed off. To celebrate this move the Great Wallenda walked a tightrope above the water. That year, more than 60 neighborhoods participated. The exhibits were bigger and better and the fair came into its own.

The fair has since remained in the Inner Harbor area, though construction and renovation have caused it to vary its exact location each year. Where the fair will be held has always presented new challenges to the organizers, and has helped give each fair a sense of uniqueness.

A show–stopping stunt has traditionally taken place at the fairs: a man was shot out of a cannon in 1972, parachutists dropped from the sky in 1974, Doug Jones dove into the harbor from an 80–foot high platform in 1979, setting a world's record. In addition to this, some nationally renowned entertainer or band has traditionally performed: Cab Calloway, Benny Goodman, the Glenn Miller Orchestra, Diahann Carroll, to name a few.

Throughout the years, however, one thing has remained consistent: the neighborhoods are what it's all about. Baltimore and its people are the stars. The fair has a certain tackiness about it; a certain corniness is central to it. Nothing commercial, nothing "slick," describes the fair. It's simply good, hometown folk "doing their thing." From first to last it is people, from the hundreds of volunteers who work weeks in advance and during the weekend of the fair, to the hundreds of thousands—millions, in recent years—who come and enjoy themselves. And

Mayor William Donald Schaefer and State Comptroller Louis Goldstein at the City Fair, 1979. Photo by John Clark Mayden

that really is what fair-goers enjoy—themselves. This is not a city government event, nor even an advertisement for local businesses—although they have always supplied the needed financial support. No one is exploited. Everything about the fair is simple and rooted in basic human values: caring, and being able to learn from others; listening, doing, eating, and having fun.

Rawley M. Grau

BLACK EAST BALTIMORE REBUILDS

In 1967, Tom Briscoe, a community organization adviser for the Baltimore Urban Renewal and Housing Agency (BURHA), received an emergency telephone call from Baltimore while he was away on summer training with the National Guard. He was told he had been picked to lay the groundwork for development of an urban renewal plan for the Gay Street area of East Baltimore. "It was put to me as though I were being sent to the front lines," he commented later. Briscoe found: "The people there had had a bellyful of redevelopment in the area south of them. They'd seen homes torn down and the new Sheraton built, and the Hopkins compound built, and parking areas for doctors where their homes had been. There were four dirty words: Johns Hopkins and urban renewal."

That part of East Baltimore contained some of the lowest-income people of the entire metropolitan area. In Gay Street I—from Monument Street north to Biddle, and from Broadway west to Eden Street—the median family income was $3,610; in Oldtown, west of Gay Street, it was $2,835, and 27 percent of the families were elderly; in Oliver, between Biddle Street and North Avenue, the median income was $5,105 but nearly half of the families were receiving welfare or Social Security assistance, and more than a quarter of them depended solely on those sources for income.

The first step of BURHA (which in 1968 became the Department of Housing and Community Development) was to work to establish confidence that something positive would actually be done.

"We were told that major changes in the housing, recreation, transportation, education,

Gay Street Before the Mall. Monument East. Old Town Mall. Photos by Housing and Community Development

Architectural Rendering of the Dunbar High School.
Photo by Cultural Arts Program.

and every other aspect of the community would
be taking place," recalls Lucille Gorham, who
became president and later executive director of
Citizens for Fair Housing, a community group
that represents Gay Street I. "The city asked us
to take part in the planning. Frankly, this was a
new experience both for the city and for us.
Never before had the city come to a community
in just that way, requesting that it take part in
planning."

The total rebuilding has taken more than
twelve years and in fact, is still not yet quite
complete.

But in that period certain developments occurred. A new Dunbar Community Senior High
School, containing social programs that served
the community literally from prior to birth
through senior citizenship, was constructed and
put in operation.

All housing in the area that was to be retained
was inspected and rehabilitated, often with use
of loans or grants through city programs.

A total of 537 units of new housing for low-
and moderate-income elderly was constructed.
"I'll never be closer to heaven until I'm pushing
up posies," said Mrs. Sarah Causion of Monument East, the distinctive public housing tower
at the end of Old Town Mall. The other developments are Waters Towers, in Gay Street I,
and Lanvale Tower, in Oliver.

Another 868 new units were built for low–and
moderate–income families. Most of these were
in the Gay Street I area. The Gay Street residents traveled to Washington at the housing
department's invitation to see a recently completed development for moderate–income families. The residents liked what they saw, and the
architect, Collins and Kronstadt, was invited to
design all the new housing for Gay Street I.

One distinctive feature of the tan "corduroy"
block houses is their orientation to open space
in the center of the blocks. The Gay Street
residents also asked that public housing constructed through renewal blend in with the rest
of the neighborhood, and consequently the 60
units of public housing are undistinguishable
from the moderate–income structures built.

In the Oldtown area, the first concentrated
homesteading in the country took place on Stirling Street.

Because the commercial strip in the 400 and
500 blocks of Gay Street was considered basically sound, although in need of assistance, the
city built Old Town Mall, the nation's first inner
city pedestrian shopping mall, and provided
badly needed off-street parking areas. The merchants spent $2 million, much of it financed by
loans arranged by the city, to rehabilitate their
stores. The Belair Market was rehabilitated.

A new stadium was constructed to serve the
community and especially Dunbar High School,

whose teams had previously been obliged to go several miles to the nearest athletic facility.

A new fire station was constructed.

Fifteen new parks or playgrounds were built to serve the area.

A federal Urban Development Action Grant was obtained that will permit rehabilitation or new construction of 252 homes in the Oldtown area, to be sold to owner–occupants.

Two privately operated medical clinics were built, one of them a health maintenance organization serving a major section of East Baltimore. The community has cooperated with the Johns Hopkins Hospital in these ventures.

A major effort was made to assure that the new housing was available to the prerenewal residents of the area. At the suggestion of the Gay Street I residents, each relocated family was given a certificate that would give it priority for the new housing as it opened.

Parallel to the physical revitalization came emergence of a new generation of leadership in the East Baltimore community: Clarence "Du" Burns, who became vice–president of the City Council and chairman of its urban affairs committee; Robert L. Douglass, a leader in Oldtown renewal who became state senator; Nathan Irby of the Gay Street I area, another city councilman; Delegate Hattie Harrison; Lee Douglass, Jr., long–time leader in the Oldtown area.

The renewal programs are not complete, but were being expanded into the Johnston Square area (north of Eager Street) and a section called Middle East (north and east of Johns Hopkins Hospital) in the late seventies. The Somerset Court public housing project, originally opened in 1943, was being prepared for total renovation as the decade closed.

Richard P. Davis

URBAN HOMESTEADING

After World War II, Baltimoreans started moving from the central city to Northwood or Edmondson Village, or to suburban bliss in Towson, Parkville, Cockeysville, Lutherville, Glen Burnie, and Randallstown, ultimately arriving at the paradise of newness at Columbia. Live in the city? Why, when suburban schools and trees and lawns beckoned, when an automobile would take you wherever you wanted, and the Beltway and Jones Falls Expressway were there to drive on?

A few, of course, still thought city life was fine. Tyson Street's petite rowhouses had attracted urban pioneers in the late 1940s; a few others spotted the beauty in the unit block of Twenty-sixth Street during the sixties and one of them thought up the name Charles Village; Bolton Hill, always a downtown residential magnet, changed from the Gin Belt in the war years and fifties into a solid middle-class rock of urbanophiles as renewal and rehabilitation took hold in the sixties. Union Square, H.L. Mencken's old neighborhood, might have grown seedy, but it still retained the charm typical of excellent old houses facing a park. And it was part of an area the city had designated for improvement through housing inspection accompanied by generous loans and grants; so in the late sixties a few property owners began to use the loans extensively to bring the houses into shape again. A community spirit began to develop. The neighborhood used monies it had raised through participating in the first City Fair to start restoring the old square itself.

Thus it had been demonstrated, by the early 1970s, that there were people who wanted to live in the central city; people who enjoyed the idea of restoring an old house for their own use; people who appreciated the value inherent in neighbors living as closely as rowhouses permit, and who saw no particular virtue in driving miles to work each day. Besides people, there were houses. Some had been left by people moving out to the suburbs, and others that older residents wanted to sell as they moved to smaller quarters. The city itself had a stock of vacant houses abandoned by their former owners.

Added to this, Baltimore had an active housing department, headed by an imaginative commissioner, Robert C. Embry, Jr., and supported by a capable staff. The first ceremonial act in 1972 of the new mayor, William Donald Schaefer, was to open an office for a program created to stimulate homeownership in the city. Mr.

Embry assigned Roger M. Windsor, director of the new Homeownership Division, to work closely with residents of in-town neighborhoods, encouraging the people of Tyson Street, Bolton Hill, Union Square, and Federal Hill to seek from the city solutions to the problems peculiar to urban living.

Beginnings of Homesteading. Mr. Windsor was also directed to establish an urban homesteading program under which the city's stock of vacant houses could be sold for a dollar to people willing to rehabilitate so that they meet the standards of the Housing Code and live in them for a specified period.

The homesteading idea, harkening back to the post–Civil War program under which the Great Plains were settled, had been bandied in housing circles in many cities, and at the end of August, 1973, Wilmington, Delaware became the first city to announce a program. They were only a few days ahead of Baltimore. On September 12, 1972, Baltimore's Board of Estimates approved a simple resolution that established the framework for the program: use of the city's tax–sale properties; sale for a nominal dollar; and requirements that the applicant show the capability to carry out the project, make the homestead structure habitable within six months, and then live in it for another 18 months.

Homesteading was announced in September, 1973, and inquiries immediately began to pour in totaling more than 1,000, with over 100 firm applications. Mayor Schaefer accepted a dollar apiece from the first homesteaders and gave each a picture of the house they were buying in its existing condition. The first homesteaders covered a wide spectrum: an army sergeant, teachers, a stockbroker, assistant principal of Boys' Village Training School, a home improver, and a recreational vehicle salesman. The houses were in East Baltimore, in Poppleton and Harlem Park on the west side, and in a neighborhood that was to become one of the most popular for homesteaders, Reservoir Hill.

Stirling Street Homesteading. Actually, Housing and Community Development (HCD) had already established a homesteading program with a slightly different thrust a few weeks before the scattered–site effort began, when a particularly attractive group of houses, all in one block, became available. Forty-two tiny two-story rowhouses face each other across the charming 600 block of Stirling Street, framing a view from Monument Street at the north end that precisely captures Baltimore's downtown skyline. In the late sixties as an urban renewal plan was being developed for Oldtown, one of the lowest–income residential neighborhoods of East Baltimore, preservationists had begged for the block to be saved from the bulldozer. But the residents wanted the street to be torn down and replaced with something new. Besides, a virtual chorus rose in response to the preservationists: you won't come here to live. As the plan was adopted, the residents prevailed. The 1969 renewal ordinance called for demolition and then construction of new subsidized housing. The city bought the existing houses (providing the generous benefits accorded to relocated families).

But in January, 1973, the Nixon Administration declared a moratorium on the construction of all subsidized housing. If the city were to tear down the now–vacant houses, it would not be able to get anything new built. On August 13, a plan to save the block was announced. If enough people could be found to rehabilitate and live in three–fourths of the houses, the city would sell the structures for a dollar apiece. Enthusiasm was immediate. The Land Development Division of HCD, which handled the entire Stirling Street sale, received 400 inquiries and eventually 63 applications. By the end of the year, houses were assigned; two apiece were combined by 18 of the homesteaders, and six others took single houses.

Again, the variety of occupations was striking. The 25 homesteaders included a doctor, the dean of students at Gilman School, an architect, a public welfare supervisor, a computer analyst, an electrical engineer, a nurse. Fourteen of the original Stirling Street group had previously lived in Baltimore City; the balance came from Anne Arundel, Baltimore, Harford, Prince George's, and Montgomery counties, with two from Washington, D.C.

The advantages to come from the mutual reinforcement by homesteading in a group were soon apparent. It may be recorded that the first general agreement among the Stirling Street

Neighbors, as the Oldtown homesteaders called themselves, was that the original facade of the buildings would be restored as well as possible to the original appearance, and that Formstone would be removed from the front of the buildings. The Stirling Streeters cooperated in such ways as buying roofing materials jointly.

Funding. Mr. Windsor believes the simplicity of the original Board of Estimates resolution provided the flexibility for the homesteading program to develop effectively, allowing experimentation to discover the best means of solving the problems encountered. A key feature of Baltimore's homesteading program, the housing department had foreseen, would be funding. One of the most successful housing programs in operation was the federal Section 312 loan program under which some owners could borrow at 3 percent interest up to $15,350 (later raised to $17,000) for rehabilitation. Baltimore had operated the program since 1966 with scarcely a default.

The problem with the Section 312 loans was that they could be used only in urban renewal areas (which would help the Stirling Street group but not many of the scattered–site homesteaders), and management of the program by the federal government was erratic. Funding was sometimes available, sometimes not. In 1972, Embry had proposed, and Mayor Schaefer had agreed, that voters be asked to support a $2 million bond issue for a fund that would supply city loans for rehabilitation anywhere in the city. Initially, the funds under the Rehabilitation Environmental Assistance Loan (REAL) program were lent out at 6 percent, representing the rate at which the city had borrowed the money, plus half a percentage point for the expense of operating the program. Later the rate was increased, but it was kept far below the rate of private improvement or mortgage loans. Through the REAL program, the Section 312 financing, and later the City Housing Assistance Program, city financing became an essential part of the homesteading program.

Homesteading Procedures. Procedures for homesteading were developed. The office at Charles and Mulberry provided homesteaders with lists of available houses that were especially suitable for homesteading, and ballpark estimates of the costs of basic rehabilitation. Cou-

Stirling Street in Need of Restoration, 1973.

ples would take the list and tour until they found something they liked. Applicants were counseled on what homesteading involved—substantial demands of money and time and extensive patience. When the homesteaders formally applied for the house, they were provided extensive financial information. Then the houses were advertised and if more than one qualified bidder wanted a particular house, a lottery was held among applicants. Once the house was awarded, the homesteader received a right to enter and was enabled to make plans and seek contractors' proposals. Steps thereafter included a first interview for discussion of costs and financing; application for a loan if needed; preparation of plans and specifications; selection of a contractor; approval of the loan and establishment of an escrow account; work by the contractor, with periodic city inspections; move–in within six months; and after completion of the two–year period, during which all code violations were corrected, deeding of the house. No city taxes were to be paid during the two–year period, since the homesteader did not own the house.

Short–term Homesteading Results. Happy as many homesteaders became with their projects, almost all found that homesteading was not a process in which one moved easily from A to B to C and then through to Z. Attrition among homesteaders was heavy. By the end of 1974, for instance, 105 houses had been awarded, 25 of them on Stirling Street and 80 on scattered sites. But at the end of 1975, two of the Stirling Street

Stirling Street Before and After, 1973–1976. Photo by Housing and Community Development

group had dropped out and been replaced (the street ended up with 25 homesteaders), and only 32 of the 80 on scattered sites were still in the program. But at the same time, the total awards in the program by the end of 1975 had risen to 127 participants, of whom 87 had obtained financing and started work.

Among those under way were seven out of eight homesteaders in the unit block of Durham Street, the second community homesteading venture, this time in the Washington Hill urban renewal area. Many of the Stirling Street Neighbors were by this time well into rehabilitation. Paul and Marjorie Gasparotti had uncovered a builder's stone dated 1829 in their house as they handled interior demolition. Richard Rohrbaugh had designed spiral brick staircases in his

own house and exciting cathedral ceilings in houses for Judy Bankhead and Deborah McMorris; the latter found herself sporting one of the only fireplaces in a Baltimore bathroom (inoperative, however).

Otterbein Homesteading. The largest group that was waiting to start work at that time was in the Otterbein community, near the Inner Harbor. Like Stirling Street, the 108 Otterbein houses, a century old, had been scheduled for demolition as a part of an urban renewal plan. But Stirling Street had provided evidence that homesteading in a community could work well, and Jane Shipley of the Homeownership Office suggested that homesteading might be appropriate for these structures as well. There were significant differences from Stirling Street. The Otterbein houses were newer, larger, had originally been built (most of them) for more affluent residents, and instead of being in a center-city,

Homesteaders in Otterbein. Photo by Housing and Community Development

low-income neighborhood, were near the beautifully redeveloped Inner Harbor, Federal Hill, South Baltimore, and downtown. The first open house in May, 1975, attracted some 3,000 visitors, and more than 700 applications were received. Applicants could bid on one house only; the most popular received 46 bids. On a hot night at the end of July, applicants packed the Old Otterbein Church, from which the community took its name, for a lottery of the houses. (George King, one of the original scattered–site homesteaders, who by that time was well on his way to completing his house in Harlem Park, was a member of the blue-ribbon committee that screened the applicants on their capability of homesteading and supervised the lottery.)

Homesteading Spreads. One more major area—Barre Circle, 125 homesteading properties southwest of downtown and near the intown campus of the University of Maryland—remained to be homesteaded on a community basis, and this went underway in 1976. In Washington Hill, another cluster of houses was marketed in 1977 and 1978, and among the scattered-site homesteads, major clusters appeared in the Ridgely's Delight and Reservoir Hill neighborhoods. Windsor and William Brosnahan, chief of the City–Owned Property Management Unit (which handled all tax–sale properties and directed all scattered–site homesteading), said that the Homeownership Office had little diffi-

culty finding takers for any houses that came up in any area where a number of homesteaders were already at work.

In 1976, Baltimore also began taking advantage of the Section 810 federal homesteading program, under which the federal Department of Housing and Urban Development turned over to cities a number of properties it had acquired (generally structures whose previous owners lost the properties through FHA mortgage foreclosure proceedings). Baltimore's participation was in the Park Heights area. Houses were generally in better condition than many of the other homesteading structures. Rehabilitation costs were therefore less, and lower-income families could participate.

Who were the homesteaders? At the end of 1977, a survey of 413 active homesteaders showed 118 standard families (husband, wife, and children), 145 singles (97 men and 48 women), 75 husband–and–wife combinations, 44 one–parent–and–children, and 31 related or unrelated adults. The head of the household was probably in his young thirties. If a scattered–site homesteader, he or she was likely to be black (121 to 55), but overall the program had slightly more whites than blacks participating. Overwhelmingly (340 to 69) the homesteaders had rented prior to taking on the homesteading role. Income varied from area to area, with the average in Otterbein, Barre Circle, and Washington Hill areas in excess of $20,000 annually, while the scattered–site homesteaders averaged $15,900. About a third of the homesteaders had moved in from outside of Baltimore.

On the question of income, both Robert Embry and M. J. Brodie, who succeeded him as housing commissioner, were candid. "We have not treated homesteading as a program for low-income families," Brodie once told a group of visiting New Yorkers who had commented adversely on the clear direction toward middle-income families. "It costs a lot to rehabilitate most houses and to make this program work we have provided financing through a generous loan program. But we consider it is crucial to the program to have the loans repaid and one thing we try to assure is that money be loaned to people capable of paying it back." However, to make homesteading achievable for families with lower incomes, the City Housing Assistance Program was established through Baltimore's Community Development Block Grant Program, providing loans at an interest rate keyed to family size and income. A large family with low income could borrow at an interest rate as low as one percent.

Were all homesteaders pleased with the program? Clearly not, as demonstrated by the high dropout rate and by the complaints expressed by many who remained active. The press provided a fairly continuous forum for the complaints, headlining "Homestead Pioneers Suffer Highway Indecision Blues," and "Delays, Errors, Red Tape Snarl Otterbein Homestead." In August, 1976, City Council President Walter S. Orlinsky held a hearing at which some homesteaders spoke out. James Moore, an Otterbein homesteader who was a professional engineer, complained of red tape and what he considered a rigid attitude toward allowing homesteaders to be their own general contractors. They complained of delays in receiving financing and of low estimates that were provided to homesteaders. The housing department responded that the city was providing the houses, cleaned, along with free estimation service, 100 percent rehabilitation loans in most cases, inspectors to assure the work was proceeding properly, professional planning for neighborhoods like Otterbein, and full–time staff assistance. Cost estimates in Otterbein, it was pointed out, had been made a year before the houses were assigned but had averaged 20 percent lower than bids, which was not bad in a period of inflation. But the department promised to take steps to improve the flow of cash to contractors as work was completed.

Commissioner Brodie added: "I know we have a good program, working better than it does almost anywhere else. I know many homesteaders have expressed their pleasure in the program to me. But the nature of homesteading simply has to result in a lot of frustration. It is a terribly difficult process. The city will do the best it can, but I'm sure we will always be accused by some of creating unnecessary delays."

One homesteader who was very pleased with the program and his house acknowledged that at each step of development it became apparent that the cost would be dramatically higher than he and his wife had believed. The cost of rehabilitation mounted from an original estimate of $16,000 to a final figure of some $68,000. "At each step we simply had to reassess and renew our commitment to what we were doing. We're glad we did," he said.

Homesteading: a Success for Baltimore. On June 11, 1978, Mayor Schaefer entertained the homesteaders at a picnic on Federal Hill and announced that Baltimore then had more than 500 homesteaders taking part in the "dollar house" program. About 275 houses were in construction, and 175 of them occupied. Statistics available for other cities showed Dallas, with 225 homesteaders, in second place. Wilmington, which had received extensive publicity when it started its program a few days before Baltimore's, had some 50 participants. Philadelphia had 91, Atlanta 68, Chicago 65, New York 22, and Boston 17. The mayor told the homesteaders that the significance of the program here is less in numbers than in the impetus given to Baltimore with the enthusiasm of homesteaders. "What you have done is to establish a mood for the city, far beyond the presence of an additional 500 families. You have said: 'Living in Baltimore is good, and we are willing to invest ourselves in this effort.' Others have heard you say it, and have followed your lead."

Baltimore has received national and even international acclaim for its urban homesteading program. A major part of Baltimore's presentation before the International Federation for Housing and Planning in Hamburg, Germany, in September, 1978, concerned homesteading—a feature that drew much praise from the distinguished planning group. But some of the highest praise came from the American Institute of Architects, which in June, 1979, made an award to Baltimore for its comprehensive urban design policies. A significant paragraph in the citation read:

Inevitably, a close connection develops between the physical revitalization of a city and a renaissance of the spirit. Civic pride and enthusiasm have also been reborn in Baltimore. In no program does this connection emerge with such clarity as in Urban Homesteading. So far some 500 citizens have agreed to pay a dollar for a vacant city-owned house, to rehabilitate it totally, and to live in it for a period of years. The real investment is far more than a dollar: rehabilitation is costly in money, in the tenacity to struggle through inherently complicated processes, in months of the homesteaders' own labor, and in the form of a total commitment to Baltimore and urban living.

Richard P. Davis

PUBLIC HOUSING

In his second inaugural address in 1937, President Franklin D. Roosevelt observed that a third of the nation was ill-fed, ill-clothed, and ill-housed. He proposed several programs to change those conditions; one of the most successful has become known as public housing.

The public housing program has been controversial from the start, in Baltimore and elsewhere. Here it was strongly opposed by real estate interests, which insisted that low-income tenants would fail to pay their rent, would fail to maintain their homes, and would generally prove a nuisance to the community. Despite such objections, the Housing Authority of Baltimore was legally established in 1937, and by October, 1940, the first development, Edgar Allan Poe Homes, opened in west Baltimore. The early residents proved the critics wrong. Baltimore's public housing program, as a consequence, won a reputation it still holds for being well-managed and well-maintained. The program grew until, by 1979, it was providing a home for more than 50,000 residents who live in 16,000 dwellings in many parts of the city.

The present residents tend to be permanent tenants—in contrast to the original concept of public housing, which was of a temporary home where families might live while in financial straits. The present population has an average income of about $4,000, compared with a city-wide average of $9,600. Nearly 60 percent of the residents are younger than 21, and more than 30 percent of families contain a member who is over 62 or disabled. Families average three persons; the racial composition in 1979 was 88.6 percent black, 11.4 percent white.

The housing takes five basic forms:

1) Low-rise developments in the central city, such as McCulloh, Latrobe, Somerset, Perkins, Gilmor, and Douglass Homes, were built primarily in the 1940s. McCulloh's three-story brick buildings, for example, were opened in August, 1941, on both sides of the 1000 and 1100 blocks of McCulloh Street.

2) Similar low-rise developments were constructed outside the central city, such as Fairfield and Brooklyn in the extreme south of Baltimore, and O'Donnell Heights and Claremont near the eastern edge of the city. Cherry Hill, south of the Hanover Street bridge, with a total of 1,597 units built between 1945 and 1956, is the largest public housing development in the city, making up about half of the entire Cherry Hill community. Several of these low-rise developments were constructed as temporary housing for war workers in the 1940s. Most of the dwellings are brick, but a few are frame; and they tend to be two-story instead of three.

3) High-rise towers for families were built in the 1950s and early 1960s. Because of their size, and the way they dominate the areas where they are located, high-rises—frequently with exterior corridors that provide a "sidewalk in the sky"—have become the public housing stereotype. In Baltimore, these high-rises actually make up only 13 percent of all units. They are in Lafayette Courts, just east of downtown; Lexington Terrace, on Lexington Street just west of downtown; George B. Murphy Homes, on George Street in West Baltimore; and Flag House Courts, near Little Italy. In each case, a number of low-rise units accompany the towers. After a few years of experience with these developments, which concentrate many low-income families in a small area, the city decided not to construct any more high-rise buildings for families. Federal policy followed suit a few years later.

4) Housing for the elderly, however, has been built as high-rises with great success. Starting with Lakeview Tower, which opened just south of Druid Hill Park in 1970, the Housing Authority constructed 15 residential buildings for the elderly during the 1970s. They range from Monument East by the Old Town Mall in the central city, to the tower of Hollander Ridge at the eastern edge of the city, and the mid-rise Bernard E. Mason Apartments west of Leakin Park, and Bel-Park Tower in the northwest. The apartments are equipped with such amenities as grab rails in tubs, ramps for wheelchairs, nonskid floors in the hallways, and extrawide doors. An early consideration was whether the elderly

wanted to live in buildings by themselves, rather than being a part of a community of all ages. The response has been distinctly in favor of the high-rises; the senior citizens have liked the security offered by the buildings; their families can always visit.

5) Vacant houses that cause blight in neighborhoods were rehabilitated so that they became community assets. Since 1970, the Housing Authority has rehabilitated nearly 1,600 units. The program has proved the most desired form of housing, since the residents become a part of the neighborhood in which they are living. This form of public housing is particularly well-suited for larger families; the need for such larger units is particularly pressing.

In addition to its conventional public housing program, the Housing Authority has been participating, since 1975, in a federal program known as Housing Assistance Payments (Section 8). Some 2,000 needy families now live in the private housing market, but pay no more than a quarter of their income for rent; the Section 8 program pays the balance.

Although the city's public housing has been generally successful, there have been some problems. For example, the open lobbies in the high-rise buildings gave nonresidents easy access to the buildings, and elevators were frequently vandalized. During the 1970s, as part of a program to modernize the public housing plant, the lobbies of the high-rises were enclosed, and residents were employed as security guards. Many of the developments, some almost 40 years old, were modernized with new electrical, gas, and water systems, new roofs, and necessary improvements to units. In Murphy Homes, for example, faster-moving vandal-resistant elevators were installed. Some residents of the older developments (notably O'Donnell Heights, Fairfield, and Westport, all constructed as temporary housing during World War II) withheld their rent at the end of 1978 and beginning of 1979 in an effort to call attention to poor conditions. In Rent Court, some of the residents' complaints were sustained, but a number of others were rejected; as the result of an appeal, the cases were ordered retried.

Residents have played an increasingly important role in decisions that affect them. In 1968, a city-wide Resident Advisory Board was established, and resident councils have been encouraged in each development. In 1976, a tenant who was president of the Resident Advisory Board became a member of the Housing Authority Commission, the citizen group that makes policy for public housing.

From the time of its establishment, the Housing Authority has considered that its responsibility toward tenants goes well beyond providing a place to live; this commitment is expressed in the phrase "shelter plus," and was previously the responsibility of the Division of Housing Management, which manages and maintains the units, collects rents, and for years maintained a staff of social service counselors. In the early 1970s, a new division of Social Work Services was established to provide such services as family counseling, youth services, child development, and senior day care for all public housing residents.

Some $21 million is spent on public housing in Baltimore each year. A substantial portion of this comes from the rents paid by residents, based on 25 percent of their income. The balance is provided by federal operating and development subsidies. Unquestionably, public housing provides a far better home than is available at nearly the same rates in the private housing market. Testimony to this is offered by the waiting list of some 25,000 families that have applied for the public housing or Section 8 programs, or both. Groups such as the St. Ambrose Housing Assistance Center demand public housing for residents because they view some housing conditions in Baltimore as intolerable, despite massive community development/urban renewal efforts. Even though Baltimore's public housing program has its problems, officials from many other cities have used it as a model.

Richard P. Davis

CPHA's IMPACT, 1941–1969: A PERSONAL APPRAISAL

In 1957, the Health and Welfare Council of Central Maryland presented the Citizens Planning and Housing Association (CPHA) its organizational achievement award for having "moved continuously and imaginatively on many fronts, and having stimulated Baltimore's businessmen, officials, school children, and citizens at large to a higher civic awareness. It has pioneered in broad human renewal, as well as in the physical rehabilitation of Baltimore, and has spurred and complemented the work of other groups with similar goals."

In 1966, on CPHA's twenty-fifth anniversary, the *Evening Sun* paid tribute to the "band of citizens who have intelligently foreseen and responded to the residential phase of this metropolitan area's desires and deficiencies...using only its own resources, but applying a strong and canny touch to the pressure points of officialdom and the public conscience, CPHA has attained a personality and influence without parallel in the life of contemporary Baltimore. It has bettered the look and the livability of the city and by its example other cities besides."

The roots of the organization go back to 1936 with the publication in the *Evening Sun* of a summary of my work *A Social Study of Wards 5 and 10,* published by the Health and Welfare Council. This survey apparently helped alert the city to its slum problems and tried to document the relationship between bad housing, disease, crime, and other social ills. The newspaper then proceeded to inaugurate an almost daily campaign of horror stories with pictures by its "architectural correspondent" highlighting individual dilapidated houses and their occupants. These pictures inspired and goaded municipal agencies (particularly the Health and Welfare Departments) into action.

The small number of citizens who started the CPHA in 1941 had literally no resources except their own enthusiasm. Their main purpose was to change the community's attitude from indifference about its slums to concern and action. They dedicated themselves to eliminating Baltimore's slums and assuring each Baltimorean the dignity of a decent home in a pleasant environment.

The scope of CPHA's activities in the housing field started with problems of low-income housing, but gradually widened to include planning, zoning, parks and open spaces, transportation, air pollution and other subjects, and covered the area of Baltimore County, as well as the city.

Through the years, CPHA never wavered in its position that citizen action is a critical element in any program aimed at better housing and planning. Widespread citizen participation in community action and the development of responsible citizen leaders to serve on key committees, boards, and legislative bodies were considered fundamental to its strength and influence.

From 1941 onward, CPHA was in the forefront of all the housing and planning reforms that official Baltimore initiated. These included the Baltimore Plan of Housing Law Enforcement (based on the 1941 ordinance on the Hygiene of Housing),* public housing, urban renewal, the development of a city planning department in Baltimore, a new zoning ordinance (in the early seventies), and a regional planning council. In 1955, it helped set up the Greater Baltimore Committee, the essential element in the rehabilitation of the downtown business area and the waterfront. CPHA was instrumental in setting up Baltimore's Housing Court that was copied in other cities. It initiated the drive (accomplished in 1947) to reform the once ineffective and politics-ridden Housing Authority and, later, lent its support to the consolidation of the city's renewal agencies into the Baltimore Urban Renewal and Housing Agency (BURHA), which was set up in 1956. In 1968, CPHA was a strong force in helping to achieve one overall housing and community development agency with a CPHA volunteer as commissioner.

Recent articles in the daily press have given the impression that the "neighborhood movement" in Baltimore began in the 1960s. This is not true. In 1937, the Health and Welfare Council formed a neighborhood group in Wards 5 and 10. This group later developed into the city's area project movement under the sponsorship of the Department of Welfare that employed at least five community organizers in blighted areas to help residents "fight juvenile deliquency." Since its formation in 1941, CPHA worked so diligently at forming and assisting neighborhood groups that by 1968 it had 146 neighborhood associations as members. In November, 1969, CPHA was so well known for its neighborhood

* As amended to include bathtubs the Bathtub Ordinance went into effect on January 1, 1956.

work that WJZ–TV said editorially that it was the "most effective private organization in the area" and hoped that it would continue its work to the point that it would become a partner with every neighborhood group in the city.

By 1969, CPHA was known as "doctor to neighborhoods." Through its experience over the years working as volunteer community organizers in blighted areas with city agencies, CPHA gained vast experience and knowledge on "improvement" tools that could be used by neighborhood groups. The main tool was expert knowledge of city agencies and ways and means to galvanize their services for the use of neighborhoods. CPHA supplied its member improvement associations with zoning and liquor–alert-

ing services. It wrote papers on zoning, how to form and operate improvement, rather than protective, associations. CPHA urged absentee churches and businesses to become active residents of neighborhoods, so that local civic groups would be stronger. It encouraged schools to be active in neighborhoods by jointly sponsoring, with the Department of Education, yearly school neighborhood improvement programs.

CPHA helped form improvement groups in many areas, especially Homewood, Mt. Vernon, Harlem Park, and in the Mt. Royal–Fremont areas. In 1955, with the help of the Episcopal

Rehabilitating Baltimore at 2300 Eutaw Place in 1980. Photo by John Clark Mayden

Diocese of Maryland, CPHA set up the Lafayette Square Community Center in Harlem Park and showed the residents how to force city agencies to plan with them and not for them. In Mt. Royal, CPHA was successful in assisting in the successful campaign for code enforcement, urban renewal, the John Street Park, and the new school. CPHA helped reorganize and strengthen the Mt. Royal Improvement Association. It joined with it in forming the Maryland Committee on the State Office Building that succeeded, after a year's campaign, in persuading Governor McKeldin in 1959 to expand the State Office Building in the Bolton Hill area. The office building complex has been the most stabilizing force in this threatened part of the city.

As a direct result of CPHA's work in South Baltimore, Pilot, Harlem Park, and Mt. Royal areas, the city (the Baltimore Urban Renewal and Housing Agency) hired a staff of professional community organizers to do what CPHA had been doing for the city in a volunteer capacity. Later another city agency (the Planning Department) hired neighborhood planners. Eventually, the city set up mayor's stations and multipurpose centers. The CPHA–sponsored Lafayette Square Center became an official multi purpose center.

In 1941, when CPHA was founded, Baltimore was indifferent to the slums and the conditions under which black people lived. One might express this attitude as "Negroes just lived in conditions like that and always would." CPHA vowed to change this. The organization was founded on a biracial basis and was the first citywide civic organization to have dinner meetings with blacks and whites in attendance. Black and white had the opportunity to work together on common interests and the satisfaction of achieving mutual objectives. As a result of good public exposure, many of CPHA's black members became housing executives, judges, members of commissions and boards, and legislative bodies.

CPHA had a very close working relationship with the Urban League. One of these joint operations was to find additional land area where black people might live. No new housing had ever been built for them (one–fifth of the population lived in one–fiftieth of the city land area). The fight to find land in the Herring Run area for black war workers was unsuccessful. Instead, Cherry Hill, a much less desirable site, was obtained and the community planned in 1943. For many years, CPHA worked with Cherry Hill residents, assisting them to improve their area and be less isolated from the general community.

When desegregation was made possible, there was no question that Baltimore's Housing Authority and School Board would comply. CPHA had influenced attitudes in both agencies, particularly the Housing Authority. CPHA helped the School Board by having held numerous biracial workshops. The first one ever held by the Department of Education was run by CPHA in the Pilot Area.

CPHA spent considerable time working on blockbusting and integration in the Bolton Hill and Mt. Royal areas. Because of this, it was asked to extend this work to other areas. Having insufficient staff for this job, CPHA joined with neighborhood groups to encourage the Greater Baltimore Committee to set up a new civic agency, Baltimore Neighborhoods, Inc., which is still working in the integration field.

Steady growth from the penniless organization of 1941 to an organization in 1969 with two offices, one in the city and one in the county, showed the effectiveness of CPHA principles and programs. CPHA raised $75,000 in 1968. It had 2700 individual members, 146 improvement associations, and 300 businesses. Five hundred people served on 50 committees, some of which (education, zoning, planning) had been in existence for over 26 years.

Probably CPHA's most lasting contribution to Baltimore's renaissance was its training of "technical" volunteers who later became community leaders. It carried on what might be called a college for adults where volunteers learned by "doing." They performed such functions as making surveys, taking appeals, public speaking to neighborhood groups and legislative bodies, watchdogging city agencies, appearing on radio and television, publishing booklets, etc. Lawyers, who made up CPHA's largest body of volunteers, did all kinds of free legal work. One large law firm sent CPHA each year its young lawyers to train in community work.

Starting with the city's present mayor, CPHA volunteers today can be found anywhere and everywhere. They have, or are serving, as members and chairmen of art galleries, historical museums, housing agencies, and planning boards in the city, county, and region. Members and chairmen of school and library boards, top planning and housing officials, presidents of colleges and civic organizations, city, county, and state legislators including a member of the United States Senate, judges, and presidents of neighborhood improvement associations—all have included CPHA volunteers.

In the late sixties, the city changed and so did CPHA. With these changes, some of CPHA's programs disappeared. As Baltimore continues its renaissance, the question arises: should any of these programs be revived and, if so, how?

Frances Morton Froelicher

CPHA SINCE 1970

The 1970s was a period of planning and housing transition for Baltimore. New developments caused new problems and the Citizens Planning and Housing Association continued to serve the changing needs of its metropolitan constituency.

Perhaps one of CPHA's most viable contributions in the seventies was helping to turn the dream of Inner Harbor revitalization into a concrete and steel reality. Harborplace opened on July 2, 1980. CPHA had supported the project on the 1978 ballot. Prior to this ratification, CPHA formed a committee that undertook an extensive study of how to utilize most effectively the entire Inner Harbor area. Through research, surveys, and debate, the Inner Harbor Committee developed recommendations for the project. It concluded that retail development should be confined to the northwest corner of the Inner Harbor. Aesthetically, the committee wanted to preserve the impression of open space throughout the design of the project. They recommended that Harborplace be limited to three stories in height. Concentrating on how the public could benefit best the committee decided that Inner Harbor development should include 24-hour, year-round access by the public and

that sufficient facilities should be provided for their use. Also, they concluded there was a need for the construction of a pedestrian bridge, as well as for the integration of a downtown people mover to make the harbor more easily accessible. The committee recommended the installation of information kiosks and directories to emphasize not only the Inner Harbor attractions but also places of interest in major downtown areas.

Besides its work on the Inner Harbor project, CPHA has been influential in planning two other recent major building ventures. The National Aquarium in Baltimore opened in August 1981. CPHA has worked long and hard to educate the public on the desirability of that project. In addition, the association's Convention Center report advocated the construction of that facility, which opened in October, 1979.

CPHA's efforts towards encouraging Baltimore's renaissance have not been limited to bricks and mortar. Late in 1969, a new group, the Committee for a Livelier Baltimore, organized to generate a city spirit. Paint-ins, picnics, and plans for a publication gave citizens a chance to participate in visible projects aimed to instill a sense of Baltimore pride. Discussion was held about organizing a city-wide neighborhood festival. Several members of that first committee went on to organize the first Baltimore City Fair.

The committee did produce an exclusive Baltimore publication, *BAWLAMER!—An Informal Guide to a Livelier Baltimore.* For many people, working on *BAWLAMER!* serves as an introduction to CPHA. In 1979, the committee celebrated Baltimore's two-hundred fiftieth anniversary with a new book, *Beyond the White Marble Steps—A Look at Baltimore's Neighborhoods.*

Although Baltimore's pride had been somewhat resurrected, housing problems persisted through the 1970s. Code enforcements and the operation of an effective Housing Court required the constant vigilance of CPHA volunteers.

In Baltimore County, CPHA continues to work in the areas of entitlement, growth management, preservation of open space, facilities usage, and open housing. As 1980 approached, CPHA continued, though unsuccessfully, its efforts to obtain grant entitlement status for the county. The grant status would enable Baltimore County to receive $6 million each year in federal Community Development Block Grant funds.

Mortgage monitoring has always been a CPHA activity. In the 1970s, the association documented that the United States government's lending practices worked against urban housing. The government was forced to change to a loan policy that would encourage rather than deter the development of urban housing.

The focus of the Citizens Planning and Housing Association in the 1980s is difficult to define. CPHA's strength for the past 40 years has been its independence and its ability to respond to the changing needs of the community. It continues to serve as a training ground for tomorrow's leaders and provides an arena for individual citizens to make an impact on their environment. CPHA's activism serves as a "catalyst for progress"—providing avenues outside of the strictures of government to utilize and channel the energy and creativity of individuals. Its wide, diverse membership reflects its commitment to better the quality of life in metropolitan Baltimore.

Leslie Rehbein Marqua and Patty Watts

OPENING
THE UMBRELLA TO PROTECT
THE NEIGHBORHOODS

Many Baltimore neighborhoods are well-organized. Citizens across the socio-economic spectrum have been collectively confronting issues affecting them. They have helped create programs for youth to meet educational and emotional deficits and to provide job training. They have pressured commercial property owners and public agencies alike into submission to the popular will and as often they have used gentle persuasion to reach their goals. They have researched and lobbied issues as disparate as school funding, housing speculation, nursing homes, and highway construction. No opponent is too large, or issue too small, to be taken on by

an effectively involved Baltimore citizenry through community organizations.

Such organizations take various forms, each suited to the needs and resources of the community. Organized groups range in scale from block clubs to corporations that deal with entire sections of the city. The latter are known as umbrella organizations because they are federations of neighborhood groups, usually employing professional organizers.

The nine umbrella groups listed below are sizable in membership and endowment. They are funded by private sources such as the Johns Hopkins University, United Fund, and others; and by public sources such as Baltimore Department of Housing and Community Development, VISTA, and others.

These umbrella groups maintain full-time professional staffs that are responsible directly to local member groups as well as to representative boards of directors.

Northwest Baltimore Corporation. The Northwest Baltimore Corporation (NWBC) was founded in 1968 through the joint effort of the Associated Jewish Charities, Associated Catholic Charities, and an informed group of Protestant ministers. Its first president was Eugene Feinblatt, and its first director was Chuck Cacace.

NWBC grew out of the recognition that there was a need to develop effective tools to preserve and improve local neighborhoods, and to promote understanding and cooperation among the many diverse groups living in the area. The residents needed a voice in decision–making in city agencies and private institutions that affected them. Existing services and programs needed improvement, and new ones needed to be developed.

Two major contracts have been negotiated by NWBC in addition to its other accomplishments. In 1974, it was one of three community groups in the city to be awarded a contract by the Mayor's Office of Manpower Resources to establish a Manpower Service Center. The following year, NWBC entered into contract with the Urban Services Agency for the administration and operation of the Pimlico Multipurpose Center.

Park Heights Community Corporation. Park Heights Community Corporation (PHCC) was chartered in 1974, to be the consultant organi-

Representatives of Community Organizations Building Booths. Photo by Documentary Photographic Project

zation to the Baltimore City Department of Housing and Community Development in the rehabilitation of the Park Heights Urban Renewal Area. PHCC is the official project area committee (PAC) for the area bounded by Northern Parkway and Druid Park Drive, Greenspring and Wabash avenues. The organization has expanded its role of services through rat control, crime prevention, neighborhood cleanups, and a community newspaper.

Communities Organized to Improve Life. Communities Organized to Improve Life (COIL) was incorporated in 1975 after a year of operation in the form of a steering committee that studied the problems of youth. Henry F. Yumatz, Olive Bugarin, and Ann Richmond were the incorporating individuals. Serious disturbances in June, 1973, had galvanized neighborhood groups in Southwest Baltimore into meeting with each other and with the city. Crime, deterioration of housing, widespread low income, and the lack of adequate health care were motivating concerns out of which COIL emerged. COIL runs a Youth Diversion Program that helps young offenders referred by the juvenile courts. It has also worked on gaining housing subsidies under HUD's Section 8.

The Greater Homewood Community Corporation. The Greater Homewood Community Corporation (GHCC) includes neighborhood groups within an area bounded by 25th Street and Cold Spring Lane, Greenmount Avenue and the Jones Falls Expressway. It was incorporated in 1969 after two years of study sponsored by the Johns Hopkins University and the United States Office of Education. Dea Kline represented the university in the initial planning process. Attention was first given to the impact on the community of expansion of the university and of Union Memorial Hospital. From this limited concern in 1972, GHCC testified before the Public Service Commission against utility rate hikes, gaining a favorable response for the organization. In 1976, various block clubs were organized.

South Baltimore Coalition of Peninsula Organizations. The South Baltimore Coalition of Peninsula Organizations (COPO) encompasses 35 member groups, eight of which have been added since its founding in 1976. COPO emerged initially out of concern with the threat of the destruction of the Sharp–Leadenhall area by the construction of an expressway. Its formation was also a response to the indifference of landlords, which led to an increasing number of housing vacancies.

An eating–together program for senior citizens was developed. COPO succeeded in the closing of a nuisance–ridden tavern. It has recently begun a program of informing residents of the problems of housing speculation in the area.

Northeast Community Organization. The Northeast Community Organization (NECO) began in 1969 through the efforts of community leaders and area churches. Monsignor Clare O'Dwyer of St. Matthew's Church was a key figure in putting the organization together. Harry Brunett was the first director.

Realtors began a blockbusting campaign in the late sixties. Because of this, NECO was formed. It approached landlords and realtors, and these racial tactics were soon curbed.

NECO was also instrumental in forming the Govans Neighborhood Housing Service.

Through Northeast, Inc., NECO continues to provide incentives to realtors to help maintain an integrated community.

Harbel. Harbel, incorporated in 1970 with 75 member organizations, covers the area of the Harford and Belair roads corridor. The first coordinator was the Reverend David Wecht and the first board president was William Clark. Representatives of 13 churches formed the original steering committee.

Motivating concerns of the founders were the inadequacy of services in the area, zoning, and the threat of racial instability as a result of realtor scare tactics and panic selling. Harbel's efforts were critical in the passage of City Council Ordinance 680, which deals with zoning regulations. Also to its credit are a drug abuse prevention program and the development of the Mayor's Herring Run Advisory Committee, a mental health center, and Mercy–Harbel Primary Health Center.

East Baltimore Community Corporation. The East Baltimore Community Corporation (EBCC) was founded in 1969. Its founding chairman of the board and president (formerly called executive director) were and are today Clarence "Du" Burns and Robert L. Douglass, respectively. EBCC was formed out of the desire to develop comprehensive health care systems for residents of East Baltimore. The corporation has worked in conjunction with the Johns Hopkins Hospital to develop such facilities as the East Baltimore Medical Center. Part of the center includes a prepaid health delivery system in the form of a Health Maintenance Organization. It is recognized as a pioneer in efficient community health care.

Southeast Community Organization. The Southeast Community Organization was formed in 1969 by Betty Hyatt, Gloria Aull, and Jack Gleason. This group came into existence out of its opposition to expressway construction that would have cut a swath across the southeastern part of the city. Since then, SECO, with its 80 member organization, has initiated a drug program and has helped bring about various block clubs. It has successfully fought to bring city funds into its neighborhoods. SECO also staffed citizens' groups that defeated the proposed prison ship and the proposed prison in the Continental Can Building. SECO has also established an inflation fighter program to help lower the cost of living to participating individuals.

Dan Mausner

THE MAGIC OF PRESERVATION

Mayor Theodore R. McKeldin had favored a city commission to preserve historical, aesthetic, and cultural properties; but before one could be created, legislation was necessary. The Historic Area Zoning Act was passed by the Maryland legislature in 1961 and the Maryland Historical Trust was created to distribute federal and state funds for historic preservation.

On May 21, 1964, City Council Ordinance 229 established the Commission for Historical and Architectural Preservation (CHAP). Composed of nine members, including architects, art historians, and citizens–at–large, CHAP was empowered to control all exterior alterations to buildings, including demolition and new buildings on vacant land in a historic district. CHAP approval was required for exterior changes, even paint color, which sometimes elicited emotional response from those standing on the principle "a man's home is his castle."

By 1966, volunteers had completed a survey of historic places throughout Baltimore city. Some historically or architecturally valuable structures were not located in districts qualifying for historic status. As a result, Ordinance 939 was effected in 1967. By creating historic preservation zoning, the sphere of the commission was enlarged to include any part of the city. And by specifying a landmark list of properties for preservation, individual structures could be designated for preservation, whether or not located in a historic district.

To allow the public an effective voice for each project, each historic district is designated by separate City Council ordinance. Such historic districts were first proposed by their own residents. Each year a new one was named: Bolton Hill (1967), Seton Hill (1968), Dickeyville (1969);

Old and New Side by Side. Photo by Betty Redifer

and others followed. By 1971, the first 12 landmarks were designated. In the administration of Mayor Thomas D'Alesandro III the commission's efforts saved historic structures in "urban renewal" (not historic) areas.

The grass–roots approach, according to CHAP staff, is the major element in the success of the preservation program in Baltimore. "It takes into account the people living in the area." Though not in the original ordinance procedure, a citizen may write to the mayor or CHAP requesting nomination of a district. A majority of the property owners, or tenants, may petition for designation. An example of this approach is Bolton Hill. A small group of residents (owners and tenants) created a revolving fund, incorporated, and petitioned the City Council to create a historic district in the neighborhood. Some private renovation was already underway. CHAP found this "a better way of doing things," and the process became a model.

CHAP obtained some grants under the "open space money" federal program. A federal grant was obtained to restore the City Hall dome. The City Hall was placed on the National Register in 1973 as a historic landmark, and the restoration was now to include the whole building. A series of time–lapse photographic slides by Fil Sibley documented the work in progress on City Hall.

The intensive period of study required for historic designation tends to impede development of urban renewal areas. Mayor William Donald Schaefer favors an extensive federally funded urban renewal building program, especially to provide public and senior citizen housing. When an area is awaiting historic designation, and at the same time is considered eligible for urban renewal funds under the renewal program, some tension results. But CHAP remains a successful operation under Schaefer's administration.

Before disposal of city-owned properties, CHAP reviews plans, surveys structures, assists in marketing historic buildings, acts as consultant to developers, performs administrative procedures, assists property owners and developers in obtaining historical status for eligible buildings, and recommends properties to the federal funding agency based upon historical review and environmental impact statements under Section

Lloyd Street Synagogue after Renovation. Photo by Morton Oppenheimer

106 environmental review compliance reports. Owners must comply with the Department of the Interior's standards for rehabilitation, under the Heritage, Conservation, and Recreation Service. Application for status is processed initially by the Historic Preservation Office at the Maryland Historical Trust. In this way, private, city, state, and federal levels act to assure that standards for historical designation are met.

Historic designation makes buildings eligible for various federal preservation program funds and protects the investment of buyers of the several thousand properties located in historic districts. Tax incentives allowed by Internal Revenue Service encourage incorporation of existing buildings with profit–generating potential into the environment. The Tax Reform Act of 1976 allows owners of income–producing certified local or national historic structures to amortize the costs of approved rehabilitation over a five–, rather than a 15–year, period; or, if the cost of rehabilitation substantially exceeds the cost of acquisition, the owner may take accelerated depreciation. Such recycling of existing buildings has proved cost–saving per square foot over erection of new "sterile" buildings.

By 1979, CHAP activity in neighborhoods was perceived in terms of renaissance rather than as a threat to long–time residents of a district. The number of historic districts was doubled (five to ten) in a six–year period; and some districts have been enlarged, such as Mount Vernon and Union Square.

The most recent revitalization is conversion of industrial properties in the Loft District, located near the harbor, into apartments. The area contains seven historic buildings, including Davidge Hall (University of Maryland Medical School), built in 1812, the oldest building in continuous use for medical education in the United States. It also includes the greatest concentration of warehouses, lofts, and "vertical manufactories" in Maryland, circa 1850–1910. The Loft District is linked to Baltimore's industrial importance and the style of its buildings exemplifies historic American commercial architecture. Development of the area is carried forward through cooperation with the city's Department of Housing and Community Development.

The Salvage Depot is another preservation activity. It was created in 1975 to recycle materials such as bathtubs, paneling, mantels, stained glass windows, chandeliers, and doors from buildings before rehabilitation or demolition. The pieces are sold to people rehabilitating homes or buildings in Baltimore city only—to "those who are making a commitment to the city."

Most recently, the commission has begun development of a program to revitalize unoccupied school buildings. Six schools have been nominated for historic status. They are scheduled to be adapted for residential use.

In addition to its preservation activity, the commission is developing educational programs. Through cooperation with the Department of Education, imaginative programs to "sensitize and educate children to neighborhoods and historic preservation," have been organized. The GATE (Gifted and Talented Education) program offers "mystery tours" where children may touch, experience, and physically explore buildings. They are encouraged to preserve textures or decoration by taking rubbings of surfaces. "Blind walks," where one partner leads another who is blindfolded and to whom he describes what he sees, provide a different sense perception of the structures and the city's heritage than a simple sightseeing tour.

A historical marker program has been instituted and integrated into the city's sign-making operation. Maps, prints of historic locations, and photographs are incorporated into small signs at appropriate locations.

Center Stage at Night. Photo by Richard Anderson

According to Barbara Hoff, former executive director of the commission, "The whole awareness of preservation has expanded. People are recognizing their own history, neighborhoods' history, and the city's history . . . that it is something unique and important to preserve. This does not preclude the new. Baltimore and its neighborhoods have to grow. Growth means change. It is a matter of bringing sensitivity to what is the best way to create change."

Marie Lehnert

The Salvage Depot

The Salvage Depot, opened to the public on November 22, 1975, was the first city-sponsored warehouse for the sale of architectural remnants in the nation. The first coordinator was Robert Hooke, a Stirling Street homesteader. He and his three-man crew rolled up their shirtsleeves and engaged in the legitimized plunder of city-owned vacant houses. They retrieved irreplaceable treasures like Victorian mantels, leaded and stained glass, squares of marble vestibule tiles, and marble and brownstone mantelpieces. They rescued Oxford gray slate fireplaces from Washington Hill, a cast-iron water heater out of the Shot Tower, and accoutrements from the now-razed old St. Mary's Seminary building.

"The idea," said Mayor Schaefer in announcing plans for the depot on April 18, 1975, "is to salvage whatever can be reused. It is an attempt to recycle our limited resources and at the same time preserve some of the unique aspects of older buildings." The depot was also established as an effort to stop illegal and dangerous pilfering by private individuals.

Numerous city agencies cooperated to smooth the way for the depot, which is operated by the city's Commission for Historical and Architectural Preservation (CHAP).

The architectural artifacts are being reused by renovators, who found them in the unpretentious depot at 213 West Pratt Street. Purchasers must show proof of city residency before they are permitted to buy anything.

Changes in the depot's operation were initiated in November, 1978, by its manager, John Friery. Although the premise for the depot remains, Friery expanded its functions to cover four new facets:

1. The depot would serve as a source of information with a bulletin board listing articles, services, and exchanges. A dentist may exchange a filling for a baluster, for example.

2. The depot would become a community place of exchange to "buy, sell, swap, and wheel and deal."

3. In a flea–market context, space would be rented for artisans to sell their crafts, thus merging the old with the new.

4. Neighborhood associations would have the option of organizing garage sales on the rear platform, free of charge, which would increase foot traffic within the depot.

Friery believes the salvaged remnants of demolished buildings are precious historic relics. Museums no longer have priority in purchasing them, because the idea is that salvaged accoutrements should be "living archives," used as they were meant to be, as opposed to being stored or displayed in an artificial environment.

It is unknown how long the articles will keep flowing into the depot. Its future is unpredictable now that the trend is toward renovation, rather than demolition. Items are becoming more scarce. But it is comforting to know that those rare, salvaged items will stay within Baltimore either way. As Friery says, "They belong to us. . .all of us."

Laren E. Stover

Downtown

A CHANGING DOWNTOWN

By the mid-1950s, Baltimore's aging downtown core faced problems that threatened its continuing economic viability. Many structures were rapidly growing obsolete due to a national trend away from manufacturing and centrally located department stores which had always been mainstays of Baltimore's economy.

The city's population base was shifting at the same time as its economy was changing. The construction of the Beltway and the availability of FHA mortgages made suburban living possible for thousands of former city dwellers. The loss of middle–income, white residents to the suburbs depressed the retail market downtown to the point where many shops were near failure. At the same time, the poor, mainly black population in the inner city was increasing. The prospects of growing social stress and upheaval faced the city's business and government leaders.

The effect of all these forces was that downtown was increasingly shunned by its former users.

It was against this backdrop that an ambitious plan for downtown revitalization was put forward by the private sector in 1956.

This plan was near realization by 1980. It is easy to forget that the course of the redevelopment of downtown in the last two decades has been marked by starts and stops, ventures that succeeded and others that failed. There has been an interplay between deliberate decision, economic constraint, and social and political movements of the times. The overall course of this redevelopment reflects the entrepreneurial dynamic that was its mainspring. The success of the partnership of business and government in the redevelopment rested on the willingness of

Downtown Baltimore, Before Charles Center, 1958.
Photo by M. E. Warren

government to tailor its development activity to the interests of business, and on the growing confidence of business that their investments would be secure. A wide array of federal aid (ranging from loan guarantees to direct grants) virtually eliminated the economic risk faced by private developers. Once given such financial assurances, the private sector joined the government in a program to revitalize downtown.

Government played a fourfold role. First, it built the physical infrastructure needed to entice private development to Baltimore. The public improvements included new streets and expressways, a rapid transit line, a pedestrian walkway system, public open spaces, and an array of special amenities. Second, government strengthened its investment in public institutions in the downtown area. These institutions—

the University of Maryland, the State Office Complex, the University of Baltimore, City Hall Municipal Center, and the Community College of Baltimore—served as anchors for private activity which helped to stabilize and improve the environment for private investment. Third, government initiated some of the basic concepts underlying the downtown development plans and offered broad administrative assistance to the private sector. This help included assembling redevelopment sites, providing low-cost development loans and loan guarantees, and coordinating the myriad interests involved in complex development activity. Finally, government integrated the citizenry into the development process through such means as conducting electoral campaigns for development loans and sponsoring festivals in downtown renewal areas.

It was the private sector, however, that was the motivating force behind the development activity. Through the Greater Baltimore Committee and the Committee for Downtown, plans

Downtown Baltimore After Charles Center, 1976.
Photo by M. E. Warren

were formalized for Charles Center, the Inner Harbor, and the entire MetroCenter area. While government might coordinate, cajole, restrain, and encourage developers, it was these private forces that ultimately determined which project got off the drawing boards.

Certain events have been critically important in the recent history of downtown Baltimore. Among them are:

Mount Vernon Renewal Project. With its fine squares, handsome monuments, and elegant homes, Mount Vernon had long been one of Baltimore's most fashionable communities. In the 1950s, the area began to show signs of the neglect and deterioration that was evident through downtown. In response, the city initiated the Mount Vernon Renewal Project in 1964. It was the first such effort in the country to use rehabilitation and restoration successfully, rather than demolition and reconstruction, as

tools for revitalizing an urban area. The project combined the incentive of low–cost home improvement loans with the powers of code enforcement to rehabilitate 1,900 residential units in the area surrounding the Washington Monument. This strategy was remarkably successful. Had this program been unavailable, one of the city's most historic areas might have suffered irreparable decay.

Charles Center. Conceived in 1956, this was the showcase project by which the business community first tested the feasibility of downtown redevelopment. Purposely limited in scale and strategically located between the financial and retail districts, Charles Center proved successful beyond expectations. Its success provided the impetus for the much larger Inner Harbor project and the MetroCenter Plan for the entire downtown area.

Inner Harbor Project. For years, Baltimore had turned its back to its waterfront, which was clogged with working commerce and polluted with industrial and commercial waste. Access to the harbor was blocked because roads were built right up to the water's edge. The Inner Harbor project changed all this. The concept for the project had been put forth in the early 1950s and remained a city objective until its realization in the 1970s. By completely rebuilding the downtown shoreline, the project transformed the waterfront into the focal point of the entire region. Moreover, the Inner Harbor project has unleashed development forces that promise to transform the entire center city through rehabilitation and new construction over the next decade.

MetroCenter Plan. Unveiled at the annual meeting for the Greater Baltimore Committee in 1970, this plan provided a framework for the development that was then occurring and projected to occur throughout downtown. It incorporated the Charles Center and Inner Harbor plans and foreshadowed the need for a retail revitalization program. It was not a traditional grand master plan, but an opportunistic portrayal showing where development was likely to take place and how various projects might be effectively coordinated. As much as anything else, its significance was that it reflected the confidence that such a plan could be put forth for the entire downtown.

Adoption of the 3A Modified Expressway System. Unlike prior proposals, the 3A configuration routed three interstate highways around, not through, the downtown. This allowed the access desired by downtown business interest without permanently scarring the city center. The Schaefer administration's dogged determination to build the system despite fierce opposition from a broad alliance of community groups effectively squelched a 30-year controversy that threatened to jeopardize development activity for many more years.

Lexington Mall. The completion of the two-block-long shopping mall on Lexington Street in 1974 marked the first step in a long–term effort to strengthen the city's traditional retail core. It set the stage for the more extensive redevelopment that is likely to occur in the 1980s around Lexington Market as a result of a concerted marketing effort and the opening of the Lexington Market rapid transit station. As of this writing, developer David H. Murdock is completing preliminary negotiations with city officials regarding the development of property near the Lexington Mall subway stop. His project is expected to include substantial office space as well as retail space.

City Hall Renovation. As important as the restoration work itself, this project demonstrated the willingness of Baltimore voters to make a substantial outlay of tax dollars for historic preservation. All $9 million—$1 million for the restoration of the dome alone—was raised through the sale of city bonds, which required voter approval.

Convention Center. The Convention Center was seen as a linchpin in the new Baltimore economy, one built on tourism and the convention trade. Without the Convention Center there would likely have been no subsequent commitments to new hotels, the National Aquarium, and Harborplace. Yet up to the eleventh hour, the state's decision to fund the center was extremely shaky. Only the efforts of the procity, probusiness, Mandel administration finally made it possible. The convention center groundbreaking occurred in 1977 and construction was completed in 1979.

Voter Approval of Harborplace. Albeit not without serious controversy, the decision of voters to devote 3.1 acres of highly prized harbor shoreline for a commercial venture dramatically demonstrated how effective the Schaefer administration and its private sector partners could be at integrating Baltimore residents into the downtown development process. In approving Harborplace, voters set the stage for the next phase of downtown development, one that would make the downtown area a year-round activity center for the entire region as well as a place where increasing numbers of middle-income professionals would choose to live.

While it is well to consider the projects that succeeded, it is also useful to remember those that failed, for their absence shapes the downtown as much as those that ultimately were completed. Downtown would have been quite different *if* a 1950s proposal to build a Civic Center and parking lot on a landfill in the middle of the Inner Harbor had not failed; *or if* the 14-lane, Lev Zetlin & Associates "tension bridge" had been built across the Inner Harbor as proposed in a 1967 expressway plan; *or if* the Maryland Port Administration's 1972 proposal for a cruise ship terminal west of Little Italy had proved economically feasible; *or if* financing had been found for the Kenzo Tenge or the Louis Kahn development proposals for the Inner Harbor. All of these were serious ventures that came close to realization. All would have had a major impact on downtown.

What about the future of downtown Baltimore? What will be the critical projects during the next two decades? No answer can be given to these questions without looking first at the project that virtually ushered in the 1980s—Harborplace—for it marks a turning point in the redevelopment process.

Harborplace symbolizes the new direction envisioned by Baltimore's business and government leaders. Their vision sees downtown Baltimore becoming a thriving center for tourist and convention trade, active 24-hours a day, year-round. Growing numbers of middle-income persons would settle in a downtown that will witness the rebirth of its retail district as in the past it witnessed the rebirth of its office and financial districts.

Harborplace is the harbinger of things to come. The immediate popularity of its many shops and restaurants is evidence of a thirst for urbanity, so often hidden in our culture but, once discovered, almost insatiable. In its dramatic setting on the Inner Harbor, Harborplace fills the need for this. Like the Piazza San Marco in Venice and the other great urban gathering places of the world, Harborplace is making downtown a destination for people with leisure time. It is a place at the water's edge where people can meet, relax, eat, buy, stroll, look, smell, taste, and see. It is a place where night and day people from all walks of life brush shoulders.

If the vision of our civic leaders is realized—and their past record leaves every reason to believe it will be—we can expect to see many projects that complement what Harborplace has begun.

There will be a growing number of cultural and entertainment activities: the Aquarium in the Inner Harbor, a new Symphony Hall in the Mount Royal area, night clubs, an expansion of the Maryland Science Center, and perhaps even a downtown stadium and a jai alai fronton.

There will be more opportunities for the middle class to live downtown around the Retail District, in the Loft District, and in Chessie's

The Completion of Rash Field Beneath Federal Hill by the Inner Harbor. Photo by Betty Redifer

Camden Station apartments; in luxury condominiums along the waterfront west of the Inner Harbor and up to and beyond Fell's Point; and in the restored rowhouses of South Baltimore, Fell's Point, Penn North, and the University of Maryland/Social Security Complex vicinity.

There will be new retail opportunities downtown as Lexington Mall is extended, a bus transit mall is created along Howard Street, and Lexington Market is renovated. To the east, Fisherman's Wharf, another retail area west of Little Italy, has been proposed. An improved transportation network—including rapid transit, an expanded pedestrian walkway system, and perhaps a space-age, monorail type people mover system—will link these new projects to each other and to the region.

Of course, this vision of the future is not without its problems. If growing numbers of people are to live, visit, and shop downtown, they will require assurances of convenience, security, and privacy. This means addressing the problems of crime, congestion, and pollution, including noise pollution, traffic congestion, and perhaps even water congestion as the Inner Harbor's popularity for pleasure boating continues to grow. Certainly, rising gasoline and energy costs will make many who work downtown consider living downtown. Even so, if the city hopes to convince these people of the advantages of in-town living, the potential problems must be dealt with.

Similarly, the public school system will have to be improved if the city expects growing numbers of middle-income families to live downtown. Efforts have been made in this direction in recent years, but far more needs to be done.

Subway Construction on Baltimore Street, 1977. Photo by Jeff Jerome

Lexington Market Subway Station, November, 1980.
Photo by Susan Bishop

The problem goes beyond simply improving the quality of education. While attempting to do this, the school system's administrators must avoid creating a dual education system—one for the children of middle–income families, another for the children of the poor.

One question—recognized but still unanswered—stands above the rest in posing a potential challenge to downtown's future: will the business and government leaders be able to retain the support of the majority of citizens of Baltimore—the black, the poor and working class populations?

From the outset, the redevelopment advocates recognized the potential problem of meeting the needs of all citizens. In a chapter entitled "The Changing Constituency," the MetroCenter Plan of 1970 states the situation quite bluntly:

It is clear that MetroCenter policies and goals to date have reflected middle–class and white values. Blacks have been asked only to affirm the programs at the ballot box and have not been involved in their formulation. Although there are already many blacks visible now in "white collar" jobs, there is a good deal of validity to the frequently expressed black attitude that expressways are being built to get suburban whites to MetroCenter jobs. Office buildings supplying white-collar jobs for white workers are replacing marginal industries, many of which provided jobs for unskilled and semiskilled blacks; the displaced firms are relocating in the suburbs—beyond the effective reach of blacks. The MetroCenter theatres, shops, and cultural activities are both too expensive for their pocketbooks and irrelevant to much of their culture . . . .

It can be and is argued that money spent for MetroCenter renewal would be better spent on in-creasing the supply of standard housing in the city; that expressways are built at the expense of unreproducible low-cost housing; and that the proposed transit system would provide few appreciable advantages over the existing bus system which it would, to a degree, supersede.

Certainly, it is to the credit of the authors of the MetroCenter Plan that they called for "programs both in and outside the ghetto far beyond the present order of magnitude" and stated that "the MetroCenter community must and can play a significant role in a partnership of black and white toward this objective."

Likewise, it is a credit to Harborplace's sponsors that their project received an award for minority employment from the U.S. Department of Housing and Urban Development. Yet, despite such recognition, the alarming and growing rate of unemployment among the city's black and white blue–collar populations and their continuing depressed income levels make the question raised in the MetroCenter plan as pressing today as when it was originally written. Making matters worse is the threat of federal and state cutbacks in vital programs serving the poor and working–class residents of the city. As the authors of the MetroCenter Plan recognized, downtown redevelopment cannot expect popular support if essential programs to meet the needs of the city at large are not forthcoming.

The ability to address this problem goes beyond the power of the city alone. Since annexation or taxation of adjoining jurisdictions is not possible under Maryland law, Baltimore by itself has no way to recapture much of the value its downtown development spurs in the form of regional growth. The burden thus falls to the federal and state governments to equalize the distribution of economic benefits derived from downtown development.

The responsibility for seeing that the federal and state governments perform this function rests with the proponents of downtown development—our government and business leaders. Their ultimate challenge of the next two decades remains the same as in the past. The success of the business/government partnership in winning the support of the city's population will largely determine whether their vision for downtown becomes reality.

Elliot Lieberman

CHARLES CENTER

Over 20 years ago, Baltimore was a city whose downtown business district was in serious trouble, beset with problems of obsolescence. Employment was on the decline and over 2,000,000 square feet of loft and warehouse space were vacant. Property values and retail services were declining at an alarming rate. No new major office buildings had been constructed since the late twenties. Baltimore was a city fast approaching the sixties without even a downtown redevelopment plan, while many other cities, experiencing similar strains, were already taking needed steps to save their downtown areas.

However, during the middle fifties, the Committee for Downtown (made up of industrial, financial, and commercial leaders) did raise $150,000 for a study of downtown renewal. The Greater Baltimore Committee also contributed $75,000 for the same purpose. With these funds, a planning council was formed, and a professional city planner was hired to draw up a plan to revitalize the area bounded by Centre Street, the Fallsway, the harbor, and Greene Street.

It was soon realized that by the time such a plan of renewal could be formulated, it might be too late because of downtown's rapid deterioration. The decision was then made to concentrate instead on a less ambitious project within the central district: to redevelop a 33–acre area between the downtown retail and financial centers, bounded by Hopkins Place and Saratoga, Charles, Lombard, and Liberty Streets.

Baltimoreans Enjoying Charles Center. Photo by M. E. Warren

By March, 1958, the concept and plan for Charles Center, Baltimore's full–scale urban renewal project in the heart of the central business district, was presented to Mayor Thomas D'Alesandro, Jr. by the Committee for Downtown and the Greater Baltimore Committee. The plan was referred to the city's Urban Renewal and Housing Agency, which contracted for a feasibility study that indicated the plan workable. The city council declared the downtown district an urban renewal area and then proceeded to pass the necessary legislation for redevelopment. At a special session, the Maryland state legislature voted to place the question of a $35,000,000 urban renewal loan on the ballot in November, 1958. The voters overwhelmingly approved the loan, thereby clearing the way to put the plan for the Charles Center project into action.

On June 1, 1959, the Commission of the Baltimore Urban Renewal and Housing Agency (BURHA) executed a personal contract for $1 per year with J. Jefferson Miller, a retired department store executive, to initiate the $150,000,000 Charles Center project. One observer noted, "Mr. Miller's business career provided the proper overture to his new job." "Jeff," as his business associates called him, had a deep knowledge of the redevelopment plan and a commitment to the Charles Center project. As a member of the Committee for Downtown, he had been largely responsible for raising the money to initiate a study on downtown renewal.

In the beginning, the execution of the plan for the project was supervised by BURHA (now the Department of Housing and Community Development), acting through the Charles Center Management Office headed by Mr. Miller. A year after the project was underway, Martin Millspaugh, then assistant commissioner of the United States Urban Renewal Administration, joined the Charles Center Management Office as deputy general manager.

With the approval of governmental agencies and the support of a large influential group of citizens, Mr. Miller and his staff began to coordinate all land acquisition, relocation, and development. Once the 350 properties in the development area were acquired, the principal problem was to interest developers in building sites.

On August 10, 1961, ground was broken for the first building, One Charles Center, on the site of O'Neill's department store at Charles Street between Fayette and Lexington streets. Designed by Ludwig Miës van der Rohe, an internationally renowned architect, this contemporary T–shaped structure is considered to be the cornerstone of Baltimore's downtown revitalization. It has been described as a "24–story chameleon" because its facade changes colors according to the angle of sunlight.

Shortly after the completion of One Charles Center in 1962, work began at developing the 16 sites in the 33–acre district. By 1975, various types of services and facilities were constructed

Summer At Charles Center, 1980. Photo by M. E. Warren

in each development area of the Charles Center project.

In areas 1, 2, 3, 4, 5, 7, 8, 12, 13, and 16, office-building facilities housing retail, commercial, and residential facilities were constructed. These buildings include: Charles Towers (areas 1, 2, and 3); Fidelity Building Annex (area 3); Baltimore Gas and Electric addition (areas 4 and 5); One Charles Center (area 7); Hamburgers and Vermont Federal Buildings (area 8); Mercantile-Safe Deposit & Trust Building (area 12); George H. Fallon Federal Office Building (area 13); Sun Life Building and Charles Center South (area 16).

Vast underground commercial and public parking facilities along with retail and related commercial activities were designed for areas 6 and 14. In areas 9, 10, and 11, the Hilton Hotel was completed; facilities for retailing and related commercial use were also included here. The Morris A. Mechanic Theatre was planned for area 15; retail services and related commercial establishments were provided here, also.

In addition to the extensive underground parking facilities in areas 6 and 14, additional parking facilities were required by Charles Center planners.

Five older structures in the 33-acre Charles Center project have remained: Lord Baltimore Hotel, Baltimore Gas and Electric Building, Fidelity Building, Baltimore and Ohio Railroad Building, and Eglin's Garage.

While the Charles Center Project was on its way to completion, Mr. Miller and Mr. Millspaugh were asked by the city government if they would also undertake the planning and implementation of the next phase of downtown redevelopment: a 20-year program of renewal projects surrounding the Inner Harbor and encompassing 240 acres adjacent to the central business district. In order to initiate this Inner Harbor program, the nonprofit corporation of Charles Center–Inner Harbor Management, Inc. was formed, with Mr. Miller as chairman of the board and Mr. Millspaugh as president. On September 1, 1965, a contract was drawn up between this corporation and the mayor and City Council, enabling the corporation to manage the planning and execution of the Charles Center and Inner Harbor projects, under the direction of the city's Urban Renewal and Housing Commis-

sion—later replaced by the Commission of Housing and Community Development.

Charles Center became the first tangible proof that Baltimore city intended an era of rebirth. Its buildings, which were soon rented, demonstrated a renewed economic vitality for the central city. Although at first many Baltimoreans remained skeptical about Baltimore's ability to return to a past age of prosperity and national leadership, from the 1970s on—when Charles Center was complete and Inner Harbor development plans announced—these structures became a vivid testimony at last that Baltimore was at the threshold of a renaissance. Skepticism has given way to belief.

Morgan Pritchett

INNER HARBOR: A NEW VIEW FOR BALTIMORE

As recently as the late 1960s, Baltimore's inner harbor was judged to be a disgrace. Baltimore had disregarded the rare blessing of a natural estuary at her central business core.

Baltimore's harbor had a proud heritage of clipper ships, steamboats, bustling produce docks, and thriving waterfront businesses. Now the pretty picture was an open sewer. Few vessels except for timeworn workboats and tugboats and their barges braved the flotsam of railroad ties, oil cans, tires, and crates. The smells of rotten fruit contaminated the spicy fragrances provided by McCormick and Company, a Baltimore institution destined to be one of the few proud survivors at the harbor's edge.

Early Plans to Revitalize the Harbor. When Mayor Theodore R. McKeldin (in his 1963 inaugural address) called for a plan to develop Baltimore's Inner Harbor, the cry was familiar. Visionaries of the late 1940s had pursued similar goals, but their pleas had evoked the laughter and ridicule of a body politic whose demand for immediate thrift far outweighed the need for civic pride, much less major improvements. The unfortunate interim compromise was Sam

Mark Di Suvero, *"Under Sky—One Family"* Near the World Trade Center. Photo by Jan Sutherland Starr

Likewise, the harbor excursion vessel, the *Port Welcome*, continued to operate from Pier 1.

In October, 1964, the planning council of the Greater Baltimore Committee finally answered Mayor McKeldin's request for a plan with a 30-year, $260 million twofold proposal. It called for both the development of the Inner Harbor and the creation of a new municipal center that would front a tree-lined boulevard extending southeast from City Hall to the waterfront. Voters killed the project the following month by rejecting the bond issue that would have financed it.

The plans for the Inner Harbor did not die, however. They called for a World Trade Center for the Maryland Port Authority, a new science center for the Maryland Academy of Sciences, a marina, parks, promenades, and playing fields. They also included a marine museum, an "aquarama," shops, restaurants, and an amusement wharf or boardwalk with commercial recreation.

Charles Center–Inner Harbor Management, Inc. was formed in September, 1965, as a non-profit corporation to manage the planning and execution of both its title projects. The new corporation would work under the Baltimore Urban Renewal and Housing Agency (later to become the Department of Housing and Community Development). Civic-minded J. Jefferson Miller, the dollar-a-year general manager of the partially completed Charles Center project, was named chairman of the board of the new corporation. Mr. Miller's deputy general manager for Charles Center, Martin Millspaugh, became president. When Mr. Miller died in April, 1972, Walter Sondheim, vice-chairman of the board since 1970, succeeded him. In April, 1975, Millspaugh became chief executive officer.

A five-step process for modernizing 108 acres around three sides of the harbor occurred after an urban renewal plan established the city's right of eminent domain. First, the Baltimore Urban Renewal and Housing Agency (BURHA) received funds from federal and local sources. Next, the city Real Estate Department bought properties around the harbor for BURHA at prices previously determined by independent appraisals. Meanwhile, Charles Center–Inner Harbor Management, Inc. located suitable developers with whom they formulated agreements

Smith Park, a metered-parking lot which, in 1950, replaced a worm-eaten, rat-infested shanty town of deserted wharves that bordered the harbor's western shore. Then in 1956, City Planning Director Arthur McVoy outlined a program to develop the harbor. Though the Planning Commission voted its approval, the project remained at a standstill.

Except for an occasional ship unloading Belgian steel at Pier 6, all foreign commerce had vanished from the Inner Harbor by 1958. Four years later, the Old Bay Line ceased its exchange of passengers and freight with Norfolk. At Pier 4, the U.S.F. *Constellation*, still looking much like a barge despite ongoing restoration, awaited a congressional directive which could move it to Fort McHenry. Fortunately for future planners, the historic warship remained in the harbor.

for the sale of land. Then BURHA approved each deal and sold the properties. The final step was construction.

Metamorphosis of the Inner Harbor. Planning gave way to action in January, 1968, upon approval of a $22 million federal renewal grant for Inner Harbor Phase I. Acquisition and clearance began immediately.

The first visible sign of revitalization occurred on September 3, 1969, when Mayor Thomas D'Alesandro III and approximately 200 other well-wishers welcomed the U.S.F. *Constellation* to its permanent home at Pier 3. Built in Fell's Point, the *Constellation* was launched in Baltimore in 1797. It has the distinction of being both the first commissioned ship in the United States Navy and the oldest American warship afloat. Even before the completion of the massive brick and concrete Constellation Dock in 1972, the vessel had become the Inner Harbor's premier tourist attraction. During the year ending July, 1978, it attracted 130,000 visitors.

Two months after the *Constellation* ceremonies, construction was underway at Pratt and Light streets on the new home office building of the United States Fidelity and Guaranty Company. When completed and occupied three years later, the structure ascended 40 stories and encased 460,000 square feet. A Henry Moore sculpture was centered on a spacious public plaza surrounding the building. In 1980, the sculpture was moved into the Convention Center.

Though begun more than a year after the

Inner Harbor, 1976. Photo by Susan Bishop

U.S.F.&G. groundbreaking, the John L. Deaton Medical Center at 615 South Charles Street was the Inner Harbor project's first completed building. Dedicated on December 10, 1972, the $7.1 million, 220-bed facility is sponsored by Christ Lutheran Church. It belongs to a complex that now includes a nine-story, 290-unit apartment building. The apartments, as well as the medical center, are for senior citizens.

Entertainment and Festivals Attract Many to the Harbor. Baltimore's first Sunny Sunday celebration in April, 1973, coincided with the dedication of a public wharf adjacent to the former Sam Smith Park. Though this area's brick promenade, kiosks, benches, and permanent park land were still two years away, that afternoon of arts and crafts, music, theatrical entertainment, and children's events drew a large and enthusiastic audience. As a result, Sunny Sundays evolved into a weekly summertime tradition.

Over the next several years, the Inner Harbor became the focal point for many of Baltimore's other civic and recreational festivities. The renowned City Fair quickly outgrew its original Charles Center location and moved to the Inner Harbor. Approximately half of the city's popular ethnic festivals—including Afram, American Indian, German, Greek, Jewish, and Polish—followed suit. New Year's Eve merriment in the harbor has become an annual tradition, as have a kite-flying festival and canoe races. Banks and other corporations sponsor free concerts—ranging from bluegrass to jazz to opera.

Bringing activities downtown and continuing the development of the Inner Harbor had been two of Mayor William Donald Schaefer's major campaign promises prior to his election in 1971. Appropriately, when Schaefer was inaugurated for his second term in January, 1976, the ceremony took place on the vast front steps of the new Maryland Science Center at the southwestern corner of the harbor.

The Maryland Science Center is headquarters for the Maryland Academy of Sciences. Dedicated in 1975, the four-story building has a distinguished exterior of massive red brick octagonal forms. It contains three floors of extensive scientific exhibits, ranging from a mechanized giant talking crab to the elaborate Davis Planetarium. The center also offers science ed-

Inner Harbor Sculpture Playground. Photo by Jake Slagle, Jr.

ucation programs and provides research and information for all of Maryland's state and local agencies. Founded in 1797, the Maryland Academy of Sciences is Baltimore's oldest scientific institution.

East of the Science Center, at the foot of Federal Hill, is the award–winning Joseph H. Rash Memorial Park. The name honors the food company executive who headed the city's Park Board between 1968 and 1974. Completed in 1975, the $2.2 million sports complex includes two playing fields framed by stands for 4,000 spectators. Additional recreational facilities include a pavilion, picnic tables, and fireplace. The field is used for games, contests, and tournaments between local and other groups. It also is the playing field for Southern High School's athletic teams.

Also completed in 1975 was the IBM Building, which faces the harbor from the north side of East Pratt Street between Light and Calvert streets.

Ships Provide Publicity. This was the scene around the Inner Harbor on July 10, 1976, when the first of the fabled "tall ships" arrived for Operation Sail. Eight resplendent sailing vessels during their 10–day stay unexpectedly developed into the grandest tourist attraction in the city's history. Over a million visitors came to see the ships. The event created among Baltimoreans and out–of–towners alike an unprecedented awareness of and appreciation for the refurbished harbor's potential. Among them were President Gerald R. Ford and Secretary of State Henry Kissinger, who visited West German Chancellor Helmut Schmidt aboard his country's Gorch Fock II. Operation Sail was sponsored primarily by Commercial Credit Corporation and the city's Bicentennial Commission.

Baltimore's annual Maritime Heritage Festival, known also as Harborfest, evolved as an offshoot of Operation Sail in 1977. This annual summer weekend is highlighted by a 155-mile race, sponsored by the American Sail Training Association between Baltimore and Norfolk. Also featured are a diversity of maritime exhibits, a regatta, concerts, and crab feasts.

Still under construction at the time of Operation Sail was the $476,000, 90-foot, 121-ton, *Pride of Baltimore*. The clipper ship replica has since become Baltimore's roving good-will ambassador to the world. Launched without its mast on February 27, 1977, the *Pride* set sail five weeks later for its maiden voyage to New York.

The Convention Center. On March 29, 1977, ground was broken at the southwest corner of Charles and Pratt streets for Baltimore's much-heralded $50 million Convention Center. Only in recent years had the city determined that the 23-room facility with 41,000 feet of meetingroom area would be part of the Inner Harbor. According to earlier plans, the Convention Center was to have been an addition to either the Baltimore Civic Center or to a new sports complex that never materialized.

Larger Plans, Larger Building. Coinciding with the Convention Center groundbreaking was the completion at the opposite corner of Charles and Pratt of a headquarters building for the Chesapeake and Potomac Telephone Company. The new structure houses 290,000 square feet of office space and offers an additional 30,000 square feet for retail use.

Because of cost overruns, the September 25, 1977, dedication of the Maryland Port Authority's World Trade Center was years behind schedule. Designed by world-renowned I. M. Pei, the 32-story pentagonal structure rises 430 feet above the harbor's northern shore. Inside are 300,000 feet of office space plus a public observation floor with exhibits pertaining to the city. Pedal boats and small sailboats are available for rental from the bulkhead flanking two sides of the building.

By December, 1977, the National Aquarium was under construction immediately east of the World Trade Center at Pier 3. The architect was Peter Chermayeff of Boston's Cambridge Seven Associates, which had designed the New England Aquarium in Boston—considered by authorities to be the world's best.

By avoiding the few proven shortcomings evident in the Boston aquarium, Baltimore's promises to be even better. It is oval-shaped and hollow, so that the visitor seems surrounded by the sea as he/she ascends. Opened in the summer of 1981, the aquarium's exhibits range from a coral reef to a shark tank. Birds, butterflies, fish, marmosets, reptiles, and other species inhabit a five-story simulated Amazon rain forest.

Extensive improvements are being made simultaneously at Pier 3. Docking is to be provided for small boats as well as the *Port Welcome* and the *Nobska*, an early twentieth-century steamship that formerly plied Nantucket Sound and that has been converted to a seafood restaurant.

Meanwhile, across the harbor, a $1.6 million city-built marina opened in March, 1978. Its 158 slips are equipped with water, electricity, and telephone. The marina accommodates local as well as transient pleasure vessels and is being expanded to include a restaurant, boating supplies shop, and fuel dock.

The first major controversy regarding Inner Harbor development blossomed in the early fall of 1978. The issue was Harborplace, a 3.1 acre two-level steel and glass eating and shopping complex proposed by the Rouse Company of Columbia. The Schaefer administration and other influential organizations and individuals viewed the proposal as a revenue-producing magnet. Others opposed the idea for reasons ranging from preserving open space to unwanted competition for area business interests. The issue was brought to public referendum in November, 1978, and won by a comfortable if not substantial margin.

When Harborplace opened on July 2, 1980, its early opponents were among more than 150,000 celebrants participating in an event that at least one newspaper columnist compared in historical importance to the great Baltimore fire of 1904. The attraction of Harborplace proved to be more than its 37 eating places, 20 food markets, 45 specialty shops, and approximately 30 kiosks. Harborplace also became a point of reference for the new downtown, a symbol of human commerce returning, after a prolonged exodus, to the urban core.

Meanwhile, Hutzler's department store opened a posh new branch in the Equitable Bank Center at the northwest corner of Charles and Pratt. Outside the building, the philanthropy of the Equitable's retired Board Chairman Robert G. Merrick, along with the Jacob and Annita France Foundation, bankrolled a fountain of granite monoliths to coincide with the Bank Center's formal opening.

All the while, along Light Street, between the McCormick and C&P Telephone buildings, the luxury 13-story 500-room Hyatt Regency Baltimore hotel was arising from ground that had been broken in 1979. The structure features a five-story atrium, garden lobby, and four glass-capsule elevators fronting on the harbor. Planned public facilities for the Hyatt include a rooftop restaurant, an entertainment lounge on the third level, and a bar and lounge in the atrium garden. The building also includes a 15,000 square-foot ballroom, four banquet rooms, six meeting rooms, and a coffee shop. Suspended walkways will link the structure with the Convention Center and Harborplace.

What seemed a fantasy in the 1950s has evolved into a $725 million undertaking. The results will be a showpiece for Baltimore's visitors and residents to savor.

Jake Slagle, Jr.

Science and Health

SCIENCE AND MEDICINE

Legend has it that the first umbrella opened in the United States was taken from a ship docked in Baltimore in 1772. The unlucky man who thought he would try it out was foolish enough to prance through the small town's streets. Soon he was followed by children who jumped in glee at the new object which was waved before them. Then a crowd of adults formed and the umbrella was quickly torn away from the man and ripped to shreds. The city, apparently, was not quite ready for such a novel gadget.

By the 1790s, however, there emerged within Baltimore a thriving umbrella business that in the 1800s made the city one of the leading umbrella manufacturers in the world. It seems that from that time on Baltimore was more receptive to scientific inventions and new ideas, especially those which might be profitable.

In the 1840s a wild-eyed young man named Samuel Morse was encouraged by the city's businessmen to tinker with his contraption. By 1844, Morse had connected Baltimore and Washington with a telegraph line. Within hours messages were clicking away. The science of communications, not only in the city but throughout the world, was revolutionized.

Another legend is that the first balloon flight in the United States originated in Baltimore in the 1780s. However, it is less debatable that Linotype was invented in Baltimore in 1884 and in 1885 the first commercially run electric cars were put into operation.

A Flourishing Science Community. Nowadays Baltimore's contributions to science are often thought of as synonymous with medical research at the Johns Hopkins Medical Institutions. Certainly the proliferation of inventions and discoveries originating at Johns Hopkins—

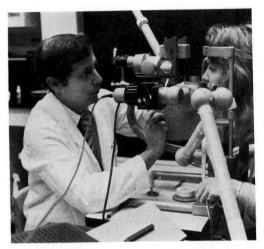

Dr. Daniel Finkelstein Using Laser Equipment. Photo by Joseph Sullivan

specialization. The former causes the need to develop novel and efficient solutions to the problem of economic adaptation in order to support large numbers of people located in relatively dense areas.

Not only is the city an enterprising area in which businessmen often were willing to encourage and finance novel but possibly profitable scientific work, but Baltimore has two other characteristics that set the stage for the emergence of science and medicine here. These are the fortuitous creation of the Johns Hopkins University by a wealthy merchant after whom the university was named and the long history of relative religious and political tolerance in Maryland.

The Johns Hopkins University. The story of Johns Hopkins' bequest to the people in this state for the founding of an institution of higher learning is well known. Even in a period of generous donations his gift was a magnificent one. Although he stated several suggested purposes of the university, his will was ambiguous enough for a clever board of trustees to interpret it broadly in order to provide maximum long-run educational gains for Maryland. Indeed, some of the board's dealings bordered on chicanery. Simply put, the decision was reached to develop, in addition to the medical school, a university that emphasized graduate training. This meant that for the first time in the United States a school was founded for the primary goal of pursuing and creating scientific knowledge instead of merely stuffing the seemingly wooden heads of undergraduates with the conventional wisdom of the day.

Hopkins became the first university with a press operating under the school's name. This was symbolically important because previously, as indicated, universities tended to limit their mission to teaching students rather than disseminating information to either the general or professional publics.

The generous funds bequeathed to the Hopkins and the goals set forth by its first board, made it possible to establish superior research facilities over the years and recruit and train the best scholars. These activities took precedence over the construction of Gothic and vulgar classroom buildings and the creation of an expensive stadium with a stable of athletes.

some of which have won a Nobel Prize, the highest award possible within the scientific world—are stupendous. Indeed, it is Hopkins that has made Baltimore a capital of science and medicine. But long before Johns Hopkins was founded in the 1870s, the city in 1792 had established the first health department in the United States. By 1807, the medical school at the University of Maryland was opened, and in 1839 the Baltimore College of Dental Surgery, the first dental college in the world, was chartered.

Since World War II, when the United States emerged as a superpower, funds earmarked for science and medicine have been immense. Baltimore's long tradition of receptivity to the novel as well as its excellent medical centers provided the city with a base from which to capitalize on the national trend of widespread federal support for medical and other research.

Why have science and medicine flourished in this city? Why not in Atlanta, Cleveland, Richmond, or other urban areas that, as rich as they might be in their particular accomplishments, are usually surpassed in science and medicine by Baltimore?

Part of the reason stems from Baltimore's being a seaport which obviously placed an emphasis on commerce and business. Historically, cities of this kind have functioned to spawn science and technology. By definition, urbanization means increasing population growth and

Thus, at Hopkins a dynamic intellectual milieu was created that had to spill over at times into the broader community making it more civilized than it might have been otherwise.

Spirit of Tolerance. Independent of the founding of the university and probably a partial cause of its creation, is the tradition of relative religious and political tolerance in Maryland. One of the clearest benefits of this tradition was the settling in Baltimore of hundreds of thousands of members of various religious and ethnic groups. Tolerance, combined with the city's economic imperative of expansion that depended on increasing labor and brain power, served to reward hard work and excellence among Germans, Irish, Italians, Poles, Catholics, and Jews—to mention only some groups. In fact, other than in its blatantly racist treatment of blacks, Baltimore generally personified the melting-pot syndrome of American folklore.

In addition to commercial and economic freedom resulting from religious and political tolerance, artistic and literary figures were also allowed to produce in relative freedom. This, too, helped create and sustain an atmosphere conducive for the emergence of science and medicine. It is probably no accident that the iconoclast, H. L. Mencken, was able to thrive in his own birthplace, Baltimore.

Since the 1950s this spirit of encouragement of ethnic groups has slowly been extended to blacks as well. However, there have been sharp exceptions to this identified pattern of tolerance during Baltimore's renaissance. For instance, in the early 1960s the atheist Madalyn Murray O'Hair was driven from the city. Harassment against this free thinker and her family culminated in a near lynch mob led by Baltimore's police with trumped up charges against her, forcing her to flee, barely escaping violence and possibly jail. Generally, however, the city has been relatively tolerant of religious, ethnic, and political minorities. Such general tolerance, as indicated, functioned to enhance scientific and medical research by creating an atmosphere for its flourishing and by rewarding members of immigrant and minority groups for their contributions.

Problems Created by Scientific Achievements. Have there been no negative effects for Baltimore resulting from its accomplishments in science and medicine? What problems, if any, might have been created during Baltimore's renaissance by science and medicine and what, if anything, is being done about them?

At least two kinds of unanticipated negative consequences ought to be identified and briefly discussed. Both are reflections of problems that exist in every urban area. There is no reason to think that Baltimore's recent history is considerably worse or significantly better in these two areas than that of other cities.

The first serious problem has to do with separation of Baltimore's great medical research institution, Johns Hopkins, from the rest of the community. The second problem is the effect of technology created by modern science on the urban environment.

The well-known elitism generated and sustained by staff at Hopkins probably has gone beyond the usual snobbery that derives from being part of a great university. Historically, the most obvious sign of such elitism is the school's racial and economic composition. Hopkins has been notorious among some for its almost completely white, upper-middle to upper-class-recruited faculty and student body. Despite claims sometimes made to justify the "purity" of the staff, the caste system there is not based on intellectual rank alone. Instead, it parallels the racial and economic inequalities within American society.

In the 1960s, this situation resulted in charges that Baltimore's poor were being mistreated in the hospital. While any university must identify with the broader, scientific community that by definition knows no local or even national boundaries, the allegations poured forth that the medical needs of the poor were not part of the concerns of either the university or the hospital.

In a June 3, 1968, *Sun* article, "The People and the Plantation: Hopkins Complex is Dependent upon, Resented by Neighborhood Negroes," former hospital president, Dr. Russell A. Nelson, said, "This institution is a product of the South and southern mores."

Although personnel at the Hopkins were aware of and concerned about the realities of racism, Dr. Nelson pointed out, "There remain as almost unconscious actions remnants of that earlier period" when Baltimore was a segregated town.

Dr. Glenn R. Mitchell, former assistant administrator for the hospital, added, "We have had great difficulty involving the community in our affairs." It was theorized that the high fence surrounding parts of the complex symbolically as well as physically created a resented barrier between the community and the Hopkins.

Internally, lower-level staff such as custodial workers, nursing assistants, and others were also treated with disdain by the professional staff. In fact, in the 1971 long-range plan, it was noted that "warm, friendly" relationships between lower-level employees and professional staff were lacking.

Almost every one of these problems, however, existed and were widely publicized in most urban hospitals throughout the 1960s and 1970s. The abysmally low wages paid to the nonprofessional staff, the claims that hospitals were attempting to "drive out" local residents whose homes border on the various medical complexes, created strains with which most administrators of large hospitals had to cope.

The professional and administrative staff at the Hopkins, as reflected in the above statements, have been remarkably candid about these problems. The 1970s were times for significant changes and improvements to remedy these strains at Hopkins. Vigorous efforts are now being made to alter the racial, if not economic homogeneity of that institution.

Dr. Levi Watkins, Jr., chief resident in cardiac surgery, was, according to an April 8, 1979, *Sun* article, "The first black to go all the way through the competitive Hopkins surgical training program." He now serves on the Hopkins admissions committee and is attempting to recruit blacks to the medical school.

In the late 1960s, community-based health care services were established. Residents who join Hopkins' Health Maintenance Organizations (HMOs) can pay a monthly set fee for medical services. However, the emphasis of the community services is to prevent illness more than actually treat diseases. It is considered one of the most innovative community programs in the nation. The idea has taken hold and several others have been organizing HMOs. Some are hospital-based, some private-based. One example is those offices run by Chesapeake Physicians, one of which is located on the grounds of

the Baltimore City Hospitals. Two other programs are currently sponsored by Hopkins under Dr. Robert M. Heyssel (who also helped establish them). One is in Columbia and the other serves the inner-city area surrounding the Hopkins medical complex.

The second negative consequence of Baltimore's scientific achievements is considerably more serious than the problems recently faced and partially solved by Johns Hopkins. Huge industries have accompanied the expansion of science and technology since World War II. These newer, larger industries result from the economic imperatives of growth and increased profits. They have added immeasurably to the city's prosperity. However, these larger industries, reflecting advances in science and technology, have also added immeasurably to the pollution of Baltimore. Their bigness and dirtiness present the city's landscape with a stark ugliness not known before. Moreover, in Baltimore there are no longer any waterways that can be safely swum in. Indeed, some water is actually dangerous to boat in or even walk too closely beside.

The full effects of carcinogenic and other pollutants on factory workers and the rest of the city remain problematic at this time. Baltimore, like many urban areas, is currently weighing the full implications of the trade-off of short-term technological and economic gains for long-run medical and other quality-of-life costs.

In spite of these observations, it seems obvious that science and medicine have contributed significantly to the current quality of life in Baltimore and are a crucial part of the city's renaissance. Within the past few years one of the most practical results of medical research has been the Baltimore shock trauma unit at the University of Maryland Hospital that has helped save hundreds of lives of those seriously injured.

The regional burn center at Baltimore City Hospitals and the kidney dialysis satellite unit at various hospitals throughout the area are also unique and have alleviated much suffering. In addition, many of the new buildings being constructed in the city are utilizing the most efficient scientific techniques recently developed in engineering, especially in the area of energy conservation. Significant technological progress based on the engineering sciences has combined to help in the renovation and preservation of many of Baltimore's fine old buildings, to mention only a few medical and technological accomplishments.

In conclusion, it probably can be said that science and medicine, along with other elements of Baltimore's social structure, combine to make the city a reasonably attractive place to spend the last quarter of the twentieth century.

Richard C. Monk

BALTIMORE HOSPITALS

From treatment for sleep disorders to open heart surgery to the reimplantation of severed limbs, Baltimore's general and specialty hospitals offer renowned medical care. They have played an important role in the city's revitalization by attracting attention throughout the world.

Both of Maryland's medical schools, the University of Maryland and the Johns Hopkins University, are located within the city limits. Baltimore boasts many other teaching institutions that keep up with the latest in medical technology. Excellent medical care is also accessible through a network of hospital-sponsored community clinics and prepaid health care pro-

Union Memorial Hospital at Night. Photo by Sussman Photography

grams throughout the city and surrounding suburbs.

Baltimore's hospitals offer an impressive showing of equipment and facilities. Provident Hospital has the only acute stroke treatment unit in the state. In 1974, Mercy Hospital was the first Maryland facility to use ultrasound to remove cataracts. The only frozen blood program in Maryland is housed at Good Samaritan Hospital. The Raymond Curtis Hand Center was first opened in early January, 1978, at Union Memorial Hospital—one of only a few in the United States. The center specializes in microsurgical techniques to reimplant severed fingers and restore injured hands. Children's Hospital has been a leader in the treatment of anterior poliomyelitis; the first respirator center for treating polio patients was developed there.

The University of Maryland Hospital hosts a wide variety of sophisticated facilities, including the Baltimore Cancer Research Center and the Center for the Study of Sudden Infant Death Syndrome. Baltimore City Hospitals offers the Sleep Disorders Center, which is only one of 11 such centers in the nation. In July, 1978, the first Maryland hospital to use the laser to treat cancer in the female reproductive tract was the Greater Baltimore Medical Center. Although most of the area hospitals offer emergency services, Sinai Hospital is the central control station for Emergency Medical Services of Maryland and has the equipment to direct ambulances to any emergency room in the area and to channel EKGs from an ambulance to a waiting physician in the hospital for instant analysis. In addition, Baltimore City, University, and Hopkins hospitals comprise the three Category I hospitals in the state that are equipped to handle any kind of emergency. These hospitals have facilities to receive helicopters. As part of this system, the University of Maryland has the shock trauma center of the Maryland Institute for Emergency Medical Services; Hopkins offers the Pediatric Trauma Referral Center; and City has the Baltimore Regional Burn Center. All three hospitals also have Neonatal Intensive Care Units that receive critically ill newborns from several nearby states as well as from Maryland.

Many of Baltimore's medical facilities offer specialized care. Mount Washington Pediatric Hospital is the only facility in Maryland dedi-

A Model of the Johns Hopkins Hospital Proposed for Completion in 1984. Photo by Documentary Photographic Project

cated solely to fulfilling all the medical, emotional, social, and educational needs of children. Montebello Center concentrates on the treatment and rehabilitation of the physically disabled. Orthopedics as well as plastic surgery and facial rehabilitation are among the specialties offered by the Children's Hospital. The Sheppard and Enoch Pratt Hospital is renowned for its psychiatric care. The James Lawrence Kernan Hospital accommodates orthopedic, plastic, neurological, and dental patients.

Procedures that were introduced in Baltimore medical institutions are used throughout the world. Hopkins' doctors Helen Brooke Taussig and Alfred Blalock pioneered the "blue baby" operation that paved the way for modern cardiac surgery. In 1976, Hopkins performed the first thymus transplant on a patient born without any natural immunities against disease. Dr. Arnall Patz, of the same hospital, developed the use of the laser beam for eye disorders, and Dr. William Kouwenhoven discovered and developed the technique of cardio–pulmonary resuscitation.

In 1955, Hopkins developed the first intensive care unit in the country. And, in 1973, the Franklin Square Hospital, Baltimore City Hospitals, the Johns Hopkins Applied Physics Lab, and the Johns Hopkins Medical Institutions jointly developed the first implantable, rechargable cardiac pacemaker.

Union Memorial Hospital physicians developed the Milan-Markley helix to aid in the detection of uterine cancer, as well as the Stone intestinal clamp for use in bowel surgery.

The first inner ear bone transplant to aid

A Baby Receiving Treatment at the University of Maryland Hospital. Photo by Philip Szczepanski

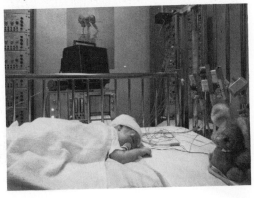

hearing loss took place at the Greater Baltimore Medical Center in June, 1973.

A history-making spinal transplant was performed in August, 1979, at the University of Maryland Hospital on a patient suffering from cancer of the spine.

Hopkins medical researchers have advanced medical knowledge considerably through identifying polio viruses (by Doctors David Bodian, Howard A. Howe, and Isabel M. Morgan); discovering opiate receptors, the section of the brain related to pain (by Dr. Solomon Snyder); culturing the first human cancer cell (by Dr. George Gey); and isolating restriction enzymes, the key to mapping complex messages of the gene strand that may lead to the prevention and treatment of many diseases. This last discovery won a Nobel Prize for Drs. Daniel Nathans and Hamilton Smith in 1979.

Baltimore's hospitals are concentrating on community programs that assure area residents of good, accessible care. Prepaid family care programs and community health centers are sponsored by Bon Secours, Baltimore City, Union Memorial, and Lutheran hospitals. Drug and alcohol abuse outreach programs are offered by many area medical institutions, including Lutheran, Mercy, and Bon Secours. Provident and Lutheran hospitals are part of a network of outreach services offering care and advice on sickle cell anemia. Sinai Hospital has a Department of Community Medicine, which includes a Drug Dependency Program and a Home Care Program; the latter is also offered at St. Agnes Hospital. The Sheppard and Enoch Pratt Hospital sponsors a community mental health center.

As Baltimore continues to grow and develop, its hospitals are enlarging and expanding to accommodate the latest in equipment and facilities. In the past few years, additions have been made to many Baltimore medical centers, including Lutheran, Sinai, Maryland General, Hopkins, University, Bon Secours, and South Baltimore General hospitals. Baltimore County General opened a new hospital in 1978.

Extensive additions are in the offing or have been begun at Kernan, Mercy, St. Agnes, North Charles General, Hopkins, and Greater Baltimore Medical Center.

Because of their world–renowned modern technology and sophisticated equipment, Baltimore hospitals can take a share of credit for the city's renaissance over the past 25 years.

Sherie Brook Libber

MARYLAND SCIENCE CENTER

The Maryland Science Center, offspring of the Maryland Academy of Sciences—second oldest science institution in the country—has overcome its nomadic tendencies and settled in an impressive new home at the Inner Harbor.

Since its birth in 1797, the academy's objective has been the encouragement of scientific interest. In the early days this meant that its museum was largely a curiosity show; managers Rembrandt and Raphaelle Peale (sons of the great painter and scientist) featured such things as a two–headed chicken in their exhibits.

The Academy eventually became firmly established as a Baltimore institution. For 21 years, from April, 1944, to April, 1965, it was housed in the Enoch Pratt Library's main branch in less than spacious quarters on the third floor. A good part of its collections had to be stored away in basements and warehouses; the "best mineral collection in the South" was entombed in a branch library basement. But despite cramped facilities, the Academy drew hordes of admiring visitors. Especially popular were the rooftop observatory and Thursday night planetarium demonstrations, as well as its outside lecture series at the Lyric.

Two moves awaited the Academy after its sojourn at Pratt Library: one to the former Cathedral School on Mulberry Street until December, 1972, and another to South Howard Street until March, 1975. The first serious steps toward securing a permanent headquarters were underway in 1961. As a result of a promotional Science and Industry Conference called by then Governor J. Millard Tawes, the state, city, and academy joined forces to create the new center. In

1965, the General Assembly provided $2 million in funds to be matched by the academy through public or private sources. The city was to donate the site, and Mayor McKeldin supported the Inner Harbor area at Light Street and Key Highway.

The new building, designed by New York architect Edward Durell Stone, consists of a series of octagonal towers or modules which are striking in red brick. Some interior exhibits—over $1 million worth—were designed by James Gardner. As construction marched into the seventies, building costs soared. Over $7 million from business, industrial, institutional, and private contributions (including a $1 million gift from Allan C. Davis, chairman of the board of the academy) helped meet these costs. The general public took part in the fund–raising spirit by "buying" various celestial bodies; the moon fetched $25,000, but a star sold for $5. On June 11, 1976, the new $10 million Science Center officially opened its doors.

Since that date, the Science Center has continued the programs that made it exciting throughout its history (such as the Round the World Adventure film/lecture series, special excursions, circulating science exhibits, seminars, and symposiums).

Its new situation has opened up still more possibilities. "Star Theatre" now appears at the Davis Planetarium under the direction of astronomer Daniel Zirpoli. These ever–changing programs of seasonal star watches and galaxy explorations are laced with "music of the spheres." Exhibits on the ecology and wildlife of the Chesapeake Bay, Maryland geology, computer games, and chemistry are presented in the "hands–on" spirit: visitors are encouraged to touch. Live demonstrations, performances at the Boyd Science Theatre, continuous films, and talking exhibits give the Science Center a flavor of immediacy and an upbeat twenty–first century bustle very unlike the museum of the past.

In fact, the center is now a dynamic, multimedia happening that would probably leave its founding fathers speechless.

Lisa L. Adams

II

SOCIAL PER

The ancient Greeks once instructed, "Know thyself." Section II helps us better understand ourselves, who we are, where we have been, and where we might be going as a people.

"Social Perspectives" attempts in 16 essays to reflect the things that make Baltimore unique. Ethnic, racial, and religious distinctions are exactly what makes cities so interesting: they create the rich heterogeneity of urban life, a mosaic of a nation if not the planet itself.

As we see it, "Social Perspectives" touches on four main classes of variables that are essential ingredients of urban social life. The first six articles deal with what we might call "the promise of pluralism." This simply has to do with various categories of people residing side by side in relative harmony within the city. The articles that deal with ethnic and religious groups and their leaders, with racial and sexual groups, and groups formed around age strata attempt to show unique contributions of each of the major groups.

The second class of articles shows the importance of transmission of culture through formal institutions. These three articles deal with education in Baltimore, both private and public. The writers cover colleges, universities, and other socializing institutions. The literal division of the word education is reflected here: e-duc-ation, 'e' is away from or out of, 'duc' is from ducir, to lead, and 'tion' on the end of a word in the English language signifies a state of being or noun status. Thus 'education' literally is to 'to lead

A Baltimore Scene by Aaron Sopher. Courtesy of Mrs. Mary Weinman. Photo by Peter Handakas

SPECTIVE

out of.' It is argued in the essays that Baltimore's educational institutions function to 'lead out of' and hence transmit the culture, ideas, values embedded within our heritage as a people, a nation, and a city.

The third class of institutions enriching social interaction and in many ways functioning as the very glue of symbolic communication is Baltimore's mass communications. Communication, like education, can also be broken into its various components capturing in the process its very social basis. 'Com' is with, 'munir' means to build. Thus communication is literally 'a state of building with.' Social interaction among humans, then, is a way of relating, building with others.

The seven essays dealing with mass communications in Baltimore document the rich forms of communication ranging from early primitive radio stations and community newspapers to modern television stations that have helped the city define itself and achieve a renaissance.

The last two essays reflect two different interpretations of the social situation in Baltimore by two writers. In many ways, such competing definitions capture the vigorous efforts of a city in flux working to reshape and redefine itself. Coincidentally, the last two essays, but especially that of Gerald Johnson, return us to the opening theme of this section of the anthology. Johnson argues (we will comment in more detail on his and the other essays directly) that Baltimore's genius, like that of America itself, rests in its terrific mix of people. We are proudly a 'mongrel' city in a 'mongrel' nation.

The lead article in "Social Perspectives" captures much of the values of ethnic diversity in recent Baltimore history. Rafael L. Cortada's "Baltimore's Ethnic Revival" traces the contributions to the renaissance of the city's Estonians, Greeks, Hispanics, Poles, American Indians, and others as well as the newly arriving Orientals. The customs, festivals, fairs, and business enterprises of many colorful groups come alive in his discussion. Cortada, however, also performs the valuable service of pinpointing important areas of strain among some. He identifies,

but without falling into a litany of despair and hopelessness, real cracks in the Baltimore melting pot. He soberly indicates that while the city has a rich ethnic heritage of which to be justly proud, there is still much to be done to enable all Baltimoreans to participate in the American Dream.

Bettye Gardner and Cynthia Martin in their "Blacks in Baltimore, 1950–1980: An Overview" identify six crucial aspects of black community development. These six fundamentals around which they delineate recent events are: neighborhood development, economic development, education advances, religious development, political activism, and cultural development. This six-pronged conceptual framework provides a handle by which to understand better the complicated and vital changes taking place in many Baltimore communities. We would argue that their model, with refinement, might also apply to nonblack communities in Baltimore and elsewhere.

Lenora Hellig Nast in "The Clergy and the Interfaith Movement: 1945–1980" also documents recent achievements of various groups of people. However, unlike Cortada, she does not concentrate on ethnic pluralism as such. Instead, Nast links the recent interfaith movement within Baltimore to the human rights movement. Her work delineates the *specific* human rights achievements of *specific* religious groups and their leaders. Nast shows that although Baltimoreans have faltered, especially during the volatile period of initial racial integration in the 1950s and 1960s, on the whole the city, and especially its major religious leaders, have been a vanguard in defending human rights.

Marianne Alexander's "Advancing the Status of Women" might very well be *the* definitive study of the women's movement in recent Baltimore history. She looks at specific women's groups, their communication networks, the legal barriers facing women, and important battles fought to help solve sexual discrimination as a continuing problem. She convincingly argues that as women obtain equality, all Baltimoreans will benefit in the process.

Betty Seidel's "Baltimore: Pioneer in Aging Services" is a moving account of how Baltimore has come to be viewed as a model city in its treatment of the elderly.

Leah S. Freedlander's "Renaissance in Public Education? . . . Not Quite Yet" is a hardhitting account of specific chinks in the renaissance armor. Yet she is able to point out areas of hope, although the main thrust of her essay is realistically somber.

M. Mercer Neale III's "Independent Schools in and Around Baltimore: A Historical Sketch" makes several important points including the fact that both public and private schools function best when education in general is doing well and not, as popularly assumed, at the expense of the other.

Dorothy Pula Strohecker and Carol Strohecker discuss "Changes on College Campuses." Their overview of Baltimore's 13 institutions of higher learning indicates that the city is serious about higher education which has significantly contributed to the renaissance.

Alice Cherbonnier's "Baltimore's Daily Newspapers in the Past Quarter-Century" is also a hardhitting account of areas of both strengths and weaknesses of Baltimore's two major dailies that have been important factors in Baltimore's renaissance.

"Community Weeklies Grow" by Sidney Kobre presents us with a different interpretation of a frequently neglected form of communication: the local publication. As a pioneer in small papers in Baltimore, Kobre brings a unique personal perspective to bear on his analysis.

"Baltimore's Alternative and Underground Newspapers" by coeditor of *Living Renaissance* Laurence Krause strikes a balance between the Cherbonnier and Kobre discussions of Baltimore's printed media. As a founder and publisher of several small papers, Krause is able to capture accurately the 1960s and 1970s as a time of ferment in Baltimore among the writers and editors of several alternative and underground papers. He documents the youthful idealism of most as well as the plain silliness of some.

"Public Broadcasting: Retrospect and Prospect" by coeditor of *Living Renaissance* Lenora Heilig Nast is possibly the most thorough treatment of the emergence of public broadcasting in Baltimore currently available.

"Commercial Television: A Window on the World" by Robert Cochrane is a factual overview of the emergence of commercial TV in Baltimore. Cochrane discusses both technical aspects and the shifting types of programs presented on commercial TV.

"Baltimore Radio During the Last 25 Years" by Tom O'Conner is a delightful article that includes a quiz for radio buffs. O'Conner wittily makes clear that news of Baltimore radio's demise is greatly exaggerated.

"Short History of WBJC" by Harvey Alexander provides a discussion of the contribution of the Community College of Baltimore to a local radio.

Peter Jay's "Political History" is a snappy piece of writing that makes you feel the enormous political changes that have advanced in Baltimore during the past 30 years. Jay's work links the political sphere with the social and shows the political contribution to Baltimore's renaissance.

"A Sage Reminisces" concludes this section. This is the late Gerald W. Johnson's touching farewell to a city he loved and served for so many years as Baltimore's outstanding philosopher-newsman.

Baltimore's Pluralism

Americans experienced intense change between 1954 and 1979, and Baltimore was deeply
affected. However, the social and cultural structure of the city provided a resiliency that enabled the area to gain a positive momentum,
while other urban centers suffered from polarization, fear, and economic malaise. This social
and cultural structure is one of the key facets of
any city's personality. It provides a unique mosaic of political balances, housing patterns, life
styles, community groups, and religious, educational, and cultural institutions. Baltimore's
black, Anglo–Saxon, eastern European, Italian,
Catholic, Jewish, Protestant, labor, management, and business groups were long accustomed
to an ebb and flow, and compromise, in their
dealings. Thus the volatile potential of the times
and the complexities of cultural fragmentation
were muted by long contact.

Baltimore's geographic position is unique. It
is a seaport, located 120 miles from the Atlantic.
It is the eastern city providing the easiest entrée
to the heartland of the American Midwest. Furthermore, Baltimore has been called "the northernmost southern city and the southernmost
northern city." In short, Baltimore defies stereotyping, and its only constant is a fluid cultural
diversity. The 1970 census population of 850,000
in Baltimore included about 13,000 Asians
(Chinese, Filipinos, Indians, Japanese, and others), about 5,000 smaller European populations
(Danish, Dutch, French, Norwegians, Swedes,
Swiss, and Yugoslavs), and 70,000 people in
larger clusters of Europeans (Austrians, Czechs,
Germans, Greeks, Hungarians, Italians, Lithuanians, Poles, Russians, Ukrainians), and Cana-
dians. The Spanish–speaking population of
10,000 was itself diverse, including Cubans,
Puerto Ricans, Spaniards, and Latin Americans.
This diversity was included in a total population
that was about half black. But the census figures
are deceptive, in that they identified cultural
roots only of persons either born abroad or who
had one or both parents born abroad. The full
diversity of the city can be appreciated when
one notes the second and third generations who
identify with the various cultural and national
groups.

The period of euphoric homogenization that
followed World War II threatened to alter the
structure of Baltimore's nonblack population.
The late 1950s and 1960s were characterized by
the flight to the suburbs. Baltimore's ethnic
groups had always gravitated toward neighborhoods in which religious and cultural institutions
developed to support the prevailing culture. For
example, today, 85 percent of the 92,000 Jews
living in the Baltimore metropolitan area reside
in the northwest corridor of the city and the
contiguous area of Baltimore County. Over the

Hopkins Fair. Photo by Susan Bishop

years, the center of this community has shifted from east Baltimore to the Liberty–Reisterstown roads corridors. The Jewish population is now growing in Owings Mills, as the community core drifts northward.

The suburban flight affected all ethnic groups in Baltimore except blacks, who were virtually eliminated from the movement by economic, social, and housing discrimination. The movement was characterized further by the fact that most new suburbanites tended to be younger married couples. Thus, during the 1960s, Baltimore city's white population declined by 130,000, while the black population rose 100,000; the black proportion of the city's population reached 47 percent. At the same time, much of the black population was of school age, while the whites who remained in the city tended to be older, well–established families. The loss of the young families of childbearing age threatened to limit the transmission of Old World culture and identity.

Jewish Community. The years from 1954 until 1979 represented a period of stabilization and consolidation for the Baltimore Jewish community. Many key Jewish educational and religious institutions relocated in the Park Heights corridor of northwest Baltimore during that period. Baltimore's Jews offered leadership in key areas that helped the city to rise above the racial tensions that characterized the era. Walter Sondheim was president of the Board of School Commissioners when school desegregation was implemented. Similarly, Robert Levi was one of the founders of the Greater Baltimore Committee. Generally, Jewish leadership has influenced every phase of Baltimore's development, from the past ownership of the Orioles to the presidency of the Baltimore Symphony.

Baltimore's Jews are also providing leadership in the city's ethnic revival. Northwest Baltimore is an aging area, but the number of young couples with children settling in the area is noteworthy. Thus there is every indication that the community will survive the threatened scattering when the general flight to the suburbs began.

Baltimore has always provided access for new populations coming into the United States. The Baltimore Jewish community has provided leadership in efforts to accommodate Soviet Jews. The "free Soviet Jewry" movement had national impact during the late 1960s and early 1970s.

These pressures helped facilitate the immigration of 120,000 Soviet Jews to Israel and, since 1973, more than 21,000 to the United States. Of this number, more than 600 have settled in the Baltimore area, supported by over $1 million from the Associated Jewish Charities and Welfare Fund. Roughly half of the employable immigrants were skilled technicians, and a quarter of them were highly educated professionals. There are indications that the Jewish community and its institutions will similarly support any Jews who might emigrate from Iran.

Black Community. No ethnic group in Baltimore experienced more tumultuous and total change than the black community. Although blacks have long been the largest ethnic group in the city, Baltimore was a rigidly segregated city until 1954. In 1940, blacks comprised 26 percent of the laborers, 30 percent of the domestics, 3 percent of the white collar employees, and 3 percent of the professionals. The civil rights movement and the rapid expansion of educational opportunity removed overt symbols of segregation and led to an expansion of the small black middle class that had long been established. By 1970, blacks comprised only 10 percent of the laborers and 6 percent of the domestics, while they constituted 19 percent of the white collar employees and 9 percent of the professionals. These figures must be evaluated, however, in the context of the movement of whites to the suburbs. The population lost included mostly young, better–educated families, leaving an older white population in the city. Conversely, much of the black population is younger and still of school age; thus they are not yet represented in the work force. A debilitating level of unemployment among young blacks was reported in 1979, indicating that problems of access remain. The city's future can well hinge on its ability to absorb these youth into its economy.

One sign of the quickening in the black community was manifested in the political arena. In 1970, a black peace activist professor from Morgan State College, Parren J. Mitchell, defeated an 18-year incumbent liberal ward politician by 38 votes in the Seventh District congressional primary election. Mitchell has, since that time, moved on to nationally visible leadership while representing Baltimore in Congress.

The quarter century before 1980 has been one

of liberation and hardship for the black community, but there remains little doubt that—with overt segregation eliminated from American life—this ethnic group has progressed. The years ahead will demand the establishment of a focus and some social, economic, and political direction in order to define the impact that the blacks will have in Baltimore during the last decades of the twentieth century.

Italian Community. The emergence of the D'Alesandro family in Baltimore politics by 1954 signaled the solid establishment of the Italian community. The absence of high–rise tenements and the potential for ownership of small homes and access to trades enabled the Italian community to develop solid roots in Baltimore, starting in the late nineteenth century. The movement into an alien, often hostile, Anglo–Saxon environment fostered a new Italian unity in America; people identified as Italians, rather than as residents of one of the regions of the old country.

The exodus to the suburbs threatened Little Italy as a community, since the second and third generations could easily have followed their peers from other groups in abandoning the city. Such a flight would have complicated any effort to maintain the extended family structure, Italian values, language, diet, and outlook on life. But Little Italy was still secure as a community in 1980. The restaurants in the area had become a resource valued by all Baltimoreans. The value of Little Italy to the city as an ethnic residential community adjacent to the Inner Harbor redevelopment area was obvious.

In 1970, the Sons of Italy had only 390 members in all Maryland; by 1979, there were about 5,000 members. Lodges were being formed in unexpected areas such as Parkville, as well as Little Italy, where the D'Alesandros had always had their own organization. The Italian community has successfully preserved its family structure and, equally important, its values. There are no organized charities to care for the elderly in Little Italy. None are needed.

The general ethnic revival in the nation, the state, and the city helped to preserve the links between generations of Italians in Little Italy and other neighborhoods. But the development of the ethnic festival in Baltimore was a special catalyst for the Italian community. This pro-vided a publicly visible project for the clubs, lodges, and parishes in which cultural heritage could be the focus. The fact that the Italian festival draws 1,000,000 people to the Inner Harbor over a summer weekend speaks volumes.

Eastern–Central European Communities. Baltimore's eastern European communities are possibly the city's most complex. Their survival in the city's ethnic revival may involve new and creative syntheses. The Byelorussian, Czech, Estonian, Lithuanian, Polish, Slovak, Ukrainian, and other eastern European communities have been deeply affected by the movement to the suburbs. For example, there are about 39,334 residents of Polish descent in Baltimore. But Greeks, Puerto Ricans, and Appalachian people are as familiar as Poles once were on Broadway, the old "Polish Wall Street of Baltimore." The Polish community has scattered from its East Baltimore core with outposts in Locust Point and Curtis Bay. Today, people of Polish descent reside all over the greater metropolitan area, in Baltimore city and County and in Harford and Anne Arundel counties. Names are no longer a clue to ethnic identity, because many are as Polish as they are Irish, Italian, or German as their surname might imply. Any census seeking to identify Polish roots may be misleading, furthermore, if it does not include Jews. Dr. Moses Aberbach, curator of the Jewish Historical Society in 1972, asserted then that 40 percent to 50 percent of Baltimore's Jewish community was of Polish descent.

One characteristic of Baltimore's Polish population that has not changed is the high rate of homeownership. The estimated 75 percent homeownership rate is among the highest of any group in the city. This is attributable, at least in part, to the building and loan associations that were unique to "Little Poland." In 1940, there were 20 strictly Polish institutions for building and loans. Today, only seven remain, but they have assets in excess of $25,000,000. They still finance home purchases in outlying areas for the children and grandchildren of people whose homes they financed years ago in East Baltimore.

An ethnic community does not necessarily need to reside near one another to be cohesive. The election of Barbara Mikulski, a former professor at the Community College of Baltimore, to the Third District Congressional seat provides one example. Congresswoman Mikulski's roots are proudly proclaimed, but it is significant to all Baltimoreans that her leadership is nationally visible, is felt throughout the city, and covers a complex web of local, regional, and national concerns. The Polish festival represents another rallying point through which the unique culture of the group can be kept vibrant and shared and through which community–based organizations and institutions can cooperate. The ethnic revival of recent years will influence each community differently. This is fitting, in view of the diversity that the city is attempting to preserve and cherish. However, the end result will be similar, as each group, Polish–Americans included, finds vehicles to preserve values and traditions vital to the integrity of the entire community.

Estonians and Lithuanians are unique, smaller eastern European communities in Baltimore which have spiritual focal points, rather than a defined locale, to keep their identity alive. Both are concerned about the Russification of their homelands. Lithuanians came to Baltimore just prior to 1900; their first settlement was adjacent to the Jewish community near Lombard Street. Lithuanians organized the Catholic parish of St. John the Baptist in 1887, then used the old Lloyd Street Synagogue from 1889 to 1905 before moving to Saratoga and Paca streets. In 1917, they settled finally in St. Alphonsus Parish. The second wave of immigrants came in 1949, after the Soviet takeover of the Baltic States. Perhaps more than many groups, Estonians and Lithuanians are able to cherish Baltimore's cultural openness and diversity. The Baltic States, many feel, are victims of Soviet cultural imperialism. Thus Baltimore's ethnic festivals represent a focus, a rallying point, and a vehicle for keeping alive the culture and values.

Greek Community. It was natural that Greeks, who never lived far from the sea, should find Baltimore a fitting place to settle. While about 18,000 Marylanders claim Greek roots, the core of this community remains in Highlandtown and the Lexington Market areas in Baltimore. In some instances, clusters of people from a given Aegean Island or Greek region have remained in close proximity. For example, families from the Dodecanese Islands have remained in the Old-

ham Street area, where the Kentrikon Music Store serves as a focus for Greek books, newspapers, and records.

While early Greek migrants came to Maryland as skilled tradesmen, chefs, bakers, tailors, and other skilled workers, they are now augmented by professionals—lawyers, doctors, teachers, dentists, and politicians. The suburban migration of the 1950s and 1960s saw a new generation of professionals move to the surrounding counties to start their families. This left older, more settled families in the city, whose children had grown up in the heretofore Greek areas of Baltimore. But the ethnic revival and the city's increased pride in its multi–cultural cuisine have strengthened the sense of identification with Greek culture. Thus, a Greek community that is scattered throughout the metropolitan area, emanating from an urban core ethnic neighborhood, remains well established.

Asian Community. Baltimore's Asian community has grown and prospered since 1954. The Chinese community was already well established at Mulberry Street in the 1920s. Thereafter, natural and external forces cultivated a slow process of change. The educational system acculturated the second generation and allowed some economic mobility. The Exclusion Acts ended in 1943, and allowed the migration of highly educated, often affluent Chinese from Taiwan. Since 1954, concentration of this community has ended, and the 2,000 or so Chinese residents are spread throughout the metropolitan area. There are Chinese cultural groups in Baltimore, but the community is not self–conscious; thus individuals tend to make their own way quite well. There is no participation, as a community, in the city's ethnic festivals. The community's outreach has been undertaken very effectively, however, through public celebration and awareness of the Chinese New Year.

Between 1953 and 1968, only 100 Koreans per year were allowed to enter the United States. Thus the immigrants were more often university students, professors, or doctors who came with exchange visas. When the immigration laws were relaxed in 1969, significant numbers of doctors, nurses, and skilled workers entered through United States–based employment agencies. Today there are over 4,000 Koreans in Maryland, and 80 percent are permanent residents. Koreans have had some success in entering the professions in Baltimore. They have also opened restaurants, Oriental grocery stores, tailor shops, wig stores, and stalls in the Lexington Market. For a new community, the educational and economic success of the Koreans is impressive.

The Indian and Vietnamese communities are relatively new. The former include many who came to the United States as students and remained to enter the professions. The Indian community today includes many practicing physicians, professors, importers, and restaurateurs. The approximately 2,500 Indians in Baltimore are viable as individuals and as a community and can be expected to grow in numbers, influence, and impact. The Vietnamese came to Baltimore after 1975. As a new community they are still in the process of mastering language and customs and becoming established. Many have gravitated into small businesses, often in black neighborhoods. This has at times caused some concern. However, the community is still too new and small in numbers for patterns and relationships to have become fully established.

Native American Indian Community. Baltimore's invisible community is that of the Lumbee Indians who came here in some numbers from Robeson County, North Carolina, after World War II. No accurate census figure of the number of Lumbees in Baltimore exists because census interviewers do not inquire about native Indian ancestry. However, the American Indian Study Center estimated a population of 3,500 in 1970, which may be the most reliable figure available. The Lumbees are unique among native Americans because they have urbanized successfully. There are Lumbee communities in every major city between Robeson County and Boston, with the most solid concentrations in Baltimore and Philadelphia. But urbanization has a different meaning for the Lumbees than for most groups. A constant flow of traffic, going both ways, continues between Baltimore and Robeson County, with many Lumbees spending part of their year in each location. The Lumbee population is concentrated along East Baltimore Street as the east–west axis, bounded by Broadway on the west, Patterson Park Avenue on the east, Fayette Street on the north, and Pratt Street on the south. This is an older area that has served as a point of entry for Germans, Irish,

Italians, and Jews since the 1880s. Thus, the Lumbees face problems of substandard housing along with other problems faced by a community in transition.

Just as one encounters certain surnames repeatedly in the Lumbee community (Locklear, Hunt, Chavis, Oxandine, Lowry, Hammond, Dial), the Lumbees have also worked in specific jobs for which they have skills. Construction work, painting, and jobs in factories and small shops have helped make the transition to city living easier. Often a specific firm will hire significantly from the Lumbee community. Koester's, a bread firm, for example, had as many as 40 Lumbees in its nonunionized work force of 500. The Schmidt Bread Company has also helped ease the chronic unemployment in the community at times. By 1980, the Lumbee community remained well established, with a migratory rhythm of its own. A few Lumbees have entered professions and small businesses. Problems remain, however, since Lumbee children sometimes adjust poorly to the educational process. The full influence, impact, and role the Lumbees will play in Baltimore has not yet been defined.

West Indian Community. West Indians represent another "invisible" community in Baltimore. These immigrants from Trinidad and Tobago, Barbados, Jamaica, and the smaller islands of the English–speaking Caribbean cannot be differentiated by language, custom, or culture. They tend to settle quietly into the social and economic life of the black community, but they will enrich the life of the city by establishing an interest in steel band and other forms of Caribbean culture as well as in West Indian cuisine. The role and the impact of West Indians has barely been sorted out and defined as of 1979. While to the casual observer the community is indistinguishable from the indigenous black community, it can be assumed that West Indian culture, values, and mores will be asserted in constructive ways.

Hispanic Community. Baltimore's Puerto Rican community is another "invisible" group that merits attention. Unlike the Vietnamese or other distinct language groups, Puerto Ricans came to Baltimore like other American citizens, without fanfare or documentation. Thus the community has grown to about 3,000 concentrated at Fell's

Point eastward to the Patterson Park area. The Puerto Rican community is plagued by problems of poverty, unemployment, substandard housing, and lack of visibility. Individual Puerto Ricans in the professions, able to leapfrog "El Barrio," have avoided these problems. Generally, however, Puerto Ricans are among the nation's poorest citizens, so it is to be expected that the bulk of the population will require special services. The city has gradually become aware of the community. A less passive acceptance of hardship among the increasing number of Puerto Ricans will inculcate increased sensitivity and the needed services. The Baltimore City Public Schools have addressed bilingual education needs for a century and are not reluctant to respond to the needs of Puerto Ricans if a coherent need is defined. The Puerto Rican community itself is striving for identity and visibility by offering its own ethnic festival in Fell's Point each year.

Baltimore also has a Hispanic community that is as diverse as the city itself. Cubans, Chicanos, Spaniards, and South and Central Americans in greater or lesser numbers, form a community of perhaps 15,000 in the metropolitan area. But the very diversity of the population, its lack of a neighborhood focus, and its newness complicate efforts to define a "community" in the traditional sense. The community is economically diverse and includes a heavy concentration in the professions. The component communities have organized social clubs, however; thus a Federation of Hispanic organizations has been working to bridge the national gaps built into the Hispanic community. The Hispanic festival in Hopkins Plaza each year has been one result of this work. Baltimore's Hispanic community has a contribution to make to the city, and it is likely that this will be defined and clarified during the coming decades. The appearance of *El Hispaño* in 1979, the Hispanic community's newest publication, is symptomatic of the progress that can be anticipated as the community defines and expresses itself within its own group and within greater Baltimore.

Implications of Ethnic Diversity. The ethnic diversity of the city might have been politically explosive because intergroup conflict or imbalance in the decision-making process could have paralyzed the system. But Baltimore has par-

layed a large black population, a plethora of ethnic and cultural groups, a strong urban Democratic organization, and an activist business community into a strong, popular, progressive mayor and the urban success story of the East Coast. Despite diversity, the city has managed to centralize power by consensus and to survive fiscally while moving aggressively to redevelop itself. This has happened while neighboring cities seem to be stagnating and attempting to manage fiscal crises instead of seeking renewal.

One facet of Baltimore's success in stitching a quilt out of its ethnic diversity has been the city's ability to avert economic confrontation among its ethnic groups. The city's economy is as diverse as its population. And, while one of the largest industrial complexes (Bethlehem Steel) is not locally owned, there are important locally based businesses in transportation and commerce. The fact that Baltimore's business community has been able to keep unemployment at fairly low levels has also helped avoid intergroup competition. The runaway unemployment among black youth has been a dangerous deviation from the historic pattern.

Baltimore's economy has also influenced the city's ethnicity by demanding a large working class; blacks were attracted to this northernmost of southern cities by the same economic opportunities that attracted European groups.

Baltimore's ethnic diversity is reflected in its political structures, both the formal and the informal. The various ethnic groups settled into neighborhoods. Thus each of the six councilmanic districts contained clearly defined ethnic neighborhoods. The election of three councilpersons per district facilitated a division of labor, rather than competition. The end result has been that councilpersons have tended to be black, German, Irish, Italian, Jewish, or Polish. Thus while no group would have a clear majority, neither would any group be excluded. Of course, blacks were relatively ignored for decades, despite the dynamic growth of the population toward a majority; but black concerns were at least acknowledged through the existence of black middle–class subsidiary organizations that related to the dominant urban political machine and its components.

Theodore McKeldin's 1963 mayoral victory was a political watershed in Baltimore's renaissance. His victory followed a feeble attempt to regain the office in 1959, when J. Harold Grady beat him by a two–to–one margin. Furthermore, no Republican had held that office since 1943 when McKeldin himself served. McKeldin's shift was that he appealed directly to the Democratic ethnic coalitions, asking them to cross over to support him as the more progressive candidate. But he also appealed directly to black and Jewish voters. This alerted the Democratic party to the disruptive potential of an alienated black vote. The McKeldin administration provided further healthy breakthroughs for Baltimore, as he introduced significant numbers of black appointees into city government. The February 26, 1964, comprehensive civil rights bill finally relieved Baltimore of the albatross of overt segregation. Thereafter, Baltimore's black community asserted itself politically. By 1970, an impressive series of electoral victories established the black political presence permanently: Parren Mitchell was elected to Congress; Milton B. Allen was elected state's attorney; and numbers of state and municipal court judges, state senators, and delegates emerged. The fact that the black community generated fewer votes in relation to population mass assured continuation of the old coalitions, leavened now with black participation; although blacks constituted a numerical majority in the population by 1970, whites held a majority among registered voters.

Baltimore's politics hinges on delicate balances and perceptions. While blacks have demonstrated political power commensurate with the population, a broader awareness of black concerns remains vital for Baltimore's political development. This is an imperfect mechanism for progress, but it represents one stage in a developmental process, since the black community is still in the process of emerging politically. Its move toward political leadership will be the next step in Baltimore's "politics of ethnic accommodation" and will establish the model for the future accommodation of other new groups.

Baltimore made a courageous choice when it opted for diversity. A lame attempt could have been made to speak of "melting pots" and oneness. But the city chose to accept itself and to revel in its many-faceted culture. There could have been fragmentation, but instead we see pride and a growing pluralistic familiarity. The

ethnic festivals each summer weekend attract millions of people to Baltimore's Inner Harbor and Hopkins Plaza and reassert the historic primacy of the urban cultural magnetism. Through the festivals, a diverse population learns alternatives to polarization. They learn one another's customs and explore each other's roots. In 1979, Baltimore festivals honored Afro-Americans, Estonians, the French, Germans, Greeks, Hispanics, Irish, Italians, Jews, Koreans, Lithuanians, Native Americans, Polish, and Ukranians. The City Fair is, in effect, a "summarizing" event.

Baltimore has made tremendous strides between 1954 and 1981, in both human and physical rehabilitation. The city's ethnic groups have visibly stated their desire to be part of this renaissance. The fact that new groups continue to come to the city shows that the nature of Baltimore will not change. There will always be a place where a group can amalgamate, achieve economic and political security, and yet maintain its essence, its historic culture, and values. Black Americans paved the way with the civil rights movement, by groping for the basic self-acceptance that must precede one's acceptance of another. If one can accept the premise that "Black is beautiful," it is axiomatic that Italian or Polish or Jewish is beautiful, too. Baltimore's ethnic groups have abandoned the mythical melting pot to reestablish their own "roots" and values. The results will provide a model for other American cities blessed with the rich diversity to create a similar orchestra.

Rafael L. Cortada

BLACKS IN BALTIMORE, 1950–1980: AN OVERVIEW

Long before 1950, Baltimore's blacks had gained distinctions. Baltimore is unique in that it had the largest free black population in the United States prior to the Civil War, in 1860, and numbering 25,680. The free blacks of the nineteenth century and blacks in the early twen-

"Hollywood Charm Center: Baltimore, 1970." Photo by John Clark Mayden

tieth century developed many social institutions and programs that left sustaining vestiges for the future. These viable social institutions and programs were often structured and implemented in spite of great obstacles and the ever pervasive institutional racism. Although the same adverse conditions existed during the period being examined, blacks in Baltimore contributed to the development of the city and at the same time created a community that was responsive to their needs. Six aspects of black community life—neighborhood development, economic development, educational advancement, religious development, political activism, and cultural development—will be discussed here.

Neighborhood Development. The population of Baltimore in 1950 was 949,701. Of that figure, the precise number of black citizens is not known. By July 1, 1959, the population had grown to 987,000 with 32 percent being black. The years 1960 and 1970 witnessed a decline in the population of Baltimore as the exodus for the suburbs escalated.

Prior to 1955, most of the city's black population lived within 10 square miles in the center of the city from Monroe Street in the west to Broadway in the east. The lower and upper sections of West Baltimore had begun to deteriorate. McCulloh Street, Druid Hill Avenue, and Fulton Avenue in West Baltimore provided housing for those who were better educated and

had better incomes. In later years, the West Baltimore communities of Walbrook, Forest Park, Ashburton, Pimlico, and Guilford would be the housing areas selected by more affluent blacks. In East Baltimore blacks had begun to move into the Second Legislative District during the early sixties. Housing in that area became the worst. Pockets of low-income houses were built throughout East Baltimore in order to impede the rapidly declining inner city.

During the years from 1959 to 1968 greater numbers of middle-class blacks moved to the outlying areas of Baltimore. The economic plight of the inner city worsened as the more affluent residents fled to the suburbs. Real estate values declined and houses, which were previously occupied by the owners, became rentals and the neighborhoods gradually became slums. Many absentee landlords would not reinvest portions of the rent money in order to maintain the property. Businesses declined in the areas as persons with low incomes moved into the communities. The housing patterns were sanctioned and perpetuated by the larger society and realtors. Local newspapers used the word "colored" to designate available housing for blacks. Often, housing was located in slum areas or areas with approaching slum conditions readily apparent.

As late as February, 1978, a survey conducted by the *Sun* showed that white realtors continued to control, to a significant degree, the housing patterns of blacks. Different advertisements, or the same advertisements with different wording, would be placed in the local newspapers. Blacks reading only the *Afro-American* would not have seen the same advertisements as the person who read the *Sun* and/or *Jewish Times.* A clear pattern of neighborhood steering was evident and the ads were ruled illegal via the Federal Fair Housing Act. The practice, however, continues to some extent even to today.

Concern for slum clearance and the preservation of neighborhoods became the central issues for the planning of Baltimore city. Blacks who were left or remained by choice in the declining neighborhoods became active participants in the planning for and renovation of the inner city. The Baltimore Urban Renewal and Housing Agency vigorously acted to halt the urban deterioration. Neighborhood organizations developed from residents' concerns and the members worked with the agencies. One such organization was the Harlem Park Neighborhood Council, which assisted in the renovation of selected areas of its community. Alleys were transformed into parks with some houses torn down and others rebuilt. An example of new dwellings in the Harlem Park area was the George B. Murphy Homes, featuring 750 low rental units.

A community to be cited for its citizens' involvement, rise from decline, and innovative growth is the Upton community. The residential neighborhood of 183 acres and 114,000 people is bounded on the south by Biddle and George streets, the west by Fremont Avenue, the north by Bloom and Laurens streets, and the east by McCulloh Street. This community has long been noted for and became nationally famous because of Pennsylvania Avenue and its entertainment center of the 1930s to the 1960s. Mrs. Lena Boone, chairperson of the Upton Planning Community Incorporated, since its inception in 1967, stated that the Pennsylvania Avenue image of the past was no longer applicable and should not be restored. The six-block strip of leisure activities was replaced in the sixties by 39 liquor outlets, drugs, and a high crime rate. The desegregation of theatre, night clubs, and other entertainment sites also shifted dollars and patronage from Pennsylvania Avenue.

In 1967, attention began to be centered upon the total Upton community and not just one street. Mrs. Boone points to a number of community "ingredients" that were part of the revitalization of the Upton neighborhood. There were a number of unified groups already present in the area; 16 churches of all denominations were active, descendants of many of the original families of the area were still residents there, and there was a movement from the alleys to the main streets. A current support factor is the presence of homes, businesses and/or interests of members of the Jackson, Mitchell, and Murphy families who are considered among the leading families of black Baltimore.

The Upton Committee, with Mrs. Boone at the helm, worked with the city in completing a marketability study that reflected the needs, goals, and concerns of the residents. The Department of Housing and Urban Development also became a pivotal unit. One of the first tasks of the involved persons was the dissolution, to a degree, of mistrust regarding governmental units and the isolation of what was no longer applicable for the area. Taking a holistic approach, Mrs. Boone states, "We provide a community that serves the total needs of a people." The approach is readily visible. Housing from garden apartments to co-op housing, to renovated houses, to houses designed with the elderly in mind is available. Schools, tennis courts, supermarkets, a sports arena, two multi-purpose centers, and a constant care unit are part of future plans or currently in existence. Glenn Doughty, member of the Baltimore Colts, has financed the Shake and Bake Family Fun Center on Pennsylvania Avenue, which represents a new form of entertainment for the eighties. The center will contain bowling lanes, fast food stands, a roller rink, and an electronic game center. All age groups will find suitable recreational activities within the center. Mr. Doughty will extend the philosophy of a center for the neighborhood by hiring neighborhood persons to staff it. All neighborhood businesses are encouraged to hire residents of the area.

The lack of employment or low-paying jobs, according to Mrs. Boone, accounts for some of the area's existing problems. Mechanisms have been developed in order to assist residents in purchasing their homes and improving the quality of their lives. Rat eradication programs, job training programs, political awareness, health

East Baltimore Youth in Track Clinic Given by John Hopkins Medical Students. Photo by Linda Wojcik

education, community meetings, and the direct passing down of knowledge from the old to the young are methods employed by the residents in keeping the community a viable and growing entity.

Madison Park, also known as Sugar Hill, is another Baltimore community that has its roots in the past and is now experiencing a renaissance. It was one of the few neighborhoods opened to blacks in the 1920s and became known throughout the city because of the middle-class persons who lived in the 1800 to 2100 blocks. Today, young, professional blacks, as part of the urban renewal and shift to the city movement, are reclaiming the area and restoring it.

Not all neighborhoods experiencing a renaissance have been black. The Ashburton section of West Baltimore began to be opened to blacks in 1959. The community starts at Wabash Avenue as the northern boundary, extends southward to Powhatan Avenue and westward to Garrison Boulevard. Ashburton has always been a relatively affluent area with professional persons residing there. In 1979, activities to retain the quality of the neighborhood began. BUILD, Baltimoreans United in Leadership Development, grew from the impetus of Our Lady of Lourdes Church headed by Father James Power. The racially mixed organization pushed for the renovation of the apartments at the corner of Hilton Street and Liberty Heights Avenue, and the leasing of vacant buildings on Dolfield Avenue between Belle Avenue and Coldspring Lane. It also maintains a close watch on the business area in the 3800 block of Liberty Heights Avenue. The approach, one which appears to be in vogue, is to monitor neighborhoods for indicators of decline.

Similar renovation efforts, urban renewal, and watchdog activities also occur in East Baltimore. The area north of North Avenue, south of Twenty-fifth Street, west of Harford Road, and east of Greenmount Avenue is known as the East Baltimore Midway. In 1979, the area was populated with 6,500 persons. As vacancy rates escalated, the East Baltimore Midway Development Association, with Ida R. Grant as the president, was founded to combat and halt deterioration. Various forms of housing and recreational facilities for all ages were incorporated into the revitalization plans. Political activism

and mobilization through the efforts of the Eastside Democratic Organization and the East Baltimore Community Corporation keep the concerns and needs of other neighborhoods in East Baltimore before the public's eye. The East Baltimore Medical Center, established in 1971 and providing vital health services, was the result of such attention and self-help programs. The East Baltimore Community Development Corporation has also initiated economic ventures, such as shopping malls, which will hopefully benefit the total area.

Economic Development. Even though many of the black communities and social institutions developed as the result of segregation statutes prior to 1965, blacks began in the sixties and seventies to redefine their neighborhoods' objectives. They worked closely with municipal officials but did not relinquish their right and responsibility to help formulate the direction that growth and revitalization would take in their communities. One of the key objectives was to keep blacks with needed skills and economic stability in the city. Caroll L. Lyles, feature writer for *Metropolitan* magazine, suggested in April, 1980, six ways of luring blacks back or keeping them in the city. They are: (1) upgrading of all city schools with an emphasis on basic skills; (2) enforcement of the housing codes; (3) positive exposure of the neighborhoods by the media; (4) development by CETA of job training programs for relevant positions; (5) nurturing of businesses in the city; and (6) development of public transportation that will take people efficiently from the city to jobs in the suburbs.

The type of employment or the lack of any job has interfaced with a number of identifiable urban problems. Many blacks in Baltimore are or have family members who are migrants from farms in the South. They came to the city seeking better paying jobs and a new way of life. During the period 1959 to 1968, blacks were hired in significant numbers by Bethlehem Steel, Western Electric, and Kennicott Refining Corporation. Some were hired as dock workers or at the General Motors Broening Highway assembly plant. The jobs that required entry into union apprentice programs or job-related training programs were kept virtually closed. Women in the city seeking industrial jobs were more often employed by the textile industries.

In 1958, 53 percent of the textile workers were women and 68 percent of the apparel group workers were women. Yet many blacks remained underemployed or unemployed.

The unemployment figures for black adults and teenagers have always been greater than those for white adults and teenagers. Blacks comprised 92.8 percent of the population in West Baltimore in 1968 with 15.4 percent of them unemployed. In East Baltimore 79.9 percent of the population was black with 10.3 percent unemployed. The figures fluctuated from 1968 onward with 8.7 percent blacks unemployed in 1974, 18.3 percent in 1978, and 17.9 percent in 1979. The city's unemployment rate in 1980 was ranked among the nation's highest. There were direct correlations between the unemployment figures and living conditions for blacks. More blacks than whites were found to live in slums. The figures for 1959 revealed that 78 percent of the people living in slums in Baltimore were black. An increase in the figures was cited for 1968 with 87.6 percent of the people living in slums being black. Exact figures are not available, but it was hypothesized that the majority of the 30,178 families in Baltimore whose incomes were below the poverty line in 1969 were black.

Racism, the high rate of black high school drop-outs, lack of skills, and the industrial job market shifts were some of the reasons given for the high unemployment rate. The number of manufacturing and construction jobs has decreased during the time period of this overview, but nonmanufacturing and service jobs have become more plentiful. At the same time, the labor force has continued to increase faster than employment possibilities.

Efforts to combat the high unemployment rates began long before 1980 and required the involvement of blacks and whites. Persons from outside the city, such as James Foreman, also became involved. In 1975, Mr. Foreman came to Baltimore to organize the unemployed workers. He was particularly concerned about the large number of black industrial workers who were unemployed. His objective was to establish a Baltimore chapter of the Unemployed and Poverty Action Council. Private businessmen met to establish the Private Industry Council that would seek to identify job opportunities for the disadvantaged. Congressman Parren J. Mitchell organized a Black Economic Summit, which was held in Baltimore during October, 1979, at the World Trade Center. The primary objective of the meeting and the follow-up conference, in April, 1980, was to develop a "5-year plan to increase minority economic development."

Many unemployed blacks took advantage of specific agency services. As of July 6, 1980, there were nine government-funded training and placement centers in Baltimore. The Mayor's Office of Manpower Resources, under the direction of Marion Pines, serves as the central clearinghouse. The CETA program, however, has come under constant attack by local black political figures because of the charged lack of sensitivity to the needs and concerns of blacks by some of its staff. Under the Comprehensive Employment and Training Act, Mrs. Pines also directed the Youth Incentive Entitlement Program for unemployed youth. The goal of the program is to keep low-income city teenagers in school. Since 1978, 18,000 youths have participated. Other unemployed persons, many of them black, have also been employed through CETA funds. While gaining valuable skills and earning salaries, the CETA workers have weatherized more than 8,000 homes of low-income and elderly residents. Some of the workers have been hired in permanent positions by the city's Housing Authority once they left CETA.

Another significant component of the labor force has been the black female. Black women in Baltimore, during the period 1950-1980, have worked in nearly every field. Over the years proportionately more black females have worked as domestics. It is difficult to get exact figures because employers attempt to avoid paying social security benefits, and some workers are illegally attempting to supplement social services grants. Service workers, including orderlies, health aides, janitors, and household employees totaled 200,003 persons in Maryland according to a 1976 count. The household employee was generally a black female over 40 years of age who had not completed high school. Some domestics have been with the same family or families for years and enjoy fringe benefits reminiscent of those for the house slave prior to the Civil War. For the majority of the household employees, there is no sick pay, and no paid vacation. The women often work at the pleasure of the employer under conditions over which they have little control. Some have expressed the desire to form domestic labor unions much like those begun during the early 1970s in New York City.

Black women are also employed in Baltimore as teachers, models, clerks, ministers, physicians, and lawyers. Their numbers are so few in the highly skilled professions that many of them are still recognized as the first and the only ones in their fields. One is Lois Young, the first black woman who was admitted to the University of Maryland's College of Medicine and is now a practicing ophthalmologist; N. Louise Young, an obstetrician and gynecologist was the first black woman licensed to practice medicine in Maryland; and Hilda Ford is the first black woman to serve as the head of the Civil Service Commission for the city of Baltimore.

In 1970, Christanta de Jesus Ricks was the first black female in the Baltimore area to become a C.P.A. Ten years later, she was appointed to the board of Advance Federal Savings and Loan. Advance Federal had recognized the ability of women to perform in the banking world, in 1978, when Carrie M. Young, Claudia Dennis, and Zelma Brown were appointed as vice-presidents. The example set by Advance has not been followed by other area banks. Cheryl Wainwright, chairperson of the Clean Up Banking Campaign Committee, in an *Afro-American* article in March, 1980, stated that black women comprise 14 percent of banking employees yet were at the bottom of the pay and promotion ladders.

Recognizing that black women often labored under two adverse labels, the Black Women's Consciousness Raising Association organized. The organization has sponsored three conferences in order to assist black women in adjusting to today's world and needs. Issues and concerns such as racism, stress, and self-concept have been explored. Hundreds of women from all social and economic levels attended the workshop sessions and related activities. The theme for the third annual conference was "Meeting the Challenge of the 80s–Part II."

Dorothy Brunson began to meet the challenge of the eighties when at the end of 1979 she purchased the WEBB Radio Station, which had been owned by James Brown. Ms. Brunson came to Baltimore with 20 years of broadcasting experience and still owns a station in New York. She was able to make the purchase under FCC's new "distress policy." Because she is a minority group member the station was sold to her at less than the appraised value. After securing the station, she hired new personnel and began to correct the financial problems that had plagued the station. She stated in an interview for *Metropolitan* magazine, "Blacks have got to understand the economics of this country if we are ever to become a part of the mainstream."

Selected black Baltimoreans serve as examples of those who not only understood the economics of the nation but also assisted others in gaining greater economic independence and stability. In 1957, Dr. W.O. Bryson, Jr. led the effort to organize the only minority–owned savings and loan company in the United States, Advance Federal Savings and Loan. Ideal Savings and Loan Association was founded, in 1920, but was not able to remain solvent. It reopened in 1962 and is also black–owned and managed. Advance, however, remains the largest and by December 31, 1979, had over $24 million in assets. Most of Advance's loans have been made to city residents, and the company works with the Baltimore City Department of Housing and Community Development in making mortgage loans available to inner–city residents.

Other efforts have been made to become a part of the banking arena. Eleven organizers, after being granted a national charter in 1974, have attempted to found the Harbor National Bank. As of April, 1980, another charter had been granted, but not enough funds had been generated in order for the bank to open. Efforts were made by selected legislators to get the state to provide subsidies to minority–owned banks. The bill was defeated in the same year.

The governmental structures of the city and state have also attempted to assist black businessmen in securing loans and/or city contracts. A survey published in the *Sun* on November 26, 1976, listed 300 black–owned businesses. The city was concerned about the number of black businessmen who were awarded contracts by it. In 1978, a report was submitted to the commissioners of the Baltimore City Community Relations Commission requesting that contracts to minorities be increased from 1 percent to 10 percent. Two years later the request was for construction and procurement contracts to be raised from 15 percent to 25 percent. Some charges still surface that the city contracts have not been awarded fairly and that whites have placed blacks in visible key positions in companies in order to get the contracts under the minority clause.

Many of the black businesses founded in the fifties and sixties began as the result of private funds, hard work, and support from the black community rather than governmental funds. William L. Adams (Little Willie) is probably the best known businessman in Baltimore because of his varied financial ventures and his support of blacks less financially successful than himself. Mr. Adams began his financial empire through the backing of numbers in 1930. From his first bar, "Little Willie's Inn" in West Baltimore, from testifying, in 1950, before a U.S. Senate Committee investigating organized crime, to becoming an advocate for his race, his career has spanned more than 42 years. He either purchased or bought shares in a number of companies. Among them are the Parks Sausage Company, Club Casino on Pennsylvania Avenue, Biddison Music Company, and a real estate firm. Probably one of his most publicized financial involvements was the Metro Plaza located in the Mondawmin Mall. Mr. Adams has not permitted his personal wealth and influence to isolate him from other blacks. He has utilized many tactics and levels of involvement with other blacks in his business operations. Henry Parks was Willie Adams' partner in the Parks Sausage Company and as a result became one of Baltimore's wealthiest men.

Charles Burns' business career was also influenced by Adams. In June, 1962, Burns along with Wesley Shelton and John Hagan opened the first Hilton Court Pharmacy in West Baltimore that led to his purchasing five other pharmacies. Mr. Burns was persuaded, primarily by Willie Adams, to take over the management of the floundering Super Jet Market in East Baltimore. His business career flourished and the market was renamed Super Pride after Burns became the owner.

Blacks have started a wide range of businesses that appeal to the special interests and/or needs of blacks. However, many of the businesses serve

the entire city and state. Leon B. Speights is the owner of Leon's Pig Pens, carry-out restaurants specializing in ribs and located throughout the city. They employed 86 persons in 1977. Roger Sanders of Roger's Beauty Supply Store serves primarily black salons and the special hair needs of blacks. Andrew McNeill, owner of AM Machine Company, Inc., which produces precision machine parts, and Robert Douglass, founder of Baltimore Electronics Associates, Inc., have extended their bases beyond the black community. The Baltimore Electronics Associates, Inc. "designs, develops, tests, and manufactures electronic equipment under military and commercial contracts." The R & R Optical Company under Roland Smith won a contract from the Defense Department to manufacture 277,000 units of basic and safety glasses. The company is the first of its kind in the nation to be owned by a black.

Although Roland Smith was able to develop his company as a result of on-the-job training and learning, formal education has traditionally been viewed by many blacks as the key to advancement and success. The Baltimore Community Relations Commission expressed the high esteem in which education was held when it commented that "considering the realities of modern life . . . education plays a major, perhaps dominant role in preparing the child to meet the challenges and opportunities of life . . . . The ability to achieve, is so dependent upon the ability of the school system to turn out useful and potentially productive citizens."

Educational Advancement. In September, 1954, the Baltimore Board of School Commissioners heeded the Supreme Court's mandate to integrate its schools. The Baltimore Plan for desegregation was heralded throughout the nation as a workable model. However, responses were mixed: northerners pointed out that not much integration had taken place since there were fewer than 2,000 black students in formerly all white schools, while 55,000 black students remained in all black schools. States south of the Mason-Dixon line, however, argued that the open enrollment policy had gone far enough since most of Baltimore's schools were of the neighborhood variety and the neighborhoods were for the most part of one race (a policy dating back to the early part of the century).

The apparently smooth transition, which

brought praise for Superintendent John Fischer in 1954, by the early 1960s was severely criticized by both black and white citizen's groups and the Baltimore Community Relations Commission. The Board of School Commissioners was accused of maintaining policies intended to preserve segregation rather than diminish it. The so-called free transfer policy, it was argued, discouraged integration. The Baltimore NAACP threatened litigation and demonstrations if the board did not begin by the summer of 1963 to press for full integration of the public schools.

The freedom of choice policy was continued in force by the school board in its 1963 policy statement, which stated in part that "the neighborhood school concept is to be preserved.... Transfers... to attend a desegregated school shall be routinely authorized on a first come first served basis. Feeling content with the policy that had been in effect for more than a decade, Baltimore filed HEW Form No. 441 in 1966 assuring compliance with Title VI of the Civil Rights Act of 1964. HEW accepted the school system's statement without reservation... and without any indication that Baltimore had taken inadequate steps to desegregate."

In an effort to halt the school board's inattention to the issues of school desegregation, the Baltimore Community Relations Commission charged it with failing to pair black and white children, to achieve faculty integration, to appoint a black principal to any so-called "prestige" school, and to appoint black male faculty to Western High School.

Baltimore's struggle with the issue of integration continued into the decade of the seventies, and was largely the task facing Dr. Roland Patterson when he came to the city in 1971. As the first black superintendent of the Baltimore City Schools, Dr. Patterson inherited a system with a number of serious problems including the need for greater desegregation. The steps taken in 1954, which were heralded as a giant step, by the 1970s were thought to be inadequate. Roland Patterson was generally viewed by the board and a community panel "as the right man with the right educational credentials and the right personal qualities." As his first task, Dr. Patterson undertook the reorganization of the school system through decentralization, a process that was criticized by persons who had traditionally

benefited by the old system.

The same concern for quality education that characterized Dr. Patterson's years in Seattle was present in Baltimore. As he began to put his plan for decentralization into operation, he began to meet with opposition. Regions were established, and for the first time there was an effort to make the bureaucratic maze more understandable and more accessible to parents. In an effort to carry out this latter concern, Councils of Parents were established with an opportunity for input.

Within two years of Dr. Patterson's coming to Baltimore, complaints about his plans for decentralization became more persistent. At approximately the same time, HEW requested information pertaining to the racial make-up of the student bodies and staff of the Baltimore City Public Schools. In responding to HEW, Superintendent Patterson indicated that a reorganization plan was then in operation and that the proposed middle-school concept would facilitate the desegregation process.

In 1974, HEW issued a directive "that Baltimore develop and implement a desegregation plan." Although the middle-school concept could have provided an avenue for integration, as it worked out in Baltimore, it simply continued the pattern of segregation because Falstaff, the school that was chosen, was to be fed by two predominantly white schools, even though there was a predominantly black school in closer proximity.

Although Dr. Patterson worked to make the predominantly black Baltimore school system one of quality, his four years were filled with controversy. One supporter of Patterson commented recently, "He was ousted before he had a chance to bring about meaningful changes. It didn't seem to matter that more and more parents were beginning to believe that they did not have to send their children to private schools." The fact that public schools would now provide quality education could be cited as a testimony to the man and his plan. By June, 1975, a school board that had generally supported the hiring of Dr. Patterson in 1971 voted "not to renew or extend any contract with him, nor negotiate a new one."

In the past six years the scope of Baltimore's Desegregation Plan has been broadened; however, many of the elementary schools are still racially disproportionate due to the residential patterns of the city that make integration extremely difficult.

The road to higher education was no less rocky for black Baltimoreans. Two predominantly black colleges have met the need: one, Morgan State University, dates back to the post–Civil War period; and the other, Coppin State, is in the eighth decade of its existence. The university, which presently has a student body of approximately 4,400 and an operating budget in the neighborhood of $22 million, began life as the Centenary Biblical Institute in 1867. Its main emphasis then was "training those men recently released from bondage for the Christian ministry." This mission was pursued until 1905, when theological courses were abandoned. The name change came in 1890 as a tribute to Dr. Lyttleton Morgan, one of the college's earliest benefactors.

In 1937, the State Commission on Higher Education of Negroes recommended "that Morgan College be acquired by the state as a means of fulfilling its obligations to provide higher education for colored citizens." On November 20, 1939, Morgan officially became a state college. That same year Dr. Dwight O. W. Holmes became the first black and the first lay president. In a Baltimore *Sun* article on November 26, 1967, Dr. Holmes is credited with bringing the college "of age" by "scouting the country for bright young faculty members who would make Morgan a quality institution."

Nine years later, upon the retirement of Dr. Holmes, Dr. Martin Jenkins became president. During the troubled decades of the fifties and sixties, Dr. Jenkins remained at the helm, expanding the curriculum and initiating the college's first masters program. The student body grew from 1,681 in 1953, to 2,570 in 1963, and the emphasis shifted away from teacher education. By 1967, the enrollment reached approximately 5,000 students, a large percentage of whom went on to graduate school.

Although the first 80 years of Morgan's existence were somewhat less than distinguished, by the 1960s positive gains were made in terms of the caliber of the faculty, of the graduate programs being offered, and the size of the student body. In a 1968 publication, *The Academic Revolution*, David Riesman in commenting on black higher education cited Morgan as one of two black public institutions that, along with such private schools as Fisk, Morehouse, Hampton, Howard, Tuskegee, and Spelman, were "at the head of the Negro academic procession."

In the past 10 years, Morgan has had two presidents, Dr. King Cheek and Dr. Andrew Billingsley, the current president. By the time King Cheek arrived at Morgan in 1971, plans were being discussed in some areas that would lead eventually to the school becoming a university. At the same time a special committee reported to the Maryland Council for Higher Education that "Morgan could not and should not become the public university serving Baltimore city, but that Morgan in cooperation with Towson State, UMBC, and Coppin should serve as a multi–university to be known as the State University of Metropolitan Baltimore."

For obvious reasons neither Dr. Cheek nor Dr. Burnett, newly appointed president of Coppin, sanctioned a merger. Dr. Cheek went forward with plans for a Center for Urban Affairs, which he commented was "one of the greatest things to happen to Morgan or Baltimore or Maryland." Not only would it serve to relate the college to the community but it would also provide a research base for ongoing analysis. Even more importantly, it was one requisite for becoming a "university" under the definition of the U. S. Office of Education.

Dr. Andrew Billingsley, a well–established scholar in the field of sociology, came to Morgan in 1975 as its eighth president. Reflecting in 1980 (in the midst of a great deal of turmoil and confusion, and a vote of "no confidence" by the faculty and students) on why he came to Morgan, Dr. Billingsley said he was "persuaded to come because the Maryland legislature was ready to grant university status to Morgan." Billingsley envisioned "an opportunity to build an urban university that would produce a cadre of black leaders." Although university status was granted in 1975, Dr. Billingsley argues that no funds were provided to implement the mandate until 1978. Even then the money received was not in the amount requested, so that the emphasis has been on graduate programs with little money being used for undergraduate programs and faculty. The 1980 budget of $22 million is approximately $2 million less than President

Billingsley feels is needed; hence, as one professor puts it, "Morgan is operating under a poverty mentality much like its fellow black colleges throughout the nation."

No effort to provide an overview of black higher education in Baltimore would be complete without some attention to the role that Coppin State has played for the past 80 years. Coppin was established in 1901 as a "normal department" of the Douglass High School "for the purpose of training colored elementary school teachers." For the first 34 years it offered first one year and then two years of training. In 1934, the curriculum was lengthened to three years and in 1938 to four years with the authority to grant the Bachelor of Science degree in education. After Coppin was on its own for almost half a century, the Maryland State Department of Education took it over in 1950. Coppin (named for Fannie Jackson Coppin), acquired a much needed campus in 1952 when the Lutheran Deaconess' Home at 2500 W. North Avenue was purchased by the Board of Public Works.

Throughout the 1950s there were discussions on the feasibility of closing Coppin, although it clearly served a need within the black community. A 1953 Coppin Bulletin pointed out that over 85 percent of the public elementary school teachers were Coppin graduates. Two years later, 57 percent of Coppin's graduates were employed by city schools. A 1956 Study of Coppin, which was designed to assess the need for its continuation, concluded that "Coppin must be commended on the excellent service it has given the community and the effectiveness of its teacher training curriculum despite the handicaps it has endured."

Under Dr. Parlett Moore, the decade of the 1960s proved to be a time of growth both in Coppin's physical plant and in the size of its student body. The numbers of students more than doubled by 1960 and the night school program leading to a B.S. degree boasted of an additional 300 students. The long–awaited "stamp of approval" came from the Middle States Association in 1962, and in 1963 from the National Council for Accreditation of Teacher Education. Ever mindful of its mission and its inner city population, Coppin has supported a day care center for retarded children at its demonstration school, a 19–month experiment in inner city teacher training, an Institute for Teachers of Disadvantaged Youth, and a summer program for Head Start Teachers.

Dr. Calvin Burnett became Coppin's third president at a time when campuses throughout the nation either had already gone through periods of student unrest or were then experiencing it. Things were not altogether tranquil at Coppin, and many students favored a change in leadership. Dr. Burnett came to Coppin believing that he could "take it from a small black college to a comprehensive urban institution, that would serve the surrounding community." Looking back, Dr. Burnett has commented that "my biggest challenge was taking the lead in converting the college from teacher education to a full fledged arts and sciences institution. As late as 1970, 85–90 percent of Coppin's students were still in teacher education; 10 years later these figures dropped to 25–35 percent.

The curriculum has undergone a number of changes designed to strengthen offerings in newer disciplines—criminal justice, rehabilitation counseling, management science, and the move of the nursing school from Provident Hospital to Coppin. The newest Coppin program, funded by a federal grant, is the Urban Economic Development Center, which is designed to help minority small businessmen solve problems. Another outreach program, the summer enrichment program for inner city youth, is funded by the city and now is in its fourth year. Tutors are provided for 150 youths who are instructed in language arts and arithmetic in the morning and have a recreational program in the afternoon.

Coppin State College has survived charges of mismanagement, threats of being closed, phased out, or merged and today continues its assistance to inner city students. Although these are extremely difficult times for all black colleges, as both of Baltimore's black presidents would attest, W.E.B. DuBois's statement in 1906 offers some hope for their future. He said, "The morning breaks, and all around us are signs of progress."

Religious Development. For nineteenth and early twentieth century black Americans nothing had more power or offered more hope for the future than religion, and no institution was of greater importance and influence in the lives of black people than the black church.

Few twentieth century black, urban communities can boast of as many churches or of a more religiously involved people than can Baltimore. A number of Baltimore's black churches provided the leadership that has inspired the community for many years—Sharp Street Methodist Episcopal, Bethel African Methodist Episcopal Church, St. James Protestant Episcopal, First Baptist, Douglas Memorial, and Sharon Baptist to name only a few. The latter church is particularly significant because William Alexander, the first minister, was founder of the Brotherhood of Liberty, an organization committed to getting black lawyers admitted to the bar and black teachers into black public schools.

Since Dr. John Bryant took over the ministry at Bethel Church in 1975, according to an April 20, 1978, *Sun* article, the membership of the congregation has grown from 600 to 4,000. Heralded as one of the "new wave of dynamic young preachers who are leading a new religious resurgence in Baltimore's black community," Bryant claims that he came to Bethel because he saw a certain potential. "I just feel," he says, "that the Lord is using our church as an example for people to follow."

In the style of the southern black Baptist minister, Dr. Bryant's sermons carry his congregation through a very emotional experience, in which many members, both young and old are moved to respond with handclapping and singing. The Reverend John Bryant feels that the black church must once again become the center of black activism, hence many of his sermons appeal to black pride. Although Bethel is involved in a number of outreach programs for the needy, a counseling center for troubled women, and a prison ministry called "The Jesus Connection," Dr. Bryant feels very strongly that the church must return to a positive spirituality.

Many of the black churches in Baltimore have undergone a "rebirth" in the past few years and young people throughout the city are returning to them. The Reverend Harold Carter is one of the new breed of young ministers who are seeking ways to make the church more relevant. Dr. Carter is very much concerned about the role of prayer in religion and sums up his concern thusly: "Prayer, rather than being a crutch, can

be a vital power in the individual and group experiences of black people."

Although black Catholic parishes existed in Baltimore and the Oblate Sisters of Providence were organized here, Protestant denominations have tended to dominate the black community for most of its existence. Black leadership had opportunities to develop within the churches that provided the only safe means of black expression. Throughout the history of the black journey in this country, often the black minister has been the one who has taken the lead, for clearly, the churches provided the only way to develop without reprisals.

Dr. Vernon Dobson, pastor of Union Baptist Church since 1969, is a community activist who, along with the Reverend Wendell Phillips and the Reverend Marion Bascom, has been involved in coordinating the role of the church in its commitment to human causes. In commenting on the mission of Union Baptist Church, Dr. Dobson has said, "Our concern for our past and its preservation shall not cause us in pride to retreat to safe places to assure our identity.... We are committed to the struggle for human causes with the high possibility that we may in the process lose what we identify, now with pride, as the church."

The renaissance in religion has fostered the growth of a rather large number of Muslims in the Baltimore black community. Bruce Robertson wrote in *Baltimore* magazine that converts are turning to Islam because it "offers them what the Judeo–Christian ethic always has offered—an all–powerful God, a strong sense of community, and hope for the future—plus the special appeal of a faith not dominated by white society."

The Black Muslims were organized in this country in 1935 by Elijah Muhammed. However, three years ago Wallace Muhammed rejected his father's teachings and founded the World Community of Al–Islam in the West. In making this change Wallace Muhammed has followed the lead of Malcolm X and has set "the course of his new movement in line with the historic Sunni Muslim tradition." Additionally, the Baltimore headquarters of the World Community of Islam is now called the Baltimore Masjid (Mosque) instead of the Masjid Muhammed No. 6 after Elijah Muhammed.

Although there is some diversity among the various mosques in Baltimore, there is an overriding sense of community, often not found among churches and synagogues.

The Baltimore Masjid of the World Community of Al-Islam in the West is the largest mosque in Baltimore with an active membership of approximately 500. Most of the congregation is black, although some foreign Muslims also attend. Even though most black Muslims are supporters of Wallace Muhammed, some local Muslims still think of Elijah Muhammed as their Prophet, and therefore remain aloof in their congregations.

The movement led by Wallace Muhammed is attempting to form a bridge between former black Muslims and the worldwide Orthodox Sunni Muslim tradition. The best known of these congregations is the Masjid Saffat in West Baltimore, organized by Imam Taif Ahmad Abdullah eight years ago.

Another very active group within the black Muslim community here is the United Moorish Moslems of America, formerly known as the Moorish Science Temple. In an effort to clarify the Moorish Science Movement, Grand Chairman Clarence Reynolds-El points out that there are twin concepts to be understood: the movement is a nationality and is not a religion; Islam is the religion.

Whatever the focus of Islam in America, it is clear that it is a major force. Dr. Harold Carter observes that the growth of Islam testifies to the "failure of the Christian church, black and white, but mostly white." Parren Mitchell also recognizes the forcefulness of Islam in Baltimore, as a part of what he calls "the growing factor of religion in the inner city." In recent years both the Christian Church and Islam have attracted black youth, and as Dr. Carter suggests, "Muslims are a people of God, too, and if they be of God, why fight them?"

Political Activism. At the same time that black churches were concerned with the spiritual growth of their congregations, they recognized that in order for blacks to achieve a more meaningful life, changes would have to occur on the secular level. Politics among black Baltimoreans has always been of key importance because of the large black population, difficulty in labeling Baltimore as a northern or southern city, and

Reuben Kramer, *"Thurgood Marshall."* Photo by Morton Oppenheimer

the opposition by the larger society to concerns and issues raised by blacks. Baltimore had elected black officials after the Reconstruction Period and during the Depression. However, blacks did not become a political force to be reckoned with until 1954. Race with all of its parameters was an issue during that year's campaigning process. Three blacks, Harry Cole, Emory Cole, and Truly Hatchett won seats in the General Assembly of Maryland, much to the dismay of the Pollack machine which had controlled the Fourth District prior to 1955. Harry Cole ran for reelection as a senator in 1958 but lost. The primary was a political battle to unseat the candidates of political boss James H. "Jack" Pollack. Verda Welcome, organizer of the Fourth District democratic organization, surfaced as a formidable political foe for a seat in the General Assembly—and won.

Dr. Carl Murphy, of the *Afro-American*, concerned about the political future of black Baltimoreans, conceived and began to implement the concept of a coalition against Pollack. Senator Harry A. Cole called the meeting which convened at Morgan State College. Three hundred persons attended, including Verda Welcome. A slate, ignoring party affiliation, was drawn up consisting of five Republicans, one for the Senate, four for the House of Delegates, one independent Democrat for the House, and Mrs. Irma Dixon, a Democrat for the House who did not cut her ties with the Pollack machine.

The concept and the desire to devise strategy for black political advancement were admirable in theory but were doomed to failure because of political naiveté. Dr. James Fleming, noted political scientist from Morgan State University, stated in his pamphlet *An All Negro Ticket in Baltimore*, "Lack of real knowledge as to what the Fourth District was ready for politically, lack of money and organization, lack of zeal for bipartisanship, and underestimation of the wiles and ways of a strong political boss may be pointed to as the major reasons for the failure of the all-colored coalition legislative ticket in Baltimore."

The failure of the coalition did not cause black political activity to stagnate in Baltimore. Henry Parks, previously cited as a businessman of note, was elected to the City Council from the Fourth District in 1963 and 1967. Robert C. Marshall, owner of the Northwestern Investigating Bureau, Inc. with 150 guards and private investigators and eight or nine administrators, replaced Mr. Parks in 1969. There was concern as to whether or not Marshall's appointment would represent conflict of interest since his company had contracts with city and state agencies. Marshall indicated he would sign his interest in the company over to his wife if conflict of interest arose. Marshall was defeated in 1971 by another black, Mary B. Adams.

In 1962, Verda Welcome ran for a seat in the Senate of the state legislature and won. Victorine Q. Adams, wife of "Little Willie" Adams, also ran from the Fifth District for the House but lost after redistricting occurred. Vernon Dobson, a black minister, and Homer Favor, professor at Morgan State University, filed a suit against the city government in 1970 because they considered the redistricting unconstitutional. Their efforts to delay the September primary failed and the Sixth District was reduced from 41 percent black to 36.6 percent. It was projected that blacks lost possibly two more seats that they could have won in the City

Council. Victorine Adams had run again in 1966 and won but decided after one year in office to run for the City Council. After Mrs. Adams' successful bid for the City Council, Lloyal Randolph was appointed to her seat in the House. Of the 18 members of the Baltimore City Council, four were black in 1969.

Part of the reason for the increase of seats in the City Council can be attributed to the activity of the political organizations that blacks developed. Clarence Mitchell III broke with Senator Welcome's club in 1963 to organize the People's Democratic Action Organization. Seven years later, William Adams and Henry G. Parks, Jr. organized the Metro Democrats, which since its inception has won seven seats in the House of Delegates. The organization also won three of the four traditionally black seats in the City Council. The Metro Democrats are composed primarily of homeowners and professional people.

A review of the districts' population figures and black delegates reveals increased participation in 1979:

District	Population	Black Population	Black Delegates
1st	145,633	24,701	0
2nd	158,370	104,742	2
3rd	125,594	18,094	0
4th	157,834	146,377	3
5th	156,900	79,739	0
6th	143,571	46,557	0

The elections of 1979 brought six blacks to the 19-member City Council. Norman V.A. Reeves and Kweisi Mfume were the newcomers.

Black representation in the state legislature also increased. Senator Verda Welcome (who by 1979) had served 16 years in the state senate, was a true advocate of the interests of blacks and the state. By 1971, there were 16 blacks besides Senator Welcome in the state legislature, three senators and 13 persons in the House of Delegates. At the same time that blacks were being elected to political offices, they were also being elected or appointed to city-wide governmental positions during the late sixties. Joseph O. Howard became the city's first elected black judge of the Supreme Bench, taking his seat in 1967. Eleven years later, the number had risen to five. Other blacks served in affiliated court positions. Three have served as the clerk of the Court of Common Pleas; Paul L. Chester was the first but was replaced by J. Randall Carroll after he was convicted of malfeasance in office. Saundra Banks was the first black woman to win a city–wide election when she became clerk. After being elected state's attorney in 1970, Milton B. Allen was noted as the only black in the nation to hold the office. Three blacks have served in the City Solicitor's office.

Even though the number of black delegates from Baltimore to Annapolis increased from 1962 to 1979, blacks still found it difficult to have their views seriously considered by the entire legislature. In order to present their views more effectively and to establish clout, the idea of a black caucus was conceived. On those issues relating specifically to blacks, the caucus, consisting of all blacks in the legislature, would vote and trade votes as a bloc. Delegate Lloyal Randolph was the first chairperson of the caucus and held the post for three years. Senator Robert L. Douglass, D–45th, succeeded Randolph.

Delegate Arthur G. Murphy, Sr., D–41st, president of the 19–member black caucus in 1978, announced the goals for the group during the legislative session. The goals clearly represent issues related to blacks. They were: (1) to secure passage of the bill to increase welfare payments; (2) to ensure that minority contractors would be guaranteed a set amount of state awards; (3) to defeat the Continental Can prison proposal; and (4) to defeat any bill attempting to bring back the death penalty. The caucus has been accused at times of being ineffective because of internal conflicts. It is hoped that as the number of black delegates increases, the caucus can be used as an internal lobby for black issues and will become known as a viable unit with meaningful clout. Delegate Frank Conaway, the current chairperson, was elected to the legislature in 1970 and served until 1975. He was reelected to the House in 1979 and elected the next year as the chairperson of the caucus.

Although population figures and other election trends indicate the results could be different, the position of mayor has remained elusive for black Baltimoreans. In 1967, Thomas D'Alesandro, III, a white, won the bid for mayor. It was in that year that blacks began to be elected as mayors in key cities throughout the United States. It was expected that Baltimore, with 47 percent of the population being black in 1967, would follow. Blacks represented 46.4 percent (325,589) of the population in 1970. Some stated the percentage was too low to carry the city.

On April 13, 1971, George L. Russell announced his candidacy for mayor. Russell was the incumbent city solicitor and had served as a state circuit court judge. Russell was a Democrat in a city that had a long history of being Democratic. He was one who was accepted by blacks and whites because of his racial and political stance.

Clarence Mitchell III announced after Russell, much to the dismay of many, that he would also run for mayor. It was felt that two leading black candidates would split the vote and cause neither to win; such was the case. Russell earned 58,223 votes, Mitchell 6,582 votes, and William Donald Schaefer, the winner, 94,809 votes. Given the attempts of leading blacks to get one of the candidates to withdraw, why did Clarence Mitchell, the underdog, continue his bid? Dr. James Fleming offered four major reasons in explanation. The Mitchell family, long recognized as one of the controlling families of black Baltimore, did not want another black to win. It was their goal for Clarence to be either the first black mayor or the first black congressman from Maryland. Secondly, it was felt that Clarence would, from 1971 to 1975, establish an exemplary record in the state legislature that would let the citizens of Baltimore know he was capable of being the mayor. Thirdly, he would run for mayor in 1975 and would be the youngest and the first black mayor of Baltimore. Finally, it was thought that by that year Russell would no longer be a threat because he would either be on the Federal Bench or heading the Maryland Court of Appeals.

Clarence Mitchell was not a candidate for mayor in 1975. With over 50 percent of the population being black four years later, no black candidate emerged as a serious contender for the position. The political game of 1971 apparently had far–reaching negative results. Dr. Vernon Gray, political scientist at Morgan State, believed that black politicians were too caught up in "factional fights and sectional self–interest to do the obvious." He commented further,

"They need to build an organization or working coalition that crosses the factional lines.... Blacks could then influence the choice of candidates for mayor and other city-wide posts even if they are not black." A number of black political scientists, politicians, ministers, and businessmen share Dr. Gray's beliefs. A group of such men, known as "The Goon Squad" with changing membership, has attempted to project, analyze, and influence black political behavior in Baltimore. The group basically fits the description given by Dr. Gray but has not come forth with a united, projected political plan for the future. The eighties may witness such a plan and a new political thrust and emphasis for black Baltimoreans.

Cultural Development. The fear of riots, such as those in 1968, has caused black and white Baltimoreans to plan more carefully for the future of the city and to pay greater attention to the need for blacks to be included in all phases of the life of the city. To what extent and how viable the inclusion will be is the key question. Generally, when people think of inclusion, they think of socially related activities. The riots did encourage various groups to initiate recreational programs for inner city youths. Most of the programs ended when the year drew to a close.

Soon it was apparent that blacks, as in the past, would have to be the catalysts for change and progress in their communities. Assistance from others was appreciated but not looked upon as a given. One way to elicit the support and assistance was through a positive projected image. Beginning in 1976 and blending the social with the cultural, black Baltimoreans became a part of the ethnic festivals sponsored by the city. Each festival was a testament to the times and concerns of blacks. In 1976, the theme focused upon blacks and their role in the growth of Baltimore and the nation. The themes for the subsequent years were: 1977-"Black Genius in America," focused upon scientific inventions and discoveries by blacks; 1978-"Afram Salutes Our Youth-The Best Is Yet To Be," focused upon educational and vocational development (business, law, medicine, and science); 1979-"The Year of the Child;" and 1980-"The Family." The Urban Services Agency-Cultural Arts Program has been the principal sponsoring agency for each year.

Cultural Arts Project Performance of *"The Nutcracker Suite,"* 1978. Photo by Cultural Arts Project

Aspects of the blacks' African heritage permeates, to a degree, every level and phase of black Baltimoreans' lives. Samuel Wilson, founder of the Arena Players, Inc., considers that two essential play themes for the group are: love among blacks and history themes relating to the United States of America. The Arena Players was organized in 1953 and presented its first plays at Coppin State College. The theatrical group utilized the facilities of other institutions before moving to its present location at 801 McCulloh Street, the Arena Players Creative Arts Center. In 1972, through funds from the National Endowment for the Arts, the Arena Players Youtheatre Workshop began and continues until today. The youngsters are taught the principles of stagecraft and receive lessons in drama. The Arena Players plan to continue their community outreach through the offering of creative writing courses at penal institutions and workshops in the public schools. Some Arena Players have joined national groups and now perform for national audiences. Other Baltimoreans, such as Trazana Beverly, Tamara Dobson, Isabelle Monk, and Howard Rollins have gained national recognition as actors and actresses.

The blending of Africa and the United States is also present in other art forms presented by Baltimoreans. The Baltimore Dance Theatre, under the direction of Mrs. Eva Anderson since 1975, has presented "universal statements about all mankind as seen through our eyes." Sixteen inner city youths, as part of the resident dance company of the Urban Services Cultural Arts Program, perform throughout the city and have travelled to Europe to present recitals. Part of their repertoire focuses upon the black experience.

The Trinidad–Tobago Baltimore Steel Band also presents a cultural blend. Lawrence Roger, manager and arranger, has led the group to London, with financial assistance from the city of Baltimore. The band is noted because it represents the diaspora from the continent of Africa and yet has great appeal to the citizens of the city and nation.

Trinidad-Tobago Steel Band. Photo by Barbara Cotell

Arena Players Creative Arts Center

Marty Brown and June Thorne Receiving the Lorraine Hansberry Scholarship Award at the 28th Arena Players' Award Night

The Left Bank Jazz Society, Inc. also draws attention from a large audience, both black and white. Performances at the Famous Ballroom on Sundays highlight local and national talents. Jazz workshops are sponsored by the society in public schools and a chapter, LBJS 954, is in the Maryland Penitentiary. Young jazz musicians, some affiliated with the LBJS, also perform at the Sportsman's Lounge in West Baltimore. Ethel Ennis, a jazz performer who started in the fifties singing at the Tijuana Club, the Comedy Club, and the Royal Theater, also continues to appear locally and has become known as one of "Baltimore's Best." Brenda Alford has come to the fore as a promising jazz singer.

Black Baltimoreans are also as interested in entertaining themselves as being entertained. Private membership clubs sprang up during the seventies where the young and not so young professionals could seek jazz, disco, food, and alcoholic beverages. Clubs, such as Gatsby's, the Ritz, the Point After, and D'Joint represent a new breed in terms of black ownership and clientele. The clubs also represent in part the economic progress made by blacks in the city.

In spite of the fact that success stories can be told and some progress can be noted, there are still many problems facing the black community of Baltimore. High unemployment rates still exist, racism still abounds, and the political clout of blacks is still limited. Yet, just as the years before 1950 laid the foundation for blacks of today, today's blacks can and must pave the way for future generations.

Bettye Gardner and Cynthia Neverdon–Morton

THE CLERGY AND THE INTERFAITH MOVEMENT: 1945–1980

All religions are like different roads leading to the same goal—Hind, Swaraj

Religion in Baltimore in the last 25 years has been many-dimensional. Volumes could be written on each theme. One momentous story, is the unheralded account of the Baltimore clergy's role in the interfaith movement.* If nothing else, I will argue, Baltimore's religious leadership has demonstrated how to do God's work in new, more dramatic ways. One major result has been the clergy's helping to make the city the American cultural pluralism success that it has become.

On November 24, 1905, Mayor E. Clay Timanus initiated an organized effort to help alleviate the suffering from anti-Jewish massacres in Russia. James Cardinal Gibbons spoke earnestly and impressively to the interfaith group of laymen and clergymen as he appealed to the Christian world "for a true exhibition of the spirit of human brotherhood." The cardinal who became the model for others enjoyed a friendship with Rabbi William Rosenau as well as Protestant ministers, the Right Reverend William Paret and Dr. Peter Ainslie. These clergymen set the example for interfaith activities that included pulpit exchanges, radio talks, ad hoc or organizational participation in times of crisis— all interwoven with friendship.

[The most effective weapon] against the misrepresentation, canards, and falsehoods that exist about Jews and Judaism is: the universal recognition that all have one Father and that one God has created us; one man shall not act treacherously against his brother. If this be so, then let it be proclaimed in season and out of season,

among us and among all others, that ill will can be cut down and good will can be enthroned when the Christian will live his Christianity and the Jew his Judiasm; and that, as a result of such living, Christian and Jew will learn to respect one another and wish one another well. [The two should] be united . . . in the eradication of all that is ignoble and vicious, and in the promotion of all that is noble and good—William Rosenau, The Rabbi in Action

While the principal victims of discrimination in employment were the blacks, the Jews were handicapped, too. Before World War II discrimination existed in Baltimore against the Jews in employment, residential restrictions, educational institutions, and public accommodations. Discrimination in housing was different in Baltimore from other cities in the United States. Whole developments such as Roland Park, Guilford, and Homeland sometimes involved hundreds of homes. Some private schools did not accept Jews on the same basis as non-Jews and most did not accept Jews at all. Swimming pools like Meadowbrook, the most notorious, actually flaunted signs on Falls Road and the Kelly Avenue bridge: "For Approved Gentiles Only."

In this setting the clergy began to play a leading role in interfaith relations. In the 1930s, the National Conference of Christians and Jews (NCCJ) organized and became active in the community. The Maryland Council of Churches, essentially a Protestant group, under the direction of Mildred Atkinson through the Christian Social Relations Division, began bringing rabbis, ministers, and priests together in community action programs.

The Years of Peace: 1945–1960

World War II brought about social changes in race relations, civil rights, and technology—particularly communications. The Holocaust of Nazi Germany shocked the democratic nations. It seared the fabric of interfaith relations and changed the entire pattern. Now interfaith efforts responded to the Holocaust and the social changes. Gradually, by the 1960s, the days of quiet in interfaith activities turned into a more complex, full-blown movement.

---

*As used in this article ecumenism is any cooperative action or unity between Catholics and Protestants.

The interfaith movement is participation between Christians and Jews to increase mutual understanding.

As they had done before the war from 1945 to 1960, individual clergymen continued to assume leadership in the moral struggle for interfaith understanding. Friendships continued to weave a touch of beauty in the interfaith fabric as the clergymen increasingly participated in organizations. It must be emphasized that the Catholic church, prior to the 1962 to 1965 Vatican Council II, participated in Baltimore and elsewhere. The clergy of the three faiths began to work toward a common goal in the areas of civil rights and interracial understanding.

Because my brother and I differ in opinions, temperament, environment and nationality is no reason that we should disagree. With all our differences, and they are as many as there are individuals, conflict with one another is an abnormal condition. The elms and the oaks do not disturb the forests by their differences any more than the gardens are disturbed by the differences between the roses and the dahlias and my brother and I are beginning to learn from the forests and the gardens that there may be differences among ourselves without disagreements. This is the message of Jesus. The practice of love, honesty, justice, liberal mindedness, and toleration sets smooth edges against the rough of the opposites and these smooth edges will wear away the roughness as drops of water wear away the stone.—Peter Ainslie, Working With God or the Story of a 25-Year Pastorate in Baltimore

---

Pulpit sharing continued with the NCCJ still influencing the interchange. Clergymen preached sermons on the theme of brotherhood. In 1958, the NCCJ established its first interfaith clergymen dialogue group.

Another activity that developed independently of the NCCJ was an interfaith organization limited in membership to clergymen, the Baltimore Clergy Brotherhood. Organized in 1955, it was the first interracial group of its kind for Catholic, Protestant, and Jewish clergymen. The goal was to create interfaith understanding among the clergy, who it was hoped would influence individual congregations.

The Christian Social Relations Division of the Maryland Council of Churches established many "firsts." In 1951, the clergy worked with the police department. In 1956, the City Council passed the Equal Employment Ordinance Bill and Mayor Thomas D'Alesandro, Jr. signed it into law, making Baltimore the first city south of the Mason–Dixon line to oppose public employment discrimination.

The Maryland Council of Churches worked on other areas of discrimination: for example, in 1946, by fighting for the repeal of the Jim Crow Law (finally abrogated in 1951); in 1948, by seeking shopping privileges for blacks in stores where they formerly had been barred in 1956; by supporting integration of city swimming pools; by organizing Educational Home Visits that included white and black families visiting in each others' homes—all interfaith clergy efforts.

In the forties the media became a more important tool for interfaith work as clergy trios began to broadcast. Actually, in 1928 and 1929, before the networks existed, many religious programs were broadcast on radio to fill in the time. When television became popular, clergy participated in "To Promote Good Will," one of the most popular television shows in the Baltimore area. The original panel consisted of the Reverend Dr. Frederick W. Helfer, Christian Church; Rabbi Abraham Shusterman, Har Sinai Temple; and the Reverend Father Richard Swift, Catholic priest, replaced by the Right Reverend William Kailer Dunn; and at his death, Father James B. O'Hara replaced him.

Judaism bases its concept of social justice upon its ideal of God as the Universal Father. Out of this religious conception grew the idea of the brotherhood of man. If all men are members of one great spiritual family, regardless of race, color, or creed, there are certain inalienable rights and privileges which in justice cannot be denied them any more than insidious discriminations can be justly made among members of any literal family, one against the other . . . .

Just as in this smaller human unit, the family coordinates without sublimation of personalities or unwarranted suppression, so in the universal family must there be freedom for minorities to develop their unique spiritual powers as a positive contribution to the larger group's life . . . . —Edward Israel in a letter to Dr. Samuel Shulman

---

The clergy worked with the Baltimore public schools. In the 1940s, curriculum and community needs began to be more interrelated. School efforts combined with other agencies for improvement of the community. Dr. Harry Bard, supervisor of curriculum for the Baltimore Public Schools, stated that World War II "practically forced the community–school idea on Baltimore." In 1946, Dr. Bard formulated an in-service training workshop that included visits to the churches, temples, and synagogues to help the teachers see how intimately religious–cultural programs affect their pupils.

The work of the Baltimore clergy in Jewish–Christian relations moved into the next decade as it faced the forces that had been developing and gathering momentum. The comparatively quiet years after World War II were leading into years of social turmoil and unrest that would sway and stir the clergy's interfaith activities.

The Years of Crisis: From Theology to Sociology 1960–1970

The interfaith movement in Baltimore from 1960 to 1970 continued to reflect the pressures that received their impetus from World War II. Heightened emotions and turbulence in race relations and civil rights provided the clergy with opportunities for leadership in attempting to improve the situation. Even though the clergy's participation in social action had been occurring in Baltimore before World War II, it became more and more important until it reached a crescendo in the 1960s during the civil rights movement. Some problems "spilled over" from the interfaith to the interracial, often making it difficult to separate the two activities. Many of the clergy were deeply affected by this and actively participated either with ad hoc groups or in formal organizations.

Dialoguing and formal organizations continued the pattern started in the pre–War period; however, in the middle of the 1960s the Catholic church announced a momentous declaration that would clear the way for many interfaith activities. On October 28, 1965, Pope Paul VI proclaimed the Declaration on the Relation of the Church to Non–Christian Religions, a document that resulted from Vatican Council II. Even though a few Catholic clergymen in Baltimore had participated in ecumenical and inter-

faith projects, now the clergy had formal approval.

Following the council, Catholics and Jews arranged and worked on ad hoc institutes and conferences that provided for the clergy a means to promote mutual understanding and respect between Christians and Jews. An example was a two–day institute at Woodstock College in January, 1966, the first "at a major Jesuit Seminary" since the Declaration on Non–Christian Religions.

Pulpit exchanges continued into the sixties either for special occasions or regular services. Sharing just for Brotherhood Week seemed ridiculous: civil rights were considered more important. One significant interfaith service, a Protestant and Catholic response to Jewish problems, occurred in 1967 on the eve of the Six Day War in Israel.

This is the first time in Baltimore and perhaps elsewhere that an exchange of pulpits between rabbis and Christian ministers has taken place on so large a scale . . . . It seems to me that this is the clearest and most definite expression that we have ever had in this country that America can be safe for religious differences.—A.W. Gottschall, Baltimore Sun, *February 12, 1937 in celebration of Brotherhood Day in Baltimore*

Dramatic events began to follow one after the other in the clergy's role in interfaith cooperation as the interracial crises developed. Included were: the civil rights movement, the crime rate, juvenile delinquency, hunger, drugs, minimum wages, Medicare, alcoholism, and peace.

Public Accommodations. Clergy and lay efforts toward ending segregation in public accommodations began before the Maryland state legislature considered the Public Accommodations Bill in 1962. Restaurant owners approved it, but the Eastern Shore legislators opposed it.

At this time, the Reform rabbis spearheaded "an effort to demonstrate publicly our protest against the segregation policy of many of our public accommodations," claimed Rabbi Abraham D. Shaw.

The three rabbis—Morris Lieberman, Abraham Shaw, and Abraham Shusterman—felt that the clergy ought to do something on the day the legislature opened (February 7, 1962) to make clear to the general public that the responsible religious elements in Maryland were behind the bill and that the public should not associate that bill with the wild demonstrations of noisy sit-in groups. Rabbi Shusterman wrote, "It was also our deep conviction that all three of us had to be in on it because of the failing of the religious groups in Germany to stand by our people at the time when it would have been most helpful."

We are often tempted to consider brotherhood merely as [a] lovely idea. It is not so much nice as it is necessary . . . . It is [a] law built into [the] structure of [the] universe by God. If it is law then it isn't a question of whether we choose to obey it or not. If it is law we obey it [or] we shall go from one tragic breakdown of society to another until we end in disaster . . . . Brotherhood is one of the conditions for the living of life. Again and again life says to us, without thy brother, ye shall not see my face. That is true of community health . . . . That is true about the full development of your personality. The exclusive people are always doing themselves harm. When during medieval times the Christians compelled Jews to live in ghettos, they did not realize that they were compelling themselves to live in a correspondingly segregated condition . . . . Strangely enough our yearning for independence makes us ashamed to acknowledge the fact that we are, all of us, dependent on others. Yet economically, politically, militarily, physically, and spiritually we are dependent for our welfare and our destiny upon our brothers around the world . . . . We believe that God has made brotherhood to be the law of life. God Himself is subject to this law. We say it very humbly He depends on us . . . . In team play and at the same time, every man bears his own burden. Victory . . . depends on the assumption of responsibility for all his teammates, and the recognition of his dependence on them. Brotherhood is the law.—T. Guthrie Speers, "Let's All Be Interdependent," February 29, 1954 (excerpts from sermon)

Father Joseph Connolly represented the Catholic clergy and Dr. Fred Webber, a Presbyterian minister, the Protestant. The five asked Dr. Furman Templeton, executive director of the Urban League, to join them for lunch. They purposely selected one Jewish-owned restaurant and one Christian-owned. The owners had stated their intentions to integrate after a state law required it. The clergymen phoned both restaurants to say that Mr. Templeton would be with them.

Rabbi Shusterman related the incident:

When we arrived at Mandel and Ballows restaurant, the Jewish-owned one, we were met at the door by Ben Belfer, vice-president of the firm and one of the owners, who informed us that he would serve us, but not because the restaurant was integrated. He was doing this, so he said, out of deference for our positions as clergymen. While we were not satisfied with this kind of rationalizing, we did accept the invitation to be seated together and ate our lunch . . . . The legal representative of the owners seated himself with us and gave a prolonged explanation as to why financial circumstances would not presently permit them to integrate their restaurant, even though it was their own wish that this might be done. We tried to point out that other places that had thus integrated in our own community had suffered no financial loss, and felt that these were mistaken fears.

Rabbi Shusterman continued:

We went to Miller Brothers [the Christian-owned restaurant], a nationally famous restaurant, and we were denied admission. I did the speaking at the door and I was told by the head waiter, "We are not integrated." I then said, "Does that mean you will not serve us lunch?" He repeated the statement, "We are not integrated." I said to him a third time, "We are here for lunch. There are five clergymen who are well-known to you and a social worker who is our guest." He repeated, "We are not integrated." We learned through fairly reliable sources that the management of Miller Bros. phoned the archbishop and tried to stop the demonstration by urging that Father Connolly be ordered to drop out. Apparently we had the full backing of the archbishop.

Rabbi Shaw in his letter wrote:

We made no protest nor any effort to force our way in, but remained in front of the restaurant long enough for reporters from several of the local papers to interview us and photograph the incident.

Our entire purpose was not self-exploitation, but to dramatize the unfortunate circumstances which exist in our state where members of different races may not be permitted to enter places of public accommodations, and be served. Unfortunately, the proposed measures did not pass the recent session of the state legislature, but as a result of the attention that was focused not only by us but by many other organizations and individuals, the effort to secure this change in our statutes will continue. Subsequently, there has been organized an Interfaith Clergymen's Committee on Human Rights and it is making strenuous efforts to secure corrections of these injustices, both before the state legislature and before our own Baltimore City Council.

Rabbi Lieberman in his letter commented, "It is interesting to note that within the last several weeks the Jewish-owned restaurant has changed its policy and is now serving all patrons regardless of color."

I give warm encouragement to these days of dialogue between Christians and Jews. At a time when religious men everywhere are striving to break down the ancient barriers of bigotry, it is good to see local efforts that promote unity of spirit and intelligent cooperation among men of good will. I pray that our common Father will bless these days together and strengthen our understanding and brotherly affection.—Cardinal Shehan's endorsement of the conference "Image of the Jew in Contemporary Culture," at Loyola College, December, 1969

Cardinal Shehan supported the clergy who traveled to Annapolis to speak to Governor Millard Tawes in behalf of the Public Accommodations Bill.

Before 1962, one of the first sponsors was Francis Gallagher whose efforts had failed. Alexander Stark, another Baltimore city delegate, encouraged the clergy to visit the governor to dramatize the "emotion-fraught and terrifying issue," as he described it. The visit proved to be just the action required to obtain the governor's open support of the legislation.

The Gwynn Oak Demonstrations. The Gwynn Oak Demonstrations provided another impetus for the clergy. "Historians writing about the struggle for racial equality in this period are going to have a number of milestones to guide them. One such, surely, will prove to be the demonstration at Gwynn Oak Amusement Park near Baltimore on July 4 which was repeated yesterday." This editorial from the *New York Times* of July 8, 1963, was only one national or international recognition of an event that was a high point in the participation of the Baltimore Catholic, Protestant, and Jewish clergy in social action.

We paid $2 for the round trip—took our lunches— and marched arm in arm. We felt that a new day of interfaith and interracial amity had come. We sang, 'We shall overcome,' as if we were singing in harmony with the Messiah. It was a new dawn of messianism which changed into night.—Abraham Shusterman recalling the national civil rights march in Washington.

The Gwynn Oak demonstrations began as an effort of the National Council of Churches and Baltimore leadership making it an interfaith effort. Organized in January, 1963, the National Congress on Religion and Race began to work on racial equality. At the same time, the National Council of Churches, the National Catholic Welfare Conference, and the Synagogue Council of America began "urging bold interfaith action against racial discrimination."

In New York, early in June the Christian Social Relations Division of the Council of Churches began planning for the Gwynn Oak demonstration. The office of the National Catholic Conference for Interracial Justice called Baltimore for Catholic involvement. Father Joseph Connolly enlisted the cooperation of Rabbi Morris Lieberman and the Reverend Dr. John Middaugh, the other two cochairmen of the Clergymen's Interfaith Committee on Human Rights, to make the demonstration an actual interfaith action. This was the first effort of clergymen anywhere at participation "on a broad front" against discrimination.

The Reverend Dr. Chester Wickwire, chaplain at the Johns Hopkins University, stated that in his opinion Walter Carter, head of the Congress of Racial Equality (CORE), was almost the major force in organizing the Gwynn Oak demonstrations. A few weeks before the much-publicized demonstrations a group of demonstrators picketed at Gwynn Oak. CORE urged the clergy to get involved.

On July 4th, Catholic, Protestant, and Jewish clergymen joined the more than 350 demonstra-

Gwynn Oak Demonstration, July 4, 1963. Photo by Catholic Center

tors, mostly whites from New York, Baltimore, Philadelphia, and Washington in the march on Gwynn Oak. One of the owners, James Price, and his aides read the Maryland trespass law to the group before him. The Chief of Police of Baltimore County, Robert J. Lally, a former Federal Bureau of Investigation agent in New York and Baltimore, told the demonstrators they could leave or be arrested. The *New York Times* described the event: "The group made no move. The ferris wheel whirled in the background and the games of petty chance went on. The police moved in politely and put the group under arrest."

Of the 36 clergymen arrested, seven (six from Baltimore, one from New York) stayed in jail. Listed among the prominent clergymen arrested were Rabbi Lieberman; Father Connolly; Dr. Middaugh; Monsignor Austin J. Healy, St. Martin's Church; the Reverend Dr. Eugene Carson Blake, chief executive of the United Presbyterian Church in the United States, former president of the National Council of Churches and one of the most respected clergymen nationally; and Bishop Daniel Corrigan, National Council of Protestant Episcopal Churches.

An article, "Civil March on Gwynn Oak Park" in *Time*, reported that in the midst of the civil rights revolution, *Time* considered the participation of the white clergy "the most significant development." Before this it had played "a sympathetic but generally nonactivist part.... Now it threw itself wholeheartedly, and even physically, into the struggle....[T]he Reverend Dr.

Eugene Carson Blake...thought more was needed than pious thoughts."

Rabbi Lieberman, Father Connolly, and Dr. Middaugh issued a formal statement:

On this Fourth of July, 1963, moved by the conviction of our faith and by the spirit of our forefathers, we have chosen to demonstrate at Gwynn Oak Park even at the risk of breaking the law.

So motivated, we reluctantly agreed to break the letter of the law in order to direct the attention of the faithful to the tragic gap between ideal and practice in our democracy a century after the Emancipation Proclamation.

Perhaps the classic statement made about the entire event was that of Rabbi Lieberman. When he was asked why he had gone to jail he replied, "I think every American should celebrate the Fourth of July."

While the clergymen (most of whom were Protestant) were in jail, they were planning further demonstrations. On July 7, more clergymen appeared again at Gwynn Oak Park and seven were arrested. White hecklers appeared at the park's main entrance. The group of demonstrators had met earlier at the Metropolitan Methodist Church for a rally—as they had for the first occasion.

There is, I hope, no need to say that in our churches and in our parochial life generally there must be not only no racial segregation, but also no distinction of rank or place or treatment based upon racial difference.... We [Catholics] have a special obligation to place ourselves in the forefront of movements to remove ... injustices and discriminations.... These problems [social problems that have had their origin in racial prejudices and tensions] cannot be suddenly solved or wiped out by wishful thinking or good intentions. They are community problems.... They call for the combined thought and planning and cooperation of all of us.—Cardinal Shehan, Pastoral Letter on "Racial Justice," March 1, 1963

Father Joseph Connolly was with the clergy again, along with members of his parish and other Catholic churches, in what he thought was the first time in the United States that "ordinary members of Catholic parishes have participated in a freedom walk." In the light of Cardinal

Shehan's Pastoral Letter, priests were encouraged to participate in the demonstrations. Cardinal Shehan's letter published in February, 1963, said, "We [Catholics] have a special obligation to place ourselves in the forefront of movements to remove the injustices and discriminations which still remain."

In the march were clergymen—and laity—of the Presbyterian, Baptist, Methodist, and Episcopalian churches, besides an observer from the Holiness churches (fundamentalist denominations that traditionally had not become involved in social issues). Three rabbis were there and arrested: Rabbi Israel Goldman, Chizuk Amuno Congregation; Philip Schecter, assistant rabbi at Oheb Shalom Temple; and Rabbi Samuel Glasner, former director of continuing education, Baltimore Hebrew College. These clergymen and the Reverend Marion C. Bascom were among the first to be confronted by the police and the park owners. Rabbi Goldman, vice-chairman of the Maryland Interracial Commission, as spokesman stated, "Our commission has been writing you and members of your family for almost a decade about this. . . ."

Colonel Lally commented that the Gwynn Oak demonstrations were "one of few national events that transpired so peacefully and orderly. Ironically, [County Executive Spiro T.] Agnew tried to forestall by having the Price brothers in to agree to integrate. They adamantly refused. If he had been successful there would have been no demonstration." Colonel Lally explained that the clergy of different denominations, Mr. Agnew, and he had many preliminary meetings to agree on the ground rules. They were more concerned with public reaction and the only reason they brought out K-9 dogs was to protect the demonstrators from the mob. The Baltimore preliminary demonstration planning probably set an example for the nation. Police and clergy felt no animosity toward each other; the demonstrations were free of adversary feelings, with many of the religious participants being good friends of the police. Dr. Wickwire stated that the clergy gave the event "the clout it wouldn't ordinarily have had." It was actually a test case, a unique issue, particularly from the law enforcement angle, in which a private owner segregated his business open to the public. The trespassing law was the only criminal violation.

As a direct result of the Gwynn Oak demonstrations, Mr. Agnew formed the Baltimore County Human Relations Commission to study what could be done "about segregation in the face of the Maryland trespass law." The commission that included Rabbi Shusterman, Monsignor Melville Taylor, and the Reverend Howard H. Ritterspusch, succeeded in getting the Price brothers, James, David, and Arthur, to agree on a date of integration.

What Protestant cooperation sought to accomplish in terms of civic influence proved impossible save on an interfaith basis, but this was a discovery tardily made. It has changed the whole character of the ecumenical movement in America.—Dr. Ross Sanderson, former Baltimore executive director of the Maryland Council of Churches

---

The War Memorial Hearings. A third dramatic ad hoc effort of the Baltimore clergy centered about the segregated housing problems, the catalyst for social concern. In 1962, the clergy of all faiths made an "Interfaith Housing Statement," the immediate spur to action. On November 29, 1965, clergymen spoke at the War Memorial on open housing in Baltimore. Rabbi Shusterman arranged for the group to speak during the City Council's open-housing hearings. Cardinal Shehan spoke first, but not until after the audience booed him. Bishop John Wesley Lord, the United Methodist Church, spoke after boos, followed by Bishop Harry Lee Doll, Anglican bishop of Maryland. Rabbi Shusterman took his turn in the same atmosphere. He reminisced:

I was greatly upset when the cardinal spoke. He's a frail man, but he stood like the Rock of Gibraltar, listening to the booing. When it stopped he spoke with a clear voice presenting his point of view and the point of view of his church.

By the time they came to me after the experience of the others, I was not too much disturbed. I almost felt it was a badge of honor because if these leaders could be booed, I would be embarrassed if I were not. It was an interesting program with interfaith overtones. The leaders spoke together in harmony on behalf of a great social benefit.

The participation of the clergymen in the issue of segregated housing was a changed climate from that of 1917. At that time, the clergy had watched the whole process without a murmur of protest against the situation.

Throughout the 1960s the clergy continued to participate in interfaith projects sponsored by community organizations, government agencies, and religious groups such as the Maryland Council of Churches, the Baltimore Community Relations Commission, the Baltimore City Police Department, and the Maryland Department of Mental Health. They may not have been as newsworthy or exciting as the restaurant desegregation efforts, the Gwynn Oak Park demonstration, or the War Memorial hearings, but they were part of the civil rights projects and important as social action in the face of social change. Some efforts included: the "Marriage Bill"; the Good Neighbor Pledge Campaign; the programs called "The Long Hot Summer"; March for Baltimore; and seminars to help the clergy study Baltimore's racial crisis, drug abuse, and alcoholism. Peace conferences met, the first one in May, 1965, at the Brown Memorial Presbyterian Church.

The Interfaith Peace Mission formed in October, 1966, consisted of clergymen from the Catholic, Protestant, and Jewish faiths. In December the mission organized a protest squad against the Vietnam War. The Reverend Philip Berrigan, a Josephite priest, the leader of the procession, was serving as curate at St. Peter Claver Church at the time. He explained that because such an

"incredible minority" of the city clergy voices protest against the Vietnam War, most Baltimore churchgoers remain apathetic toward pacifist issues....The church is moving more slowly into the anti-Vietnam War movement. The Protestants are especially vulnerable in [civil rights] because their livelihoods are at stake. Of Baltimore's Catholic church...the freedom is there, I'm sure. I think it's the default of responsibility on the part of the clergy rather than on the part of the cardinal.

Representatives of all faiths had met together informally in 1965 with a concern for Vietnam, poverty, and civil rights. This group, believing the clergy had to respond, was ahead of labor and business and political parties. Then, on the first Sunday of May, 1967, the members held a

conference on Vietnam at which Rabbi Shusterman, Bishop Lord (from Washington), and the Reverend John C. Bennett (Union Theological Seminary) asked that President Johnson stop the war completely. The press decided to ignore the conference of 400 people of whom 75 to 80 were clergymen. The Reverend Ellsworth Bunce (Methodist, later executive director of the Maryland Churches United) remarked that it was a "historic occasion; Brotherhood Week or Christian Unity Week have been easy to get together, but here we got together over an occasion."

The clergy sometimes responded to issues with conferences that resulted in new organizations, such as the Clergymen's Interfaith Committee for Human Rights, mentioned earlier in the Gwynn Oak demonstrations. The group began in 1962, at the peak of the civil rights movement, as an ad hoc committee of nearly 200 clergymen. One important activity was to sponsor a lecture by Dr. Martin Luther King.

Another new organization, Clergy for Community Understanding, formed as a result of the riots of 1968. Members of the clergy met at the Council of Churches and concluded that the clergy had a responsibility in this area. That same year, black and white ministers, priests and rabbis participated in an overnight retreat called the Black and White Confrontation. Mr. Bunce was chairman of the retreat whose purpose was for the clergy to get to know each other and "discover their own prejudices."

... Those present ... agreed that more and more there is an awareness of our need for a continuing dialogue with the broader clergy groups, for the problem of race is immense, and solutions can come only through a total involvement of the religious community.—Ellsworth Bunce, spokesman for the Black and White Confrontation

---

Rabbi Goldman discussed the antipathy and tension between blacks and Jewish merchants. As Mr. Bunce describes it, "It was a tense moment in which it became obvious this was a trouble area." Out of the discussion came the idea to bring clergymen and merchants together and the Clergy for Community Understanding (CCU) came into being "to implement an ongoing program in community dialogue." The chairman was Rabbi Howard Simon, assistant at Har Sinai Temple, and the Reverend O. St. Clair Franklin, Mt. Zion United Methodist Church, was cochairman. In 1969, Father Michael Mueller joined the executive committee as cochairman with the Reverend Harold Dobson, Interdenominational Ministerial Alliance and Union Baptist Church.

CCU was highly significant in as much as it went beyond the clergy and was not just ceremonial. It involved itself in a tough issue and worked at it. Merchants even developed a symbol and agreed to contribute to community activities, one being the youth program. Merchants had certificates of membership and this encouraged neighborhood people to buy from these stores. Mr. Bunce concluded, "For a couple of years it was a very viable program."

After many committee meetings, which consisted of the three faiths and merchants and the black consumers, many changes took place. Some of the black citizens in the beginning refused to sit next to the merchants at our committee meetings, but because of merchants' (one in particular) willingness to listen to the complaints and find some of them valid . . . not only did they sit next to each other—talk to and not at each other—but ate together. One merchant rounded up others and gave generously to support a recreation program for the black youth in the Pennsylvania Avenue area. If the program did not continue, it was not the fault of the merchants. We at the council went out of business and so did the program.—Mildred Atkinson, executive director, Christian Social Relations, Maryland Council of Churches

---

Mr. Bunce joined with Rabbi Shusterman; Bishop David K. Leighton, bishop coadjutor of the Episcopal Diocese of Maryland; the Reverend Vernon Dobson; and Bishop Joseph Gosman, assistant to the cardinal, to plan "the Hunger Banquet" that resulted in the Maryland Food Committee.

The fact that a group of religious leaders could accomplish something on an issue like open housing had made them realize they could meet periodically and work toward the resolution of other social issues.

In 1965, the Interfaith Urban Committee was one such joint effort that centered in downtown Baltimore with the purpose of getting together people concerned with the urban minority problems. Because there was no Jewish center of worship in the area, the Baltimore Jewish Council became part of the committee with Executive Director Leon Sachs as the representative. The members met for a short period and then realized that they needed the executives or heads of the judicatories to work across religious lines. The work did bear some fruit: the U Vote Campaign (in which whites helped blacks to vote through registration, education, or getting out the vote, in cooperation with the League of Women Voters), problems of the aging, and minimum wage. Any urban problems became their concern.

The Interfaith Urban Committee led into a new group: the Executive Heads of the Baltimore Judicatories in Conference. Harry Mills, a layman from the Episcopal Diocese, spoke with Bishop Doll about such a group. The Reverend Fred Webber, Synod of the Chesapeake United Presbyterian Church, became the driving force and assembled a group with the impetus from Cardinal Shehan (before he was cardinal), Rabbi Morris Lieberman, and others. There had never been a meeting like this before: a meeting to explore areas of common concern and to act in social situations. The religious voice would speak in unison.

During the years the group met informally, it involved itself in several projects: Project Equality, a vehicle for getting various private businesses to use fair employment practices in their hiring; Baltimore Interfaith Housing Council that encouraged different churches to sponsor low-and-moderate income housing construction (including Madison Square Housing, a low-cost 63-unit project); lower-cost housing in Columbia City; and the Joint Office of Urban Affairs.

Social Welfare. In the area of social welfare the first landmark occurred during the Depression when the government stepped in to lend its assistance. The creation of the Health and Welfare Council was a second landmark in terms of early joint cooperation of Catholic and Jewish agencies along with the Community Chest. The needs of the Depression of the 1930s had shown the importance of the various groups working together.

At that time the needs were different from those clarified 30 years later by "A Letter to Ourselves." It was a joint effort in 1960 by the Archdiocese of Baltimore, the Associated Jewish Charities, the Community Chest, and other human services agencies under the auspices of the Health and Welfare Council. The latter produced on paper a true beginning of an urban program of human renewal, a third landmark in interfaith cooperation.

The approach of the 1960s led to the more current historical developments in interfaith work more than the methods of Depression welfare groups. The earlier period concerned itself with the basic needs. In the sixties, the charities expanded their social action to a wide range of social concerns: nursing service, chronic care, housing needs, welfare rights, food stamps, and other issues of this kind.

Following "A Letter to Ourselves," between 1962 and 1964, a community action program was being planned on the problems of Baltimore's disadvantaged people. In that same year, the Congress voted for a national Office of Economic Opportunity (OEO) and, by 1965, the federal plan went into action. At the same time, Baltimore created the Community Action Agency, later renamed the Urban Services Agency.

The last major landmark occurred in 1969, with the creation of the United Fund, an amalgam of funding agencies of Central Maryland: Associated Catholic and Jewish charities, the Community Chest agencies, Anne Arundel County Community Chest, and Red Cross. The United Fund became one of the agencies of participation in social welfare. The explicit reason why the archdiocese cooperated was for ecumenical and interfaith implications: it believed that cooperation with various beliefs and backgrounds would be a positive step in bringing about a greater sense of cooperation in the community. Clergy and laymen responsible for the move included Cardinal Shehan, Father William Dumps, Bishop Francis Stafford, Mr. Nicholas Muller, Mr. Henry J. Knott, and Mr. William McQuirk. (In 1978, the United Fund assumed the national name, United Way.)

In the sixties a major interfaith effort in education was a formal institution for ecumenism and interfaith understanding called the Ecumenical Institute of Theology, a graduate school in theology. Protestant and Catholic clergymen and laymen founded the institute at St. Mary's Seminary in September, 1968. The purpose of the institute is "to provide the best possible graduate theological education available in metropolitan Baltimore and surrounding areas for all interested persons, lay, clerical, religious, men and women of all faiths." Its aim is "to offer courses of instruction in theology that will meet the demands of a public interested in theological inquiry."

The institute began as an ecumenical endeavor; however, with Rabbi Lieberman's association it soon became an interfaith institution.

Aftermath: 1970–1975

The fever pitch of Jewish–Christian clergy activities in response to the turbulence of the sixties subsided and eased into a quieter period in the seventies. The clergy continued to work in areas they had been developing, with friendship still being an integral aspect.

[The group planned to concern itself with] issues of ethics, and the responses that Jews and Christians make from their own traditions in matters of public and private morality; Israel as a phenomenon in world history and as a present political entity; questions and problems posed by Zionism as a phenomenon; the meaning of "revelation" in the two traditions; the way in which the two traditions handle religious training; the crucifixion narrative; the problem of "two covenants" and the whole matter of messianic expectation.—Jewish–Christian Seminar, Minutes, October 25, 1973

One dialogue group that received its impetus from St. Mary's Seminary and University, the Jewish–Christian Seminar, came into existence in the fall of 1973. The motivation stemmed from a conference that Father Addison Wright, professor at St. Mary's Seminary, attended. The seminar participants planned to concern themselves with issues of ethics and the responses that Jews and Christians make from their own traditions in matters of public and private morality; Israel as a phenomenon in world history and a present political entity; questions and problems posed by Zionism; the way in which the two traditions handle religious training; and other areas of similarities and differences.

Ad hoc conferences and institutes continued into the seventies: one was a one–day seminar on "Prospects for Peace in the Middle East," held at the Johns Hopkins University in May, 1974, sponsored by the American Jewish Committee, the Archdiocesan Commission on Ecumenical and Interreligious Affairs, the Baltimore Board of Rabbis, the College of Notre Dame, the NCCJ, and the Office of the Chaplain at Johns Hopkins. Clergymen from the different faiths addressed sisterhood interfaith conferences at the various temples. B'nai B'rith Women held interfaith meetings with clergy from the different faiths as speakers. Invited to the program were the Federation of Maryland Women's Clubs and the Jewish Federation of Women who had worked together since 1943.

... The seeds of that hatred were planted by the writers of the Gospels, watered and nurtured by the early Christian Fathers, and kept alive and growing by almost all Christian leaders for two thousand years from the time of the death of Jesus right down to the sermons that will be preached in many a Christian pulpit this coming Friday....

The Fourth Gospel is the real source of shame in the Christian religion. It is the largest and most poisonous of the seeds that led to the death of 6,000,000 Jews in Germany, to say nothing of untold millions of Jews killed in earlier Christian pogroms. Through this book, backed by the twisted history of the other Gospels, a Roman error of justice became a source of sanctified hatred against a whole race of people for two thousand years.

I use the words "sanctified hatred" deliberately. The record is there for any who wish to take the trouble to read. It became the holy obligation of pious Christians to hate the Jews, and this hatred was preached over and over again by the leaders of the church, including almost all of those who now have the pious title "Saint" attached to their names....

I see no way to avoid the truth that hatred has been continuously nurtured by Christian leaders for two thousand years and it continues to be taught by our New Testament. Anti–Semitism is the shame of

Christianity. It is our religion that prepared the way for Dachau....

Maybe it isn't words of apology that are important. What is really needed is to stop teaching anti-Semitic lies—even ones sanctified by Holy Scripture. What is needed is words and deeds that make certain that all of this filthy inhumanity will stop with each of us individually; that no one of us will be guilty of passing on any further to any man, woman, or child, the idea that the Jews killed Jesus of Nazareth and that God hates them for that crime.—Alfred B. Starratt, sermon in Emmanuel Church, Baltimore on Palm Sunday, March 26, 1972

The second wide area of clergy participation in interfaith activities in Baltimore continuing in the seventies was pulpit sharing. On January 14, 1971, the St. Thomas More Society of Maryland sponsored a highly significant service, the thirteenth annual Red Mass, at the Basilica of the Assumption, the older of Baltimore's co-cathedrals and the first Catholic cathedral in the United States (begun in 1806). Rabbi Goldman was the first Jew to speak from that pulpit. He expressed his deep feelings about being able to speak at the Basilica and praised Cardinal Shehan for his strong stand on behalf of the Soviet Jews.

Another "first," the Centennial Interfaith Service, occurred at the Chizuk Amuno Congregation on Friday, February 12, 1971. Cardinal Shehan and the Right Reverend David K. Leighton joined Rabbi Goldman in the pulpit. Other church dignitaries from all of the religious judicatories from the Baltimore metropolitan area participated in the processional and sat on the platform of the sanctuary "in seats of honor." A special new ritual emphasized the "ecumenical character and spirit." Rabbi Goldman spoke on "What Every Christian Should Know About Judaism;" Cardinal Shehan "What Every Jew Should Know About Christianity;" and Bishop Leighton "Jewish Roots in Christianity."

Special Interfaith Services. Two memorable services took place in September, 1972, to commemorate the men who died at Munich during the Olympics. The first occurred on the playing field of Loyola College. "The students spontaneously decided they wanted a religious service the day before Rosh Hoshanah," wrote the service and requested that Rabbi Shusterman ap-

Chizuk Amuno Congregation Anniversary Celebration. (left to right) Lawrence Cardinal Shehan, Rabbi Israel Goldman, the Reverend Fred M. Webber

prove it. He commented that the service might have been taken from any Jewish prayer book; it was universal.

To be sure it was universal enough and not weighted on the side of Christianity. The service might have been taken from any Jewish prayer book. I caught phrases like those in the Union Prayer Book and some other prayer books. At least 1,000 students attended the service at which Father Joseph Sellinger, president of Loyola College, read a declaration proclamation that the service would be held. Then came the religious service conducted by the young people. I spoke, a student spoke, a priest spoke. Led by the faculty the entire group marched with great dignity around the playing field and met again at the platform where I gave the benediction.—Abraham Shusterman, September, 1972

The second service took place at noon before Rosh Hoshanah at the Federal Building on Hopkins Place. Rabbi Shusterman, representing the Baltimore Jewish Council, arranged these services with other clergymen participating: Rabbi Nahum ben Natan, Beth Jacob Synagogue, and representative of the Orthodox rabbinate; the Reverend Vernon Dobson, president, the Interdenominational Religious Council; Bishop Austin Murphy, for the Catholic church; Bishop Leighton, then auxiliary bishop of the Episcopal church. Rabbi Shusterman read a prayer, others read scriptural verses and recited prayers, and Mayor William Donald Schaefer spoke.

Interfaith Organizations. In 1970, the organization that had spearheaded many of the social

actions of the previous decades, the Maryland Council of Churches, yielded to the pressures of the emerging form of ecumenical relationships. For example, (1) projects went more to the grassroots, approached more from the local community level; (2) the Council of Churches had been basically Protestant and Orthodox, without Roman Catholics; and (3) the interfaith aspect was not provided for structurally, even though as far back as the 1930s and 1940s the leadership of the council included it. As a point of continuation of some of the more vital ministries of the council, the Maryland Churches United began its work in January, 1971. This group promised to be a coordinating center, a community link, and a clearinghouse concerned with seeking answers to the problems they were facing.

One activity in which Mr. Bunce, the executive director of the organization, played an active part, was the Maryland Food Committee. In the spring of 1979, the committee headed by Ann Miller (former nurse and social activist) started the Maryland Food Bank. The only such nonprofit organization on the East Coast, it has distributed about 75 percent of the food to needy people in Baltimore.

The importance of the Brotherhood Clergy has been fellowship, theological and educational enlightenment, not social. We have had good, strong fellowship over the years. It has, I think, done as much for the interfaith movement as anything else. It has set a base for getting to know the other clergy. Contacts have been made throughout the city. It has been a tremendous spiritual force.—Eric Peacher, assistant pastor, Grace United Church

---

Three organizations that continued from the earlier periods were the Baltimore Clergy Brotherhood, the Archdiocesan Commission for Christian Unity, and the Interdenominational Ministerial Alliance. The BCB had a membership in 1974 limited to about 150 men, with an average of 75, and still used the format of a speaker or a panel, presenting a topic or issues related to the group. Monsignor Martin Gamber, assistant chaplain at Stella Maris Hospice, said, "It seems to be a threat to be involved in anything controversial. Issues examined are not too explosive although in recent years they have been more bold. The constitution projected some committees, but they never developed." Evidence of fellowship has included increased friendships between Jews and Catholics, Jews and Protestants, and Protestants and Catholics. The brotherhood has stimulated pulpit exchanges and people of the different faiths have increased visits to each others' churches and synagogues or temples.

The Archdiocesan Commission for Christian Unity began in January, 1962, encouraged by the Holy See as far back as 1948. Cardinal Shehan established the commission, the first one of its kind in the United States, to develop local ecumenism. In 1973, Father Rafferty suggested the name of the commission be changed to the Commission for Ecumenical and Interreligious Affairs because the group had become "involved so deeply with our Jewish friends."

Rabbi Israel Goldman (the Jewish member), and the Reverend Hugh Dickinson (Christ Episcopal Church) helped the commission understand how Jews and Protestants feel about issues. The commission began in the 1970–1975 period to renew its guidelines in the light of the progress of the years since Vatican Council II.

The third organization was the Interdenominational Ministerial Alliance, an ecumenical group that had started in the mid-thirties. In the sixties it became an interfaith group of 100 to 200 clergy members. Rabbis joined the alliance in response to the inner city crises. In the seventies, leadership in interfaith efforts began to emerge with an aim to bring together rabbis, priests, ministers, black and white, from the inner city with those from the suburbs to look at religion in Baltimore.

The organization that reached into the seventies and seemed to be the culmination of all the efforts that had gone before was the Executive Heads of the Baltimore Judicatories. On October 30, 1970, the Heads formed a formal organization, the Interfaith Council of Metropolitan Baltimore. The three cochairmen were Cardinal Shehan as Catholic Archbishop of Baltimore; Rabbi Goldman as president of the Baltimore Board of Rabbis; and the Reverend Fred M. Webber as assistant Synod executive of the United Presbyterian Church.

... very enriching to see these fine scholars and

humanitarians from all the faiths come together to face human tragedy and problems on an interfaith basis. It is a fledgling organization, groping its way in the area of services. This is the most important area with worship being second.—Oscar Bonny, former executive secretary of the Religious Society of Friends, Homewood

The leaders generally conceded that the most important facet of ICMB was that an individual church did not have to participate in an activity or decision that it opposed. Mr. Jack Carr, secretary of ICMB, emphasized "the reason for ICMB is to generate action which is carried out at staff level by such interagency consortia as the joint Office of Urban Affairs and the emerging interagency staff dealing with welfare policy; and, of course, permanent incorporated agencies like Project Equality."

ICMB projects continued into the seventies, including Project Equality, but the problems engendered by the group became more serious. The Jewish representation was concerned that it was not working and asked that a study be made. The Baltimore Jewish Council decided to make a recommendation to withdraw its support, but with the small amount of money it cost to stay in, the council, wanting to avoid community disruption, remained in. Some of the smaller groups had already withdrawn and after another year, the Baltimore Jewish Council decided not to be a member. Actually, the Jewish groups were among the few that had continued, although Mr. John R. Burleigh, executive director of Project Equality, did not mention this in a public statement about Project Equality. He said that the Jewish community showed little or no interest in Project Equality, which aroused bad feelings between the two.

Father John Cronin—active in national civil rights activities—said there were misunderstandings about who ran the project and its goals, that the project was understaffed, and that led to "some sloppiness at this level." He added that the "pullout of the Jewish community came as no surprise."

Other problems accompanying the project caused its demise: Project Equality took much of the time of the ICMB and kept it from working effectively; it was too much to organize and educate the religious community on the type of buying required; and besides, at this time there were federal and state antidiscrimination laws. One accomplishment was its pinpointing the problem of discrimination by the business community against anyone because of race.

As far as ICMB was concerned, it also highlighted the conflict that developed from the presence of staff and other representatives. Regardless of their "ranks" within judicatories, stronger personalities began to dominate meetings, which discouraged some judicatory heads from attending sessions. What had obviously happened was a breakdown in communication between the judicatory executives and their staffs.

The fact that so many church dignitaries meet frequently in common causes and get to know each other, inevitably results in a feeling of mutual trust and confidence between the leaders of the various religious denominations. I can cite my own experience in relation to Cardinal Shehan. It was he who authorized my appearance at the Red Mass . . . . I had the great privilege of speaking from the pulpit of the Catholic Cathedral.
This has never happened before in Baltimore history. Likewise, when I was requested to obtain from the cardinal a statement in behalf of Soviet Jewry, he did so with the greatest courtesy . . . . Likewise he accepted readily my invitation to speak from my own pulpit . . . February 12, at the Centennial Interfaith Service of my congregation. If it were not for the Interfaith Council of Metropolitan Baltimore and for the opportunities for personal contact, it is very unlikely that these things would have come to pass . . . .
—Israel Goldman

Ecumedia was another important project incorporated in ICMB. In January, 1969, the Reverend John Paul Davidson, director of the Maryland Council of Churches' Department of Radio, and Father Casimir Pugevicius, head of the Office of Radio and Television for the archdiocese, formed Ecumedia to develop radio and television programs. It was the only one of its kind in the United States: the only agency that works "for and with" Roman Catholics, Protestants, and Jews. In spite of being affiliated with ICMB, after Mr. Davidson and Father Pugevicius left Ecumedia, the group lost its impetus until a new board attempted to revitalize it in 1974. After

several serious meetings and plans to develop new programs, the organization received a staggering blow to its progress when the treasurer absconded with the funds. As with Project Equality, Ecumedia suffered from a lack of leadership and insufficient funds.

There is now a serious reexamination of ICMB to see what can be done on the level of intergroup understanding where the influence of church and synagogue will mean something. With the tension in the schools recently and the threats of violence a joint statement might be calming. This is only one area. The ICMB is attempting to be more than just a verbalizing group.—Abraham Shaw

---

In June, 1973, ICMB decided it could not handle many issues at the same time. It then studied and acted on only one social problem at a time, for example, prison reform. In 1973 to 1974, it aided the state in establishing community correction houses, one at the west end of the city, one at the east. In 1974 and 1975, the project was concerned with city and suburban tension.

However, working with one problem at a time had disadvantages for ICMB: The council did not become well–known even among the local clergy. Dealing with only one issue at a time was not compatible with high–profile visibility; besides, ICMB could not respond to immediate crisis needs as could the Maryland Churches United, even though it was basically a Protestant organization open to Catholic but not Jewish membership. Furthermore, the working force of ICMB found it difficult to sustain interest and commitment to one project over a long period of time. Recognizing this, the ICMB made the decision in the spring of 1975 to return to its original activity; that is, simply to provide the occasion for judicatory heads themselves to meet periodically for the fellowship and the sharing of concerns.

The pressure of the times had compelled the creation of an ICMB, but as part of the evolutionary process, the times were not really ripe for such an organization. Project Equality and Ecumedia were a part of the same problems. One clergyman commented that the deep trust and confidence necessary for a viable interfaith group were not there. He believed time and continued interfaith activities will eventually help an organization like ICMB succeed. In spite of its failures, some clergymen evaluated ICMB as an interfaith method that had accomplished the goals of the clergy's activities.

This group holds the promise for the future. The heads of the denominations and the staff met. They never knew each other before and after a year called each other by first names. This is the best example of the clergy "doing its thing" in interfaith understanding. It exemplifies the finest kind of interfaith when the mingling is natural, not for purposes of interfaith understanding.—Leon Sachs

---

Social Welfare. The most outstanding recent development in the interfaith work of the clergy has been in the area of social welfare. As we have seen in the sixties, the consortium of interfaith agencies dealt with welfare problems that included health problems. In the seventies, the agencies had to deal with the Vietnamese refugees. Wherever there was a specific need and a common interest, the charities worked together. Because of the mechanics involved, they found working through an organization less effectual than acting directly through their own groups. Programs and activities were necessary rather than dialogue per se to satisfy the needs.

Along with working on problems, the joint welfare groups have opened doors and made progress in interfaith relations. Actually, in Baltimore, the Jewish clergy has not been active in social welfare activities because the clerical setup is different from that of Catholics and Protestants. The work has been an interfaith project mainly because the Jewish laity of the Associated Jewish Charities has cooperated with the Protestant and Catholic agencies.

The necessity of the Catholic church's involvement with races other than the Caucasian helped increase the extent of the church's concerns over the years from 1965 to 1975. The Methodists have increased their work and have expanded, although not at the same rate as the Catholics. Actually, the Jews did not need such expansion since they already had a most comprehensive "Jewish welfare system." Representing the different agencies were: Bishop J. Francis Stafford, director of the Associated Catholic Charities; the Reverend William Black, for the Lutherans; the Reverend Wayne Moulder, for the Presbyterians; and Mr. Robert Hiller, director of the Associated Jewish Charities.

Several areas of participation in social welfare developed in the 1970 to 1975 period. For example, the Interfaith Committee for Social Welfare was a combination of Protestant, Jewish, and Catholic service agencies; in 1973, the second project, the Maryland Association of Residential Facilities for Youth, or MARFY, began as a combination of religions, some with clerics at the head, including Kids in Need (KIN); begun in 1972, the Center for Metropolitan Research and Planning for the Johns Hopkins University had a committee called the Interfaith Committee on Religion and the Metropolis; the St. Ambrose Housing Association, headed by Father Vincent Quayle, worked to enhance the level of home ownership among the city's poor; and the Criminal Justice program headed by Father Joseph Wenderoth worked on community correction proposals.

Formal education in interfaith understanding still remained the province of the Ecumenical Institute of Theology continually plagued with "financial uncertainty." In 1970, summer sessions became a part of the calendar. The Jewish–Christian Seminar enabled the interfaith group to exchange views on biblical religion. The "Historical Survey" summed up the progress of the institute "from one manila folder to a filing system jealously guarded by the efficiency of our secretary...."

The Administrative Advisory Board enabled the institute to keep contact with the community needs and interests and to provide services not necessarily academic. Beginning in 1974, Gerson and Sandy Eisenberg funded a professorship in classical Hebrew taught by eminent professors and/or lecturers. Included were Dr. Jimmy Roberts, Father Addison Wright, Fr. John Kselman, Rabbis David Goldstein, Jacob Agus, and Donald Berlin, Dr. Moses Aberbach, and Dr. Leivy Smolar. The Eisenberg–Dunning lecturer in 1980 was Dr. Hiltgunt Zassenhaus. In the same year, Peggy Obrecht, a graduate of the institute, established a chair in Jewish studies in honor of her husband, Charles Obrecht. Rabbi Berlin was the first professor in the spring session of 1981.

The women's movement in the 1970s brought about a significant innovation in the role of the clergy in Jewish–Christian relations. Before that time, lay women like Mildred Atkinson as a representative of a church–related organization, the Maryland Council of Churches, had provided a leadership role. However, now in the seventies, as women entered the ministry, a new group developed.

In 1977, the Task Force on the Status of Women in the Catholic Church—a lay and religious group—provided the impetus. Flo Bunja, president of Women Together and a Catholic, and Sister Mary Eileen McNamara, of the Carmelite Monastery, organized a meeting in October at the College of Notre Dame to bring together women in ministries to "discover how women are ministering in the other churches and synagogues today." The women would then go out to their neighborhoods with more awareness of how the spiritual can affect our attitudes.

Women in the ministry spoke of their experiences to religious and lay leaders. At the time, Ann Zibelman, cantorial soloist at the Har Sinai Congregation, was the closest to a female rabbi in Baltimore. "A Spiritual Encounter" was planned to be the only meeting; however, the group became an ongoing organization called Women of Faiths. Since then, Catholic, Protestant, and Jewish women have had public meetings in churches and synagogues to emphasize the spiritual significance of the group.

Established organizations continued their interfaith activities. In 1978, Rabbi Mark Tanenbaum (director of the Interreligious Department of the American Jewish Committee and a former Baltimorean) spoke at the Cathedral of the Incarnation for a meeting of clergy and educators. The AJC and the Commission for Ecumenical and Interreligious Affairs have worked together on programming on Soviet Jewry and Middle East concerns. Ten years after Vatican Council II, Cardinal Shehan received an award from the AJC honoring his work on the council. AJC, the Baltimore Jewish Council, and the Northwest Corporation have initiated steps toward a dialogue for clergymen in the northwest area of the city. The aim is to have the clergy get to know each other and then use their pulpits to talk about interfaith understanding.

Lois Rosenfield, executive director of the AJC and Stanley Sollins, executive director of the Baltimore Jewish Council, have been spearheading such interfaith efforts with other groups in the city as their predecessors had done in the years before them. Leon Sachs had been director of the council during the dramatic years of the civil rights period.

Conclusion

In Baltimore the interfaith movement grew from seeds—some national some international—that rooted and budded and blossomed into healthy, viable plants in the local soil. True, some offshoots have withered and died, but the roots are firm. Many times Baltimore was the first, or among the first, particularly in the cooperation of Catholics with the Protestants and the Jews. We have traveled from the fear that each denomination had of losing its own identity and a policy of proselytizing toward a greater unity among Christians and Jews, with a growing respect for each other. The influences were the leadership and the model of Cardinal Gibbons and his interaction with Protestant and Jewish clerical leaders. These relationships set a pattern that Cardinal Shehan continued and the movement burgeoned.

I have no desire to persuade my fellow countrymen all to become Jews .... I am just as anxious to preserve the Christian tradition as the Jewish tradition. I believe that Christians have so much of truth and beauty and goodness in their own tradition that it is worthwhile to preserve it all in its variety. I feel the same about my own Jewish tradition. I may not believe in the ideas of Christianity about Jews, but I can understand their compelling challenge to Christians and to that challenge Christians will yield. I do not worship God through Christian forms, but I can stand with bowed head and moved heart before the profound reverence of the Christian approach. They have color, mystery, drama, profound sanctities, and high achievements behind them. They should keep them. So have we. And we shall keep ours. And each shall influence the other and share what is beautiful and best. And there shall be give–and–take and mutual modification and interpenetration between us and the differences, the conflicts shall be softened and civilized, but the rivers of thinking and practice shall flow on and empty into that great ocean of human aspiration into which the hearts and souls of men have poured their holiest dreams. And the world will be better and happier for us both.—Morris Lazaron, Common Ground

---

It is important to emphasize certain statistics: in Baltimore in 1975 there were 761 priests and 41 rabbis; the Protestant figures are difficult to obtain. From these numbers we can see what a small number of clergymen were active in interfaith activities. We know from membership lists of various interfaith organizations, task groups, and newspaper articles that more of the clergy participated than just those named here. Aware of their moral responsibility for fellowship and human rights needs, some of the clergy became more active. Evidence of discrimination still persists although it has much diminished or disappeared as the climate of Christian opinion has changed. Restrictions on residency are illegal now and there have been vast changes in educational opportunities for Jews due to the efforts of the clergy. There have been great advances in employment and in the area of public accommodations: no hotels or restaurants keep Jews out today. However, few changes have taken place in social clubs. The clergy helped to effect the changes in the situation.

In the sixties, the clergymen were busy running to caucuses, strikes, one crisis after another—like on the battle line. The Reverend Mr. John Sharp (Govans Presbyterian Church) remarked that some ministers suffered breakdowns from the pull of pressures from all sides. All were overworked with the combination of activism and congregation responsibilities. Then the swing of the pendulum began to return again to conservatism. Mr. Sharp also observed that Vietnam and issues like Cambodia were settled and the times were like a breath of fresh air when people asked for Bible studies.

Yet, the activism helped to bring about the changed climate in interfaith relations in Baltimore. That cooperation was sometimes Catholic–Jewish–Protestant, sometimes Jewish–Catholic, sometimes Jewish–Protestant. The Jews have had misconceptions about Christians generally; the Christians have had misconceptions about Jews. Interfaith cooperation in dialogue, worship, education, and social action strengthened Jewish–Catholic–Protestant relations and mitigated some of these misunderstandings. In spite of impediments, the clergy has made some progress in Baltimore in lessening anti–Semitism.

Have those hopes been fulfilled? Not completely, I am sure. With the difficult circumstances that have developed since the publication of the Declaration, it would have been a miracle if all hopes had met complete fulfillment. But the very fact that we are all gathered here in this synagogue tonight, to pray together and to discuss our present religious situation, is an indication that those hopes have not been completely unjustified.—Cardinal Shehan on "The Statement on the Jews" at Beth El Synagogue, February 14, 1975

The spirit of brotherhood and sisterhood permeates the renaissance of Baltimore, a unity of efforts to improve physically and spiritually. The interfaith movement reflects that spirit.

Lenora Heilig Nast

ADVANCING THE STATUS OF WOMEN

A review of the progress of women in Baltimore since 1965 reveals a remarkable record of achievement. However, this survey of recent advancement must acknowledge that distinguished accomplishments by Baltimore women is a tradition dating back to the beginnings of Baltimore.

Baltimore's first newspaper, the *Journal*, was published and edited by Mary Katherine Goddard, who also headed the city's early postal service until 1789. A century later the personal philanthropy and fund-raising efforts of Mary Elizabeth Garrett and a committee of other Baltimore women enabled the Johns Hopkins Medical School to open and guaranteed that women as well as men could gain admission.

Early in this century Baltimore suffragettes such as Emma Funck, Bessie Ellicott, and Edith Hooker led the campaign to gain the vote for women, which was finally granted by constitutional amendment in 1920. In the decade that followed, civil engineer Olive Dennis oversaw the B & O Railroad's passenger service; Katherine Mahool established and ran a Baltimore advertising agency; and Lulu Dryden, known as the "Iron Woman of Baltimore," operated her own iron and metal brokerage firm.

In the 1930s, Angela Bambace launched her Baltimore career with the International Ladies' Garment Workers Union, which brought her national prominence as a labor leader. She was best known to Baltimoreans, however, as a civic leader who boosted the symphony and advised the city's antipoverty program. In 1944, Dr. Helen Brooke Taussig, the Hopkins pediatrician, developed the world-famous "blue baby" operation with Dr. Alfred Blalock. By the end of the 1950s, Baltimore could boast of women in the business community who were bank officers, advertising executives, stock brokers, and business owners.

Working for Social Change. Despite this impressive record of individual achievement in Baltimore, the 1960s brought a growing recognition that opportunities for many women were limited by traditional attitudes and by laws and policies that discriminated against women. Baltimore women's groups urged Governor J. Millard Tawes to address the problem statewide through the creation of a special commission to examine barriers to the advancement of women. In 1965, Tawes responded by establishing the Commission on the Status of Women. He appointed Baltimore attorney Jeanette Wolman as its chairman. An outstanding civic leader, she had been active for 40 years in the public affairs of the city prior to this appointment, and in 1937 had been further distinguished as the first female member of the Baltimore Bar Association.

The creation of the commission marked the beginning of public awareness that a women's movement was being launched in Maryland, and that its base was in Baltimore. The commission was directed to study and recommend ways to eliminate discrimination against women in the areas of employment and of civil and property rights. The report released by the Wolman Commission in 1967 became a blueprint for governmental actions aimed at improving opportunities for Maryland women. Its impact contributed to the reestablishment of the commission by Governor Spiro Agnew in 1968.

Early in the work of the first Commission on the Status of Women, the issue of equal pay for equal work received special attention. The commission recommended state legislation to correct salary inequities. The principal sponsor of the legislation was commission member Verda Welcome, Baltimore's first woman member of the Maryland Senate. Her bill provided that employees of one sex be paid wages equal to those paid employees of the opposite sex for comparable work. Following strong support by the commission, as well as a coalition of women's groups and a variety of labor, civic, and professional organizations, the bill was approved by the legislature in 1966.

By the late sixties, Baltimore women became active in a national movement dedicated to changing society's traditional image of women. The local leaders of the women's liberation movement—like feminists elsewhere—blamed the widely accepted stereotype of women as housewives and mothers for hindering the acceptance of women in other roles. Founded in 1968, the Baltimore Women's Movement organized consciousness-raising groups, published a newsletter, distributed leaflets for women's causes at public events, and established a Women's Liberation Center on Greenmount Avenue as a focal point for their activities.

The Baltimore Center for Victims of Sexual Assault, formerly known as the Baltimore Rape Crisis Center, originated at the Greenmount Avenue Women's Liberation Center, where volunteers responded to calls from rape victims who needed a sympathetic ear as well as advice on reporting the crime to the police and receiving medical attention. Today the center is an independent entity with its own board of directors. It has received an emergency grant from the city's Coordinating Council on Criminal Justice and seeks community support through fundraising events. The center, at the Central YWCA, receives approximately 1,400 calls annually relating to rape and other types of sexual assault. It provides victims with information on the help available from medical and law enforcement agencies.

The project of the Women's Liberation Movement in Baltimore that perhaps gained the most attention in the 1970s was the publication of a periodical called *Women: A Journal of Libera-*

tion. Dee Anne Pappas, a college English instructor, joined forces in 1969 with Donna Keck and Vicki Pollard to edit and publish the first editions of the *Journal*, which printed articles addressing the question of "What is Liberation?" and the issue of whether behavioral differences between the sexes were the result of inherent characteristics or cultural conditioning. Articles on women in history and in the arts also appeared. Interest in the journal extended beyond Baltimore, with distribution along the East Coast. The 3,000 copies of the first edition, published in the fall of 1969, were insufficient to meet the demand. An additional 10,000 were printed to fill requests. By February of 1972, 20,000 copies of the journal had been printed.

Unlike the Feminist Press (which left Baltimore in the early 1970s with one of its founders, Florence Howe), *A Journal of Liberation* has retained its Baltimore base. It continues to be published at least twice a year by a volunteer staff operating as a cooperative. Considered the oldest continuing national magazine by and about women, its 1979 edition marked the publication's tenth anniversary. The Women's Union, formed in 1972, is an outgrowth of the *Journal*. A socialist feminist organization, it began as a study group and has sponsored a series of educational programs on women. It annually observes International Women's Day in March.

Women's Groups Fight Legal Barriers. While some Baltimore women were working to change social attitudes toward women, others directed their efforts toward eliminating legal barriers to the advancement of women. In 1971, a group of women attorneys and law students in Baltimore founded the Women's Law Center for the purpose of eliminating sex discrimination in law. The center continues to provide legal representation for individual women who encounter discrimination and maintains a hotline to answer questions and give legal advice. The center also offers information to the public on the legal rights of women through a speakers' bureau and a series of booklets; it offers publications on the credit rights of women, marriage and divorce laws in Maryland, and legal advice for battered women. Evidence of the success and effectiveness of the Baltimore center is the recent establishment of a Women's Law Center in Annapolis.

A substantial barrier to the progress of women in Baltimore was removed in 1971, when the city enacted one of the strongest prohibitions against sex discrimination of any municipality in the nation. The law, which amended the city's 1966 Community Relations Ordinance, bars race discrimination and guarantees equal treatment in education, job training, health and welfare services, employment opportunities, and public accommodations regardless of sex. The bill had been introduced by City Council President William Donald Schaefer at the request of Baltimorean Anne Boucher, chairman of the Commission on the Status of Women under Governor Marvin Mandel.

Further progress was made at the state level in 1972, when the state legislature approved an equal rights amendment to the state constitution. It ratified the proposed equal rights amendment to the United States Constitution at the same time. Maryland voters approved this legislative action in a November referendum on the issue. Baltimore attorney Katie O'Ferrall Friedman, one of the founders of the Women's Law Center, chaired a special gubernatorial commission charged with the responsibility of recommending legislation to implement the state's equal rights amendment. Many of its recommendations to place men and women on equal footing in Maryland law earned legislative acceptance by 1978, when the commission wrapped up its work and was dissolved.

The 1972 session of the legislature also yielded a new political group devoted to the advancement of Maryland women. Led by Senator Rosalie Abrams of Baltimore city, the women members of the state legislature formed a Women's Caucus for the purpose of seeking leadership responsibilities for women in state government. The Caucus has grown in numbers and effectiveness. It had 28 members in 1979 and added the goal of enacting legislation to remove discrimination against women in the law. Current membership in the caucus includes Baltimore city's Senators Rosalie Abrams and Verda Welcome, and Delegates Hattie Harrison, Lena Lee, Margaret Murphy, and Anne Perkins.

Two important women's groups were founded in the city in 1972, Baltimore New Directions for Women (BNDW) and the Baltimore chapter of the National Organization for Women. New Directions was created as a career counseling service aimed at helping women gain equal employment opportunities and at assisting them in marketing their skills to maximum advantage. By 1973, it offered a wide range of services to women seeking employment, including individual and group job counseling and workshops to help applicants identify their skills and present them to prospective employers in resumés and interviews.

While continuing these basic services, BNDW has also branched out to serve the special needs of women who must, because of divorce or widowhood, become the main breadwinner in the family. Known as "displaced homemakers," these women are counseled and are given job training and help with job placement at the Displaced Homemaker's Center, which was first funded by 1976 state legislative action. This center is the second of its kind in the nation and is considered a model for programs elsewhere in Maryland and in other states. BNDW also

helped establish in 1977 the Executive Women's Network in Baltimore with the goal of assisting the career advancement of business and professional women in Baltimore.

The Baltimore chapter of the National Organization for Women, organized in 1972, refers to itself as a "civil rights organization" dedicated to achieving equality for women. In 1974, Baltimore NOW was active in the successful campaign to gain admission of young women to Baltimore's Polytechnic Institute, renowned for its technical training of male students. Through the Battered Women Task Force, NOW was instrumental in making the public and the legislature aware of the need for services to victims of domestic violence. The House of Ruth, a shelter for battered spouses in Baltimore, received state funding support in 1977.

Working in tandem with the Women's Law Center, Baltimore NOW has helped bring sex discrimination cases to the courts. While the

Workshop for Displaced Homemakers, Baltimore New Directions for Women, Inc., 1980. Photo by Frankie Payne.

Women's Law Center provides the legal counsel, NOW funds many of the procedural costs of litigation—such as court recorders' fees, preparations of depositions and duplication of legal documents. For example, one case initiated several years ago but still pending against Bethlehem Steel, contends that the company has employed too few women and kept women employees in low-paying jobs without providing opportunities for advancement.

In June, 1979, the Baltimore chapter sponsored the first Women's Health Conference in the city. Baltimore NOW keeps its estimated 400 members informed on women's issues with its newsletter, the *Equalizer*.

Improving Communication Among Baltimore Women's Groups. The creation of groups like Baltimore New Directions for Women and the Baltimore NOW indicated a growing interest in women's issues and increased the need for closer coordination and communication among women's groups in the city. Women Together was created to fill this need in 1973. The first of the annual Women's Fairs in Baltimore was the result. Attendance and participation at these fairs has increased each year; since 1978, the fair has been extended to a second day. More than 100 exhibitors participated in the 1979 fair with booths that showed the wide variety of educational, health, and other services available to women in the Baltimore area.

Women Together also initiated the *Women's Guide to Baltimore*, which is compiled annually by volunteers from member organizations such as NOW and New Directions for Women; it is supported financially by local banks. The guide, a directory to women's organizations and service agencies for women in Baltimore, is available at the Women's Fair held each February and from any of the 33 organizations of Women Together.

Further efforts to increase cooperation and communication between women's groups throughout the year have resulted in the 1978 establishment of the Women's Resource and Advocacy Center on East 25th Street near Charles Street, in the same neighborhood as the House of Ruth, the Women's Law Center, Baltimore New Directions for Women, the Displaced Homemakers Center, the offices of NOW, and the League of Women Voters.

The Resource and Advocacy Center, designed to be a focal point and central resource for women's groups and service agencies, maintained a library on women's issues, including the materials collected by Women Together that were formerly housed at their Women's Resource Center. In the fall of 1979, the Advocacy Center phased out and its work is still being carried on by OPENLINE, a part of New Directions. The collections of the Career Counseling Center and the Center for Displaced Homemakers are also available. Women's groups use the center for meetings and support services such as printing and phones. Initially funded for 1978–79 by a federal grant from ACTION, the center has been staffed by volunteers, many of whom are displaced homemakers receiving stipends while gaining work experience. The center is attempting to obtain funding from other sources to continue its work now that its grant has expired.

Establishing a communications network between women has been a recurring theme for Baltimore women in the 1970s. For example, women officeworkers in the city have formed Women Employed in Baltimore, an organization working to improve the economic status of working women; and the Women's Executive Network was formed.

Baltimore County Delegate Bert Booth and Baltimore city Councilwoman Mary Pat Clarke spearheaded organizational efforts in 1979 to build a statewide network of women in elective office known as the Maryland Association of Elected Women. In 1976, women artists of Baltimore formed the Women's Art Community. Black women in the Baltimore community met in 1975 to share their feelings on family and work responsibilities and decided to form the Black Women's Consciousness–Raising Association. In 1977, Baltimore women representing Catholic, Protestant, and Jewish religious traditions created a group known as Women of Faiths to explore the spiritual concerns they share as women.

One organization that has facilitated the building of communications networks among Baltimore women is the Maryland Commission for Women, known in its early years as the Commission for the Status of Women. Although it serves the entire state, its influence in Baltimore has been particularly strong. The commission is headquartered in the city and, in all but two of its 15 years of existence, has been led by a resident of the Baltimore area. Baltimoreans Jeanette Wolman, Anne Boucher, and Shoshana Cardin (a delegate to the Maryland Constitutional Convention from a Baltimore suburban district) served as chairwomen of the commission, and Kay Carter of Baltimore served as vice-chairwoman. Jo-Anne Orlinsky, also a Baltimore resident, was appointed by Governor Harry Hughes to be the chairwoman in the summer of 1979.

Solving Problems Particular to Women. The commission has encouraged the creation of Baltimore-based groups to meet the special needs of women. For example, Baltimore New Directions for Women emerged from an initiative by the commission to establish a program in Maryland similar to WOW (Washington Opportunities for Women). The commission also played an important role in the creation of Women Together. WISH (Women in Self Help), a telephone service offering counseling to the housebound woman with personal, social, or emotional problems, was begun with the cooperation and support of the Maryland Commission.

The commission also serves as a statewide information and referral service for women seeking help, and provides a communications link with women throughout Maryland in the form of a newsletter. It brings together representatives of women's groups from all corners of the state as a legislative coalition that discusses and keeps track of state legislation affecting women.

Governor Marvin Mandel Signs Maryland's Equal Rights Amendment, May 26, 1972. Photo by Lee Troutner.

The commission frequently plays the role of advocate for women, testifying for bills that its members believe will improve the status of women in Maryland.

Workshops and courses designed to further women's understanding of their roles and issues that affect them are other projects supported by the commission. One of the first courses offered in the Baltimore area was cosponsored by the Commission for Women and the College of Notre Dame in 1971. Called the "Woman in Perspective," the course was developed by Sister Kathleen Feeley, now president of Notre Dame, and Lenora Nast, a commission member. Mrs. Nast coordinated the course, which featured talks by outstanding women on the position of women in contemporary society. Verda Welcome, state senator, and Mildred Otenasek, a political science professor and Democratic committeewoman from Maryland, discussed women and politics. Baltimore lawyer Connie Putzel spoke on women and the law; Johns Hopkins gynecologist Georgeanna Jones, the psychology of women; and Dean Elizabeth Geen of Goucher College, women in higher education. More recently, the commission and Goucher College cosponsored a conference on barriers to career advancement of women working in government.

Although it has played a significant role in advancing the status of women in Baltimore, the Commission for Women has been only one facet of the women's movement in the city. The movement also has consisted of other individuals and groups who, with special skills and interests, have perceived particular needs of women in the community and have succeeded in creating ways to meet them.

Women psychologists, counselors, and therapists in Baltimore—concerned that the special mental health needs of women were not being satisfied—in 1972 formed the Women's Growth Center to offer individual as well as group counseling for women. That same year another group of Baltimore women, concerned about the effects of racial stereotyping in reading materials used by the city's schools, secured funding for and conducted a study of elementary level reading materials. The 130–page report that resulted is credited with sensitizing Baltimore's school system to the detrimental effects of sex and racial stereotyping. In 1974, Francine Brown and

Betsy Milleman recognized a need in Baltimore for a place where women could meet and find books of particular interest to them. Thus they established the 31st Street Bookstore.

The common theme in the wide range of activities by Baltimore women since the sixties is women working together to help women, whether establishing a rape crisis center, creating a program for displaced homemakers, or seeking to fund a shelter for battered spouses. Undoubtedly, these and the other efforts that make up the contemporary women's movement in Baltimore have resulted in advances for women. However, they have also enriched life in Baltimore and contributed to a more humane environment for both men and women.

Marianne Alexander

Baltimore: Pioneer In Aging Services

A lofty senior citizens' dwelling now rests on the site where a historic Baltimore landmark, the North Avenue Market, once stood. Viewed from its glass–walled nineteenth floor, the city skyline is silhouetted with a variety of new buildings that house living quarters, services, and activities for the city's elderly. This changing skyline is a reflection of the changing patterns of life for Baltimore's 60–plus citizens, who now represent over 15 percent of the total city population.

During the past quarter of a century, programs designed to offer the elderly the fullest opportunity to continue playing a productive role in the life of Baltimore city have blossomed. This renaissance has evidenced itself in a growing awareness of the needs of older citizens and in the discovery of creative ways to meet these needs.

What was the impetus for these changes? The stage was set by early pioneers: Judge Thomas J. S. Waxter; Drs. Mason F. Lord, Herman Seidel, and Matthew Tayback, geriatricians; Esther Lazarus, social worker; and Mazie Rappaport and Wilmer Bell, adult educators. These visionaries and other community leaders, with the support of city administrations led by Mayors Theodore R. McKeldin, Thomas D'Alesandro III, and William Donald Schaefer, provided the stimulus to translate the public concern for the needs of the elderly into action.

Mobility was a factor. Nowadays, children often live far from their parents. This prevents their caring for elderly relatives. In addition, more people are living longer. Thus there is a need for shelter and care for America's growing aged population.

Programs for the Elderly. At the beginning of the 1940s, some observed that recreation buildings were not being used during the school day. Recreation programs for the city's elderly grew out of this concept. The first such program was the South Baltimore Golden Age Club at 1010 South Light Street; it was followed by similar clubs in Hamilton and Patterson Park. The Bureau of Recreation developed a network for the elderly throughout the city. Selma Gross was appointed coordinator of the programs; she was later to become the first executive director of the Commission on Aging and Retirement Education.

In the early 1950s, West Baltimore retirees, seeking the companionship of their peers, spontaneously gathered at the benches along the promenade of the Edmondson Village Shopping Center. Their presence led the merchants to provide a meeting hall, a professional adviser, and financial support. The social club which was formed developed into an active community service organization.

In 1957, the Jewish Community Center gave impetus to the movement toward increasing programs for the elderly by establishing a full-time Senior Adult Department that provided social, educational, and recreational activities under the leadership of Leon M. Woolf. Mr. Woolf later guided a city-wide comprehensive center known as the Metropolitan Senior Center, a pilot program started in 1964.

With the passage of the federal Older Americans Act of 1965, Baltimore was awarded the first senior center grant in the United States. It was used to construct the Waxter Center, which opened in 1974. It is the largest and most comprehensive senior citizen center in the country. Free and open to all city residents 60 years of age and older, the center operates seven days a week. It provides a full range of activities as well as health, legal, social, employment, and food services. The physically disabled elderly and residents of nursing homes have not been neglected; they are brought into the mainstream of activity by specially designed programs which transport them to the Waxter Center and involve them as participating members.

The Commission on Aging and Retirement Education. The Waxter Center is a component of CARE (the Commission on Aging and Retirement Education), developed by city ordinance, in 1973, under Mayor William Donald Schaefer. CARE's function is to coordinate government programs and develop public and private resources to enable the elderly to remain full participants in the community. Its first executive director, Selma Gross, still serves in that capacity, and is a member of the Mayor's Human Resources Cabinet.

Another aspect of CARE is the Area Agency on Aging, the planning arm through which federal funds are administered for such programs as sheltered housing, information and referral, telephone reassurance, and a network of neighborhood senior centers.

Still another function of CARE is the coordination of pre– and postretirement education for city employees and the community. This Baltimore retirement program has been recognized as the first in the country to be offered by a government unit.

Some of the special programs by CARE include Salute to Seniors, an informational festival held each spring; Senior Hall of Fame, an annual event honoring senior citizens for community service; and the publication of a Senior Citizen Discount Directory of services and merchandise.

Service Agencies. During the 1970s innovative programs for the elderly have grown rapidly. Mayor Schaefer established the Mayor's Office of Human Resources, headed by Quentin R. Lawson. Health Services for the Aging are administered by the Baltimore City Health Department, whose current commissioner is Dr. John B. DeHoff. Scores of "Eating Together In Baltimore" nutrition sites offer daily meals along with supportive services. The Bureau of Special Home Services provides home visits to make sure older people are safe and well and receiving escort, transportation, and other help they may need. RSVP, the Retired Senior Volunteer Program, provides opportunities for meaningful community service. Geriatric Evaluation Service studies the needs of persons being considered for nursing home care. Employment opportunities in community service are made available by the Mayor's Office of Manpower Resources for persons of limited income over 55. To make the homes of the elderly weather-tight, comfortable, and energy-efficient, weatherization is available through the Urban Services Agency.

Educational Programs. Mental stimulation and physical fitness are not neglected. The Community College of Baltimore offers tuition-free courses, a community-based lecture series, and cultural events designed for the older popula-

A Senior Citizen Attends the Community College of Baltimore. Photo by Sidney Kobre

tion. Its gerontology curriculum—training professionals in the art of working with senior citizens in health, recreation, and counseling programs—was one of the first of its kind in the nation. The Baltimore Museum of Art brings slide presentations, classes, and museum tours to senior adult groups throughout the community. The Enoch Pratt Library presents free multi-media programs called "Gray and Growing." The Baltimore City Police and Fire departments make specialists available to show films, give demonstrations, and speak with groups of senior citizens on personal and community safety. Performing arts groups offer free tickets or reduced admissions programs, promoted by the Mayor's Advisory Committee on Art and Culture.

Services for the Elderly. To offer elderly people comfortable homes in which to enjoy retirement, federally funded subsidies help with moderate rent apartments. These are operated by HCD (the city's Department of Housing and Community Development) and by concerned local organizations. Baltimore is among the first cities in the nation to institute the pioneering concept of sheltered housing, which provides housekeeping, personal care, and meals to the physically impaired, frail, and elderly.

To promote all possible opportunities for independent living, day care programs are offered by Project SAGA; Meals on Wheels volunteers bring food every day to the elderly who are unable to cook for themselves; and the Department of Social Services supplies community home care, foster care, and protective services.

Transportation needs are a major concern for the elderly. These have been addressed in several ways: the MTA has a reduced fare for persons 65 and older; specially equipped buses for the handicapped are available; shuttle services are offered by neighborhood organizations; and the Baltimore City Health Department provides escort to medical appointments. The Mayor's Office of Human Resources coordinates group transportation with trips arranged for shopping, sightseeing, cultural, and sports events.

The National Institute on Aging's Gerontological Research Center is located on the grounds of the Baltimore City Hospitals complex. Its study of the basic biological processes and social phenomena which contribute to aging—directed by Dr. Nathan W. Shock—seeks to acquire knowledge to enhance the quality of life in later years. Its Baltimore Longitudinal Study of Aging has been observing over 150 male volunteer subjects for the past 20 years and in 1978, women were added to the study. The Robert Woods Johnson Foundation and others have selected Baltimore city to receive grants for the study and provision of aging services.

Baltimore is also a leader in the development of hospice care, designed to enable the terminally ill to come to the end of life in a comfortable, supportive setting, and—when possible—in familiar home surroundings.

A recent study by the United States Conference of Mayors showed Baltimore to be a model in the delivery of services to its aged citizens. A major factor in this success story must surely be the decision–making role played by senior citizens themselves, through senior advisory councils whose elected representatives plan, promote, and establish policies that govern the operation of many of the projects for the elderly.

Baltimore has become a "good news" city for its elderly population, who have lived its history and contributed to its progress. Heritage projects are gathering artifacts and recording oral history, reminiscing about the past, and thus preserving for tomorrow the living social history that has shaped the city of Baltimore.

Pathways have thus been established. Innovation has resulted in an improved quality of life for the city's older adults. From present indications, the citizens can look forward to continued consciousness–raising concerning the needs and rights of an ever–increasing older population. The image of vitality, creativity, and independent spirit of Baltimore city's elderly people sets the pattern for future generations to face aging with dignity and joy.

Betty Seidel

Schools and Colleges

RENAISSANCE IN PUBLIC EDUCATION? ... NOT QUITE YET

Public education in Baltimore has undergone many changes since 1954. The effects of the Supreme Court desegregation ruling resulted in a shifting student population with diverse needs. This presented enormous challenges to the schools. The positive attitudes and community support of the fifties gave way to confusion and frustration in the sixties and seventies. Only in recent years has public education in Baltimore regained a direction and continuity for meeting the needs of the community, but there is still much more to be accomplished if a renaissance is to come about.

Curiously, Baltimore's schools were integrated with relative ease and a minimum of time largely due to the efforts of three men: Mayor Theodore R. McKeldin; Walter Sondheim, Jr., president of the school board; and Dr. John H. Fischer, superintendent of schools. Community involvement with the schools was strongly encouraged following Dr. Fischer's announcement that integration would be effectuated immediately to aid in a peaceful acceptance of the new policy.

Public education was highly regarded and actively supported during the period from 1954–1965. The curriculum was diverse, including special programs for accelerated children and the handicapped. The leading universities in the country favored Baltimore's graduates and there

David von Schlegell, *"Ship's Prow"* at Southern High School. Photo by Joanne Rijmes.

demands in education. The decline in the status of the family unit resulted in numerous disciplinary and motivational problems among students. Schools were forced into roles other than educational and teachers became surrogate parents. Parental participation in the schools sharply declined as many white children and middle class black children were enrolled in private and parochial schools to avoid the turmoil of public education.

Out of necessity, the emphasis was often on discipline rather than education during this time and security personnel became a priority. The schools were grossly overpopulated; teachers were fatigued and frustrated. A large number of qualified, dedicated teachers left the public school system and the new teachers were unprepared for the demanding new roles in which they found themselves. Many left after only a few weeks. The turnover rate amongst teachers, school board presidents, and superintendents was extremely high, placing the schools in a state of constant change and instability. School board meetings turned into shouting contests among board members and visitors.

Baltimore's schools benefited from federal grants under the Johnson administration and Ford Foundation grants, but problems persisted. Funded by a Ford grant, the Head Start program originated in Baltimore and was headed by Katherine Brunner, who became a national figure as a result of this. The program was designed to bridge the gap between the home and the school by teaching preschoolers health and study habits in preparation for kindergarten and first grade. Unfortunately, some public school teachers were frightened and intimidated by these culturally disadvantaged children when they entered their classroom; "prepared kids" encountered unprepared teachers. Ultimately, teachers were blamed for the "flop of the Head Start program."

The Ford Foundation also funded Project Mission, which was developed to deal with the deficiencies of the teacher training programs at the time. Project Mission involved a college consortium consisting of Morgan, Coppin, and Towson state colleges and represented the first time that colleges were actively involved in Baltimore's public school system. Despite many obstacles, Project Mission was considered a

was a general sense of pride in the schools on the part of parents, teachers, and children. Parents supported tax increases for building construction and raises in teachers' salaries. They favored "teaching character"—defined as loyalty, honesty, respect for others, respect for truth, self-discipline, and personality—as opposed to the fundamental three Rs.

However, as integration progressed into the sixties, the vast changes resulted in a different student population with the need for new programming and teaching methods. Teachers were unprepared to deal with these changes, and local colleges and universities contributed little towards training teachers to cope with the new highlight in public education during the sixties as it proved the need for better teachers if public schools were to survive the problems of the inner cities. The Ford Foundation also partially funded a third program to educate pregnant teen-agers, who had been segregated and excluded under the old system. The federal government continues to fund this program at the Lawrence Paquin School. In its first year, the program enrolled 450 girls; 700 are now enrolled.

Another addition to public education in the sixties was the Family Life Curriculum. This course was designed to meet contemporary needs in the areas of early sexual awareness and involvement, health care education, and the importance of a stable family unit.

Citizen participation increased under superintendents Lawrence Paquin and Thomas Sheldon in the early seventies with the planning and construction of the new Dunbar High School. This program was designed to prepare students for higher education and to provide skills in the open market. Agencies to combat absenteeism such as juvenile services, day care, social services, probation, and legal aid were located at the school. The community decided that health careers held the greatest career potentials for youth in the eighties since the largest private employer in Baltimore, the Johns Hopkins Medical Institutions, were nearby. The curriculum at Dunbar was to emphasize science and it was hoped that the school would attract students from all over the city. A dearth of teachers adequately qualified in the health curriculum was Dunbar's greatest problem. In 1979, a joint cooperative effort with the University of Maryland School of Medicine was established, and Dunbar is now beginning to attract a greater number of highly qualified students.

A lowered birth rate and the exodus of whites and middle–class blacks from the public schools resulted in a drop in school enrollment concurrently with huge school building programs in the seventies. Whereas 193,000 students were enrolled in the public schools in 1971, only 139,000 were enrolled in 1979. Many new buildings constructed out of the needs of the sixties were underutilized in the seventies. Desirable class sizes were finally achieved as a result of the demographic changes that had occurred.

The introduction of middle schools in Balti-

more was advocated by Dr. Sheldon in 1968 to relieve crowded elementary schools. Middle schools have proved to be at least a partial solution to the problems related to junior high school education, and may eventually replace all junior high schools in Baltimore.

Decentralization was once considered to be the solution to urban school problems, but this has not proved to be so. The new administration is returning to an emphasis on discipline, on proficiency and competency testing, on making diplomas meaningful to the student and industry, and on teaching what the student needs to survive. Reading skills are once again a top priority in the schools, which include reading programs for all levels to assure literacy and the ability to cope in society.

The Baltimore school system now has beautiful new buildings and exciting new programs. Alternative educational programs have been im-

Mural on a Hampden Elementary School. Photo by Laurence Krause.

plemented in numerous schools in such areas as specialized career education, as seen in the secretarial sciences and marketing curriculum at Eastern High School and the School for the Arts; the Gate Program for the gifted and talented has been operating in selected schools since 1975; and the liberal arts bastion of City College has gone through refurbishing. Integration, for example, is no longer the prominent issue it was in 1954 as the former "minority" now comprises 75 percent of the school population.

The Baltimore schools of the eighties have the added problems of dealing with a constant flow of new laws on the local, state, and federal levels, as well as adapting to numerous court decisions. The city must cope daily with the "municipal overdrawn concept" as needs exceed the tax dollar's support. Baltimore's public schools have survived some critical times during the past quarter of a century.

The local public schools finally reached a point where they are once again being regarded in a favorable light. The possibility of a renaissance in Baltimore's public schools does exist but can only come about with much effort and cooperation. Local institutions of higher education must design their teachers' education programs to meet the current needs of the schools; teachers must accept the challenge of working a minimum of five years in the "tough schools"; materials must be upgraded to be relevant to contemporary life; and parents and teachers must join together as they did in the fifties and early sixties if there is to be any kind of "true" renaissance in Baltimore's public educational programs.

While progress has been made in Baltimore's public schools since 1954, the citizens of Baltimore will need a vision going beyond the improvements that exist today if a true renaissance in the schools is to be achieved.

Leah S. Freedlander

INDEPENDENT SCHOOLS IN AND AROUND BALTIMORE: A HISTORICAL SKETCH

Private schools, or perhaps more accurately— independent schools—are governed by self-per-petuating boards of trustees who delegate broad powers to the headmaster or headmistress. These institutions, which have long been an alternative to public schools, abound in the Baltimore area. The earliest in Baltimore to open its doors was Friends in 1784. Boys' Latin was probably next in 1846, and a number of others, notably McDonogh (1873), Bryn Mawr (1885), Roland Park Country School (1894), and Gilman (1897) all began before the twentieth century. All of these schools, with the exception of Friends, came along after the inception of the public school system in 1829.

Several of the schools began in what is now the center of the city and moved to newer locations during the twentieth century. Gilman, Bryn Mawr, and Boys' Latin are three examples. But they, like their neighbors, now all draw substantially upon the entire metropolitan Baltimore area for their students. Today, the enrollment is perhaps higher than ever before. In 1977, nonpublic, non–Catholic school enrollment in Baltimore city was over 6,000, and nearly a fourth of the 26,000 students attending nonpublic schools in Baltimore County were attending independent institutions.

Independent schools were started for a variety of reasons, and they have continued to develop in different ways. Naturally, there is a tradition of college–preparatory day schools. Gilman was founded for the purpose of being the equivalent of " . . . Exeter or Andover." At least one purpose for the founding of Bryn Mawr was to create a preparatory school for Bryn Mawr College. Roland Park Country School was designed to prepare students for Radcliffe, and for the year 1907–08 only one student of four in the senior class could meet the stiff requirements for graduation. McDonogh, however, began as a school for poor and destitute males in the Baltimore area who were to "labor at husbandry or farming as well as study the science of agriculture." Park School was a product of the educational theories of John Dewey and quickly became known as a "center of innovative pedagogy."

Some schools (Garrison Forest, St. Timothy's, and Boys' Latin) started as single–sex institutions and have remained so; others, McDonogh, for example, have joined the recent trend toward coeducation. Still others, Friends, for example, have always been coeducational. Several schools that once started as single–sex institutions, Gilman and Bryn Mawr, for example, are now offering coordinate programs in their upper schools that enable students to take a number of courses of interest at either school. St. Paul's School and St. Paul's School for Girls are actually separate schools after the first four grades, yet their campuses are contiguous. Nearly all are day schools exclusively, although Garrison Forest and McDonogh still have thriving boarding departments. Although many have broadened their traditional college–preparatory programs, Park has remained true to its progressive philosophy, and Boys' Latin has identified itself as a school for a limited number of boys needing a "second chance." Finally, most of the schools remain nondenominational or without any religious affiliation. Friends, however, still reflects its religious heritage.

This diversity in educational philosophy and/or identity has not gone unreflected in the student bodies. Although McDonogh was founded with the goal of admitting students "of all colors," the independent schools were not really alternatives to many ethnic or religious minorities until after the *Brown* decision of 1954. Friends School responded immediately; others followed suit. Today, minority enrollment at many of these schools exceeds the National Association of Independent Schools' regional average of 10 percent. Many of these schools are actively seeking to enroll minority students who will fit into their programs. In these efforts independent schools are currently attempting to enlist both the support of the community at large and the support of the surrounding public schools.

This last point about cooperation with surrounding public schools is one consistent feature of the Baltimore independent schools that consider themselves alternatives to, not replacements for, public schools. Each institution has its own identity and tries to enroll students who show promise of being able to contribute to the school and to whom the school has something to offer. There is virtually no evidence that any of these schools mentioned has ever profited from troubles in the public sector. Both systems seem to operate best when each is healthy.

Although most independent schools are at full enrollment, some are experiencing difficulties. Inflation and high energy costs, specifically, are creating hardships. These factors may force greater cooperation in the form of scheduling, transportation, and curriculum development. In-creasing operational costs have resulted in higher tuitions and have also imposed hardships on scholarship programs. Most schools have sought to increase the amount of financial aid available to their students and most have sought to increase the amount of financial assistance through endowment. Indeed, Gilman has been successful in increasing the amount of money available for aid and in 1978–79 budgeted $146,000 for that purpose. Other schools, Friends, for example, use other resources including tuition revenues to help support their financial aid program (8 percent in 1977–78). Thirteen independent schools are cooperating with the Baltimore School Independent Fund, which has a 1979 goal of $44,500 for scholarship aid. Additionally, A Better Chance has recently begun to help fund a limited number of scholarships for day school students who have a demonstrated financial need.

Certainly the future is not without grave concerns, but with the continued support of the Baltimore community, it is very likely that many of these independent schools will continue to thrive and offer viable educational alternatives.

M. Mercer Neale III

CHANGES ON COLLEGE CAMPUSES

The quest for knowledge and the good through higher education has a rich history in the Baltimore area. As Baltimore grew into a boom town that centered around its world–famous port, philanthropists like George Peabody and Johns Hopkins who had made their fortunes as a result of Baltimore commerce gave grants and legacies for the development of institutions of higher learning. These institutions early contributed to making Baltimore a culturally advanced city. During the past 25–30 years the picture of higher education here has changed dramatically through the diversification and expansion of existing colleges and the opening of new ones. Like the man who came out of the shadows of Plato's allegorical cave, we are dazzled by the new realities of the emergent educational scene.

Sociological trends such as the demands of

the veterans returning from World War II, the coming of age of the baby boom, combined with the civil rights movement of the fifties and sixties helped to focus on the need for colleges to add programs and expand physically. The community college concept rose in direct response to these needs. Government grants, loans, and research programs also increased the availability of funds for attending college so that for some, the right to go to college became a matter of justice. The idea of adult or continuing education also became extremely popular. Colleges sometimes found it necessary to share programs, curriculums, and physical facilities to hold down some of the soaring costs which, in some cases, forced merging and absorption: Mt. St. Agnes College merged with Loyola; Baltimore College of Commerce was absorbed by the University of Baltimore; Eastern College and the Mt. Vernon Law School merged with the University of Baltimore; and the Peabody Conservatory became affiliated with the Johns Hopkins University.

The Johns Hopkins University and Peabody Institute of Music. Already opened for instruction in 1868, Peabody impressed Peter Ilyich Tchaikovsky in 1891 with its "enormous building, marvellously arranged classrooms, music library ... and faculty." Visitors today find a world–renowned music conservatory that has grown by adapting to the ever–changing needs of American society.

The Peabody Library has become part of the Enoch Pratt system; together they cooperated with institutions such as the Maryland Historical Society, the Peale Museum, and the Walters Art Gallery in exhibiting George Peabody's rare art collection. The conservatory joined with other Baltimore institutions such as the Baltimore Symphony Orchestra, Goucher College, and the Baltimore Civic Opera to give the city many fine musical performances. The Ford Foundation sponsored a program to benefit young conductors, utilizing the newly created Peabody Art Theatre. The American Conductor's Project gave young conductors the combined education–performance program that had not been previously available, though European student conductors enjoyed such an opportunity.

The sixties' expansion in the form of additions

and other changes to the buildings such as the dormitory–cafeteria–garage complex, gave way to the inflation–spurred financial crisis in the mid–seventies. But Baltimore did not ignore Peabody. Without charging for his work, one contractor undertook the job of replacing antiquated plumbing; in addition, cash donations poured in from many citizens. The ultimate solution was a merger with the Johns Hopkins University in July, 1977. Through this affiliation Peabody maintains considerable autonomy while continuing its many programs. (The close intellectual and artistic association has proved to be of mutual benefit to both prestigious institutions.) In short, Peabody continues to offer to Baltimore the cultural enrichment intended by its founder. There is something poetic about this alliance of Peabody and Hopkins whose names are synonymous with Baltimore.

Like George Peabody, Johns Hopkins loved Baltimore and wanted to leave something to benefit the town. His philanthropy made possible the establishment of the hospital as well as the university, whose recently celebrated centennial climaxed a century of progress in all divisions. One of the most visible changes is the admission of undergraduate women, begun in 1970.

During the past two decades, undergraduates at Johns Hopkins have inaugurated two programs that involve the Baltimore community. The annual Milton S. Eisenhower Symposium features internationally known speakers on such topics as the arms race, violence, creativity, human sexuality, the media, and the 1960s. "3400 on Stage" is an annual spring fair which brings hundreds of thousands of Baltimoreans to the campus for a large outdoor arts and crafts exhibition.

Morgan State University. Morgan State University was founded in 1857 by the Methodist Church to provide an opportunity for blacks to get a college education. It grew to become part of the State College System in 1939 and expanded during the Baltimore renaissance to university status in 1975. Its scope was broadened to include studies about city concerns.

In developing its urban thrust, Morgan strives to serve the educational needs of persons living in urban areas. Its programs include studies on improving the quality of life in the cities and learning about their nature, history, problems, and assets. Ways to contribute to the solution of urban problems are also examined.

The most recent development at Morgan is the doctoral program which comes at the heel of the launching of four new MA programs in economics, sociology, music, and environmental studies. (Morgan is also known for its outstanding dance company.) Signs of Morgan's exciting growth into a university are also evident in several magnificent new buildings.

College of Notre Dame of Maryland. Since its founding, Notre Dame has been an institution that has been broadening its physical structure to meet the growing needs of the community. Founded in 1848, Notre Dame became an academy in 1863, a collegiate institution in 1873, and a four-year college in 1895. The College of Notre Dame takes pride in its being the first Catholic college for women in America to award the bachelor of arts degree.

Caught in the same bind as other small private institutions of higher learning, Notre Dame was one that determined not only to survive, but to maintain its characteristics as a college for women and to continue to grow. In the seventies the college met changing needs in the community by going beyond its initial offering of an undergraduate education in the liberal arts with appropriate career preparation, to establish the Center for Continuing Education. Its purpose was to help women to return to school and/or employment after an absence spent raising families. In 1971, it was the only such program locally in an independent college. The Weekend College, established in 1975, has similar goals. It is structured to take into account an adult's multiple responsibilities to family and job by placing emphasis on independent work and self-directed study.

Goucher College. Another growing women's college is the famous Goucher, which is preparing for a centennial celebration in 1984. "In the 1940s and 1950s many people thought the college wouldn't survive the move from St. Paul Street to Towson; by 1960 it was evident that they had been successful," said past President Dr. Otto Kraushaar. During the period from 1955 to 1965,

course offerings were expanded in the fine and performing arts and the old physiology and hygiene departments were upgraded into the modern department of biological sciences.

In the seventies Goucher entered the familiar, difficult era for private colleges and for single-sex institutions in particular. During the decade between 1966 and 1976, more than half of the nation's women colleges closed and many more opted for coeducation. "Co or no" was a much debated issue on the Goucher campus during the seventies, but, in 1974, the college reaffirmed its commitment to women's education by deciding to remain a single-sex institution. "This is a good time for women's colleges," said Goucher's president, Dr. Rhoda M. Dorsey in a *New York Times* article. "Suddenly more women are interested in women's colleges and the strengths of these institutions are more widely recognized. We have turned the corner."

Loyola College. At the same time that Goucher decided to remain a women's school, Loyola College of Maryland decided to admit women registrants. During the past quarter-century, Loyola has grown in size and quality far beyond its achievement in its first 100 years. People began to realize in the 1950s that Loyola had maintained since its beginning a steady and traditional interest in science. Loyola was listed among the top 10 percent of American schools for the high rate at which its graduates went on to earn science doctorates.

As on many campuses across the nation, courses in specialized "relevant" areas were introduced in the sixties. By the seventies, Loyola stood apart from many other institutions by maintaining a stable financial position without sacrificing quality.

Some of its outstanding recent accomplishments are the successful merger with Mount Saint Agnes in 1971; the opening of the first joint library with the College of Notre Dame in 1972; the opening of Loyola College centers in Columbia, Maryland, and in Baltimore, Montgomery, and Anne Arundel counties; the receipt of increased financial aid and other assistance for minority and disadvantaged students; the victory in the United States Supreme Court case which challenged state aid to church-related colleges; and the introduction of resident students along with the construction of apartment complexes for undergraduates.

Towson State University. What began as a small two-year teachers' school—State Normal—of little more than 1,000 students, expanded in 1963 to become Towson State College. In 1976, it grew further to become a university. Today, Towson State University has 45 different undergraduate majors and 14 master's degree concentrations. It offers student exchanges through cooperative programs within the state university system as well as the private institutions in and around the Baltimore area.

The new face of the campus reflects the changes the school has enjoyed. From Stephens Hall's distinguished clock tower to the streamlined Administration and Fine Arts buildings, the campus has grown steadily. Towson is particularly proud of its fine theatre arts and dance programs, its Asian and African art collections, and its status in the First Division of National Collegiate Athletic Association.

According to John Wighton of the Office of Public Relations and Development, Towson is fortunate that it can draw from its heritage the benefits as a small liberal arts college and combine them with the diversified resources of a large university.

University of Baltimore. Change at the University of Baltimore is best represented by the difference between its modest beginnings on Howard Street, and the award-winning conversion of an automobile showroom to a classroom and office building in 1960.

It has grown to a well-accredited university of more than 5,500 undergraduate, graduate, and law students in its day and evening weekend divisions. The Eastern College and its Mount Vernon School of Law merged with UB in 1970. This merger was followed by the absorption of the Baltimore College of Commerce in 1973, which put all three of the local private evening schools under a single administration.

Famous for its Business and Law schools, UB is also developing its liberal arts programs. Among the 13 masters' degrees it awards, are those in taxation, applied psychology, public administration, and urban recreation. UB cooperates with Morgan State University in offering

an M.A. in sociology, and with the Maryland Institute of Art in offering an M.A. in publication design.

Maryland Institute College of Art. The Maryland Institute offers other exchange programs with Goucher College, the Johns Hopkins University, and the Peabody Institute, which expand students' choices at all participating institutions and reduce duplication of course offerings.

In 1826, the famous art college began as the Maryland Institute for The Promotion of the Mechanic Arts. In addition to the core courses in the industrial and fine arts, the diverse program included bookkeeping, chemistry, and music. As other institutions of higher learning were founded in Baltimore, the Maryland Institute became more and more dedicated to the fine and applied arts. Today the college remains a private, nonprofit institution which trains professional artists and art educators through courses in drawing, painting, graphic design, illustration, printmaking, interior design, ceramics, photography, sculpture, crafts, art teacher education, and liberal arts.

Only the institute's main building was originally built to house an art school. Its other buildings represent an architectural mixture of recycled structures ranging from converted factories and townhouses, to the highly acclaimed renovation of the Baltimore and Ohio station. This adaptation of the B&O train station to a library, gallery, and classrooms was a model of urban rehabilitation in the transformation of an existing old structure to a new use. The old Cannon Shoe Company was the institute's most recent candidate for structural transformation, the very act of which was a celebrated artistic endeavor. Thus, the Maryland Institute of Art, long considered one of the finest art schools in the country, seeks to maintain its reputation by expanding its facilities as well as its programs.

Coppin State College. Also experiencing structural changes is Coppin State College. A new ten-story office/classroom building and a new administration building accompany the other renovations and expansions on the North Avenue campus.

Coppin, begun in 1900 as a training course in

cooperation with the Baltimore City Public Schools to train black elementary school teachers, became a multipurpose institution in 1963, when it began to prepare liberal arts majors in a variety of disciplines and to offer a program of secondary education. In 1970 Coppin became a full-fledged liberal arts and sciences institution. Since that time, it has grown rapidly in program offerings, facilities, and student enrollment. In fact, Coppin's enrollment surged past the projected figure for the eighties, possibly in part because of their efforts to make education accessible to blacks and other minorities, to the financially deprived, to the physically handicapped, and to anyone seeking professional skills.

Even though the word "Teachers" was dropped from the name of the college in 1962, Coppin continues to graduate a large number of education majors each year. The special education program is particularly well known. New undergraduate majors, as well as new masters' degrees, are designed to provide skills for administrators, counselors, and teachers.

Community College of Baltimore. From its beginning in 1947 as the Baltimore Junior College with only 57 veteran and nonveteran students, the Community College of Baltimore became the first community college in the Baltimore area. It started on the third floor of the City College building as "Veterans Institute." As such, it reflected a growing national trend to-

A Community College of Baltimore Graduate. Photo by Sidney Kobre

wards two–year schools offering vocational programs, two–year degrees, and certificates.

In 1951, (when it went to Liberty Heights) the college established its evening division and WBJC, the first junior college radio station in Maryland. The station now broadcasts jazz and classical music on a 24–hour basis from the Liberty Heights Avenue Campus.

One of the more conspicuous developments of Baltimore's Inner Harbor project was the construction of the twin red brick, modern design buildings which constitute CCB's Harbor Campus. The construction ws necessitated by the growing number of students to enroll at CCB. Today, the community college serves more than 10,000 students of all ages, races, and socio-economic backgrounds, offering more than 50 career–oriented programs and 250 liberal arts and transfer courses. The Office of Continuing Education also offers more than 250 credit and noncredit courses each semester at both campuses and at more than 20 off–campus locations.

Other community colleges in the Baltimore area, such as Essex, Catonsville, and Dundalk community colleges have followed CCB's lead by growing with their acceptance in the scholastic community. The concept of the community college has become one of the landmarks in education during Baltimore's renaissance.

Less successful was Bay College, which was founded in 1969 as an independent two-year college to provide an opportunity for higher education, a second chance for inner-city Baltimoreans. In 1978 it closed its doors for the last time. Students, faculty, and administration felt that students would now miss "a second chance."

St. Mary's Seminary and University and Ecumenical Institute of Theology. Although the staid grandeur of the massive building in Roland Park belies change, St. Mary's Seminary and University has enlarged from its intense focus on the formation and education of seminarians, to a broader inclusion of philosophical and theological studies that reaches out to the layman as well as the religious, Protestant and Jew as well as Catholic. In response to the Second Vatican Council and its resultant emphasis on ecumenism, many changes took place in what seminaries taught and how they taught it. A great transition of lifestyle at St. Mary's occurred. The laity, men and women, and religious women began to register for classes leading to the doctorate as well as masters' degrees. One of the most noted changes was the beginning of the Ecumenical Institute of Theology in 1968 as a graduate–level evening school for qualified students of all faiths.

The diversity of St. Mary's programs continues to reveal itself. In 1973, the Institute for Continuing Education began as a two–year program that brings to a convenient center in Baltimore a curriculum designed to fill local needs. By 1978, the program was operating in full swing.

Ner Israel and Baltimore Hebrew College. Two prominent schools in the Jewish community continue to provide higher education opportunities in the Baltimore area. Ner Israel Rabbinical College was founded in 1933 as a religious school that trains men in rabbinical studies and for spiritual leadership in congregational service and educational institutions as teachers, administrators, and chaplains.

The Baltimore Hebrew College provides secular studies as well as religious, with courses in Bible, archaeology, rabbinical literature, Jewish history and philosophy, Zionism, Hebrew, and Yiddish. It also engages in many cultural activities to which the public is invited to hear speakers and view films pertinent to the Jewish experience. In addition to the Jewish studies, there is a program that combines the M.A. in social work at the University of Maryland with the M.A. in Jewish studies. The college also provides a Ph.D. program.

University of Maryland. The University of Maryland system of higher education is well–represented throughout the state and in the Baltimore area. The schools of Law and Dentistry, as well as the Nursing and Medical schools, are located in the hospital complex downtown. The School of Social Work and Community Planning is the largest in the nation.

The Baltimore County campus is known for its science programs and for its developing arts programs, including music and the film arts. The very construction of UMBC was an admission that the University of Maryland had to expand in the Baltimore area to meet the increased demands of commuter students. The county campus came about when a group of state legislators and the city and county and the Greater Baltimore Chamber of Commerce asked the University of Maryland to expand in Baltimore as a research university to old industries.

The fifties ushered in a time of change in education that fomented expansion and diversification. For example, social sciences have developed faster than fine arts. Having met the calculated risks of these years, the challenges of the sixties and urgent needs of the seventies, Baltimore area institutions of higher learning look to the eighties with confidence and great expectations.

The presence of so many fine institutions of higher learning in Baltimore has made it a good city culturally. In their number and scope in the past 30 years, these institutions have increased educational opportunities and contributed to making our city culturally better for all. Perhaps in making higher education more available to more people, Baltimore has even moved a step closer to Plato's dictum that knowledge is necessary for justice.

Dorothy Pula Strohecker and Carol Strohecker

Media

BALTIMORE'S DAILY NEWSPAPERS IN THE PAST QUARTER CENTURY

In 1956, Baltimoreans could buy a daily paper for a nickel, and a Sunday paper for 15¢. But, by 1980, the daily price had tripled, and Sunday's had quintupled.

Despite the rapidly growing population of metropolitan Baltimore, newspaper circulation has dropped off, as it has in most urban areas nationwide. In 1956, *Sunpapers* circulation for the morning *Sun* was 186,320, for the *Evening Sun*, 213,695, and for the Sunday *Sun*, 320,243. By late 1980, these figures were 177,980, 172,868 and 374,989 respectively. The average circulation of the Hearst Corporation's Sunday *News American* dropped more than 100,000 from 330,231, and the daily paper hovered around 140,000.

Despite drops in readership, both of the city's dailies have seemed as profitable as ever, if not more so. Yet sustaining journalistic prestige has been a different matter.

The *Sunpapers* won three Pulitzer prizes in the 1930s and six more in the 1940s, but not until 1979 did they win another—and this one in a new category, feature writing. The honor went to the *Evening Sun*'s staff writer Jon Franklin. This award reportedly met with the silent consternation of the *Sunpapers'* management, which has traditionally lavished more money and perquisites on the more staid morning *Sun*.

As for the *News American*, it has followed the traditions of its parent, the Hearst Corporation, by seeking preeminence in stories other than those gauged to win national standing among peers.

Time magazine, which every decade traditionally lists what its editors judge to be the 10 best newspapers in the nation, listed the *Sun* among them in 1964, with this characterization: "aloof, aristocratic, affluent, acerb." However, the *Sun* was dropped from this list without comment in 1974. It may be back on that list by 1984 if its current self-improvement efforts in news and editorial coverage are sustained.

Baltimore's dailies are household words, but there used to be many more such newspapers before the advent of radio and television. Today's *News American* was forged from such predecessors as the *Baltimore American* (1773), the *Baltimore News* (1872), and the *Baltimore Post* (1922). The *News* and the *American* were bought by the Hearst Corporation in 1923 to compete with the Scripps–Howard syndicate's *Post* (a tabloid), which was acquired by Hearst in 1934. The resultant hybrid was called the *News–Post and Sunday American*. It wasn't until Mark Collins became publisher of the paper in 1964 that the name was simplified to the *News American*. An editorial at the time explained that the former name had become "just too unwieldy and too complicated."

The *Sunpapers* have undergone no such name changes since the first of the three papers was founded in 1837 by Arunah S. Abell. However, the three papers' editorial content has undergone metamorphoses. On through the 1960s, the former "penny dreadful" *Sun* seemed to print more and longer stories than the average reader was generally able to get through. Its staid journalistic image was further augmented by the establishment of foreign bureaus: Bonn (1955), Moscow (1956), Rio de Janeiro (1962), and others. In an article in the *National Review* (2/15/56), Jonathan Mitchell said that the *Sun* "is one of the best written papers in the country," yet he did not give it high marks for foreign coverage. The *Sun* now syndicates articles by its foreign correspondents, but it does not share its local columnists with other papers in like manner—indeed, the *Sunpapers* seem intent on keeping their writers out of the limelight. Their by–lines in other local publications are scarce.

The same cannot be said for the *News American*, whose writers' by–lines appear in many other local publications.

Both the Hearst and Abell companies have invested heavily in modernizing their facilities. The *Sunpapers'* Calvert Street building cost $8 million when it was opened in 1950. At that time, it was a "hot metal" plant, with Linotype equipment that was in use until July, 1974, when the papers began converting to "cold type," bringing with it video display terminals and increased computerization of the editorial departments. The papers' $50 million changeover from the letterpress printing system was to be completed in 1981, when the new south wing of the building with automated offset press equipment became operational.

The *News American* took occupancy of a new five–story addition to its plant at South and Lombard streets in September, 1962. The new facility was hailed by one of the paper's writers at the time as "the most modern plant in the world." However, though it was at last air–conditioned, the plant was not equipped with computer printing equipment until March, 1975.

Despite the heavy expenditures for facilities, the employees of Baltimore's dailies were not as well paid as their counterparts in cities of comparable size until the strike that began at noon on April 17, 1965, and continued for over 40 days. The strike was instigated by the Washington Newspaper Guild, which was bargaining for 657 *Sunpapers* employees. At the time of the strike, weekly wages ranged from $64.75 for copy boys to $150 for experienced reporters.

The management of the *News American*, which dealt with the unaffiliated News Union of Baltimore, suspended publication and laid off most of its employees on April 20. Teamsters Local 3551 charged that this was an illegal lockout, and the International Typographical Union Local 12 and four other unions filed charges against the *News American* with the National Labor Relations Board. The paper's rationale for closing down was that the typographers and teamsters who were on strike at the *Sunpapers*

had violated a joint contract between the two publishers.

During the strike, 2600 employees at the two papers were out of work. The strike was so seriously deadlocked that Mayor Theodore McKeldin and Governor J. Millard Tawes designated Goucher College president Dr. Otto F. Kraushaar to be their personal representative in an attempt to reach settlement.

The strike was the first interruption of publishing for the *Sunpapers* since the founding of the company. One reason given for the peaceful negotiations of the past was that prior to 1965, contracts between the company's management and the guilds were often negotiated far beyond the terminal date called for in the preceding contract. When finally signed, the new contracts provided for retroactive pay in lump sums that the employees looked forward to receiving. They therefore might have been willing to accept less over the long term. However, this friendly paternalism changed in 1965, when the rather weak local guild at the *Sunpapers* merged with the Washington Guild local. This proved to be a militant move.

Baltimoreans, bereft of their dailies during the long strike, learned of the news through the *Catholic Review*, the *Daily Record* (the state's five–day–a–week legal paper), neighborhood weeklies, and several interim independent publications staffed by strikers and students. The most notable of these was the *Baltimore Banner*, published six days a week by unpaid striking guild members. Other efforts included a three-day venture called *Sports Scope* by locked out *News American* staff; a ten–day appearance by the *Baltimore Herald*, published by students from the Johns Hopkins University; and a four-day stint of the *Daily Tribune*, put out by *News American* staffers in conjunction with a Detroit syndicate.

These efforts to fill the print void attempted to explain the strike to the public as well as to fill the news gap. The long–term consequences of the strike, however, were wider in scope, due to the attention that was focused on Baltimore's dailies by the national media. This attention was generally not favorable to the papers' publishers. For example, in the May 3, 1965, issue of *Newsweek*, a reporter revealed the following conditions at the *Sunpapers:*

Despite a net worth of more than $20 million,* the *Sun*'s prestige over the years has been matched by management's reputation, among many staffers, for penuriousness. There is no employee medical program; company life insurance policies pay only $500; and even to park on the paper's lot costs an employee $9 a month. "They treat us," said one editorial page writer, "with calculated contempt."

So touchy was president [William] Schmick about the publicity the *Sun*'s other reputation was getting last week that he refused to talk to reporters about it. One newsman, Ben A. Franklin, covering for the *New York Times*, was asked to leave the *Sunpapers* building. His presence, according to a company spokesman, was "awkward and embarrassing."

An unsigned article that appeared in the *New Republic* on May 15, 1965, called "The Eclipse of 'the *Sun*'," related that:

> The modern–day *Sun* spares no expense in its news-gathering activities. But there the munificence stops. No matter how much they enjoy working for one of the 10 best newspapers in the country, *Sun* reporters, rewrite men, copy readers, and editorial writers are not happy with their pay.

The strike ended with a two–year contract that boosted the guild members to pay levels commensurate with those at papers in comparable cities. Since then, there was a 77–day shutdown in 1970 by web pressmen that caught Baltimore unaware. Another guild strike in 1978 only lasted three days and did not stop publication. As of this writing, a reporter with five years' experience can expect to earn about $500 a week on Baltimore's dailies.

The dailies have been gradually changing their formats and their coverage during the past 25 years. The *News American*, which for many years followed the Hearst formula of sensational news coverage of crime, has seemed to soften its focus towards more positive ends during the past decade. However, this softness has sometimes taken the form of feature stories, at the expense of news and investigative reporting. Front page lead stories about the weather and about sports are not uncommon.

News American editor Ron Martin (who took over the job in June, 1978, and left that position two years later), stated that his paper was seeking "to take advantage of new things" in order to capture and retain its share of the shrinking market for dailies in Baltimore. One step taken was to subscribe to the Independent News Service, in addition to the news services of the *Washington Post*, the *Los Angeles Times* syndicate, the *Sunday Times* of London, and United Press International (UPI). The paper dropped coverage from the Associated Press (AP).

Mr. Martin maintained that his paper's circulation was "holding steady" as he and his staff strived to "reflect Baltimore's spirit and identify with its renaissance." Under the leadership of editor Jon Katz and publisher Maurice Sparby, the *News American* sought to be a viable alternative to the *Sun*.

A one-sided rivalry has sprung up on the pages of the graphically updated *News American*, whereby references are made in print about the "gray neighbor" or "The Unpapers." Readers are alerted to times when the *Sunpapers* have missed a story or made mistakes.

The *Sunpapers*, however, have generally ignored the presence of the *News American*. Instead, after years of passing over investigative stories about Maryland's politicians (Spiro Agnew was first exposed by the *Wall Street Journal*) and analyses of controversial subjects such as race relations, the *Sunpapers* seem to be giving more attention to such stories. Some staffers believe that the papers' exposure of the Pallotines was a breakthrough in investigative reporting. The *Sunpapers* are also emphasizing local news, and have set up metropolitan area bureaus in county seats (begun in 1975). Further, local news has been given more prominent positions, with sports being relegated to the inside of the paper's daily third section.

Also, the *Sunpapers'* largely white, male staff of the 1950s has become more integrated, although Mr. Martin of the *News American* asserted that his paper employs a higher percentage of blacks and women in managerial positions than do the *Sunpapers*.

The *News American* also has a younger staff than the *Sunpapers*, in part because of the massive staffing upheavals that accompanied the coming of Mr. Martin. Only a few of the "old retainers" of the paper are still working there, while the *Sunpapers* seem reluctant to ease anyone out, although they have finally adopted a policy of forced retirement at the age of 70.

*The *Sunpapers* in 1981 would be valued more likely at $100 million.

Both papers have recognized the need to reach the so-called youth market. The under-30 reader is being wooed, not by hard news and stellar reporting, but by features on popular night spots and rock music.

Concurrently, the "society set" is being given less prominence in both papers. The last vestige of the social order is the Sunday *Sun*'s layout of brides and brides-to-be, where the astute reader can readily ascertain the social standing of the families mentioned by the position and length of the coverage. The *News American* gives no such signals in its truncated layout.

In fact, neither paper seems as intent on mom, flag, and apple pie as it was in the 1950s. However, the *News American* has been much more aggressively self-promotional in these matters than have the more reserved *Sunpapers*. The Hearst paper has offered Oriole booster bumper stickers ("The Birds Belong in Baltimore"), colored posters of the city, and other visible signs of civic support. However, the paper no longer sponsors the Highlandtown-based "I Am An American Day" parade, as it had done for 40 years. A staff member explained that some of the employees who had worked on the project retired, and that the event had become very costly—up to $10,000 per year by the time the sponsorship stopped in 1976.

The parade is now being backed by several sponsors, including the *Evening Sun*. In fact, the *Sunpapers* are involved in many projects that serve the community, but for some reason the public is seldom aware of the papers' good works—such as the highly regarded program that assists secondary school journalism classes, and the papers' subsidies for advertising for certain cultural events. Still, the Abell papers do not seem to measure up to the boast made in the company's 1962 promotional booklet, which stated, "There is hardly a worthwhile undertaking from sandlot athletics to book and author luncheons to which the *Sunpapers* does not lend support."

In fact, if generalities might be permitted in an otherwise objective evaluation, it might be said that the morning *Sun* is popularly perceived as being intellectual, conservative, and middle and upper class in tone, while the *Evening Sun* does not have the "Ivy League" image, and serves as a counterpoint to the market targeted by the *News American*, whose strongholds are reputed to be in heavily populated, blue-collar East and South Baltimore. None of the dailies, in a city that is heavily black in population, seems to reflect that fact. However, this may not be due to prejudice against blacks, but instead be due to the fact that all three papers are heavy with syndicated features that have little to do with the people who live in the papers' circulation areas. There is little space for community news and notes of any kind, unless the stories are unusual enough (or sensational enough) to merit coverage. One who reads the dailies in Baltimore must come away with a picture of a city that is heavy on crime and accidents, because these are the stories that are given prominence over other local news. The other main thrust is reporting on government—leaving out stories on people and small businesses.

Though Baltimoreans may at times differ with what they perceive to be editorial perversity, laxity, or obtuseness on the part of their newspapers, they are fortunate at least to be residents of one of the few American cities where there are two viable independent daily newspapers, so that they might benefit from different perspectives on the same news. Even the most persuasive critic, such as Michael Kelly, dean of the University of Maryland School of Law, admitted in a scathing op-ed page commentary called "What Ails the *Sun*?" (January 12, 1978):

> I confess that any time I travel to other parts of the country I come back with a greater appreciation of the *Sun*. To live in San Francisco, for example, is to live without news.

However, in the same article, Dean Kelly called the *Sun* "irresponsible to the community," among other allegations, and accused the paper of misusing its "power to affect the way the community feels about itself ... "

The *Sun* printed this long and detailed criticism of itself with characteristic lack of editorial comment or rebuttal.

Dean Kelly is correct in stating that newspapers can have powerful effects on the community—positively as well as negatively. The daily newspapers have done much to mold public opinion, garner support for projects, and inform. They have also increasingly seemed to abdicate their potential for generating a sense of worth among members of the community by acknowledging their existence and their good works.

Curiously, none of the dailies has exhibited a dedication to one kind of journalism that "sells" very well, and that is responsible investigative reporting coupled with strong editorial backup. Perhaps such stories are seen as troublesome and prone to lawsuits, but they are a necessary public purgation.

This problem of an unresponsive press is not new, nor is it confined to Baltimore. In a special issue of *Newsweek* devoted to "What's Wrong With Newspapers?" back in November, 1965, the editor of the *Raleigh News and Observer* is quoted as saying:

The press, like some other American institutions, has grown fat and proud at the same time. Today, newspapering as a business is as anxious as any other business not to make anybody in the immediate neighborhood mad . . . . As the American press has become more and more aware of its dignity, it has become less and less able to go baldheaded after the whole truth, and not merely the released fact.

On balance, Baltimore's dailies are probably better than most. Whatever their future may be—and there are many technological advances in store, including the possible phasing out newsprint in favor of cable television—Baltimore's dailies should be ready. The question remains, however: will the papers of the 1980s strive for reportorial depth and comment, or will they continue the national trend to popularize the news at the expense of public understanding?

Alice Cherbonnier

COMMUNITY WEEKLIES GROW

Beginning in the 1920s, a number of community newspapers caught hold in Baltimore. These weeklies, semi-weeklies, and monthlies reflected the changing city and its growth. They provided news, features, and photos of neighborhood or district people and their activities. The expansion of the city and the increase of organizations limited the amount of space that editors of dailies could devote to a particular neighborhood. Besides, the number of dailies decreased because of mergers, reducing further the chances for intensive local coverage. To large

measure, then, the economic factor was the major stimulus for a number of the new publications. Their editors also conducted campaigns for civic improvements in their areas of circulation.

Another important reason for the growth of the community press was that merchants in the district stores and shopping centers could not afford the advertising in the daily press. These daily newspapers had citywide circulations, reaching customers who would not patronize these neighborhood establishments.

In the city, as merchants became more advertising conscious, the weeklies issued in various neighborhoods grew stronger. New publications were launched. With the spread of population into the outlying sections of the city and adjacent Baltimore county, new community papers sprang up like weeds.

In the older sections of the city, established weeklies added experienced news and advertising personnel and developed into solid, successful publications. For instance, in 1929 the *Shopper's Guide* emerged as a response to the need for merchants in the Monument and Gay streets areas to have a newspaper circulating among their customers. The C. W. Boone Company, a printing concern on Barre Street, issued the paper. Later, finding the South Broadway and Highlandtown residents and merchants responsive, the publisher added circulation in those areas. An editor, who also served as advertising manager, built up readership with many local news articles and a column, "Across the White Steps," symbolizing the homes in East Baltimore.

In 1938, the brothers Nelson and Milton Lasson bought the *Shopper's Guide* and brought me in to serve as managing editor. To widen the paper's scope and appeal, he changed the name to *East Baltimore Guide* and embarked on a stronger news and feature program.

The *Guide's* influence resulted in various civic campaigns to improve the neighborhood, including better transportation and health facilities. Traffic was improved because the *Guide* emphasized the need for Eastside residents to reach Sparrows Point steel mills more easily. As a result of the paper's campaign, the Baltimore City Health Department opened a better facility in Highlandtown, which later led to the construction of a new building. A campaign begun in 1937 for the opening of a Baltimore junior college resulted in one being started on the third floor of the Baltimore City College building 10 years later. This grew into the Community College of Baltimore.

Meanwhile, in 1932, in the southern part of the city, the *South Baltimore Enterprise*, a weekly, was launched to serve the needs of residents and merchants in that section. In the late thirties, Lola Watson, pen name for Lola Rivkins, edited the paper. She was joined later by Colonel Harvey Rivkins, her husband. The *Enterprise* won a strong foothold in the area by providing news and features about local people and their organizations. Much attention was given to schools and the paper backed the development of the Community College of Baltimore, particularly the building of the Harbor Campus, adjacent to South Baltimore.

In 1973, Delegate R. Charles Avara and Bryan Moorhouse joined the colonel as coowners. Mr. Moorhouse serves as publisher. The paper continues in the colonel's tradition of being opinionated, highly vocal, and generally conservative on political matters.

Meanwhile, the belief that a citywide weekly, focusing on news of neighborhoods with some general articles appealing to all districts, was conceived by Howard Burman and Seymour Goodman and the Goldstein brothers, owners of the Twentieth Century Printing Company on Redwood and Eutaw streets. In the 1930s, they launched the *Home News*, a free–distribution weekly with experienced news and advertising personnel. Arnold Landau, in charge of advertising display pages, served as the production chief. The *Home News* distributed 100,000 copies, printed on the presses of the parent company. A campaign to lower gas and electric rates was carried on the front page of the *Home News* for several years. Finally, a $1 million reduction occurred for which the paper felt it could take partial credit.

In the 1930s and 1940s, the population of Baltimore began to move north, northeast, and northwest. Suburbs expanded within the city and then in Baltimore County surrounding the city. The *Suburban Times* was published in 1941 to reach people in the Pimlico section and in the Forest Park and Waverly districts. The paper also covered Hamilton and Parkville in the extreme northeast area. I edited and published and

Anne Albaugh, who had served on the *Home News* as a reporter, was managing editor and woman's page editor. In addition to publishing news of the areas, campaigns were carried on to improve the bus service across town, from Forest Park to Hamilton, and from these areas to the steel mills and shipyards working at capacity during World War II. (Hamilton and Parkville were almost considered suburban areas.) A contest to select the "Most Popular Mother of Hamilton" drew 5,000 coupons. The *Suburban Times* closed down in November, 1942, but it had foretold the growth of the area and the need for publications in the postwar period.

In 1955, at the request of merchants in the northeast section of the city, Sarah Burdette, who had had some experience in the business department of the *East Baltimore Guide* and also in an advertising agency, issued the *Parkville Reporter*, a monthly. The highly successful publication furnished the residents with a newspaper that concentrated on their activities, organizations, and churches. The Belair Road merchants saw the success of the *Parkville Reporter* and requested that Mrs. Burdette publish a newspaper in their area. She complied with the monthly *Belair Road Booster*. After several decades, Mrs. Burdette sold out to the Stromberg Publications, but she remained as a consultant.

Maurice Shochatt, editor of the *Jewish Times* for 19 years, between 1935 and 1954, saw the

East Baltimore Guide Reports Success of Community College Campaign in 1949. Photo by Sidney Kobre

growth of the Northwest suburbs and decided to launch a weekly publication for the area. He therefore issued the *Suburban News* in January, 1947. This biweekly newspaper circulated in the Park Heights, Pimlico, and Upper Park Heights areas. It also covered Arlington, West Arlington, Mt. Washington, Pikesville, and Forest Park, and even went out as far as Owings Mills.

Mr. Shochatt campaigned for various civic improvements, including the removal of the street car tracks from Park Heights Avenue, as buses had been installed to transport residents.

He became editor and publisher of the monthly *Baltimore Beacon* in March, 1948, and Julia Yon Pickett served as the managing editor. The *Beacon* was a slick-page publication and aimed at civic improvements. It played a prominent role in founding the Safety First Club of Maryland, which grew to 200 members, and in forming the Sports Boosters of Maryland, which became widely known for its program to advance amateur and professional sports. The paper also supported the Metropolitan Civic Association that five years later established a Municipal Complaint and Information Service known as the Customer Service Division of the Department of Public Works.

Gustav Berle, former general manager for the *East Baltimore Guide*, discovered that the Northwest Baltimore suburbs lacked a weekly and that the area's growth showed a prime newspaper market existed. Mr. Berle brought out the *Northwest Star* on October 18, 1966, to fill this need. Mr. Berle used his flair for makeup on both the outside and inside pages. He covered the Liberty and Reisterstown roads sections of the city and moved to a limited extent into the Baltimore County areas, including Randallstown and Pikesville. Berle was strongly supportive of local organizations, particularly schools, and gave much space to the growing Community College of Baltimore located on Liberty Heights Avenue, with a branch at Northwestern High School where college classes were conducted in the evening. Arnold Landau, who had experience on the *Home News* and later worked for a local food chain, served as advertising manager. Desiring to publish in a warmer climate such as Florida, Berle sold his interest in the *Northwest Star* to Jeffrey Pollack, a New York City advertising agent. Continuing to expand the *Star*, Mr. Pollack bought out the *Valley Voice*, in 1978.

The *Voice* was a failing weekly owned by Nathan Goldberg and served the Towson–Timonium areas. Although Mr. Pollack made some progress with this publication, he continued the expansion of the *Northwest Star* by adding a sister edition, the *Northeast Star*. That paper circulated from Towson into the northeast part of the city. Advertisement revenue could not keep abreast of the wide circulation that Pollack offered.

In the spring of 1980, Gustav Berle, the founder and original publisher of the *Northwest Star*, returned to Baltimore, and resumed publication of the weekly. His son, Jon, served as his assistant and worked in the production of the paper. Arnold Landau remained as director of advertising. The *Northwest Star*, under the new Berle management, emphasized news of the community and focused on features relating to organizations and residents of the area. Particular stress was laid on school news on all levels— elementary, junior high, and high school as well as college.

In April, 1973, the *City Dweller* made its appearance by defying journalistic trends; it sought an urban market in a period when nearly all publishers avoided such an audience. Just the same, the publisher, Laurence Krause felt that there was a need for this publication. This monthly tabloid went through a youth-oriented editoral phase before settling into its role as a community newspaper serving mid–city neighborhoods. This change began in late 1974 when Mr. Krause took over editorial functions. In the following year, Alex Hooke, a recent college graduate, became part of the newspaper and his one–year stay helped make the *City Dweller* more appealing to community readers. Later that year, Alice Cherbonnier joined the small staff and a new level of professionalism began.

Then in April, 1977, the staff decided to change the name of *City Dweller* to the *Baltimore Chronicle* because it was felt that the newspaper's broadened editorial focus merited a name more suited to its purpose and goal. The paper emphasized the positive aspects of city living, chronicling Baltimore's rebirth. The *Chronicle* became the first community newspaper to reach beyond local news items—covering the arts, cultural affairs, social issues, and even some national news. On several occasions, the *Chronicle* scooped the dailies on its coverage of the Kennedy assassination hearings. It was also the first city community newspaper to bring a number of neighborhoods of diverse social and economic backgrounds together under one banner.

In 1978, Mr. Krause was asked by merchants of the East Monument Street area to publish a newspaper for them. He agreed and the *Monument Street News* was born in May, 1978. Dick Budd, owner of an advertising agency that had handled accounts in that area, worked along with Mr. Krause in establishing the publication. Because of the paper's attentiveness to community concerns, the Johns Hopkins Hospital (located in the area where the paper serves) permitted the *Monument Street News* to be distributed within the hospital. Serving an area of high crime and extensive social problems, the *Monument Street News* chose for its editorial slant positive and uplifting aspects of that community. Between the newspaper and several of the area's merchants, a number of efforts were made to benefit the community, such as a community fair and a free turkey giveaway for Thanksgiving.

In 1973, Patricia Brain edited the *Govanstowne Courier* to fill the gap for a newspaper to serve the north central section of Baltimore. She intensified her coverage of people and events in that area and secured a strong foothold among residents of the section. Mrs. Louise Reynolds, advertising manager, helped promote the paper. Mrs. Brain terminated her activities with the paper in winter, 1979. Two months later members of the Community Council of Govans approached the *Chronicle*, inquiring if it would continue to publish the newspaper. It was agreed, providing the name could be changed to the *Courier* and the readership expanded to nearby northeast neighborhoods.

Meanwhile, Charles Carroll, who had extensive advertising experience on the *Miami Herald*, saw the possibilities for a monthly in the Roland Park area and launched the *Messenger* in December, 1976. Filling a need for a publication to furnish news of residents and feature articles about organizations in North Baltimore, the *Messenger* soon developed a strong following as residents could not get their news into the columns of the dailies. Mrs. Frances Burke served as editor. Mrs. Toni Rehrig, advertising manager, built up a large clientele. Advertising

rates on the *Messenger* were kept low for the merchants and service companies and they produced a steady revenue for the publisher. The *Messenger* expanded its territory to include other higher-income neighborhoods nearby. Then in March, 1979, Alterwood Publications bought the *Messenger* and a month later it became a weekly.

From 1928 through the 1930s, the Stromberg Publications in Ellicott City began to circle Baltimore city until they owned a ring of 15 weekly newspapers printed in standard size. (The original newspaper, the *Howard County Times*, had been started in 1840 by Matthew Fields and Edward Waite.) Then, in 1966, Philip Thompson took over from his father-in-law, Paul G. (Pete) Stromberg. The company began to expand and, known as the *Times* chain, extended from Dundalk, on the eastern end of the city, to Pikesville on the north; it even invaded—with the *Towson Times*—the area of the *Jeffersonian*, established weekly in Towson. A merchant could get a special rate by advertising in various Stromberg weeklies; the classified ads ran heavy in these papers. Throughout the years of his management, Mr. Thompson maintained a policy of publishing only local news. The publications and their staffs won 25–30 awards a year—locally and nationally.

Eventually, the Minneapolis Star and Tribune Company bought the Stromberg weeklies and sought to strengthen them by stepping up local news and feature coverage. James Schafer became publisher, Lowell E. Sunderland served as the executive editor, and Francis Toole, the advertising director. The *Times* chain actively participated in community relations projects such as teaching offset printing to college and high school students, printing high school newspapers, and providing speakers for community organizations.

The profit picture did not, however, vastly improve and in November, 1979, Minneapolis sold a number of its publications to Whitney Communications from New York. Whitney then created Columbia Publishing Corporation that in turn became Patuxent Publishing Corporation. Zeke Orlinsky was head of Patuxent. Included in the group of papers were the *Howard County Times, Catonsville Times, Arbutus Times, Parkville Reporter, Belair Road Booster, Laurel Leader*, and *Columbia Flyer*.

Three Baltimore publications that are not strictly community-oriented like those above also serve a specific audience.

Competing with the dailies and the weeklies, the *Baltimore Afro-American*, a chain of five weekly's and *Dawn* magazine, was one of the largest black newspapers in the United States. It began in the last century, when John H. Murphy, Sr., a whitewasher by trade, and part-time superintendent of the Baptist Sunday School of the St. John's African Methodist Episcopal Church, published the *Sunday School Helper*. He printed the paper on a small press in the basement of his home. In the meantime the Reverend William M. Alexander had launched the *Afro-American* to help advertise a store he operated.

Borrowing $200 from his wife, Murphy acquired the name *Afro-American* and the equipment at an auction, and began to publish on August 13, 1892. Then, in 1907, he merged his paper with the *Baltimore Ledger*, issued by the Reverend George F. Bragg, then pastor of St. James' Church. Murphy became publisher of the *Afro-American-Ledger* and Bragg wrote the editorials. Murphy met the needs of his subscribers and the paper expanded slowly.

In this new period the *Afro-American* grew steadily as thousands of blacks migrated from southern farms and towns to Baltimore to work in the steel mills and shipyards, and the city's black population expanded. With the coming of the New Deal in 1932, a more humanitarian attitude was taken toward all minority groups, and the first of various civil rights acts was enacted, providing for greater employment opportunities for blacks in business and in federal agencies. They were able to join labor unions. Blacks thus had a greater income than in the past, thereby creating a better advertising market than ever before. Because of the United States Supreme Court decision in 1954, schools were ordered to be desegregated. Although many were desegregated, the great advance came in the improvement of educational facilities for blacks. Illiteracy was cut remarkably, resulting in more readers for the *Afro-American*.

The *Afro-American* gave readers thorough coverage on the activities of the blacks in Baltimore. The city editor featured one or two crime stories on page one, but the remaining pages were devoted to news and constructive articles about blacks in the community. Extensive articles on the black clubs, organizations, and churches were printed. A special section was devoted to sports. During World War II the *Afro-American* sent correspondents to all fronts.

The paper carried on a continual battle for black political rights, better economic opportunities, and the reduction of discrimination. Among the more successful local campaigns carried on yearly was the Clean Block Campaign, founded by Francis Murphy in 1934, and conducted by Ida Murphy Peters. Thousands of dollars were collected for prizes for the cleanup and beautification of blocks in the black sections of the city. The Baltimore City Council provided $500 and the remainder of the funds came from black and white residents, merchants, and other organizations. The *Afro-American's* special supplements devoted to education and career opportunities were very successful. A special edition was issued on the silver anniversary of the Community College of Baltimore.

The *Afro-American* remained principally a family institution. When founder John Murphy, Sr. died, his son Carl, then a professor of German at Morgan State College, went into the business as publisher. One of his daughters, Elizabeth Murphy Moss, who studied journalism at the University of Minnesota, went from reporter to publisher. A second daughter, Mrs. Peters, became entertainment editor. A nephew, John Murphy III, became vice-president, president, and later chairman of the board.

Another publication that served a specific audience was the *Catholic Review*, the official newspaper of the Baltimore Archdiocese. Founded as the *Catholic Mirror* over 100 years ago, it changed its name in 1913 and served the parishes which extend from Garrett County to Havre de Grace to Anne Arundel County. The largest weekly in the state with a circulation of over 55,000, it went almost entirely by mail to members of parishes on Fridays. Since 1978, the editor has been Robert L. Johnston, who works with a staff of about 20.

The *Catholic Review* was geared mainly to families—mostly middle-aged and older. Fifty years ago it covered mostly national and international news, but in the eighties focused more and more on local developments in the parishes.

The publication covered the Catholic Center's different departments such as charities, personal development, pastoral counseling , and the various bodies that advise the archbishop or others in the hierarchy. Besides news articles on the activities of the Catholic church, the *Catholic Review*'s feature stories included personalities, church leaders, adoption of foreign-born children, the Basilica of the Assumption, and social issues such as hunger, poverty, racism, prolife and abortion, disarmament, and the peace movement. The main focus in covering legislation was on state issues relating more directly to local needs: tax credits and food stamps.

Editor Johnston commented, "The staff wants to reflect what's happening in the archdiocese and build an awareness of what's happening in the world as well. Only then can the church in Baltimore become educated and sensitized to respond to the variety of issues that face us. The church is one voice in the community and it is a voice for moral concern."

The third publication that served a specific audience was the *Baltimore Jewish Times*. The Alter family began publishing it 60 years ago. Known as the "largest weekly publication in the nation," its reputation clearly soared in the nine years after Charles A. Buerger and Susan A. Patchen took over as publishers. Gary Rosenblatt was editor and Kim Muller-Thym associate editor and graphics design editor.

The *Jewish Times* aimed to educate, inform, and enrich its readers on all significant aspects of Jewish life—cultural, social, and political, as well as religious. Concerned with the quality of Jewish life, it included stories on how Jews live and how they fit into the larger communities around them. A typical issue covered life in Baltimore and in communities around the world; Jewish religious practice and philosophy; historical and contemporary anti-Semitism; local support for Israel; fundraising activities such as walkathons; interviews with guest lecturers; and a review of the arts in Baltimore.

The *Times'* strongest appeal was general feature articles relating to the family, professional, and commercial lives of Baltimore Jews: care for the elderly, stress, marriage and intermarriage, career and the workaholic, and Jewish country clubs.

Wherein lay the difference between the *Jew-ish Times* and the general press? In learning and reporting facts "ever mindful of the Judaic concept of responsibility of one Jew for his fellow Jews" said editor Rosenblatt. This mission, he added, should be carried out "in a sensitive, responsible, and ultimately constructive manner." The *Jewish Times* did not hesitate "to write articles of a controversial nature, forcing the reader to grapple with real situations, to rethink his positions," Mr. Rosenblatt emphasized.

And not only was the Jewish community informed and affected, for news items from the Baltimore *Jewish Times* crossed the desk of the president of the United States. The publication's editor and staff won many journalistic awards, such as the Smolar Award for Excellence in North American Jewish Journalism and honorable mention in the Newspaper Guild's Lowell Mellett Award for Improving Journalism Through Critical Evaluation.

Sidney Kobre

BALTIMORE'S ALTERNATIVE AND UNDERGROUND NEWSPAPERS

Up to 1968, a number of Baltimoreans, particularly the younger ones, had concluded that the city was not part of mainstream America. Through national media they had become aware of a "hippie movement" and of "flower children" chanting and preaching various cults. They knew that many cities had underground newspapers that freely used four-letter words, castigated police departments, vehemently criticized the "establishment," and paid tribute to pot and other drugs. But since Baltimore could neither boast of nor damn a local underground newspaper, many suspected the "revolution" was bypassing the city.

This changed dramatically at the time of the 1968 April riots, when Herman Heyn, Alan Kaplan, Walter Shook, Gren Whitman, and Evan Wilson published *Peace and Freedom News* (*P&F*). The paper's primary focus was unabashedly left; it featured such stories as the Baltimore riot, the Catonsville Nine, and welfare mothers' groups. After eight issues, however, the paper folded. "When it didn't click, we decided to quit," Whitman wrote. He and others continued their political interests in other arenas.

In May, 1968, another radical paper, the *Baltimore Free Press* (*BFP*), originated from the suburbs when a Catonsville Community College teacher, Jack Kicks, and one of his students, John Walsh, along with Stuart Cooper, decided the city needed another paper. *BFP*'s content was limited and aimed its appeal at a readership between the ages of 17 and 30, which Cooper defined as "that segment perennially referred to as 'freaks.'" The editors felt that its pages provided an open forum: if the contributors had "credibility" and met the editors' standards, the material would be published. *BFP* stressed ideas at variance with the "establishment" viewpoint, but unlike *P&F*, it had a "satirical slant." *BFP* also included Bob Hieronimous' graphics. Regardless of its differences with *P&F*, *BFP* only lasted a few issues longer than its sister underground newspaper, *P&F*.

The darling of Baltimore's underground newspapers was *Harry*. It began in the autumn of 1969 when a group of students under the leadership of Michael Carliner, Tom D'Antoni, and P. J. O'Rourke, felt Baltimore needed a daring and dynamic alternative publication. *Harry* embodied all of the stereotypes of its journalistic genre. In describing his publication, Tom D'Antoni wrote, "What was it like? I think it was like being with the original–original cast of 'Marat/Sade' inside the revolving drum of a cement mixer careening wildly out of control the wrong way down Charles Street in a rush hour." *Harry*'s wild ride lasted two years.

By the end of 1969, Baltimore's underground press had succeeded in arousing the public's damnation or praise. Among those who damned were many who believed that Baltimore should have a serious, responsible alternative paper. These thoughts were put into action when the *Paper* appeared in April, 1970.

Under the direction of Jerry Litofsky, Bruce Schwartz, and Larry Singer, the *Paper* won several local awards. This tabloid published articles of broader community appeal: it covered the arts, cultural events, personalities, and other topics of political and civic interest. The editorial philosophy was summed up by Mr. Singer when he said, "We want to make more people see what this city has to offer. We definitely want to be a positive, not a negative force."

A number of Baltimore's leading writers, artists, and photographers contributed to this twice–monthly paper. It was noted for its outstanding graphics and layout. Toward the end of the *Paper*'s two–year existence, the *News American* contracted with the staff to produce *EXTRA*, a Sunday supplement to the *News American*.

Although revenues from advertising, street sales, and subscriptions had been sufficient to meet costs, the *Paper* was terminated because of poor cash flow. The staff also felt that, for the long hours spent in producing the paper, their remuneration was inadequate.

Six weeks after the *Paper* began, another serious publication made its debut, the *Chesapeake Weekly Review*. This publication was oriented more to literary interests, as opposed to news and issues. It ran music and movie reviews, prose, and poetry. John Bunting was its publisher and Denis Boyles its first editor. When Boyles left to study at Oxford University, John Herman took over as editor.

After six issues, at 20 cents per copy, the insufficient income did not justify a continued weekly printing. By midsummer of 1970, the decision was made to publish every other week. However, the Baltimore market was unresponsive and the *Chesapeake Weekly Review* folded soon thereafter.

Undaunted by the failures of Baltimore's underground and alternative press, William Bray published the first issue of *Performance* in June, 1972. Mr. Bray, though not a native Baltimorean, thought of all the cities that he had visited or lived in this city was the finest. Two editorial guidelines were followed: positivism, because it was perceived that people were tired of negative journalism; and entertainment, because the city offered a variety of worthwhile cultural events and provided an active night life.

After seven months of producing a weekly newspaper, Bray realized that more income was needed to sustain the effort and pay for several full-time employees. Steve Cardin, from a locally prominent family, invested in Bray's publication. Two conditions of Cardin's investment were that editorial functions should be shared and that Bray would be responsible for advertisement while Cardin would be in charge of all other publishing aspects. Cardin's goal was to make *Performance* closer to becoming "a cross between the *New Yorker* and *New York* magazines and *Rolling Stone*."

Although *Performance* did an admirable job in trying to fulfill its goals, a year and a half later, after reportedly losing $80,000, *Performance* passed into history as another valiant attempt to provide Baltimore with a serious alternative publication.

In April, 1973, another paper joined in the uncertain Baltimore market—*City Dweller*. As publisher, my goal and that of my staff was to combine all of the positive elements of the *Paper*, *Chesapeake Weekly Review*, and *Performance*; it also intended to be a community-oriented publication. The publisher took a cue from his paper's predecessors and eschewed the college and youth market. Instead, I asked my staff to concentrate on producing a community newspaper—one emphasizing local and neighborhood news. The first staff, which was more interested in creating an intellectual digest, balked and seven months later a second staff was formed. This staff wished to turn back the clock and make *City Dweller* an underground publication. After heated arguments, the second staff walked out and began its own newspaper. *City Dweller* continued as a community paper, and in 1977 changed its name to the *Baltimore Chronicle*.

Richard Bronson and Robert Waldman and other disgruntled *City Dweller* staff members founded *Port City News*, which was first printed in September, 1974. Unlike other underground publications, it was a standard size instead of the familiar tabloid. *Port City News* tended to be sensationalistic in content. It sold for 10 cents a copy, but did not prosper and went out of business in February, 1975.

Messers Bronson and Waldman shortly thereafter published a free paper called the *Newsprint Co-op*. All space in this paper, including editorial content, was sold to whoever wished to purchase it. Mr. Bronson eventually dropped out, while Mr. Waldman continued the effort for about another year. Both of these publications thus followed the prediction *Port City News* warned about in one of its earlier issues, "There are others [newspapers] in the graveyard and there are sure to be more."

The *City Squeeze*, started by undergraduate Johns Hopkins students as an offshoot of the University's *Newsletter*, began in May, 1977. Its early issues were youth-oriented and sensational, with emphasis on rock music and other timely interests of a young audience. Its calendar appealed to many readers.

The staff temporarily suspended publication after trying to continue publishing after graduation. During the hiatus, they sought to redefine their paper's goal and purpose and to acquire capital for their enterprise. In February, 1978, the *City Squeeze* reemerged as the *City Paper*, under the sole ownership of Alan Hirsch and Russ Smith. Despite the new name and a broader focus, the paper made few changes in its editorial content format (which resembles the *Village Voice* and *Rolling Stone*). At this writing, *City Paper* publishes every other week, and sells for 35 cents per copy, though it continues free distribution on local college campuses.

Baltimore had one other major alternative newspaper—the *Unicorn Times* which originated in Washington, D.C. The publisher of this paper felt a Baltimore edition could succeed. In early spring, 1978, Geoffrey Himes was hired as the Baltimore editor.

This monthly tab generally ran in excess of 48 pages and was viewed as a significant supplement to those wishing to know more about the entertainment scene in both cities. Most articles were features dealing with music, theatre, dance, art, and their respective reviews. Owing to financial mismanagement, the Baltimore edition of the paper folded in spring, 1980.

Though Baltimore had a late-blooming youth market, it still had its share of underground newspapers. However, these had, by their nature, a fatal flaw—they aimed at a limited, younger audience. The alternative papers, in contrast, approached publishing from both an editorial/artistic and business viewpoint. Regardless of the quality some of these alternative papers provided, Baltimore's business community and the readership as a whole did not respond to or support an alternative press.

Laurence N. Krause

PUBLIC BROADCASTING: RETROSPECT AND PROSPECT

Efforts to develop educational broadcasting in Maryland took longer than to put a man on the moon. The movement unfolded slowly: it began in Baltimore in 1948, was interrupted, began again in 1952, was interrupted, resumed in 1954, was interrupted two years later in 1956 only to begin again in 1961. This pattern is not unique to Baltimore since it occurred throughout the United States. Indeed, the story has been the same in most of the world as each locality established noncommercial broadcasting in a way peculiar to its own needs. In Baltimore, a single experimental program led the way to a fully equipped broadcasting center 20 years later.

I will share with you my own experiences as well as my observations and historical studies of this period.

From a Book Report to Public Broadcasting. In spring, 1961, Hervey Brackbill, book editor of the Baltimore *Sunday Sun*, requested that Minna Shulman, president of the Child Study Association of Baltimore, select a member to review *Television in the Lives of Our Children* by Schramm, Lyle, and Parker. I was delighted with the opportunity to express my thoughts publicly. In my review, I pleaded for some action:

Baltimore, one of the largest cities in the United States, has no educational television. What a project for us to encourage with demands, gifts, and subscriptions! If television could portray reality rather than fantasy to an important extent, what cultural and intellectual growth would we see!

Afterward, the board of the Child Study Association asked me to chair a research committee to discover why Baltimore lacked an educational station. The committee soon realized that research was not enough and that it had to take action. To include the entire state was another important decision. Repeated conversations with Dr. Wesley N. Dorn, director of the Division of Research and Development of the Maryland State Department of Education, convinced him to cooperate with the citizen efforts.

On May 2, 1962, the committee called together a meeting of representatives of organizations, institutions, and individuals interested in developing educational television (ETV) for Maryland. That day the Maryland Committee for Educational Television organized. Coincidentally, just the day before, President John F. Kennedy signed a bill to authorize that the federal government grant funds to the 50 states for expansion of ETV facilities.

Donald Kirkley, television critic of the Baltimore *Sun*, wrote that the new group "set in motion something of which many a frustrated parent and hopeful teacher have dreamed: the fuller use of television in its great, barely touched capacity for teaching young and old, and creating a kind of cultural awareness never before attained."

Wilmer V. Bell, director of adult education for the Baltimore Public Schools, became the president of the organization and I was honored as vice–president and later became (1966) president. A steering committee met with Governor J. Millard Tawes in June, 1962, to petition him to designate the State Department of Education as the official agency, appoint an advisory committee, and authorize the state ETV agency to engage a professional staff and provide the funds from the governor for work on this project. In September, the governor complied and designated the State Board of Education as the official agency and created the advisory committee.

By August, 1964, the committee ended its studies: Maryland would have a seven–station network—one for the Baltimore area, the others for the rest of the state. The State Board of Education asked the governor to include the necessary funds in the 1965 budget. The legislature refused. The Maryland Council for Educational Television (the name now changed) realized it had to strengthen its efforts for the next session in Annapolis.

The legislature had authorized the Legislative Council's Education Committee to study ETV. Senator Mary L. Nock of Wicomico County was the chairman. The Maryland Council for Educational Television (MCETV) provided the committee with materials that might convince the legislature of the value of ETV.

Other efforts included a campaign for public enlightenment. The press, radio, and commercial television stations were remarkably cooperative. Maryland was especially fortunate to have the assistance of commercial television, which offered spot announcements, editorials, and programs specifically produced to tell the public about ETV. By then the MCETV had help from the National Association of Educational Broadcasters (NAEB) whose representative was Dr. Frederick Breitenfeld, Jr. William McCarter, executive director of Washington's ETV station (WETA), and Dr. Robert Hilliard, director of the Federal Communications Commission (FCC), also assisted the campaign. Freddie Loiseaux, president of the Maryland Congress of Parents and Teachers, gave support and the Maryland State Teachers Association (MSTA) under Dr. Robert Dubel, and Phyllis Brotman Community College of Baltimore student, lobbied in Annapolis. The Greater Baltimore Committee provided the services of Eugene Petty (Assistant Director of GBC), clerical help, and a meeting room for MCETV. Many Baltimoreans and other Marylanders joined in.

Those involved, including members of the legislature, had fought a long battle. Victory was finally theirs when in 1966 the necessary legislation was passed.

Now another battle had to be fought. Who would be the official ETV agency? Controversy split the enthusiasts into two camps. In 1962, when MCETV began meeting, some members hoped for a citizen-controlled agency. The University of Maryland had ideas of being the agency. However, the Maryland State Department of Education had been developing ETV plans and moved forward aggressively when the opportunity presented itself.

In 1966, after the state legislature studied the plans, it decided that too much power would be centered in one agency like a state department of education. Legislators believed ETV in Maryland should be broader than just that. Senator Harry Hughes wrote a compromise bill with Dr. Breitenfeld's assistance. Senate Bill 24 passed the legislature and Maryland ETV joined the

other 115 stations already existing in the United States.

Baltimore's Pioneers in ETV. Although the efforts took five years to reach the goal, the entire process had begun 15 years earlier. In 1946, predating the opening of the first commercial television in Baltimore, the Johns Hopkins University was already studying the mechanics of television. Their aim was to determine "the technical potentials and limitations of the medium" before putting it to some educational uses. In March, 1948, Lynn Poole, public relations director for the university, appeared on WMAR-TV from the campus at Remsen Hall with the first of an eight-week series called "The Johns Hopkins Science Review." The Columbia Broadcasting System, WAAM-TV, and the DuMont Network (now WJZ-TV of the Westinghouse Broadcasting Co. in Baltimore) broadcast the program. Twenty-four cities viewed it.

Along with WBAL-TV, the commercial stations in Baltimore were broadcasting many educational programs, a possible reason why Baltimoreans were not actively seeking an educational station. Baltimore City and County Public Schools also developed some programs, as well as closed-circuit installations in the county schools: Washington County Closed-Circuit Television System (funded by a Ford Foundation grant), the Delmarva Educational Television Project broadcast by WBOC-TV in Salisbury, and WETA that served schools in Maryland as well as Washington and nearby Virginia. In 1961, the University of Maryland presented courses on closed-circuit television to 40 classrooms on the College Park campus.

Early in 1952, several educators organized because they realized that the FCC was creating special wave lengths to help increase ETV channels. At first, the Citizens Temporary Committee on Educational Television consisted of educators from the parochial schools, Baltimore Public Schools, Maryland State Department of Education, and Loyola College; it then added business, professional, civic, as well as other educational organizations. Dr. Katharine Whiteside-Taylor, director of Adult Education, Baltimore City Schools, was chairman. The members were convinced that "serious educational objectives could not be in the main interest of commercial television interests." After appealing unsuccessfully for city funds to establish a publicly owned and operated ETV station in the area, the group folded by the end of 1952.

A temporary organization called Baltimore Community Television was launched in May, 1954. Sponsors included Lynn Poole; Thomas Van Sant, director of Adult Education of the Baltimore City Schools; Fr. John E. Wise, S.J., president of the Baltimore Association for Adult Education; and the Reverend Leo J. McCormick, Archdiocese of Baltimore, Department of Parochial Schools. The group later incorporated as Baltimore Community Educational Television.

In 1955, commercial television stations broadcast programs to show the promise of ETV. Mayor Theodore McKeldin even wrote a certificate of commendation for those civic-minded individuals who were trying to bring ETV to the city. Charles P. McCormick, Sr., chairman and president of the board of the McCormick Tea and Spice Co., chaired a dinner for business and industry. In spite of such intensive efforts the group failed to raise funds. Then, Mr. Poole traveled across the country to investigate educational television stations and returned to warn the group that if it opened a community ETV station in Baltimore, it would be "saddling the city with a white elephant." In 1956, the Baltimore Community Educational Television Committee, Inc., collapsed because of a lack of funds.

The Baltimore City and County Public Schools continued to develop programs. Dr. Thomas G. Pullen, the state superintendent of schools, formed a committee of local superintendents to study the possibilities of developing a state network.

Finally, in February, 1961, Baltimore lost channel 24 to a commercial organization and gained the unwanted ultra-high frequency channel 66. In 1953, the FCC had granted the Citizens Temporary Committee on ETV channel 24 for at least one year that actually extended for eight years. The FCC then dealt Baltimore a heavy blow when it assigned an even higher frequency band. By 1965, the FCC again changed the channel—to 69—and again a year later to the 67 the station now holds.

Few gains were made in generating noncommercial broadcasting in Maryland from January 16, 1956, until May 14, 1961, when the book

review appeared in the Baltimore *Sunday Sun*. Some joined the new MCETV; those remembering the frustrations and heartbreak stayed away. Five years later, the state would finally be looking ahead to its own network. When planners included all of Maryland, ETV had more chance. State and federal funds (available in 1962) made it a reality.

From Legislation to a Broadcasting Center. In July, 1966, Governor Tawes appointed the commission that began its assignment to establish ETV for Maryland. Herbert B. Cahan, area vice-president, Group W Westinghouse Broadcasting Company, was chairman and Fred Archibald, former Baltimore *News American* publisher, vice-chairman. Dr. Frederick Breitenfeld, Jr. was selected to be the executive director. The State Department of Education appointed James Petersen as director of instructional programming. Housed temporarily at 1101 St. Paul Street, the staff began its assignment.

The 1967 Maryland legislature changed the name to the Maryland Educational–Cultural Broadcasting Commission to include radio in the future. That year the commission received its license from the FCC for channel 67 to cover the Baltimore area. Federal funds followed from the Department of Health, Education, and Welfare (HEW) for equipping the station. The same year the legislature again changed the name: Maryland Public Broadcasting Commission. In October, 1969, the station went on the air at Gwynbrook State Park in Owings Mills.

In its tenth year the Maryland Center for Public Broadcasting joined the world's most extensive system for distributing television programs via domestic communications satellite. Dr. Breitenfeld commented, "Satellite communication is one of history's greatest technical accomplishments." By January, 1979, the system linked all television stations in the 50 states, Puerto Rico, and the Virgin Islands.

A New View for Baltimore. What happened between 1969 and 1979? In 1964, the State Committee on ETV Planning had listed the kinds of programs that characterized ETV. The center has indeed been broadcasting almost every suggestion included in the committee's report. All the expectations of those who worked so hard had begun to be a reality. Dr. Breitenfeld had hoped to produce 40 percent of the programs at the center; in 10 years the actual production was 30 percent.

Programs distinctly catering to Baltimore have been "Baltimore Clipper: The Ship That Launched a Port"; "Strategy for Action," that explored the problems of urban living; "Our Street," a family situation drama depicting the struggle of an East Baltimore family coping with the problems of inner-city living; "Point Blank: Shock Trauma," a documentary about the University of Maryland Hospital's Shock Trauma Unit; "Basically Baseball," featuring the Baltimore Orioles; "The Critic's Place," a program on cultural events in the Baltimore and Washington area; "A-Rab Summer," a program on the fading art of street huckstering; "Make a Loud Noise," on contemporary local black theater in Baltimore; and "In Search of a Maestro," a documentary on the Baltimore Symphony Orchestra's first young conductors competition. The Maryland Public Broadcasting Center holds many awards, including one from the Baltimore Ad Club for the "Best in Baltimore Show," "Promo Art," and "Ascent of Man."

As cultural television was developing, instructional television (ITV) was moving ahead. "In the fall of 1969 a red light came on over a camera, a teacher fresh from the classroom began to talk, and Maryland Instructional Television was born," according to an excerpt from a report for the Instructional Television Office of Maryland Public Broadcasting. Many months of planning went into that birth. Many people were involved and their enthusiasm was exceeded only by their pride.

Ten years later in 1978, channels 28, 31, and 22 had joined channel 67; 65 series were available; color generally supplanted black and white. ITV provides programs that deal with "the new emphases of public instruction—basic skills, parental involvement, and quality instructional materials."

Under Angela McDermott, assistant superintendent for instructional television, the division won many awards, including the John Cotton Dana Award in 1976 for "Book, Look, and Listen," "Spinning Stories," "Once Upon a Town," and "Readers' Cube," and the Ohio State Award in 1977 for "Book, Look, and Listen."

In 1980, Dr. Michael F. Sullivan replaced Ms. McDermott. The Maryland Public Broadcasting Commission has selected an advisory committee of 44 citizens required by the Corporation for Public Broadcasting. The chairman is Dr. Renwick Jackson, president of St. Mary's College.

A national directive for the formation of a citizens advisory group has significant implications for Maryland public broadcasting. Maryland already had such a group—the Maryland Council for Educational Television—that was greatly responsible for getting public broadcasting for the state. After its successful campaign in 1966, the council still existed until 1969 when outside pressures snuffed it out.

Two of its purposes—similar to those of the present federal law—were: "(1) to offer advice and assistance to the State Educational Television Agency and other public agencies on utilizing the full resources of the state; and (2) to serve as a citizen's voice for educational television," according to the by-laws of the Maryland Council for Educational Television. A continuing Maryland Council for Public Broadcasting could have been fulfilling the needs of the recent national requirement.

To add to state-given funds the center has held auctions-on-the-air and a direct-mailing campaign; local businesses and institutions have given grants and corporations have underwritten program services. All of these funds have helped the center to lead nationally in the field of underwriting.

The Maryland Public Broadcasting Commission has been adding stations until now six of the seven planned for the state form appendages of the network. The last station will be in St. Mary's County in the near future.

Dr. Breitenfeld commented that the worst problem in Maryland public broadcasting has been the channel offered to Baltimore—channel 67, "an incredibly high frequency." The short wave length prevents the signal from bending around telephone poles or buildings. The transmitters in Annapolis providing Baltimore with channel 22 have helped, but there are still difficulties in some spots; special wiring on the roofs of buildings could help. As for the impact of public broadcasting on Baltimore, Dr. Breitenfeld would hope that it is in "conjunction with our impact on the rest of the state. We'd like to think of some of the services we provide as bridging the various cultures that Maryland includes. Somehow an urban program about Baltimore's problems should be seen by Salisbury or Pocomoke City residents. Hagerstown's rich farm land should be aware of a tennis program or a flood somewhere else in the state. We may find the inferiority complexes helped; I like to think that public broadcasting can assuage these feelings."

Telecommunications, the Wave of the Future. On March 1, 1974, the Maryland Center for Public Broadcasting opened its own Telecommunications Office headed by Sidney Tischler. The office has been helping to guide Marylanders into the telecommunications era. Radio, television, two–way radio in mobile vehicles and walkie–talkies, satellites, and, over the last 20 years, cable television provide the means to send, store, and receive information. The key: the individual can push buttons. The future in communications lies with the videodisc and videotape. Broadcasting will mean that anyone can use the retrieval system of playing whatever program at anytime the person wishes.

In spring 1981, the new wing added to the center was ready for the Telecommunications Office to move in. The wing also houses the ITV division, giving it one roof instead of the temporary arrangements it had been using. Eventually radio will be added. The new building is twice as large as the old.

The city itself has had the Mayor's Office of Telecommunications since September, 1973. Dr. Marvin Rimerman, director, oversees the city's radio, cable, TV, and audio–visual program. The office has already engaged in several innovative projects, including the discussion via satellite between the mayors of Baltimore and Columbus, Ohio.

Telecommunications developments in Baltimore reflect the needs of a city that has turned more and more from blue–collar workers to white–collar whose need is information. The new products are information. Producing and distributing goods and commodities still continue to be important to the economy of Baltimore. "However," according to Dr. Rimerman, "layered upon that type of economy is the newly emerging post–industrial age service sector economy. We are following along with the entire nation in this regard, where more people are engaged in providing services than in farming or manufacturing

Employee at the Mayor's Office of Telecommunications. Photo by Mayor's Office of Telecommunications

things. Communications systems are required for the production, distribution, and use of information."

In 1971, Mayor William Donald Schaefer acted on suggestions that the city consider cable television. A year later he appointed a committee from the general community chaired by Everett Goldberg (then law professor at the University of Maryland Law School, now associate dean). The mission of the CATV Committee was to determine whether Baltimore should have a cable television system. In January, 1973, the committee reported that the focus of cable television should not just be entertainment, but should concern itself with information for a changing community. The committee recommended an office of telecommunications to be funded by the city to assess the needs of the people in Baltimore.

That spring Mayor Schaefer appointed another committee which looked at two–way landmobile radio that at first had been a police service. Baltimore was in the vanguard of cities in using two–way communications.

In May, 1979, the mayor and City Council created the CATV Commission. By January, 1980, the mayor appointed the nine members who decided in April that the industry (cable television) from "local and national interests would be economically feasible and desirable."

These steps—as well as all the public broadcasting activities—to meet the needs of its citizens have been a part of Baltimore's renaissance.

Lenora Heilig Nast

COMMERCIAL TELEVISION: A WINDOW ON THE WORLD

By 1956, commercial television was already a factor in Baltimore life. There had been a postwar informational vacuum, teased by newspaper and magazine stories of experimental telecasts that followed actual demonstrations at the 1939 World's Fair. When the Maryland public had seen the new video fare, they liked it.

Small fortunes were made by appliance dealers who quickly began to sell, deliver, and install the receivers which became (in the words of a now-failed network) "Your Window on the World."

Television's camera crews roamed Baltimore's streets to picture disasters and debates, politics and people, sports and spectacles of any available kind. And, by 1956, elections, parades, and Preaknesses had become commonplace in local living rooms, where television sets had become a "must buy" item.

Television had come to Baltimore in October, 1947. By then there were already more than 1,000 homes prepared to receive local programs. The availability of telecasts from the District of Columbia had begun some months earlier and provided the Baltimore stations with a ready-made, albeit tiny, welcoming audience.

The Tools of Baltimore's Television. Channel 2, the *Sunpapers* station, was the first TV station to air in Baltimore. It installed its transmitters atop what is now the Maryland National Bank building at Baltimore and Light streets, one block from the *Sunpapers* building (then at Baltimore and Charles). Curiously WMAR–TV elected not to build TV studios then, but invested instead in two mobile units that it sent skittering through the area to telecast parades, horse racing from Pimlico and Laurel, wrestling and basketball from the Coliseum, and baseball from Memorial Stadium. WMAR televised foot-

ball from Annapolis, as well as other Naval Academy sports such as swimming and basketball.

Channel 11 was second on the scene, with studios at 2610 North Charles Street, where it shared space with its sister station, WBAL–Radio. Channel 11 was created by the Hearst Corporation, which published the *News-Post* (now the *News American*). WBAL–TV operations began in March, 1948, specializing in studio–type presentations.

Channel 13 (now WJZ–TV, but originally WAAM) had the distinction of having Baltimore's first built-for-TV building on a hilltop in Northwest Baltimore, an area which then became known as "Television Hill." Its main studio was, by the standards of November, 1948, huge and spacious. Its transmitting tower was just outside the building. Channel 13 was created by Ben and Herman Cohen (now owners of Pimlico Race Course).

A fourth powerful TV voice came into the picture considerably later, when WBFF–TV signed on channel 45 in April, 1971. It is located adjacent to Television Hill, and is owned by Chesapeake Television, Inc., whose president is Julian S. Smith.

Because of poor reception, pressures to centralize broadcast antennas were being felt in the late fifties. The three early stations planned a consolidated tower. This effort gained impetus when WAAM was sold by the Cohen brothers to Westinghouse Broadcasting in 1957. Westinghouse had acquired considerable real estate in the WAAM purchase and made enough of its land available on "Television Hill" for all three stations to be accommodated.

The planning began, and with it came a few problems. The simplest engineering construction would have been to have the three stations' antennas stacked, one atop the other. But every foot of antenna height is something very precious to the individual station. Height, with power, means more homes served and more people reached. None wanted to be low-man-on-the-antenna-stack. None wanted his competitor to be able to say, "My antenna is higher than yours." A way to resolve the dilemma was found when the antenna–makers developed the triangle–in–the–sky design; it was tricky and very expensive, but it worked—and still does.

One further word on the triple antenna tower: it was built to a height of 750 feet, and put into service in 1959, strung with huge cables designed to hold it erect against 165–miles–per–hour winds. When it became feasible in the early 1960s to elevate the three station antennas another 250 feet—to 1,000 feet above ground—the stations decided to go ahead with the project. Again, it was expensive and tricky. The center shaft was elongated and, in a breathtaking moment, the triangle–in–the–sky was cut loose and hoisted to its new level, bolted in place, and broadcasting resumed. The date was August 26, 1964.

Meanwhile, other structural changes occurred in Baltimore's video stations. WBAL–TV built a handsome new studio and office building near WJZ–TV on Television Hill, and began using it in 1962. WMAR–TV had built studios in the old *Sunpapers* building in 1949. When the *Sunpapers* moved to a new building on Calvert Street in 1950, the station took over what had been the morning *Sun* newsroom for its main studio. These quarters were used for about 12 years, until the station moved to its new, spacious studio and office structure on York Road, just north of the city line, in May, 1963.

What Baltimore Watched on Television. Not surprising, perhaps, the average viewer certainly cared very little for those precious feet of antenna heights. What came on the screen was what attracted viewers, and the story of Baltimore programming is a fantastic mix of big stars and little shows. The networks were off on their gilded flights by the year 1956, and they haven't been grounded since.

In the past quarter–century, television has brought hitherto unknown worlds of entertainment, information, glamour, culture, and counterculture to the home. Baltimore's own star performer, Garry Moore, was one of those who led the video parade, especially for the CBS network. (Moore began as a staff announcer on WBAL–Radio.) Milton Berle was "Mr. Television" on Tuesday nights at eight o'clock, and it seemed that he would be a permanent fixture on the tube. Arthur Godfrey, who began as a banjo–plucking entertainer on Baltimore's WFBR, also became such an attraction that competing networks programmed around him. Ed Sullivan's "Toast of the Town" at 8:00 Sunday night was "must" viewing. Today it still evokes "do you remember . . . " quotes wherever older TV viewers discuss the medium.

Television has always been competitive. Baltimore TV was even competitive in the public service area. Each of the four stations in the city has extensive displays of awards and citations. Early examples are WMAR–TV's two unpretentious programs: "Comeback!," devoted to achievements of the handicapped; and "Your Family Doctor," devoted to health care, which ran for 20 years. In 1962, WMAR–TV started a documentary team that turned out a film a month on such topics as vandalism, overuse of drugs, life in Maryland prisons, the operation of the Maryland legislature, and a variety of other subjects. WJZ–TV won Ohio State University awards in consecutive years, and WMAR–TV won Gavel Awards from the American Bar Association.

Along with these programs in the public service area (which, frankly, never attracted the huge viewing audiences that entertainment programs did), were scores of afternoon programs for general viewing, morning programs for children, midday cooking–and–interview programs for the housewife, amateur talent shows, and afternoon dance programs where dozens of high schoolers gathered in studios to dance to station–provided records while cameras showed their skills. Buddy Deane conducted one of the more successful of these on channel 13. (Deane now runs a radio station in Arkansas.) Another such program was hosted by Al Ross.

Nick Campofreda provided an afternoon live entertainment program on channel 13 and Bailey Goss presided over a three–hour mélange of sports results, skits, music, and race results on channel 2. Goss was assisted by former *Sunpapers* reporter Jim McManus, who is now better known as Jim McKay on ABC's "Wide World of Sports."

Nibbling into afternoon time half hour by half hour, the locally produced afternoon shows began to dwindle as the networks switched to serial dramas and "soap operas." Now local entertainment programs are disappearing. They are replaced by superior production and more professional talent brought by tape and cable from the centers in New York and Hollywood.

Surveys showed that by 1970 the majority of

Royal Parker in Early Television Days in Baltimore.
Photo by John Kelly

people nationwide got most of their news from television first, and read about it later in print. The people have learned to trust the TV medium. This trust began, possibly, with TV's coverage of the Army–McCarthy hearings in the early 1950s. Together with Joseph Welsh's excoriation of Senator McCarthy and Edward R. Murrow's program, TV coverage helped expose McCarthy's tactics and led to his censure by the Senate.

National anchormen Howard K. Smith, Walter Cronkite, and Eric Sevareid have become father figures to the nation, as have John Chancellor and David Brinkley. One wonders if Barbara Walters or Jane Pauley will become comparable mother figures.

Local Television Performers. In the last 25 years, local television gave Baltimore something priceless: a sense of unity, a oneness generated by the daily exposure of virtually every problem and controversy of the area. Every part of the city became known to all others as television camera–reporter teams searched the communities for each night's news.

Anchormen Dave Stickle, Rolf Hertsgaard, Jerry Turner, and weatherman Al Herndon were—or seemed to be—personal friends.

With the pressure from national networks to usurp local time and programming, Baltimore's TV tradition has been an unusual one. Observers have often exclaimed over the amount of local programming shown by the composite Baltimore TV schedules.

This account could not be complete without recalling some names that are linked with the growth of TV in Baltimore. Channel 13's early managers included Sam Carliner, a former Baltimore city judge. Since the Group W purchase of the station there have been possibly 15 managers, most of whom remained here a year or so, then were moved to other assignments by Westinghouse. The station's programs included performers such as Ken and Lou Calfee; Lynn Poole, who did "The Johns Hopkins Science Review," first on channel 2 and then for a much longer period on channel 13 and the ABC Network; Pernell Roberts, who was a cameraman at WAAM and then became one of the stars of "Bonanza"; and Keith McBee and the late Wiley Daniels, the newsmen.

Channel 11 has had six managers, beginning

Eleanor Arnett Nash Interviews Her Brother Ogden, November, 1965. Photo from Channel 2 Files

June Thorne, Hostess for *"The Woman's Journal,"* Interviews Brock Peters. Photo from Channel 2 Files

with the late Harold Burke, who had also managed WBAL–Radio; Leslie Peard, who managed from 1951 to 1959 and then went to manage a station in Fresno, California; Brent O. Gunts, who managed from 1959 to 1973 and is still active in local television; Jack Beauchamp, 1973 to 1976; and Larry Carino and Malcolm Potter, both of whom are still active here. J. Sydney King is the dean of the city's public service directors; John Frankenfield was program director for about 20 years. Among the performers were Happy Johnny, Kitty Dierken, Mollie Martin, Gene Klavan (now a radio star in New York), and Miss Nancy of "Romper Room."

Channel 2 has had three managers. First was E.K. "Jack" Jett, who left the FCC to become WMAR–TV's first manager in January, 1948, and served until his death in 1965. Don Campbell took over then and served until his retirement in 1976, while Dale Wright still serves. Before then, I was recalled by the *Sunpapers* from my assignment in Tokyo in 1946 to start construction of the station and served as program director until retirement in 1975. Performers to be remembered from channel 2 would certainly include Stu Kerr, who created and performed as "The Janitor" and the clown "Bozo"; George Rogers, longtime anchorman and news chief; and Ann Mar and Sylvia Scott who, between them, did "The Woman's Angle" weekdays at 1:00 P.M. for 20-odd years.

Baltimore has originated several programs that have been seen nationwide, but probably none has had the basic, everyday influence of "Romper Room," originated by Bert and Nancy Claster. Bert, an old–style showman from vaudeville days (he managed the stage shows at the Hippodrome in downtown Baltimore), developed the show at channel 11; it later moved to channel 2, where it still telecasts five days weekly and is conducted by "Miss Sally," daughter of the originators. It is still syndicated into more than 50 American cities and is or has been seen in two dozen nations around the world.

Robert Cochrane

BALTIMORE RADIO DURING THE LAST 25 YEARS

After World War II, Baltimore had only five AM radio stations: WBAL, WCAO, WFBR, WCBM, and WITH. Ten years later, there were eight AM and three FM stations. In 1955 alone, three new stations joined the Baltimore broadcasting community: WAYE, WTOW, and WEBB. Ironically, radio was supposed to be dying as television's popularity rose. However, Baltimore's radio investors and listeners did not seem to have been told about the impending funeral. More stations were to come.

Program listings in the mid–fifties are filled with personalities—some nostalgic, some still familiar: Al Ross, Galen Fromme, Jack Wells, Al Stevens, Buddy Deane, Jay Grayson, Mollie and the Captain (and their dog, King), Lee Case, Bailey Goss, Martin Edwards, Ralph Phillips, Hot Rod, Eddie Fenton, Ted Phillips' Hawaiians, and Homer Todd (Baltimore's original "Mr. Fortune"). The new major league Orioles were on WCBM, where Chuck Thompson was broadcasting an afternoon record show. Sports were covered by Nick Campofreda for WFBR and Roger Griswold for WCAO. The afternoon record shows of Joel Chaseman and Nelson Baker of WITH and WWIN were competing with Chuck. Late–night listeners tuned to Harley Brinsfield on WCBM; Chuck Richards on WBAL; and Charles Purcell and "Nocturne" on WCAO, with Roland Nuttrell at the organ.

Although radio networks were losing their sponsors and some of their talent to television, many of the old established entertainment programs were still on the city's stations. Baltimoreans heard "The Lone Ranger," "Fibber McGee," and "The Great Gildersleeve." Long–run programs like "Amos 'n' Andy" and "The Voice of Firestone" were still on, and new ones were aired, such as Danny Kaye and "Arthur Godfrey's Talent Scouts." Different programming on the weekends began, including the debut of NBC's "Monitor." The daytime hours were still filled with soap operas on WCAO and WBAL. The famous national commentators held on to their 15–minute programs in the early evening: Edward R. Murrow (WCAO), Morgan Beatty (WBAL), Lowell Thomas (WFBR), and Fulton Lewis, Jr. (WCBM).

However, traditional programs like these were soon to disappear, as Baltimore radio restructured itself as a medium for a variety of music, news, and sports presentations. This change was accomplished by 1960, and the number of stations continued to grow. That year alone five new FM stations began broadcasting: WFMM, WSID-FM, WCBM-FM, WRBS, and WAQE-FM.

No WBAL names are on the trivia quiz list because in 1961 the station was in the midst of its flirtation with "Beautiful Music."

DJs' names disappeared from the newspaper listings, replaced by titles like "Morning Overture," "Serenade in the Afternoon," "Carousel," and "Limelight." However, the DJs were still

Baltimore Radio Trivia Quiz #1

This list of sixteen names was taken at random from Radio Program listings in 1961. What station did each of these people work for then? A perfect score automatically makes you one of "Baltimore's Best" Radio Trivia Experts.

John Jeppi	Joe Knight	Jack Gale
Buddy Young	Bill Jaeger	Bob Adams
Gil Kriegel	Ray Davis	John Dark
Dennis Hill	Herb Carneal	Mike James
Larry Monroe	Jay Neely	Dave Robinson
Les Alexander		

there. These personalities included Perry Andrews (who had taken over the morning program from Frank Hennessey), Jim West, Paul Shields, Mollie Martin, and Jay Grayson. In addition, Conway Robinson dispensed his rural philosophy in the very early morning, and in the evening Baltimore's first stereo programs (AM and FM, then) of concert music included live broadcasts of the Baltimore Symphony Orchestra with Bob Benson.

The early fifties had seen the beginning of rock music, too. As this new music grew in favor and the number of broadcasters increased, specialization became the order of the day. In the past each station had prided itself on its wide variety of programs. Each has specialized in one type of music, and Baltimore now has "Top 40," "Good Music," "Country and Western," "Soul," religious, classical, and "middle of the road" stations. New formats are constantly vying for a place in the market. "Album Rock" (WIYY) and "Rhythm and Blues" (WXYV) are the latest successes.

Most of these music formats have been enhanced by multiplex stereo broadcasting on the FM stations, which—after years of struggle—are now competing on an equal basis with their older AM counterparts.

Women broadcast regularly from the very start, but 25 years ago they were uniformly consigned to homemaking programs, gossip, and "culture." Baltimore radio is now liberated; women are working in every aspect of all operations. Modern Baltimore radio even includes women executives. Denise Oliver, the inventive program director of 98 Rock, is prime among them.

And, of course, there was news. WITH had pioneered "News on the Hour" in Baltimore. As programming changed, the networks restructured their service to supply news for the new formats. Radio news names to remember include Charlie Roeder, Lou Corbin, Eddie Fenton, Al Quinn, and Ian Ross MacFarlane. Many familiar television newsmen started as Baltimore radio reporters: Richard Sher, Jack Bowden, the late Wiley Daniels, George Baumann, and Ernie Boston, for example. Jed Duvall, who started at WBAL-FM, is now with CBS-TV; Bob Matthews is at NBC-Radio. First and foremost among local news personalities, of course, is Galen Fromme, whose morning newscasts on WBAL became a Baltimore tradition during his 40–year career, from which he has only recently retired.

"Prime Time" for radio listening has changed from evening to the morning and afternoon periods of heavy commuter traffic. Radio is the only medium that can reach that audience in their automobiles, and these listeners need new and different services. Baltimore stations have responded with a variety of reports on area traffic conditions—gathered by the state police or the city's Department of Traffic and Transit, or reported from planes, helicopters, and a variety of radio station–based "Traffic Centrals."

As Baltimore radio developed new programming, there was continuing emphasis on sports. The Orioles spent most of the last 25 years on WBAL, but have now moved to WFBR. The Colts were a WBAL fixture, too, during their glory days; they have now moved to WCBM. Sports names from the period include: Ernie Harwell, Bailey Goss, Bill O'Donnell, John McClain, and—of course—Vince Bagli, and Chuck Thompson.

During this quarter century, Baltimore has experimented with other sports. In their time ice hockey, basketball, and soccer have been local radio features. As the teams folded or moved, radio coverage followed. Even the great Baltimore amateur sport, lacrosse, has never proved to be much of a radio attraction, either. By contrast, racing—another favorite local sport—is given considerable continuing coverage on many local stations.

Specialized programming within the various formats still exists—mainly as five–minute talk features. These, too, are most frequently sports features, with John Steadman, Tom Davis, Ted Patterson, Neal Eskridge, and Charlie Eckman. Other existing talk features are provided today by Elane Stein, Clark West, Bill Shriver, Jesse Webster, and Don Spatz.

Baltimore radio has frequently been at its best in emergencies. Local stations have demonstrated this many times in the past 25 years whenever "Charm City" has been subjected to blizzards, floods, hurricanes, civil disturbances, gas shortages, and other emergencies. In these situations, the city's radio stations have performed "beyond the call of duty." Staffs have worked around the clock for days on end, sometimes at physical risk, to serve the community and keep the public informed.

Stations have enthusiastically participated in the Baltimore renaissance, too. The success of Trash Ball, Baltimore's Best, the Walkathon, the Preakness, and ethnic festivals, and—above all—the City Fair, has been in large part due to radio's promotion efforts. WBAL has invented its own unique projects to serve Baltimore including the Marathon, Call For Action, and the Auction for Center Stage. Its "Kids Campaign" has collected and distributed hundreds of thousands of dollars to send city children to summer camp, to supply them with needed clothing, and to provide them with other services and pleasures which would not have been possible without the station's efforts.

Long before 1954, Baltimore stations were featuring regular programs for the German, Italian, Jewish, and Polish communities. During recent years, stations have added programs for other ethnic groups: black, Greek, Irish, Lithuanian, and Spanish.

Four stations now devote their full attention to the needs of the black audience: WWIN, WSID, WEBB, and Morgan State University's noncommercial WEAA. Black entertainment pioneers include: Fat Daddy, Rockin' Robin, O.J., Anthony, and Diamond Jim, as well as Al Jefferson, Bob Greene, Don Brooks, Larry Dean, Larry Wilson, Russ Johnson, and Eddie Morrison. Among black women radio personalities are Kitty Broady, Mary Clayburn, and the much-loved Pauline Wells Lewis.

Gradually, Baltimore radio's offerings came to include more than music, news, sports, and service. There are now "talk" programs as well. WFBR's noontime "Conference Call" features the opinions of the station's news staff. Alan Christian's popular late-night program on WBAL features the people in the audience on the phone—asking questions, arguing with guests, giving their opinions, and debating with each other and with Mr. Christian.

More competition and much greater variety exist in Baltimore radio today than 25 years ago. For instance, WBJC–FM was Baltimore's only noncommercial, educational station. Now it shares that audience with six other stations, including the area's newest station, WJHU–FM at Johns Hopkins University.

Baltimore Radio Trivia Quiz #2

Stations now on the air in Baltimore once used different sets of call letters. Can you name the present-day descendants of the stations which were once known by the following calls? WCBC WAQE WFDS WYOU WDJQ

Matching names and programs to dates was comparatively easy for the early years of this report. They were then listed daily in the local papers. In recent years, reporting on personalities is more difficult. The daily listings now report only the stations' call letters, dial position, and format. There is no record of the names. Any list of today's radio personalities would not be complete, but let's mention the following: John Sterling, Johnny Walker, Thom Thompson, Ted Steele, Ron Riley, Bob Jones, Ron Matz, R. C. Allen, Tom Lattanzi, Jack Elliott, Jack Lacy, Paul Berman, Ole Dirty Shirt, and Terry Johnson.

As Baltimore stations converted from programs of live music, audience participation, and drama to programs of records, their physical needs changed drastically. WCBM moved from its historic old building at North and Harford to Charles Street and then to its transmitter in Owings Mills. WFBR closed up its elaborate art deco North Avenue entrance, and eliminated the big studios that once housed "Club 1300" and "Quiz of Two Cities." WCAO gave up its fifth location in a Charles Street brownstone and moved to its transmitter site. Only WITH, of all

the "old–line" stations, still maintains its original location on Lexington Street.

One important change in Baltimore radio has gone largely unnoticed by the listening public. More and more stations have passed from strictly local control to ownership by "chains" or "groups." WCAO, WCBM, WITH, WLIF, WFMM, and WAAM–TV have all gone through this change. Some of them have changed hands several times, and the prices paid keep escalating. Whatever else this may mean, it indicates that Baltimore radio is economically stronger than ever.

The reported death of Baltimore radio has turned out to be greatly exaggerated. Baltimore radio today serves and employs more people than ever before. It has succeeded by changing, adapting, expanding, and specializing. These same features will probably sustain Baltimore radio's status as one of the city's most viable institutions in the next 25 years.

Tom O'Connor

Answers to quizzes
Jeppi, WWIN; Knight, WFBR; Gale, WITH; Monroe, WCAO; Young, WEBB; Jaeger, WFBR; Adams, WITH; Alexander, WCAO; Kriegel, WITH; Davis, WBMD; Dark, WCAO; Neely, WITH; Hill, WWIN; Carneal, WITH; James, WFBR; Robinson, WFBR. WCBC:WRBS; WAQE:WTOW (or WLIF); WFDS: WIYY; WYOU:WLPL; WDJQ:WBSB.

SOUNDS AND SWEET AIR: A SHORT HISTORY OF WBJC

Every hour on the hour (except the hours between midnight on Sunday and 6 P.M. on Monday) a voice at 91.5 proclaims, "This is WBJC, Baltimore. The Radio Service of the Community College of Baltimore." Within the meaning of those letters and words there is a history far removed from the static ordering of events and people, for WBJC—like the Community College of Baltimore—has undergone a sea change, and the names of both institutions were once different in time and place.

And the history of Baltimore's fine arts radio station goes something like this: in September of 1948, a radio production course began at the

Baltimore Junior College, located on 33rd Street on the third floor of Baltimore City College. This course was designed by the Department of Speech to prepare students for jobs in commercial radio. Then in the summer of 1949, talk started about building a studio and control room for broadcasting these efforts within the school. But as luck would have it, someone noticed that the tower at City College stood 135 feet above the ground and that a transmitter could be installed for about what it would cost for an on-the-campus broadcasting system.

These plans were carried forth and a proposal was submitted to the Board of School Commissioners in May of 1950. Permission was granted, bids were let, application was made to the Federal Communications Commission (FCC), and construction was begun in August, 1950. While the transmitter was being built, students in the radio production course changed a small classroom into a studio, using castoff rugs and a salvaged stage curtain to improve the sound quality of the room. During the time of construction and renovation, the students trained to become the radio station's announcers, writers, and engineers. But the Korean War made it difficult to obtain the electrical equipment in order to put the station on the air. Finally, and with borrowed phonograph records, all of the necessary equipment was available. Program tests began on April 6, 1951, and on April 19 the FCC approved the college's radio license.

At that time the radio station called itself WBSC–FM, and it was the only licensed educational radio station in the area, including Virginia, Delaware, and the District of Columbia. What then was so new and important spoke in a voice of 125 watts. Small and tiny. The course of the radio station, however, was set—with classical music, jazz, drama, public affairs, and educational programs—operating from 2:00 P.M.–3:30 P.M. on school days and from 7:00 P.M.–9:30 P.M. on Thursday. Baltimore could hear WBSC–FM by tuning to 88.1. Membership to the station cost a dollar and included a program guide.

Shortly thereafter, the call letters of the radio station became WBJC in order to reflect the name of the college, and its place on the FM dial was 91.5, with a voice of 800 watts.

In 1961, things began to change: the Baltimore Junior College moved to the grounds of the old Park School on Liberty Heights Avenue, bringing with it the radio station and housing it in a wooden shack on the campus. In 1968, the college changed its name to the Community College of Baltimore. Since the call letters WCCB were assigned to another radio station, WBJC remained the designation of the college's radio service.

Another major change occurred on April 4, 1966, when WBJC went stereo and increased its broadcasting strength to 17,500 watts. By the autumn of 1978, WBJC's power grew to 50,000 watts.

At every step in WBJC's struggle to increase its power, new towers have been built to replace the older and weaker ones. Now sitting in back of the Liberty Campus of the Community College of Baltimore is a 20–foot diameter dish-shaped antenna, constructed to receive programming via satellite. The antenna picks up programs from both National Public Radio (NPR) stations and the rest of the world. Satellite reception is superior to the telephone cables and recording tapes formerly used. Now "Live from the Met" sounds as though you are actually sitting in the Metropolitan Opera House in New York's Lincoln Center.

While WBJC has moved in name and power in its 32 years, much of what was started in 1948 remains the same: a classical music station with a rich interest in public affairs and educational programs, serving the Community College of Baltimore and the people of Baltimore city, with a subcarrier to serve the needs of the visually handicapped.

Now WBJC, with a membership of some 7,500 subscribers, occupies a part of the art wing on the Community College of Baltimore's Liberty Campus, with a modern control room and a spacious and generously stocked record library. Schubert, Bach, Ellington, a Cole Porter tune, or a college course on "The Poem," can be heard on WBJC, Baltimore.

Harvey Alexander

Contemplating Baltimore

POLITICAL HISTORY

The best way to consider the history of Baltimore, political or otherwise, over the last 25 years is to begin in the middle, which also happens to be the bottom.

For the dozen years before 1968, the city was on the skids, and this was reflected in the nature and tone of its politics. In the years since, things have been looking up. 1968 is a sort of benchmark. That terrible year—the year of the riots, the year of the breaking of young Tommy D'Alesandro's political career, the year the crooked star of Spiro Agnew reached its apogee—is the place to begin.

What happened in Baltimore in the spring of 1968 was not, in retrospect, as bad as it might have been. It was not as bad as what occurred simultaneously in many other cities in the wake of the assassination of Martin Luther King, Jr., and it was not as bad as it was portrayed in the press (by myself, among many others). But it still came as a shock to the city, a blow as devastating in its own way as the great fire of 1904. It meant that life in Baltimore would never again be quite the same.

There was gunfire in the streets. There were arson and looting. Federal troops—1,900 men from the 197th Infantry Brigade—were flown in from Fort Benning, Georgia, and other military posts. They joined national guardsmen and state and city police; at one time there were more than 12,000 armed and uniformed men stationed in Baltimore during the riots.

This was an unparalleled opportunity for demagoguery. Black and white politicians jeered at one another across a gulf of hatred and mistrust. Many of those in responsible positions, the ones who had to help make crucial decisions about the handling of the disorder, were shattered by the experience.

Thomas J. D'Alesandro III, the young mayor who had been in office only a few months, had thought he understood Baltimore's politics, thought he knew how a political leader could get things done. He had grown up watching his father, a three-term mayor, at work—knowing everyone in all the neighborhoods, working the political clubs, doing a favor here and calling in an old obligation there. Through a haze of cigar smoke, the municipal wheels could be made to revolve.

But suddenly the old ways didn't work any more. People screamed at you; they wouldn't listen to reasonable talk. One side was all "burn-baby-burn," the other urging the police to shoot to kill. Young Tommy flew over his burning city in a helicopter and felt himself close to tears. He would never run for office again.

For others, though, the riots and their aftermath represented a shimmering opportunity. They were, along with plain dumb luck, the making of Spiro Agnew.

Agnew was the Republican governor of Maryland that year, 15 months into his first term. He had been elected as a progressive, and for the most part had lived up to his reputation. But 1968 was a national election year, and he was ambitious. When his overtures to his party's moderate wing, personified by Nelson Rockefeller, were rudely ignored, the riots suddenly suggested to him that there might be some running room on the right. The governor suddenly reversed his field.

He summoned a number of eminent black Baltimoreans to his Baltimore office, and there, with abundant publicity, he flayed them verbally. He as much as said the riots were their fault; the rioters were black, after all, and weren't they the black leaders? Where had they been? Why hadn't they prevented the violence?

That simple but carefully calculated action

Voters Sign Petition in opposition to Inner Harbor.

did two things. It ignited Agnew's career, sending him into the embrace of Richard Nixon and on to the vice-presidency of the United States until his earlier venality (and the Department of Justice) caught up to him in 1973. And it brought the new politics of racial confrontation to Baltimore. It would be a long time before whites and blacks, collectively if not individually, would begin to trust one another politically again.

Thirteen years later the wounds have healed and city politics are remarkably free of Agnewvian racism, but the scars are there. These years following the riots have been a very different period, politically, from the 13 years that went before.

When Thomas (Big Tommy) D'Alesandro, Jr., the 1968 mayor's father, was elected to his third term in 1955, Baltimore politics was not

the same game. The senior D'Alesandro was a highly traditional politician. He knew his wards and precincts, and he knew that if you were after power, it was often helpful to deal with a broker. That meant, among others, Jack Pollack from Northwest Baltimore and the Trenton Democratic Club. It also meant a continuing suspicion of Mayor D'Alesandro on the part of reform types and *Sunpapers* editorialists.

Reporters assigned to City Hall in the first D'Alesandro era found the mayor both colorful and irascible—unlike Theodore R. McKeldin, who was only the former, and William Donald Schaefer, who is only the latter.

There is a famous anecdote about the time a young *Sun* reporter was sent to the mayor with an editor's query.

"Sir," he quavered, "my desk wants to know

if you'll sign the transit bill," or whatever the burning issue of the day actually was.

The mayor laid his ear against the blotter in front of him, looked thoughtful, and then declared, "My desk tells your desk to go to hell."

The D'Alesandro collapse came suddenly. In 1958, the mayor announced his intention of running for governor, but the J. Millard Tawes forces persuaded him to run for the United States Senate instead. "They want a strong Baltimore man on the ticket to help drag an old nag across the finish line," said the mayor, with characteristic modesty.

But as it happened, he barely squeaked through a four-way Democratic primary, and then—in a year of great Democratic successes in Maryland—was defeated by Senator J. Glenn Beall by 15,000 votes. That was the beginning of the end. A year later, as he was seeking his fourth term as mayor, he was defeated by the reform Democrat, State's Attorney J. Harold Grady, by 33,000 votes.

But the elder Tommy D'Alesandro was, in retrospect, a competent mayor as well as a gifted and effective politician. At least, he was competent enough for the times; it's arguable that the turbulence of the 1960s, which overwhelmed his son, would have overwhelmed him, too. Cigar-chomping tough guys weren't any better off during that period than were hand–wringing liberals.

Times have been changing since 1954. That was the year of *Brown v. Board of Education*, the Supreme Court's landmark desegregation decision; it was also the year that blacks in Baltimore began, at long last, to make themselves felt as a political force. (Blacks served on the City Council between the 1890s and the 1930s.) In 1954, three blacks cracked Jack Pollack's iron control of his West Baltimore district and won election to the state legislature; by 1958, leading black politicians saw further gains as inevitable.

However, the blacks hadn't reckoned with the enormous adaptability of Jack Pollack. When Harry A. Cole, a black Republican elected to the state Senate in 1954, fielded an all–black coalition ticket in 1958, Pollack was ready. His integrated Trenton Club slate swept to victory, giving his somewhat battered organization a much-needed shot in the arm.

When Harold Grady unseated Big Tommy D'Alesandro in Baltimore in 1959 and went on to defeat former Mayor and Governor Theodore McKeldin in the general election that fall, it was considered a serious and perhaps fatal blow to the Pollack organization. But things didn't work out that way.

Grady had enormous problems, not the least of them the city's fiscal condition, which was dire. The municipal debt had been soaring throughout the D'Alesandro period, and revenue was dwindling. Grady hung on for three years and then threw in the towel, accepting a judgeship from Governor Tawes and turning over the mayor's office to Philip H. Goodman, the City Council president.

In 1963, the Pollack organization (and the old D'Alesandro forces) threw in with Goodman and helped him win the primary. Some of the Pollack people in the precincts, though they had been with Big Tommy for years, refused to go along with his son. Little Tommy was running on the Goodman ticket for president of the council, but many sample ballots circulated on election day by Pollack workers carried the name of Solomon Liss instead.

Goodman came up in the general election against McKeldin, who was giving it a last hurrah. With the *Sunpapers* inveighing against Goodman's Pollack connections, McKeldin won by less than 5,000 votes, and began yet another era in city political history.

Young Tommy D'Alesandro was also elected City Council president that year, as was Hyman A. Pressman, who had lost the Democratic primary for comptroller, but who accepted a Republican offer to fill that vacancy on the GOP ticket.

Theodore Roosevelt McKeldin was an extraordinary figure. He had been mayor 20 years before as a young man; now he was the old veteran, magic–tongued, almost eerie in his resemblance to the character Frank Skeffington in Frank O'Connor's *The Last Hurrah*. Some called him a charlatan, and surely he was, to a degree. But he gave politics a zest, in the years when he was on the scene, that no one has approached since.

Much of the Republican party despised him, partly because of his refusal to pay even lip service to conservative Republican policies, and partly because he was always ready to lecture his party about its need to reach out to blacks and Jews and other minorities—something he devoutly believed and fervently practiced as both mayor and governor.

But while McKeldin was fun and refreshing, his city was still in trouble. He decided not to challenge Little Tommy in 1967—he would almost certainly have lost if he had—and the election of a second D'Alesandro was accomplished without more than token opposition. But the seeds of trouble had been planted for a long time, and it wasn't long after McKeldin bowed out for the last time that trouble, big trouble, appeared in the shape of the 1968 riots.

William Donald Schaefer had succeeded Tommy D'Alesandro III as City Council president. When Tommy declined to run for a second term in 1971, the top job was Schaefer's for the asking, as it turned out.

For a while, though, it seemed as though the hour had come around at last for black Baltimore to win one of the city's top offices. Certainly black Baltimore thought so. George L. Russell, Jr., the city solicitor, ran against Schaefer in the 1971 primary. There were many people who thought Russell would be Baltimore's first black mayor.

He spent $250,000. So did Schaefer. And when the dust of the primary settled, there was William Donald Schaefer, mayor of Baltimore. It was assumed by those who followed municipal politics that his victory was an aberration, and that Baltimore, like Cleveland and Detroit and Atlanta and Los Angeles, would shortly elect its first black mayor.

And in fact it may, but it hasn't happened yet. We are now 10 years beyond 1971, and William Donald Schaefer coasted to a third term. He dominated city politics during the decade of the 1970s, and there are few signs that his authority is waning.

To dwell on the failure of black candidates to get elected to the most visible city-wide offices— mayor, council president, comptroller—is, however, to miss a key point. Black politics has come a long way.

The key election for blacks in Baltimore was not George Russell's loss. Nor was it Milton Allen's 1970 election as state's attorney, nor his defeat by William Swisher, a white Pollack-

Congresswoman Mikulski Talks With a Constituent. Photo by Peggy Fox

backed candidate, when he ran for reelection four years later. The key election came in 1968, with the election of Joseph Howard to the Supreme Bench of Baltimore.

The Howard election showed that blacks, if they wanted to, could do a political job. Howard, who was recently appointed to the federal bench, bucked the city bar association and virtually the entire white establishment (which liked to call him a racist) in order to become a judge.

In addition to the slow awakening of black Baltimore, another important political phenomenon was taking place in the late sixties and early seventies. This was the rise of neighborhood and issue-based politics, replacing the old political clubs as the most dynamic force in city politics.

Neighborhood issues helped ignite the political career of Barbara Mikulski of East Baltimore, among others. People would get together, for example, to fight an expressway, and from their efforts would grow a vital and effective political organization. Mikulski, who served on the City Council before her election to Congress in 1976, was one of the first major city politicians to come from this sort of background.

With Mikulski and Parren Mitchell in the House of Representatives and Paul Sarbanes in the Senate, Baltimore's current Washington representation is cerebral, generally well-respected, and firmly liberal. That in itself reflects a considerable change in city politics from that of a decade ago.

In the 1960s, the city had three veteran congressmen who were all products of the old politics—just as Mikulski, Mitchell, and Sarbanes are products of the new. They were George Fallon in the Third District; Edward Garmatz in the Fourth; and Samuel Friedel in the Seventh. Each was white, powerful in Congress, and apparently unbeatable. But by 1972, all three were gone.

Sarbanes, a lawyer and former Rhodes scholar who had served in the legislature, defeated Fallon in 1970. The same year, Mitchell, a member of one of Baltimore's best-known black families, edged out Friedel. Two years later, when the city lost a district, Garmatz retired; he would have had to run against Sarbanes and chose not to do so. Then, in 1976, when Sarbanes moved to the Senate by defeating J. Glenn Beall, Jr., Mikulski won Sarbanes' old seat in the House.

In the mid-1960s, after a major legislative reapportionment, it was said that Baltimore had finally lost its historic dominance in Annapolis to the fast-growing suburbs. And, in fact, that seemed to be true for a while, even when Marvin Mandel, a Northwest Baltimore politician, occupied the governor's office.

Today it certainly isn't the case. The city, helped by the lobbying of Schaefer and Council President Walter Orlinsky, has done well with the legislature in recent years. And it has continued to produce influential politicians, including Stephen Sachs, the current attorney general; Benjamin Cardin, the speaker of the House of Delegates; Rosalie Abrams, the state Senate's majority leader; and Harry McGuirk, chairman of the Senate Economic Affairs Committee—known in Annapolis as "Soft Shoes" and respected for his ability to get things done.

As the city moves into the 1980s, Baltimore politics continue to evolve. Due to Mayor Schaefer's virtually uncontested third term, there is something of a lull. But the pot still simmers, and the next quarter-century isn't likely to be any less eventful than the last.

Peter A. Jay

Poster at the Johns Hopkins University Fair, 1979.
Photo by Ric Bartter

A Sage Reminisces

"Baltimore," said Henry Louis Mencken just after the population of the inner city had passed the half-million mark, "is now twice too big to be rated as a decent place for civilized people to inhabit." Nevertheless, all of his 70 years he remained a resident of the city. Even until the five years of his married life with the charming Sara Haardt were ended by her death, they occupied an apartment on Mount Vernon Place, architecturally of the very essence of nineteenth-century Baltimore.

Oh, well, ever since the days of Juvenal, satire has been recognized as a distinct, but definite branch of philosophy, and Mencken handled it with a brilliance that is, in my opinion, unmatched in American literature. The only American writer who, as a satirist, can be regarded even as a close rival of Mencken was Edgar Allan Poe, not a native, but resident here for a part of his most active life, and who died here and is buried in old Westminster churchyard.

Incidentally, the oft-repeated story that Poe was left to die in a Baltimore gutter is a brazen libel not only of the city, but of the business organization that brought me to Baltimore, and the craft that I have followed through most of my active life, that of newspaper worker.

The known and proven facts are these: at three in the morning of October 7, 1849, a type-setter employed by the Baltimore *Sun* knocked off work at his usual hour and started home, but on his way stopped off at his customary oasis for a nightcap—no inconvenient closing laws in those days. The place was nearly empty at that hour, but after he had been served, the printer noticed a man slumped over a table across the room and inquired of the bartender. "Passed out, I guess," was the indifferent reply. But in those days you couldn't—and in these you can't easily—fool a newspaper printer about the difference between being merely passed out and something more serious. So the printer walked over and took a closer look. A mere glance was enough.

"This man isn't drunk," he told the barkeep. "It's worse than that. I'll see if I can catch a hack outside."

He was lucky enough to find one quickly and back at the saloon he and the bartender hustled the customer outside and into the hack. "Washington College Hospital [now Church Home and Hospital]," said the printer, naming the nearest hospital.

So Edgar Allan Poe died, not in a gutter, but decently in a hospital bed with a doctor and a nurse in attendance. And the reputation of Baltimore was saved from one disgrace by a news-paper printer working for the same newspaper that I served, nearly 100 years later.

A triviality? Certainly, but it is precisely by such small and apparently trivial incidents that one comes closest to a true estimate of the real philosophy of a city—or of a state, or a nation, for that matter.

To turn, then, to an event far more dramatic but, I think, revealing far less of the dominant spirit, the ruling philosophy, of the town. My house is built on the south slope of Bolton Hill and from the kitchen window one looks across an alley to a tennis and swimming club whose premises include several tennis courts, a large swimming pool, and a larger children's play-ground, but no buildings except one-story dress-ing rooms and offices. From our kitchen window the eye has a clear view to the grounds of the Fifth Regiment Armory, 200 yards away, and a semicircular panorama of Baltimore city, with the Washington Monument looming up clearly in the middle distance and the skyscrapers of the downtown financial district behind it. That is by day: by night the semicircle takes on the sparkle of an artistic triumph of some master jeweler working with rubies, emeralds, sap-phires, and flashing white diamonds. My wife and I stood looking out of that window on the Sunday night after the cold-blooded murder of the Reverend Dr. Martin Luther King, the great-est American black leader, certainly since Booker T. Washington, creator of Tuskegee In-stitute, and possibly since Frederick Douglass, most famous native of Tuckahoe, Maryland, and most celebrated of black agitators just prior to the Civil War.

Looking out of our window and scanning the semicircle from left to right, we could see the glow from seven huge fires set by rioters stirred to madness by the murder, and we learned later of twice as many beyond our sight. Something of the sort was going on that night in 28 other American cities, including the national capital. To assist the Washington city police, troops had been drawn from the army divisional headquar-ters at Fort Meade, between Baltimore and Washington. The governor of Maryland had sent National Guard units to assist the city police, but they had not been enough, so he had ap-pealed to the national authorities and in the end they had sent in troops from as far away as Fort Bragg in North Carolina and an army post at Anniston, Alabama. The troops that did come, though, were splendidly disciplined. Gradually, they pushed the mob back by sheer weight of numbers without firing a shot. During the whole night only one black was killed, and he for pulling a knife on a city policeman trying to arrest him.

All night the radio kept repeating warnings to all law-abiding citizens to get off the streets and stay off—wasted advice in our house, for neither of us felt the slightest impulse to indulge in any heroics, and I had long since surrendered my newspaper job and so was under no compulsion to turn in a story in time for the next edition. I distinctly remember thinking, and possibly muttering aloud, "This is intolerable. This is a reversion to barbarism that must be put down with a high hand, and fast." Yet at the back of my mind a small voice kept insisting, "But the insult was deliberate and deadly. Dr. King, always the man of peace, always the wise counselor urging his people to make their appeal to the best, not the worst, always remembering that it is the just man who is entitled to receive justice, Dr. King, finest hope of all the black men and women in our country, this highly civilized man to be shot down like a mad dog by a creature half man and half gorilla, lurking in a house across the alley. I can't help being glad that the black people of Baltimore would not take that insult lying down."

I do not know how it can be proved, but I have a strong conviction that the smaller voice came nearer to reporting the true philosophy of Baltimore than did the louder one. I am confirmed in this opinion by what happened during the great blizzard at the end of February, 1979, when all traffic, including police cars, was stalled or at most proceeded at a crawl, and the looters had a field day, carrying off much valuable property and damaging more. I have yet to hear any Baltimorean, white or black, voice anything but the bitterest condemnation for that affair. The real nature of the raids is exposed by the fact that the liquor stores were the first establishments to be looted. That was not the work of anyone who was either starving or freezing. It was thievery unadorned and Baltimore condemned it with a vigor that was utterly sincere.

These two incidents do little more than point the way to discovery of what it is that makes Baltimore tick with a speed and at a value measured in decibels that are all its own. All its values are American, but that is merely a description, not a classification. Ethnically, Baltimore is as variegated as most large American cities.

The composition of the city's population, except for a recent influx from the Baltic and Scandinavian countries, is today rather old American. The Germans and the Irish, for instance, arrived long ago. The bulk of the city's Jews are at least second or third generation Americans. The characteristic of a population including a substantial contingent of every great

ethnic strain in the world makes Baltimore undoubtedly American, but is it typical? I don't know. After having visited every city, St. Louis and San Francisco excepted, of more than half a million population, I am not sure what constitutes a typical American city, unless it is the marked disparity between the development of its science and technology, on the one hand, and its philosophy on the other. This freakish development pervades the whole country, but its cause was nothing ethnic; it was the result of a mere accident of history.

The Europeans who first colonized the Western Hemisphere were the Hispanics (Spanish and Portuguese) who pretty well monopolized South America and came into North America as far as Mexico up to the present northern boundary of Texas; and North Europeans (French, English, Dutch, and Scandinavians). Germany was then fragmented into small principalities and was not counted as a nation. The earliest Americans were largely refugees from the incessant wars that had convulsed Europe for centuries with intensified savagery ever since the rise of Protestantism had vastly intensified the hatreds that politics had already raised between the nations, or, rather between the families who ruled the principalities, dukedoms, and church domains into which the continent was split.

William E. Gladstone, one of the most memorable of British prime ministers, called the Constitution of the United States "the most wonderful work ever struck off at a given time by the mind and purpose of man," and he might have added that the most wonderful point in it is reached, not in the main body of the instrument, but in the first words of the first of the ten amendments that the common people demanded should be added to the document before they would consent to its ratification. Those words are: "Congress shall make no law respecting an establishment of religion, or prohibiting the free exercise thereof." Those are the words that made the government of the United States forever secular; yet Christians may reasonably argue that they are obedient to the injunction of the Founder of their Faith, "Know the truth, and the truth shall make you free." Yet our relative obedience to these words is what has made the United States—since the decimation of the Jewish population of Russia—the biggest

Jewish nation in the world. It is the reason why a Jewish citizen of Baltimore may rest assured that if a gang of hoodlums contemptuous of all religions, should burst into a synagogue and interrupt the religious service being conducted there, the Baltimore city police would come just as fast, and swing their espantoons just as heartily as if the outrage had been perpetrated in the Cathedral of Maria Regina or in the University Baptist Church.

The freedom of religion, guaranteed by the secular state, is, in fact, the massive foundation stone of all our other freedoms.

The city of Baltimore, I am fain to believe, is slightly, if only slightly, in advance of most American cities in the value it sets upon the local freedom of religion. But I am aware, of course, that we have our need of zealots who regard such tolerance as not praiseworthy, but heathenish. Well, many a dish is enlivened by a judicious measure of pepper.

Candor, though, compels the admission that Baltimore carries its full share of the great fault of the nation, to wit, the intellectual inertia that has allowed its science and technology to outstrip its philosophy. In the beginning the situation was less distorted, for in 1607, when Jamestown was first settled, the Industrial Revolution was as yet unheard of, and even at the outbreak of the Revolution, in 1776, industrialism was barely a quarter of a century old, even in England, its point of origin. The early settlers faced the task of domesticating a savage wilderness, three thousand by eighteen hundred miles in extent. In such a situation, the first demand is necessarily for muscles, rather than minds.

Yet among the very first settlers of Jamestown was an ex-soldier of fortune with the name of John Smith who claimed the rank of captain, and who was considered a man of genuine intelligence. In an eight-oared barge he explored the Chesapeake Bay as far north as a river that still bears the Indian name of "Patapsco." Captain John Smith rowed up the estuary to its end where, on his left a hill of some height was built of a clay so red that it reminded him of rouge; he named it "Bole Armaniac." Thus the future site of Baltimore received its first English name, which the Calverts, 121 years later, replaced with the name of their Irish estate, "Baltimore."

Later Captain Smith returned to England and appointed himself a propagandist for the New World. He was a good one, too, for he developed a simple and agreeable English style which is easily readable today. The colony had been named "Virginia" in honor of Elizabeth the Great who never married and accordingly was known to the populace as the Virgin Queen. As long as Captain Smith was describing the landscape and products of Virginia, and what was to become Maryland, he was definitely more reliable than most of his contemporaries; it was only when he was relating his personal adventure that he took to literary embroidery in a really big way. His tale, for instance, of his rescue from imminent death by the Princess Pocahontas, daughter of the Indian Emperor Powhatan, may have had a basis of cold fact, but was pretty surely touched up to improve the dramatic effect. Nevertheless, the book had a resounding success in England and vastly increased Englishmen's interest in the New World.

Almost 25 years later a Yorkshire gentleman named George Calvert, by nature an adroit politician and by training a smooth diplomat, for valuable services rendered to Kings Charles II and James II was knighted, and later after his conversion to the Catholic religion, was made Baron of Baltimore in the Irish peerage. Then his son, Cecilius, second Baron, also with the consent of the King, sent a colony of Catholic refugees to settle on a grant of land from the north bank of the Potomac to Penn's grant.

But the conquest and development of a raw, new country left little time for purely speculative thought, so the province, while developing a tremendous demand for science and technology, had little interest in abstract philosophy. Hence was created an imbalance that now threatens the future of the country, Maryland included. What is worse, when the people are so obsessed by admiration of their own wisdom that they ignore the injunction of the greatest philosopher of them all, "Ye shall know the truth, and the truth shall make you free," I am persuaded again that the Baltimore philosophy of "pause and consider" may be the strongest means of defense that a city can possess. At least it has served us well for nearly 300 years, and can you beat that?

Gerald W. Johnson

III

In the 1960s there was a catchy song, "Downtown," which celebrated the city as a place to go to do things. For years, Baltimore was thought of as "Sleazeville," with its cultural attractions primarily housed behind red lights and 24-hour flashing neon signs.

Strippers, massage parlors, peep shows, porno stores, and backrooms with fat ladies languishing on cots, waiting to be spanked, constituted Baltimore's contributions to the arts in the national mind. Now, however, word is getting out that the city has things to do besides catering to the erotic needs of rotund businessmen, the S & M crowd, or those enjoying the company of male hustlers.

The contrast is astounding. Baltimore's support of "high culture" nowadays rivals its support of the "sweet life." Operas, symphonies, art galleries, live theatres, music groups, serious film–makers as well as hundreds of writers, poets, and other artists have found a home in the city. Since the beginnings of its renaissance, Baltimore no longer primarily provides needed sensual services for tourists and others. Instead, its widespread achievements in theatre, music, dance, architecture, and the visual arts, according to some, rival what took generations to accomplish in Paris, Budapest, and Florence.

This section documents a few outstanding examples of this achievement in aesthetics (of which Baltimore has always had some examples but had been ignored). Seven areas in the arts are identified: theatre, music, visual arts, dance, films, architecture, literature, and poetry. A perusal of the six articles on theatre, or the five articles on Baltimore music, leaves one with a sense of amazement at both the quality and variety of artistic talent existing in one city. The energy of a people who are encouraged to do

Sylvester Campbell and Camille Izard of the Maryland Ballet—Hopkins Plaza, 1977–78 season. Photo by Eric Feinblatt.

THE ARTS

their best has created a new and more beautiful milieu. It has also permanently torn asunder old images of urban decadence and death.

The first of the 20 articles on Baltimore's artistic renaissance is "Small Theatres" by Laurlene Straughn Pratt and Earl Arnett. Pratt and Arnett provide a rich, detailed account of the rise and fall of several Baltimore theatres capturing the volatile and chancy nature of this segment of the art world. Pratt and Arnett also convey a genuine feel for theatre life and its goals.

Lou Cedrone's "Mechanic Theatre" is a brief case study of Baltimore's most famous live theatre, its rise, fall, and subsequent rise.

Ron Israel's "Center Stage" describes the many awards and literal rise from the ashes of Center Stage.

Cathy Dryden's "Children's Theatre Association" is a sad story of a form of theatre that has yet to be incorporated into Baltimore's renaissance.

John Strausbaugh's "Theatre Project: Alternative Visions" is a useful overview of an alternative entertainment media.

"The Only International Theatre Festival in the United States in Baltimore" by Al Kraizer describes another Baltimore "first" which has won world acclaim.

Stephen J. Gordon's "Filmmaking in Baltimore: 1956–1979" traces early film producers in Baltimore through the present, commenting on both educational and commercial film making.

Elliott Galkin's "Other Classical Groups" is a brief overview of increasing musical support in Baltimore. Galkin documents that until very recently, Baltimore did not even have full-time newspaper music reviewers, but this has changed dramatically as accentuation of the classical replaces the "sleaze."

Rawley Grau in "Baltimore's Music: A Wild Crescendo" gives a detailed account of the emergence of classical music groups in Baltimore including the Chamber Music Society, Summer Chamber Music Festival, Baltimore Choral Arts Society, and the Greater Baltimore Flute Club, to mention a few. Grau indirectly reveals why Baltimore's music renaissance has been a success: it has benefited from not only a few elite patrons financially supporting music but, perhaps even more importantly, the widespread participation of thousands of Baltimoreans with musical interests and talents in making music.

John Brain's "The Baltimore Symphony Orchestra" is an example of a real entertainment success story. Baltimore's orchestra, Brain points out, is one of the best supported orchestras in the nation and has accomplished much since its founding in 1916.

Mark Miller's "The Baltimore Opera" documents one of Baltimore's most outstanding contributions to formal musical culture, its opera.

"The Left Bank Jazz Society" by Dianne King outlines the emergence in South Baltimore of an unusual group of jazz buffs that provides a spark for Baltimore's musical soul.

Lenora Heilig Nast graphically identifies several facets of Baltimore art. "Spirit," or attitudes toward art in recent history through its institutions: art schools, art museums, galleries, art organizations, both private and public, are discussed definitively.

"Baltimore Art Collectors and Patrons: City and Citizen" by L. H. Nast and Jacqueline Nast Naron is an unusual account of a neglected area, another art institution: patrons and sponsors of great and not-so-great artists.

Bernadette Trattner's "Commercial Art Galleries: the Dealers" is a succinct history of Baltimore's many galleries and their multiple functions. For the uninitiated, Trattner indicates exactly how broad galleries are.

"The Baltimore Arts Festival: Reshaping the City's Image" by Sandra Sugar is a brief history of the GBAC and the Baltimore Arts Festival, an additional city contribution to the world of beauty.

Edward Lyell Gunts in "Urban Alchemy: Baltimore Architecture" is an unusually frank account of architectural failures and successes in Baltimore since the 1950s. His article is also an elegant explanation of the importance of the city's buildings for its renaissance.

Clarinda Harriss Lott's "Poetry and Literature" is a definitive account of the literary and art world in Baltimore, its major representatives, and their recent contributions to the renaissance.

Lori Jackson Marble in "Renaissance of Baltimore Dance" identifies several outstanding individuals and studios and discusses their influence on dance in Baltimore.

Janice D. McCrory's "Baltimore on its Toes" is a brief outline of dance. For example, it includes comments on the School for the Arts and Baltimore Ballet.

In combination, all the articles clearly document our claims for the city's artistic renaissance and ought to dispel forever former stereotypes of the city's lack of artistic potential.

Theatre

SMALL THEATRES

An average weekend in Baltimore usually offers more than 20 theatrical possibilities, about evenly distributed among professional, university, and amateur groups. There are probably more community theatres and performers in and around Baltimore than at any other time in the city's history.

To understand this recent burst of activity, we should recall the groundwork of innovative playwrights like Eugene O'Neill and the enthusiastic, dedicated workers in the little theatre movement of the early 1900s—when theatre groups sprouted around the country in barns, college buildings, warehouses, and a host of other makeshift spaces. They didn't always succeed, but their vision helped successors develop a clearer notion of what native American drama could be.

Baltimore can trace its theatrical origins to the 1770s, but the decades leading to this century were dominated by European imports and commercial considerations that prohibited the kind of imaginative experimentation so necessary for creating art. The early twentieth century playwrights and amateur performers spurred disciplined craftsmanship among the professionals and paved the way for what we now label the nonprofessional community theatre—an awkward, somewhat redundant term that encompasses a wide range of stage activity.

What follows in rough chronological order and necessary brevity is a summary of the past 60–odd years of such theatre in Baltimore and a peek into its tantalizing future.

The Vagabond Players

Founded in 1916, the Vags claim to be "America's oldest continuous little theatre," with the emphasis on "continuous." They began their travelling, roller–coaster life in a spare room on West Centre Street with "The Artist," a forgotten one–act by H. L. Mencken. Other locations and plays followed: O'Neill in a carriage house on West Read Street.

The names associated with this theatre include a long list of nationally known performers: Mildred Natwick, Mildred Dunnock, Garry Moore, Chester F. Morrow, Evelyn Varden, Charles Marquis Warren. Add to them the dedicated people who remained amateurs: Helen Penniman, Naomi Evans Brightfield, Harry Welker, Walter Pearthree, Patti Singewald, Hilary Hinrichs, Virginia Robinson, Carter Wallace . . . the list goes on and on.

The thirties and forties are regarded as the Vags' artistic heydays, the great flowering pe-

Fifty–Ninth Season Opener for the Vagabond Players Performing "Rain," 1974–75. Photo by John Yusaitis.

riods marked by truly distinguished productions. They had to move again in the early fifties and changed to an arena format during their residence in the basement of the Congress Hotel. Incidentally, this had been the old Kernan Hotel that had housed the University Players in 1931 while they performed next door at the Maryland Theatre, and had hosted the wedding of Henry Fonda and Margaret Sullavan on Christmas Eve while Jimmy Stewart played his accordion! They moved three more times before finally settling in their present Fell's Point location (808 South Broadway) in 1974.

With the acquisition of their own building, augmented by ambitious plans for renovation, the Vagabonds are now showing new vitality. They're not as experimental as during their adolescent years, but their "mid–life crisis" seems abated, and a new period of maturity looms ahead.

Theatre Hopkins

Baltimore's second little theatre was established in 1921 on the campus of the Johns Hopkins University. Originally called the Homewood Playshop, the theatre was a joint project of the university's English department (Drs. John C. French, John Uhler, Morris Cushing, and later, N. Bryllion Fagin) and community enthusiasts such as Harry Pouder, Donald Kirkley, and Louis Azrael.

Like the Vagabonds, the organizers planned to produce plays not risked by commercial theatres, to present the classics, and also to encourage the introduction of new playwrights. Theatre Hopkins has probably had more success in these first two purposes than the Vags, although neither group has had remarkable success with brand–new plays. Two factors account for this theatre's tradition of excellence: a permanent location and the practice of hiring a paid director. The theatre has only moved once, from a little clapboard building just behind Homewood House to the old (1803) Carroll barn in 1942.

Dr. Fagin, its first director, molded the theatre for almost 30 years and became its strongest influence. Frances Cary Bowen directed it from 1955 to 1965. Edward J. Golden was director from 1965 to 1969 and gave the group its present name. Laurlene Straughn Pratt, the fourth director, has continued the tradition for the past decade.

More often than not, the level of excellence achieved on the Barn Theatre stage exceeds that to be found in many "professional" productions.

Theatre Hopkins remains a joint enterprise of university and community, with a strong corps of experienced nonprofessional actors. It has become a community standard–setter for disciplined acting, intelligent direction, and restrained diction.

The Spotlighters

Like many other theatre groups, the Spotlighters, launched in their small theatre at 817 St. Paul Street in 1962, have earlier origins. Under the guidance of Edith Gorsuch Onion, a group called the Stagecrafters was organized within the Baltimore Bureau of Recreation in 1944. They performed throughout the city until finally moving into their own quarters at 4 West Eager Street in 1955, when they opened with three Shaw plays in repertory.

The Spotlighters grew out of the Stagecrafters, who disappear from record about the same time the former moved to St. Paul Street. By 1963, the Spotlighters had outfitted their new space with seats from the demolished Century Theatre and were going strong.

Under the direction of Audrey Herman, for the past 15 years, the Spotlighters are still flourishing. They produce a play a month, including Broadway–style musicals which they are frequently able to adapt very imaginatively to the requirements of their tiny stage.

Both skilled and novice performers need regular places in which to play before audiences. This theatre promises to continue such valuable and persistent service for the upcoming generations.

Arena Players

When Samuel H. Wilson, Jr. returned to Baltimore from Boston University in the 1950s, he found a rigidly segregated city where Afro-American theatre lovers could not sit together with their white counterparts. In response to this grew the Arena Players. Founded by a group of 10 led by Mr. Wilson in 1953, Arena Players was the first integrated theatre in Baltimore.

Their first performance, William Saroyan's "Hello Out There," took place in a loft on the campus of Coppin State College. "We had more people on stage than in the audience," Mr. Wilson recalls, "but we just kept on going, not thinking too much about the limits of what we could do."

Along with people like Irv Turner, Camilla Sherrard, Harvey Denmark, June Thorne, Vacountess Payne and many others, the Arena Players kept their "possible dream" alive. In 1962, they located a former church and casket warehouse on Orchard Street, which they personally converted into a theatre. By the end of the decade, they had bought the building. In 1975, a combination of private and public funding made a complete renovation/reconstruction effort possible.

The Arena Players opened their new theatre at 801 McCulloh Street in 1976 with a production of the comedy "Little Ham" by Langston Hughes, their patron theatrical saint. Supported by a staunch backbone of black social groups, the Arena Players continue to grow; plans for expansion include workshops, studios, and a school. With their youth training program, the Arena Players are already several steps toward their goal of creating an arts center.

NEW PLAYers Company

Theatre is a place where dreams are born, nurtured, and transformed into surprising reality. Just ask Ray Hamby, who helped put the NEW PLAYers Company together with Don Swann in 1953 in nearby Ellicott City. It began as a nonprofessional arm of the Hilltop Theatre, a stock company which played the Green Spring Valley in the summer and the Belvedere Hotel in the winter. Within two years, these Hilltop Players began touring the state and eventually became known as the PLAYers Company, which presented a series of summer productions through 1963.

Then, like so many other theatrical ventures, the company died away—but not Mr. Hamby's dream of directing his own theatre on his own terms as a vehicle for his own and other unproduced plays. Thus, in the spring of 1978, the NEW PLAYers Company emerged like a crocus after a long winter.

With the assistance of Ralph Hostetter, Mr. Hamby bought a building at the corner of Madison and St. Paul streets, fixed it up, and opened on April 28, 1978, with "Collateral," his own play.

He hopes the 75–seat, basement theatre will eventually develop into a professional repertory company devoted to new work. The response thus far, in his opinion, indicates that Baltimore "is in a theatrical renaissance."

Baltimore Actor's Theatre

Helen Grigal, founder and artistic director of Baltimore Actor's Theatre (BAT), occupies a special place in the modern history of musical theatre in Baltimore. She began her brainchild in 1959 with an acclaimed performance of "Kismet" in the Maryland Casualty auditorium. Since that time, this enthusiastic woman and her dedicated followers have come a long way toward their initial stated goal of "a membership both professional and nonprofessional, a children's theatre, a school of drama for adults and children, a dance department, and a playwrights' workshop for the development and presentation of original works."

BAT companies have performed in many of the city's major theatres, including the old Ford's Theatre in the early sixties. The organization conducts a summer arts program at the Hannah More Arts Center at St. Timothy's School in Stevenson, Maryland and has just opened a full time conservatory on the campus of the School Sisters of Notre Dame outside Baltimore. The conservatory is Maryland's first, fully accredited school for the theatre arts, grades four through twelve. It will also house BAT's weekly academy for children, established 18 years ago to give avocational training to musical theatre. In 1979, for the fourth time, BAT also assembled a 40–member touring company which performed during August in the Fort Lauderdale–Miami area.

Considering the winter performances at Shane's Restaurant in Timonium; the big band under the direction of Walter Eugene Anderson (also BAT's executive director); the touring Wixie Children's Theatre under the direction of Martha Anne Sherman; and the operation of its Educational Repertory Theatre, the overall record of energy and enterprise of Baltimore Actor's Theatre is remarkable.

BAT has also managed to be self-sustaining

for more than two decades and has never missed a season. Mrs. Grigal, ably supported by her husband Vic, still dreams of a performing arts center in downtown Baltimore, a place where children of all ages could learn, play, and entertain audiences. With her record of accomplishment to date, this possibility should not be discounted. She believes that Baltimore is a city where artistic visions can come true.

Corner Theatre

The sixties changed the tempo of community theatre in Baltimore. There was a sudden awareness of the theatricality of reality, and young people felt a strong desire to repossess body and soul from what they perceived as stifling politics and social practices.

Corner Theatre was born in the midst of this change in 1967 as a local response to such New York experimental groups as Café La Mama. Les Irons and others staged John Osborne's "Look Back in Anger" as their first production at 853 North Howard Street. Actor Larry Lew-man served as artistic director from 1969 to 1971, during which time the theatre moved to a small, narrow space in "Antique Row" at 891 North Howard.

Then Foster Grimm assumed artistic control, producing plays by Gordon Porterfield and other local writers, trying to establish "a clearing-house" for student talent. Under Grimm's direction, Corner was sometimes raunchy, rambunctious, and always yeasty, a lively but struggling little theatre blessed with both the strengths and weaknesses of youth.

When the theatre moved to the undercroft of the Cathedral Church of the Incarnation in 1977 under the presidency of John Alan Spoler, it had already changed its course slightly. Still dedicated to local talent, it restricted its efforts to fewer and "better" plays. By 1979, through the efforts of people such as Theodore L. Manekin, Bruce Godfrey, and Barry Feinstein, the theatre made a regional name for itself as a center for new playwrights, producing works by writers from New York, Washington, Baltimore, and even the Eastern Shore.

"Seer of the Highlands," at Corner Theatre, Baltimore's First Experimental Theatre, 1970 Season. Photo by Theodore L. Manekin.

Corner Theatre apparently survived a serious threat to its existence. In the fall of 1979, it left the church abruptly in search of a permanent home. It located at the Community College of Baltimore, where it became part of an unofficial performing arts consortium, the Puddingstone Group. The Free Spirit Theatre and the Movement Arts Parasol were part of the group. The three groups separated in 1981 and Corner moved to 100 East Madison Street to continue its performances of new works.

Fell's Point Theatre

This distinctive theatre, located near the Vagabonds in a rented building at 814 South Broadway, traces its origins to 1969 and the Bristol Players, who first produced Larry Eisenbert's "Catonsville Act" in 1972. The group moved to its present location the following year and has since produced a wide variety of plays. Al Tyler, the managing director, has been particularly successful with Preston Jones' Texas trilogy plays and has consistently demonstrated an ability to select plays that fit the theatre's ambience. He has been ably assisted in these

Two Actors in Fell's Point Theatre Play, "When Did You Last See My Mother?" 1973. Photo by William Lockwood.

efforts by such mainstays as Brian West, Bill Lockwood, and Kathleen Duffy.

The theatre produced its first original work in 1978, Robert Minford's "The Bird Is on the Wing," and plans to continue this effort with readings and future productions. "FPT intends to remain active in innovative local theatre," say the Fell's Pointers. "We're proud to be part of the excitement, the revitalized Charm City theatre scene which is now possibly greater than when the old Ford's Theatre was going strong, and Baltimore was considered a major try out town."

Colleges and Universities

Some of the best theatre work in the past two decades has occurred on the campuses of the numerous schools of higher learning scattered throughout the Baltimore metropolitan area.

Towson State University is a good example of how dedicated amateurs helped create a first-rate department of drama. In 1948, a remarkable group of students under the direction of Harold C. Paul organized the Glen Players, who produced such substantial works as "Dr. Faustus," "Antigone," and "Winterset." Their success encouraged Towson to establish a theatre department in the fifties. A group of graduate students later organized under the name Baltimore Theatre Ensemble in 1970, the year that Dr. Paul Berman arrived to transform the theatre department with imaginative dramas that explore the contemporary malaise of the mind.

Dr. Berman staged American premieres from the canon of Witkiewicz, the madcap Polish playwright of modern insanity; and produced eloquent treatments of Lorca, O'Casey, and Ibsen as well as a world premiere of Israel Horovitz's translation of Ionesco's "Man With Bags," featuring Towson graduate Dwight Schultz.

A year after Dr. Berman arrived in the Baltimore area, Philip Arnoult organized the Theatre Project, which Herbert Blau has called the "Finland Station of the new theatre movement." Dr. Blau, who collaborated with Arnoult in creating the New Theatre Festival in 1976, arrived in Baltimore in 1974 to teach and administer an arts and humanities program at the University of Maryland Baltimore County in Catonsville.

A visionary and theorist, Dr. Blau had co-founded the Actor's Workshop of San Francisco during the 1950s and later codirected the first Repertory Company at New York's Lincoln Center. During his four-year residence here, Dr. Blau compared Baltimore's artistic ferment of the 1970s to similar developments in San Francisco during the 1950s. He predicted that Baltimore could become an international center for new theatre culture. His presence spurred much creative thinking about theatre in this area and gave the UMBC campus impetus for subsequent achievements, which included a nationally recognized, 1978–79 student production of four recent plays by Samuel Beckett, under the direction of Xerxes Mehta.

While such innovators were getting their acts together, a more conservative but equally significant development occurred at Essex Community College in 1973, when F. Scott Black, William P. Ellis, and Robert Stoltzfus organized a summer theatre program entitled "The Cockpit in Court." By the 1980s, this annual event expanded to include simultaneous productions of cabaret theatre, large-scale musicals, and outdoor Shakespeare, nearly all performing to capacity crowds.

The College of Notre Dame of Maryland has had an active drama department under the direction of Sister Kathleen-Marie Engers and Alice Houstle. The program at Goucher College, long under George Dowell, has become more oriented toward the work of new playwrights under the direction of Barry Knower. The Ira Aldridge Players at Morgan State University, relatively inactive in recent years, promise new and more frequent offerings with the presence of Dr. Samuel Hay and Michael Joyce. Loyola College has its Evergreen Players, and Catonsville Community College has its Barnstormers. The list goes on, adding up to ever-widening diversity as these institutions reach out more to their surrounding communities.

Early Musical Theatre and Operetta

The year 1946 marked the establishment of both the Valley Players and the Alamedians, two groups that spurred postwar Baltimore interest in theatrical music. Blanche Bowlsbey and Clarence de Haven led the latter, which

grew out of the City College and Eastern High School glee clubs. The Alamedians opened their brief life with "The Vagabond King," were active during the fifties, and closed in 1958 with a production of "The Song of Norway" with Spiro Malas.

Virginia Irene Owen began the Valley Players, who were known after 1960 as the Metropolitan Musical Theatre. They performed in many Baltimore-Washington locales and boasted productions of "South Pacific" with Earl Wrightson and "The King and I" with Lois Hunt. Mrs. Owen introduced dinner theatre to local audiences at the Southern Hotel, and toured Pennsylvania dinner theatres during the early 1970s.

The Comic Opera Company, organized in 1962, originated with the St. David's Players in the church of the same name on Roland Avenue. They mounted 17 major productions of Gilbert and Sullivan and other light operas for the next eight years with Edward Leonard, William Hyder, and Arnie Lindquist as stage directors and Carl Dietrich as musical director. Their work included an acclaimed production of the first G & S collaboration: "Thespis; or, the Gods Grown Old." The most recent development in this community fascination with light opera is the Young Victorian Company, founded in 1978. It grew out of the Gilman Summer Theatre, which existed from 1971 to 1977. The Young Vic staged an impressive production of "The Mikado" in the Gilman Auditorium and promises to keep the tradition alive in fine fashion.

Other Groups

The oldest performing group still active in Baltimore is the Paint and Powder Club, founded in 1893 as an all-male vehicle for social satire in the mold of Harvard's Hasty Pudding. Its annual spoofs provide useful funds to city charitable organizations.

The Matthew Players have trained some of the best voices in Baltimore under the baton of Joseph Senatore.

The Jewish Community Center, under the watchful eye of Leon Siegel, has a long history of successful productions, first on Centre Street and later in the center on Park Heights Avenue.

During the mid-sixties, Barbara Copanos ran

a successful production of "The Fantasticks" in a cabaret theatre at the Stafford Hotel. Several independent productions staged by Dr. Ron Israel at the New Belvedere Hotel indicate that this type of entertainment may flower further.

Under the direction of Barbara Turk, the Brown Memorial Players turned to a modernized Biblical drama, which caused a stir in 1965 but has yet to be explored much further.

The Free Spirit Theatre, founded by Percy W. Thomas in 1975, hopes to "achieve institutional status as the Black National Historical Theatre," and has performed throughout the Baltimore area.

The Lovegrove Alley Theatre, established in 1978 by a small group of young actors, produced several little-known works by internationally famous writers before internal squabbles dissipated its efforts. One offshoot of this group, the Baltimore Esoteric Theatre, held its first production in 1979 and promises unusual work in the future.

The Baltimore Theatre Company, begun by Steve Yeager, promises to develop a nucleus of talented repertory players to perform the most recent, off-Broadway style plays from New York.

The Harbor Shakespeare Festival indicated that Baltimore is ready for the Bard as a regular attraction at the Inner Harbor.

Then there's the Mansion Theatre, Theatre-on-the-Hill, Ruxton Players, Texas Boots, and Double Joints Women's Theatre Company and . . . There's no room to provide a complete list of all the enterprising organizations active in Baltimore during the sixties and seventies. Some have already foundered; others won't survive much longer. Still others have the look of winners. "From their fruits you will know them."

Individuals

Dale Edward Fern deserves special mention for his spectacular productions, first at Mount St. Agnes College in the late sixties ("Mourning Becomes Electra"), at Loyola College in the early seventies ("More Stately Mansions"), and at the Cathedral Church of the Incarnation ("Hamlet"). Debbie London, active in Baltimore dance circles for 40 years, continues her service to all groups with her Cultural Arts Institute, founded in 1978 as both a school and musical theatre production center.

There are theatre "families" too, husband-and-wife teams who have worked hard and made a mark: Robert and Ruth Lawson Walsh, Audrey and Joseph Cimino, David and Martha Keltz, Bruce and Ruth Duncan. Alfredine Brown made valuable contributions to the theatre program at the Cultural Arts Project of the Urban Services Agency during the late seventies; her husband William has also added valuable technical expertise in his theatre work at UMBC and service with community groups in the summer.

Thousands of people in the Baltimore area labor every year as unsung heroes in amateur productions that are almost always marked by hard work and sometimes by true artistic distinction.

It would be a mistake to label such activity a renaissance yet. Too much work has yet to be done. For example, no significant local playwright has yet emerged, although a few, such as poet Daniel Mark Epstein, show promise. The theatres have yet to take advantage of the artistic collaborations inherent in the presence of the Maryland Institute College of Art and the Peabody Conservatory of Music. And local actors and directors still show the need for more extensive training.

The notion of artistic renaissance—an old American dream—has reemerged in the 1970s. It reflects Walt Whitman's statement in the 1870s that "the work of the New World is not ended but only fairly begun."

Eugene O'Neill hoped in 1931 for an "imaginative theatre" in America, "a theatre returned to its highest and sole significant function as a Temple where the religion of a poetical interpretation and symbolical celebration of life is communicated to human beings, starved in spirit by their soul-stifling daily struggle to exist as masks, among the masks of living!"

There is no reason why such theatre cannot grow in Baltimore, particularly among the amateurs who work out of a true love of the art. The seeds are already here. They await only the nourishment and nurture of human enterprise and imagination in the 1980s.

Laurlene Straughn Pratt and Earl Arnett

MECHANIC THEATRE

In 1959, playwright William Inge called Baltimore "the worst show town east of the Mississippi." Twenty years later, New York producers would be hailing the same city's audiences for their support of Broadway's offerings. During those years, commercial theatre had a bumpy existence. It was, in every sense of the phrase, the "Fabulous Invalid." Season–ticket subscriptions went from 4,700 during the 1958–1959 season, to nothing in 1975–1976 when there was no Broadway theatre here, to the current levels of about 17,000.

It was Baltimore's fate to be left with a sentimental favorite, but ancient playhouse, as the city entered the second half of the twentieth century. Ford's Theatre, which opened in 1871, was a relic by 1900. But in 1964, it was the city's only legitimate house. Oddly enough, it survived many of its competitors. Gone were the Holliday Street and Maryland theatres; the Academy of Music fell to become the Stanley, a movie palace that briefly served as a legitimate house; and the Auditorium, that still stands, but as a third–rate movie house.

Ford's, built by the family who owned the Washington house of the same name where President Lincoln was assassinated, had been purchased in 1942 by Morris A. Mechanic. He was a man who entered show business indifferently in 1929, when he purchased Lexington

Mechanic Theatre. Photo by M. E. Warren.

Street's New Theatre (a movie house) as a temporary investment. When he died in 1966, he was remembered as one of local theatre's foremost proponents and an astute businessman.

Ford's was well remembered by the generations of Baltimoreans who saw such performers there as Katharine Cornell, Tallulah Bankhead, Mae West, Judith Anderson, Henry Fonda, and Eva Le Gallienne. The place seated 1,800 persons in a rather compact area. This intimacy imparted good acoustics and sight lines. There was little thought given to restore this antique when in 1964 Mechanic announced its demolition. The final production was the musical comedy, "A Funny Thing Happened on the Way to the Forum."

Mr. Mechanic, who was born in Poland and immigrated to Baltimore as a child, was a graduate of City College and the Johns Hopkins University. He had scores of real estate interests in Baltimore—including the Hotel Belvedere, apartment houses and garages and major downtown movie theatres. When the city started massive urban renewal projects in the 1950s and 1960s, Mechanic stated he wanted to be a part of the rebuilding.

He was sensitive to the nostalgic sentiments of audiences who stuck by the old Ford's, but he said the building must go. He believed that it was no longer safe; it was unsound and was a fire hazard. In the early months of 1964, only a few years before Washington's Ford's Theatre would be restored to the legitimate theatre it was, Baltimore's Ford's was torn down and replaced by a parking garage.

The city was now without a live house, and those groups who had worked to prevent the demolition of Ford's wondered if Baltimore would ever have another live theatre.

The answer lay with the builders of Charles Center which was, at the time, several years underway. Those behind the project said that the new center would include a legitimate theatre and only required a builder.

Meanwhile, the Painters Mill Music Fair presented shows that might have played Ford's. After lengthy discussion about the possible conversion of the Hippodrome or the Stanley into a temporary live house, the Stanton (formerly the Stanley) was chosen and used as a live theatre for one season.

The Stanley, however, was much too large for

(1869)... the time when... was very... management prom-... condition... a... from two-thirds of the way back; ... Final of Virginia... Window Shade ... among the ... On the ...

The ... World, however, was not ideal, and the city was again faced with the possibility of ... At this point ... Morris Mechanic announced that he would build a new theatre as part of Charles Center ... he intended to lease the ground, the site of the old Sunpapers ... for 75 years at $35,000 a year. He also pledged to raise the money himself, and he ... It was all private capital.

The groundbreaking ceremony took place on November 15, 1964. Anticipation was high as construction continued according to plan. The new Morris A. Mechanic Theatre opened January 16, 1967, with Betty Grable starring in "Hello, Dolly."

The opening, unfortunately, was too late for Mechanic, who had died six months before. His widow, Clarisse Mechanic, assumed command ... project. The theatre, when finally finished, cost approximately $4.3 million.

The shops and the restaurant that were part of the complex were designed to produce approximately $400,000 in annual rentals that would enable the managers of the Mechanic to operate so long as the income offset expenses.

It did for several seasons. The James Nederlander Corporation, based in New York, leased the theatre from Mrs. Mechanic for ten years, and the future held promise. The subscription list reached 18,000, one of the highest in the country, and the Nederlanders proceeded to bring a succession of quality productions to Baltimore.

Community response remained high for a few seasons, but then lessened. When the operation was no longer profitable to them, the Nederlanders announced that they would prefer to break their lease. If that could not be arranged, they would have to convert the Mechanic into a movie house, they said.

The uncertainty of the Mechanic Theatre's future in this period was reflected in the commercial outlets that surrounded the playhouse.

In particular, the Charcoal Hearth Restaurant, which occupied the southern half of the structure, was in and out of business. Its closings disappointed many theatregoers who enjoyed a full night out, with dinner before and drinks after a performance.

Mayor Schaefer and the downtown merchants were not pleased with the Mechanic's demise. Three leading citizens, organized as Baltimore Theatre, Inc., assumed control of the theatre. The late Howard Owen, who was married to a niece of Mrs. Mechanic and was head of the Fire Board at the time, was one of these three. The others were Jack Fruchtman, the owner and operator of a chain of movie houses which included the New; and the late Frank Roberts, a businessman and sports promoter.

Baltimore Theatre, Inc. managed the Mechanic for two years. Then they, too, announced that the operation was unprofitable and that they would have to use the house for the showing of films.

Once more, civic leaders and owners of the downtown restaurants protested. They reasoned that they didn't want movies shown at the Mechanic because film patrons wouldn't be likely to patronize other businesses already in the area. They said they preferred a live theatre, which they hoped would be attended by patrons who would visit restaurants for dinner before or after the show.

It was at this point that the city became involved in the operation of the theatre at the cost of $600,000 to settle the debts of Baltimore Theatre, Inc. During that time, the Mechanic remained closed for 18 months.

The city, under then Housing Commissioner Robert C. Embry, Jr., invested $500,000 to improve the Mechanic with better lighting, seating, and acoustics. It also completely revamped the old Charcoal Hearth restaurant into the now-popular Café des Artistes and Food Bazaar—a row of small eating spots that do a brisk lunch-time business.

When the Mechanic reopened on November 1, 1976, with George C. Scott in "The Sly Fox," Alexander Cohen, New York impresario, was in control. The city had made an arrangement with Cohen, who pledged to promote theatre in Baltimore. He began by bringing a number of personalities to town for a gala luncheon at the Hilton Hotel.

Among the shows that were brought here under the Cohen aegis were "Anna Christie," "Hellzapoppin," "Bed Before Yesterday," "Equus," "Same Time, Next Year," "A Matter of Gravity," and "Golda."

The arrangement was a profitable one for Cohen. He received 12 percent of the box-office gross plus $5 for every new subscription and $4 for every renewal. His estimated "salary" was $180,000 for the first season and a similar figure for the second. When the city asked him to revise his contract for a third season, he declined and withdrew from the operation.

The theatre is currently under the management of a group of people employed by the city. Working in association with the Theatre Guild, their first season, 1978-1979, was a success. Carol Channing's "Hello, Dolly" played to full houses, "Music Man" did excellent business, and "The Kingfisher," starring Rex Harrison and Claudette Colbert, did equally well.

The theatre continues to operate at a loss, but the management says it can cope with the deficit. The first year Cohen was in charge, the deficit was $711,000. The following year, when the theatre became a property of the municipal government, the loss was reduced to $300,000.

Barring unforeseen circumstances, the Morris A. Mechanic Theatre should be at a break-even basis within a few years, as the Inner Harbor development attracts increasing numbers of visitors to the downtown area.

Lou Cedrone

CENTER STAGE

"Neither way out or way in" is how one critic described Center Stage in March, 1963. At that time it was Baltimore's newest and only professional little theatre. In January of that year, Center Stage had opened its doors at 45 West Preston Street, in a second floor walk-up of a remodeled gymnasium. The Greek Orthodox Cathedral of the Annunciation had once used the auditorium. The theatre-in-the-round seated 241 people and suggested "an air of quiet affluence with its carpeting and chandeliers."

Sixty-five businessmen decided that the city needed a good resident professional theatre. Center Stage Associates, Inc. was the name of the profit-making corporation that founded the theatre and sold shares of stock.

About an hour before the first performance of its initial performance, "La Ronde," the new theatre was inspected by the Baltimore city fire chief, who insisted on cancelling the opening because of the lack of a necessary fire exit. After some last-minute negotiations with Mayor Thomas D'Alesandro III, Center Stage opened as scheduled. The next day construction began on that additional exit. Unfortunately, the back of a bank vault—about which no one knew—blocked the exit. Thousands of dollars later, the exit was completed.

The opening night incident was the first in a series of unexpected expenditures that escalated until by the end of the second season Center Stage was $90,000 in debt. The first season had operated on a $45,000 budget for an eight-play, five-month season. All the original investors lost their money and then realized that the only way to survive was to become a nonprofit organization. Each investor did become a founding member of the new group. As a nonprofit corporation, Center Stage was eligible for support from government agencies and private individuals through tax-deductible charitable gifts.

On Preston Street, a new play opened every two weeks—an ambitious undertaking for any theatre. Despite the strain, under the direction of Edward Golden the theatre struggled to im-

"Measure for Measure" at Center Stage. Photo by Richard Anderson.

prove its professional standards and to build an audience.

By 1965, Center Stage needed more space. The old Oriole Cafeteria on North Avenue became the second home. About $85,000 was spent to convert this building into an intimate 296-seat thrust stage. (These seats, incidentally, were purchased for five dollars each from Lincoln Center, which was having acoustical problems and wanted to get rid of them.)

During the ensuing years, Center Stage developed a resident company and attracted about 5,700 subscribers. By 1971, the theatre had presented over 60 productions, two of which were moved to New York ("Slow Dance on the Killing Ground" and "Park") and the Young People's Theatre was touring schools throughout the state of Maryland. The total budget was up to $450,000, but the accumulated deficit had reached its highest point ever. However, the theatre had reached a turning point in its history. Based on its growing reputation for fine quality theatre and management, Center Stage began to meet its fund-raising goals and, for the first time, its operating needs. Through the help of a major grant from the Ford Foundation, the accumulated deficit was eliminated and the theatre moved forward.

On January 9, 1974, following the opening of "Who's Afraid of Virginia Woolf," the theatre on North Avenue burned to the ground. Donald Rothman, current chairman of the board and one of the original founders, recalls his feelings when he first learned of the fire: "Everything was lost in the fire—props, costumes. . . . I thought the fire was the end of Center Stage. . . . Eleven years of work to bring the theatre to a peak of artistic achievement and community support seemed destroyed in the fire. . . . I didn't see how we could go on."

The community recognized the theatre's value and importance to the city and rallied to its support. The next day the show reopened at the Baltimore Museum of Art after missing only one performance. The following week, the production was moved to the College of Notre Dame, where the 1973–74 season was completed.

Instead of planning a 1974–75 season, all energy went into locating a new home for Center Stage. The century-old Loyola College building at Calvert and Monument Streets, adjacent to St. Ignatius Church, became the new home. The building had been vacant and for sale for five years. Baltimore city paid $200,000 to the Jesuits (the owners), who in turn donated the money to Center Stage. The city then sold the property to Center Stage for five dollars. Additional money came from the National Endowment for the Arts, the Ford Foundation, Baltimore city area banks, and private contributions.

A $1.8 million Center Stage officially opened its new building on December 9, 1975, with a production of "Tartuffe." It had 11,500 subscribers, more than twice the number it had before the fire.

In the 1978–79 season, after 13,000 subscriptions were sold, sales had to be stopped. During the 1979–80 season, each play was performed an additional week, or five weeks altogether in order to sell a larger number of subscriptions. Over 120,000 theatregoers attend Center Stage each year.

An original production of "A Christmas Carol," "Scrooge and Marley," an adaption by Israel Horovitz, premiered in 1978 and repeated in 1979. In addition, in 1978, Center Stage collaborated with the Maryland Center for Public Broadcasting on a television version of "Bartleby the Scrivener." It was broadcast nationally and won many awards, including Best Dramatic Program in 1978 from the Public Broadcasting System.

The Young People's Theatre, which is part of Center Stage, tours schools in Baltimore city as well as the counties; it has played to over 100,000 people. Several internship programs and theatre classes have been started at the theatre.

Besides the six-play mainstage subscription series, the theatre offers the Center Stage Hands, "Summer Cinema," the Baltimore Film Forum, fashion shows, jazz concerts, and other community events. Orchestra Piccola performed there. A 1980 innovation was First Stage, a program designed to provide workshops for new scripts as well as the means of testing new conceptual approaches to proven texts and the discovery of performance styles appropriate to them.

In 1978, the completed building received a national award from the American Institute of Architects (AIA) for outstanding "adaptive reuse of an old building, one of the ten leading architectural achievements in Maryland in the past five years."

Center Stage has become one of the top 10 resident professional theatres in the country. Restaurants and retail stores in the area have increased their business drawn by Center Stage theatregoers. From its humble beginnings on Preston Street, it has become a major force in American regional theatre today. Center Stage is now firmly established as one of Baltimore's major cultural institutions and remains an integral part of the continuing renaissance of the city.

Ron Israel

CHILDREN'S THEATRE ASSOCIATION

The Children's Experimental Theatre began in 1941 as CET, but later changed its name to the Children's Theatre Association. Isabel Burger began CTA as an educational experiment in creative drama. It was listed as the only member of the Baltimore Council of Social Agencies designed to serve youth through drama.

The uniqueness of this designation highlights the distinction between children's theatre and creative drama for children. The former is theatre tailored for children's entertainment and performed by adults; the latter refers to drama by and for children.

Though in existence for nearly four decades, CTA has yet to find a permanent home. From 1944 to 1949, CTA was located in the Vagabond Theatre. It was during this period that CTA grew from an educational experiment. It was invited to become a member of the Baltimore Council of Social Agencies, incorporating as the Children's Theatre Association, Inc.

From 1949 to 1963, CTA was located on Ploy Street at the old Carriage House, the group's first real theatre, which seated 70 people.

From 1949 to 1950, CTA was asked to experiment with the medium of television by presenting three 20-minute episodes of "A Christmas Carol," sponsored by the McCormick Company. By 1950, the calendar of events included drama classes, rehearsals for major productions, Min-

Children's Theatre Association's Performance of "Black Moses," 1976–77. Photo by Jerry Woods.

iature Matinees performed by the children, Teachers' Training classes in creative drama, and scene-building sessions.

This was merely the beginning of CTA's recognition as a major force in children's creative drama. In 1953, Ms. Burger was invited to attend UNESCO's International Theatre Institute's Fifth World Conference in The Hague as a delegate from the United States to the Commission for Theatre and Youth.

Though the next five years brought similar international acclaim, local support in Baltimore and the surrounding counties was lacking. Financial difficulties, lack of staff, and the inability to sell Baltimoreans season tickets led to a suspension of all CTA activities in 1959. A Ways and Means Committee sought to determine if CTA was in fact fulfilling a need in the city and if, through state or private subsidy, financial assistance to the association could be found.

An Honorary Advisory Board, headed by Grace Campbell, was created, private donations were increased, and the findings of the Ways and Means Committee were acted upon. Plans were formulated for producing three plays in four high schools, with the hope of encouraging a wider audience. The efforts brought success: the 1961 to 1962 season resulted in substantial increases in both subscription audience and class waiting lists.

Showmobile, a touring company on wheels that took live children's theatre to the rural areas of the state, was begun in 1962. By the end of 1963, subscribers were still increasing, performances were crowded or sold out, and WBAL-TV was sponsoring eight Showmobile performances. Calls for benefits, lectures, and other services were pouring in.

However, the ensuing years, with their awakening in youth of political and social consciousness, brought about a dwindling in the number of applicants for membership in CTA. Children were more politically active and had less time for theatre. As participation dwindled during the remainder of the decade, the quality of the plays dropped, as did community support.

A new era for the Children's Theatre Association began in 1972, accompanied by another relocation, this time to the Baltimore Museum of Art. The next year CTA began using actors from Actors Equity Association. The basis for the change to Equity was then-director Carl Pistilli's belief that theatre for children should be performed by professionally trained creative actors. Pistilli and others within CTA felt that Equity, though expensive, would not only assure high quality drama, but would give a new credibility to children's theatre. Main stage performances by the children became limited to a final class play. The plays performed by the adults became more sophisticated in subject matter.

Impractical logistics and expenses led to the demise of the Showmobile in 1973. The Equity group, however, began touring schools again in 1974, in addition to performing main stage productions.

In 1975, the Board of Education and the City Council passed a proposal providing that, in exchange for use of stage facilities, CTA would begin a theatre arts program at Lake Clifton High School. The city-funded pilot program was to run for three years. Though successful, the city's unexpected cancellation of funds in the fall of 1978 brought an abrupt end to the program.

A further setback was a fire at the high school on March 13, 1979, that caused the loss of Lake Clifton as a performance center. The fire also destroyed $20,000 worth of CTA equipment.

However, CTA continued offering classes and touring schools with professionally produced plays for children. As the 1980s decade began, class attendance doubled and performances of the CTA increased. Under the artistic direction of Jason Rubin, in the 1980–81 season the troupe performed 154 times in 11 counties and Baltimore city. Although CTA dropped Equity affiliation in 1981, another professional company was formed. Also, the hopes of finding a new home in close proximity to the other arts organizations was on the horizon as CTA shared in the arts renaissance.

Cathy Dryden

THEATRE PROJECT: ALTERNATIVE VISIONS

Theatre Project opened in 1971 under the aegis of Antioch College. Since that time it has become an independent entity. It bought its 100-year-old building from the city of Baltimore, established itself as a major link in an international network of "alternative" theatre and dance groups, and offered nearly 2,000 free performances by 300 professional companies.

Founder/director Philip Arnoult had a vision of his theatre as a meeting place where artists, students, and audiences could gather to share their knowledge, ideas, and art. This vision infuses every aspect of the Theatre Project's many activities.

At Theatre Project, the traditional mechanisms that distance artists from those around them have been eliminated. The hat (a floppy leather one) is literally passed at the end of each performance. No box office or ticket sales are needed. The suggested donation is three dollars—but members of the audience are free to give more, less, or nothing. The seating arrangement also offers choices. There are normal seats, lofts, and cushions on the floor. And there is no formal stage; instead, the artists are free to choose the size and shape of their performing area. Over the years, the "stage" has ranged from a tiny black-curtained box to the entire room.

Theatre Project's audience profile reflects this

Mime Performs in a Series of Concerts at the Theatre Project, 1976.

theatres and companies, "the flagship of alternative theatres" (*Milwaukee Journal*, 5/1/77). These groups share Mr. Arnoult's vision that their art is generated by and for the great majority of people who don't or can't normally attend live performances. Their goal is to "bring the people into the theatre." Failing that, they are quite willing to "take the theatre to the people"—by performing in churches, schools, prisons, hospitals, on street corners and river rafts, or in parks and in circus-like caravans.

Largely through Mr. Arnoult's efforts as an organizer of the New Theatre Festival '76 at the University of Maryland, Baltimore County, alternative theatre groups are forming regional networks for touring and information-sharing. And, as the United States delegate to the International Theatre Institute's New Theatre Committee, Mr. Arnoult is a link between this United States network and the rest of the world.

Presentation in the main space is only one of the Theatre Project's functions. It has become an interdisciplinary community arts center. The dance studio offers a wide range of low-cost classes (from modern to tap to yoga and more) and is becoming a center for local dance artists. The Baltimore Neighborhood Arts Circus trains some 60 city youths each year in performance skills and then tours Baltimore throughout the summer, bringing performances and workshops to over 170,000 city residents. And, for the Baltimore Neighborhood Heritage Project (a joint venture with the University of Baltimore), the Theatre Project developed theatre presentations based on oral histories gathered in six city neighborhoods. These theatre pieces were presented at the project itself, on television, and—like the circus—toured the city extensively, as part of a traveling neighborhood museum.

There was a time, not so very long ago, when "alternative theatre" meant esoteric, avant-garde, experimental. Theatre Project is one of a growing family of theatres and companies around the world that is changing that definition.

John Strausbaugh

informal, unusual atmosphere. The traditional "theatre crowd" is predominantly white, well-off, and well-educated. A 1978 survey shows that 54 percent of Theatre Project's audience hold blue collar or clerical jobs; 69 percent earn under $15,000 a year; and 84 percent are under 40 years of age.

Theatre Project rarely mounts its own productions; it is a host theatre. In eight years it has presented groups from over 23 states and 12 foreign countries. In this way, as well as through Mr. Arnoult's ceaseless touring and proselytizing, it has become a nexus for a wide family of

THE ONLY INTERNATIONAL THEATRE FESTIVAL IN THE UNITED STATES IS IN BALTIMORE!

International Theatre Festival Comes to Baltimore, 1977.

Nowhere is the spirit of Baltimore's renaissance more clearly captured than in its festivals, the largest of which is the Baltimore International Theatre Festival. Each June Baltimore hosts an unprecedented three–week celebration of the world's finest theatre. Downtown Baltimore becomes the stage for America's only international theatre festival with performances offered from Mt. Vernon to the Inner Harbor, utilizing such institutions as Center Stage, the Walters Art Gallery, the Baltimore School for the Arts, and the Morris A. Mechanic Theatre, as well as the city's streets, parks, and plazas.

Modeled after such classical European festivals as Edinburgh, Avignon, and Belgrade, the Baltimore International Theatre Festival provides a unique opportunity for local, national, and international audiences to experience the world's finest theatre, ranging in style from classical to contemporary to the avant–garde. During the festival there are performances by some of the world's most distinguished theatre companies, an ongoing program of children's theatre, a "solo series" of one person performances, daily workshops, and seminars exploring the process of theatre, and a nightly cabaret featuring everything from vaudeville to musical theatre. In short, the festival is the largest single theatrical event in the United States!

It is the only international theatre festival in this country and fulfills two vital functions. First, it provides a rare opportunity for international cultural exchange, where audiences are able to experience the finest international theatre and where theatre artists and students from around the world can share and explore their craft. Secondly, the festival makes a major contribution to Baltimore's economic development as a unique national cultural event that attracts tourists from all over America and abroad.

The Baltimore International Theatre Festival is a nonprofit cultural organization which is

"TNT," 1979. Photo by Ric Bartter.

made possible with the support of the National Endowment for the Arts, the Maryland Arts Council, the Mayor's Advisory Committee on Art and Culture, the Mayor's Office of Manpower Resources, the Baltimore Center for the

Performing Arts, the Baltimore Office of Promotion and Tourism, national and local foundations and corporations, private contributors, and numerous Baltimore cultural and educational institutions. The festival's precursor was the New Theatre Festival, which began on the campus of the University of Maryland, Baltimore County. From 1976 to 1979, it brought together over 100 theatre companies from 17 nations in a convocation of new and experimental theatre artists. In 1980, the festival's board of directors decided to broaden the range of theatre presented and to establish the Baltimore International Theatre Festival as a major national event.

The 1981 Baltimore International Theatre Festival featured some of the world's most prestigious theatre companies, such as the Abbey Theatre from Ireland, the Habimah National Theatre of Israel, and the Greek Art Theatre from Athens. Companies came from England, Africa, Spain, Japan, India, Canada, the U.S.A., and even a one-ring family circus from France. It was the largest gathering of theatre ever in our country's history.

The goal of the Baltimore International Theatre Festival and the city of Baltimore, working together, is to enhance what is already in place: the city's commitment to culture, its history of celebrations and festivals, and its great ethnic heritage. It is altogether fitting that Baltimore is known across the world as America's International Theatre Festival City.

Al Kraizer

Filmmaking in Baltimore: 1956–1979

Mention the word "movies" and what flashes to mind? A strip of celluloid? A movie house? A huge, moneymaking industry?

And what cities does one associate with filmmaking? New York? Los Angeles?

How about Baltimore? It's no Hollywood, but the fact is, this city *does* have an active film community.

Film today means different things to different people: independent features—feature-length films produced by independent filmmakers; documentaries; industrial training films, films for any of the numerous governmental agencies; film exhibitors—film exhibitions, festivals, and competitions.

Baltimore is fortunate to have talented filmmakers here, but it is unfortunate that the filmmaking community itself happens to be splintered. In fact, it is so splintered that any definitive list as to who's who is impossible. Yet, there are some names that repeatedly stand out: Monumental Films, Milner-Fenwick, Vince Clews &

Associates, B F & J Productions, Mike Lawrence Films, Stan VanDerBeek, and John Waters, among others.

By 1956, a number of film companies were already established in Baltimore. Both Monumental Films and Milner-Fenwick had been in operation for over five years. Monumental, established in 1947, now works in both industrial training and governmental film areas. Milner-Fenwick, established in 1949 as a production house for advertisers, now focuses on the health education field. In addition to this work, Milner-Fenwick also handles marketing and distribution of its films.

Side-by-side with these long-established companies is the newer Vince Clews & Associates, which is also involved in educational and training films. Clews is a veteran of the media in Baltimore. Before starting his own company, he was a producer with the Maryland Center for Public Broadcasting for 10 years. He was the creator and producer of the center's nationally carried "Consumer Survival Kit." Today, after four years of business, Vince Clews' roster of clients includes more than 15 government and business organizations.

As the medium of film grew technically over the years, so did the producers' finesse. Films as a whole have changed people into moviegoers, but more importantly, they've changed the way we see things. Television commercials are a prime example of a producer's cinematic dexterity.

In 1964, B F & J Productions was established. Four years later, the firm won a Cleo Award, the advertising industry's most prestigious honor. B F & J won a second Cleo in 1974, this one for a commercial on the Mayor's Trash Ball campaign.

B F & J is not alone in excellence in commercial production. In 1967, Academy Film Productions was established. Six years later, they won two Cleos—one for Best Demonstration and one for Best Home Furnishings.

While client–related productions were thriving, so too was an almost diametrically opposed field—documentaries. In 1973, Mike Lawrence of Michael Lawrence Films produced "Spacecraft America," a satirical look at this country at the time of President Nixon's reelection. The film won awards in Atlanta and Baltimore. In 1975, Mr. Lawrence produced a documentary on a "new age" educational center. "The 30 Second Dream" was next, produced in 1977. "Dream," a film funded by Mass Media Ministries in Baltimore, discusses television commercials. Mr. Lawrence's fourth work, "The Shared Experience," was written by Arthur Seidel and Terry Brandon. The film focuses on the transmission of human experience throughout the ages. It was shown on public television in New York. Mr. Lawrence, who studied music at the Peabody Institute, is currently working on a film about music.

Two years after Mike Lawrence began working on films, Stan VanDerBeek came to town. Mr. VanDerBeek fills a category all by himself; only a handful of people have his background and expertise in experimental film. He sees film as the most significant art form of our time, and his concern is with the aesthetic. An instructor at UMBC who teaches classes on approaches in film and film theory, Mr. VanDerBeek tries to integrate technology into art. He is now working on computer graphics, which is actually a branching out of traditional animation. His works have been in major festivals all over the world.

At the other end of the scale from the aesthetic film is the film produced as a commercial venture. John Waters has been producing independent commercial films in Baltimore since 1964. He has completed 10 films to date, each more popular than the last. Mr. Waters usually has no problem booking his films into a theatre and he now finances a new film, in part, with the profits from the others.

Another local firm, Cinemonde International, produced a feature film on Benjamin Banneker, an early black scientist, in 1978. The film was televised and marketed to educators.

But what if, as a filmmaker, you *can't* get films into theatres? The Baltimore Film Forum, the Maryland Film Guild, and the Chaplain's Office of the Johns Hopkins University fill the need. Each organization exhibits films, but each is a distinctly different group. The forum, which began about five years ago, is a cultural organization that promotes the art of film. It sponsors a film festival as well as an independent filmmakers' competition. The guild, on the other hand, exhibits strictly local films. In addition, the guild exists to bring Baltimore filmmakers together. However, not many producers take advantage of the guild; today it remains merely a loose association of filmmakers. The Chaplain's Office is an institutionally motivated group, with a somewhat different goal than either the forum or the guild. The Chaplain's Office film series, a nonprofit organization, is one of the best in town.

Many other people are involved in the Baltimore film community; not all could be covered here. No list, though, would be nearly complete without including the noteworthy contributions of Harvey Alexander, Leroy Morais, Michael Frommeyer, and Rachel Wohl.

Stephen J. Gordon

Music

RECENT CLASSICAL GROUPS

Since World War II, music and the sponsorship of music in the United States have flourished as in no other period of American history. One index to such prosperity is the increase in the budget of the National Endowment for the Arts. In 1963, when it was created, barely $3 million was allocated. The budget in 1979 was approximately $150 million. From a local perspective, another indication of such growth is the operational budget of the Maryland Arts Council. In 1967, when it came into existence as a result of an order by Spiro Agnew, then governor of the state, its budget was approximately $50,000; in 1979 it rose to $1.7 million.

From 1950 to 1961, a typical concert season in Baltimore consisted of approximately 60 events, as reported in the pages of the local newspapers. With such a limited number of presentations, it was possible for the *Sunpapers* to allocate the responsibility for music criticism to a writer who was also delegated various nonmusical journalistic duties. From 1962 to 1977, as the number of events increased, criticism in the *Sun*, whose coverage of the arts has been the most comprehensive of all newspapers in the city, became the responsibility of a writer, an individual who was also a faculty member of two local colleges. Because of Baltimore's dynamic calendar of events during the past two years, it was necessary in 1977 for the *Sunpapers* to engage a full-time critic.

The expansion of the musical season in the city has been consistent and vigorous. By 1974, the number of public musical events was six times more than it had been a decade earlier, and double the number in 1969. Since 1974, it has not increased dramatically; it has reached a plateau of about 600. Examination of the present annual musical calendar in Baltimore reveals the existence of a wide variety of performers, ensembles, and repertories. The musical season consists of programs that range from medieval and Renaissance repertories, to opera, symphonic, and chamber music, as well as electronic and experimental works.

In its "rug concerts" the Peabody Conservatory's Contemporary Music Ensemble has presented unusual programs, preceded by talks by distinguished composers—for example, a program of the works of Elliott Carter, with the composer as commentator, and a Varèse program with remarks by the venerable Otto Luening.

Similar sponsorship by music departments of area colleges in Baltimore and throughout the nation has become a unique phenomenon since World War II, and confirms the observation of Harold Taylor, former president of Sarah Lawrence College, that it is the colleges and the universities who have developed into "the true impresarios of the arts in America."

Elliott Galkin

BALTIMORE'S MUSIC: "A WILD CRESCENDO"

Classical music in all its forms has come into its own in Baltimore. Today the concert–goer may choose from a wide selection of events, ranging from intimate trios to hundred–voiced choirs. Devotees of both baroque and contemporary music will be equally satisfied; and those who care about authenticity may attend concerts of Renaissance music performed on lutes, sackbuts, shawms, and virginals. Lovers of choral music may hear masses, motets, cantatas, and oratorios from the past six centuries sung by excellent choirs. And all of this is in addition to Baltimore's nationally acclaimed symphony orchestra.

Baltimore's music calendar was not always so full, however, nor so varied. Most of the current ensembles and concert series were established in the past twenty years, creating what Lubov Keefer, the "grande dame" of Baltimore's music community, describes as "a wild crescendo." In the 1950s, the symphony's season lasted only six months and, besides the newly formed Chamber Music Society and the two or three performances of the Handel Choir, there was little else of note. Newspapers listed about 60 events in the average season. Today, in contrast, there are nearly 600 events throughout the year.

The Chamber Music Society. The founding of the Chamber Music Society of Baltimore in 1950 by local music lovers was the first effort after World War II to develop the city's musical life. It began as an idea shared by a local pianist, Richard Goodman, and composer Hugo Weisgall, then teaching in Massachusetts. In July, 1950, they brought together local musicians and music–lovers to organize a society with a twofold purpose: to attract first–class performers to Baltimore, and to offer the community programs of chamber music not feasible for the symphony to present. A three–man committee was chosen to supervise the project—Mr. Goodman; Dr. Edward Davens, a local pediatrician; and James Winship Lewis, then director of the Handel Choir.

The first concerts, a series of four, were given on successive Wednesday nights in April, 1951, in the Catherine Hooper Hall at the old Goucher College. They were very well received. Local performers, conducted by the society's music director, Hugo Weisgall, played music that ranged from Schubert to Stravinsky and Hindemith. One of the four concerts was devoted entirely to vocal music, and included both early madrigals and modern songs by Poulenc and Ravel.

Richard Goodman presided over the society until he was replaced by Randolph S. Rothschild in 1954. Under Mr. Rothschild the society began inviting more out–of–town ensembles to Baltimore, introducing local audiences to the nation's best musicians. Nevertheless, at least one concert a year has been devoted to local artists.

Also, the society has consistently encouraged local composers, premiering works by Gordon Cyr, Lawrence Moss, Robert Hall Lewis, and others.

The Chamber Music Society has always been committed to fostering public interest in contemporary music. It was the first organization in the country to invite composers to talk regularly about their music before it is performed. Among the many who have done this are Aaron Copland, Karel Husa, George Rochberg, Roger Sessions, and Gunther Schuller.

In the late fifties, as other chamber music series developed in the area, the society began to devote its programs exclusively to twentieth–century music, and since 1961, has given at least one concert a season which consisted entirely of the most recent music. Also in the sixties, the society expanded its range to include international as well as American contemporary music. For example, it sponsored the American premiere of the Czech composer Jindrich Feld.

In honor of its tenth anniversary in 1958, the society awarded its first commission. This went to Leon Kirchner for his "Concerto for Violin, Cello, Ten Winds, and Percussion" that was performed in 1959 with the composer conducting. A second commission was awarded in 1962 to Hugo Weisgall, then still music director. When Dr. Weisgall left Baltimore in the mid–sixties, he was replaced by Robert Hall Lewis, who was awarded the commission for the society's twentieth anniversary.

Under Dr. Lewis' direction, an annual commission for chamber music has been awarded in recent years, thanks to grants and private donations. Thus the Chamber Music Society of Baltimore has become one of the nation's foremost organizations encouraging young composers.

After the first concerts at Goucher College, the society's programs were regularly held in the auditorium of the Baltimore Museum of Art, excepting the 1977–1978 season when they were at the Langsdale Library of the University of Baltimore. Due to the museum's renovation in 1979, the concerts were temporarily moved to the Harvey M. Meyerhoff Center for the Performing Arts at the Park School in Brooklandville, Maryland.

Summer Chamber Music Festival. The first

serious attempt in recent times to provide musical refreshment during Baltimore's muggy summers was the Summer Chamber Music Festival, founded in 1961 by harpsichordist Shirley Matthews. Performers came from all over America to play at the weekly concerts held at the Park School, though many local musicians participated also. Primarily baroque and classical, the concerts ranged from duo recitals of cello and harpsichord to chamber orchestra, and included the first Baltimore performance since 1792 of Pergolese's chamber opera "La Serva Padrona." This series lasted four summers before it was ended by a long newspaper strike which cut off all publicity.

Ms. Matthews' company then changed its name to Festivals, Inc. and began a series devoted to baroque chamber music, giving four or five concerts per year at Goucher College in Towson during the regular season. The artists were mostly faculty and students from the Peabody Conservatory. This series ran from 1965 to 1972.

In 1974, Shirley Matthews formed another group, the Musicians Company, which sponsored a series of mostly baroque and Renaissance concerts at Goucher College. In 1978, the Musicians Company was incorporated into the recently formed Pro Musica Rara.

Pro Musica Rara is one of the very few chamber orchestras in the country playing on authentic Renaissance and baroque instruments. At their first concert, however, they used modern instruments. This free, 2½-hour concert was given on April 20, 1975, at the Mt. Vernon Place United Methodist Church. Calling themselves "The Baroque Soloists," the musicians, most of whom were from the winds section of the Baltimore Symphony Orchestra, had simply decided to put on a concert for their own enjoyment. This met with a great success, so oboist Joseph Turner and trumpeter Rob Roy McGregor began to advertise their fifteen-member orchestra. With the new name, Pro Musica Rara, the group played for various local concert series during the next two seasons. They also gave a special free Christmas concert at the Walters Art Gallery with the Baltimore Choral Arts Society in 1975. This has since become an annual tradition. Mr. Turner served as the ensemble's music director, and Mr. McGregor was its manager.

Pro Musica Rara Performers.

In the spring of 1976, the musicians began to experiment with authentic Renaissance and baroque instruments, which are constructed and tuned differently from modern ones. Soon they became committed to the idea of approximating as nearly as possible the original sound, modeling their orchestra after the Viennese company Consentus Musicus of Nikolaus Harnocourt.

A year later, having nothing lined up for the next season, Pro Musica Rara decided to initiate its own concert series. These were held at Loyola College and were free, supported by voluntary contributions and the Musicians Union. The next season, 1978–1979, the series was moved to Lovely Lane United Methodist Church, and, due to the company's expanding budget, admission was charged. In the spring of 1979, a two–concert Renaissance series was begun under the leadership of the company's lutenist, Roger Harmon. These compliment the four baroque concerts. In both series Pro Musica Rara provides Baltimoreans with a musical experience found in only four or five American cities.

Orchestra Piccola. A significant role in Baltimore's musical life was filled in 1976, when Saul Schechtman organized Orchestra Piccola (Italian for "small orchestra"), a chamber orchestra of winds and strings consisting of twenty–four musicians, most of whom also play with the symphony. Many musical works, especially from the classical and romantic eras, were written specifically for ensembles of this size, and are not suited for performance either by the large symphony orchestra or by the smaller chamber music groups. Mr. Schechtman is a conductor of international repute, having conducted the Philadelphia Symphony Orchestra and the Danish and Norwegian State Radio orchestras, among others. He had recently moved to Baltimore when the intimate setting of the new Center Stage theatre inspired him to form a chamber orchestra.

Local musicians were enthusiastic, and major financial support came from Sigmund M. Hyman and Robert L. Williams, both of the S. M. Hyman Company. The first season opened on a Monday evening at Center Stage, November 15, 1976, with the orchestra playing the music of Mozart, Haydn, Handel, and Dvorak.

Although there is a definite emphasis on music from the eighteenth century, especially Mozart, every concert of Orchestra Piccola includes at least one twentieth century work, and usually something from the romantic and baroque eras.

In addition to its regular three–concert series at Center Stage, Orchestra Piccola presents the same series at the Harford Community College.

Festival Chamber Players. In 1978, a new chamber music group was formed by Arno Drucker, the Baltimore Symphony pianist and head of the music department of Essex Community College. Called the Festival Chamber Players and funded by Baltimore County and the Maryland Arts Council, its original purpose was to fill the gap left in the summer music calendar when the Harford Opera Company went out of business. The three free concerts, all held in July at the Park School, were devoted to the music of Franz Schubert, commemorating the 150th anniversary of his death. Mr. Drucker's wife, soprano Ruth Drucker, was soloist at the second of these, which featured Schubert's lieder. Following the success of the Schubert festival, four free concerts of French chamber music were given the next summer. A summer Festival of Viennese chamber music was held in 1980, though for this series admission was charged.

First Tuesday Concert Society. The newest chamber society in the city is the First Tuesday Concert Society, founded by noted violinist Berl Senofsky and his fellow artists. They simply wanted to play the kind of music they enjoyed,

and they organized the society and gave four concerts at Goucher's Kraushaar Auditorium in the spring of 1979. The concerts were so well received that six concerts were planned for the 1979–1980 season. For both seasons Goucher College developed lectures for each concert. The repertoire of the players, who are all local artists, consists primarily of romantic and modern chamber works.

The Handel Choir. Alongside this dramatic increase of chamber music, Baltimore's choral offerings have developed significantly in the past 20 years. The Handel Choir, the city's oldest chorus, was founded in 1935 under the direction of Roman Steiner, and from its beginning has given at least two concerts a year, one of these being its annual Christmas performance of Handel's oratorio "The Messiah." The choir did not really gain any stability, however, until James Winship Lewis assumed its direction in 1948. By that time there had already been four conductors since Steiner.

Under Mr. Lewis' direction, the choir comprised at different times from 50 to 70 voices and awarded its first commission in 1958 to Alan Hovhaness for his oratorio, "Look Towards the Sea." This experimental work received mixed critical reactions. In 1964, Saul Lilienstein replaced Lewis as artistic director. Under his leadership a chamber ensemble was formed in 1966, which received a special award of merit in the 1969 Parade of American Music from the National Federation of Music Clubs. In 1967, the choir performed Handel's oratorio, "Israel in Egypt," as its first pre–Passover concert. It was accompanied by the Baltimore Symphony at the Chizuk Amuno Congregation synagogue.

Mr. Lilienstein left the choir in 1971 and was replaced by Ronald J. Gretz, who served as director and conductor for four years, and who greatly developed the contemporary repertory of the chorus. Darrold Hunt, then assistant conductor of the Baltimore Symphony, took over for two years after Mr. Gretz' departure. Herb Dimmock became the choir's artistic director in 1977.

Throughout its history the Handel Choir has given the city excellent performances of the music of George Friedrich Handel and has also developed a wide repertoire of other choral works, both sacred and secular, ranging from baroque to the present day. It has significantly encouraged local composers, singing the works of Baltimoreans such as Louis Cheslock, Thomas B. Dunn, Katherine E. Luck, and others. The Handel Choir usually performs at the Lyric Theatre and in various local churches and synagogues.

The Bach Society. The performance of Johann Sebastian Bach's motets and cantatas was the main reason for the founding of the Bach Society of Baltimore in 1959 by Dr. Wolfgang Christian Schroeder, a German physician then residing in Baltimore. Upon Dr. Schroeder's return to Europe in 1962, George R. Woodhead became director of this small choir of 20 to 30 singers. Following Mr. Woodhead's resignation in 1971, Ann Flaccavento, then concert mistress of the society's orchestra, assumed the position of music director. The small orchestra was soon disbanded, and the choir began to rely on piano, organ, or violin when accompaniment was required. Under Mrs. Flaccavento's direction, the singers have developed into a choral group of professional caliber.

Although still dedicated to Bach—they perform at least two new cantatas and two new motets a year—the repertoire of the chorus includes both sacred and secular music from the Renaissance to the present day. Four or five concerts are given each year in local churches and auditoriums; one of these has traditionally been devoted to instrumental music. From 1965 to 1979, harpsichordist Joseph Stephens gave an annual recital under the society's sponsorship.

Sacred Choirs. Baltimore is the home of one of the nation's finest sacred choirs, the Men and Boys Choir of the Cathedral of Mary Our Queen, which sings music from the Roman Catholic and Anglican traditions. Developed in the tradition of the English school of choral singing, it was founded in 1960 by the late Dr. Edward Cordon. Robert Twynham, the present director, assumed that position in 1961. The Cathedral Choir, in addition to singing the liturgy for Sunday Mass, gives two or three special concerts a year, including its Christmas Festival of Lessons and Carols, which it has presented annually since 1962. The choir also tours once a year, and has performed in every major cathedral from Hartford, Connecticut, to Richmond, Virginia.

Usually the men and boys perform together,

but the boys' choir occasionally sings separately. It has sung at both Baltimore's Lyric Theatre and New York City's Carnegie Hall. Nationally prominent, the choir sang at Lucy Johnson's wedding in 1966 and at the ecumenical service for Pope John Paul II on October 7, 1979, in the Trinity College chapel in Washington, D.C.

The Baltimore Choral Arts Society, the city's largest chorus, presented its first concert in the spring of 1967, performing Bach's "St. John Passion" at the Kraushaar Auditorium of Goucher College. Theodore Morrison, one of the founders of the company and its music director since its beginning, conducted the chorus. He is a native Baltimorean, organist, conductor, and composer who had served as choir director and organist for Baltimore's Episcopal Cathedral of the Incarnation for 10 years before becoming director of the Choral Arts Society.

The society was founded to fulfill two main purposes. The first was to give Baltimore audiences professional performances of major choral works written during the past 400 years, while adhering as nearly as possible to the composers' intentions. Thus, the size of the chorus may vary from a chamber ensemble of 20 voices to the majestic sound of 150 singers, though the chorus usually consists of about 100 voices. The second purpose was to bring internationally renowned soloists to Baltimore. Since its beginning, soloists from the New York City Opera, the Metropolitan Opera, and other major companies have sung with the choir. These include Elaine Bonazzi, Patricia Brooks, Thomas Paul, Charles Bressler, and the Metropolitan's leading baritone, Sherrill Milnes.

In the past four years, the society has begun to commission works. The first work commissioned was Norman Scribner's choral setting of Richard Crashaw's poem, "The Nativity," premiered by the chorus December, 1975, in honor of the society's tenth anniversary. Commissions have recently been awarded to Twynham, Morrison, and Scribner.

Various orchestras and chamber ensembles regularly accompany the group in their concert series, expanded in 1979 from three to five concerts. These accompanying groups include the Baltimore Symphony Orchestra, the Concerto Soloists of Philadelphia, and Pro Musica Rara, with whom they perform the annual Christmas concert at the Walters Art Gallery. Regular concerts are given at Kraushaar Auditorium, local churches and synagogues, and occasionally at the Lyric Theatre.

No review of Baltimore's music would be complete without mention of the Peabody Institute, which in 1977 became affiliated with the Johns Hopkins University. One of the nation's leading conservatories, the Peabody has over the years consistently offered Baltimoreans a large selection of concerts and recitals, featuring its orchestra, chamber ensemble, and contemporary music ensemble made up of faculty and gifted students. Many of these events have included talks by distinguished performers and composers.

In addition to the Peabody, the music departments of Catonsville Community College, Goucher College, Morgan State University, Towson State University, and the University of Maryland Baltimore County have developed significantly in the past 15 years. They have attracted many of the country's best musicians and composers to the area, as well as promoted local talent.

One group that meets in a college setting is the Greater Baltimore Flute Club. It meets and holds free recitals and lectures at Peabody Preparatory-Goucher College. The group includes other instruments than the flute in programs.

Concert series sponsored by local colleges and universities make up an important part of the city's cultural life. Perhaps the most noteworthy of these is the Shriver Hall concert series, sponsored by the Johns Hopkins University. Since its founding in 1965, this series has featured such outstanding artists as the Juilliard String Quartet, Rudolf Serkin, Jean-Pierre Rampal, and Mstislav Rostropovich.

As is evident from the number and variety of music organizations formed in the sixties and seventies, Baltimore has thrived in its musical offerings of recent years. This brief survey has touched only the highlights of the city's music calendar, which, though still centering around the fine symphony orchestra, radiates in all directions and virtually covers the entire field of classical music. Emerging from the culturally bland years that followed World War II, Baltimore has acquired a rich and varied cultural life that continues to offer newcomers and natives musical alternatives to Memorial Stadium and Pimlico.

Rawley M. Grau

The Baltimore Symphony Orchestra

The Baltimore Symphony Orchestra was born 65 years ago when it performed its first concert in Baltimore's Lyric Theatre on February 11, 1916. At that time, it was a municipal agency of the city—the first orchestra in the United States to be supported by public funds. The BSO's first music director was Gustav Strube, a former assistant conductor of the Boston Symphony and a faculty member of Baltimore's Peabody Conservatory. The BSO's first season comprised just three concerts, performed by 53 musicians, some of whom were imported from Philadelphia and other neighboring music centers.

Today, the BSO is one of America's busiest orchestras, performing more than 250 concerts a year to an audience of over 400,000. Its nearly 100 full-time musicians play a 45-week season under Maestro Sergiu Comissiona, Resident Conductor William Henry Curry, and Exxon-Arts Endowment Conductor Alan Balter. An administrative staff of 30 is needed to "keep the show on the road." Little did the Baltimore City Board of Estimates realize in 1915 that their initial grant of $6,000 would build into the multi-million dollar operation that it is today.

"Keeping the show on the road" is not an empty figure of speech as applied to the BSO. The 56 major subscription series concerts performed in Baltimore's Lyric Theatre are only a fraction of the total number of concerts the orchestra performs annually throughout Maryland. The hosts are symphony societies which cultivate their own audiences and enrich the cultural life of their communities. The BSO travels to Frederick County in the west and Queen Anne's County on the Eastern Shore, northeast on the Pennsylvania border, and to Montgomery County in the Washington suburbs. Ninety concerts a year are now played outside Baltimore, including those at Carnegie Hall and the Kennedy Center. The BSO also performed in Mexico on its first international tour prior to opening its 1979–80 season in Baltimore, and traveled to East and West Germany in 1981.

Music education is one of the orchestra's most important functions, both in terms of the state of the audience served and as a long–range audience development investment. The BSO performs 22 "Music for Youth" concerts in the Lyric Theatre, 43 concerts in city and county schools, and 26 Tiny Tots concerts annually, as well as a number of free family concerts to which children and parents are invited. Over 140,000 school children attend BSO youth concerts during the course of each school year. Children's programs have been part of the orchestra's activities since 1924, and were greatly expanded under the music directorship of Ernest Schelling in 1935.

In addition to its educational and community responsibilities, the BSO has been making a major effort in recent years to build its internal resources and make a name for itself in the world of music. The appointment of Sergiu Comissiona as music director in 1968 was seen by many as heralding a new era in the orchestra's development. For the first time, the BSO was able to perform at Carnegie Hall and Kennedy Center and return with glowing reviews, reviews that proved invaluable in awakening Baltimoreans to the increasing stature of their own orchestra.

The slow, painstaking process of improving an orchestra is not one that lends itself to dramatic "before and after" demonstrations. It is more akin to the uncertain flowing of a tide, a process of incremental advances and recessions that conceal the cumulative progress. What may be imperceptible to the regular concert audience in Baltimore, however, becomes very noticeable to New York and Washington critics reviewing an annual performance, particularly when every effort is made to achieve the highest standard of which an orchestra is capable for such showpiece performances.

When Joseph Leavitt became general manager of the BSO in 1973, Sergiu Comissiona's leadership had already made great strides in improving the quality and consistency of the performances. It soon became clear to him that the orchestra, even as it was then, was undervalued and underexposed, and that the road to "greatness" for the BSO was not simply a matter of making further incremental musical improvements. A systematic strategy of exhibiting the orchestra to the world by means of tours, broadcasts, and recordings was needed. This was easier said than done: the half-dozen most eminent United States orchestras have a virtual monopoly on these resources, not because they are party to some insidious orchestral cartel, but because the media machine that characterizes modern society acts in such a way as to publicize what is already well-known and to keep what is not in obscurity. For example, orchestras well-known for their many recordings are sought after by recording companies; their contracts are lucrative, their recordings sell, and their recording sessions may be fully paid for by the record company. By contrast, orchestras that are relatively unknown will sell fewer records, are unlikely to receive more than a pittance by way of royalties, and must advance all the considerable production costs of recording.

When weighed against such inertial forces acting against any challenger for the big time, the BSO's accomplishments during Leavitt's administration have been substantial. The BSO has begun recording with two major companies (Vox and Columbia), and the records produced to date received excellent reviews. The BSO's concerts are now syndicated by Parkway Productions, Inc., and are broadcast by many radio stations nationwide, including WGMS in Washington and WBJC in Baltimore.

The orchestra also served as subject for two public television documentaries, "In Search of a Maestro," a blow–by–blow account of the BSO's first biennial Young Conductors' Competition; and "Music for Prague, 1968," a video fantasy by Allan Miller built around the music of Karel Husa.

As can be imagined, the cost of upgrading the BSO's visibility in this way, coupled with the rising cost of musicians' salaries, increased rehearsal time, and other operating expenses, has been considerable. To bring the orchestra's deficit under control and reestablish a firm financial base, BSO President Joseph Meyerhoff launched a massive fund-raising campaign in 1976 called "Threshold of Greatness," with the aim of raising $3.4 million over a three–year period. Under the chairmanship of Frank A. Baker, Jr., this program has now been brought to a successful conclusion, but inflation has caused operating costs to increase so much that financial stability is as elusive as ever.

Outwardly directed though they may appear to be, the primary effect of image–building efforts has been to increase the orchestra's audiences in the greater Baltimore area. Baltimoreans are now beginning to show the kind of pride in their orchestra that Chicagoans show in the Chicago Symphony. (Interestingly, the Chicago Symphony never succeeded in selling out its hall on subscription basis until it made its great European tour in 1969 when rave reviews from European capitals turned on the audience back home.) The increased regard Baltimoreans show for their orchestra is reflected in the steadily rising numbers of subscribers: 7,000–plus in 1974–75; 8,000–plus in 1975–76; nearly 10,000 in 1976–77; 11,000 in 1977–78; over 12,000 in 1978–79; and continues to increase.

Of course, the rising tide of subscribers cannot be wholly ascribed to the orchestra's broad image–building. Comissiona's introduction of the "Friday Favorites" popular classic series gave subscriptions a big boost in 1976–77. The Saturday Pops series has been selling out for the past three seasons. Dividing the 16–concert midweek "Classical" series into two eight–concert sections has also added new subscribers. The Summer Festival concerts at Merriweather Post Pavilion, at Goucher College, in the city parks, and more recently under the stars at Oregon Ridge Park in Baltimore County also have had the effect of introducing the orchestra to new audiences who later joined the "Baltimore Symphony Family" at the Lyric Theatre. In 1981, the BSO participated in the "Harborlights Music Festival" at the Inner Harbor music pavilion on Pier 6.

Occasionally, in the history of an institution, an event occurs that marks a turning point and initiates a whole new phase of development. Such a turning point for the Baltimore Symphony will be the opening of the orchestra's new Symphony Hall, now being constructed at Cathedral and Preston Streets. This monumental project, made possible by grants from the state of Maryland and the city of Baltimore, as well as from BSO President Joseph Meyerhoff, is expected to open during 1982. It will not only provide a permanent home for the orchestra, but will also symbolize its growing stature and recognition.

A new concert hall for the BSO was among the first things Maestro Comissiona discussed with Mr. Meyerhoff when he joined the orchestra in 1969, and this project has moved steadily forward since that time. Plans were announced in 1974, and a long campaign ensued to enlist the support of state and city authorities. Finally, in March, 1978, after Mr. Meyerhoff had personally guaranteed $5 million in addition to the city's grant of $2.5 million, the Maryland legislature approved $7.5 million to enable construction to begin. Ground was broken on November 10, 1978, at which time Maestro Comissiona said:

One of our great dreams is about to become a reality—the dream of a new concert hall for the Baltimore Symphony.

What does it mean for the orchestra, this new concert hall?

It means a new permanent home at last, an end to the gypsy life. It means a coming of age in every way...a place to showcase the Baltimore Symphony's magnificent sound. It also means strength, stability, and an assured future. It symbolizes our resolve to become a great and world–renowned orchestra....

The outlook for the BSO is excellent. That $6,000 appropriation for a municipal orchestra in 1915 may be the best investment the Board of Estimates ever made!

John V. Brain

THE BALTIMORE OPERA

Opera has been described as the "queen of the arts" because it combines the ingredients of drama, music, prose, and choreography into a magnificent recipe for entertainment. As with certain foods, opera requires a cultivation of taste. In the last decade, Baltimoreans in increasing numbers have tasted and enjoyed samples from the likes of Verdi, Puccini, Bizet, Mozart, and Wagner, presented by the Baltimore Opera Company.

This opera company, considered one of the best–managed arts organizations in the country, has been actively engaged in promoting opera to the city for more than three decades. The company's current success and national recognition are products of an evolution of dedication and patronage that began some 50 years ago.

The founder of this heritage was Eugene Martinet, who established a school of opera bearing his name in 1924. In those early years, a 25-cent ticket gave an audience performances of "scenes from operas" staged in different local auditoriums including the Lyric Theatre. Under Mr. Martinet's conducting and coaching, the infant company had an extensive operatic repertoire, an advisory board, and a new name, all by the mid-1930s.

The Baltimore Civic Opera Company was incorporated in April, 1950, with provisions that excluded profit for corporation members and emphasized the development of musical talent and public education. Charles B. Duff became the company's first president; Leigh Martinet, its musical director; and the late Rosa Ponselle—who earned international acclaim during her brilliant 30-year career at the Metropolitan—accepted the post of artistic director. Except for his father, Eugene Martinet, Leigh Martinet has conducted more performances for the company than any other conductor.

The new company's first decade was one of tremendous growth, due primarily to increased patronage from prominent Baltimoreans and Miss Ponselle's tireless efforts in preparing new artists for roles. Also, the establishment of a union with its particular criteria for professionalism changed the status of the house from amateur to semiprofessional.

President Russell C. Wonderlic's direction and a grant from the Ford Foundation set off major innovations in the early and mid-1960s. These included the hiring of professional management, the establishment of an annual national vocal competition, the staging of a new production of "Aida" at the Lyric, and an expansion of the company's format to include three productions a season. In March, 1967, the Rosa Ponselle Club was formed to "perpetuate the name of our beloved artistic director." The 1968–69 season was especially productive because the Opera Education Program expanded and the Baltimore Civic Opera Guild was formed.

By 1970, the opera company that began from the ideas of Eugene Martinet had come of age. At the annual meeting that year, President Harry B. Cummings suggested that a name change to the Baltimore Opera Company was necessary to enable the company to attract wider financial support.

In 1972, the establishment of the Eastern Opera Theatre, the educational touring subsidiary of the BOC, was probably the most significant development in the past decade. An inspiration of the Baltimore Opera Company's general manager, the late Robert Collinge, Eastern Opera Theatre makes opera accessible to Maryland students who might otherwise never see an operatic performance.

Succeeding Collinge, Jay C. Holbrook assumed the position of general manager in August, 1980. He served formerly as production assistant and assistant manager.

Mark Miller

THE LEFT BANK JAZZ SOCIETY

The Left Bank Jazz Society, Inc. was founded in 1964 by a group of men who met in a south Baltimore night club to discuss jazz in Baltimore. Among those present were Benny Kearse, Vernon Welsh, Phil Harris, Charles Simmons, Eugene Simmons, Joseph Simmons, Gilbert Rawlings, Earl Hayes, Benjamin Kimbers, Glen McGill, James Dunn, Harold Bell, Charles Brice, Robert Brice, and Lionel Wilson.

The idea of forming an organization devoted to perpetuating and emanating a strong awareness of jazz as an art form was born at this meeting. Lectures, concert sessions, and field trips to festivals and nightclubs where jazz is featured were planned. Within two weeks of their original meeting, the group met several more times to draw up a final constitution and decide upon a name for their group. Benny Kearse was elected president at the final meeting.

Since the Left Bank Jazz Society's birth in 1964, it has had, like anything else, good times and bad times. For the past 10 years, the group has had 600 to 700 subscribers. The society was running a bit dry financially in 1977, but that situation has since improved.

The Left Bank holds weekly jazz sessions every Sunday from 5:00 P.M. until 9:00 P.M. at the Famous Ballroom, 1717 N. Charles Street.

Internationally and nationally known musicians are featured. Auxiliary organizations have been founded, including the Left Bank Jazz Society of Washington, D.C.; the LBJS at the Maryland State Penitentiary; and the LBJS at the Jessup House of Correction. The Society has also participated in the Eastern Conference of Jazz Societies since 1967. The LBJS has established a "Jazzline," a 24–hour taped telephone message which lists coming jazz attractions.

The Left Bank Jazz Society has also sponsored and produced a jazz radio program since June of 1967, on station WBJC–FM (91.5 mh). The program, called "Jazz Extravaganza," broadcasts on Saturday evenings from 7:00 until 11:00 P.M. The program was hosted for the first eight years by Vernon Welsh and the past five years by Benny Kearse. The cooperation of Kenneth Stein, general manager of WBJC, and Tim Owens, of National Public Radio, resulted in the taping of two of the society's Sunday concerts at the Famous Ballroom for national broadcasts on National Public Radio's "Jazz Alive" program.

Jazz lecture series and fund–raising concerts for the following organizations in the community have also been sponsored by LBJS: Provident Hospital's Development Fund; Morgan State University's ROTC Fund; the Department of Recreation's "Street Club Service"; CORE; the Community Action Agency's "Project Survival"; the Activists; Model Cities (John Coltrane Jazz Society); Target; Neighborhood Youth Corps; Martin Luther King Community Center;

WBJC–FM Public Radio; Rosewood School for Mentally and Physically Handicapped Children; Homestead–Montebello Center of Antioch College; and the Third World Museum. The list could go on.

Unforgettable appearances for the Left Bank Jazz Society include performers such as Pharoh Sanders, who plays tenor sax; Clark Terry, who was at one time a member of the stage band for the Johnny Carson Show and who plays flugelhorn; Sun Ra and his Mystic Science Cosmos Swing Arkestra; Arthur Prysock with his velvet voice; Sonny Fortune, innovative saxophonist and flutist; and Stan Kenton and his orchestra, which entertained at the society's twelfth anniversary celebration at the Eastwind.

Thad Jones and Mel Lewis have also performed at the Famous Ballroom for the LBJS, as has the Don Ellis big band. Roland Kirk, who used to play three saxophones at one time, has played for the Left Bank; the great Richard Groove Holmes and the legendary Horace Silver have also. Silver, an outstanding pianist and composer, reported that when he came to this city in 1978 he felt it was hard to compare other jazz communities to Baltimore's because the crowd here seemed so receptive. He indicated that where jazz is concerned, Baltimore is "the Europe of this country."

A new generation of jazz enthusiasts is being groomed by the founders of the society. It appears that as long as jazz has vitality its Baltimore audience will too.

Dianne King

Visual Arts

The young Baltimore mother stands at the Baltimore Museum of Art's Wurtzburger Garden entrance, child in hand, and surveys her city's most recent boast of a rich art heritage. It is a scene repeated from a previous generation when that mother, then a child, was exposed to the beauty of color, form, and space fashioned by the masters. In time, the scenario will repeat itself as it has for hundreds of years. Art flourishes in Baltimore!

It flourishes in the wealth of world–

renowned collections. It buds in the rich endowment of the Walters Art Gallery. It grows in the breeding ground of the Maryland Institute College of Art, the numerous colleges, the private instruction classes.

Baltimore's love of art is irrepressible. In the 1880s, while traditionalists held to their old mores, a vitality in art sprang forth reflecting the self–reliant voices of poets Emerson and Whitman. By 1890, a golden age existed and clubs like the Sketch Club (eventually the Charcoal Club) sprang up.

Despite a tendency of some conservative viewpoints to keep the *status quo*, by the 1920s art institutions reflected the industrial and educational progress. The automobile provided easier access to art schools, museums, organizations, and exhibitions. Travel to Europe opened up new art vistas. Technological inventions, economic prosperity, and increased leisure time contributed to art appreciation in Baltimore.

Ultimately, art passed from the exclusive privilege of the aristocrats to the average citizens. In Baltimore that process led to a new kind of art collecting, the only avant–garde activity between the two World Wars.

Baltimore artists financially thwarted by the Depression of the 1930s received assistance from the Works Project Administration's (WPA) nationally subsidized art projects. Some Baltimore artists got their start through WPA.

As leisure time grew in the fifties and sixties, more people turned to the arts as an avocation. Art organizations proliferated with one difference: in the twenties fine arts groups were mainly women's organizations, but in the recent years men joined.

By 1956, when Baltimore struggled to renew itself from urban decay, art was mirroring the milieu of which it was a part. Television helped spread the interest: children and adults saw art in their living rooms, widened their interests, and then visited art institutions either to see the exhibits, attend lectures, and/or participate themselves in drawing, painting, or sculpturing.

Out of the chaos of the 1960s—the confusion of a Sargasso Sea, that place of formlessness but still fertility—the 1970s witnessed the changes. By 1980, art institutions

Art Benson Sculpture in Front of a Maryland Institute College of Art.

had expanded their size or renovated existing space to accommodate more spectators and artists. The 1920s, that blooming period in America when art burgeoned as never before, again bloomed as never ever before.

Public patronage (local, state, and federal) existed early in American life and developed as the country grew. Unlike other cities in the United States such as Boston, Minneapolis, or Pittsburgh, art institutions in Baltimore had to be supported by taxes in the absence of corporate backing. Private philanthropy provided much of the financial assistance to the Baltimore Museum of Art and to the other arts including Center Stage, the Baltimore Symphony Orchestra, and the Mechanic Theatre.

The generous gift of the Walters family fell short of the mark. Public funds were drawn from and corporations also contributed. As a result, the Walter J. Jeffery Gallery opened in December, 1979, the gift of the United States Fidelity and Guaranty Company. Mr. Jeffery was chairman of the company and also a member of the Walters board.

The Peale Museum renovation is financed by city funds, a state bond, an anonymous donor, and the Jacob and Annita France Foundation. The Maryland Institute College of Art gained corporate help also: 13 corporations along with city cooperation sponsored the exhibit, "Sculpture 1980."

The history of art is the history of civilization. Baltimore's history radiates with the glow of its art schools, museums, galleries, dealers, and collectors.

Baltimore Art Schools

The art school should be the life–center of a city. Ideas should radiate from it. Everyone would know of its existence, would feel its hand in all affairs. Such a school can only develop through the will of the students. Some such thing happened in Greece. It only lasted for a short time, but long enough to stock the world with beauty and knowledge which is fresh to this day. Robert Henri, *The Art Spirit*

Baltimore artisans in the nineteenth century needed schools of design to teach the distinction between the crude and the beautiful in articles used everyday. By 1967, art curriculums again responded to career needs when students studied art education. The trend moved slowly until it reached a crescendo in the late seventies when the need to prepare for varied art careers surged forward. Even interest in art itself became more serious. Whatever the trend was, the art schools grew in number, expanded physically, and increased enrollments.

Baltimore was in the vanguard in the early years (around 1826) when the Maryland Institute for the Promotion of the Mechanic Arts opened to teach artisans. Towson State University also taught industrial drawing techniques when it opened as the Maryland State Normal School in 1866. At the beginning of the twentieth century freehand drawing, sketching, and painting outdoors supplanted them. After other higher institutions of learning were founded in Baltimore, the

A Lithographer at the Maryland Institute College of Art.

Maryland Institute College of Art (as it came to be known) replaced general with fine and applied arts.

Two streams converged in the last 25 years as students became more serious about their commitment to art. Sister John of Notre Dame College commented that students became less concerned with fashions and more interested in looking and seeing. Schools taught studio art techniques; but they also included the humanities to teach self–awareness, how the arts form the individual's personality and environment, and how the arts and society are interrelated. Techniques were less rigid and students were encouraged to express their own individual creativity.

Community colleges, a new phenomenon, reflected many of the trends affecting the other art schools. The Community College of Baltimore opened in 1947 and like most of the other colleges experienced rapid enrollment increases. Students included older women motivated by career goals, and senior citizens seeking an avocation.

The trends from manual training to the study of art for art's sake to art as a career again occurred in broader terms than previously. By 1967, increased need for elementary and secondary art teachers attracted students to major in art. For example, at Towson State College there were 200 art majors. As the need for art teachers decreased, commercial art related areas began to draw students. By the end of the seventies, undergraduate programs included studio art, art therapy, crafts, art administration and conservation, photography and film techniques, as well as traditional art education.

Dr. Lincoln Johnson of Goucher commented that a golden age for the visual arts at Goucher set the pattern in the sixties for the turbulent seventies when survival was a problem for many colleges.

Notre Dame, Goucher, University of Maryland Baltimore County (UMBC), and Essex provide film courses. UMBC, the newest of the four-year colleges in the area, added a second instructor in 1968, Leroy Morais, to set up a film program that came to be "the fastest growing department at UMBC and the only advanced film department on the East Coast." Professors Fred Stern and Stan VanDerBeek brought art and technology together by using film, computer, and computer graphics.

Reuben Kramer, Baltimore Sculptor and Teacher.

Robert Henri's idea of the art school as the life-center of the city is realized in Baltimore as art departments provide lectures, exhibitions, film showings, receptions, concerts, and festivals. The University of Baltimore, Theatre Project, the Lyric, the Baltimore Ballet, and the Baltimore Opera form an indigenous cultural-educational center.

The colleges collect art including textiles, modern, Oriental, and African. Galleries provide exhibition space that are as much a part of the art school as the courses—with two exceptions. One is Morgan State University where Professor Scott Oliver is director of the art department and Professor James Lewis director of the gallery. The other is the gallery in the library at UMBC under the direction of Sara (Cynthia) Oeschle. Loyola College's exhibitions preceded its art department. The alumni sponsor the invitational art exhibitions to show who the area's artists are and what their work is like.

Physical expansion marked the growth of college art departments. When Eugene Leake became president of the Maryland Institute in 1961, the magnificent old Baltimore and Ohio station (closing for economic reasons) would be the solution to the college's need for expansion. Since the first classes held there that same year, the station has provided a place for exhibitions, lectures, dinners, receptions, fashion shows, concerts, film festivals, poetry readings, and drama production. The use of the station itself was an inspiration imitated nationally. In 1980, the Fox Building, former home of the Cannon Shoe Company, joined the cluster of Institute buildings to house studios and liberal arts classrooms, graduate painting schools, and exhibition areas including three galleries.

UMBC, Notre Dame, Goucher, Coppin, Towson State, Catonsville, and Dundalk added new buildings or space for their galleries.

Other Baltimore Art Schools. One school dependent on the leadership of the founders, the Schuler School of Fine Arts, opened in 1959 to teach academic and realistic methods of painting and the mediums (of the masters) that Maroger had rediscovered. Ann Didusch and Hans C. Schuler (son of Hans Schuler, former president of the Maryland Institute) founded the school.

In 1957, George Horn and Bennard Perlman established and directed the Metropolitan School of Art where a group of well-known Baltimore artists taught adults, teenagers, and children. The school included branches in Pikesville and Towson before it closed in 1961.

A full-time high school, the School for the Arts, opened in 1980 with David Simon as

Gina Wendkos, *"The Cat,"* Photo by Ric Bartter.

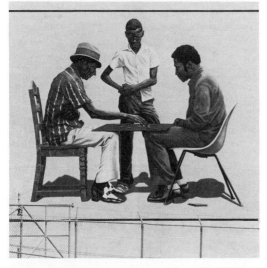

James Voshell *"Checkers Players,"* Beautiful Walls of Baltimore Mural. Photo by Ric Bartter.

head, and is supported by the Baltimore Public Schools and federal grants. The same ideas influencing the Baltimore Arts Festival are reflected in this school. The path led through the Mayor's Advisory Committee on Art and Culture (MACAC). Mrs. Marion Pines through the Manpower office cooperated with MACAC on the murals, Beautiful Walls for Baltimore. The Baltimore Comprehensive Employment and Training Act (CETA) project developed the only and biggest mural program anywhere. Seventy-two artists painted over 100 murals. Other cities in the United States and foreign countries as well came to Baltimore to learn. A spokesman from MACAC commented, "In terms of courageous programming in the arts, Baltimore was number one for its time in the world."

Then Jody Albright followed Richard Micherdzinski as MACAC director. Summer arts programs, the Mayor's Ball, the Children's Museum, the annual Baltimore Arts Festivals, and the sculpture symposium, resulted in convincing Mayor William Donald Schaefer of the need for a school for all the arts.

Dr. Luke A. Shaw, artist and chairman of the Coppin State College art department, believes that the artist needs an art teacher who takes an interest, one who "has the charisma to generate the art interest in a student." With such teachers at Baltimore art schools artists should help keep the city alive.

Baltimore Art Museums

Men, women, and children flock to the museums and galleries. Many discuss art knowledgeably. The symbolic high flight of steps to reach the temple of culture is no longer viable.

Formerly, Baltimoreans were less interested in what they had than what was available in other cities like Cleveland or St. Louis. However, in the last 25 years the audience changed more than the museums. The museums performed a significant part in the reawakening of the city as they, too, enjoyed a renaissance.

Richard H. Randall, former director of the Walters Art Gallery, described the renaissance as a rebirth in architecture and a reawakening of the museums. The new wing at the Walters in November, 1974, made Baltimoreans more conscious of the gallery's gigantic collection and its importance. Since the Walters opened as a gift of Henry Walters to the city of Baltimore in 1934, it has been enriching the adults and children who have visited it. Today the Walters is considered to be one of the six greatest collections consisting of art from the last 6,000 years and only one of three comprehensive museums in the nation.

Rebirth can also describe the Baltimore Museum of Art (BMA) and the Peale Museum. Both went through massive renovations.

The Peale is essentially a historical museum. The late Wilbur Hunter, director for over three decades, defined history as including more than just art. The Peale's mission is to show people through artifacts on display what life in Baltimore has been like and is today. It represents the only museum in the city that is devoted entirely to interpreting the city's history. The Peale considers a gift of even one object from an individual of importance. The collections multiplied 25 times in the last 25 years.

Another historical museum—the Museum and Library of Maryland History, the Maryland Historical Society has grown into an art museum. Artifacts are continuously added. They include furniture, paintings, pottery, watercolors, sketches, prints, jewelry, clocks, maritime prints, letters, sheet music, papers, books, and manuscripts. (These items, of course, are representative of the entire state of Maryland.)

The Jewish Historical Society of Maryland started a museum in the basement of the Lloyd Street Synagogue. Wilbur Hunter played a vital part in preserving this building, the third oldest synagogue building in the United States. The museum also collects artifacts and art objects owned by Baltimoreans and the rest of the state. The exhibits quickly expanded into the corridors—perhaps presaging a new building in the future called the Jewish Museum of the Arts.

Exhibitions at the museums showed treasures owned by the institutions and local collectors, works of noted Baltimore artists and sculptors such as exhibits at the BMA of Morris Louis, Herman Maril, and Reuben Kramer. The Walters Art Gallery's collections proved that they can compete with foreign "name" exhibits like the "The Treasures of Tutankhamen." The Peale exhibited winning works of artists chosen for the Maryland Arts Council's traveling shows. Actually, the Peale participated in almost every conceivable exhibit in art, city planning, and history that included documents, pictorials, engravings, and prints. In 1980, the Maryland Historical Society showed the works of the city's noted sculptor, Grace Turnbull.

Besides new buildings and exhibits the museums' educational projects played a role in Baltimore's renaissance. The Walters activities service schools, universities, and colleges in the area and even out-of-state locations. Series include lectures, concerts, dance performances, films, and demonstrations. At the BMA Belle Boas guided the education department to national acclaim and in her memory a memorial library was established by Saidie A. May in the Young People's Art Center.

Museums sponsor trips to foreign countries throughout the United States. The Walters was the first museum in the United States to sponsor a trip to Europe. In 1967, the first foreign trip for the BMA was to the Soviet Union. The Maryland Historical Society arranged a trip on the Delta Queen before President Jimmy Carter made his much-publicized tour.

The Walters was the first museum in the United States to take responsibility for a permanent television program. For a time television grew cool to art programs, but stations began to show interest again and the staff of the gallery made a 27-minute film about what a museum is.

All these institutions maintain libraries. The Walters library contains many rare, valuable books used by researchers from near and far. Of particular note is the Peabody collection, a part of the Enoch Pratt Library that is housed in the Peabody Conservatory complex.

Under Gertrude Rosenthal's guidance the BMA's periodical became a serious art journal combining the new and the old arts. Publications of the Walters include catalogs of exhibits, the *Journal of the Walters Art Gallery*, the *Bulletin*, picture books, pamphlets, and monographs. Through the past years under the guidance of its directors, Harold Manakee, P. William Filby, and Romaine Stec Somerville, the publications of the Maryland Historical Society achieved national recognition with the *Maryland Historical Magazine*, the *News and Notes of the Maryland Historical Society*, the *Maryland Magazine of Genealogy*, and other publications including some of art interest.

Other activities included in museum art contributions to the city are volunteer women's committees. The BMA formed an Artists' Committee composed of representatives of local artists' organizations and Maryland artists–at–large. Committees add new members, raise money for exhibitions and publications, maintain and run the café, operated the Rental Gallery, hold lecture series, arrange trips to other art centers in the city, and entertain children. Women's committees at the Walters and the Maryland Historical Society perform similar functions that add to membership and attendance.

During the McKeldin administration the Peale restored and preserved the Carroll Mansion on Front and Lombard streets. The museum directed the Old Town Meeting House and the information booth at the Washington Monument. The renewed interest in preservation generally brought a tremendous increase in attendance at the Peale.

The Black History Committee was an additional effort to reach the people. It sponsored exhibits and seminars, for example, at Dunbar High School in October, 1979, and another in 1980, that documented contributions of black teachers and principals to the housing reform movement in the forties and fifties.

Two other activities of the BMA were conservation and branches. The last attempt at a separate gallery closed after five years at Charles and Redwood streets; the Downtown Gallery suffered from an overburdened staff. As for conservation, the Walters also had a conservator, Victor Cory, who began his work around 1960.

In the last 25 years, Baltimore museums added new buildings, restored existing space, added to collections, conducted educational programs, gained wider exposure, and generally expanded.

Galleries

Galleries do exist apart from schools and museums, some to exhibit works of local artists; others are businesses not limited to local artists. These galleries and dealers have the advantage of presenting small exhibits where people can concentrate on a few art objects at a time.

One gallery of particular note is the Morgan Gallery of Art, opened in 1951 at the Morgan State University in the Carl Murphy Building. Professor James Lewis identified its two purposes: (1) to have a continuing program of exhibits drawn from a number of sources, including works of local artists; and (2) to collect art for teaching purposes.

The Morgan Gallery attempts to show our uses of the planet from historically and socially oriented exhibits to purely aesthetic or

Art Exhibit at the Community College of Baltimore Liberty Campus. Photo by Sidney Kobre.

innovative exhibits. One, in May, 1960, was called, "The Calculated Image," an attempt to focus upon another direction for contemporary art away from abstract expressionism prominent then. A few years later the Museum of Modern Art in New York City had an exhibit like the one at Morgan, except larger.

The nature of the collection is broad, including works from Europe, America, and Africa—both period and contemporary—and New Guinea. The traditional African collection is more extensive than in any other institution in the Baltimore area. Professor Lewis lamented that the great expectations for the gallery were not realized, "not even a justifiable portion." Reasons involved several areas: bureaucratic, political, social, and racial.

The second gallery in the Baltimore area that is attached to a university is the University Library Gallery at the University of Maryland Baltimore County. Under the direction of Sara Oeschle it became a center for important exhibits of both American and foreign artists. These exhibits extend classroom instruction by showing art works to the university and the community. The varied exhibits have included photographic materials particularly: Roland Freeman in 1978; James Van Der Zee; Walter Rosenblum; continuing exhibits from the Edward L. Bafford photographic collection; and the history of photography including one of the largest collections of photographs by Lewis Hine, the famous documentary photographer of the National Child Labor Committee. Some other exhibits were contemporary Chinese prints from the People's Republic of China, Tadaeusz Lapinski's retrospective prints, and Voice Beyond the Vail, Afro-American artists from the United States and the Caribbean.

Various innovative galleries sprang up in Baltimore. One was the City Hall Courtyard Galleries, the responsibility of the Art Commission of Baltimore. The galleries were created with the idea that City Hall is the place where people go. It happens to be the only city hall in the United States to have anything like it. These galleries serve an educational purpose as well as a place for government functions, a place for and about people, where the beautiful and the functional can be displayed. There are three formal exhibition spaces: the North and South Courtyard Galleries and the Circular Gallery on the lower level. The exhibitions have not been purely art shows but have included a history of local transportation. Choir and chamber music have enlivened the building. In December of 1980, the Baltimore Patchwork Quilt of Neighborhoods opened as a continuing exhibit showing artifacts, photographs, and community art work.

In 1977, Ruth Corson became the first part-time curator. Margaret Daiss, working full time since 1979, plans the displays of local untouched resources and explores the possibilities of the City Hall Courtyard Galleries. Ann Spooner became the assistant curator in 1980.

Even barrooms have exhibits and are a kind of gallery. Three such places are Bertha's, the Mt. Royal Tavern, and the Dead End Bar. The Baltimore City Police hold exhibits at the Baltimore Police Library Galleries. The Fell's Point Gallery was significant as a place for Maryland Institute alumni and alumnae to exhibit. It closed in July, 1980, because of financial reasons. Another group opened there as the Art Gallery of Fell's Point. Another exhibition place is the Proposal Gallery whose purpose is to promote a community spirit for nongallery-type shows.

The Kromah Gallery is unique as the first such contribution of a black businessman. Mr. and Mrs. Ernest Kromah opened the gallery to ensure a place for black artists to exhibit, although their goals do not state for black artists only. The Kromahs just wanted to help "towards eliminating elitism in the arts." Black artists—like women—have often been outside the art establishment. Opened in 1978, the Kromahs have included poetry-reading sessions, theatre performances, photography classes, black history exhibits, slide presentations, workshops on practical aspects of an art career such as grantsmanship, arts management, arts and the law, and marketing. Serving the Upton community, the gallery is funded by a city arts grant and the National Endowment for the Arts.

The Mechanic Theatre under Susan Kroiz displays arts and crafts in the lobby to show the community the works of Baltimore artists.

The St. Ignatius Center on North Calvert Street revitalized itself and the community 10 years ago in an attempt to bring the people back to the church. At that time it became an "artsy" parish as it opened the Loyola Art Gallery. Other arts were included in the center: the choir gives concerts; Peabody students perform in recital there; poets recite their writings; and religious dancers have performed. Added to these art activities are all kinds of social services to make the church and parish a community center.

Since 1974, the Reverend Jim Dockery, director of the gallery, has exhibited paintings, photographs, and sculpture, all created by the Jesuit Order and guest artists. The gallery consists of two showrooms that are next to the Center Stage and opens 45 minutes to an hour before the evening performance.

Other galleries in the last 25 years, and even some dating before then, include the Peabody Bookstore, the Playhouse Theater Lobby, WCBM (radio) Gallery, Charcoal Gallery (part of the Charcoal Club), and Haussner's Restaurant. The Jewish Community Center Gallery exhibits art of local, as well as national and international, artists. Even though universal themes are included, Jewish works are particularly emphasized.

One young Baltimore artist, Yvonne Everett, who painted a large–scale mural in the Bethel A.M.E. Church sanctuary, expressed the thought that an art work exists for a creative release, but it is also a statement to be seen and the artist needs recognition. Joyce Scott and Duane Thigpen joined Ms. Everett in speaking of the need for some new creative thought about the art institutions that they call "the old boy system" (even the young follow it) that exists nationally.

Gladys Goldstein spoke for artists when she commented that because Baltimore is close to New York and Washington, D.C., it

Yvonne Everett Mural in the Sanctuary of Bethel A.M.E. Church on Druid Hill Avenue. Photo by Jan Sutherland Starr.

is a "marvelous place for artists." But this city should be "lined with places to show art." Then we will hear the artists' voices.

The small Baltimore galleries are some answer; they serve as angels for artists who need them. The innovative galleries also are proof that art is proliferating in Baltimore and filling our lives more than ever before. Culture seems to appear in every nook and cranny. The city is alive with art.

Baltimore Art Organizations

Baltimore is alive with art: murals, sculpture, paintings. Some of these stem from efforts of the men and women who belong to art organizations. Some groups are community, some public. Whatever they are, they give us a picture of life in this city. They provide numerous examples of attempts to bring together various communities.

Baltimoreans imitated national trends and

founded art organizations. Artists and students found a common cause: they realized the importance of cooperating with each other. The organizations could promote art education, improve conditions for artists, mold public taste, serve as a clearinghouse, and organize exhibitions.

That was exactly what the Baltimore art groups did. The Charcoal Club's influence reached into the management of every art institution in the city; for example, the initial and combined efforts to open the Baltimore Museum of Art came from members of the club. That influence reaches down to the present generation that benefits from the museum. The Charcoal Club itself is enjoying a rebirth, "new, robust life," as described by Robert Brown, vice-president in 1979.

Women's groups such as the National League of Pen Women (professional artists, writers, and composers), the Three Arts Club of Homeland, the Baltimore Weavers Guild, and the Potters Guild exhibit, publish newsletters, aid talented young artists, hold workshops and lectures, and demonstrate their techniques. The Pen Women sponsored the first exhibit at a restaurant in Baltimore: Gladys Goldstein and Ona O'Connell prepared the display of paintings in the fifties. Members of the Weavers Guild made a duplicate of the original Star Spangled Banner for the Maryland Pavilion at the New York World's Fair (1964–1965).

Several other art groups in the Baltimore area have similar characteristics. The Baltimore Watercolor Society (before 1957 known as the Baltimore Watercolor Club) began as a reaction to the all–male Charcoal Club, but unlike its predecessor by the turn of the century admitted men. The Maryland Crafts Council lent its expertise to the American Crafts Enterprises Winter Market in Baltimore. The Maryland Art League, Etchcrafters Guild, the Pastel Club, and Baltimore Arts Community were all models of the more social–based groups, all usually limited to one art form, and devoted to increasing communication with each other as artist members.

The art organizations reflected some of the general trends of society in the sixties when legislatures declared discrimination illegal.

William Leizman, *Wind Screen* at Penn Station. Photo by Joanne Rijmes.

For example, geographical boundaries restricting membership were eliminated by the Three Arts Club of Homeland. Men and women were admitted to groups like Artists Equity and the Greater Baltimore Council of the Arts and Sciences.

Artists Equity was a different kind of group: it was a place where artists could voice their problems and work together politically, if necessary, to grow stronger and more effective. Besides the typical format of art groups, it drafted material and lobbied for a one percent ordinance for art imposed on municipal buildings. Bennard Perlman wrote the pamphlet that was instrumental in the final success of the legislation. Councilman William Donald Schaefer introduced the bill and worked with the American Institute of Architects to pressure for its passage. The Civic Design Commission resulted. The group eliminated entry fees for juried shows at the Baltimore Museum of Art, supported George Sugarman's sculpture, and organized a "Friends of Artists Equity" in 1975 to help with educational projects. Dr. John Blair Mitchell, former Equity president in Baltimore, served as president of the national group.

Another kind of art organization appeared in 1980: Fusion Enterprises, a profitmaking corporation, whose purpose is to provide management and technical expertise to individual artists. The group believes there is art talent that needs help with business and

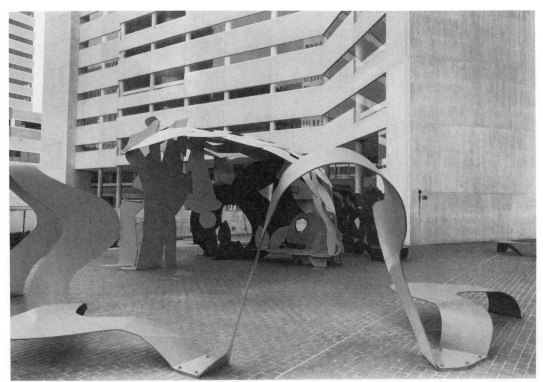

George Sugarman, *"Baltimore Federal,"* at the Garmatz Federal Court Building. Photo by Jan Sutherland Starr.

career development. Art organizations could
use this assistance as well as individuals.
Bernette Jones, president of Fusion Enterprises, described the company as a counseling service for all the arts.

Public Art Organizations. By the end of
the 1970s, the Art Commission of Baltimore
City had had a checkered history. With
Mayor Schaefer's assistance, for the first
time in over 10 years, the commission became active. Michael F. Trostell, Baltimore
architect and chairman of the commission,
commented, "Because there is little new art
in the city that falls under the Art Commission's review, Mayor Schaefer urged the
commission to accept the responsibility for
the restored City Hall, to keep it in its present handsome condition, and to be responsible for the two galleries that were created
during the restoration."

Another group, the Municipal Art Society
of Baltimore, is not technically a public or-

ganization, but it contributed primarily to
murals and statuary in public places. Beverly
Compton, president of the society whose
members lost interest through the years, still
attempts to continue spearheading projects
for which the city would hopefully assume
responsibility.

The most recent public art organization is
the Mayor's Advisory Committee on Art and
Culture (MACAC) whose seeds were planted
with the one percent ordinance as well as the
floundering of the Greater Baltimore Arts
Council. Jody Albright as director oversaw
the funding, planning, and implementing of
community art projects that may never have
been given a chance.

Finally, one organization is concerned with
the entire state, the Maryland State Arts
Council. It benefits Baltimore in various
ways, for example, grants to the Baltimore
Museum of Art for a summer art program;
exhibitions; workshops; adult and children's

Henry Moore, "*Conception*," at the U.S.F. & G. Building Before Removal to the Convention Center. Photo by Carol Strohecker.

film programs; community programs; grants to the Walter Arts Gallery for nine exhibitions and restoration of a pair of portraits; and many other projects.

The public art organizations play an important part in bringing art to the attention of Baltimoreans. In the streets and public buildings of every neighborhood a mural or a statue or a painting belongs to the people. At the same time, the public organizations like MACAC gives artists support for their creativity and additional income in administrative positions in art organizations.

Lenora Heilig Nast

Baltimore Art Collectors and Patrons—City and Citizen

The social and economic history of the United States includes art collecting. The earliest collectors were financial giants. In the 1870s and 1880s the wealthy were building up vast stores of art, mainly looked upon as an investment. E.P. Richardson, author of *Painting in America: The Story of 450 Years*, commented, "They were the earliest of those waves of uncritical snobbism, so typical of this country, which have marked the subsequent history of collecting in America."

Baltimore has had its share of collectors, two of the earliest being Robert Gilmor, Jr. (1774–1848) and Dr. Thomas Edmondson (1798–1856). They patronized struggling American painters and accumulated works by Thomas Doughty, the first American to devote all his time to landscape painting. Another famous collection, the Peabody Collection, was a good example of the history of taste in Baltimore, according to art historian Anna Wells Rutledge who wrote: "The collection is one of the few left in the country that clearly traces the development of local connoisseurship."

Of inestimable importance is the collection of the patrons and connoisseurship of inter-

Gabrielle Clement, *"The Battle Monument,"* 1927.
Courtesy of Mr. and Mrs. Mose T. Speert. Photo by
Peter Handakas.

national fame, William T. and Henry Walters.

Not only did the father go afar to amass art treasures, he recognized talent in William Rinehart. Walters, Sr. became his friend and business administrator, and as executor to the renowned sculptor, saw to the establishment of the Rinehart School of Sculpture at the Maryland Institute.

The beginning of American collecting can be traced back to the Armory Show in New York in 1913. The new collectors, unlike Henry Clay Frick, Andrew Mellon, and J.P. Morgan, who had spent fortunes on European art treasures, learned about the art they collected and spread the word about it. They were connoisseurs as well as patrons, giving their works to museums or establishing them to house their collections.

By 1930, Baltimore displayed evidence of breaking with the tradition of art for the aristocrats. Some well-to-do aristocrats and a growing middle class enjoying prosperity and increased leisure pressed for additional exhibition places—local as well as national and international. These new art patrons also became collectors from whom the museums would profit.

An important factor in the rise of collecting occurred in the 1950s. The machine technologies were mass-producing magazines, films, and records that became easily available to the masses. Baltimore benefitted along with the rest of the nation as America discovered art.

The American press provided another impetus for art collecting by writing more about art. Kenneth Sawyer, art critic for the *Bal-*

timore Sun from 1954 to 1961, played a major role in inspiring Baltimoreans to become collectors. Sawyer wrote his column of art criticism every Sunday for the seven years he was at the *Sun*, and also wrote occasional side articles on art.

Another factor important to the rise of collecting in Baltimore was the efforts of Adelyn Dohme Breeskin, former director of the BMA. In her 32 years there (1930–1962) she inspired collecting and stimulated interest in modern art at a time when museums generally ignored it. Mrs. Breeskin and Dr. Eleanor Spencer, former Goucher College professor, helped significantly the city's artists and collectors. Dr. Gertrude Rosenthal also played an important educational role as a member of the museum staff. Mrs. Breeskin provided the impetus for Baltimore collectors to give their art treasures to the museum.

Perhaps the most famous gift to the BMA was the Cone sisters' collection. These women were probably the first of the new collectors. They enjoyed friendships with artists and knew something about art. In 1949, when Etta Cone died, she left the collection (sought after by New York dealers and curators) and $100,000 to the Baltimore Museum. In addition her will provided $400,000 for a wing to house the collection. Thus, modern art came to the museum and to all Baltimoreans.

The BMA received other collections. The Saidie A. May Wing opened in 1950 to house the May collection. Other collections included works given by Nelson Gutman (1953), Edward Joseph Gallagher, Jr. (1953–1961), the Alan Wurtzburger primitives (1953), George Siemonn (1954), William Woodward (1956–1957), Harry A. Bernstein (1958), Thomas C. Benesch (1959), Philip P. Perlman (1960), Abram Eisenberg (1967), and the Wurtzburger sculptures (1973). As these gifts arrived, the BMA expanded physically to house some of them, for example, the May and Cone Wings and, most recently, the Wurtzburger Sculpture Garden.

At the same time, the Peale Museum under the directorship of Wilbur Hunter received another kind of collection. Acquisitions included a single art treasure that be-

longed to someone not necessarily wealthy or famous. The donor may have had only one valuable item. Or the collection may have been tne photographic collection of A. Aubrey Bodine, noted Baltimore photographer.

The BMA has received one–item gifts, too, as has the Walters that has also accessioned larger collections such as Alexander Griswold's Oriental treasures.

Other factors instrumental in inspiring Baltimore collectors could include national and international travels, the growing number of art dealers, courses in art history at colleges and universities, classes in painting, drawing, or sculpturing, groups like the Friends of Modern Art, or even other collectors. Dr. Israel Rosen, retired Baltimore physician and collector, started the Friends at the BMA in 1972. This group arranged visits to collectors' homes and encouraged people either to collect or contribute money to buy works at the museum. Dr. Rosen has himself inspired others to collect.

Some Baltimoreans collect art works and display them in nontraditional ways. The Haussner Collection of Art represents the most extensive collection of any restaurant in the world. Robert G. Merrick, retired banker, is another Baltimore collector whose gallery consists of an unorthodox but now–growing–commonplace exhibition place—a commercial establishment—the Equitable Trust Bank. Mr. Merrick's prints tell the story of Maryland; many are of the city of Baltimore. They formed the basis of the book *Mary-*

Cloisters Children's Museum. Photo by Jerry L. White.

land Historical Prints 1752 to 1889. Thus two other dimensions were added to art collecting and the connoisseurs who play the important role in the collecting of art—the commercial institution and the book as galleries.

Unusual or different kinds of collectors are themselves institutions: churches, temples, and synagogues. Whether the art is sculpture, paintings, stained glass, or ceremonial objects, each church, temple, or synagogue collects such objects—and religious institutions of Baltimore are no exception. In a booklet, *Art and Architecture,* available at the St. Vincent de Paul Church, is the statement: "Art came into the church because it is man's expression of beauty that reflects and reaches for the supreme Beauty that is God." Other religious places may have similar statements about their collections.

Public patronage by the city must be mentioned: monuments, sculpture, murals, the city-owned and/or supported museums and galleries at City Hall, School 33, the Cloisters Children's Museum—all form the city's patronage and/or collections. The display of artists' works in the streets, public buildings, and soon the subway helped and should continue to influence the bringing of art to the attention of the citizenry and visitors.

As the wealth of Baltimore grew, whether private or public, the number of collectors mounted and artists had increased opportunities for recognition and sale of their works. As Baltimoreans collected, their homes became art centers, and the collectors were in direct contact with artists on a one-to-one basis. The institution of collecting and patronage and the artist came together. The collectors' gifts in the last 25 years reflected the rebuilding and rebirth of the art institutions.

The impetus for the collecting by city and citizen was all a part of the process leading to a growing democratization of the arts. Even the growth of investing in paintings as a way to overcome inflation is a part of our modern society. Collecting continues in Baltimore.

Lenora Heilig Nast and
Jacqueline Nast Naron

Commercial Art Galleries—the Dealers

As part of its support of the arts, Baltimore has traditionally sustained a variety of commer-

cial art galleries, both old and new. The oldest gallery is the 120-year-old Bendann Art Gallery. David P. Bendann, third-generation owner of the gallery, is continuing a family tradition which dates from 1859. The first Bendann photographed many prominent leaders (including Robert E. Lee, Jefferson Davis, President James Buchanan, Johns Hopkins, and Enoch Pratt) in what was originally also a photographic gallery. The establishment promoted, published, and popularized etchings of Baltimore scenes and marine life. Today, the Bendann Art Galleries (including a branch in Towson) exhibit traditional realist paintings and limited edition graphics from England, France, and Germany. Works range in style from that of French Impressionist Gerard Passet to those of American artists Adolph Sehring and Cygne. Dutch and Oriental works are also represented. Local artists James Iams (known for water scenes) and Peter Egeli (known for portraits), as well as American and English wildlife artists, are familiar exhibitors.

The Purnell Galleries, begun 60 years ago, offer a wide variety of original works. Purnell, at 396 North Charles Street, has been a showcase for the arts (particularly nineteenth century arts) of English, French, and American sources. Unique to Richard Harwood's gallery ownership is that he owns all exhibited works. Included is a variety of original contemporary works—etchings, paintings, treasured objects of fine china, glassware, and statuary. A collection of liturgical reproductions and small tapestries, against a backdrop of velvety walls trimmed with heavy wood paneling, provides a secure, monastic atmosphere. The gallery also serves as appraiser, consultant, investigator, and restorer. Artists featured have included Passet, Alyse Lord, A. Dusservais, and Henry Wo. In March, 1979, Purnell held a show of Trafford Klots—the first artist since 1923 to be individually presented at the gallery.

The Katzenstein Gallery, 202 West Pratt Street at Hopkins Place is owned by Gertrude Katzenstein. In 1942, Ludwig Katzenstein opened an art gallery in the eighteenth century, Federal-style brick cluster house built as the home of Moses Sheppard. He actively operated the gallery until his death in 1977. Linked to the new direction of Baltimore's revitalization, the Katzenstein site was approved for preservation by the City Council in 1980. The Katzenstein Gallery specializes in duck-stamp prints, hunting prints, and prints of Baltimore scenes as typified by artists Melvin Miller and Skip Barry.

The B. R. Kornblatt Gallery, Inc., opened in 1975, was the first of the new-era art galleries in Baltimore to show modern art. It was owned by Barbara Rodbell Kornblatt. Unlike the older galleries it changed shows every four to five weeks. Set among long-established downtown businesses, the newly renovated gallery served as a modern backdrop for the display of large, contemporary canvases and three-dimensional art. A second, more intimate, room held smaller works, while a variety of selections was exhibited on the second floor gallery. Mrs. Kornblatt, combining her love of art and business, realized a need to "provide Baltimore with an important gallery for American artists with a unique statement to make." Her gallery of contemporary art featured new, rising artists and those of worldwide acclaim. Selections were made with the new or young collector in mind. Included in past shows were Baltimore's Morris Louis, Hilton Brown, Amalie Rothschild, and Lila Katzen, as well as such other renowned artists as Hans Hofmann, Robert Motherwell, Frank Stella, Sol LeWitt, Kay Freeman, Roger L. Nelson, Donald Shaw, Dorothy McGahee, Ben Woitena, as well as Louise Nevelson, and Lowell Nesbitt.

The building that housed Mrs. Kornblatt's gallery was renovated starting in 1980, and she moved her business to Washington, D.C.

Costas Grimaldis opened the Grimaldis Gallery in 1977 in a century-old neoclassic structure. The garlanded bas-relief on the ceilings, walls, and window frames provides an interesting contrast to the art work of silk-screens, lucite or metal sculptures, and expressionist paintings. Grimaldis is especially willing to show the works of local artists as well as the work of recognized artists from outside of Baltimore. The gallery has shown the work of local artists Eugene W. Leake, Raoul Middleman, Keith Martin, Stephanie Scuris, Bill Schmidt, Christine Neil, Jane Frank, Allegra Ockler, and Mary Biron, among others. Grimaldis' expansion to include an upstairs gallery indicates the positive public response that the gallery is receiving.

The Arts Gallery opened in 1978 and encourages a mingling of the less-known local artists with those more renowned. It is located in an 1865 brick rowhouse that was originally built for private optometric services; its russet marble and antique furnishings contrast attractively with contemporary art works. Owner Judith Lippman sees her gallery as part of an educational process that creates a greater awareness of aesthetics by teaching people to look and discover as they are enjoying the works of art. Her gallery offers a varied range of affordable works. Special interest shows, such as portraiture, monoprints, and contemporary tapestries, are featured. Shows at the Arts Gallery have included the work of Reuben Kramer, Calder, Warhol, Baylard, Solman, and DeNiro. The gallery's goal is to offer a complete slide collection of art works, including a growing number of drawings, that are available for purchase.

Since 1979, no less than five galleries have emerged. Galleries of longer duration experienced a rebirth of attention stemming from new ideas, future plans, and exciting shows.

The "409" Gallery on North Charles Street offers a variety of mixed media and promotes a developing Cultural Arts Center. The purpose of its program is to train the up and coming artist in an experience of varied art media. Under the Youth Entitlement Program of the Urban Services Agency, courses in painting, drawing, silkscreen, photography, crafts, and dance are held. Center Director Jeanetta Jones indicates that the public is invited to participate. Coordinator Guy Jones, Baltimore city muralist, is a graduate of the Hoffberger School of Painting of the Maryland Institute College of Art. Mr. Jones explained the gallery's function is exhibitions. Besides artistic exposure, the rising artist is educated in surviving the rigors of the gallery experience, including contracting. Future plans include initiating courses in grantsmanship and other areas of need in furthering the career artist. An example of an exhibit was the center's faculty exhibit, followed by a photography show: "The Black Baltimore Hall of Fame."

At 914 North Charles Street, Gallerie de l'affiche exhibits works of the art deco and art nouveau periods. Carolyn Frazier, graphic artist and collector, opened a gallery of original poster lithographs. Availability of works varies, based on the fluctuation of the art market. A catalogue of complete works is printed every six months. Artists have included Mucha, Babcock, Christy, Beardsley, Parrish, Berthon, and others.

In August, 1979, the Lily Gallery, Inc. opened at 2442 North Charles Street. It features original European and American etchings, woodcuts, and lithographs. Owner Pat Hart, former manager of Roten's, remains open to explore a broad appeal of works, from introducing new artists to uncovering old manuscripts. One Lily show was "Orient Express" that included nineteenth and twentieth century Japanese woodcuts and contemporary Chinese watercolors.

The Tuppenny Gallery, North Charles at 26th, opened in September, 1979. Uniquely set up in a former carriage house, this graphics gallery was named to create an awareness that art need not be expensive. Owner Muff Weil explained the purpose of her gallery is an aid in developing individual tastes in art. Ms. Weil is open to ideas from the community and encourages browsing. Original lithographs, etchings, and stonecuts are featured. Many works come from a primitive co-op of the Hudson Bay Area of Quebec Province. Shows have included a large collection of primitive Eskimo art and artists: C. Reiseweber, K. Girard, and B. Ruben.

The Framemaker at 820 South Charles Street opened in November, 1979. Owner Peter Owens is an avid art promoter who recognizes the need for giving new artists gallery exposure. The first show, Baltimore Historic Drawings, featured colored inks of Jim Walsh. Mr. Owens features a variety of media.

Bernadette Trattner

The Baltimore Arts Festival: Reshaping the City's Image

Early in 1964, the Greater Baltimore Arts Council (GBAC) was born. It is a nonprofit, educational organization of some 60 institutions, professional associations, and a complement of diverse groups supporting the visual and performing arts.

Later that year, the first project of the council was a monthly calendar listing the cultural events sponsored by the member organizations. Another contribution was the groundwork for the

establishment of the Governor's Council on the Arts in Maryland that led to the Maryland State Arts Council. The GBAC was responsible for inaugurating a downtown Baltimore arts festival. Initiated in 1967, Richard L. Micherdzinski, a member of the council, served as the festival's first director.

The first festival was held in May at the Hopkins Plaza with the seed money from the premiere showing of the film, "The Agony and the Ecstasy." Elane Stein, local radio personality, had encouraged WCBM to raise the funds for the festival. Ms. Stein almost singlehandedly worked to make the film a successful fundraiser.

From the first festival, artists and art students were invited to hang their art; groups of musicians performed; writers gave readings; craftsmen demonstrated their works; school children even exhibited their art works. The festival soon became an annual tradition in Baltimore. Due to subway construction, however, the festival moved from Hopkins Plaza to the Inner Harbor promenade in July, 1978. In addition, it now also boasted "stage barges" and dancing on the promenade.

Karen Little, the festival coordinator since 1978, introduced arts demonstrations called "Artists in Action," chaired by Fred Lazarus, president of the Maryland Institute College of Art. Faculty members publicly conducted classes for their regular students, such as figure drawing and weaving.

In 1979, a new approach to crafts was made; crafts people exhibited at the Science Center. Other additions have been added to the format, such as displays arranged by state-wide cultural institutions. Howard Hubbard, chairwoman of films and lectures, presented a series relevant to the arts at the Enoch Pratt Central Library. The Johns Hopkins University and Morgan State University exhibited at City Hall.

The success of the festival can be measured in terms of its established and growing list of volunteers; its increasing number of entries (originally there were 200 entrants, now grown to 500, and requests come in from out-of-state artists, also); its physical expansion; and its impressive community and political support.

Sandra Sugar

Urban Alchemy: Baltimore Architecture

Urban renaissance means more than bricks and mortar, glass or steel. But in Baltimore—where the construction dust still hasn't settled after 20 years of rebuilding—no facet of the city better sums up its past achievements and potential for future growth than the increasingly rich architectural environment in which all else takes place.

Buildings completed since 1956 have dramatically reshaped the center city, turned it around—literally and figuratively—so it can capitalize on its own unique form and waterfront location. They also have reshaped the public's perception of the city by providing powerful images of renewal. In many ways, Baltimore's architecture *is* the renaissance, the spirit of rebirth made flesh.

Those who expect the unprecedented amount of rebuilding to have transformed Baltimore into an architectural mecca, however, are likely to be disappointed. While the city has gained dozens of serviceable, even handsome new buildings in the last two decades, few stand alone as distinguished works of architecture. The effectiveness of Baltimore's rebuilt environment comes not so much from individual structures as from the goals set by urban planners striving to produce a whole greater than the sum of its parts.

The process is comparable, in a sense, to the medieval science of alchemy, in which base metals were said to be transformed to gold. For Baltimore's urban alchemists, working with the chaos and grime of an aging inner city, the gold is imageability, a highly prized but elusive design characteristic that separates America's overgrown tank towns from their more distinctive urban counterparts. Massachusetts Institute of Technology professor Kevin Lynch defined imageability in 1960 as "that quality in a physical object which gives it a high probability of evoking a strong image in any observer."

Some would argue that the goal of creating an entirely beautiful and delightful city, like turning base metals to gold, is impossible to achieve. "Any great city is a tapestry of success and failure," Boston Mayor Kevin White said in 1980.

But the rebuilding of Baltimore has had more than cosmetic significance. Psychological and economic benefits have been derived as well from Baltimore's refurbished waterfront, images of which now appear on placemats, postcards, even billboards. Redevelopment instills civic pride, and for many residents, viewing the city with that pride heightens the sense of "place" that always has been one of its greatest attributes. From the heart of the old Baltimore, Mount Vernon Place, to the heart of the new Baltimore, Harborplace, the city simply *seems* more inviting because it is being rebuilt.

"To some degree, the very process of reshaping a city to improve its imageability may itself sharpen the image, regardless of how unskillful the resulting physical form may be," Mr. Lynch wrote in his book, *The Image of the City*. "Although such a process can become sterile if not accompanied by increasing control and judgment, even awkward 'beautification' of a city may in itself be an intensifier of civic energy and cohesion."

Physical improvements have drawn professional praise as well. During a visit to Harborplace in July of 1980, for example, the noted city planner and author, Edmund Bacon, said Baltimore has "the finest urban waterfront on the East Coast."

As it entered the eighties—with its image enhanced by the Convention Center, Harborplace, and the National Aquarium in Baltimore, among others—Baltimore reached a turning point in its redevelopment, architecturally. Planners say the city is about halfway through the rebuilding process that began with the ground-breaking for One Charles Center in 1961. Both for planning professionals and those affected by their decisions, this midpoint represents a fitting time to examine the rebuilding effort and what it says about the city and its renaissance.

Becoming a Modern City. The surge of re-building can be traced to 1955, when a group of business leaders formed the Greater Baltimore Committee to decide how to revive the dying downtown area. Their first challenge was to develop a master plan for the city—not merely a mapped-out receptacle of all that had been built before, but a comprehensive plan that set overall priorities for future growth and averted the wheelspinning of piecemeal development.

The goal then was much the same as it is now: to make the center city a magnet where middle-class Baltimoreans would want to live, work, and shop. If the city were more attractive, planners reasoned, those who could leave would remain and those who had fled to the suburbs would return.

This was easier said than done. Despite growing concerns on one hand that change was imperative to bring Baltimore out of its doldrums, there was on the other hand a reluctance to change, a remnant of the provincialism observed by writer Gerald Johnson before World War II: "Baltimore is unquestionably the great harker back," he wrote. "Baltimore is becoming a modern city, but gosh, how she dreads it."

Like the alchemists with their base metals, the initial planners of Baltimore's renaissance had to work with limited financial and physical resources. Baltimore was a conservative southern city in many respects; there was no guarantee it would go for expensive works of modern architecture when a cheaper, plainer product would do. Few national corporations—traditionally patrons of quality architecture—had headquarters in town. Baltimore didn't even have an accredited architecture school until Morgan State University established one in 1979.

"Somewhat before the last quarter of this century, the understanding of the high style of architecture being practiced nationwide had not taken hold in Baltimore," noted local architect Alexander Cochran. "There was not the kind of knowledgeable self-confidence here that there was in Philadelphia, Boston, or San Francisco. Local architecture firms—many of which weath-ered the Great Depression—had built up after World War II, but their clients needed assuredness."

That assuredness came in the form of a plan for Charles Center, proposed to the city in 1958. Developed with the help of J. Jefferson Miller, a local businessman, and David Wallace, a professional planner on leave from the University of Pennsylvania, it led to the creation of (so far) 15 new buildings—including the Morris A. Mechanic Theatre, the downtown Hilton Hotel, two high-rise apartment buildings, offices, and shops—on 33 acres that had been a center-city slum. Individual buildings were mounted on a

Charles Center: the Old and New. Photo by M. E. Warren.

continuous urban base with piazzas, overhead walkways, and underground garages that accommodate, on separate levels, movements of people as well as vehicles.

The unique aspect of Charles Center, according to Charles Lamb, a principal of RTKL Associates, Inc., design consultants for Charles Center, was the high percentage of private developers involved. "We had private parking garages under public streets and private buildings over public plazas. It is very complicated to build that way. In its time, the plan was unheard of—eons ahead of what other cities were doing."

Total investment to date has been estimated at $180 million, mostly in private funds. More important, however, Charles Center was the first in a chain of projects that radically improved the public's perception of Baltimore and created investor confidence in the downtown. With Charles Center well underway in the mid–sixties, city planners turned to the even more ambitious redevelopment of the 240–acre Inner Harbor area nearby. By 1980, with developers identified for more than half of the Inner Harbor sites, the city gave top priority to revitalization of the Howard Street retail district. Encompassing all three areas is MetroCenter, a guidance program for more than $1 billion worth of investment over 1,076 acres of downtown city property.

MetroCenter was developed by the city's planning department in conjunction with several quasi–public agencies that oversee much of the actual work. One result of this approach, especially at the Inner Harbor, has been a set of urban design principles that subordinate individual buildings to the overall composition so that they function as backdrops for people and events rather than as monuments fighting each other for attention. Generally, the forms of Baltimore's new buildings reflect more concern for siting, density, scale, and other basic considerations than for momentary stylistic exigencies.

The urban frame for the Inner Harbor is formed by relatively low buildings along Pratt and Light streets that make essentially recessive statements and are punctuated only at strategic locations by towers such as the World Trade Center and the United States Fidelity & Guaranty Company headquarters. Along the Pratt Street boulevard, the horizontal office buildings—built at a consistent height and distinguished primarily by facade details—form a quiet outline, tending toward monotony. They are complemented, however, by the aquarium, the Harborplace pavilions, and other unique, decorative objects along the Inner Harbor promenade that enliven the scene and help define the water's edge. By keeping the frame low and the occasional towers slim and far apart, planners also have given taller and more massive buildings several blocks from the water views of the harbor they otherwise would not have had.

Adherence to this plan has been crucial to the renewal effort's success, according to architect George Pillorge of RTKL: "Baltimore's city officials and design review boards have been rigorous in seeing to it that the Inner Harbor plan and urban design principles have been consistently followed. The result is an urban environment of considerable architectural sophistication and control. It is no wonder that the harbor skyline is photographed from a distance. It is a very attractive composition and one that is growing more attractive as these principles are followed."

During the rebuilding, four trends have emerged that reflect the extent to which architecture has become intertwined with Baltimore's renaissance image. The city, as represented by the public and private sectors, has commissioned architects of international stature for some of the most prominent projects; looked to other cities for design ideas; increased efforts to restore or recycle historic structures; and established overall design standards for ongoing development.

Brand–Name Architecture. Over the years, Baltimore has become a repository of buildings designed by such masters as Benjamin Latrobe and Stanford White. From the start of the current phase of rebuilding, planners also have attempted to attract architects of international stature.

The pristine One Charles Center was designed by Ludwig Miës van der Rohe, one of the luminaries of modern architecture. The concrete-clad Mechanic Theatre reflects the "functional expressionism" of John M. Johansen. I.M. Pei and Partners left their indelible stamp on the World Trade Center, the pentagonal tower that overlooks the harbor. And the National Aquarium—perhaps the city's most spectacular new building inside and out: part zoo, part natural history museum, and part botanical garden—

was designed by a firm that began building its reputation with that type of structure, Cambridge Seven Associates.

Hiring a design firm with a national reputation—like buying brand-name toothpaste—provides some assurance of quality and translates, to a limited degree, into the big-league stature city planners are seeking. While such commissions afford the opportunity for name-dropping, however, they don't always guarantee superior work.

The late Edward Durell Stone produced a mediocre dormitory complex for the Peabody Institute in Mount Vernon and, later, an austere brick fortress for the Maryland Academy of Sciences. Half the residents in Coldspring New Town have filed suit against architect Moshe Safdie for alleged heating and plumbing defects in their homes. The two-building Inner Harbor campus of the Community College of Baltimore, designed by the Los Angeles firm of Daniel, Mann, Johnson and Mendenhall, fits uncomfortably with its neighbors.

Along with a recent proposal they submitted for building a hotel and office complex near Harborplace, former federal housing officials Robert Embry, Jr. and David Cordish outlined some of the problems Baltimore has had in obtaining first class architecture: "Developers, attempting to maximize profits and often unconcerned or insensitive to design, have often failed to select architects of the highest calibre," they wrote. "In the past, when a first class architect has been selected, the marriage has often been a forced one and the developer expends much effort and time attempting to discredit the architect to justify switching to a more pedestrian but pliable firm....A second problem is that, when an internationally known firm is selected, the acting architect working on the project is generally a staff architect of no extraordinary competence."

Awards of choice commissions to out-of-state architects also have frustrated local practitioners, who feel they are more sensitive to the Baltimore landscape. The argument has been put forth most persuasively by members of the Baltimore chapter of the American Institute of Architects, which has done more than any other local group to inform Baltimoreans about architectural issues through free lectures, house tours, and other events.

In some instances, however, local architects have undertaken important jobs with disappointing results. One unfortunate example is the 1963 Chesapeake and Potomac Telephone Company building on North Charles Street. A windowless, 13-story tower whose granite slabs at one point started coming off the exterior and had to be replaced, it brutally violates the more human scale created by shops to the north and south. The headquarters of the Municipal Employees Credit Union, completed in 1981, affronts the grandeur of nearby City Hall.

Other projects by local architects have been more successful. Warren Peterson and Charles Brickbauer have produced the handsome Sun Life, Vermont Federal, and Mercantile-Safe Deposit and Trust Company buildings in Charles Center, as well as a mirrored cube in Towson for Blue Cross & Blue Shield of Maryland and the sweeping new terminal for the Baltimore-Washington International Airport in Anne Arundel County. Cochran, Stephenson and Donkervoet, Inc., working with a Seattle firm, contributed the low-slung Convention Center, whose chief attributes are its unimposing profile and interior flexibility.

And downtown Baltimore is a veritable gallery of works by RTKL, with the Garmatz Federal Court building, Charles Center South and the Hyatt Regency Baltimore hotel typifying the crisp, consistently high-quality product that helped make this firm the region's largest. These and other projects demonstrate that builders need not always look outside the city's boundaries for design talent.

Urban Cloning. An extension of the idea of importing good designers to create the city's new image has been the importing of good design ideas. From Harborplace, whose precedent was the Faneuil Hall Marketplace in Boston, to Coldspring, whose theoretical roots can be traced to the Habitat project built for Montreal's Expo '67, planners have not hesitated to adopt workable ideas when they see them elsewhere.

As a result of this practice, the *Boston Globe* chided Baltimore in 1980 for being an "urban clone" of its sister city to the north. To some extent, though, replication of ideas is unavoidable whenever cities rebuild. The ultimate test is not whether Baltimore lacks originality by not being the first city to try an idea, but how well it implements that idea once it is pursued. And

Equitable Bank Center in Construction Behind the
Chesapeake and Potomac Telephone Building. Photo
by Bethlehem Steel Corporation.

planners have proved they can adapt different
building types to Baltimore's unique geographical and functional needs—from the aquarium,
which "sits on a prow over the harbor like the
Sydney Opera House," as architect Werner Se-
ligmann put it, to the eight–mile subway, whose
stations were designed by different architects in
an attempt to reflect the different neighborhoods in which they are located. Harborplace,
by Benjamin Thompson Associates, represents
a particularly successful solution to a problematic site and program.

Another case in point is the Top of the World
observation deck in the World Trade Center. A
mere 27 floors above sea level, it cannot match
the views of New York's World Trade Center or
Chicago's Sears Tower. But in its own way, with
its plexiglass posters of city natives, nautical
knickknacks, and push–button displays, it is distinctly Baltimore. And that isn't bad.

Reaching Back. Concurrent with the importing of new ideas and design talent has been a
drive to reach back into time and preserve the
best of the old Baltimore along with the new. It
is important to understand, Mayor William Donald Schaefer told a meeting of Historic York,
Inc. of York, Pennsylvania, "that the fabric of
the city is woven with threads which represent
different periods and different outlooks."

Many of Baltimore's most successful projects
have involved adaptive reuse, rehabilitation, and
restoration, jobs left mainly to local firms. These
projects have served a dual function of invigo-
rating the city economically while promoting
awareness of history and a positive self–image
for residents. Baltimore's initially conservative
approach to rebuilding has helped it avoid some
of the mistakes of other Northeast cities, whose
more vigorous land clearance efforts left little to
preserve.

The office of James R. Grieves and Associates, Inc. stretched limited construction funds to produce handsome homes for Center Stage and the Baltimore School for the Arts, both in Mount Vernon. Meyers, D'Aleo and Patton helped preserve the Second Empire facade of City Hall while making the interior more efficient than ever. Edmunds and Hyde, Inc. salvaged the "Mansion House" at the Baltimore Zoo. Cochran, Stephenson and Donkervoet transformed the Mount Royal train station to a sculpture studio, gallery, and library for the Maryland Institute College of Art. The firm also planned the conversion of the Belvedere Hotel to luxury apartments and the restoration of the Peale Museum.

The preservation climate has not been entirely favorable, however. At Charles Center and the Inner Harbor, preservation sometimes has been forsaken for "urban removal" of historic cast-iron structures. Other notable buildings, including Hansa Haus and Camden Station, remain unprotected by any kind of historic landmark designation. Arson remains a problem for old buildings, too; the vintage President Street train station next to Little Italy was nearly destroyed by fire in 1979, and a nine-alarm fire in 1980 obliterated much of the fine architectural detail inside the old City College building near the retail district.

But as energy resources diminish and the cost of new construction soars, adaptive reuse will become increasingly important. This is one area where Baltimore, with its plentiful housing stock and recyclable industrial buildings, enjoys an advantage over other cities.

Retaining Sensitivity. City government has been a prominent patron of architecture in its own right, but Baltimore's rebirth has largely been the result of the public-private partnership cultivated at Charles Center. While city planners don't have as much control over private development as their own projects, they have established overall design standards to insure adherence to planning goals. Two city panels play a crucial role in design supervision: the Architectural Review Board, which scrutinizes plans for the Charles Center and Inner Harbor areas, and the Design Advisory Panel, which reviews proposals for other parts of the city.

Another secret behind Baltimore's redevelopment is that improvements have been spread over such vast areas that virtually no part of the city has escaped at least the semblance of change. "Now that enough new construction is in place and enough old structures are left, we can see pretty well where we stand," said city planning director Larry Reich. "We must make sure what we build doesn't destroy our views or obliterate the human scale of what we already have."

Yet the construction pace has not been too fast to monitor, said Reich, who has overseen the planning department since 1966. "I believe we've gone slowly enough and developed enough of a planning framework that we can retain sensitivity in our decision-making. If anything, I think our goals have been refined as a result of the constant rethinking that takes place each time a new project is completed. Instead of being nibbled away, the overall plan has become clearer and sharper."

Rigid in some respects, local planning guidelines also have been flexible enough to accommodate important individual buildings throughout the area. Major additions to college campuses, for example, include the joint library of Notre Dame and Loyola colleges; Goucher College Center, a complex containing a gallery, auditorium, bookstore, cafeteria, and offices; and the Carnegie Institute Laboratory at the Johns Hopkins University. Still to be completed at Hopkins is the Space Telescope Science Institute, whose importance comes not so much from its form as from its contents: state-of-the-art equipment that will link astronomers in Baltimore with a giant telescope launched into orbit by the space shuttle.

Additions in the health field industry have included Turner Auditorium and the Harvey and Nelson towers at the Johns Hopkins Medical Institutions; additions to Union Memorial Hospital and the Greater Baltimore Medical Center; and South Baltimore General, Mercy, Sinai, and Provident hospitals, all part of the health field's building boom.

Most of the ecclesiastical architecture completed in the city since 1956 is not as daring for its time as earlier edifices such as the Basilica of the Assumption and Lovely Lane United Methodist Church. Two exceptions are the Church of the Redeemer by Pietro Belluschi and Temple Oheb Shalom by Sheldon Leavitt and Walter Gropius.

In the area of housing, the Rouse Company's Village of Cross Keys, a residential community for 2,500 built on 72 acres of former country club turf, helped set a new standard for in–city living and served as the prototype for the new city of Columbia between Baltimore and Washington. Israeli architect Moshe Safdie has seen completion of the first several hundred units of Coldspring, his proposed community for 12,000, but many intriguing aspects of the plan have yet to be constructed.

The city also has started to rebuild existing neighborhoods as Baltimoreans have rediscovered the virtues of rowhouses and white marble steps. Some of the most creative design work has come in the rehabilitation of eighteenth and nineteenth century dwellings—and the recycling of nineteenth-century industrial buildings such as those in the loft district—for contemporary residential use. Whole neighborhoods have been upgraded with the help of design consultants such as Land Design/Research Inc. of Columbia, which provided a sensitive master plan for the Otterbein homesteading area. At the same time, unique individual houses by local architects such

B'nai Israel, Neighbor of Lloyd Street Synagogue, Waiting to Be Restored. Photo by William Weiner.

as Charles Richter, Jr. and Alexander Cochran have added to the potpourri of residential styles.

Finally, four one-of-a-kind projects prove, if nothing else, that Baltimore is a place where designers have the opportunity, if they wish, to push unorthodox design ideas to the limit.

The headquarters of the Mid-Atlantic Toyota Company, hidden within an Anne Arundel County industrial park, represents California architect Frank Gehry's special brand of "invisible architecture." The spacious, two-story office complex is a striking fusion of High Tech, delicate colors, ambient light, and punctured planes—complete with an exclusive collection of Japanese art and an authentic Japanese tearoom—camouflaged as a mundane auto parts warehouse.

Towson's Eudowood Plaza contains the "tilt building," one of a series of works of "de-architecture" by New York architect James Wines for the Best Products Company. The eye-catching feature is a 450-ton wall, detached from the building and tilted at an unsettling angle to reveal the contents of an otherwise conventional merchandise showroom.

Near the Inner Harbor, the somber Holocaust Memorial by Arthur Valk and Donald Kann is a three-dimensional allegory of the Nazi annihilation of one-third of Europe's Jewish population during World War II.

And on Pier 6, a soaring fabric pavilion, designed by Future Tents of New York for symphony concerts and other live entertainment, reflects the spirit of Baltimore-as-urban-resort that city planners have attempted to foster.

Open-Ended Order. Although its image has improved significantly as a result of recent physical changes, Baltimore still is evolving in detail. And that is all to the good, urban planner Lynch argues: "An environment which is ordered in precise and final detail may inhibit new patterns of activity. What we seek is not a final but an open-ended order, capable of continuous further development."

One of the primary reasons that continued development in Baltimore seems a certainty is the momentum that has built up over the years; even if one developer bows out of a project—as with the Inner Harbor hotel proposed in 1979 for the abandoned power generating station on Pier 4—another is likely to come along and take his place.

Ultimately, when an environment becomes better organized visually, users are more inclined to make changes to suit their needs. In the development of a city's image, Mr. Lynch says, the process of seeing is just as important as the reshaping of what is seen: "They together form a circular, or hopefully a spiral, process: visual education impelling the citizen to act upon his visual world, and this action causing him to see even more acutely."

As Baltimore's planners reshape the retail district and guide development east and west of the Inner Harbor in the eighties, the city's needs likely will change from what they were during the previous decades. The increasing importance of mass transit and energy conservation and the growth of the convention industry and downtown retail activity, among other factors, will shape the city's future image in ways that couldn't be predicted today.

But by all indications, Baltimore has forever emerged from its pre-renaissance doldrums. "You've always got to keep pushing," said architect Lamb. "Cities either go forward and change or settle back and lose position. There's very little in between."

Edward Lyell Gunts

Poetry and Literature

"A real writer has more ideas than he could conceivably write in a life time. I have one famous author in mind who has two hundred different plots well-worked out for his novels; I am writing several books now and have planned many more; but death will render them incomplete."

There is the essence of a writer, as witnessed by Henry L. Mencken, renowned opinionative author of Baltimore. Thirty-five years of intimate association with writers has convinced him of the importance of having something to say.

Writing is exhausting. Henry Mencken claims that no man can write at his top form more than three hours a day. This judgment is qualified to mean writing from the intellect. Mr. Mencken has often written twelve hours a day, but "not from the head." That was newspaper work, where the material constantly pours in and needs only skillful selection and orderly composition. Consequently, without good health, your best writing cannot be produced. The author of Happy Days *insists that if your body is slowed down the slightest degree, your mind cannot give birth to vigorous literature.*

"I can write anytime I feel good. At sixty-two, that isn't often. Good health is most important."

If you are a good writer, you'll never have to starve. Mr. Mencken can sell any article he writes. Though Mr. Mencken edits his writing, he seldom rewrites. To him, rewriting is a false system of writing. The reason people rewrite is because they don't think first.

Excerpts from an article by George W. McManus, Jr. in the Loyola College publication, Greyhound, *February 13, 1942.*

A post-Mencken generation of Baltimoreans—such as John Barth, Anne Tyler, Daniel Mark Epstein and Josephine Jacobsen—looms large in contemporary literature. Readers all over the country must wonder: Is the Eastern Shore some mythic modern Avalon? Can places so Gothic as Roland Park, so exotic as The Block exist?

Baltimoreans, however, have the opposite problem. Here, where Roland Park and Hargrove Alley are as matter-of-fact as old tennis shoes, it is Barth, Tyler, Jacobsen, Randall, Epstein, *et al*—in their role as Known Writers—who seem mythic. One sees them in the Acme, at the PTA, or the Southern States Cooperative, trundling the *New York Times* home from the drugstore early on a Sunday morning; they can't be "stars." It must be somebody else with the same name.

Nationally acclaimed black poet Lucille Clifton has lived in Baltimore for more than a decade. Author of *Good Times, Good News About the Earth, An Ordinary Woman*, and other collections, as well as 16 children's books, she recalls a telling incident. Shopping at the Hecht Company with her six children, she was pleasantly startled to come upon a prominent display of her most recent books, a great pyramid of volumes, each bearing a large photo of herself. "My God!" she exclaimed, "I wrote those books!" "No, you didn't," a nearby salesgirl firmly replied.

Asked to comment on Baltimore's "literary scene," noted poet Julia Randall, a lifelong Baltimorean who wrote *The Puritan Carpenter*, *Adam's Dream*, and *The Farewells*, says, "Honey, I don't think there *is* one." She adds, "Thank God." Clifton concurs: "Baltimore is a good place for what I do. It leaves me alone, gives me space, allows me to write poems instead of 'Be a Poet.'"

Josephine Jacobsen's literary reputation has enhanced Baltimore's for several decades. She has published many volumes of poetry, recently completed a term of office as Poet in Residence at the Library of Congress, and made the National Library Association's list of *Most Notable Books of 1978* with her collection of short stories *A Walk With Rachid*. Jacobsen says that her writing "is saturated with the atmosphere of where I live, of course," but that she has "always been a private, noncommunal–minded writer, private though not isolated."

"Writers don't need a 'literary scene,'" claims Randall. "They need themselves."

Although her grandfather lived with Justine and made all those moves with her he called it visiting; he considered himself a citizen still of Baltimore, his birthplace. All other towns were ephemeral, no–account; he shuffled through them absent–mindedly like a man passing a string of shanties on the way to his own sturdy house. When he arrived in Balto. (for Thanksgiving or Christmas or the Fourth of July) he would heave a sigh and lower the sharp narrow shoulders that he held, at all other times, so tightly hunched. The brackets around his mouth would relax somewhat. He would set his old leather suitcase down with finality, as if it held all his earthly goods and not just a shirt and a change of underwear and a scruffy toothbrush. "There's no place in the world like Balto., Md.," he would say.

Anne Tyler, SEARCHING FOR CALEB, Alfred A. Knopf, New York, 1976.

Baltimore fiction writer Anne Tyler, whom Clifford A. Ridley of the *National Observer* calls "one of our finest novelists" in the United States today, uses Baltimore as the setting of many of her works. Among these are *Searching for Caleb* and *The Clock Winder*. Another novel is currently in progress. Raised in pacifist communes across the country, Tyler says, "In my writing I use whatever city I'm in at the time—it's convenient—but Baltimore, especially Roland Park, satisfies one of my lifelong fantasies: to be in a time machine." She plans to make Baltimore her permanent home, calling it "a good place for a writer—it has a lot of depth and color." Tyler shares with Randall, Jacobsen, and Clifton the view that another good thing about Baltimore is that it allows her the privacy she needs. "I don't know *any* writers, *any* place," Tyler says, but adds that she suspects "there *is* a literary scene of sorts in Baltimore, especially among the poets."

Though these major writers deny being part of a community of literatae, they regard each other warmly as colleagues, sometimes teach workshops, run seminars, or give readings jointly, and help guard each other's right to be private people. They might be considered part of a Working Galaxy—stars over Baltimore in the post–1950s era.

Within this galaxy, probably the individual most clearly visible to the naked eye is John Barth. Born on the Eastern Shore of Maryland, Barth is an alumnus of the Johns Hopkins University, where he currently holds the Centennial Chair in the Writing Seminars. After two successful earlier novels, *The End of the Road* and *The Floating Opera*, Barth rocketed to stardom with *The Sot–Weed Factor* (a comic epic concerning the settlement and questionable civilizing of the Eastern Shore) and *Giles Goat–Boy*. Both are overwhelming, not only in size but in stylistic inventiveness. A measure of Barth's stature as Man of Letters is the nationwide attention received by an interchange at Hopkins in 1978 between Barth and John Gardiner, prominent author of *The Sunlight Dialogues*, *Grendel*, and many other works. Barth emerged as curator of the Writer as Teller–of–Tales tradition, while Gardiner represented the position of Writer as Moralist. Critics and students all over the country took what was essentially an informal exchange as a debate of major literary themes.

Poet and playwright Daniel Mark Epstein is indisputably the shiniest nova in the Working Galaxy. Almost everything else about this young writer, however, initiates dispute of the most vituperative kind. To have published three major volumes of verse (*No Vacancies in Hell, The Follies*, and *Young Men's Gold*) and two successful plays; to have won the Prix de Rome (1977–78); and to have been favorably compared by a Baltimore *Sun* reviewer to John Donne seems, somehow, suspect—like Bob Dylan's getting rich. The fact that Epstein's artistic merits have won him a visiting professorship in the Hopkins' Writing Seminars for 1979–80 may remove one main source of people's grudgery against Epstein: if, up till now, he did not *entirely* support himself and his family by his writing alone, he at least made a remarkably good shot at doing so—something which, it is universally agreed, cannot be done in this time and place.

FIRST PRECINCT FOURTH WARD

Every bar on The Block shut down,
Villa Nova, the Crystal, the Ritz and Midway,
dead neon, night flowers gone day blind,
eyes like a gutted steeple,
streetwalker with her make-up peeled clean.
. . . .
Blaze Star, where has she gone,
 and Lola, that up–side–down girl
and a hundred others that dance the drinks off the
  bar–tops,
 and the topless shoe-shine girls,
and the shades of countless women trapped in the
  photo
 peep shows?
They have all gone to the polls.

Jimmie the Greek is laying one hundred to one
 The President can't lose,
and the action is slower than a drugged clock,
 and may be slower.
But some people will bet on anything.

—from NO VACANCIES IN HELL, poems by
Daniel Mark Epstein, Liveright, New York, 1971.

Epstein, who has lived here for 10 years "by chance," calls Baltimore "a good place to work: it's friendly, and there aren't many distractions." Its low cost of living—relative to New York—made it possible, in the early 1970s, for him to "work" part time and write all the rest of the time.

"It's an illusion that there's no 'literary scene' in Baltimore," he asserts. "During the mid–seventies, when the Maryland Writers Council still had its own building, with a bookstore and presses and readings, there was really a very intense literary community. Things were, and still are, very lively here." Epstein feels that "if a renaissance exists—here or anywhere else—it has to do with people communicating." At present, Epstein is busy communicating professionally with William Arrowsmith, of the Johns Hopkins University, a well–known classicist whose translations of Euripides are, themselves, becoming classics.

GOUACHE

*ah golden and shimmering small and profound
childhood luminous island of night purples and fog,
green rippling arches vault that trembling air… by
Marion Buchman, Grand Prix Award, Penn State
Poetry Society*

In the category of international prize winners—in fact, probably heading it—is poet Marion Buchman, "a Baltimorean for over a hundred years—at least that's when my people came to live here." Buchman has, as of this writing, won over 90 national and international awards, including the Cheltenham Prize (from the Arts Council of Great Britain) in 1969 and the John Masefield Award. Her book, *A Voice in Rama*, published in 1960, was prefaced by William Stanley Braithwaite (mentor of Amy Lowell) and reviewed by Carl Sandburg.

Almost as vigorously as they deny the existence of a Baltimore literary scene, many Baltimore writers express unwillingness to isolate "trends" in literary developments since 1956. Two significant developments do, however, appear to have been happening during this time-span; these are closely related both to each other and to more general artistic–social developments in the United States as a whole. One is the rise to respectability of writing—as a vocation, an avocation, a serious pursuit, and a joyous amusement. The other is the emergence (or reemergence) of Art as Craft.

No, it is not the local habitation—
Cedars by white washed fences, some half gone
With honeysuckle: And not Chesapeake, the
name.
No, it is knowing them somehow for one's own.
Environs of the single history
That matters, and a force in it. Thus,
One could wear sneakers on the rue de
Rivoli, but never on Charles Street, for they look,
Those doctors' offices, and those sad apartments.
The Sheraton–Belvedere, and those purveyors
Of reproduction antique furniture,
They look with Grandmother's eyes, and they
carry the news
Home to one's conscience. Or say that one should
meet
Mrs. Lenhart in Cleveland. One would say "How
dull,"
And be right. But in the A & P
At Roland and Deepdene, one somehow
remembers
Those who were nice to Father, those who sent
A bouquet at graduation, those whose sons
Are missing since Korea, those who fix
Clocks, those who know the recipe
For cucumber aspic.

—from "Maryland," THE PURITAN
CARPENTER, poems by Julia Randall, University
of North Carolina Press, 1965.

"These days *everybody's* a poet," sighs Julia Randall. "Writers are *everywhere!*" says Sister Maura, long-time professor of creative writing at the College of Notre Dame of Maryland. Both Randall and Sister Maura lament what they see as a resultant dilution of discipline and standards in the literary arts; but both admit to being gratified by the fact that in the sixties and seventies the literary arts have acquired a wider, more varied, and perhaps more intimately informed audience than they have ever had before. During the last few decades, and the seventies in particular, there has been interest in the so-called "nonperforming arts" such as poetry and

fiction. Interest has increased to such a degree that the city sustains, through community support, several on–going series of readings at which literature is, in fact, performed. Such series include most notably the Poetry Project, an off-shoot of the Theatre Project; the Maryland Writers Council's Friday night readings (which provided Baltimore in the mid–seventies with something approximating a literary salon); and the extremely durable "Poetry At . . ." readings, sponsored by the New Poets Series, Inc., a Baltimore small press. This last group has continued every Sunday night for years ("Poetry at The Angel Tavern," "Poetry at Bread and Roses Coffeehouse," "Poetry at the Loyola Gallery"), and is still going strong.

The Red Door Hall, part of the Maryland Writers Council's present quarters at Christ's Church, frequently stages "big readings" by famous nonlocals, such as Lawrence Ferlinghetti, as well as by confirmed locals like Roxy Powell (author of *Step–Dancing, Kansas Collateral,* and other works) and Clarinda Lott.

Barriers between audience and poet, and between poet–as–writer and poet–as–performer, seem to be loosening. For example, Fell's Point resident David Franks, formerly a teacher at the Maryland Institute but now attempting to, well, make bread by poetry alone, calls himself a "performance poet." He has, in turn, been called by Allan Austen, District of Columbia editor of the distinguished *Black Boy* series of recorded readings, "a genius—totally mad, and maddening to work with, but a genius." In one of his more recent metamorphoses, Franks performs from a wheelchair accompanied by a slide show, using as props test tubes and foot–long hotdogs (franks, get it?). In one stand–up routine, Franks announces that ever since he came to Baltimore he has "found it impossible to make a mistake." Thus, he comforts himself with nostalgic reexamination of past mistakes, of which this is an example:

RE: "REJECTS" (A WORK IN PROGRESS) :
"FRANKS":

For about two years I have been saving my mistakes
on KO–REC–TYPE.

For the past several months I have been absolutely
unable to make anymore. I don't know what to

attribute this "block" to: personal problems, dislocation, lack of inspiration, and so forth.

Finally I have decided to stop bemoaning my perfection; to accept it, however much it displeases me, to get on with other things and be grateful for the mistakes I have made.

Therefore I think it is time to present a few of my favorite mistakes in this Anthology. I usually read the "REJECTS" aloud—more or less left to right— weaving really and including words, phrases, word fragments, letters, spacing, punctuation etc. The lettering on the KO-REC-TYPE forms a leitmotif.

Since I have destroyed the Archetypal Narcissistic Image by making love (fusing) with Xerox Machines (see last issue of ASSEMBLING), I can't easily believe in a concept of individual identity. So despite the fact that I do, at moments, tend to think of the "REJECTS" as a confessional sound work, I really believe that others may identify with my mistakes—if read aloud they may be shared. It is my hope, equally, that others may learn from them, and I would be both interested and very grateful to hear from people who have experienced them.

—David Franks

MISTAKES

. . . It's not easy being a Perfect Master. For 7 years, I was unable to make a mistake. The more I tried, the harder it got. It was a lonely life. Finally, to make a long story short—out of desperation—I decided to accept my perfection and move on. I moved to Baltimore, and I've never been happier. The first day I arrived, I realized I made a mistake! . . .

—David Franks

Many other Baltimore writers are currently engaged in furthering the cause of "holistic art" (a parallel to the national trend toward holistic medicine?)—in which there are no clear-cut dividing lines between the Word and the Word Made Flesh via performance. The most obvious area in which this is true is, of course, the writing of drama. The Corner Theatre has, from its beginning in 1967, provided a very immediate link between writing and performance, with heavy emphasis on local playwrights. Balti-

moreans Dr. Murray Kappelman (*The Medal Winner, The Clinic*), Gordon Porterfield, Richard Gillespie, John Alan Spoler, James Cary, Percy Thomas (of "Free Spirit Theatre"), Martha Keltz, Barry Knower of Goucher College (winner of the Stanley Award for his play *Cutting Away,* later changed to *Cleaving in Summerlight*), Patricia Motley, Carol Weinstein, and Chris Dickerson have all had their plays performed at the Corner Theatre.

On a smaller scale, local playwright Ray Hamby's organization, the NEW PLAYers Theatre, also provides a showcase for Baltimore drama writers' talent.

Gordon Porterfield and George Gipe are noteworthy among contemporary Baltimore playwrights. The city can also boast a recent Pulitzer prize winner: Donald Coburn, a former Highlandtown resident, who wrote *The Gin Game* (1979). Inspiration for this prize–winning play came from visits with his 87–year–old aunt at the Belair Convalesarium in northeast Baltimore, according to Coburn. Other Baltimore writers who are not known primarily for playwrighting—Sara deFord and Daniel Epstein, for example—have had successful plays produced both locally and nationally.

Similarly blurring the line between the written word and other media is poet Gloria Oden, author of *Resurrections* and teacher of creative writing at the University of Maryland Baltimore County (UMBC). She appears with May Swenson and Ed Field in a film entitled *Poetry is Alive and Well and Living in America.*

Percy Thomas's "Free Spirit Theatre" provides a striking example of Word Made Flesh and of disappearing dividing lines, for—within its framework—the performers, drawn from the Cherry Hill community, act as both writers and actors, delving into black history for dramatically explorable material. Much of this material is extemporized to create a sort of Encounter Theatre, an intense and direct experience for both performer and audience. The drama that emerges sometimes develops into fully formed theatre pieces.

An important factor in helping to give Baltimore writers, especially the young and new, some sense of community has been the Maryland Writers Council (MWC). An accidental outgrowth, during the past decade, of the now-defunct Maryland Inter-University's Writing

Seminars (MIUWS, founded by Peter Cosgrove, Michael Lynch, Joe Carderelli, and Grace Cavallieri), the Maryland Writers Council for some years enjoyed its own building and its own resident magician, Denis Boyles.

Boyles is a poet in the Teller-of-Divine-Lies tradition who could talk the A.B. Dick Company into lending him a million-dollar computerized printing machine just like that. As emergent head of MWC, Boyles performed, with poet/printer Stephen Wiest, his most spectacular sleight of hand trick, *The Instant Book*, which, in the words of its preface, was "published at two o'clock on April 12, 1975, at the Maryland Institute, without fuss." It was "printed, bound and published out of thin air. Transcripts of the first exchange at the Coleman Symposium were taped and rushed to a waiting and eager typist who captured the spoken words and set them down on direct image masters. The plates were slapped on the press and published. The supplement of contributions was both printed in advance at various presses and printed on the spot at the hour of publication."

Having done it, Boyles then vanished into the thin air from whence came *The Distant Book*. After that, MWC fell on evil days, until it was resuscitated in 1977, more or less accidentally, by Paul Bartlett, then an unemployed chef. On the suggestion of Robert Waldman, a writer whose efforts had helped maintain some sort of existence for the writers council during its darkest hours, Bartlett set himself up with a typewriter and some plumbing on the second floor of the semideserted Franklin Street building and soon found he had become "executive catputter: the one to open and lock the doors, answer the phone, and put out the cat." Muses Bartlett: "At that point in my life, I was packed up and ready to leave town. I got as far as Leakin Park, where I camped for a while. But somehow I just couldn't go."

Under Bartlett's leadership, MWC, now housed at Christ's Church, has become, in his words, "the traffic desk for Baltimore's literary community." Its main vehicle is a publication called *Hard Crabs*, which supplies the city with a monthly schedule of readings, workshops, seminars, and the like; a classified section to help writers locate things from used typewriters to furnished rooms to sure-fire places to get their work published; broadsides and graphics by emergent artists; and—perhaps most important—a way for other local literary organizations to get their material mailed out to a very large, computerized list of people. For $20 per thousand sheets of paper—on which can be printed whatever—any arts group can have its flyers stapled into *Hard Crabs* each month. "It's working!" says Bartlett with justifiable glee, for dissemination of information seems always to have been a problem in the development and maintenance of a sense of literary communality in Baltimore.

Meshing neatly with the upsurge in popular support for the literary arts over the past several decades has been an increase in institutionalized support for the arts. Many Baltimore literary organizations are now being partially funded by the National Endowment for the Arts and/or by the Maryland Arts Council. In 1979, under Jody Albright (director of the Mayor's Advisory Committee on Art and Culture) and Deborah Birnbaum (project director), CityArts came into being, a program designed to foster art in the urban communities—storefront theatres, salon/saloon readings, and more. A particularly hopeful sign has been the increasing effort at reaching the local communities and the burgeoning talent within them. This effort is being made by well-established organizations such as the Maryland State Poetry Society, the Lizette Woodworth Reese Association, and the Edgar Allan Poe Society. The latter, up till recently, had tended to play a primarily curatorial role. Other "old" organizations, notably the Three Arts Club of Homeland, have quietly encouraged developing artists for many years by awarding sizable cash prizes to college-level writers.

A second, related trend—developing since the fifties—might be described as an emerging guild system, in which the gap between Art and Craft becomes appreciably narrowed via the Small Press. More and more Baltimore writers are combining inspiration and printers' ink, setting the Muse to work running machinery. "Even a poet can do it," says Denis Boyles; the fact is that "a poet had *better* do it," in the words of Paul Bartlett, "because the commercial presses won't." Whatever the reasons—snubs by the big publishers or the sheer delight of making something or both—the "small press movement" may well be the most significant development in Baltimore's recent literary life. Seems as if almost every writer runs a small press. There's Kraft Rompf, whose Broad Sheet/Baltimore series has just handsomely printed the work of former Baltimorean Anselm Hollo (noted multilingual translator and poet). David Beaudouin, who established the Tropos Press in 1976, has recently published a major work by rising Baltimore poet Rodger Kamenetz, *The Missing Jew*. Others include Victoria Crenson's Lark Press; Kirby Malone of Co–Accident and Pod Books; Dorothy Alvez, Macmillan/Taylor Publishers; Joe Carderelli, Phantom Press; Cherry Valley Editions, formerly published in Baltimore by Charles Pleymel and Josh Norton; and Robert K. Rosenberg's durable Linden Press. Out of the old Franklin Street offices of MWC came *Port City News* and Stephen Wiest's Print Co–op, which published over two dozen volumes.

For the uninitiated, it is important to note that "running a small press" does not always mean actually cranking the machinery; it means establishing a corporate entity, a format, an editor, and editorial board; reading, rejecting, accepting, and editing manuscripts; seeing to it that the books or periodicals do, in fact, get printed; paying the printing bills; and attending to the distribution of the products. Some of the small presses do their own printing, and, in the case of at least one Baltimore poet, Stephen Wiest (a teacher of poetry and fiction in the JHU Writing Seminars from 1970–75), the printing aspect has become focal. A poet who is "as much interested in the visual aspects of poems as the auditory," Wiest got into printing via editing; he apprenticed with an experienced printer, and in 1976 founded his own printing company. Wiest's company now does the printing for many of the Baltimore small presses listed above. "It's nice to have a poet printing your book," says Jan Mitchell Sherrill, one of the latest poets to be published by the New Poets Series, Inc. "They kind of have a feel for it." "I still write a little bit," says Wiest.

Though the effluorescence of small presses seems a development of the seventies, the small press tradition in Baltimore goes back to well before the time spanned by this book. Mary Owings Miller, a gifted Baltimore poet, founded the Contemporary Poetry Series in 1944, and ran it singlehandedly until ill health made her stop in 1961. During that period, this highly prestigious series published approximately 30 handsome hardback books of poetry by writers including Elliott Coleman, Josephine Jacobsen, Richard Macksey, Richard Hart, Charles Glenn Wallis, Merrill Moore, David Heminway, and Tom Boggs. The New Poets Series has attempted to take up where Miller left off by providing a way for outstanding young writers to get collections of their verse published without having to use up their youth knocking at New York publishing–house doors.

Magazines as well as books have also been on the Baltimore small press scene for some time. Margaret Diorio's poetry magazine *Icarus* began in Baltimore in 1973. The Enoch Pratt Library also publishes a magazine called *Chicory*. Its first issue was brought out in November, 1966, under the editorship of Sam Cornish. Its aim continues to be what Cornish set forth in the preface of that first issue: "to publish work which reflects the music of language in the inner city." A periodical that comes out 10 times a year and is distributed free of charge throughout the city, *Chicory* comprises literature and artwork by predominately black artists representing a wide range of educational and artistic backgrounds. Cornish and the two subsequent editors, Lucien Dixon and, for the past five years, Melvin Brown, have made a point of seeing to it that submissions are printed in *Chicory* precisely as they are turned in—even down to misspellings. At first *Chicory* was funded federally, through the Community Action Program; now it is financed by the city, through Pratt, as part of its urban services. *Chicory* won a beyond–Baltimore readership when Association Press published a book of selections from the periodical called *Chicory: Young Voices From the Black Ghetto*. Edited by Cornish and Dixon, this book attracted national attention.

The Maryland State Poetry Association, initiated in 1962, publishes *Maryland Musings*; the Edgar Allan Poe Memorial Association, founded in 1907 by the Women's Library Club of Baltimore, adds to its published collection of Poe lectures every year and, under the editorship of Baltimore poet Laurence Wayne Markert (*Riddle and Incest*, the New Poets Series, 1974), is bringing out a monograph series named *Stylus*, after the journal that Poe had always wanted to edit but never could afford. Markert also edits *The Contemporary Poets Series of Recordings*, which has issued readings by Elliott Coleman,

Josephine Jacobsen, Henry Rago, Haydn Corruth, James Laughlin, Stephen Wiest, and Paul Zimmer.

As part of Baltimore's literary–magazine scene, well–known Baltimore journalist R.P. Harriss inherited a monthly magazine (called, rather unfortunately, *Gardens, Houses, and People*) in the 1940s; it ran through 1958 and carried poetry and prose by Josephine Jacobsen, Ogden Nash, William Manchester, and Gerald W. Johnson. H. L. Mencken's chapter on regional speech—part of his giant opus, *The American Language*—was first published in *G. H. and P.* Mr. Harriss is known to have been so diffident as to reject work by poet Eleanor Glenn Wallis on the grounds that it "ought to be sent to the *New Yorker*"—which promptly, and without diffidence, added Wallis to its stable of regulars.

Traffic sweats and stalls on Oliver Street,
and Hargrove, Dolphin, Bethel Streets; the
dirty bars sweat, and the usual accidents
in the accident–rooms are glazed by July,
as are the gutters and the junk–man's
horse, jerked up the tar–soft mountain of July.
My cousin, however, is in
the green city of the dead.

—from "Arrival of my Cousin," THE ANIMAL
INSIDE, poems by Josephine Jacobsen, Ohio
University Press, Athens, Ohio, 1953–66.

A few college and university literary magazines have blossomed during recent decades into noteworthy public literary forums; Loyola's *Unicorn* for example, under poet/professor Philip McCaffrey; UMBC's *Maryland Poetry Review*, under influential Baltimore poet Michael Egan (author of *The Oldest Gesture*, New Poets Series, 1970); and Towson State University's *Grubb Street Wit*.

One can hardly fail to notice that a large proportion of the Baltimore writers and publishers dealt with so far are women. It is not surprising, then, that feminist small presses have been significant in Baltimore. The Feminist Press and Diana Press, both founded in Baltimore, have gained nationwide eminence. Mary Jane Lupton, professor of English at Morgan

State University and one of the early movers in the Diana Press, now runs her own publishing house, the Bloomery Press. These small presses publish a variety of books from poetry anthologies through historical monographs to children's books.

A handful of influential writers and/or professors constitute what might be called the "Major Mentors" of literature in Baltimore. John Barth, as head of the JHU Writing Seminars, is the city's current unofficial Mentor–General. The Writing Seminars, under the leadership of poet/scholar/gentle man–about–town Elliott Coleman, became a dominant force in Baltimore letters after they began in the 1940s. The staff of the Writing Seminars has included such well–known authors and scholars as Richard O'Connell, Richard Macksey, Leslie Epstein (author of *King of the Jews*), Ed White (*Nocturne for the King of Naples*), Dick Kim (*The Martyred*), Richard Howard, Cynthia McDonald, and many others. However, it was Coleman who provided the seminars' spiritual center. A gifted poet and translator, author of many volumes of poetry (including *Rose Demonics, The Tangerine Birds, The Mad Poet, Pearl Harbor, A Glass Darkly, Mockingbirds at Fort McHenry,* and *Broken Death*), Coleman was an eminence whose guidance warmed many Baltimore writers. During Coleman's tenure, the Writing Seminars staged two Bollingen Festivals (in conjunction with the Turnbull Lecture Series) that attracted widespread public attention by bringing to the Homewood campus such world–famous poets as Robert Frost, Yvor Winters, Marianne Moore, and Mark Van Doren in 1958; and, in 1962, Robert Lowell, Richard Wilbur, Richard Eberhart, John Holmes, and May Sarton. When he retired in 1975, there was fear that the seminars might crumble. A number of faculty members left when he did; however, at latest report, the seminars are alive and well in the hands of John Barth, David Saint–John, Daniel Mark Epstein, Frederick Breitenfield, Jr., and Robert Arellano.

Unprepossessing as it had been from afar, the town
of Cambridge was even less impressive at close
range. There was, in fact, no town at all: a small
log structure visible farther inland Burlingame

identified as the Dorchester County Courthouse, which had been built only seven years before. Nearer the river was a kind of inn or ordinary of even more recent construction, and at the foot of the wharf itself was what appeared to be a relatively large warehouse and general merchandise store combined—a building which outdated both town and county as such, and which doubtless had been known to Ebenezer's father as early as 1665. Other than these no buildings could be seen, and there were, apparently, no private houses at all.

Yet at least a score of people were strolling on the wharf and about the warehouse; the sounds of general carouse rang down the roadway from the tavern; and in addition to the numerous small craft moored here and there along the shore, two larger ocean going vessels—a bark and a full-rigged ship—lay out in the choptank channel. The activity, so disproportionate to the size and aspect of the town, Ebenezer learned was owing generally to its role as seat of the county and the convenience of its wharf and warehouse to the surrounding plantations, and specifically to the fall term of court currently in session, which provided a rare diversion for all and sundry. Since the day was warm, the courthouse small, and litigation such a popular entertainment among the colonials, the court was sitting out of doors, in a little valley just adjacent to the building, in order that the greatest number of spectators might observe the proceedings. Ebenezer found nearly a hundred of the audience present already, though the court had not yet reconvened; they were engaged in eating, drinking heartily, calling and waving to one another across the natural amphitheater formed by the valley, wrestling playfully on the grass, singing rowdy songs, and otherwise amusing themselves in a manner which the poet deemed scarcely befitting the dignity of a courtroom. Notes for tobacco were everywhere being exchanged, and Ebenezer soon realized that virtually all the men were making wagers on the outcome of the trials.

—from THE SOT-WEED FACTOR, John Barth, Grosset and Dunlap, New York, 1966.

North of Homewood campus, two other widely influential postmentors have been at work for an equally long time: Sister Maura, of the College of Notre Dame of Maryland, and Sara deFord, of Goucher College. Both widely published poets themselves, these two women have helped grapple many new poets into existence. Sister Maura, author of *Bell, Sound and Vintage; Walking on Water*; and *What We Women Know*, describes herself as "just a hard-working teacher," but as such she has shown an uncanny ability to produce prizewinning poets; her students have been particularly successful in the annual *Atlantic Monthly* contest. She has helped countless young women decide upon writing as a career. Similarly Sara deFord, who publishes globally from Baltimore to Japan, has produced a spate of working poets—including Jan Beeler, Ellen Bass, and Baltimoreans Bonnie Towner, and me.

Mentor Emeritus Richard Hart (now retired head of the Humanities Division of the Enoch Pratt Library system) encouraged several generations of poets, including Daniel Epstein, to take writing seriously. A working writer himself—author of *Papers of Identity* and many monographs—Mr. Hart took an intensely practical approach to helping fledgling authors. (On one occasion he made me a gift of 20 dollars' worth of postage—in order to send poems to magazines.) He built at Pratt one of the most complete collections of "little magazines" in the country, and made sure his pigeons saved themselves postage by looking their work over before they sent out their work for publication. He mimeographed and distributed specific instructions in the fine art of sending out manuscripts in proper form, and he kept an up-to-date address file of Baltimore writers, professional and amateur, to enable these people to reach out to each other.

Despite the large number of serious writers and small press publications in the Baltimore area, distribution remains a major problem. The villain named by every writer, printer, and serious reader interviewed for this chapter was the Commercial Bookstore. True, the same Baltimore Street bookshop that gave me the bum's rush in 1974, when I attempted to place a few volumes of the New Poets Series on consignment, now features a small "Baltimore Authors" section. But for every bookstore (such as the Thirty-first Street Shop in Waverly and the Little Professor in Timonium) that really makes local products visible, there are half a dozen that still operate on the principle enunciated by Lucille Clifton, "If you're a Baltimore writer, you've got to be bad."

Not surprisingly, publications by local authors

and presses are most likely to be taken by shops that specialize in handcrafted products—shops that may not be primarily bookstores at all—or by bookstores that cater to college–age readers. "Go for the bookstores with bongs," is the rule of thumb of one Baltimore small–press distributor. Feminist bookstores also tend to respond favorably to local and small press offerings, no doubt on the fellow–underdog principle. Oddly enough, college bookstores, with a few exceptions, are among the most reluctant to take books by local authors, even when the author is a student or teacher at that college. "They just don't sell," apologizes one college bookstore manager. Apparently the new respectability of writing has not yet been matched by new salability.

Of course respectability—the critical kind or the social kind—is something that many a Baltimore writer doesn't give a fig for anyway. Some, like the late Richard Ireland, gleefully courted its opposite. A painter and teacher of painting at the Maryland Institute and a gifted poet as well, Ireland—until his death in an auto accident in 1978—headed the notorious Worst Verse Society, along with men–of–letters John Stoneham (chief librarian of the Maryland Institute) and Dan Jones (English department chairperson at Towson State University). The Worst Verse Society was dedicated to desecrating Mother's Day, Valentine's Day, the Fourth of July, and other such holidays by giving public readings of appallingly bad serious verse, mostly Victorian, that has been inspired by these occasions. The New Poets Series holds an Annual Dick Ireland Memorial Dirty Limerick Contest in his continued honor.

Andrei Codrescu, author of *License to Carry a Gun: Poems*; *The Life and Times of an Involuntary Genius*; and *A Serious Morning*, as well as many other works in poetry and prose, furthers the image of the poet as a somewhat sinister Romantic figure by playing his Transylvanian origin to the hilt. He is unoffended when the response to his widely attended public readings is "You sound just like Dracula."

Best known for his graphic erotica, writer and political activist David Eberhart has spent time behind bars for his antiwar protests, while Harvey Alexander revivifies his own writing by conducting unorthodox poetry–writing workshops in Maryland prisons. Others flout contemporary traditions by reverting to older ones— Father Joseph Gallagher (author of *Painting On Silence* and other works) as poet–priest; Michael Egan (author of *The Oldest Gesture*, head of the Irish Studies Institute, and original head of the New Poets Series) by bending early traditional verse forms to modern uses.

The narrator of John Barth's *The Sot–Weed Factor* quotes the following bawdy epitaph written by Ebenezer Cooke, fictional first poet–laureate of Maryland and Barth's answer to Candide ("begotten by Don Quixote upon Fanny Hill," says the *Kenyon Review*):

Here moulds a posing, foppish Actor,
Author of THE SOT–WEED FACTOR,
Falsely prais'd. Take Heed, who sees this
Epitaph; look ye to Jesus!
Labour not for Earthly Glory:
Fame's a fickle Slut, and whory.
From thy Fancy's chast Couch drive her:
He's a Fool who'll strive to swive her!
    E.C., Gent, Pt & Lt of Md

Comments the narrator, "Regrettably, his heirs saw fit not to immortalize their sire with this delightful inscription, but instead had his headstone graved with the usual piffle. However, either his warning got about or else his complaint that Maryland's air—in any case, Dorchester's—ill supports the delicate muse was accurate, for to the best of the Author's knowledge her marshes have spawned no other poet since Ebenezer Cooke, Gentleman, Poet and Laureate of the Province."

But *The Sot–Weed Factor* is merely fiction.
Clarinda Harriss Lott

Dance

RENAISSANCE OF BALTIMORE DANCE

The growing popularity of dance can be attributed in part to the fact that dance is a unique means of physical expression. A dancer can create a mood or tell a story that cannot be told in words. Every talented dancer has within his or her power the ability to convert the products of the imagination into a reality on stage.

The rebirth of dance in Baltimore is also the regeneration of a dream for many artists who chose this city as a home for their professional schools and dance companies. In seeing their dreams realized, these dance artists spawned a new generation of Baltimore dancers and dance companies. Many of these dancers are related, not by blood but by dance training with the same teachers.

Dance can preserve "old-fashioned" traditions or it can create statements of new values for society. Estelle Dennis, director of the Estelle Dennis Dance Theatre, and her assistant, Louise Muse, keep the old-fashioned ballroom dances and ballets alive at their studio located at 13 Mt. Vernon Place. A trip to Ms. Dennis' studio, equipped with mantelpieces and antiques, is a journey into the 1930s. From 1927 to 1928, Ms. Dennis was a member of the Denishawn Dance Company. In 1979, Baltimore dance companies such as the American Dance Heritage Company, directed by Mino Nicolais, have sought Ms. Dennis' help in the reconstruction of the work of early modern dance pioneers such as Charles Weidman and Ted Shawn, (the father of modern dance in America). In 1934, John Martin of the *New York Times* described the Estelle Dennis Dance Theatre as "the first dance theatre in the United States." It is certainly the oldest in Baltimore and still holds ballet classes. In 1980, Ms.

Dennis received the Maryland Council for Dance Award for her contributions to dance in Maryland.

Another prominent figure in the rebirth of dance in Baltimore is Carol Lynn. Ms. Lynn arrived from New York in the 1920s when her sister married a Baltimorean. Ms. Lynn was the administrative assistant to the late Ted Shawn at Jacob's Pillow in Massachusetts from 1943 to 1960. In Baltimore, Ms. Lynn served as a chairman of Peabody Conservatory's Dance Department for many years. Her ballet company of advanced dancers performed at the Lyric Theatre and the Baltimore Museum of Art. One of her ballet students at the Peabody Conservatory was Dr. Helene Breazeale, who became the director of the Towson State University dance core program and the TSU Dance Company. "The Rosenkavalier Waltzes," choreographed by Ted Shawn in 1936 was restaged by Ms. Lynn for the Dance Company in 1978. The energetic nine-year-old company presents a variety of works and gives lecture–demonstrations in elementary and secondary schools as well as concert performances in the Baltimore area.

Goucher College's dance program is unique in that it not only offers a major in dance with a choice of emphasis in dance education, choreography and production, or history and criticism, but the college offers a master's program in dance therapy as well. Chrystelle Bond, director of the dance program at Goucher, feels that her greatest contribution to dance in Baltimore is her effort to develop an intelligent audience by training future dancers, artists, and critics. When the American Ballet Theatre in New York was unable to rehearse because of financial problems with the company management, the company came to Goucher College's Kraushaar Auditorium to perform on November 25, 1979.

In 1979, Goucher dance graduates, Diana Curran and Robin Williams, formed their own dance company, "Naked Feet." These young artists have staged works for Essex Community College's resident dance company, "Dimensional Dance Media," directed by Carol Drake. Their approach to dance centered around developing a new stage environment through unusual design.

One of the more enthusiastic groups that have just begun to benefit from the rebirth of dance in Baltimore are handicapped. The blind, deaf, elderly, cerebral palsied, and disadvantaged–gifted enjoy dance classes provided by the faculty members of the Cultural Arts Institute, Inc. Deborah London, director of the Cultural Arts Institute on the campus of the College of Notre Dame, has been actively teaching dance and dance workshops in Baltimore for the past 40 years. In 1949, Ms. London had the first multi-racial dance school in Baltimore. Her rebirth of a dream is the fact that she is able to see that many handicapped nonwhites have an opportunity to develop their talents through dance. The Cultural Arts Institute was the recipient of a Comprehensive Employment and Training Act

Dance Arts Ensemble, Members of Cultural Arts Institute, 1980. Photo by Harry Marble.

(CETA) award for the third year from the Mayor's Office of Manpower Resources under CETA Title VI for the "Rehabilitation Through Cultural Enrichment" project. Ms. London and her program director, Rita Abel, offer the program with the most variety of dance in Baltimore. In 1980, Ms. London won a silver and blue "Baltimore is Best" award for her contributions in dance to the handicapped community. The Dance Arts Ensemble, the institute's resident dance company, performs lecture–demonstrations for area schools and gives concert performances in the Baltimore area.

Oriental philosophy and dance find their union in the work of Peggy Myers. Ms. Myers, who has been on the faculty of the Atlanta Ballet School, the Alvin Ailey American Dance Center, and Towson State University, directs her own Baltimore group, "Movement Arts Parasol," which she founded in 1978. Several of the performers of the Movement Arts Parasol were Towson State dance majors.

The growing practice of incorporating dance into the liturgy has given new spiritual depth to church services in Baltimore. Ms. Myers performs liturgical dance for services at Corpus Christi Church, where the Parasol offered classes in T'ai Chi Chuan, modern dance, ballet, and mime. Patricia Enoch of the Peabody dance faculty directs a liturgical dance group that has performed for the 1978 Cathedral Arts Festival at the Cathedral of Mary Our Queen on North Charles Street. Several dance companies consist of dance faculty and students from the Peabody Preparatory Department. They are: the Peabody Chamber Ballet, the Maria Morales Spanish Dance Company, and the "Pas de Six" company.

Some dance studios in Baltimore have programs with appeal to the beginner. One of these is the Theatre Project Dance Studio, which holds "carry–out exercise" lunch hour dance classes. Director Shelley Walpert Fineman and coworker Diane Ramo combine modern dance and yoga principles to produce classes that provide a dance experience that is not overly tiring to the beginner.

Other companies preserve the heritage of black Americans. Norman Ross, the father of music and dance for inner–city blacks in Baltimore, founded the Urban Services Cultural Arts

Project in 1971. Eva Anderson directs its resident dance company, the Baltimore Dance Theatre, which concentrates much of its work on parables.

In 1978, New York choreographer Jeff Duncan chose Baltimore as the home base for his dance company, "Impetus." Mr. Duncan became the artist-in-residence in dance at UMBC in 1979. He became the vice-president of the Maryland Council for Dance in 1980.

The Maryland Council for Dance is also Baltimore's own dance organization. It is a statewide, nonprofit organization that provides a spectrum of services for Baltimore dance companies. The council publishes a newsletter of dance events, and offers opportunities for master classes and dance festivals around the region. It sets standards for dance in education and acts as a voice for the state in matters pertaining to dance. The council's business office is located at Slayton House in Columbia. As Baltimore continues to be an attraction spot for touring dance companies, the council offers out-of-town companies much assistance.

The Maryland Dance Theatre, founded by Dorothy Madden, is the modern dance counterpart of the Baltimore Ballet. It is a professional modern dance company formed by the faculty of the dance department of the University of Maryland, College Park.

There are many other important contributors to the rebirth of dance in Baltimore. Baltimore has its own dance critics, historians, and dance TV programs. The Baltimore list of community centers, private dance studios, and small companies is endless thanks to the spirit of the renaissance in Baltimore.

Lori Jackson Marble

Members of Impetus, the University of Maryland Baltimore County Dance Company. Directed by Jeff Duncan. Photo by J. B. Schamp.

BALTIMORE ON ITS TOES

Nationwide, dance has become the fastest growing of all performing arts. Baltimore, which has become an art-oriented city much like Washington, Philadelphia, or New York, reflects this trend. Baltimoreans now have the opportunity to learn and enjoy dance at all levels and in all forms.

The opening of the School for the Arts in February, 1980, in the Alcazar Hotel at Cathedral and Madison streets has underscored the city's commitment to the arts. There students are able to combine scholastic endeavors with artistic ones on an on-going basis. Among other courses, the school offers classical ballet under the direction of Sylvester Campbell of the Baltimore Ballet Company (formerly the Maryland Ballet Company).

Admission to the School for the Arts is by audition only, the yearly auditions are held each spring. The school enrolls students from grades 9 through 12, and since it is a public high school, charges no tuition to city residents. Leslie Seyffert, specialist for the school, states that the curriculum is evenly divided to allow equal time for academic as well as artistic pursuits.

Dale Sehnert, an alumnus of New York's Martha Graham Company and presently chairman of the dance department of the Peabody Institute points out that "although it takes several years to realize appreciation from a program such as offered by the School for the Arts, the results are well worth it. You cannot expect progress in dance unless you are schooled daily. It's not like playing a musical instrument; dance is a specialty unlike any other."

The Peabody Institute, established in 1857 by philanthropist George Peabody and located in the historic Mt. Vernon area, has fulfilled Mr.

Modern Dance in a Local Bar, 1975. Photo by Betty Redifer.

Peabody's dream of creating a focal point that "may become useful toward the improvement of moral and intellectual cultures ... and also toward the enlargement and diffusion of a taste for the fine arts."

Forty–one years later, the Preparatory Department was opened to enable students to prepare for entrance to the conservatory. The Preparatory Department has a branch completed in 1958 and located in Towson on the Goucher College campus.

Although the Peabody is perhaps most recognized for its classical ballet, it also offers a wide range of diversified dance classes, including character dance (traditional dances of national origins based on ballet techniques), modern dance (introduction to modern dance through advanced levels), and Spanish dance (including classical and Mexican, jota, and flamenco).

Several Peabody graduates have furthered their education at Juilliard School of Music; others have performed with the Alvin Ailey Company and Pilobolus, while others have taught at New York University.

One aspiring group, the Baltimore Ballet, has become one of the nation's outstanding regional ballet companies after a modest beginning in 1961 under the tutelage of Danny Diamond. Kathleen Crofton, artistic director, helped the group, then called the Maryland Ballet, reach international recognition when two of its dancers won awards in competition in the Soviet Union.

Petrus Bosman, artistic director following Ms. Crofton, brought quick recognition to the company for its artistic strength. Two years after Mr. Bosman joined the group in 1979, Maryland Ballet made its New York City debut.

The company suffered a severe setback that year when a fire destroyed its headquarters. Public and private support has enabled the company to survive and continue to practice in temporary quarters; it eventually found a home on Mount Royal Avenue. In January, 1980, Charles F. Fischl became president and general manager. Under Fischl the company presented its most ambitious project, the world premiere of "Equus—The Ballet." In July of that year, Alphonsus Cata, joined the company as artistic director; he left less than a year later.

The Baltimore Ballet offered three subscription series, as well as 10 performances of the "Nutcracker" at the Lyric Theatre. At Goucher College, six subscription series were offered and three other performances were given at Oregon Ridge. The group performs in hospitals and prisons, as well as other community places.

The company's dancers, former members of the American Ballet Theatre, the San Francisco Ballet, the Harkness Ballet, and other European and American companies, built a repertoire of ballet of such notable choreographers as Sir Frederick Ashton, George Balanchine, Ruth Page, Kenneth McMillin, Jack Carter, and others. They performed to live music when possible and to taped selections otherwise.

The company was practically defunct in 1981 except for its ballet school.

Since dance depicts a story, presented in one form or another, it would seem to be a natural progression to combine mime with dance. One person who recognized and sought to pursue the possibilities of the dance/mime concept is Robinne Comissiona, who directs a dance troupe called Collage. Collage is a company of six, which offers classical, modern, jazz, and ethnic interpretations. They have performed in prematinee entertainment at the Mechanic Theatre, the College of Notre Dame, the Baltimore Museum of Art, and with the Baltimore Symphony at Oregon Ridge.

Collage understandably prefers performing to live music, but it often must rely on taped selections due to its budget limitations. The company is funded partially by private donations along with grants from Baltimore city and County.

Robinne Comissiona has long been involved with dance in London, Switzerland, and Israel. She stresses the fact that no one actually knows just how much mime can be developed because of the different personalities of each choreographer and the ability to expand his/her concepts beyond conventional limitations. "Mime has always been considered the inferior sister to dance, but we feel they are equals that can complement each other beautifully."

Janice D. McCrory

IV

Analytically, we would argue, our conceptualization of various aspects of Baltimore into "Baltimore Builds," "Social Perspectives," "The Arts," and now, "What Makes Baltimore, Baltimore," makes sense. There does exist a defensible logic to this arrangement. However, in reality these convenient cutting points of the face and heart of a city are not so tidy. There is much overlap, some glaring omissions as well as room for serious disagreements as to proper labels and section assignments. This is a problem which we are aware of and have touched on before.

This last section attempts to do two things. First, without functioning as a grab bag for things accidentally left out, efforts are made to describe important institutions and people who logically do not fit well in earlier sections but are too essential for omission from an anthology on Baltimore's renaissance. Second, four specific classes of Baltimore's renaissance that we see as vital to the city, its shape and identity, and not directly touched on before, are developed in these last essays. These are specific businesses with comments on their public and private promoters, Baltimore's politicians, and discussions of recent governmental processes. The third class of Baltimore life dealt with in this section is Baltimore recreation, including its nightlife and sports and racing. Finally, six Baltimoreans and/or Baltimore families are taken as prototypes of the many outstanding people who have contributed to the renaissance. In addition, Joseph Arnold provides an overview of the six biographies searching for common themes in these uncommon lives.

Bennard B. Perlman, "Sunday Morning," Oil 20 x 24, 1980. Courtesy of Dennis K. McDaniel. Photo by William L. Klender.

WHAT MAKES BALTIMORE,

BALTIMORE

Dorothy Pula Strohecker's "Tommy's Two: The D'Alesandros" is a rich and factual account of what many describe as Baltimore's greatest political family.

"Theodore Roosevelt McKeldin, 1900–1974" by Morgan H. Pritchett is a concise summary of the two terms as governor and two terms as mayor of the man said to have started Baltimore's renaissance.

"Political Aspects—William Donald Schaefer" by Larry Krause describes councilman, city council president, and since 1971, Mayor William Donald Schaefer. Although mistakes made by Schaefer are identified, Krause generally links the renaissance with the work of the city's mayor.

Joseph Arnold's "The Politics of the Baltimore Renaissance" is a glowing account of the obstacles, including democracy itself, that have been overcome, according to Arnold, by Mayor Schaefer.

"The City Council" by W. Theodore Durr is a trenchant discussion of democracy's greatest "failure": the Baltimore City Council. He also provides illustrations of some positive contributions and suggests that with recent elections there is hope for the future of the Council.

"Baltimore's Financial Institutions" by Gary L. Browne documents rapid changes among banks and savings and loan associations in Baltimore. Browne also discusses new banking structures and services that help support the city's renaissance. In the next article, also by Browne, "Small Business in Baltimore," statistics on the changing number of small businesses in the city are identified and analyzed along with the city's role of promoting small businesses.

Alison Brawner's "The Mayor's Advisory Committee on Small Business" is a short account of concerned merchants working through governmental agencies to obtain funds to salvage declining business districts. In the process, she shows how they contribute immensely to Baltimore's renaissance.

Victoria B. Obrecht's "The Greater Baltimore Committee" analyzes the GBC, its merger with the Chamber of Commerce and its essential contributions to the city's financial evolution.

Barbara Bonnell's "Charles Center–Inner Harbor Management, Inc." traces the creation of Charles Center–Inner Harbor and shows how its accomplishments parallel the renaissance itself.

"What Makes Baltimore, Baltimore" is a multiauthored article. Ric Bartter, Stephen J. Gordon, Frederic Kelly, Mark Miller, Bernard Penner, Jake Slagle, Jr. and William Weiner that along with Slagle's "Baltimore Night Life" show that the city in its evening entertainment as well as in its contributions to the arts has evolved significantly beyond the sleaze of the 1940s and 1950s. Yet it is shown that Baltimore's renaissance is capable of supporting beautiful office buildings, high culture, and a variety of evening good times unlike many areas such as Northern Virginia or Atlanta that become virtual tombs after the 6:00 P.M. rush hour. Slagle also documents important changes in both types of night spots and clientele, which also indicates a changing Baltimore. "Tourtapes of Baltimore" describes how one Baltimorean's inspirations helped make his city more known.

John F. Steadman's "The Colts" is an action-paced history of the city's famous football team.

James Bready's "The Orioles" is a study of what makes Baltimore, Baltimore in sports.

Gilbert Sandler's "Black Baseball in Baltimore" is an interesting account of a frequently neglected area of Baltimore sports.

Lisa Kirshner and Jacques Kelly's "The Preakness" demonstrates the role of this horse racing event which has been part of Baltimore intermittently since 1873.

Joseph Arnold provides us with an introduction to six lives.

R. C. Monk and Blaine Taylor document the many achievements of Walter Sondheim, Jr.

Nicholas Varga's "Lawrence Cardinal Shehan" is a brief account of Baltimore's popular and courageous religious leader who helped cement the ecumenical and interfaith movement in Maryland and was in the vanguard for racial equality.

Dorthy T. Apgar's "The Mitchell Family" is an account of Baltimore's most well-known black political-real estate family.

Jane Sellman's "Barbara Mikulski" sets out to capture Baltimore's daughter, Congresswoman Mikulski, who has brought politics to the neighborhoods.

Morgan H. Pritchett's "Harry Bard, 1907–1976" is a moving study of one of the city's best-known educators.

Ric Bartter's "Robert C. Embry, Jr." is a portrait of the accomplishments of former Baltimore Housing Commissioner (1968–1977) Robert C. Embry, whose energy and foresight helped reverse the city's decline.

In the appendix of this work is Joseph Arnold's "How to Write about the History of Baltimore." This is a concise overview with step-by-step instructions on how *you* can contribute to preserving Baltimore's history.

The "Chronology" by Richard P. Davis gives some of the important rebuilding events.

Political Aspects

TOMMYS TWO: THE D'ALESANDROS

For many years, "mayor" in Baltimore was synonymous with "D'Alesandro." Both "Tommy the Elder" and "Tommy the Younger" served the city well as mayors, initiating and implementing programs that contributed to the city's revitalization, sometimes dramatically paving the way for Baltimore's current renaissance.

When asked to look back to assess Baltimore's shiny new look and revived personality, Thomas D'Alesandro III gave a comprehensive explanation:

"One of the most important aspects of the revitalization and rebuilding of downtown Baltimore concerns itself with the joint effort between the private sector led by the Greater Baltimore Committee (at that time chaired by Clarence Miles) and the city government at the time that my father was mayor in the early 1950s. What transpired was a realization that the downtown area of Baltimore, if it were to be allowed to exist as is, would die; that there was no growth potential; that it was a downtown for another era, the old Baltimore. But something had to be done to revitalize it and it meant the complete demolition of many downtown acres and a precise plan for reconstruction.

. . . Once this plan was agreed to between the Greater Baltimore Committee and the mayor, the legislation was introduced in Annapolis, passed in Annapolis and also passed by the Baltimore City Council, placing this renewal project on the ballot. It was subsequently passed by the voters. All this was accomplished in record breaking and unprecedented time. (I think it was less than 60 days before the legislative aspect of this was approved.) And with the voter's approval, all this came into being very rapidly. I think (and I don't say this braggadociously for my father) as a former mayor myself, I couldn't comprehend anybody getting legislation through the General Assembly and the City Council within 60 days. It couldn't be done now, so that's to his credit. It's the kind of thing that people today I don't think realize or understand or appreciate, but it was a herculean task in those days.

"The Greater Baltimore Committee conceived the idea and my father had to get the

Mayor Thomas D'Alesandro, Jr.

Mayors Thomas D'Alesandro, Jr. and Thomas D'Alesandro III. Receiving an Award from the Italian American Charities of Maryland, Inc.

Harbor, which meant in essence that the Charles Center was completed and now we move on to our natural base, the harbor.

"When the mayor showed it [the inaugural address] to me for review, I think he was asking me to read it but also to see whether or not I would support it and I told him at the time I thought it was a natural. And so he planted the seed. Then during his four years we had the benefit of the experience that we gained in the creation of the Charles Center so we could expedite the procedure by which we were going to move towards the Inner Harbor.

"And when I became mayor I brought into government some very talented people, but one of the real shining lights in which I take pride is the selection of Bob Embry as the Housing and Community Development commissioner. And we picked up where McKeldin left off and started to sign the disposition agreements for most of the major construction you see down there today. When I left office the pendulum shifted to Mayor Schaefer and he continued and added to portions of the development of the Inner Harbor."

The frequent references to his father's talents and accomplishments indicate the pride that Tommy the Younger took in Tommy the Elder. "He was the greatest natural politician Maryland ever saw," he beams, corroborating what Ernest B. Furgurson of the *Sun* said of Tommy the Elder when speaking of him as a "Maryland Model":

"He is politician right down to his metatarsal phalanges, and he can laugh about it—has been, for half a century, since he first ran for the legislature."

The story of Tommy's running for the legislature in 1926 and winning, to become, at 22, the "baby" member of the House of Delegates points up the idea that he was a born politician. From this first victory, he went on to win 23 consecutive elections, serving in the House of Delegates, City Council, United States House of Representatives (three terms), and as mayor of Baltimore (three terms).

As congressman he was known to President Franklin Delano Roosevelt as "Tommy." (D'Alesandro named a son, born within 24 hours of Roosevelt's inauguration as president, "Franklin Delano Roosevelt D'Alesandro.") Because he did so much in both people projects

necessary legislation and appropriations to move it. It couldn't have worked if it had been done by the private sector alone or if it had been done by the government alone. It had to be a realization by all segments of the community that something had to be done and done quickly and we really were in the forefront of all the cities in redevelopment because we moved quickly. And as a result of moving quickly, we now are the beneficiaries of a lot of federal funds that come into Baltimore because we're a showcase.

". . . The momentum that had been built by my father's administration was being carried on by the Grady administration. In other words, the entire aspect of urban redevelopment in Baltimore was never jeopardized by a change of administrations. Administrations have come and gone and all of them have supported the urban redevelopment. So Grady picked up where my father left off and carried it. And then when I came onto the scene as council president, McKeldin came in as mayor. And I remember very vividly Mayor McKeldin allowing me to review his inaugural address in which he called for the creation of the development of the Inner and public works as chairman of the House Committee on the District of Columbia, he was unofficially known as "the mayor of Washington." Tommy reminded Baltimore of this when he ran for mayor, citing the Washington experience as good preparation for becoming mayor of Baltimore. In his first inaugural address, he promised that he would turn the city into marble. Later, he commented that he had to take a lot of kidding because of that remark. A Richard Q. Yardley cartoon in the *Sun* of October 21, 1947, depicted Tommy at his desk, above which could be seen a framed scroll satirizing that same remark: " 'Augustus Caesar found Rome a city of stone and made it one of marble.' Hope to do same for hometown. Tommy." Tommy explained that "this was only a figure of speech meaning that I would make many improvements."

He did just that as mayor of Baltimore from 1947 to 1959.

In September of 1947, the morning *Sun* already stated:

"Mayor D'Alesandro yesterday took major steps toward the realization of long-discussed public works proposals and the furtherance of plans for the improvement of one of the city's present assets—the port of Baltimore."

He inaugurated a study that advocated "combining the overlapping" duties of the Port Development Commission, the harbormaster, the police harbor patrol. . . and the Bureau of Harbors under a single port authority, emphasizing that "such an authority could supervise and coordinate various activities—and should have sufficient authority to develop the harbor in a comprehensive manner to the benefit of the whole community."

He said then that he was looking to the future, just as he had claimed as Representative D'Alesandro when he initiated the plan "to convert the Light Street waterfront into a national park commemorating General Sam Smith, local hero of the War of 1812." On March 3, 1964, Representative D'Alesandro is quoted in the *Sun* in an article dealing with this D'Alesandro plan for the conversion of Light Street's waterfront into a memorial park: "We are building for the future of the city, not for today."

This vision was evident in other legislative and imaginative projects for the city. In 1941, following a City Hall conference that was attended by heads of municipal government as well as the state congressional delegation and WPA officials, after referring to the present airport as a mudhole, he said:

"Let's do something toward getting a real airport for Baltimore."

By the time Tommy came to run for a third term, his campaign press could boast an impressive list of accomplishments for his first two terms in office. The campaign slogan claimed the mayor had made "50 years of progress in 8 years." Indeed, the comprehensive list makes the boast believable.

Based on actual physical facts, the following took place or were constructed during his first eight years in office:

30 new schools (64 buildings)
25 new recreation centers and swimming pools
1400 miles of streets and highways
7 new hospital buildings and health centers
18 off-street parking garages
4 new firehouses
3 new library branches
21,947 new street lights
New People's Court building
Reconstruction of Memorial Stadium
Development of Druid Hill Park Zoo
City program for slum clearance
Best garbage system Baltimore ever had
Fight to bring big league baseball back to Baltimore
Fluorine in city drinking water
Modern solutions to city's traffic problems
Plans for municipal convention center

When contemplating running for mayor the first time, D'Alesandro claimed that he had become a candidate for the nomination "because of the overwhelming number of requests from all sections of the city, . . . from all types of citizens who believe, because of my congressional record and because of my earnest willingness to make the city a better place in which to live, that I should be elected mayor of Baltimore city. . . ." They continued to want him, electing him to three terms. He became known as a peppery, hard–working mayor who also liked hilarity and created it in his colorful speeches and off-the-cuff comments. His press conferences were known as "rough and tumble, wall-rumbling talks."

It is said he turned all his children into cheerleaders, who sang together to the tune of the rousing Notre Dame victory song:

Cheer, cheer for Tommy Dee Ay
He is the winner of every fray;
Cast your votes for Tommy Dee Ay,
The defender of the U. S. A.

To some the man with the black mustache and mangy cigar was jester and buffoon, but all would agree with the people in Little Italy who still call him "Signor Sindico" (Mr. Mayor).

Tommy the Elder was happy in 1967 when Tommy the Younger also became mayor. At the swearing in of his son, the old mayor presented him with a Bible that had been inscribed to Old Tommy when he was sworn in in 1947: "To The Honorable Thomas J. D'Alesandro, Jr. from your devoted family." He told his son with pride that now his name would be put in the Bible, too. "Seldom if ever in city history has a new mayor been installed with less political bitterness, or with more popular unanimity, or with a faster running start on his job than the 33-year old taking charge today," said the *Sun* on December 5, 1967. "This man . . . has a rendezvous with destiny."

The young mayor was described as having "his father's pizzazz but his own ideas." Yet there was a similarity of feeling for the city in the upbeat, optimistic tone of Young Tommy's inaugural address. "There are many among us who despair of the future of our city. Some flee. Others are despondent and feel that this is a time of hopelessness. I do not share these views." He went on to profess that he saw it as a time of opportunity, calling Baltimore "the city of our hope." There was high idealism in his promise "to root out every cause or vestige of discrimination" as the most fundamental commitment of his administration. To this day he believes that his civil rights package was one of the most important pieces of legislation to come before him. Because problems dealing with the educational system in Baltimore also received his special attention, educators in the city considered him a special friend. Probably he felt most strongly the concerns of poor people. Like his father, he was a grass-roots politician, with a belief in getting at problems at their source in the neighborhoods. Often characterized as sensitive and altruistic, he was still classified as an activist.

His progress report, "The Emerging City," published near the close of his term in office in 1971, claimed that "Baltimore today is a city emerging from its past toward what I believe will be one of the nation's strong and vital urban centers in the decades ahead." He explained the immediate and critical problems that met him at the outset of his administration. Citing "unprecedented efforts to rebuild our city in both physical and human terms," he gave a checklist of proud accomplishments: the Inner Harbor renewal program to transform Baltimore's waterfront; construction begun on the USF&G skyscraper, the Maryland Academy of Sciences center, the downtown campus of the Community College of Baltimore, etc. "We have made quality education the number one priority. We have established one of the nation's leading Model Cities' Programs, which aims to rebuild slums, to provide fuller services. As I have said many times, Baltimore is the one city in America that has 'turned the corner' and is on its way."

In a recent interview he said that there was, at first, a great negative consensus prevalent in Baltimore, that "we would never live to see it happen." Yet it did and the dramatic proof that Baltimore was not a dying city came with the establishment of the Baltimore City Fair, "one of America's most exciting events." Its purpose was to bring the people from all neighborhoods together to the center of the city to celebrate their city and themselves. "Baltimore became the first city in the nation to have a city fair designed to throw the spotlight on its people and its neighborhoods."

From the time he became City Council president in 1962 during the unexpired term of Mayor Grady which was being completed by Philip Goodman, he believes that the momentum from his father's administration could be felt. He insists again that urban redevelopment in Baltimore was never jeopardized by a change of administrations. "Administrations have come and gone and all of them have supported urban redevelopment. So Grady picked up from where my father left off and carried it. I would say in all fairness to all the mayors dating back to my father—Grady, Goodman, McKeldin, myself and Schaefer—the commitment was always there. It never deviated—and maybe I got credit for some of the things McKeldin did and McKeldin got credit for some of the things my father did. But in essence, I don't think it's a question of who gets the credit. It never affected me that way. I was just happy to see that we could follow through, you know?"

Followthrough is what both Tommy D'Alesandros had plenty of. Whether it's the father who was the natural politician, interested in politics before he could vote, or the modest son who says, "I'm not my father. I don't profess to being the politician he was. I just inherited a lot of what he laid the groundwork for." They were both intensely involved with programs for the people of a city whose future they believed in. Both get a lot of the credit for the beautiful rebirth of Baltimore.

Dorothy Pula Strohecker

THEODORE ROOSEVELT McKELDIN, 1900–1974

"People are not inclined to remember that I kept the tax rate down. But rather, they will ask

Theodore Roosevelt McKeldin, 1900–1974. Courtesy of Enoch Pratt Free Library.

what did he do?" was the way Theodore Roosevelt McKeldin felt he would be evaluated by posterity, for he often expressed this point of view and firmly believed that people would assess his years as governor and mayor by such a question.

The achievements of Mr. McKeldin compiled from 16 years in office—two terms as mayor (1943–1947, 1963–1967) and two terms as governor (1951–1958)—were, according to a contemporary news analyst, "formidable for any man in Maryland political history and incredible for a Republican."

Born on November 20, 1900 in South Baltimore at the corner of Eutaw Street and Stockholm Street (now Ostend Street), Teddy, of Scotch–Irish descent, was one of 11 children of James A. and Dora (Greif) McKeldin. His father, an admirer of Col. Theodore Roosevelt (the great Rough Rider, who had just been elected vice–president of the United States), named his son after this famous American.

Mr. McKeldin's father was a stonecutter turned policeman with no schooling, and his mother had completed only the third grade. Ted attended public schools Nos. 9 and 24, and often referred to himself during this period of his life as a school "walkout" at age 14. By law, boys and girls were required to go to school to age 14, then by custom, especially in Ted's neighborhood, they went to work. Often Ted McKeldin fondly related how he obtained his first job and how that caused him to speak proper English.

A friend and neighbor, who was a clerk in a bank, advised the young McKeldin that the Citizens' National Bank needed an office boy. All of his brothers had taken hard labor jobs, but Ted accepted the bank job and was, as he said, "thrown in with people who had gone to school." As a result, others working at the bank made fun of his English usage and such incorrect English expressions as "ain't got none" and "have went." On the advice of a fellow worker, young Ted enrolled in an English course at the City College night school. As a new, eager student, Ted McKeldin thought that to learn was to memorize, so he memorized everything—including poems, quotations from speeches, ideas of great men, and even the alphabet backwards. This exercise in mental gymnastics was later to hold the young McKeldin in good stead as a speaker and an orator.

During his first week of vacation from the bank, he got a job at Loudon Park Cemetery as a gravedigger at $2.50 a day. A remark by his father that young Ted would not last a day gave him the determination to stay on for the full week.

Young Ted went on from the Citizens' Bank to a better job at Alexander Brown and Sons and then to a still better job at Fidelity and Deposit Company. After he left City College and the old Milton Academy (which was a combination pharmaceutical and preparatory school), he attended evening classes at the College of Commerce, the Johns Hopkins University, and then finished his studies at the University of Maryland Law School.

On weekends he studied and later taught in the Sunday School of Bennett Memorial Methodist Episcopal Church in South Baltimore where at age 10 he watched his father march to the mourner's bench and swear off liquor. At that tender age he vowed never to touch the stuff himself, and though he opposed prohibition, he never allowed a drop to enter his home.

While at Fidelity and Deposit Company, he became a member of the American Institute of Bank Clerks which has been described as a "sort of combination labor union and Chautauqua Association." Here he took a leading part in organizing debating clubs among bank clerks, and these clubs were forums in which he gained a reputation for his oratorical ability.

In 1925, he graduated from the University of Maryland Law School, demonstrating his oratorical skills by winning the honor case, a mock trial argued by the graduates' brightest legal minds.

A year earlier he had married Honolulu Claire Manzer, whom he met while working as a bank office boy earning $20 a month. They had two children, Claire and Theodore, Jr.

Shortly after finishing law school, the young McKeldin began his political career as secretary to Mayor William F. Broening during the latter's administration from 1927 to 1931. Mr. McKeldin once said that, "Mayor Broening was the greatest politician I've ever known. He was a great human being, 100 percent honest man. He was a plumber who became a lawyer. He came out of poverty, and he never forgot it."

All the while he was becoming acquainted with the political scene at City Hall, young McKeldin was also achieving recognition as the Boy Orator of the Republican Party. As a young teen-ager, he had taken a Dale Carnegie Course in public speaking (25 lessons for $20) at the Baltimore College of Commerce. This class in public speaking prepared him so well that several years later he became the teacher. As a result of his ability as an orator of note, Mr. McKeldin was asked in 1952 to deliver the address that placed the name of Dwight D. Eisenhower in nomination for the presidency of the United States. In the ensuing campaign, he was active in promoting the election of General Eisenhower, not only in Maryland but in various states, particularly throughout the South.

Mr. McKeldin made his first run for mayor in 1939 and was beaten by Howard W. Jackson, the Democratic incumbent. Then, in 1942, Ted made the first of two unsuccessful bids for the governorship but succeeded in being elected mayor the following year by beating Mr. Jackson by a rousing 20,251 votes. As a wartime mayor, Mr. McKeldin could do little but keep essential services running and help draw plans for the postwar era. During this period, he incurred the wrath of the old guard of the GOP by awarding top municipal jobs to Democrats. His own party opposed him in 1946 when he made his second try for the governorship. Ted licked the Republican put up against him in the gubernatorial primary so badly that he was never again the object of an attempted primary purge. He then lost the following general election for governorship to William Preston Lane. Mr. McKeldin settled back to serve the one remaining year of his term as mayor. At the end of this year in 1947 he temporarily bowed out of the political arena knowing full well that the Democrats, with their 4 to 1 registration margin over the Republicans, were united and would kill off any chance he had for reelection.

Governor Lane, confronted with tremendous postwar money problems, was able to push through the General Assembly legislation for a sales tax. This gave Mr. McKeldin an issue that he effectively used in his third gubernatorial campaign. He stumped the state in 1950, promising first to cut, then to abolish the then–unpopular two percent sales tax and was elected governor by a landslide. As governor, Ted found quickly he was unable to eliminate the sales tax. In fact, during his last year in office, the two percent levy became a three percent one, and the state income tax was also raised 50 percent.

In reply to the pledge he made in 1950, Mr. McKeldin would simply say, "I made a mistake."

Probably no Maryland governor got more sheer fun from his job than did Ted McKeldin. He loved meeting people and talking with and to them. He was a vivacious and exuberant campaigner who could and would use bare knuckles when necessary. This he demonstrated in 1954 when he ran for reelection against Dr. H.C. Byrd, former University of Maryland president. It proved to be one of the roughest campaigns in recent times, but he came out of it with dignity ready to dig in for another four years. In his last term of office, he was able to get through the Democratic legislature a remarkable amount of legislation. Though more of his vetoes were overridden than of any other twentieth century Maryland governor, his crucial and important pieces of legislation had a way of sliding through the Maryland General Assembly.

During his administration as governor some of his major achievements included the new State Office buildings for Baltimore and Annapolis, Friendship International Airport (now Baltimore–Washington International Airport), Baltimore Harbor Tunnel, Baltimore Beltway, Liberty Dam, Maryland Port Authority, home rule for municipalities, Susquehanna Water Development Project (this ensures Baltimore a continuous water supply until the year 2000) and— possibly the most significant for the future of Baltimore and the state—the vast Inner Harbor Redevelopment Project. This listing does not take into account the improvements made in the state training schools, the establishment of the Patuxent Institute for Mental Defectives, and the enlargement and building programs at state schools of higher learning.

As one contemporary put it, "These are only the major bits and pieces, and they represent to some extent the ordinary building and constructing achievements of government."

Ted McKeldin was limited to two consecutive terms as governor; he had senatorial aspirations that did not materialize politically. The only option open to him at this time was to return to the local political arena. He suddenly found himself pitted in the mayoralty election against J. Harold Grady, a "new face" with the glamorous

background of being a former FBI agent. Mr. McKeldin took the worst licking ever administered a candidate for mayor. This he took gracefully as he had taken past honors, and, with his interest in practically everything unimpaired, went on to make his speeches, distribute autographed pictures, add to his collection of antiques and gold coins, and to build his law practice. He remained aloof from city and state politics from 1959 to 1962.

Then Mayor Grady resigned in 1962 to become a judge of the Supreme Bench of Baltimore. Philip H. Goodman, president of the City Council, was elevated automatically to mayor, and it became evident he would run for an elective term of office. The Republican State Central Committee voted overwhelmingly to ask Ted McKeldin to run in opposition to Goodman.

Mr. McKeldin campaigned on his record as governor and wartime mayor, raising the cry of "bossism" at City Hall. Just a month before balloting was to begin, the Republican candidate for city comptroller resigned, and, in his place, Mr. McKeldin persuaded Hyman A. Pressman, the self–appointed watchdog over city affairs who had barely lost out in the Democratic primary for city comptroller, to become Republican candidate for the post. This so–called "fusion ticket" was very attractive to the voters, and both Ted McKeldin and Hyman Pressman went on to victory in the general election. Thomas D'Alesandro 3rd, who was a landslide winner of an elective term as City Council president, immediately developed a working agreement with Mr. McKeldin.

This new administration got off to a harmonious start—despite the fact that Mr. McKeldin was the one Republican in a city government in which all other elective jobs were held by Democrats.

During this term of office, Ted McKeldin proposed the historic park which is now taking shape in downtown Baltimore. This includes the Carroll–Caton Mansion, the Flag House, Shot Tower, St. Vincent de Paul Church, and other historic buildings.

The new City Charter, which he approved in 1964, had such important provisions as creation of a Department of Finance, a requirement and provision for program budgeting.

Actually, Mr. McKeldin's accomplishments cannot be restricted to bricks and mortar: he carved a niche in the records of the state for his championing unpopular but just causes, his concern for social justice, and the political courage to lead a populace into securing that justice for all citizens. "I hate injustice and I have dedicated my entire life to fighting injustice," he said. His commitment to this ideal, though a master politican, was not a vote–earner. At times, his staunch belief in social justice led to hate letters (one depicting a man urinating on Mr. McKeldin's grave), obscene phone calls or a cross burned late at night on his lawn. His record of achievements in the realm of social justice is evident in his efforts to eliminate racial barriers when he appointed the first black to the Baltimore City Public School Board, the city solicitor's office and the mayor's staff; eliminated racial designations on state employment applications; had blacks admitted to Baltimore Polytechnic's A Course which was a full two years before the Supreme Court's antisegregation ruling; appointed the first Jew to the Court of Appeals; integrated state–owned beaches and parks; eliminated the policy of the Baltimore Transit Company not to employ black bus and trolley operators; integrated Baltimore hotels. One of his outstanding accomplishments was the creation and signing into law of the first comprehensive public accommodations law in Baltimore.

A number of colleges and universities honored him with honorary degrees, and he was also the recipient of four Freedom Foundation Awards, the Sydney Hollander Foundation Award for promoting better interracial relations, and the Histadrut Award for outstanding aid and service to the state of Israel. He was selected the 1953 "Man of the Year" by the Advertising Club of Baltimore and the same year also awarded the citation of the National Conference of Christians and Jews for his accomplishments in the interests of brotherhood and "an enduring democracy."

Mr. McKeldin attributed the success he had while in political office to the fact that all major issues were always taken directly to the people well in advance of legislative action: "A well–informed public giving expression to its sovereignty is the best guarantee of good government."

Morgan H. Pritchett

WILLIAM DONALD SCHAEFER

Beginning in the late 1940s, Baltimore was thought of as "that dirty city on the way south." Now it is considered one of the most successfully revitalized cities in the United States. Many Baltimoreans credit Mayor William Donald Schaefer with being the foremost agent of Baltimore's renaissance. However, Schaefer, now serving his third term as mayor, is quick to recognize correctly that the renaissance began with the efforts of former mayors. Schaefer, however, has played a significant role in its unfolding.

Today's burgeoning Baltimore almost concedes the fact that, during Schaefer's first few years as mayor, he was criticized for accomplishing little. He was then best known as Baltimore's "biggest booster." Most of his public pronouncements were simply varieties of the theme: "Baltimore's a great place." Many people laughed and sniggered at this man as they waited impatiently for tangible city improvements. However, Schaefer was a seasoned politician by this time and had learned to promise little publicly. Meanwhile, his administrations, bolstered by hard work and diligence, ultimately established clear goals and plans for the city that are now emerging.

William Donald Schaefer was born in Baltimore on November 2, 1921. He grew up in West Baltimore, where he still lives, and attended local schools: P.S. #88, P.S. #91, and City College High School, class of 1939. He was graduated from the University of Baltimore in 1942. He later received a law degree from the same institution.

In the late 1940s, after serving in the army during World War II, Schaefer's interest in civic affairs began with his involvement with the Allendale–Lyndhurst Improvement Association. This interest was stimulated by a situation he viewed as being grossly unfair: his church wished to purchase some land from the city and submitted a bid. The land was sold, however, at a lower price to another party, and the young Schaefer suspected political hanky–panky in the decision.

Schaefer later became president of the association. He also became a member of Citizens Planning and Housing Association (CPHA). It was through CPHA that he met Joan Bereska, who has since become his chief political assistant. His CPHA activities broadened his political scope from neighborhood issues and problems to city-wide concerns.

Out of these experiences Schaefer learned that groups and associations can have significant political impact. Schaefer also believed that more can be accomplished by being "for" something rather than "against." Throughout his entire political career he has stressed this belief. He has had angry conflicts with those he perceived as being "against." Often, reporters have caught the mayor's wrath for their alleged negativism.

In 1950, and again in 1954, Schaefer ran for a seat in the Maryland House of Delegates. He ran as an independent, without machine backing, and was defeated in both elections. In 1955, he accepted support from Democrats and was elected to the City Council from the Fifth District.

Although Schaefer embraced machine sup-

Mayor William Donald Schaefer. Photo by Kenneth M. Brooks Studios, Inc.

port, he quickly established a reputation for being a maverick. This trait endeared him to some while it antagonized many others. It wasn't unusual for the council to vote 16 or 17 against a bill, with only one or two in favor, with Schaefer's vote in the minority.

Urban renewal and housing conservation, both for the inner and outer city, were among Councilman Schaefer's primary concerns. He argued that home ownership, maintenance, and rehabilitation were keys to strong neighborhoods. He determinedly backed antiblockbusting legislation, called for an urban renewal agency with genuine power, and asked for inspection programs with strict code enforcement. These views established Schaefer's liberal credentials, and made him a minority voice in council chambers. Nevertheless, he was respected by his peers for his hard work and devotion to the job. When he became mayor, many of his neighborhood policies were finally implemented.

Councilman Schaefer was also interested in education. (Even today he has very fond memories of his teachers and schooling.) He has held strong views on transportation and the road system, but throughout his political career, he has changed his position several times on the extension of interstate highways through the city—losing, and then gaining, political support with each change.

City Council President: "Strictly By The Rules"

In 1967, after 12 years in elected office, William Donald Schaefer was elected president of the City Council on the ticket of Mayor Thomas D'Alesandro III.

The new council president witnessed with distress the continued exodus of middle- and upper-income city citizens to the counties. The city's tax base was reduced, which resulted in a decline of such city services as health, housing, fire and police protection, recreation, and education. This heightened Baltimoreans' negative feelings toward their city.

Another concern of Schaefer's was that Mayor D'Alesandro didn't ask the council to do more work; nor did that mayor actively seek the council's cooperation. Schaefer also believed that entrenched bureaucracy was holding the city

City Provided Activities at War Memorial Plaza, 1976.
Photo by Maurice Dixon.

down. He stated in a published interview in 1968, "I am so tired of red tape." Under his leadership the City Council became less of a rubber stamp for the mayor. Schaefer believed this political freedom would increase the likelihood of the council's assuming a positive role in tackling municipal problems. (A curious reversal has occurred, however, since Schaefer became mayor. He has been widely accused of demanding that the City Council be his personal rubber stamp; council people who do not "go along" have complained that city services have been cut back in their districts in retaliation).

Schaefer took a strong hand in running the council meetings. First, and to the surprise of many council members, he ran the meeting strictly by the rules. He even required that the pledge to the flag be recited at each meeting. He sought unity and a consensus on issues. Here is how he accomplished this: if he knew a bill he favored was not likely to pass, he would hold "mini-meetings" prior to the open council meeting to iron out disagreements. If a consensus were not reached, the bill or topic would be postponed until the next open meeting, to allow time for further behind-the-scenes manipulation.

Despite his desire for unity and democratic procedures, William Donald Schaefer seemed

determined to have his own way—a trait that has characterized his entire political career. One of the better known examples of this occurred in 1969, as reported by David Ahearn in the *News American*, when he failed to get a bill passed on a tough law for pool hall regulations. Schaefer appointed various officials from different agencies to "form an inspection team that would deliver a joint jolt to the formerly free-and-easy billiard parlors. Asked if he had the authority to do so, he bluntly shot back, 'Damn it, I did it.' "

His term as president of the City Council was called an "iron rule," but through this approach, Schaefer believed Baltimore could begin to reverse its negative trend and start to solve its many problems.

Schaefer's leadership was typified by other changes. One of the first things he did was to streamline the council itself. He also helped eliminate bureaucratic inefficiency. He emphasized the hiring of competent department heads—people possessing positive attitudes and having team work loyalty. He encouraged the financing of many professional studies. Lastly, Schaefer supported increased expenditures, even though city funds were limited. His energy was directed toward lobbying for more state and federal money.

Although he had strong ideas of his own, and often did not see eye-to-eye with Mayor D'Alesandro, Schaefer worked closely with the mayor as much as possible.

Schaefer's civic views as president of the City Council are reflected by an observation he made about the school system's failure: "We have reached a low ebb. What destroyed the school system was that everyone started to down the system by talking it down." He saw many other city problems in the same simplistic terms of positivism versus negativism.

Schaefer believed that the three major ingredients for urban engineering were a positive attitude, competent personnel, and increased spending. This philosophy guided him when he became mayor.

The New Mayor: "... the engineers will fix the bridges, but not the potholes."

In 1971, William Donald Schaefer was elected mayor when Tommy D'Alesandro declined to run for a second term. What struck the newly elected mayor most was the belief that "people were not proud of their city or of being called Baltimoreans." Baltimore was then experiencing severe urban problems.

On the positive side, Schaefer knew that Inner Harbor development, many housing programs, a road system, and other building projects were already in various stages of implementation. These physical structures would represent a major accomplishment for his administration. Schaefer felt that time was not yet ripe for grandiose plans to cure the most serious social problems plaguing Baltimore.

The first step of Schaefer's new administration was to build pride in Baltimore. During the previous 16 years, he had visited many other cities and found that Baltimore compared favorably to most of them. If his strategy of pride-building was to work, he knew he had to communicate his travel experiences to the city.

Schaefer was comfortable with boosterism. Besides public declarations about how great Baltimore was, Schaefer insisted on buttons for the City Fair that said, "Smile—You're In Baltimore." The "Charm City" slogan and bracelets soon followed (though so did national publicity on Baltimore's sanitation strike at the same time). Other public relations gestures were developed, including Department of Public Works signs proclaiming the name of Mayor Schaefer as well as information about the repair or project being performed. However, by the end of the decade the bottom of the signs would read instead: "Mayor William Donald Schaefer and the citizens of Baltimore."

Schaefer stressed from the onset of his administration that "little things are important. We know the engineers will fix the bridges, but not the potholes." Without subtlety, Schaefer wanted these "little things" attended to immediately. This attention, he believed, would demonstrate to city residents that their government was responsive to their needs. Another "little thing" that the mayor did was to sign many of his own letters personally. The mayor frequently walked through neighborhoods taking notes of local problems. He would listen to residents' complaints and jot them down in his pocket notebook. If the problem was small and could be readily rectified—such as trash removal—he had his staff contact the appropriate agency; if

the problem was major—such as physical decay in a shopping district—he informed his staff, "We have a serious problem here, let's develop plans to solve it." Out of this approach, programs such as the Mayor's Advisory Committee on Commercial Revitalization were born.

Schaefer knew that Baltimore's greatest strength was its neighborhoods. Improvements here could help build urban pride and be the first step toward overcoming years of urban decay. During his first two administrations, Schaefer encouraged an extensive program of building multi-purpose centers, mayor's stations, health clinics, and senior citizens centers, all of which were located in the neighborhoods.

Another change reflected in the mayor's attitude was, "It doesn't cost any more to have a pretty city than it does an ugly one." He enthusiastically endorsed a 1 percent for art in public buildings program and offered his office's support for the creation of the Mayor's Advisory Committee on Art and Culture.

Mayor Schaefer appreciated that Baltimore's many cultural institutions were major assets. He strongly supported increased funding for such projects as new wings for the Baltimore Museum of Art and the Walters Art Gallery, and the construction of a new symphony hall. When the Mechanic Theatre was closed, the mayor became the talk of the town when he went to New York City to pitch Baltimore to scores of producers, directors, and actors in an effort to assure the theatre world that Baltimore could and would support professional live theatre if it were performed at the Mechanic. When Center Stage's theatre burned down, Schaefer lent city support to help that company raise money and find a new home.

"People want more for their tax dollars than just basic services. People do not want to just exist in their city; they want to *live* in it," said the mayor. He called for many municipally sponsored programs: the Beautiful Walls for Baltimore mural program; War Memorial lunchtime activities (frog hops, chess and checkers, scrabble tournaments, miniature golf, and hog-calling contests); nature programs at Cylburn Park; Sunny Sundays; outdoor music programs; and the now–famous ethnic festivals.

By 1976, Schaefer believed that the two turning points in development of civic pride were the City Fairs and the tall ships. The former demonstrated that neighborhood pride is valued and that people would come downtown to discover, or rediscover, the diversity of their city. The visit of the tall ships gave Baltimore national and international attention. Baltimore began to become a point of destination rather than a city to pass through on the way to Washington or Philadelphia. By the time the city's Convention Center opened in 1979, it already had an impressive number of prior bookings—testifying to the success of the city's self-promotion effort locally and nationally.

Meanwhile, boosterism was proving to be infectious. In 1976, when Schaefer announced the "Baltimore Is Best" program (which recognizes Baltimoreans who promote good things in the city), there was little laughter, ridicule, or cynicism. Baltimoreans were clearly becoming proud of their city.

However, the mayor realized that city pride alone could not solve urban problems. For too long, Baltimore's tax base had been declining; businesses and industries were leaving the city; many neighborhoods were blighted; the bureaucracy was too often ineffective; and the school system was failing.

One of the first things Schaefer did when he was elected mayor was to streamline the bureaucracy. Many department heads were eliminated, resulting in a more efficient, smaller cabinet. From past political experience he knew that "the bureaucracy will move as *slowly* as you let it." Schaefer had little intention of letting this happen in his administration—which he promised would be "a City Hall you don't have to fight."

His next step was to hire executive personnel who were held in high professional esteem. Experts in city government were needed, in part because Schaefer accepted the fact that he was not a brilliant innovator of ideas, nor a technician aware of the latest concepts of urban engineering. He was, rather, an observer who could identify problems and could motivate a staff that would find solutions and then execute them.

Schaefer, however, was not a pawn of his experts or staff, regardless of the esteem in which he held them. He tried to seek consensus among them, but if he were not persuaded by his professionals, he would insist on his own policy or program. He had no intention "about reading of a new city program in the newspaper the next day" without his prior knowledge.

Schaefer made it clear to his staff that he demanded hard work and loyalty. He also expected this from the City Council as well. He was "married to his job" and expected his staff to have close to the same devotion. Disagreements were expected to be kept at a minimum and performance was expected to be maximum. When staff members "fouled up," or even if there was just a disagreement, the famous Schaefer temper was exercised.

How did the Schaefer administration go about problem solving and developing goals and programs? It followed this procedure: at a staff meeting, Schaefer or his staff would identify the problem, general discussion would take place, and then Schaefer would direct the appropriate department to develop a solution. One example was the Old Town Mall project, which helped Baltimore win an All-American City Award in 1977; it evolved through this decision-making process.

The same method was used to solve economic problems. Baltimore faced strong industrial competition from the surrounding counties and from southern states from the 1960s on. To keep industries in Baltimore and to bring new ones in, Mayor Schaefer encouraged the development of new industrial parks and instituted an aggressive program to entice corporations to locate in Baltimore. Results of this are seen in the Quad Avenue, Union Stockyard, Canton, and Holabird industrial parks. BEDCO (Baltimore Economic Development Corporation) is largely responsible for these developments, but it was through the mayor and his staff that BEDCO came into existence as a bulwark against continued economic decline.

To expedite city progress, by Schaefer's second and third terms, a "shadow government" (as it was called when its existence came to light) was created. It was an ad hoc group of facilitators whose job was to cut red tape and financial restraints to accomplish ends that might not have otherwise been possible. In effect, the city had two governments—one operating as a representative body (City Council) and the other acting as would the controlling officers of a large private corporation. The "shadow government" circumvented council approval on certain mat-

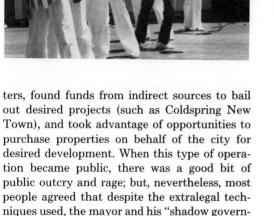

Festivals and Fun for Baltimoreans, 1980 and 1981.
Photos by Ric Bartter.

ters, found funds from indirect sources to bail out desired projects (such as Coldspring New Town), and took advantage of opportunities to purchase properties on behalf of the city for desired development. When this type of operation became public, there was a good bit of public outcry and rage; but, nevertheless, most people agreed that despite the extralegal techniques used, the mayor and his "shadow government" accomplished a great deal.
Structures ride but not all spirit soars.

Mayor Schaefer began his first administration facing four major problems: economic decline, lack of pride in the city, a failing school system, and a relatively low quality of city life. By the end of his second term, the school system had begun to improve, but it was generally agreed that it was far from the zenith it had once reached. Schaefer has been successful in building pride and improving the quality of city life.

People are beginning to enjoy living in the city, or coming to visit it. Despite two recessions during Schaefer's administrations, the overall economic health of Baltimore has been favorable; it has a blue–chip bond rating among cities. Lastly, Baltimore has been recognized worldwide as an example of successful city revitalization.

The task of running a city seems almost insurmountable; myriad demands for quick solutions to municipal problems frequently conflict. Thus, time has taught many politicians that the window–dressing remedies are politically safest. This short–sighted approach ignores the pathos of many city residents.

With this idea as a backdrop, there is another side of the Schaefer coin, which in the eyes of many, is tarnished. Baltimore still has massive urban problems (crime, unemployment, poor housing and education, and racial inequality). Many observers have criticized the Schaefer administration for laxity in dealing with these so-cial problems. But it must be added that though these problems still exist, Schaefer has taken many positive steps, with the use of federal and state funding, to work toward solutions.

Many Baltimoreans are willing to call William Donald Schaefer a great mayor, but most profes-sional observers feel that still more attention must be given to human services before such a title can be rightfully bestowed. Few would dis-pute, however, that Mayor Schaefer has been an outstanding leader and public servant who has done much to make Baltimore a viable city in an age when cities were supposed to be dying.

Laurence N. Krause

THE POLITICS OF THE BALTIMORE RENAISSANCE

It was fashionable a few years ago to say that American cities have become ungovernable, but this generalization certainly doesn't apply to Baltimore. Through most of the post–World War II era this city has been governed by mayors who kept the municipality financially strong, held it together during moments of social crisis, and pushed it through an extraordinary period of physical reconstruction and human service expansion. Baltimore has been able to do this because it has had two mayors in the 1947–1980 era who between them have controlled city gov-ernment for two-thirds of that time, and were able to overcome the grave weaknesses of mu-nicipal democracy. These two men were Thomas D'Alesandro, Jr. and William Donald Schaefer. Of the two, Schaefer looms larger. He is, in fact, the greatest mayor in the history of the munic-ipality. They were able to exert their authority over a municipal political system that, left to its own devices, would probably have bungled many of the city's projects and failed to initiate many others. Mayor Thomas D'Alesandro, Jr., whose administration began the Baltimore renaissance in the years 1947–1958, was an old-line political boss who brought a remarkable degree of order

Mayor J. Harold Grady. Photo by James Karmodt Lightner.

to the city's Democratic ward–boss system, end-ing a 20-year period of interward fighting that swirled around William Curran and marking the rise of James H. "Jack" Pollack. From 1971 to the present, the city has been ruled by William Donald Schaefer, another product of the city's machine politics (he came out of the Irv Kovens and Marvin Mandel faction), who has wielded more absolute political power than any politician in the city since the great boss Isaac Freeman Rasin in the 1880–1905 era. Rasin, however, never held the mayoralty and had only a fraction of Schaefer's long–range vision for the city. D'Alesandro ruled for 12 years and began the Baltimore renaissance; Schaefer, who will gov-ern for 12 and possibly 16 years, will preside over its climax. During the interim between these two long reigns, the city was actually rudderless for only a short period of time. Only during the terms of Mayors J. Harold Grady, Philip Goodman (who served out the last five months of Grady's term), and the bizarre four years under ex-Governor McKeldin, was there a real vacuum of leadership. Mayor Tommy D'Alesandro III's term in office (1967–1971) was a far more positive contribution to the city than he has been given credit for, but fate played some of its worst cards on Tommy D'Alesandro, for his term in office coincided with the darkest days of modern Baltimore history. The municipal employees were restless because financial problems prevented the city from giving them much in the way of pay raises or benefits. There were strikes and great acrimony. The City Council under McKeldin had become terribly difficult to manage and it took City Council President Schaefer some time to create order so that important business did not get ignored or cut to pieces in the petty intercouncilmanic squabbles. Most serious of all, racial tensions in the city reached their highest point in the entire postwar era, culminating in the five days of rioting following the assassination of Dr. Martin Luther King in April, 1968—a bloody event that substantially deepened hostilities and resentments in a city whose population was moving steadily towards a black majority. In addition to these extraordinary factors, the city's now long-established white middle-class exodus increased its tempo and the numbers of poor immigrants continued to spiral upwards. While federal money was increasing, city expenses seemed to increase even faster. The city budget doubled during D'Alesandro's term. The numbers of new problems, projects, state programs, federal programs, protests, court orders, and union demands appeared almost to overwhelm D'Alesandro and his advisers. "During the first two-and-one-half years of office," he told a reporter, "we had crisis after crisis . . . we got hit with everything except the kitchen sink." He spent much of his time, he said, dealing with "people problems . . . mainly getting suspicious blacks and whites together again after the riots . . . getting black and white citizens to understand each other." It was, he reflected, "like getting hit on the head with a hammer." Long before his first term ended he decided to return to private life, but his sense of honor and responsibility kept him beating away at the city's problems until the end of his term—

Henry Cooper, Portrait in Oils of Mayor Philip H. Goodman of Baltimore, Maryland.

long after his heart and spirit had gone out of the job.

The office itself had become a mind-numbing and physically crushing responsibility for anyone wishing to do a conscientious job. Unlike the state governors or even the president, city mayors are held *personally* responsible when specific services and facilities go wrong. When the trash isn't collected on some alley, its residents go to the mayor's office and really expect *him* to correct it. Cities, unlike state and national levels of government, are in an almost continual state of financial crisis, increasingly dependent on state and federal grants that may be withdrawn the next year. They depend for their economic health upon middle-class residents who can always pull out for the suburbs if they find the city too difficult, and many businesses can (and do) the same thing. Increasingly, both groups look to City Hall for solutions. In too many of those city halls, political leadership is so fractured and weak it cannot respond with either vigor or with rationality—sometimes it is incapable of any response. Urban politics has always been the weakest link in the whole American political system because the central political issues are often struggles between classes and neighborhoods that cannot become very adequately reflected in the regular two-party system. For the past 150 years most American cities have moved between a chaotic, local-ward boss dominated system of democracy and a highly centralized rule of a single city-wide boss. Chicago under the late Mayor Richard Daley weathered quite well the shock waves of the 1960s and 1970s in some large measure because it was ruled rationally (and at times ruthlessly) by that single political figure. New York, during these same years, staggered along under a succession of coalition front men as mayor, none of whom could control the city government or city politics. As a result, New York slipped into financial irresponsibility and ultimately into de facto bankruptcy. To rule a large American city today, it seems, calls for a person with the mind of Machiavelli, the spirit of St. Francis, the physical stamina of a horse, and the epidermis of a Maryland crab.

By blind luck Baltimore obtained something like this in Mayor Schaefer. Mayor D'Alesandro complained to reporters in 1971 that he and his top aides had to work many nights until eleven o'clock and regretted the high price his family paid for such grueling hours. Mayor Schaefer, without the private responsibilities of a family, normally works 14 or more hours per day. He does this because he continually attempts to keep in hand an enormously broad range of city affairs and to keep in personal touch with a substantial number of the city's people and problems. If he were mayor of New York, Chicago, or Los Angeles he would, one suspects, have by this time drowned in the details of such supercities or dropped dead of heart failure in the attempt. Baltimore is about as large as a city can get and still allow the mayor to have the range of detailed knowledge and personal involvement that Mayor Schaefer evidences here in Baltimore.

The fact that Mayor Schaefer is possibly the hardest working mayor in the history of the city

would not account for the success of his administration. He is a man who stepped onto the stage of Baltimore history at the exact moment when someone with his vision and skills could seize the strings of the city and pull most of them together. He is by temperament a classic political boss. His philosophy of government was aptly summarized to a *News American* reporter in 1978: "Somebody has to be in charge." That has been a constant thread in the mayor's political thought. Back in 1968, when he was City Council president, he expressed his frustration with "red tape" and the accompanying attitude that some worthy goal was just too complex and difficult to attain. "The most depressing thing," he told the writer, "is to know something is right and there's a simple way to do it, and be unable to do it. I am tired of hearing that it can't be done." The mayor's now famous temper stems from the same basic attitude. Walter Sondheim was reported to have said of Schaefer, "He's a perfectionist. And one of the prices of being a perfectionist is losing your temper when you don't get perfection." His frustrations with "red tape" clearly extend to the City Council and he has, over the past 10 years, attempted to rule as much as possible without them—most controversially with the establishment of appointed city trustees to preside over millions of dollars of city expenditures that would normally come under the control of the City Council. His problems with the council stem from a basic desire to make it a creature of his own power.

Some have seen Schaefer's courting of the city neighborhood associations as a means of undercutting the council. One frustrated councilman told an *Evening Sun* reporter in 1979 that neighborhood associations in his district continually went around him directly to the mayor, and did so with Schaefer's encouragement. "From the morning he got elected [the mayor] eliminated the middleman." There seems little doubt that Mayor Schaefer has a low opinion of municipal democracy as it presently exists in Baltimore, and he has accumulated enough political power to overwhelm any direct challenges to his rule. The city councilmen who cross the mayor, like anyone else who publicly challenges him inside or outside the government, is considered disloyal and un-Baltimorean. Criticism of the mayor is equated with criticism of the city. Schaefer's long-running warfare with local reporters stems largely from the same problem—criticism of the mayor or his administration was looked upon as unpatriotic, harmful to the city's image, and, by implication, to its credit rating on Wall Street and its attractiveness to potential businesses and back-to-the-city folks. In short, Schaefer is a classic city boss who is authoritarian in philosophy and more comfortable with private negotiations than with the rough and tumble of open decision-making.

The fact that Mayor Schaefer has succeeded in becoming the most powerful city boss in Baltimore's entire history and works constantly to extend this power into every area of the city obviously troubles many people. Yet more troubling is the fact that without the strong hand of the Schaefer administration, the Baltimore renaissance could easily have ground to a halt—or fallen far short of the goals it is now reaching. The view that the city improvements would have come about under any mayor seems overly optimistic. While Baltimore forged ahead in the 1970s, cities like St. Louis, and Cleveland (not to mention New York) slipped further into decay and financial impotency largely because they lacked strong imaginative mayors. There was no assurance that the momentum of the Baltimore improvements would have been sustained under some less powerful administration. An aide to former mayors McKeldin and D'Alesandro III said recently, "People assume once the impetus gets moving, things get easy. That's not true ... the bureaucratic machinery can grind to a halt." Not only has Schaefer kept the bureaucratic machinery turning, he has improved its performance considerably—largely by attracting and holding a staff of extremely bright and hard-working people who follow the mayor's example of working 14-hour days and striking terror into those who are not pulling their oar hard enough or who try to pull in some other direction. One immediately thinks of Charles L. Benton, Joan Bereska, Francis Kuchta, or Robert Embry; but there are many other men and women around the mayor who are of equal zeal and ability. It is hard to believe that these people, all of whom could be earning considerably more money in private business, would have remained in city government if they were constantly wound up in the red tape that multiplies when a weak exec-

utive is in office, or who would have been continually whiplashed by the petty politics of a typical city council attempting vainly to rule the city over the mayor. Further, it should not be forgotten that many of the key decisions that brought important new facilities and investments into Baltimore (or kept important businesses from leaving the city) were the result of strong and convincing personal appeals from Mayor Schaefer and his chief aides.

Schaefer's ability to push things through in Baltimore has undoubtedly been an important factor in winning new investment in the city. The mayor has unquestionably restored confidence in the city and its future—a confidence that suffered very severe blows by the racial and economic problems of the 1960s. The racial cleft in American life falls most heavily on cities like Baltimore, where the largest concentrations of low-skill black people compete with hard-pressed whites in a difficult job market. Riots, high city taxes, crime, schools, the expansion of low-income and/or black residential areas all continued to drive tens of thousands of white (and now increasing numbers of middle-income blacks) out of the city. The influx of the back-to-the-city people, never equalling the outflow, was hardly assured in the 1970s since these people have the money to pull out if the atmosphere changes.

Mayor Schaefer is the city's most successful promoter because he is the one man at the center of the city's power structure. Mayor McKeldin was perhaps more eloquent than Schaefer in singing Baltimore's praises, but Schaefer is far more convincing because people realize the speaker is in fact the real voice of the city. In his long support for both urban superhighways and neighborhood level revival he has attempted, with a large degree of success, to bring into some harmony two opposite poles of the urban environment. The superhighway, so obviously destructive to much of the fabric of neighborhood life, was essential if Baltimore was to survive as a major port and commercial/industrial center. It would have been politically popular to cave in on the highway issue; but he refused to do so. His refusal to compromise on some issues of the specific siting of the highways was wrongheaded, but his dogged effort to drive the highway program through over widespread opposition was courageous, and Baltimore as a whole will benefit enormously from that effort.

The same is true of the Charles Center–Inner Harbor effort. It would have been far more popular to have invested the money in a variety of very worthy neighborhood projects; but without the leading edge of investment in the central district, the city's entire economic position would have remained questionable. Charles Center–Inner Harbor was the visible symbol of Baltimore's revival—it had become the central focus long before Schaefer entered the mayoralty; but once the die was cast in this spot it *had* to succeed—indeed, it had to be a smash hit to compensate for so many other aspects of Baltimore's life that could never undergo the same type of swift, dramatic transformation. Long before he became mayor, Schaefer was acutely aware that the city is an utter prisoner of private investors. If the businessmen found it unprofitable or disagreeable to remain in the city, they would simply leave—and the city would die. Schaefer stated the matter concisely in 1979.

In the first place, two thirds of the city's budget, $800 million, goes to human services, schools, recreation, parks, housing, health, rat eradication, and so on . . . And in the second place, people don't understand how the city works *economically*. No convention center: no new money. No new money: no medical center. No hotels, no Inner Harbor, no transit system: no new jobs attracted, no public housing, no future. It's as simple as that.

A great measure of Schaefer's success has been due to the fact that he has maintained a clear direction and a consistent set of priorities. The economic health of the city has been the first priority, but it is not his only one. The promotion of Baltimore's neighborhood life has been a second priority. The rise of the new neighborhood associations coincided exactly with Schaefer's rise in Baltimore politics. He began his political career with the Allendale–Lyndhurst Improvement Association and then quickly established himself in one of the older traditional political organizations. But as the old political clubs and organizations faded before the rising neighborhood associations, Schaefer's original affiliation with the associations allowed him to straddle both movements. It has remained the key to his political power in Balti-

more and has provided a philosophy of action exactly suited to the city's social structure.

Human services have been the third priority in terms of the mayor's attention, although they have clearly always ranked first in the city budget. If one includes education within the human services area, almost two-thirds of the city budget goes to this area. Tragically, the problems in this area are largely beyond the scope of even so powerful a municipal leader as Schaefer. With the surrounding counties careful to keep their housing at a price level beyond the reach of poor families, Baltimore city becomes the dumping ground for multiproblem, low-skilled people and their children. The strain on the city's social service system is staggering. The city school system, struggling to educate thousands of badly nourished, culturally deprived and psychologically wounded children, is under-staffed and underfinanced. These are really national problems. The city by itself cannot hope to make dramatic progress in these areas. That any progress at all is made is remarkable testimony to the effectiveness of the educational and social service systems. If the mayor can make substantial progress with these two areas, he will become more than a brilliant leader—he will rival Houdini.

As the downtown renewal projects near completion, all the highways finally link together, and the revived neighborhoods begin to generate their own private investment, Baltimore will have recast itself in the form it will maintain into the twenty-first century. This greatest and most dramatic transformation in the entire history of the city will be presided over by Mayor Schaefer and his name, far more than any other, will forever be linked to the Baltimore renaissance. For that reason alone his place is secure as Baltimore's greatest mayor. History is always unfair in its judgments—it tends to personify in one person the work of a whole generation. And so it will be with Mayor Schaefer. Nevertheless, no man better deserves to have the credit gather about him, for no other individual has so steadfastly stamped the city with his personal vision. Perhaps a man of lesser strength and vision could have done nearly as well, or perhaps even the City Council, given its freedom, could have muddled through. Municipal democracy would today be considerably stronger if the council rather than Schaefer had led the city during the past decade; but the chance is very great that the Baltimore renaissance would have foundered in a sea of neighborhood rivalry, racial mistrust, business disillusionment, and political anarchy. The Constitution of the United States provides for a quasi-executive dictatorship during wartime, and Franklin Roosevelt in the crisis of 1933 invoked much of the same level of emergency powers. The Baltimore City Charter makes no such provision for municipal crises. Mayor Schaefer, inheriting in 1971 a still seriously sick city, assumed powers not specifically granted him. One hopes that there will come a day in the city's future when it can afford the slow, erratic process of local municipal politics—the luxury of hesitant and compromising democracy. However, during the last 30 years the city's problems have been too large, and the inherent divisions within the city too deep, to allow it to move forward without a person of power, determination, and vision in the mayor's office.

Joseph Arnold

THE CITY COUNCIL

The Baltimore City Council was originally founded as part of an experiment. Until 1796, Baltimore Town was part of Baltimore County, under the legislative authority of Maryland's General Assembly. On December 31, 1796, the General Assembly passed an act "to erect Baltimore Town, in Baltimore County, into a city . . . " and place the whole idea on trial for 20 months. The council's principal duties concerned police power, the collection of taxes, supervision of the harbor, and general legislative powers required for the "good order, health, peace and safety" of a large city. The 16 members and mayor evidently performed successfully for, not waiting for the experiment to end, the General Assembly in 1797 made the council a perpetual body.

After the current City Hall was constructed in the nineteenth century, council debates took place in a room with a high ceiling, tall windows,

a spectator balcony, lots of marble, dark veneer furnishings, and a stately presidential seat. It all suggested a moderate Old World elegance as interpreted by Victorian Americans.

Elegance did not always describe what happened inside the council. For instance, on July 12, 1962, it met in special session to consider prayer, bar-girls, and redrawing the boundaries of the city's councilmanic districts. The first subject, prayer, involved a resolution that denounced the Supreme Court ruling against state-imposed prayers and called for a constitutional amendment to override the court. Eventually the resolution was withdrawn and the council adopted a unanimous declaration supporting the court ruling. The bar-girl issue concerned solicitation of customers in Baltimore's bars. Action on the bill that would ban solicitation was deferred and a hearing was scheduled. The problem of drawing new boundaries for councilmanic districts came up because of the Supreme Court's "one man, one vote" ruling. Mayor J. Harold Grady presented a bill to the council that led to a long debate and a series of actions continuing until the fall of 1966. If anything had been resolved, the meeting on that day in July would not have been typical. As things turned out, the chamber was filled with rhetoric and indecision. All decisive votes were put off, making it a typical day.

The subsequent paragraphs will examine how the council conducted itself in the face of a basic constitutional issue during the sixties: civil rights. Then the redistricting issue will be reviewed, for it shows how politics and constitutional issues get mixed up in the heat of a body whose members are concerned about self-preservation.

The city used to hold elections in May and celebrate with installation of the winners shortly thereafter. At the May, 1959, opening session the council chambers were flower-bedecked and filled with a 300-person audience. Yet, true to form, the council began to fight immediately over political patronage. At the time, the forces of political boss Jack Pollack numbered six. A reform group led by Mayor Grady and Council President Philip Goodman set out to deprive the "Pollackians" of any patronage. The immediate issue was selection of 13 clerks, including the first black clerk. During the debate, 300-pound

Councilman Solomon Liss addressed a young, newly elected law student named Peter Angelos. Said Liss, "I am quite a sizable dragon and would like to admonish the new councilman he is too small to be a St. George and accomplish my demise. I expect to be here after he is gone." Angelos, a quick student, replied that Mr. Liss would be there long after he (Angelos) had moved to higher office. Thus was a newcomer initiated to council debate while the newcomer, in turn, implied his disdain of the council with his first remarks.

During 1961 a film was proposed that would show the City Council at work. Advocates quickly passed the measure and stated that the film would be useful in schools where it could be used to demonstrate democracy in action. Some council members called on the Women's Civic League to support the idea but were quickly rebuffed by the league president, who said she was against it and that the funding resolution had not been advertised for a hearing and no public hearing had taken place. This was hardly democracy in action. Democracy lived, the film died, and the council continued in its ways.

Anyone who looked at the government of Baltimore could quickly discover that it had a so-called strong mayor–weak council form of government. This came about because mayors controlled the city's purse through the Board of Estimates. The mayor "owned" three of the five votes: his own, the city solicitor, and the director of Public Works, who were appointed. The other two people were elected at large: the president of the City Council and the city comptroller. There are also more subtle ways the mayor dominates the city. These will be discussed later. This kind of government is, however, the context in which the City Council must be viewed.

On January 20, 1964, Republican Mayor Theodore R. McKeldin made an unusual appearance before the council, asking for it to pass his administration's civil rights bill that would establish a fair housing law and expand coverage of an equal accommodations law which, at that time, did not include bars. Although McKeldin got a standing ovation when he came to and as he left the council chambers, his proposal received a cool reception and was defeated. In November of that year, a rent aid bill on behalf of the city's poor also lost. Detractors believed

that this was an attempt to integrate certain parts of the city through economic support of the poor, who were predominantly black. Proponents did not surrender but reintroduced the civil rights measure and in January, 1965, a number of prominent clergy appeared before the council to urge passage. Lawrence Cardinal Shehan was the most prominent spokesman, appearing in spite of a threat on his life. The January 13 session was held at the War Memorial to accommodate an overflow crowd. The cardinal, small and delicate in stature but resolute in countenance, entered amidst jeers and boos from many in the crowd. One of the council members reported that he was "startled and frightened" by the reception. Four days later the bill was again defeated by a vote of 13–8. Not until the federal courts and Congress acted did open occupancy become the law in Baltimore. Even then financial institutions, realtors, and individual owners restricted equal treatment for black citizens. The council, with its two black members, in a city which was almost half black, continually rendered itself powerless to bring a policy change to the city. In January, 1967, the *Sunpapers* wrote about the "same old problems" that faced the council, chief among them open-occupancy, and in June of that year the editorial writers called the council "bad as ever" and "twenty-five years behind the times."

Back in 1954 the Junior Association of Commerce called for council redistricting. Their plan suggested a reduction of membership from 21 to 19 with three council members elected from each district and a president elected on a city-wide basis. While the council rejected the plan, the Junior Association of Commerce obtained enough signatures to put its plan on the November ballot, where it was rejected by the city's voters. In 1959, Council President Philip H. Goodman appointed a committee to study the problem. No success. The issue lay dormant until pressure mounted from the Supreme Court decision and a study published in the newspaper pointed out that population in the districts varied so greatly that some councilmanic districts contained more than one and one-half times as many voters as other districts. At the heart of the matter lay three issues: 1) the city's black population was severely underrepresented, 2) the Pollack–Reed political machines that often controlled the council were threatened, and 3) every council member was willing to have some other member's district (i.e. political base) redrawn, but not his own, lest he, in effect, be voted out of office. In 1965, Mayor Theodore R. McKeldin turned to a citizen group, headed by Harry Bard, president of Baltimore Junior College (now the Community College of Baltimore). The Bard Commission produced a plan painstakingly developed. The Pollack–Reed forces countered with a gerrymandered plan of their own that gave an extra seat to the two districts their forces would control. Both plans ended up on the November, 1966 ballot. The League of Women Voters campaigned for the Bard plan and it passed. Some machine politicians challenged the Bard plan in the courts, but it was upheld in May, 1967. Twelve years, hundreds of fights, fifteen council votes, and three councilmanic elections passed while the city's elected representatives tried to determine how to have themselves elected. They were unable to come up with a solution. Instead the mayor, a citizen commission, and the courts brought about the necessary plan.

The council's record on redistricting and civil rights would seem to justify its critics' complaints that it was a useless body. Could it do anything right with any degree of speed and resolution? The answer is a qualified yes.

In 1958, Councilman Liss proposed that the council appoint a full-time fiscal research director. By 1962, the office was created and Janet Hoffman, who had served as a financial adviser to the General Assembly, was installed. In 1966, it established its own Department of Legislative Reference. The council regularly cooperated with the mayor in appropriation of urban renewal funds. For instance, in June, 1967, it unanimously approved a $14 million bond issue and a $36 million receipt of federal urban renewal money to develop the Inner Harbor. By 1968, the council adopted a new master zoning plan with the aid of the Citizens' Planning and Housing Association. The council could and did accomplish results, but too often it moved at a snail's pace and required that it be led or pushed.

In 1960, Council President Goodman appointed a special committee to study how the council functioned. Little came of it. Fourteen years later Council President Walter S. Orlinsky

appointed a similar committee. In its report the committee noted that "the normal legislative function of originating and passing bills is not a prime feature of today's council." This weakness is inherent in the city's government. On the one hand it means that the council can afford to go on with its petty politics and patronage games as usual without doing much harm to the city as a whole. On the other hand it means that the city administration is seldom checked or prodded into action by the citizens' elected representatives.

In an effort to find the significance of council actions, a study was made of all legislation prepared in one councilmanic year (1973). The information revealed that of 437 bills introduced, 128 involved condemnation, zoning matters, or land sales. Another 41 dealt with supplementary appropriations to city agencies, while 54 involved parking regulations or lots. Fourteen involved health and welfare legislation and the remainder covered governmental organizations, urban renewal, and corrections. Over half (251) the bills were introduced by the administration. Eighty percent of these passed, while bills requested on behalf of constituents or citizen groups passed only 37 percent of the time. The City Council as a body referred most of its bills (through its committees) to the administration's agencies for recommendations. Usually they were followed. Thus the council in 1973 was dominated by an administration that proposed most of the legislation, evaluated virtually all of the laws, and had its advice followed most of the time.

Mayor William Donald Schaefer knew the council well, having served for many years as a member, the latter ones as its president. Upon becoming mayor he took no steps to increase the council's power but moved instead to exercise the power granted him. As a council member, Schaefer consistently voted with the reform wing of the council: *for* civil rights, *for* equitable redistricting, *for* better housing, *for* improved zoning. Schaefer also frequently saw the causes he espoused lose or become compromised. This experience undoubtedly gave him cause to view the council with care. During the seventies the council elected some new talent which fit the reform mold: Barbara Mikulski, Mary Pat Clarke, Thomas S. J. Waxter, Donald Hammen, and Norman Reeves were examples. These people could communicate with constituents in enlightened ways and frequently deliver limited services to their districts. They, with their colleagues, could set the city's tax base and trim (but not expand) its budget. Yet the larger political issues of the governance of a metropolitan area of over two million were left to the mayor, the county executives, and officials of the state of Maryland.

W. Theodore Dürr

Business

BALTIMORE'S FINANCIAL INSTITUTIONS

Baltimore is the principal financial center of the southeastern region of the United States, and the development of its financial institutions reflected the city's renaissance during the generation that followed World War II. Concentrated growth characterized that development. The number of institutions became fewer, but they accounted for ever-greater amounts of assets. The electronics revolution enabled branch banking to alter the structure of the industry, and certain institutions benefited at the expense of others. And finally, the state-chartered savings and loan institutions were brought under state regulation in 1961 to better serve the needs of savers and home buyers.

Baltimore Clearinghouse records illustrate many of these trends. The number of banks and trust companies shrank steadily from 14 in 1950 to 6 in 1975, while the total resources of these institutions increased more than five times. The number of mutual savings banks declined from 8 in 1950 to 3 in 1975, though their total resources increased nearly three times. Credit unions also reflect these trends: their number dropped from 47 in 1955 to 32 in 1977, but their total resources increased nearly 14 times.

The changing position of various institutions within these general trends demonstrated the human capital—management—of Baltimore's financial institutions. Throughout the 1950s, the Mercantile–Safe Deposit and Trust Company increased its share of the total banking resources, the Equitable Trust Company maintained its position, and the Union Trust Company declined. But dramatic changes then occurred during the 1960s and first half of the seventies. By 1970, Equitable emerged as the leading state–chartered bank or trust company, and five years later its total resources virtually equalled those of the First National Bank of Maryland, one of the two federally chartered banks in the city, for second position. The Maryland National Bank maintained its first rank throughout the 1960s and 1970s, and even increased its lead. In 1975 its total resources were double those of its nearest rivals, the First National or Equitable.

The city's mutual savings banks developed somewhat similarly. Throughout the fifties, sixties, and early seventies, the Savings Bank of Baltimore maintained, and slightly increased, its lead over the others. By way of contrast with the commercial banks and trust companies, SBB held over 50 percent of the total resources of Baltimore's mutual savings banks in 1975 compared with Maryland National Bank's 40 percent among the bank and trust companies. Like the SBB, the Provident Savings Bank increased its share of the total resources among mutual savings banks, while the Central Savings Bank declined slightly and the Eutaw Savings Bank declined significantly.

Technically speaking, savings and loan associations are not banks; they originated as building and loan associations as early as 1849 in Baltimore; and today they serve as lending institutions for would–be home buyers. More than any other types of institutions, the growth of S&Ls has underpinned the purchase and sale of homes. Because of their unique function, even giants such as Loyola Federal, the largest in terms of assets, Baltimore Federal, the second largest, and Vermont Federal are affected by changes in the interest rates in the capital markets, and the ebb and flow of savings deposits. Disintermediation occurs when savers withdraw their deposits from S&Ls, as they are called, and invest them elsewhere for higher interest rates. Such individual savers may thereby benefit, but reduced deposits force the S&Ls to curtail mortgage loans or borrow from one another and increase mortgage interest rates.

Because branch banking increased profits, it has characterized the development of the S&Ls as well as the banks and trust companies. During the fifties and sixties, such branches commonly appeared in the new shopping centers that ringed Baltimore's suburban development. But in the seventies, the electronics revolution introduced a new kind of branch bank, the "satellite" branch in department stores and supermarkets. These terminals for deposits, withdrawals, and transfers are not full–service branches: they do not take mortgage or loan applications; they are open only when the stores are open; and they do not have automatic teller machines. Nevertheless, such branches are beneficial because they are less expensive to install than building new, full–service ones, they have lower overhead costs, they are located where there is high shopper traffic, and they provide people with a useful range of immediate services.

Baltimore's financial institutions also have broadened their services in other new and non-traditional ways during the 1970s. "Free checking" for patrons who maintain a minimum balance in their savings account appeared early in the decade. Bank credit cards such as Bank-Americard appeared in the mid–seventies. Maryland's Equal Credit Opportunity Act in 1975 ended discrimination on the basis of sex or marital status. Overdrafting policies for checking accounts appeared about the same time. Also, the speed of electronic data processing has enabled banks and S&Ls to offer automatic trans-fer of funds between checking and savings accounts. EFT (electronic funds transfer), as it is called, has led many to proclaim the dawn of the "checkless society."

Gary L. Browne

SMALL BUSINESS IN BALTIMORE

Small business has had a checkered career in Baltimore since World War II. Statistically speaking, no definitive statements emerge from the data. However, certain patterns are quite clear. The number of manufacturing firms, retail and wholesale outlets, and the number of employees in those units declined from 1950 through 1977. However, their volume of sales rose, certain kinds of establishments flourished, and black businessmen found unprecedented opportunities opened to them. The accompanying tables, compiled from various issues of the *Maryland Statistical Abstract* published by the Maryland Department of Economic and Community Development, reveal some of these various ambiguities.

Table 1. Number of manufacturing firms in Baltimore City

1950	1738
1960	1513
1970	1100
1977	860
1978	841

Table 2. Retail trade in Baltimore City

year	no. of estab.	no. of employ.	sales (in 1,000)
1963	6291	57,193	$1,268,191
1967	5518	56,392	1,472,960
1972	4744	52,393	1,719,471
1977	4212	43,692	2,030,106

Table 3. Wholesale trade in Baltimore City

year	no. of estab.	no. of employ.	sales (in 1,000)
1963	1906	26,629	$2,682,029
1967	1700	25,484	2,823,661
1972	1400	23,892	3,497,791

Shopsteader in the Water Street Mews: Before and After.

Table 4. Selected businesses in Baltimore City

category	1963	1967	1972	1977
personal services	2642	2592	2103	1348
miscellaneous	712	882	1102	1355
amusement (nonmotion picture)	319	400	362	671
repair auto, services, garages	657	595	522	355
repair services, miscellaneous	526	515	423	352
hotels, motels, camps, tourist parks	64	68	48	62
motion pictures	80	69	73	38

Other developments of small business in Baltimore followed social, political, and legal changes in the broader community, and these occurred chiefly during the 1960s and 1970s. In 1968, for example, the Council for Equal Business Opportunity came into being as a two-year Ford Foundation project designed to assist blacks who wished to begin their own businesses. Working through the newly created Small Business Development Corporation, this council soon acquired the best record of helping to start and expand black businesses of all of the 22 cities in which the council was involved. The *Sun* reported that by November of 1971 the gross income of Baltimore's black business community had grown from about $100,000 annually to an incredible $43 million. About 1,000 new jobs and 115 new businesses had been created in that three-year time period, and 47 existing businesses had expanded. There were only five failures.

Such success prompted the Economic Devel-

opment Administration in the Department of Commerce to open the Minority Business Enterprise Project in Baltimore in October, 1971. This was mainly a technical assistance program that was coordinated through Morgan State University. Loans and other forms of credit were not offered to minority businessmen, but such businessmen were given leads to sources of start-up capital, and they were given help with their applications. Maryland's first community-operated Minority Enterprise Small Business Investment Company opened its office in Mondawmin Mall after being licensed by the Small Business Administration in June, 1970.

The Small Business Administration encouraged other entrepreneurs as well. A Baltimore chapter of SCORE—Service Corps of Retired Executives—appeared in 1965. Concerned about the 50 percent failure rate of new businesses in their first year, and the 75 percent rate by the end of the third year, this progam provided consultants having wide and deep business experience to neophytes who were encountering difficulties. The consultants, retired executives and small businessmen, volunteered their time. So successful was this program by 1974 that the Baltimore chapter was averaging merely two cases per month.

One of the continuing problems that has plagued small businessmen has been a lack of long-term credit. Commercial banks are short-term lenders; savings and loan institutions are restricted by law to home financing; and insurance companies do not provide small business loans. To correct this chronic problem, the federal government, Baltimore city, and local lending institutions initiated new policies during the late 1970s that have underpinned Baltimore's renaissance for its small businessmen.

The first of these new policies was part of President Jimmy Carter's National Urban Policy. The Neighborhood Business Revitalization program began in September, 1978, when the Department of Housing and Urban Development, the United States Small Business Administration, and the Economic Development Administration within the Department of Commerce signed an interagency agreement to coordinate their services to assist cities in establishing self-sustaining local economic development systems. The interagency activity was guided by the National Development Council, a private, nonprofit foundation whose task is to coordinate federal resources in specific projects, to train city staff in loan packaging and business finance, and to provide mechanisms to make federal agencies more responsive to community needs.

This new program was premised upon the statistics that small businesses—those employing 150 to 400 people—generate more than 65 percent of the private employment in most American cities. Yet, because of their size, most financial institutions were unwilling to loan them between $150,000 and $1 million. The social need to preserve small business was made clear by the fact that about 50 percent of the economic base in cities—jobs, industry, spending power, and commercial businesses—was generated by small business. Baltimore, with two-thirds of all of its businesses employing 400 or less, epitomized the small business city.

The second policy that has underpinned Baltimore's small business renaissance has been the "shopsteading" program of Mayor William Donald Schaefer. Analogous to the city's famed "homesteading" program, shopsteading started in 1978 and aimed at the restoration of commercial property and at the attendant revival of business enterprise. Through the city's Commercial Revitalization Environmental Assistance program, a shopsteader could borrow up to $50,000 at 7 percent interest for 20 years. He

Ships in Drydocks, 1980. Photo by Bethlehem Steel Corporation.

or she could also borrow from the state's Home Rehabilitation program and the HUD's section 312 program that provided 3 percent money for 20 years.

In June of 1979, Nelson Bolton opened the Ice Cream Review at 1501 West Baltimore Street as the city's first shopstead. Several others opened two years later. About 40 other shops would shortly be opened in the 1400 and 1500 blocks of West Baltimore, the 600 blocks of North Chester and North Duncan and the 800 and 1600 blocks of East Baltimore streets. The average shopsteader had borrowed $65,000, and renovation costs had averaged about $25,000 per floor in buildings that usually contained three floors and a basement.

The third policy was an amalgamated effort by federal and local financial institutions. Essentially, the United States Small Business Administration, the Department of Housing and Urban Development, and the Economic Development Administration coordinated eight Baltimore banks and savings and loan institutions (the American National Bank of Maryland, Baltimore Federal Savings and Loan, First National Bank of Maryland, the Maryland National Bank, the Mercantile–Safe Deposit and Trust Company, Loyola Federal Savings and Loan, Suburban Trust, and Union Trust) to provide a pool of $35.5 million for long term—15 to 25 years—financing for medium and small businesses. This, too, was part of President Carter's National Urban Policy, and Baltimore was the first American city to adopt the program.

Gary L. Browne

THE MAYOR'S ADVISORY COMMITTEE ON SMALL BUSINESS

The Mayor's Advisory Committee on Small Business was formed as a result of mounting concern over the increasing commercial blight in the city's retail areas. Store vacancies were cropping up regularly by the late 1950s.

Affiliated Merchants, Inc. was formed in response to this concern, under the leadership of Herman Katkow, a small businessman. The new organization had 17 neighborhood merchants' groups as members.

Katkow met with then–City Councilman William Donald Schaefer to discuss the group's purpose. Statistics were assembled to prove that the erosion process was already well under way. As expected, the figures revealed an acceleration in store vacancies, a sharply eroding tax base, a steadily increasing crime rate, and more and more problems relating to the general welfare of both the business and residential communities in the inner city.

At Schaefer's request, Mayor Harold J. Grady appointed an Advisory Committee on Small Business in June, 1960. Schaefer was designated to serve as liaison between the mayor's office and the committee. For four years, the committee met irregularly and operated with no budget and no office space. Its biggest accomplishment during that period was being granted a public hearing on the plight of small businesses.

In 1965, Mr. Katkow, committee chairman Rubin Levinson, and Schaefer went to Washington in an attempt to obtain funds for their revitalization project. The committee's leaders were dealt a setback when their request was turned down. Later, in 1965, the committee leaders applied to the Department of Housing and Urban Development (HUD) for a demonstration project grant which, if approved, would be used as a model for the whole country. The application to HUD stressed working with city planners regarding slum clearance, neighborhood conservation, traffic improvements, and industrial development.

HUD granted the committee $108,000 for urban revitalization. This marked the first time anything had been done to meet the need for such an effort.

A massive self–help program among merchants (a hallmark of the committee's approach) was necessary to attain maximum economic productivity in the city's business districts. Public improvements, such as improved parking facilities, new lighting, and street landscaping would be made if merchants would make their own private commitments to revitalization.

The committee selected Candeub, Fleissig and Associates as prime consultant for the HUD–funded demonstration project. A planning program for three shopping districts was developed: the districts were Light Street, Monument

Street, and Pennsylvania Avenue. These districts were sufficiently varied to result in findings that could have validity in other communities.

In 1969, after all the information had been gathered, a report was published on the findings of the study. The project drew national attention, but unfortunately attracted little notice in Baltimore.

Included in the demonstration project's recommendations were the following: identification of the role of the business center; concentration and expansion of centers so that linear distances could be decreased; land consolidation; and implementation of these recommendations through concentrated urban renewal projects.

When City Council President Schaefer was elected mayor in 1971, the implementation began. Baltimore was unique in that the city enjoyed an enviable financial rating. It was retiring the public debt at a greater rate than it was accumulating debts. In 1974, a $2,000,000 bond issue was passed for public improvements. Long-term, low-interest improvement loans were made available to merchants.

The first physical evidence of cooperative revitalization efforts was the construction of a parking lot on East Monument Street. Merchants in this area decided to erect canopies over the sidewalks and generally improve the appearance of their shopping area.

From 1976 to 1978, additional bond issues for public revitalization and loan funds were approved at the polls. Baltimore's voters are given credit for contributing to the project's goals. Other shopping areas benefiting from this project have been Hampden, Highlandtown, Mount Washington, West Baltimore, and Waverly.

For every dollar of public money used in commercial revitalization projects in the city, four to five dollars are generated in the private sector. As usual, Baltimoreans recognize a good bargain.

Alison Brauner

THE GREATER BALTIMORE COMMITTEE

A driving force behind Baltimore's heralded rebirth is an organization called the Greater Baltimore Committee (GBC). Its objectives include the development of both the economic and the cultural life of the city. Its philosophy is that what helps one is good for the other.

From its beginning in 1955, the GBC had strong lay leadership. James Rouse, Robert Levi, and Louis Kohn were among the young businessmen who first felt a need for such an organization. They went to established businessmen for advice. They first approached Clarence W. Miles, a lawyer who had just brought the Orioles from St. Louis to Baltimore. Miles became the GBC's first chairman, and Tom Butler, president of the Mercantile–Safe Deposit and Trust Company, the first vice–chairman.

"What's happened to Baltimore?" This is the usual question of anyone who returns after an absence of a few years.

The things that have "happened," things for which the Greater Baltimore Committee takes full or partial credit, cover a wide range of accomplishments. To mention the most obvious ones, they include: the building of Charles Center; the development of the Inner Harbor; the construction of a rapid transit system and an interstate highway system; the rebuilding of the Baltimore–Washington International Airport; the establishment of the Adopt-a-School program; plus helping to institute an urban renewal program and human and civil rights legislation. The formation of the Maryland Port Administration was also a high–priority project of the GBC.

William Boucher III, a man who refers to his heritage as "several generations of small business," retired in 1981. Robert Keller succeeded him as director of the Greater Baltimore Committee. H. Vernon Eney, a senior partner and former managing partner of the law firm of Venable, Baetjer, and Howard, held the volunteer position of chairman until his death in 1980. Mr. Eney, who headed the constitutional convention in the late 1960s, succeeded W. Wallace Lanahan, Jr. as GBC chairman. Mr. Lanahan, chairman of the board of trustees of the Johns Hopkins Hospital, is a retired attorney who was formerly president and chief executive officer of Stein Bros. and Boyce. Present chairman is Mr. Bernard Manekin, chairman of the Manekin Corporation.

The GBC is 25 years old. When it merged with the Baltimore City Chamber of Commerce in January, 1978, reactions varied from criticism and apprehension to applause.

The first suggestion of a merger had come from the Chamber of Commerce. Chris Hartman, executive vice-president, and Edgar M. Boyd, president—as well as some of their predecessors—felt that this was the practical, and perhaps the only way, to achieve their goals for Baltimore city. The interests of the two organizations overlapped, with some businessmen belonging to both. While some projects were getting a great deal of attention, others were in danger of being overlooked.

Many businessmen wondered whether this newly merged organization would be able to solve the problems of Baltimore city. From some Chamber of Commerce members, the most often heard criticism was that the Greater Baltimore Committee (the name under which this new union would operate) would concern itself only with big business, neglecting small- and medium-sized ones. On the GBC side, formerly a group of only 100 members, there was fear that a merger with the 1,000-member Chamber of Commerce would generate too many issues. The result would be that efficient resolution of even major ones would be difficult or impossible.

The bottom line in everyone's mind was the big question: Can this newly merged organization bring new business and more jobs to Baltimore?

The importance of economic development in Baltimore city tipped the scales in favor of the merger. It was the result of a comprehensive study involving both professional and volunteer leaders of each group, as well as professionals from outside the city. Carrying their investigation still further, Baltimore businessmen checked with other cities that had merged such organizations, visiting some—such as St. Louis—where three groups with similar interests had been combined.

In the words of Mr. Hartman, now press secretary to Mayor William Donald Schaefer, the advice boiled down to this: "You can do it in Baltimore. You've got everything needed to attract business, but you are going to fail unless you merge your Chamber of Commerce and Greater Baltimore Committee. You have got to tightly focus the concentration of your business leaders in an intensive effort."

There was careful planning as the merger went into effect to insure that all bases were covered. In the first place, the GBC, although now many members larger, would continue to discharge its traditional role, a role that has been described as that of a "rifle shot" approach. The method is to seize onto a certain objective, zoom in on that particular target, and pursue it to a successful finish. The development of Charles Center is a classic example.

Great hopes and expectations are pinned on the GBC's Economic Council, which is an important division headed by Donald Moyer. This council, with the high-priority responsibility of promoting new industry, business, and jobs, was implemented. The private sector contributed $500,000 in cash and pledges payable over three years to fund its efforts. The GBC budget for other activities amounts to about $700,000.

The Business Services Division of the GBC, set up at the time of the merger, is a continuation of the highly successful services that the Chamber of Commerce rendered directly to its members. It includes finding out about legislation, following legislation, and getting information for business people on a variety of topics. It is a service to which a businessman can turn for answers and assistance. It is set up with the interests of the small business, as well as the medium and larger ones, in mind.

The Maryland Chamber of Commerce, created by the Baltimore City Chamber of Commerce during its last three years of existence, was retained as a division of the Greater Baltimore Committee. With offices in Annapolis, it represents the interests of the business community before the legislature and regulatory agencies.

Asked about failures, former GBC director, Mr. Boucher replied: "We've had plenty of them. A new stadium in downtown Baltimore in the Camden Station area probably tops the failure list. We got the hotel and the convention center, but we didn't get the stadium."

The GBC succeeded in getting the public to support a $3 million bond issue to develop the Jones Falls stream valley into a public park, but could not get the city administration to implement it. Neither was able to get a "new town" like Coldspring, which members recommended be built adjacent to the park.

In the late sixties and seventies, the GBC spent a lot of time and money in an effort to get low-income housing built through the private sector. They succeeded only in building fewer houses than were needed and spending a great deal of money. Taking this philosophically, Mr. Boucher commented: "We found that wasn't our area of expertise, but if you are not ready to take the risk of failure, you don't do much."

Revitalization of the downtown retail district is a big problem. Business leaders realize the extent of the undertaking and acknowledge that it will be a difficult task to finance, and that it will take years to achieve. Former GBC Chairman Lanahan would like to see, among other things, more assistance for minority business people.

The prognoses for Baltimore city have changed radically since the founding of the GBC. Mr. Boucher and others remember the ultimatum delivered years ago by the old commission on Governmental Efficiency and Economy. That dire warning predicted that Baltimore would be facing municipal bankruptcy within a generation unless it could reverse the decline of the city.

Former GBC Chairman Eney spoke out enthusiastically in support and praise of his city. He considered the port, one of the biggest in the world—although never developed to its full potential—to be far superior to others in many ways. And, speaking for many Baltimoreans, he continued: "In its people, its attitudes, in its cultural advantages, in its ability to offer many things to many different kinds of people, Baltimore is very definitely superior to many, many other places."

As for the occasional person who may still think in terms of "Chamber of Commerce," there is no problem. The Baltimore telephone directory still lists a number for the Chamber of Commerce as well as a number for the GBC. The numbers are identical.

Victoria Boney Obrecht

CHARLES CENTER-INNER HAR-BOR MANAGEMENT, INC.

The renaissance of downtown Baltimore was initiated in 1956 by a group of businessmen, members of the Committee for Downtown and the Greater Baltimore Committee. Their mission was to reverse what was then considered the inevitable decline of the center city. With the encouragement of Mayor Thomas D'Alesandro, Jr., the business community established its own in-house planning firm, headed by David A. Wallace (now with Wallace, Roberts & Todd of Philadelphia) to prepare a master plan for the deteriorating central business district.

In 1958, the planners developed the Charles Center proposal, covering 33 acres of strategic land. The plan was practical enough economically to gain the support of the business community. The potential tax revenues and employment opportunities, as well as the change it would make in the spirit of downtown, appealed to the city administration. And the voters of Baltimore city were sufficiently impressed to support a bond issue covering the city's share of development costs.

To implement this first phase of downtown renewal, the Charles Center Management Office was created in 1959, with J. Jefferson Miller as general manager. Mr. Miller, former executive vice-president of the Hecht Company and first president of the Committee for Downtown (which had helped launch the Charles Center plan), came out of early retirement to head the organization for $1 a year. He remained on the job until his death 15 years later in 1972.

By 1963, it was evident that Charles Center would be a success and that it was time for the next phase of downtown revitalization. Mayor Theodore R. McKeldin, in his second inaugural address, called for redevelopment of the 240-acre area surrounding the historic harbor basin. Once again, the business community responded with more than half of the planning money needed, and Wallace and his associates were hired to prepare the master plan. Morton Hoffman Associates of Baltimore supplied the required economic and market studies, and the ambitious Inner Harbor program was unveiled in 1964.

Shortly thereafter, the management organization was incorporated and its name enlarged to the Charles Center–Inner Harbor Management, Inc. (CCIHM). Over the years, this unique public/private organizational system has come

Harborplace, 1980. Courtesy of the Rouse Co.

to be regarded as a model among the large cities in the United States. Funded under a contract with the city's Department of Housing and Community Development and operating directly under the authority of the HCD commissioner, the management organization makes available to city government the skills and experience that are needed to perform the city's role in large commercial development projects. The city establishes development policies, while the corporation negotiates agreements with private developers and supervises the design and implementation of publicly financed projects.

While the corporation normally represents the city in dealing with developers, it can also represent developers in dealing with the city—when a third party having nonfinancial interest in the outcome can help achieve the desired result. This is the unique feature of Baltimore's downtown redevelopment program, which has been indispensable to the city's success in attracting developers and enabling them to achieve the city's objectives in a mutually profitable manner.

A major factor in assuring excellence of design in Charles Center and the Inner Harbor has been the Architectural Review Board, created in

1959 to evaluate all proposals—public and private—for architectural quality. Original Review Board members were the deans of the schools of architecture of Harvard, the Massachusetts Institute of Technology, and the University of Pennsylvania: Joseph Hudnut, Pietro Belluschi, and Holmes Perkins, respectively.

Design of pedestrian open spaces and walkways throughout the projects was entrusted to RTKL and Associates, Inc. of Baltimore, a firm which is also credited with designing several major new downtown office buildings.

What has the Charles Center–Inner Harbor Management, Inc. achieved over the past 20 years of its existence? In addition to 18 national awards for design excellence, in 1978, Baltimore was selected by the International Federation for Housing and Planning as the American city with the best urban revitalization program.

The 30–year program for renewing downtown, which is costing more than $1 billion in public and private investment, means that Baltimore broke into the 1980s widely regarded as the most sparkling center city in the United States. Says developer James W. Rouse, Easton–born, "There is pride and excitement about what the city is today compared to what it was two decades ago. The city is infused with a new life at its heart."

Barbara Bonnell

Around Town

WHAT MAKES BALTIMORE, *BALTIMORE?*

Sometime in the mid–1960s, the *Washington Post* sent a reporter to Baltimore to do a story on the city. The paper's editors were pretty sure they already knew what the reporter was going to find: "a seedy, mildly amusing hick town full of strip joints and people with crooked politicians."

The reporter gave his editors pretty much what they expected—not, he confessed years later, from any lack of objectivity but "through man's age old tendency to find supporting evidence for his preconceived notions."

Now, of course, the perception of Baltimore has changed, not only in Washington, but also across the nation. She is no longer the faded old town by the bay where, as F. Scott Fitzgerald once said, "everything is civilized and gay and rotted and polite." She's become positively chic.

Washingtonians come here to see and be seen. They spend $200,000 on a Federal Hill rowhouse with a view of the harbor and consider it a bargain. They stroll through the Otterbein community, shop at Harborplace, see the Orioles, and complete their day with a quiet drink on the thirteenth floor of the stylish old Belvedere.

A dozen national magazines have discovered Baltimore and sung her praises in stories and pictures. She's "one of the most livable cities in America," "the city that works," "the urban future."

Why? What makes her so special? What makes living and working in Baltimore today so much better than living here 10 or 20 or 30 years ago? Obviously, there are as many answers to that question as there are people living here. One writer grappled with the problem and concluded that "a city is a complex organism composed of so many elements that pinpointing the real Baltimore" is impossible.

For him—and obviously thousands of other Baltimoreans—it had a lot to do with two admittedly overworked symbols—the Orioles and Harborplace. For others, however, Baltimore is The Block or Street Arabs or Druid Hill Park. Its uniqueness to them is forever exemplified in its food, its markets, its streets, or its characters, probably one of the most famous of whom is its

"BALTIMORE IS BEST" PROGRAM
AWARDS PRESENTATION - AUGUST 1979

AWARD WINNERS & STEERING COMMITTEE
LEFT TO RIGHT:

Reverend George A. Wichland - St. James
  and St. Johns
Dr. Frank Barranco - "Baltimore is Best"
  Steering Committee
Mr. Harold Flecker - "Baltimore is Best"
  Steering Committee
Ms. Christine Moore - "Baltimore is Best"
  Steering Committee
Mayor William Donald Schaefer
Mrs. Floraine Applefeld - Director,
  "Baltimore is Best" program
Ms. Tammy Marble - "Miss Baltimore, 1978"
Ms. Kathy Lynn Wienecke - "Miss Baltimore,
  1979"
Ms. Jardiolyn Valino - "Miss Charm City"
Mrs. Ruth Epstein - Community Involvement

"Baltimore Is Best" Program Awards Presentation,
August, 1979. Photo by Dennis Doda

"Baltimore Is Best." Photo by Janenne Corcoran

No. 1 news dealer and resident curmudgeon, Abe
Sherman.

Sherman, who is now in his eighties, continues
to put in a 12-hour day, 6 days a week at his
store on the corner of Mulberry Street and Park
Avenue. There, surrounded by newspapers and
magazines from all over the world, and an enormous selection of paperback books and posters,
he wanders up and down the aisles greeting
browsers with, "Get your hands off that unless
you want to buy it."

He started with a $15 pushcart and bought his
first stand in 1919. He served in both World War
I and World War II, but is convinced it's a
different world today. "The battlefields were
safer than the streets are now," he says. Still, he
has unbounded faith in the city.

"It's the best city I've ever been in. I wouldn't
live anywhere else. It's a city of hundred thou-

sand dollar millionaires. Sure, it's a nickel town,
but it's a good town. This is a town where ethnic
groups are respected . . . . I just want to die here
with my boots on."

The plaque in the radio station's foyer reads:
"To Harley Brinsfield for thirty years of dedication and devotion to jazz through your incom-
parable style of radio broadcasting. You have
truly earned the name 'Mr. Jazz'. Presented
April 8, 1978, at the Benny Goodman concert by
Firstnighters, Inc."

On Tuesday through Saturday evenings, Harley Brinsfield plays two hours of jazz records—
roughly 30 to 40 cuts of music—on WITH Radio
for all of Baltimore to hear. He has been doing
this since 1945, though not all of those years
were on WITH. He drifted from WITH in 1950
to WCBM, where he stayed for about 10 years,
to WBAL for 17 more years, then back to WITH,
where he continues to broadcast.

"Music," says Harley, "is the most beautiful
of all the arts." The problem today, he feels, is
that people don't give sentimentality a chance.
And that's where jazz comes in. Jazz has sentimental tunes as well as "hot" ones.

Harley has been in love with jazz ever since
he heard it 60 years ago, when he was a boy on
the Eastern Shore, in Dorchester County. He
was 10 years old then, and his radio consisted of
a crystal set constructed out of a Quaker Oat-
meal box. Harley became increasingly en-
chanted with jazz as he grew older. He met Louis
Armstrong, "the greatest trumpet player who
ever lived," in Culver City, California and they
became good friends. Over the years, Harley

developed close relationships with other jazz greats as well, such as Duke Ellington, Benny Goodman, and Eubie Blake.

Today, Harley, who resembles actor Burgess Meredith, boasts one of the greatest jazz collections in the country. In his five-day-a-week radio program he shares not only this collection, but also his wisdom, experience, and enthusiasm.

Baltimore may be the birthplace of such jazz artists as Cab Calloway and Billie Holliday, but it is also the residence of jazz broadcaster Harley Brinsfield. Cab and Billie may have sung it, but Harley plays it.

Morris Martick couldn't have said it better. Martick's restaurant, just up Mulberry Street from Sherman's newsstand, still has a bohemian flavor to it, although the avant-garde crowd of the fifties has vanished and the few true eccentrics that are left now mostly work for Martick.

It began as a bar, a place for people who didn't fit into the mainstream of life, and later became the city's first French restaurant. It was a haven for writers and journalists and artists and students and, while it may not have been exactly in the mode of an eighteenth century French salon, it was a magnet that drew the intellectually curious.

"These people were at odds with themselves and the world," Martick once said of some of his early patrons. "Most writers feel rejected. This place gave them an identity . . . it had its own vitality."

"It was a community," said noted black poet Sam Cornish. "You could have a drink and talk with people from all walks of life. There were no racial, social, or political boundaries at Martick's."

The same could be said, more or less, of that other Baltimore institution, The Block. Always loud, gaudy, and bawdy, The Block added a new dimension of sleaziness a few years ago, eschewing scantily clad ladies in favor of drugs, pornography, and almost rampant prostitution.

World War II brought the raffish Block its greatest period of prosperity. But what the government gives, it takes away. By the early fifties, the soldiers and sailors were gone and nightclub owners were blaming anyone who was handy— the government, television, even installment buying—for their woes. One by one, the old burlesque houses went dark.

Striptease artists were replaced by go-go dancers, and top bananas became doormen and bouncers. Murderers, muggers, and bookmakers, gamblers and flimflam artists walked the streets; cops were hauled in and quizzed about taking bribes and the grand jury launched major investigations into narcotics and prostitution.

The Block has calmed down considerably since then. Major efforts have been made to stamp out drugs and prostitution, and the city has moved to improve the general appearance of Baltimore Street, an irony that did not escape an editorial writer on the *Baltimore Sun*, who noted The Block "spent 30 years cultivating a sleazy look, only to be overtaken in the end by urban renewal, which required clubs to clean and paint the upper stories of their buildings and refurbish the street-level fronts."

While the Read Street area, especially the four blocks between Howard and Charles streets, is hardly in the same category as Baltimore's Block, it has its own special charm. It's one of the city's trendier streets, a Kings Road in microcosm.

In the 1920s, it was home for a famous speakeasy and a famous bookmaking shop, both of which were raided frequently; a few generations later, it housed one of the first "head" shops in Baltimore; still later, it was home to the Read Street Festival, notorious for its ear-shattering rock bands, large-scale drug consumption, and general all-around rowdiness.

Like The Block, Read Street has combed its hair and brushed its teeth and cleaned up its act. But there are still unmistakable traces of the past up and down the tree-lined street. The bookmaking shops and the head joints are gone and so is the late, largely unlamented Read Street Festival. In their place are trendy leather shops and natural food stores and bakeries— check-by-jowl with the Maryland Democratic Party headquarters.

Miles away, as sylvan as Read Street is urban, is Druid Hill Park, 500 acres of rustic charm that includes one of the nation's first zoos.

The city of Baltimore purchased Druid Hill from the Lloyd N. Rogers family in 1860, but it wasn't until after the Civil War that George A. Frederick, the architect who designed City Hall, submitted a plan to add various structures, including the oriental pavilions, the boathouse,

Northeast Market. Photo by Joe Kohl, Jr.

Edmund's well, and a conservatory, which contains many fine examples of tropical plants.

Deer and various birds were kept in captivity at Druid Hill as early as 1865, although the zoo was not formally organized until 1876. It wasn't until 1948, however, when Arthur Watson was appointed director, that the zoo realized its full potential. Under Watson's leadership, it was recognized as one of the 15 best in the country.

Today, Druid Hill Park is trying to overcome an unsavory reputation as a dangerous, crime-ridden area. The park is still beautiful; its facilities are still intact; all that is missing are the people who once found refuge there from city life, strolling its English-style open spaces, picnicking on its grassy knolls, sleeping through the hot summer nights beneath the branches of its majestic old trees.

If Druid Hill is avoided by some, few avoid the city markets. Shoppers from all over sample everything from mangoes to muskrats in the eight city-sponsored markets. At one time, however, there was some question whether the markets would survive or, indeed, if they were even worth saving.

But as revitalization of the city progressed through the 1960s and 1970s, it enhanced the value of neighborhood markets. For many, they are the last remaining link with the "old neighborhood."

Except for prices, the experience of shopping in city markets is remarkably similar to 1785, when the city's oldest market, the Broadway Market in Fell's Point, was built. Later came the world-famous Lexington Market and the Cross Street, Belair, Hollins, and Northeast markets.

The Wholesale Fish Market, which once depended almost exclusively on fishermen to bring their catches to Market Place, now relies on refrigerated trucks from as far away as Maine and Florida to deliver millions of tons of fish annually.

But Market Place still lives up to its name every Sunday morning from July to November, when the square adjacent to the fish market becomes a true Farmers Market. Farmers from across the state truck their fresh fruits and vegetables to the outdoor market where swarms of Baltimoreans start arriving as early as 6:00 A.M.—something that would have seemed impossible only a few years ago but reflects, today, a significant improvement in the quality of city life.

Some things never change, however, and one of the constants around Baltimore is its seafood. While Bostonians must resign themselves to baked beans year–round, the seasons allow Baltimoreans greater variety. Accordingly, the local seafood industry focuses more on consumption than packing, processing, or canning.

Oysters and crabs from the Chesapeake Bay have long been local favorites. Shrimp from farther south is also popular, even among those who usually disdain seafood. Shad, prized for its roe as well as its flesh, is a spring delicacy while diamondback terrapin is a traditional winter favorite.

Baltimoreans also enjoy clams, lobsters and—of late—mussels. They consume immense quantities of hake, whiting, steakfish, shad, bluefish, rockfish, flounder, sea bass, and lake trout, most of which are available at local supermarkets. True connoisseurs, however, depend on either Lexington Market or the Wholesale Fish Market for much of their fresh seafood.

Similarly, many Baltimore housewives still count on Arabbers for their fresh fruits and vegetables. How long they will be able to do so is open to question, for the so–called Street Arabs (hucksters who peddle their goods from horses and carts) are a vanishing breed. Baltimore is the only large American city today with a sizable number of Arabs still plying their trade, and even here their numbers are slowly dwindling.

Where once there were hundreds, today there are dozens, mostly black (although Arabbing was once dominated by whites with central or eastern European backgrounds), who took to Arabbing when they found other avenues of employment above menial labor closed to them.

The city must take some of the blame for the decline of these colorful, hard–working, street–wise vendors. It has tried on a number of occasions to stop Arabs from stabling their ponies in residential areas, something they have done for two centuries.

"Baltimore Arab" Wooden Photograph by John Clark Mayden, 1972.

Arabs still rise before dawn, still fill the streets with their distinctive songs. But instead of going to the old Camden produce market to buy their fruits and vegetables, they now go to Jessup. And where they once had regular routes, they now range across the length and breadth of Baltimore, a vanishing breed battling time and age and a city that has seen the future.

Contributing to this article were:

> Ric Bartter,
> Stephen J. Gordon,
> Frederic Kelly,
> Mark Miller,
> Bernard Penner,
> Jake Slagle, Jr., and
> William Weiner

TOUR TAPES

TourTapes of Baltimore. "TourTapes of Baltimore," a self-guided automobile tape tour opens up the city, allowing explorers to "Discover Baltimore." "Historic Baltimore" and "Cultural and Religious Baltimore" along with accompanying brochure and maps serve to guide seekers to the hidden treasures of the Monumental City.

The idea for "TourTapes" came from Gerson G. Eisenberg, a native Baltimorean of many avocations whose travels throughout the United States and other countries acquainted him with a variety of tour facilities. In 1968, Mr. Eisenberg found that Baltimore had no tour–guide operations at that time. A few years earlier, a horse–drawn carriage departing from the Lord Baltimore Hotel had given a brief tour of the downtown district.

As a long–time enthusiast of tape recording, Mr. Eisenberg thought that a tape tour of Baltimore taken at his own convenience and speed would be valuable. Encouraged by many city and state officials, he proceeded with the project. A full year was spent planning and writing the scripts, preparing the maps and brochures, and devising the "TourTapes" logo. In April, 1969, under the auspices of Algerson Enterprises, Inc., the first "TourTapes of Baltimore" were made available to the public. The format was one tour emphasizing Baltimore's history and another its cultural and religious institutions.

In 1970, "TourTapes of Baltimore" had a booth at the city's first City Fair and the first Art Festival. The Automobile Club of America's Tour Book and the Mobil Travel Guide began to list "TourTapes" and continued it throughout the years. In 1971, The Baltimore Area Convention and Visitors Council promoted the tapes with the funds provided by Mr. Eisenberg.

The next year, a matching grant from him was planned to equip Baltimore city school buses with "TourTapes" for student trips throughout the city. When vehicles were not available, narrated filmstrips were produced for the students. Anna Fehl, radio and television media specialist (who also helped prepare the original "Tour-Tapes"); Dr. Rebecca Carroll, assistant superintendent; Larry Elbogen; and other social studies specialists from the Baltimore City Public Schools helped Mr. Eisenberg produce the three–part armchair tour, "Discover Baltimore" film-strip series. Released in 1974, the initial strip focused on the historic Fell's Point and the following two featured downtown Baltimore. All city schools, the Enoch Pratt Free Library, and others interested in the series received copies of

Robert Hieronimus, *"Coldspring, New Town, 1980"*
Watercolor. Photo by Blow Up Studio. Courtesy of Lynn and Harvey N. Meyerhoff

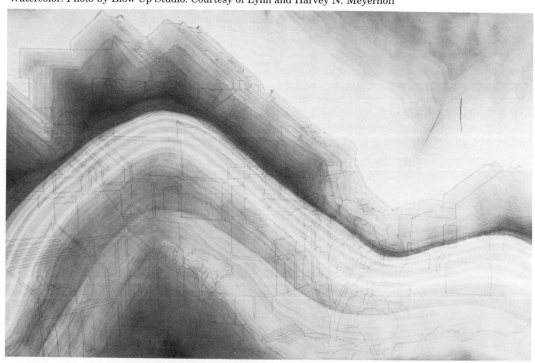

the film along with audio cassettes and teachers' guides.

As the face of Baltimore changed and as new "gems" worthy of notice were discovered, "TourTapes" kept pace. Elane Stein, media personality and critic, recorded a second version (on cassettes) and assisted with script revisions. A third set of tapes was recorded by Arnold Zenker, who was then with WJZ-TV. The 1980 set, released by the Eisenberg Educational Enterprises, was narrated by Stanley Morrow (of the Maryland Automobile Club) and his wife Rosalind.

Because of the role that "TourTapes of Baltimore" has played in exposing Baltimore's secrets to appreciative visitors and residents, Mayor William Donald Schaefer proclaimed April 1, 1979, as "TourTapes Day in Baltimore." He proclaimed them as "an invaluable resource for information about the Monumental City and as such serves as an integral part of our campaign to enhance the general perception of Baltimore." On this occasion Mr. Eisenberg presented sets of the tapes to the Waxter Center, the Child Study Association, and the Baltimore Council for International Visitors. Among others who received the sets were the Baltimore Convention Bureau and the Women's Civic League.

"TourTapes," the first visitors' guide of its type in the continental United States, has served as a model for cities such as Philadelphia and San Francisco. As new buildings rose and old sites were rebuilt, as Baltimore changed, "TourTapes" continued to change.

Gerald Z. Levin and Sandy F. Eisenberg

BALTIMORE NIGHT LIFE

During the fifties and sixties, Baltimore's night spots were dying a slow death. The action was following the population toward the suburbs.

It left behind a legacy of Dean Martin, Jackie Gleason, Tony Bennett, Pearl Bailey—all performed during the forties on North Charles Street at the Club Charles or the Chanticleer.

Less than a decade later, much of Baltimore's former café society was watching its idols on television.

Black Baltimore's equivalent of North Charles Street was the entertainment mecca along Pennsylvania Avenue. "The Avenue," however, remained prosperous throughout the fifties as Billie Holiday packed the house at Tijuana and Ethel Ennis sang her way to stardom at Red Fox. Then urban blight and its associated problems began to take their toll, while integration lured away much of the talent.

On East Baltimore Street, The Block was no longer what a local columnist remembered as "the type of place you visited on New Year's Eve in a tuxedo." Its transition into a seedy adult entertainment area was complete by the mid–fifties. Unfortunately for the city's image, many out-of-towners continued to link The Block with Baltimore as they associated the Loop with Chicago and the French Quarter with New Orleans. Albeit, the lure of The Block continues, enhanced by a facelift, which began in the late seventies.

The Club Charles had stood at 1300 North Charles Street, southernmost in a stretch of establishments known as the "Junior Block." Surviving it through the early sixties at 1308 North Charles Street was the Spa, a musical lounge best known as home base for "top-forty" artist Ronnie Dove. Along with the Carousel at 1815 North Charles Street and the Celebrity Club at 21 East North Avenue, the Spa was part of a circuit for which Cal Bittner's on Fayette Street was a popular starting point.

Last stop on this circuit was likely to be Sweeney's on Greenmount Avenue in Waverly. Owing much of its popularity to the colorful personalities of its owner Manuel DiPaula and manager Gabby Mancini, Sweeney's was Baltimore's undisputed haven for the "twist."

Sharing the uptown spotlight with Sweeney's during the late sixties was the Cavalier Lounge of the Pimlico Hotel at 5301 Park Heights Avenue. Fresh from downtown at Cy Bloom's Place in the Alley, vocalist Bruce Wescott distinguished himself here as "Baltimore's answer to Frank Sinatra." Wescott and his band continued to play engagements at the Pimlico throughout the seventies. Even today, the Pimlico remains as busy as ever.

No less enduring has been Stabile's at 3919 Eastern Avenue, Baltimore's country music stronghold. Owner Chris Dardamanis proudly recalls Loretta Lynn's first appearance here in 1968 "when she was struggling to make ends meet." Mel Street, Billy "Crash" Craddock, Guy Mitchell, and Ernest Tubb are but a few names on a long list of country music greats who have performed at Stabile's.

More temporary were the bohemian–oriented coffee houses that came into vogue for a brief period during the early sixties. They included the Check Mate in the 800 block of Park Avenue, the Florentine Caffe Espresso at 520 North Charles Street, the Zen Den in the 900 block of Cathedral Street, Café Flambeau on West Twenty-fifth Street, and the Blue Dog on York Road near Belvedere. Patronage was about evenly divided between beatniks and tourists who sought to emulate the former.

A somewhat older crowd of beatniks, artists, and intellectuals imbibed stronger libations at Martick's. The former speakeasy at 214 West Mulberry Street is doubly distinguished as Baltimore's first bar to display art (in the forties) and to feature dixieland jazz (in the fifties). Martick's closed in 1968 while its unique proprietor, Morris Martick, learned to cook in France. He returned in 1970 to reopen Martick's as one of Baltimore's first French restaurants.

Another notable former speakeasy—owned by Rose—is the Peabody Book Store and Beer Stube, which survived the nocturnal famine of the fifties and sixties as easily as it did Prohibition. It provides an opportunity for musicians and performers with little experience to play to an audience. Neither the dark but friendly cave-like pub, nor the dusty bookshop behind which it hides ever changed significantly in over half a century.

Another landmark was the Owl Bar, a bastion of masculine conviviality on the ground floor of the Belvedere Hotel. Closed in 1971, it reopened six years later to share its ambience with members of the fairer sex.

Worlds apart in spirit if not geography, the beat of black soul music beckoned through the mid–sixties. Braving some of the city's meanest streets, patrons of all descriptions flocked to the Club Casino on Pennsylvania Avenue and to the North End Lounge, a former jazz mecca near North and Gay streets. Further uptown was Lenny Moore's at 4723 Gwynn Oak Avenue and Brice's Hilltop Inn at 5440 Reisterstown Road, both of which endured through the seventies. A favorite for jazz was Henry Baker's Peyton Place, which thrived in the 2600 block of Pennsylvania Avenue from 1966 until the riots of 1968.

Surprisingly, the integration of Baltimore's night life was never more complete than during the two years following these riots. Most of it was at the Gentlemen II in the 200 block of Cathedral Street and the Tomfoolery in the Park Plaza Hotel at Charles and Madison streets. These oases for conversation and dancing were precursors to the singles bars and discothèques of the seventies.

In 1974, approximately five years after the Tomfoolery closed, Longfellow's (the Park Plaza was once called the Longfellow) opened in the same building. Less than two years later, Bumper's (later Casablanca) opened in an adjoining structure. That the former became known as a singles bar and the latter a discothèque was sheer coincidence. Live jazz finally won out at this site, however, when Café Park Plaza opened in December, 1979.

During the Tomfoolery era, the Bumper's-Casablanca-Café Park Plaza structure had housed the Schoolery (later the Classroom) where antique school desks served as tables. It and the ever popular No Fish Today, which opened in 1969 at 610 North Eutaw Street, bridged the gap between Baltimore's beat and hip populations. The stripped–back–to–basics–with–art look of the No Fish set the norm for dozens of pubs which later opened in Fell's Point, South Baltimore, and elsewhere around the city.

One of the first emerged in 1971 when the former Thames Café in Fell's Point became Leadbetter's. Where the Schoolery and the No Fish had fused beat and hip, Leadbetter's added an element of the bizarre with a touch of Alice Cooper. In its early days, Leadbetter's literally shook as wall–to–wall patrons of questionable gender boogied atop the bar, tables, and barstools, as well as the floor. Providing the beat was high–energy rock which blared from stereo speakers instead of a juke box.

Within a year, young new owners had similarly converted another Fell's Point Tavern on Aliceanna Street into Rupert's (later Good Master Mustard Seed). Around the corner at 710 South Broadway, the irrepressible Turkey Joe Trabert took over the Parisian Café and christened it with both his nickname and his beer can collection. Al's and Ann's on Thames Street became The Horse You Came In On and expanded to include an outdoor café, which *National Geographic* mentioned in a 1975 article. Meanwhile, Baltimore's renowned offbeat filmmaker John Waters and some of his cast were hanging out at Bertha's (formerly the Lone Star) on the corner of Broadway and Lancaster. Soon, more than a dozen new youth–oriented watering holes were peacefully coexisting with rough and tumble seamen's haunts, several ethnic discothèques and some older bars which featured go-go girls.

During the second half of the decade, a similar destiny befell quite a few neighborhood bars in conjunction with the gentrification of streets near the Cross Street Market in South Baltimore. Barbara Ann's (now Regi's) at 1002 Light Street was the first such bar to draw a young crowd from outside the neighborhood. Next was Sticky Fingers on Cross Street, followed a few doors away by Lush's with its huge fireplace. On the same block at 10 East Cross Street, the former Dew Drop Inn became Jo's Organic Bar and later booked some of Baltimore's best rock'n roll bands. Largest of the new South Baltimore operations is at 1024 South Charles Street, where Hammerjack's opened in November, 1977, and grew to include upstairs and downstairs bars, an upstairs lounge, and a glass–roofed atrium.

As night life proliferated around its periphery, however, the downtown business sector with its burgeoning after–work crowd remained largely ignored. One of the few spots that prosperously catered to such persons from late afternoon until closing was O'Henry's. It opened in 1973 at 15 East Centre Street.

By 1977, the Crease and the Brasserie in Hopkins Plaza were effectively filling this void; and by 1978, Peter's Pub at 21 South Calvert Street had already become a Friday night tradition for all who could squeeze through the door. Within two years, Dunhill's at 32 South Calvert Street was picking up a hefty overflow from Peter's by

Musical Offering at a Baltimore Night Spot. Photo by Stephanie Lawrence.

providing dining and disco in slick surroundings.

Despite the emergence of successful pubs and lounges, Baltimore suffered a dearth of dance places. A notable exception, the Hippopotamus, opened in 1972 at Charles and Eager streets in the building that once housed the Chanticleer. Not only was the Hippopotamus Baltimore's most successful dance spot, it served, along with nearby Leon's, as the after–dark headquarters of her gay community. Though several clubs had attempted disco earlier, the craze did not catch on in Baltimore until the Hippo made the switch from live music in the mid–seventies.

Disco gained just as much momentum with the January, 1975, opening of O'Dell's at the former location of the Celebrity Club. Because no alcoholic beverages were served, its predominately black clientele was able to dance the night away until much later than Baltimore's conventional 2:00 A.M. closing time. Two months later, Gatsby's opened where the Carousel once stood at 1812 North Charles Street. A posh private club with three stories, many–mirrored walls, and a mostly black membership, Gatsby's features a disco on its first floor, jazz room on its second floor, and hair stylist on its third floor.

Though it had reached Baltimore later than other metropolitan areas, disco established itself in grand style with the April, 1978, opening of Girard's in a former automobile showroom at Cathedral and Eager streets. Lighting and stage effects were created by the same engineers responsible for those at New York's renowned Studio 54, of which Girard's became Baltimore's undisputed counterpart.

Disco had contributed little, however, to the welfare of live music in Baltimore. As records increasingly replaced bands for dancing, a lot of musicians found themselves out of work. To their rescue in March, 1978, came the *Unicorn Times*, a monthly arts tabloid, which focused heavily upon Baltimore's contemporary music scene.

The *Unicorn Times* emerged as the Marble Bar was failing. After decades of dormancy, the ancient and cavernous nightclub beneath the crumbling Congress Hotel at 306 West Franklin Street had reopened in late 1977. Despite performances by Muddy Waters, James Cotton, and others of national stature, it folded in June, 1978. Three months later, under new ownership, it began to feature different local bands nightly. As rock'n'roll's new-wave phenomenon came into vogue, the Marble Bar became its showcase.

By now, Baltimore had nightspots offering music for nearly everyone. Traditional Irish music drew a substantial following at several Baltimore pubs, among them the Cat's Eye in Fell's Point and the Gandy Dancer in Southwest Baltimore on McHenry Street. And since 1975, the revival of big band music has flourished in posh Cross Keys at a nightclub called Perry's Ordinary.

Very significantly, jazz made a comeback. Though Sunday afternoon Left Bank Jazz Society concerts had long been popular, live jazz had not been well supported in Baltimore night spots for more than a decade. Only Elzie Street's Royal Roost at 4227 York Road, bringing in such talent as James Moody and Fuzzy Kane, had been able to subsist on jazz alone between 1970 and 1976. Then, a couple years later, the Closet at 211 West Franklin Street successfully featured local talents. Finally, after opening in 1978, the Bandstand at 1616 Fleet Street in Fell's Point distinguished itself with such acts as the entire Lewis Hayes Quartet, Charlie Rouse, Curtis Fuller, and Clifford Jordan.

Atmosphere rather than entertainment spelled the success of Baltimore's biggest newcomers of 1979. First to open was the Chart House, a restaurant with extensive cocktail lounge facilities affording a view of Baltimore's rapidly developing Inner Harbor. And uptown, the Pimlico Hotel management opened a posh glass-walled lounge from which patrons could gaze down upon the city from atop the newly renovated Belvedere Hotel.

The following year marked the greatest resurgence in nocturnal activity that Baltimore had ever seen. The catalyst was Harborplace, where dozens of restaurants and diners awakened thousands of residents to a downtown they had previously ignored at night. Several of the restaurants, notably the Black Pearl, City Lights, and Phillips, featured live entertainment in their lounges and drew standing-room-only crowds.

Nightspots in the immediately surrounding city enjoyed the overflow, which included tourists and conventioneers as well as Baltimoreans. For the first time ever, the downtown sector was alive seven nights a week and new spots quickly appeared.

First and westernmost of the larger new establishments was the Baltimore General Dispensary. It opened on December 15, 1980, in the magnificently renovated shell of a building once the site of a free medical clinic with the same name. On the second floor, above the bar and dining room, was an entertainment area where a comedy review soon drew large audiences.

Approximately a month later, the Water Street Exchange opened at 110 Water Street in a building that once housed Baltimore's first indoor miniature golf course. Located at the vortex of the Crease, Peter's, and Dunhill's circuit, the Water Street Exchange became an immensely popular rendezvous for affluent prime-of-lifers.

Third within two months among architectural triumphs in which patrons could toast the renaissance was P. J. Cricketts at 206 West Pratt Street, which opened on February 8, 1981. Inside the preserved cast-iron confines are a lobby, bar, and dining rooms, all furnished with elegant late nineteenth century decor.

Undoubtedly, more spots will continue to open, while many of those established are likely to change. Indeed, because of fickle public tastes in entertainment and decor, Baltimore's nighttime scene is likely to change more rapidly than any other aspect of the ongoing renaissance. What may be permanent, however, are the people from all over Baltimore and beyond who now go out into the public sector at night not just to dance or to listen to music but to socialize. What other phenomenon, one might ask, better reflects the spirit of our city's rebirth?

Jake Slagle, Jr.

Sports

THE COLTS

It's a team ranked among the elite, one of the five best in the history of professional football. The Baltimore Colts of 1958–1959 won consecutive world championships with an ideal packaging of power and finesse that made them both explosive and artistic. Trying to control them was about the same as fighting a field fire with a whisk broom.

They were endowed with a precious skill, like John Unitas delicately timing a pass to Raymond Berry on sideline pattern or Lenny Moore swinging wide of end, kicking his legs free of tacklers and vanishing into faraway places or Jim Parker straightening up a charging lineman with a devastating block, or Arthur Donovan and Gino Marchetti hoping the opposition might come their way so they would, in effect, be wasting another play.

Those golden names out of Baltimore's past became more than provincial heroes. All six, along with the coach, Wilbur (Weeb) Ewbank, are enshrined in the Pro Football Hall of Fame, the highest honor that can come to a man who makes his livelihood on Sunday afternoons in the fall and winter trying to cross a goal line or keeping others from doing the same.

The Colts were part of the greatest game ever played, the first sudden–death event in the storied pages of pro football. It all unfolded December 28, 1958, where they prevailed over the New York Giants 23–17. But most of the players and some observers in the press box felt a game that was exceedingly more important was played a

month earlier, when the Colts erupted from a 27–7 half-time deficit to defeat the San Francisco 49ers by 35–27 for the Western Division title.

Had it not been for the win over the 49ers, there may not have been a playoff against the Giants. The divisional crown was indeed something special. It proved to the Colts they had the capabilities to win against a quality foe, the 49ers, and to come from behind to do it. They attained maturity that day and with that came an awareness of how good they were as a team.

They met the Giants on their field, Yankee Stadium, and rallied against the clock and scoreboard to win a classic confrontation that for pure excitement, if not play execution and error–free football, became a historic occasion.

It was more than a game as far as the National Football League was concerned. The event became its showcase for prestige and public acceptance. The Colts were a colorful, exciting team, led by a once obscure quarterback named John Constantine Unitas, who had been rescued from an old waiver list by General Manager Don Kellett for the price of an 85–cent long distance telephone call. That was in January, 1956.

The Colts' emergence as a team with championship possibilities started the following year, 1957, when a controversial loss to the 49ers in Kezar Stadium bitterly eliminated them from contention. But, as often happens in sports, a team or individual, after once being denied, attains the title objective a year later when increased confidence enhances the ability that's already there.

When the Colts won it all in 1958, they became the first world professional championship team to earn such distinction for Baltimore since the "old Orioles" of 1894–95 and 1896 earned the

What Makes Baltimore, Baltimore / 269

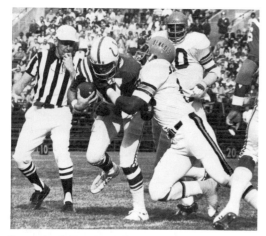

Quarterback Bert Jones Tries to Allude Tackler in a Game Between Colts and Bengals. Courtesy of Baltimore Football Colts Club. Photo by Joe Giza.

Temple Cup, forerunner to the World Series. Baltimore was ecstatic over the Colts. Parents named children after their favorite players and fans traveled on air excursions to all parts of the country to watch them perform.

The welcome-home of the Colts, after they whipped the Giants for the championship, found a mob scene waiting at Friendship Airport. Police estimated 30,000 men, women, and children in a state of frenzy, gathered there to greet the team. They climbed atop police cruisers, crushing one of the cars much the way you would collapse an empty tomato can, and crawled to the roof of the team bus, all for the chance to see their heroes.

The "sudden death" game in 1958 found the Colts tying the score, 17-17, with a Steve Myhra field goal of 19 yards with only nine seconds remaining. Then the Giants won the coin-toss for the first sudden-death contest ever played. They took the kickoff, couldn't manage a first down, and punted to the Colts on their 21-yard line.

In 13 plays, Unitas orchestrated a drive that was culminated on a one-yard touchdown by Alan (The Horse) Ameche, behind clearing blocks delivered by Moore, George Preas, and Jim Mutscheller that ended the overtime at 8:15. Unitas was superb in sudden death, just as he had been in the final drive of the last quarter that saw him bring the Colts from their own 14, fighting the clock, to tie the score and then win it all.

It's a game that will always have a special meaning among exceptional sports accomplishments. And the next year, 1959, the same two teams won their divisions again. This set up a rematch, played in Memorial Stadium, and the outcome was the same, the Colts winning, 31-16.

John Sample played an extraordinary game at safety, intercepting two of Charley Conerly's passes and standing out on defense as few men ever have. The Colts as a result of their back-to-back titles, established themselves as a team to be ranked with the Chicago Bears, Cleveland Browns, Los Angeles Rams, and Green Bay Packers when it came to grouping the all-time great championship outfits.

The Colts probably would have made it three in a row except for what happened when they literally collided with the Chicago Bears at Wrigley Field in 1960. The Colts won in the last 19 seconds when Unitas, bruised and bleeding about the face from the Bears' strong pass rush, "loaded the gun" for a 39-yard passing shot to Moore in the end-zone that was one of the most pulsating finishes ever produced.

Donovan and Marchetti, coming away from Wrigley Field and a 24-20 victory, said it was the most physically draining game they ever played. Both teams battered themselves and each other into such a state of collapse that neither the Bears nor Colts won again the rest of the year. They were spent.

The Colts just didn't win two titles, come close to a third, and then flatten out. They remained one of the dominant teams for more than the next decade. It was an era of disappointment, too, as they were frequently shot down by serious injuries, controversial calls, and even a quirk in the playoff rules.

A coaching change was made after the 1962 campaign. Ewbank was being dropped and Don Shula (a former defensive halfback with the team), who had been an assistant with the Detroit Lions, was appointed to replace him. The team won eight and lost six in Shula's first season, despite being without Berry for five weeks because of a shoulder injury and getting little help from Moore, who had a head ailment.

Then in 1964, Moore came back to score 20

touchdowns and the Colts put away the Rams, 24–7, for the Western Division title as the defense sacked quarterbacks Roman Gabriel and Bill Munson 11 times. But in the championship game against the Cleveland Browns, the Colts, although heavily favored, didn't score a point and were totally embarrassed, 27–0. Three TDs came via the combination of Frank Ryan throwing and Gary Collins catching.

Although there was a period in 1964 when the Colts won 11 games in a row—a club record—they came up dry against the Browns in the one that counted the most. What was an otherwise exceptional season ended in dejection. The pattern was the same in 1965, only there was still greater disappointment and disillusionment.

The Colts lost both quarterbacks, Unitas and Gary Cuozzo, to late-season injuries, yet still tied the Packers for the Western crown with a record of 10–3–1. In the playoff with the Packers, the Colts were forced to improvise. They turned Tom Matte into an instant quarterback. Matte had been a split-T, QB at Ohio State University, and was one of the few options Shula had after Unitas and Cuozzo were wiped out.

He fitted Matte in at the position and put a plastic-covered band containing the ready list of plays on his left wrist. The Colts scored early when Don Shinnick converted a fumble into a touchdown and held on tenaciously. With only 1:58 left to play, they had a 10–7 lead. But what appeared to be a surprising Colts' upset, considering they were using a converted halfback at quarterback, became a different story when Don Chandler missed a field goal from the 27-yard line.

The ball sliced to the right, but official Jim Tunney, underneath the goal post, signaled the kick was good. It was human error on Tunney's part. The Colts complained, but nothing changed. Movies later showed the kick did not go through the uprights. Because of the subsequent controversy, the next year the NFL extended the posts ten feet higher and stationed two officials, instead of one, in the end zone on field-goal attempts.

After the debatable FG tied the count, it forced sudden-death and the Colts played the Packers for another 13 minutes, 39 seconds before Chandler drove home another kick from 25 yards away. This one was straight and true,

giving the Packers a 13–10 win that was as crushing as any the Colts have had to accept.

Still another set of unusual circumstances blocked their way in 1967. They completed the campaign with an 11–2 record, the same as the Rams, but newly devised rules by the league decreed a tie-breaker would be decided by the team that scored the most points in games played in head-to-head competition. The Colts and Rams had deadlocked in Baltimore, 24–24, but the Colts lost in Los Angeles, 34–10.

The Colts had the best offense in the entire league and the defense had allowed fewer points than any team in club history. Still, they weren't going anywhere for the playoffs, except to watch on television. It was as if the Colts were traveling under a dark cloud. Something was continually happening that proved frustrating.

The same pattern held again in 1968. Unitas tore a muscle in his pitching elbow in the final exhibition game, but Shula had fortunately picked up Earl Morrall from the New York Giants. It was Morrall who filled the void when Unitas couldn't play and they won 13 of 14 games, including a 34–0 rout of the Browns in Cleveland for the NFL crown. This sent the Colts on to the Super Bowl for the first time since the extravaganza had been conceived. The outcome proved to be a shock. More of the negative was to be the rule.

The Colts somehow lost to the New York Jets, 16–7, after being favored by 16 points. Jimmy Orr was open near the end of the first half on the old standard flea-flicker play, but Morrall "lost" Orr in the backdrop of a band—dressed in blue uniforms, too—and elected to try to pass down the middle to Jerry Hill, but the ball was intercepted.

It was the first time in Super Bowl play an AFL team had whipped an NFL representative and, to this day, the upset ranks with some of the most famous or infamous in history—depending on your point of view. Joe Namath of the Jets predicted the upset prior to the game and the Colts laughed. But it was Joe who won the bragging rights and new credibility when it was over.

The Colts felt ashamed at what happened and vowed they'd come back to square the account, but it was under different circumstances. Shula got the chance to become both coach and general manager of the Miami Dolphins and decided to leave. He believed owner Carroll Rosenbloom, disenchanted over not being able to win the title, was getting ready to fire him so he wanted to make a move on his own, before it happened. Shula got permission from Steve Rosenbloom, a son of Carroll, to talk with the Dolphins and accepted the position, which made the Colts' boss most unhappy.

He later cried foul and charged tampering. This resulted in Commissioner Pete Rozelle granting the Colts the first round draft choice of the Dolphins. Shula's replacement was Don McCafferty, who had been the backfield coach and offensive coordinator.

McCafferty was known as the "Easy Rider" and in his first try accomplished something the Colts had never done before—won the Super Bowl, 16-13, over the Dallas Cowboys. Jim O'Brien's field goal of 32 yards in the last minute decided the issue. The game was far from an artistic presentation. There were 11 turnovers, including three intercepted passes thrown by the Colts and four fumbles.

Baltimore got its final chance after Craig Morton of the Cowboys had a pass tip off the hands of receiver Dan Reeves and into the grasp of Mike Curtis at the 41, Curtis ran to the 28 and, two plays later, O'Brien split the uprights with the winning kick. It was a day of vindication for the Colts and their first outright championship since 1959, despite the fact they had come so close so many times.

In 1971, the Colts almost duplicated their success of the year before, coming within one game of a return to the Super Bowl. Again, they had a bitter demise, losing to the Dolphins in the Orange Bowl and being blanked 21-0, the first time they had been shutout in 97 games, or going back to December 13, 1965. Before another training camp started, Rosenbloom traded himself to the Los Angeles Rams.

It evolved this way: the family of the late Dan Reeves, owner of the Rams, wanted to sell the franchise. Joe Thomas, who had been a Colts' line coach in 1954 and later a personnel director of the Minnesota Vikings and Dolphins, decided he would try to put a package together. He interested Bob Irsay, an air-conditioning executive from Skokie, Illinois, in buying the Rams for a record $19 million. Then Irsay would trade

the Rams to Rosenbloom for the rights to the Colts. The transaction, as bizarre as it sounded, came into being and the league gave its approval.

Thomas' agreement with Irsay was he would become the general manager with unlimited authority. The Colts, in 1972, opened by losing four of their first five games and Thomas relieved McCafferty of the head job, appointing line coach John Sandusky on an interim basis. Thomas ordered Unitas be benched to see what Marty Domres could do. At season's end, Unitas, after saying he wanted to play elsewhere, was sold outright to the San Diego Chargers for $150,000, completing a Baltimore stand for him that started when he joined the club as a little known rookie in 1956 and continued through all-pro accomplishments and most valuable player awards. Unitas only played one more year in San Diego and then retired to Baltimore and the operation of his restaurants.

Other Colts, such as Matte, Bill Curry, Dan Sullivan, Fred Miller, Tom Nowatzke, Jerry Logan, and Norm Bulaich, were dealt away. Thomas had traffic moving. The Colts were being dismantled and, subsequently, reshaped. Thomas gave up tackle Billy Newsome and a fourth-round draft choice to the New Orleans Saints for their first-round draft choice and selected Bert Jones, a multitalented and much-coveted quarterback from Louisiana State University.

Jones was an impressive natural athlete, gifted with all the necessary skills. But he was still a rookie and the Colts had to wait for Jones to get playing time and the seasoning he needed. Howard Schnellenberger, a member of Shula's staff in Miami, was named head coach and suffered through a 4-10 season in 1973. The next year's schedule was only two and a half games old when Irsay went down on the field as the Colts were playing the Eagles in Philadelphia. Words ensued between the owner and the coach and it was no surprise who won—Irsay. The coach was gone and Thomas finished out the year handling the team.

The next season, another new coach, Ted Marchibroda, arrived. He had been an assistant for 14 years in the NFL. The chance to be a head coach had long evaded him. Actually, he admitted he was never as much as interviewed for a head position until Thomas knighted him.

Marchibroda established an excellent rapport with his players, spent long hours working with Jones, and the Colts were the surprise of the league. From a 2–12 dead–last position in 1974, they had a 10–4 season. Marchibroda was named "coach of the year;" Thomas was voted "executive of the year."

The Colts were applauded for their turnaround but lost to the Pittsburgh Steelers, 28–10, in the playoff elimination, an afternoon when Jones was injured and couldn't go all the way. But the Colts' general performance was entirely unprecedented. No team had ever been 2–12 one season and 10–4 the next.

Thomas continued to add good draft choices, but all was not tranquil within the organization. After the final exhibition of 1976, a poor performance against the Detroit Lions, Irsay entered the locker room and berated the players and coaches. Two days later, as a result of the stormy scene, the coach quit. Players protested and Jones was especially vocal.

It was apparent Marchibroda, somehow, would have to be induced to return to the team. Thomas didn't like it, said he was backed into a corner, and ridiculed Marchibroda for "jumping ship." "As far as I'm personally concerned," said Thomas, "he can keep on walking." Support of the players, public and press in behalf of the coach were too much for Thomas and Irsay to offset so they brought Marchibroda back. The coach was given full power to make decisions on team personnel. It also was the beginning of the end for Thomas.

The Colts had another excellent season in 1976, earning a playoff berth but, again, fell to the Steelers. They were bombed out, 40–14 as the Terry Bradshaw–led team cranked out 526 yards to only 170 by the Colts. The game was more memorable for what happened when it was over. That's when a small plane, piloted by Donald Kreiner, crashed into the upper deck of the horseshoe–shaped stadium. Kreiner suffered only minor injuries. Most of the crowd of 60,020 had left early because of the way the Colts were losing—or else a major tragedy might have occurred.

There was more to come later in the stormy aftermath of the campaign. Irsay decided he would listen to quarterback Jones, who advised him Marchibroda was more important to the Colts than Thomas. But Irsay had solicited his opinion—an unusual thing for an owner to ask of a player. Thomas was fired, Marchibroda was granted full control of the team and a coach (who only five months before had quit) was now entrenched in a power position.

Dick Szymanski, one of the best all-around players the Colts ever had, and later a personnel director and scout, was named general manager with Ernie Accorsi, former publicity director and an aide in the league office, the assistant GM. On the field, under Marchibroda, the Colts continued to win but, per usual, had trouble in the first game of the playoffs. They played the Oakland Raiders to a 31–31 deadlock at the end of four quarters. Then they went into overtime, and after an extra period the score was still tied.

It wasn't until 2:17 of the second extra session that Ken Stabler completed his third touchdown pass to Dave Casper to end the most frustrating afternoon the Colts had ever known. The score had been tied or changed eight times in what rates as one of the most unforgettable games the Colts have ever played, even though they came away the loser.

There were aspirations to come back and do it all over again, but 1978 wasn't to be the year. Jones suffered a shoulder separation in the final exhibition and the Colts, using backup Bill Troup, were never a threat in the regular schedule. Another 5 and 11 showing in 1979 and an alarming decline in attendance brought about the firing of Marchibroda, who still had three years remaining on his contract. Jones suffered an injury-plagued season again, which added to the woes.

In a realignment of authority, Dick Szymanski, the general manager, assumed the control of the football operation. Szymanski gave consideration to hiring Frank Kush, the deposed Arizona State coach, but backed off and then appointed Mike McCormack, a personable former all-pro tackle with the Cleveland Browns, as the team's new head coach. He had been a headman with the Cincinnati Bengals.

The Colts have known the heights of ecstasy and also the depths of despair. It has been a franchise that has had talented, colorful players, success and failure, controversy on and off the field, exceptional support at the box office, and a storied history few professional teams could ever match, going all the way back to the organizational year, 1920, of the National Football League when it was founded in a Canton (Ohio) garage. Baltimore's football past is part of that rich tradition.

John F. Steadman

THE ORIOLES

The single greatest high in Baltimore's post-World War II experience, the one happiest time of all for city and suburbs together, happened Sunday, October 9, 1966, from 3:50 P.M. on into the night. It began with the third and final out in the top of the ninth inning in a baseball game at Memorial Stadium. The full house streaming out the exits, joined by the far vaster crowd that had been watching on television, proceeded to whoop it up, and up, and up.

Baltimore's Orioles, representing the American League, had won the fourth and final game in that year's World Series. A rarity, the series sweep—the most devoted fan hadn't really expected his or her Orioles to do that well. After winning a big league pennant for the first time in this century, Baltimore was squared off against the redoubtable Los Angeles Dodgers, headed by the awesome pitcher Sandy Koufax. Yet, there the Orioles were, winning two games in California, then two more in Maryland; in the last three games, not allowing their foe so much as a score.

So, on an afternoon and evening of balmy early autumn, and 22-cents-a-gallon gasoline, the town turned out. The biggest mill-around of all was downtown, along East Baltimore Street; but everywhere, car horns sounded, strangers embraced, all Baltimore was asmile.

On another October day in 1979, very likely this high mark in celebration would have been topped, had the Orioles only won. After five innings of the deciding World Series game, again it was being played in Baltimore, the home team led Pittsburgh's Pirates. But by the end of nine, all was lost. Another epochal date: December 28, 1958, after the Baltimore Colts beat the New York Giants in that year's National Football

Wild Bill Hagy—Oriole Parade, October, 1979. Photo by John Clark Mayden.

League playoff. The celebrating then was boisterous enough to establish this vicinity's previous morale maximum. Yet that glorious 23–17 victory in overtime, chapter headed, "The Colts" was an away game, with some hundreds of Baltimoreans as eyewitnesses. Winter darkness was also a restraining factor. On baseball's great day, after the stadium had been reluctantly vacated, someone rang the bell in City Hall's dome 66 times. You could scarcely hear it, there on The Block, amid the whoopee.

For an Oriole fan, emotional overflow is a frequent condition. Ironically, of the 4,100 championship-standings games played by the modern Orioles through 1979 (including postseason games) one run has meant the difference between winning and losing almost exactly 30 percent of the time. Here perhaps is a clue to what otherwise mystifies: how the same flushed, hoarse spectator can be committed as well to that passionless occupation, arithmetic.

Evidences of this duality have been widespread. Mark Belanger, the post–1966 shortstop, and a nonpareil at nipping off the batter in his hurried trip to first, himself often found it hard to get a hit. As the 1979 season neared, Belanger promised to hit a home run; indeed, two homers! He had of course no idea in which game this would happen. He was luring his incredulous public into buying tickets for as many as all 77 home dates. And indirectly, he was reminding Baltimoreans of an embarrassment: the attendance statistic, which year after year has recorded a higher head count for Oriole road games than those at home. As it turned out, in 1979, what Belanger smote was two triples and his alternate Kiko Garcia hit homers. (Objection? Belanger could simply point to three games left unplayed: it rained so much that year.) In any case, paid attendance at home did for once out-total that for Oriole games everywhere. Nay at 1,680,561 it set an all-time record for Baltimore. (The record was broken the next year, with home attendance at 1,797,438.)

With equal statistical ease, the Oriole fan will recall that April 13, 1954, marks the first pennant-season game played (in Detroit) by this team after its readmission to the American League, which in 1901 it had helped found; and April 15, 1954, a Thursday afternoon, the first home game (against Chicago), in the entirely rebuilt, city-owned baseball park at 1000 East 33rd Street. These dates matter. To baseball's broad following, 1954, with its end to 51 years' existence in the pleasant but inherently ignominious minor leagues, was the start of modern times in Baltimore; 1954 brought the resumption of national acceptance, national importance.

Accordingly, the 1978 season closed out 25 years' play. Of those 4,010 games, 2,181 had happy outcomes. Seventeen times, Baltimore finished in the first division; eight times, in the second. Never did the team incur the indignity of last place. Many another set of fans would have been willing to swap particularly for the four pennants and two World Series triumphs (the Os, as headline writers dub them, won again in 1970, over Cincinnati, in five games; they lost in five to New York in 1969, and in seven to Pittsburgh in 1971). By 1978, the American League had expanded from eight clubs to 14; in that league and the century, New York was the only other city to win as many pennants. Of the 24 cities with franchises in the American or National League or both, only New York, Los Angeles, Oakland, St. Louis, Cincinnati, and Pittsburgh won as many World Series.

Then, in 1979, as if to mark the anniversary, a set of almost ordinary Orioles walked right away from their hugely salaried, loudly ballyhooed rivals. In the course of winning the East-

ern Division race, by eight full games, they electrified their fans. An upperdeck rooter named Bill Hagy led everybody in a body-language cheer: O-R-I-O-L-E-S. Then Baltimore took the pennant playoffs, three games of four, against favored California. Then, just as in 1971, came a showdown with powerful Pittsburgh, and a sorrowful home-field, seventh-game defeat.

The proportions of this success have had an almost classical symmetry: long and arduous climb, followed by dizzying double summit, followed by a high yet peakless plateau. In 1954, when the American League finally unfroze the alignment in effect since 1903 (when Baltimore's original franchise was snatched away so the league could put a team in New York), the team moved east was St. Louis', the last place team. The danger was that Baltimore, too, would be stuck with perennial tailenders. Instead, the determined manager-general manager combination of Paul R. Richards and Lee McPhail, Jr. gradually, painfully assembled a lineup of pennant contenders.

A single dazzling trade made the final difference and brought about 1966: the obtaining of right fielder Frank Robinson from Cincinnati. Stung by his former club's low assessment of him, F. Robby now displayed his capabilities for all to behold. On Mother's Day, at the stadium, against Cleveland, he hit a home run that sailed not into, but over the left-field bleachers and out into the parking lot. It was, it still is the only homer ever to carry clear out of the park. He went on to win that year's league championship in homers, in runs batted in, in batting average. This is the so-called triple crown, the only time an Oriole had or has won it. His final, fourth-game homer provided the 1-0 edge enabling Baltimore to sweep the 1966 World Series. And his return in 1979 as a coach had something to do with that year's happy surprises.

In the lull following 1966, Manager Hank Bauer was replaced by Manager Earl Weaver and the club reverted, for its strong point, to the pitching excellence that has been its clearest characteristic. Two of its young, farm-system pitchers matured, Dave McNally and Jim Palmer; and another masterful trade netted Mike Cuellar. One year the Oriole pitching staff included four 20-game winners. Meanwhile, its tide again cresting, the team won pennants in

Oriole Parade, October, 1979. Photo by John Clark Mayden.

three consecutive seasons with games–won totals of 109, 108, and 101. The nearest enemy team was 12 games behind. Unbelievable years, those of 1969, 1970, 1971 or they would have been, but for the tendency of the World Series, in odd-numbered years, to be won by the National League.

For the rest of the 1970s, the Orioles won, but never quite often enough. Their assets including fielding, with three infielders and center fielder Paul Blair winning more Gold Gloves than any other whole team did; and shrewdness, with cantankerous Earl Weaver generally recognized as the No. 1 manager in all baseball, and other teams grabbing Oriole coaches for their managers; and Brooks Robinson.

As far back as 1955, when he played in a few Oriole games as an 18–year–old, Brooks looked good. In the 1960s and 1970s, it became evident that here was the best all-around third baseman so far, anywhere. For his defense against bunts, grounders, line drives, and pop flies, the Gold Gloves given him should have been platinum. Fifteen times, Brooks was on the American League's All–Star Game squad. He was the hero of the 1970 World Series. In all, he played 23 years with one major league club, something no one else has ever done. In a 1975 understatement, the fans voted him the "most memorable Oriole."

What kept a team with these strengths from making it clear to the top? A succession of slow starts, for one thing, with too much of a Boston

or New York lead to overcome in its customary August–September sprint. Another setback was 1975's court–ordered relaxation of the reserve clause. The effect was to free star players (most noticeably, in Baltimore's case, Reggie Jackson) to decamp for larger cities and wealthier franchises.

And, growing uncertainty as to the club's future ownership and location was distracting to player, to fan, to all Baltimore. Unimportant, the feeling used to be, that the attendance was moderate: across the first 25 years, 974,912 persons a year came to home games—the year's profit or deficit was small enough to be inconsequential. Beer was the big thing: brewers and breweries owned most of the stock, and quips went the rounds when inside dealing gave Gunther's the TV rights, or switched them to National. Now the camera could roam the outfield; now it must never, never show the scoreboard, dominated as that was by a Hamm's or Schaefer's beer ad. From 1965 on, with Jerold C. Hoffberger as chairman, the beer (as well as the new electronic scoreboard) was National.

In the seventies, however, the national corporate pastime came to be merger, or engorgement. Big business swallowed small, and even other big business. Regional and local breweries disappeared, alarmingly. The Hoffberger family, investing in activities unrelated to promenade-concession thirsts, lost interest in a chronically low–return enterprise. The club was announced for sale. (What had cost $2,475,000 in 1954 proved to be worth $12,000,000, a quarter century later.) Would a buyer leave it in Baltimore?

Having just seen their soccer and pro tennis franchises die, their (minor league) ice hockey franchise fold, their National Basketball League franchise moved to Washington, Baltimoreans anguished. Ever vaster, ever more moneyed, Greater Washington from 1971 on had no baseball team of its own, and lusted for one. Other metro areas issued siren calls. Ordinary Baltimoreans, those with a feeling for yesterday and tomorrow, for physical exertion, and the three-and–two pitch, lost sleep.

A first ownership crisis, in 1975, abated. A second, boiling up after the 1978 season, was more serious, especially as it transpired that, around town, a few businesses and individuals were willing to contribute, but only modest sums. Those who could afford the purchase cared more about earnings prospects. The small investor, in his and her large numbers, was ignored.

Early in August, 1979, with some suddenness, a purchaser stood revealed: Edward Bennett Williams, a Washington lawyer with a name for crafty maneuvering in the trials of prominent defendants and for sports enthusiasts at the control level. Because his Baltimore venture coincided with a season of fan frenzy and black-ink ledgers, there was no threat of the club's immediate removal. Over the long run, however, Oriole diehards could discern the grisly likelihood of an attempt to—the very least—make over the Orioles into some kind of two-city hybrid.

Amid such excitements, anniversary observances paled. Yet many a person harked back to close games across the years, to laughter, to disgust and despair and hope eternal. Mornings, on the *Sun*'s front page, Jim Hartzell's bird told how the Orioles had fared the previous night—as it winged high over the Statue of Liberty (we beat the Yanks) or stood on a pier labeled Fell's Point and debated jumping off (we didn't even score). Afternoon, the *News American* savored the scene in Baltimore's zingiest headlines ("Delirium," said its one-word front-page bannerline of fan fever; another day, following another phenomenal come-from-behind Oriole victory, "Madness"). Bob Maisel, Bill Tanton, John Steadman, Gordon Beard, Sam Lacy, Lou Hatter, Ken Nigro, Jim Ellis, Doug Brown, Jim Elliot, Neal Eskridge, ultimately even women reporters and columnists went into the locker room. They noted how much Boog Powell appeared to weigh by now, whether it was true that Bob Nieman might be traded, what Earl Weaver had to say about Jim Palmer and what Palmer had to say about what Weaver had to say, and what kind of pitch it was that Gus Triandos or Jim Gentile, Lee May or Eddie Murray, had hit far off into the night.

How great it was, as Chuck Thompson once more bade Miss Agnes to go to war, as Ernie Harwell and others left and Bill O'Donnell arrived and Brooks himself became an announcer. What fun for the memory freaks, poking through 253 player names: what position did George Werley play? Name two Whiteys and five Millers. What was Hoyt Wilhelm's nickname? What did these have in common: Mabe, Young, Adams, and Avila? And what was there in common about these two: the resident major league Orioles and Baltimore's best quarter century so far?

James Bready

BLACK BASEBALL IN BALTIMORE

"Most people my age is dead," ole Casey Stengel of the New York Yankees used to say, "and you could look it up." Well, don't try looking up anything on black baseball in Baltimore, at least not before 1950—pretty late in the game at that. White newspapers gave it scant coverage; black newspapers were not much better.

But if you were to look in the *Sun* on May 19, 1950, you'd find this: "ROMBY HURLS ELITES' OPENER." And the story on the sports page went on, "The honor of hurling the Elites Giants' first game goes to Bob Romby on Sunday when the champions of the Negro American League meet the Philadelphia Stars."

That was almost 30 years ago, and mention of that story today stirs Bob Romby to reminiscing. "I began with the Giants as a starting pitcher. We only had starting pitchers; you started, you finished. We played most of our games at Bugle Field, out on Edison Highway near Biddle where the Lord Baltimore Press is today. And we played good baseball! Henry Kimbro, the player manager, was hitting .419; Finney, .356; Pee Wee Butts, .315. We even played against Sachel Paige. Satch threw everything—fast balls, curves, sinkers. He used to strike me out on three swings."

The ageless Paige may have humiliated Romby but not first baseman Hubert Simmons. "I remember one game, "Simmons recalls, "We shelled him pretty good. I hit a single off of him myself."

We have to take the words of Romby, Simmons, and one-time owner Richard D. Powell for the life and times of the Baltimore Elite (pronounced "Ee–lyte") Giants; almost no records were kept of the earlier years. Nothing shows up until the team's last year—1950. But reports of those who were there and research by buffs have turned out a sketchy history: black baseball in Baltimore began with the Lord Hamiltons and the Orientals playing each other in South Baltimore as far back as 1874. The first black baseball league included a Baltimore team, the Lord Baltimores. That 1887 league folded in June of its first year—a very short season in the sun. The next one, the Negro Eastern League, started in 1920 and fared better. The Baltimore Black Sox were members and in 1929 won the pennant; but that league disbanded the following year.

As the Depression lifted, new leagues were formed. In 1938, the Nashville (Tenn.) Elite Giants franchise was transferred to Baltimore. This was the Negro National League, whose 1939 pennant was won by the Elites. That team had many first–rate players, but all have been subsequently outshone by the 17–year old catcher—Roy (Leroy, then) Campanella.

Under a different name, Negro American League, the clubs resumed play after World War II. When the year again ended in a nine—1949—Baltimore again finished first. And, in a post–season world series, the Elites took four straight from Chicago's American Giants, representing the western black league. But by then, organized baseball was raiding the black clubs of all their best players, and 1950 was the last year for black league baseball.

Baltimore teams had played hundreds of games in a variety of cities across the years. There were, undoubtedly, pitcher's battles and slugfests, moments of high drama and lots of laughter. But don't try looking it up. It's not here.

Gilbert Sandler

THE PREAKNESS

A tough and honest contest between horses and their owners has lured Marylanders to race tracks since 1743, the date of the first Maryland Jockey Club–sponsored race. In the intervening

Henry Cooper, *"Jockey Lafitte Pincay."* One of the 25 Portraits in the National Jockeys Hall of Fame at Pimlico, 1978.

years, horse racing has fascinated generations of writers, politicians, socialites, and devoted fans of the sport.

In pre–Revolutionary days, Maryland aristocrats maintained stables that, according to one newsman, rivalled the best in England. Quarterhorse and Thoroughbred matches became so popular (any public gathering was a likely occasion) that an act of the General Assembly was required to prohibit the competitions on Sundays, Saturday afternoons, and at Quaker meetings.

With such a tradition, it is fitting that Baltimore's Pimlico Race Course should host the annual Preakness Stakes, a two–minute spectacle witnessed by huge crowds every May. Should the weather be in this race's favor, the Preakness can draw the largest audience of any Baltimore sporting event.

In the past decade, the city, the owners of Pimlico, and other commercial interests have used the Preakness as the focal point of a major springtime festival and promotion. A week's worth of outdoor picnics, parades, festivals, and civic promotions help boost the race and Baltimore itself. Television coverage of the Preakness has also brought the race into a national sports perspective.

More than a century of racing history has established the Preakness Stakes as one of the high points of the Baltimore scene. It is often called the second hurdle of racing's Triple Crown. The three contests are held each spring, beginning with the Kentucky Derby at Louisville, followed by Baltimore's Preakness, and end with the Belmont Stakes at Belmont Park on Long Island.

The first Preakness was held May 27, 1873, before a crowd of 12,000 who traveled out from the center of town by horse and train. Pimlico, named after a section of London, also came to be named Old Hilltop for the rise of ground that once existed in its infield. A bay colt, Survivor, reached the wire ten lengths ahead of the next best of a seven-horse field to win that first Preakness Stakes.

The annual spring contest continued over the years, save for an erratic period when the race was stopped, then transferred to the Brooklyn Jockey Club in New York. In 1909, the Preakness returned to Baltimore and Old Hilltop. Racing enthusiasts followed the race, which has been run on Saturdays since 1931.

The Preakness, which retains many traditional elements, has seen change. For decades, the choice spot to view the race was the old Clubhouse, a frame Victorian building with a dining porch. Racing's oldest edifice burned June 16, 1966. Its historic cupola and weathervane were preserved however. As soon as the result of the Preakness is announced, the metal jockey on the weathervane is painted with the winner's racing colors.

In 1967, the management of Pimlico began a concerted effort to boost attendance at the Preakness by promoting the track's infield as a popular place to watch the race. It brought in bands, entertainment, lacrosse games, and encouraged all Baltimore to make a day of it. By 1978, some 81,000 persons would be at the Preakness.

The upsurge in attendance was coincidental with the Preakness Cultural Festival, a week of city-wide festivities that have included a huge pasta party in the Inner Harbor, fireworks, downtown parades, and a hot-air balloon race across the Chesapeake Bay from one of the city's parks. All the merriment serves to put Baltimoreans in a positive mood to appreciate one of America's best known thoroughbred racing contests.

Lisa Kirshner and Jacques Kelly

A Multitude of Givers: The People of the Baltimore Renaissance

The city is the people. Baltimore without its people is like a stage without the actors—an empty space. Even the city's buildings, streets, and parks are a reflection of human ideas and labor. The Baltimore renaissance is therefore essentially the story of Baltimore's people— from the thousands who have participated in neighborhood activities or cast a ballot to the several hundred who have played leading roles. To single out any among these multitudes for special praise is impossible, but the following six brief sketches may indicate the range and diversity of people who have taken major roles in uplifting Baltimore during the last several decades. In reading over the many great gifts these individuals have bestowed on the city, it is hoped that the reader will be reminded of the hundreds of others whose time, energy, talents and money have enriched this city in many hundreds of ways.

WALTER SONDHEIM, Jr.

Before John F. Kennedy brought Camelot to America with his appeal, "Ask not what your country can do for you, but what you can do for your country," Walter Sondheim, Jr. already had devoted much of his life to public service in Baltimore in several roles including promoter of the city, businessman, and school board president. In the 20 years since Kennedy, Sondheim's contributions to his city and his country continue to match those of any citizen.

He "has made a difference to our city," Mayor William Donald Schaefer says of the 73-year old Sondheim who often still walks daily from his Bolton Hill home to his office at the World

Trade Center. Among his many tasks on behalf of Baltimore, Sondheim chairs the board of Charles Center–Inner Harbor Management. Charles Center, of course, as well as the renewal of the Inner Harbor are only a few of the more well-known achievements that Walter Sondheim significantly contributed to during the past several decades.

Exactly who is Walter Sondheim and why has it been possible for him to do so much for the city and its people?

He graduated in 1925 from Park School and in 1929 from Haverford College. According to friends, Sondheim originally planned to minister to the medical needs of individuals as a physician instead of the educational, housing, and architectural needs of a city. However, his plans to enter medical school were dashed by the Depression. Sondheim went to work for Hochschild Kohn in 1929, a company which his father had helped found many years before. Sondheim remained at Hochschild Kohn for over 40 years, finally retiring in 1970 to devote all of his time to Charles Center–Inner Harbor activities. He was senior vice-president and treasurer for the retail corporation at that time.

In recent times, Sondheim has held directorships of Chesapeake and Potomac Telephone Company, Baltimore Gas and Electric Company, Provident Savings Bank, and Baltimore Life Insurance Company. As will be shown, these extensive business contacts have been vital for his work in changing the face of the city. Sondheim has also served on boards for Goucher College, Sinai Hospital, the Citizens Planning and Housing Association, League of Women's Voters, American Red Cross, and the National Alliance of Businessmen. He has received various honorary degrees: the McCormick Civilian Award, the Interfaith Award, and various "Man of the Year" awards. These achievements, however, constitute only a small part of his efforts for Baltimore and explain little about the man.

During World War II, Sondheim was director of the United States Employment Service for Maryland and assistant state director of the War Manpower Commission for Maryland. He also served in the Navy.

Shortly after the war, Sondheim combined his demonstrated leadership abilities in both the private and public sectors to become president,

Jewish Family and Children's Service; director of the Association of Commerce; and a member (1948–1954), then president of the Board of School Commissioners (1954–1957). Sondheim assumed leadership of the city's school system the day the Supreme Court's school desegregation ruling was handed down (1954). His primary task was to help desegregate the city's schools while maintaining quality education. His work was successful and stands in sharp contrast to the many failures since then of America's schools.

During the 1950s Sondheim expanded his civic contributions to become chairman of the Baltimore Urban Renewal and Housing Commission and Housing Agency (1957–1963). In this role he was able to execute vigorously his ideas for seeing Baltimore advance from its primary efforts at housing to the commercial revitalization and the downtown renaissance of the 1970s and 1980s.

The Three Secrets to Sondheim and Baltimore's Success

Sondheim's achievements, in both education and urban renewal, remarkably parallel the three characteristics that seem to underlie those rare instances in which an American city, such as Baltimore, has been successfully revitalized.

First, there has to be a recognition that a city is in trouble and something more than the ritualistic litany of complaints is drastically needed to reverse increasing deterioration, unemployment, and the growing exodus of businesses and educated population.

"Back in the early 1950s, there was a good bit of dissatisfaction in Baltimore with the disjointed nature in which development, which was just beginning, was going," Sondheim disclosed in an interview. "'Urban renewal' was hardly a word. It was known as redevelopment."

The second characteristic of a successfully revitalizing city is a strong commitment to *planning* among its leaders. This is in marked contrast to the usual variant of 'laissez faire chaos' in which governmental agencies and the private sector are more or less allowed to work haphazardly—sometimes with disastrous results for the people and environment. Very early Sondheim and others realized the folly of either government or businesses independently "doing their own thing" without judicious administration based on sound theory and planning.

"The City and the Greater Baltimore Committee," Sondheim explains, "got a group of distinguished people in housing and fiscal administration to come to Baltimore to make a study. It came out in 1956 and was a real landmark. It recommended a unified agency that would pull together efforts in housing and urban development. This led to the Urban Renewal and Housing Agency" (a predecessor of today's city Department of Housing and Community Development).

Baltimore shares with many other cities an awareness that something has to be done and that that something ought to be based on rational planning. Yet there is a third factor that is equally important and one, largely due to efforts such as men like Sondheim, that distinguishes this city from dozens of others whose pursuit of a renaissance have thus far been failures.

In a nutshell, this third characteristic of a successfully revitalizing city is the meaningful combination of leaders from both the private and public sectors with a hardheaded recognition that any long –term accomplishments without a marriage of the two is impossible.

It is surprising how often American cities refuse to enter into this arrangement or in how many ways the private and public sectors have worked to sabotage one another. For instance, in cities such as New York and Cleveland flash-in-the-pan charismatic elected leaders tried to make a career out of denouncing bankers and landlords. Routinely, governmental officials in many parts of the West Coast and other areas assume the silly posture of 'moral superiority' to those not serving in government. Even in those areas where such artifical schisms are not as pronounced, as in Richmond and Philadelphia, there often appears a reluctance to admit that segments from the private or public sectors may have something to say to each other. In these situations, the typical consequence is a crippling of much–needed programs and long–lasting resentments.

On the other side of the coin, there often exists the situation, as in smaller cities, in which the commercial–industrial sectors have been allowed to dominate the scene, and do so almost exclusively for their own gain. Such private sector leaders typically are philistines manifesting disdain for idealism and social equality. Cities of this type, such as New Orleans and Kansas City, might have a flashy stadium, an antiseptic giant mall, or a plaza or two, usually owned and managed by one or two real estate dynasties, but citizen participation is negligible. In the long run, it is the very few who most benefit from the rare changes that occur.

By contrast, one generally finds in Baltimore in recent history not only a much greater likelihood of the private and public sectors combining their efforts, but, comparatively speaking, an almost uncanny willingness to subordinate egos to the task of getting the job done.

Walter Sondheim's genius lies partially in his ability to merge successfully the idealism of the times with the practicality of the business community. He does this by utilizing his extensive contacts and friendship networks linking all layers of Baltimore society. Also, by knowing his limitations as well as his strengths, and consistently working within that understanding, he shows other leaders the difference between intelligence and wisdom.

"I'm not a technician, but a generalist," he states. The reason that his talents are relied on while those of perhaps equally knowledgeable others have been ignored is partially found in his comment, "A lot of my job is not a matter of skill, but of experience."

Of course other men and women also have been commendably aware of their limitations, have had friendship networks possibly as deep and as extensive as those of Walter Sondheim, Jr. But their ideas, their visions, and their programs never got off the ground while many aspects of the Baltimore renaissance are a partial monument to Sondheim's ability to translate ideas into action.

Perhaps without even realizing it, Sondheim himself comes closest to unraveling for us the secret of his genius. Specifically, to Sondheim, "Liking people is not as important as understanding people. This is a skill that is not born; it's trained."

Achieving *verstehen,* or sympathetic understanding, has been a central task of serious twentieth century social sciences and possibly of philosophy itself throughout history. Yet few social scientists, political leaders, or philosophers ever gain this insight or consistently apply it, once gained. It has been Baltimore's good fortune that its school board president, housing renewal chairman, businessman, friend, and citizen, Walter Sondheim, acquired this wisdom at an early age and has applied it over a lifetime for the betterment of the city.

R. C. Monk

Blaine Taylor, local freelance writer, contributed the interview sections to this article.

LAWRENCE CARDINAL SHEHAN

Lawrence Cardinal Shehan's contributions to the revitalization of Baltimore are rooted in ideas that predate the city's founding. As Archbishop of Baltimore from 1961 to 1974, he served not only as a moral and administrative leader in the movement for renewal within the Roman Catholic church but as a champion of religious unity and opponent of racial discrimination.

Born in 1898, Lawrence Shehan studied for the priesthood at St. Charles College and St. Mary's Seminary, and spent several years in Rome. Returning to the United States after ordination, he became an assistant to Monsignor Cornelius Thomas. Because the structure of the Catholic charities recently had been centralized, Father Shehan was named an assistant and later a director of this archdiocesan office.

In 1945, he was consecrated an auxiliary bishop of Baltimore and served as pastor of St. Philip and St. James Church. As an auxiliary bishop, he was attentive to institutions and groups that previously had only sporadic contact with the Catholic hierarchy, including the Johns Hopkins University. Numerous speaking engagements made Bishop Shehan a familiar and welcome presence in the civic life of Baltimore.

This growing rapport was interrupted from 1953 to 1961, when he served as bishop of the newly established diocese of Bridgeport. Then in 1961, he returned permanently to Baltimore when Pope John XXIII named him coadjutor to Archbishop Francis Keough. When the latter

died shortly afterwards, Lawrence Shehan became the Archbishop of Baltimore, a position he held until 1974.

Archbishop Shehan became a major force in the revival of the Baltimore community. His most important contributions came in joining other religious and civic leaders in openly attacking laws and practices that perpetuated racial discrimination and in encouraging Catholic priests, nuns, and lay people to cooperate with like-minded Baltimoreans.

This was a significant change in the way Catholics interacted with their neighbors. Previously, they had cooperated as individuals or through some liaison structure, but the weight of the Catholic church as an organized group rarely was volunteered even for admittedly worthy causes.

One of Archbishop Shehan's earliest acts was to proscribe discrimination based on racial or social origins in all Catholic institutions, organizations, and activities. He appealed to the long history of prejudice that Catholics had suffered as the reason they had a special obligation to place themselves "in the forefront of movements to remove the injustices and discriminations which still remain."

He joined with Protestant and Jewish leaders in urging both the state and city governments to enact laws that would eliminate racial segregation in housing and public accommodations. At a public hearing on segregated housing in 1966, Archbishop Shehan's testimony was interrupted by jeers and catcalls from opponents. This raucous treatment of the archbishop convinced a number of civic leaders that further delay was dangerous, and the legislation he wanted finally was enacted.

First among the Catholic hierarchy in America, Lawrence Shehan also appointed a commission of theologians and clerical leaders to guide the local effort toward unity with other Christian churches. He helped work out an agreement between the archdiocese and the United Way to combine fundraising efforts and accepted invitations to address groups of all faiths.

His bold and effective moral leadership recommended Archbishop Shehan to Pope Paul VI, who in 1965 named him a cardinal of the Roman Catholic church—only the second archbishop of Baltimore to receive such an honor. As Cardinal Shehan he continued to demonstrate the breadth of his vision in interracial, ecumenical, and interfaith concerns.

Cardinals, according to formal protocol, are addressed as "Eminence." Even without such a warrant, his fellow–Baltimoreans would willingly use it in addressing Lawrence Shehan. This customary honorific carries a special warmth and conviction when applied to him because of the courageous, apt, and steady leadership he offered at a crucial time in the life of the city.

Nicholas Varga

HARRY BARD
1907–1976

When students walk into the beautiful buildings of the Liberty Campus and the Harbor Campus of the Community College of Baltimore, few are aware of the significant contributions to the development of these campuses made by the late President Harry Bard.

He was the spark plug that ignited the interest of the public in the importance of providing low-cost college education beyond the high-school level for Baltimoreans. Dr. Bard had to fight every inch of the way and had to overcome many obstacles to build up the community college. More than 50,000 Baltimoreans have attended the college since 1959 when Dr. Bard became associated with it as dean. Many of the graduates have entered directly into careers in Baltimore's business and industry, professional and governmental life. Others have continued with their education at four-year colleges and universities.

The Community College of Baltimore was but one of Dr. Bard's contributions to education, political, civic, and cultural life in the city. He taught in public schools and became a supervisor and an administrator. He also conducted classes at local universities in the evening and summer sessions. A political scientist, he served on important governmental commissions and sought to improve our governmental structure and its operations. A fighter for social justice, and a promoter of interracial harmony, Dr. Bard

worked on biracial committees and developed workshops for blacks and whites. Some have commented that he did more for the interfaith movement in Baltimore than anyone else. While carrying on all his professions and civic activities, he found time to write a number of solid books on government and to contribute to a variety of magazines. A hard worker, an industrious one, he was a warm human being with hundreds of friends who called him Harry. He took delight in his family: his wife, two children, and his grandchildren.

A native Baltimorean, Dr. Harry Bard was one of nine children of Rubin and Fanye Bard, who operated a general merchandise store in East Baltimore. Encouraged by his parents, who believed that the security and destiny of an individual rests on a sound education, Dr. Bard began at an early age to prepare himself for a career in education.

After being graduated from the old City College at Howard and Center streets, he set out to become an educator by completing studies at the Maryland State Normal School (now Towson State University) and by earning a bachelor's degree from the Johns Hopkins University. With this solid foundation, Dr. Bard went on to earn a master's degree at Columbia University and a doctorate in education from the University of Maryland.

His educational background qualified him to hold responsible administrative positions in the Baltimore City Public Schools until he was appointed dean of the Baltimore Junior College in 1959. A year later, he was named president of this struggling two-year college. His personality, hard work, and conviction regarding the value of the community college concept made Baltimore an acknowledged pioneer and leader in this aspect of higher education.

The creation of the main campus at Liberty Heights Avenue and later of the Inner Harbor facility was a dream come true for Harry Bard. The Inner Harbor Campus was a solution to the imbalance of undergraduate enrollment between the rest of the state and South and East Baltimore. Dr. Bard always maintained that "this imbalance was due to the lack of an undergraduate institution accessible to these areas of Baltimore." He believed in providing a quality education to the working and middle class at low tuition costs.

While very much involved in his career as educator, he found time for other civic endeavors, from working for racial and social justice and the United Nations, to reforming local and state government.

In 1964 he chaired the Baltimore Charter Revision Commission and three years later the Commission on Councilmanic Redistricting. Dr. Bard also headed the Legislative Committee of the Maryland Constitutional Commission, and in 1969 was a convention delegate.

A prolific writer on educational and governmental matters as well as international politics, Dr. Bard was the author of several books. His last published, in 1974, was *Maryland State and Government: Its New Dynamics*, which is considered by many to be the best book yet written about the government of Maryland. Dr. Bard often said, "The wonderful thing about books is that the story they tell in all ages is that men *do* ultimately listen—if perhaps far too reluctantly."

During his career he received honorary degrees from Morgan State University and Loyola College. For his dedication and devotion to his profession and the city and state, he received awards from the Maryland state legislature, the Baltimore City Council, the *Afro-American* newspaper, the National Conference of Christians and Jews, the Metropolitan Civic Association, the Jewish Community Center, and the Young Men's Christian Association.

Mayor William Donald Schaefer summarized Dr. Bard's achievements by saying, "He was a significant and dedicated force in the educational communities of both our city and nation."

Morgan H. Pritchett

BARBARA MIKULSKI

Barbara Mikulski, the Democratic congresswoman from the Third District, was born in Baltimore in 1936. The granddaughter of Polish immigrants, she grew up in Highlandtown where her parents ran a grocery store. She remembers fondly the "Old Baltimore ... Howard Street and shopping with my mother.... I knew it

before they tore it down in the name of progress."

Congresswoman Mikulski attended parochial schools and was graduated from Mount St. Agnes College. She then became a child-neglect social worker and community organizer. She recalls that she and her colleagues in the Department of Public Welfare had difficulty finding places where they could have lunch together. "In 1956, while they were planning the great One Charles Center, black people and white people could not sit down in downtown Baltimore and have a beer together.... "

Mikulski obtained a master's degree from the University of Maryland School of Social Work in 1965, worked for a period as chief social worker in a program for the elderly, and then became a sociology professor at Loyola College.

Mikulski's activism began when she was assigned to the Pennsylvania Avenue area during her second-year field placement in graduate school. "It was a rough, tough survival neighborhood.... If you had the money you could buy anything and I was supposed to bring urban renewal policies to the people's attention. Well, I did something else. I worked out of a lunchroom, where I set up my own information and referral service and got people to the services they needed."

During this period, the Office of Economic Opportunity had been established by congressional order. "It changed for all time how people would be involved.... It said that there had to be 'maximum feasible participation' of the people affected in the policies." Mikulski and coworkers took the idea of "maximum feasible participation" to heart and worked to get people to take a more active role in the development of urban renewal programs and strategies, believing that "intelligence is randomly distributed through the population, a principle that seems either to be ignored fundamentally or even dismissed when policies are made."

In the late sixties, when an interstate highway threatened to destroy the neighborhoods of Rosemont ("the first black home ownership neighborhood in Baltimore") in the west and Canton and Fell's Point in the east, Mikulski helped organize a coalition of neighborhood groups that "used every democratic tool" to block it. This coalition evolved into the Southeast Community Organization (SECO), which is still active today. Also, out of this effort to stop the road came "a vast grass–roots network of community organizations, civic groups, improvement associations. . . . "

Ms. Mikulski believes that the most important development in Baltimore has been the "grass–roots citizen movement." That, combined with a "sympathetic mayor," a "gifted housing commissioner," and funds for neighborhood projects, have all contributed to making Baltimore a better place to live.

That grass–roots movement also helped Mikulski get elected to the Baltimore City Council as an independent candidate. On the council she received national attention as a spokesperson for ethnic Americans, women, the elderly, and the working class. While devoting herself avidly to the concerns and problems of her constituents, she became noted for her advocacy of neighborhoods. She continuously promoted the idea that all Baltimore citizens should have a voice in the direction Baltimore will take in the future.

In 1974, she was the Democratic nominee for United States Senator; her opponent was Republican incumbent Charles McC. Mathias. Although she lost that election, she received 43 percent of the vote. In 1975, she won reelection to the City Council and in 1976 she was elected to Congress.

In Congress, as well as in her personal life, Mikulski has reaffirmed her commitment to Baltimore and her support of neighborhoods. Her opposition to the Panama Canal Treaty—which surprised liberal supporters—was based on her belief that the treaty would adversely affect Baltimore's port.

Mikulski is currently a member of the House subcommittee on merchant shipping. She is also a member of the Steel Caucus and has staunchly sought "more equitable trading rules" for the steel industry. The congresswoman is credited with causing the amendment of the National Energy Act of 1977 to help local governments conserve energy in municipal buildings.

Barbara Mikulski resides in the 600 block of South Ann Street in Fell's Point, and commutes to Washington, D.C. when Congress is in session. "The great thing about Baltimore," she says, "is that we are a federation of neighborhoods and that we were never a monolothic geographic area."

Jane Sellman

ROBERT C. EMBRY, JR.

Robert C. Embry, Jr. played a major role in the rebirth of Baltimore as housing commissioner from 1968 to 1977. He directed programs that have won Baltimore a reputation as a city that is making a major effort to deal with its urban distress. The National Neighborhood Commission cited Baltimore as the prototype of a city that has worked effectively with its neighborhoods. And in June, 1978, in Hamburg, Germany, the International Housing Association termed Baltimore an outstanding example of redevelopment in the world.

Robert Embry and his staff have had much to do with the success of these and other projects: the Inner Harbor renewal project; the revivals of the Morris A. Mechanic Theatre, Center Stage, and Theatre Project; the Baltimore subway; and the homesteading program, to name only a few.

Who is Robert Embry?

Robert C. Embry, Jr. was born in Baltimore on September 7, 1937. After attending high school at City College, he graduated from Williams College in 1959 with a degree in political science. He then attended Harvard Law School (LL.B., 1964). During the summer of 1963 he clerked for the Baltimore law firm of Venable, Baetjer, and Howard, and began working as a volunteer for the Citizens Planning and Housing Association (CPHA), then directed by Frances Froelicher. He continued to work closely with CPHA for three years, and during this time got what he has described as "the best education that I received in urban and neighborhood problems." Mr. Embry clerked for Judge Simon Sobeloff, chief judge of the Fourth Circuit Court of Appeals, and was a city councilman. He then worked for Venable, Baetjer, and Howard. During the Carter administration he served as assistant secretary for Community Planning and Development of the United States Department of Housing and Urban Development. He has since returned to Baltimore and established his own development firm.

In a March, 1979, interview at his Charles Village home, Mr. Embry discussed some of the problems he encountered as Baltimore's housing commissioner. His comments reflect both his keen perceptions and dynamic leadership qualities.

"Housing in Baltimore is typical of older Eastern cities: "rowhouse stock, most of the housing built before World War II, very little vacant land, very little new construction going on, and also a certain amount of abandonment going on, as the population of the city decreases. Most of the slum housing, if not all of it, has been removed, so that the housing stock that remains, while there is a large part of it that is substandard, can be rehabilitated and doesn't have to be demolished."

The main problems he encountered were: first, to prevent sound buildings from deteriorating; and second, to upgrade buildings in poor condition. From an economic point of view, a major problem for Embry was to attempt to provide more low–income housing for the large low–income population of the city, while holding and attracting middle–income people.

One of Mr. Embry's chief causes was to end demolition and clearance projects, this for a number of reasons. First, Baltimore housing stock is better built and more commodious than what would replace it. Second, demolition and rebuilding take time. Third, demolition totally disrupts neighborhoods and scatters people, thereby disrupting other neighborhoods.

Elaborating on the city's efforts to hold and attract middle–income people, Mr. Embry specified a number of efforts he made, among them "emphasizing neighborhoods and the uniqueness of the city. This we did through the City Fair and also through a series of mortgage programs to provide low–interest loans to people who either wanted to buy a house or fix one up. Another method was the Homesteading Program; the plan was to take vacant houses that were costing the city money and to attract middle–class people back into them who would fix them up."

Mr. Embry seemed especially proud of his efforts to revive the theatre of downtown Baltimore. He pointed out that the city first was able to get the Morris Mechanic built in Charles Center and then, when the theatre went under, the city took it over and provided management. The city also played a large role in the relocation of Center Stage in the Mount Vernon area. The present building on North Calvert Street was bought by the city and given to Center Stage. When Theatre Project was evicted by its landlords, Baltimore bought its building and donated it to them, then helped the company renovate. Finally, the city built a new home for the Arena Players on Madison Street.

Mr. Embry discussed the decision–making process he utilized as commissioner: "A first principle was to make sure that no neighborhood project was undertaken without full community support. Second, I consulted with the City Council and with the mayor, depending on what the decision was. Nothing was done without the mayor—there were different mayors, but Mayor Schaefer was in office most of the time. And I consulted with the business community if the issue was one involving downtown or economic development, and with the artistic community if it involved something in the arts."

As for the problems, he said, "The issue that was most important was the balancing of the competing, both legitimate, needs of low–income and middle–income people. Most people when they think about cities think of one or the other. In fact most *cities* do that—they either devote themselves to attracting middle–income people or they devote themselves to low–income programs. One of the secrets of Baltimore's success has been pursuing both of these [sets of needs] very vigorously."

Ric Bartter

THE MITCHELL FAMILY

In the 1950s, Clarence Mitchell, Jr. and his younger brother Parren J. (now congressman) Mitchell were not allowed in Baltimore's better restaurants, hotels, theaters, schools, or any other areas designated "for whites only." Due in part to the efforts of Clarence M. Mitchell, Jr., long–time chief lobbyist for the National Association for the Advancement of Colored Peoples (NAACP), it's no surprise that today either of the two politically astute brothers might be seen in any of those places that were still off limits to blacks less than 15 years ago.

The Mitchell brothers are members of a prominent black family that has sometimes been referred to as the "black Kennedys." They are part of an elite black middle class that emerged in Baltimore in the forties and fifties. When Clarence Mitchell married Juanita Jackson 42 years ago, two famed black families were united. The bride's mother was the redoubtable Lillie May Carroll Jackson, staunch civil rights activist and head of the NAACP in Baltimore for many years.

Clarence Mitchell, 68, is now considered the elder statesman of Baltimore's black community. Retired in December, 1978, from the post he held at the NAACP in Washington since 1950, he has returned to the private practice of law in Baltimore. A lecturer in the Distinguished Lecturer Series at Morgan State University, he continues to work for passage of legislation designed to insure enforcement of fair housing and employment codes, equal rights for women and minorities, minimum wage standards, and reduction of unemployment.

Parren J. Mitchell, 58, was elected to Congress in 1970. He is now serving his sixth term as representative from Maryland's Seventh District. He serves on the following congressional committees: Banking and Currency; Democratic Policy Steering; and the Permanent Select Committee on Small Business. He is also a member of the Congressional Black Caucus. A bachelor, he lives in Baltimore and commutes to Washington as his brother did. He also maintains an office in the Federal Building at Hopkins Plaza.

As a family of seven children, the Mitchells were poor, though not dirt poor. The children were given the best schooling then available to blacks. Their mother was born Elsie Davis. Their father, Clarence M. Mitchell, Sr., was a waiter at the old Rennert Hotel and an amateur musician. His favorite axiom was, "Don't ask anyone for anything."

Because the University of Maryland was still segregated in the 1930s, Clarence, Jr. went to Lincoln University in Pennsylvania. It was Parren, a graduate of Morgan State, who broke the color barrier at the University of Maryland graduate school in 1952, when he received a master's degree in sociology. Later, both Clarence and Juanita received their law degrees at the University of Maryland.

The brothers became activists for civil rights while still schoolboys, when they picketed Pennsylvania Avenue merchants who refused to employ blacks at that time.

Clarence joined the NAACP in 1945 as labor secretary and became director in 1950. During his years in Washington, he dealt with eight United States presidents; Franklin Delano Roosevelt was the first under whom he served on the Fair Employment Commission. As the NAACP's chief lobbyist, he worked behind the scenes in the halls of Congress, persuading congressional leaders and the presidents to achieve passage of the Civil Rights Acts of 1957, 1960, 1964, and 1965. He helped to engineer passage of the 1965 Voting Rights Act and the landmark 1968 Civil Rights Bill.

Before joining the NAACP, he was on the War Manpower Commission and the War Production Board under President Dwight D. Eisenhower. A high point in his long career was when President Gerald Ford appointed him a member of the United States delegation to the United Nations.

The Fair Housing Act of 1968 was the toughest legislation he lobbied for, he has said. "We were up against well-organized groups. It took three years to get that law passed. We were up against not only southern racism but business groups that opposed it. We didn't have as many people working for it as in 1964, when the Civil Rights Bill was passed."

The three laws he considered most significant for blacks were those calling for public accommodations, equal employment, and fair housing: "I think these are the firm foundations."

Clarence Mitchell was sometimes called an "Uncle Tom" by militants because of his quiet, reasoned approach. "I think my way worked. Working within the law is an orderly approach. It is not necessarily moderate," he has said. "I always tried to work on the issue—not on people or person."

Of all the presidents he dealt with, he considered Lyndon Johnson the most cooperative. "He had the strongest commitment to civil rights."

Parren Mitchell has long been noted for feisty speechmaking and arguing to implement laws for minority rights that had already been passed. He is chairman of a House subcommittee on housing, minority enterprise, and economic development.

Before entering Congress, he was a professor of sociology at Morgan State University, and assistant director of that school's Institute for Urban Research.

Parren first came to public attention when he was made executive secretary of the Maryland Commission on Interracial Problems and relations. His two-year stint was marked by the development of programs designed to promote black welfare and to improve interracial relations. In 1965, then–Mayor Theodore McKeldin named him executive director of the Community Action Agency, the government arm which administered the city's federally funded "War Against Poverty."

Parren Mitchell continued to teach when he began his political career as a probation officer with Baltimore city. In 1957, he became supervisor of a program of casework for the Domestic Relations Division of the Supreme Bench of Baltimore. He also served in the United States Army as a commissioned officer, executive officer, and company commander. He received a Purple Heart. As a result of the Vietnam War he became an ardent pacifist, and was one of 23 congressmen who tried to halt the bombing and mining of Vietnam ports in 1972. He is a lay reader in the Episcopal Church of St. Katherine in Baltimore.

Juanita Jackson Mitchell's mother, Lillie May Carroll Jackson (1889–1975), was a guiding light of the Baltimore NAACP, which she reorganized in 1935 after it had dwindled to a mere five members. For the next two decades she fought to break segregation in Baltimore. In 1951, the first breakthrough came with desegregation of public golf courses and some tennis courts. Black transit drivers were first hired in 1952. That

same year, Ford's Theater ended segregated seating. (The Lyric did not allow black artists to perform until 1964.)

Mrs. Jackson, who claimed descent from Charles Carroll, Maryland signer of the Declaration of Independence, was a lecturer and teacher with her husband, Keiffer. They were lifetime members of the Sharp Street United Methodist Memorial Church, where Clarence and Juanita were married in 1937.

Juanita Mitchell, who practices law privately, argued many of the Baltimore desegregation cases on behalf of the NAACP. A graduate of the University of Pennsylvania, she holds a law degree from the University of Maryland. She and her husband continue to live in the Druid Hill Avenue house that they purchased in 1941.

Michael Bowen Mitchell, Clarence M. III, Keiffer (a physician), and George are the four sons of Clarence and Juanita Mitchell. Two are following the family's political tradition: Clarence is a state senator and Michael, a lawyer, is a city council member.

Clarence III was elected to the House of Delegates in 1963. He was appointed majority whip in the Senate. He founded the state office of Minority Business Enterprise.

Michael, youngest member of the city council at age 30 in 1976, was first appointed as assistant state's attorney by Milton B. Allen in 1970. He practiced law with his mother and brother and has since become a partner in the law firm of Mitchell & Pettit. He has been a prime mover for low-cost loans from the city to poor blacks for rehabilitating old homes.

Dorothea T. Apgar

HOW TO WRITE ABOUT THE HISTORY OF BALTIMORE

Many people have become interested in Baltimore's past or at least some aspect of its history. They would like to learn what their neighborhood was like in 1900 or in the 1850s or they would like to know who the black community's leaders were in the 1870s and 1880s or how the city's synagogues developed. Most of these people have no training in historical research and haven't had a United States history course since high school or college. This guide is written with these people in mind. I hope it will get them well launched on that local history project they have had in mind for some time but just never knew how to begin.

Doing research on some piece of Baltimore history is rather different from working on a more general subject like the Civil War or the Great Depression. There are many excellent general and specialized histories of the Civil War and many published guides to the detailed literature on every aspect of this conflict. Not so with the history of Baltimore. Sherry Olson's book, *A History of Baltimore* (Johns Hopkins University Press, 1979), is an excellent general history of the city, but hundreds of important people, institutions, and events could not be covered because space was limited and also because surprisingly few really detailed and thoughtful studies have been written about those smaller aspects of Baltimore's past that allow one to draw broader conclusions. For example, it would be impossible to write a comprehensive history of Roman Catholicism in Baltimore because so few parish churches and other Catholic institutions have adequate published histories or well-organized records. Therefore it is essential that interested amateur historians learn about all the little pieces of Baltimore's past so that others, both amateur and professional, can use these threads to reweave the larger fabric of the city's past. Without the pieces we cannot see the wider picture and without the more general knowledge, no one can fully understand any of the pieces.

The three secrets of success in writing good history, whether it be *The Decline and Fall of the Roman Empire* or the decline of Baltimore's trolley car system, are: (1) learn how to find and use all the best raw data on your subject, (2) find out the right questions to ask about this data, and (3) get the right sort of help in presenting your conclusions in a clear, organized manner that relates your specific topic to the general history of the city.

Finding the Information. Locating the "raw data" or, as historians call it, the "original documents," is the first step in any project. Perhaps there are almost no documents dealing with the person, place, or event that you hoped to learn about. Possibly there are thousands of documents, reports, and other materials that would take months or years to examine. How do you find out? You go, of course, to those institutions scattered around the city and state that hold these specialized materials.

Unlike most public libraries, the specialized departments, libraries, and archives holding major collections of materials on Baltimore require special instruction if they are to be used efficiently. At each library there are well-trained and knowledgeable staff members to aid you in locating the material you want. Even the most experienced academic researcher relies heavily upon these staff members for help because they know how difficult it is to use all the catalogues, indexes, lists, and other aids that will guide you ultimately to the books, documents, or photographs you are seeking. If you are serious about your research project, be prepared to spend a considerable amount of time hunting down the items you need. This is particularly true in the area of local history—in this case the history of Baltimore and its urban region. There is a vast amount of information about Baltimore's past, but it takes more effort to locate this information because much of it has never been written about or organized in a card catalogue or index.

There are several dozen libraries, archives, museums, and historical societies that hold materials relating to the history of Baltimore. Many of them are small and specialize in the history of only one or two aspects of the city's past. They are often very valuable to the researcher but not usually the proper place to begin work. It is best to start at one of the four major institutions having extensive collections of historical materials in a variety of subject areas. They are as follows:

Maryland Department, Enoch Pratt Library, 400 Cathedral Street, Baltimore. Telephone 396–5468. Hours 9:00 A.M. to 9:00 P.M. Monday through Thursday, 9:00 A.M. to 5:00 P.M. Friday through Sunday. This is the logical place for most people to begin their research on Baltimore. The Maryland Department has in its collection several thousand books, photographs, and maps of the city and also contains an extremely useful vertical file of newspaper clippings and other materials organized alphabetically into thousands of topics. One floor above the Maryland Department is the microfilm room where one can find the state's largest collection of Baltimore newspapers from the eighteenth century to the present.

Library of the Maryland Historical Society, 201 West Monument Street, Baltimore. Telephone 685–3750. Hours Tuesday through Saturday 9:00 A.M. to 4:30 P.M. This library also contains a very large collection of books, photographs, and maps of Baltimore and in addition it holds approximately 1.5 million manuscripts dealing with all aspects of the city's history. It is especially strong in family records and its collection of genealogical materials is the best in the state. This is a highly professional research library operating with a small staff and very limited resources so you need to have a rather clear idea of what you are looking for to use the library and especially the manuscript collection. The MHS is a private institution with chronic financial problems and thus it charges all non-members $2.50 a day for the use of its facilities.

Baltimore City Archives, 211 East Pleasant Street, Room 201, Baltimore. Telephone 396–4861. Hours Monday through Friday 8:30 A.M. to 4:30 P.M. This giant archive holds most of the official records of the city government of Baltimore from its founding in 1730 to the present. Until recently, many of these records were scattered around the city and uncatalogued because the city had never bothered to hire a trained archivist to organize them. Richard Cox, the city's first archivist, has created order and efficiency over nearly 2,000 cubic feet of records which include the records of the city council, the mayor's office, tax department, and many other city agencies.

Maryland Hall of Records, P.O. Box 828, Annapolis, Maryland 21404. Hours Monday through Saturday 8:30 A.M. to 4:30 P.M. This excellent archive is the official repository of the records of the state of Maryland, and it holds thousands of documents, reports, and other papers relating to Baltimore city from its founding to the present. These records are briefly described in a publication entitled *A Series Summary Guide to the Public Records of Baltimore City,* which is available from the Hall of Records. The archive building is located on the campus of St. John's College in the center of Annapolis and its well–trained staff is prepared to answer your inquiries in person or by mail.

From this initial survey of the "raw data" you can determine in a rough way how large and difficult your task will be. Do not, however, dive into these documents and begin feverishly making notes. These documents do not speak for themselves. You need to have enough knowledge of your subject to ask the right questions and to know whether each piece of data is important, trivial, misleading, or inaccurate. There are three ways to prepare yourself. First, locate, with the librarians' help, all the published books, articles, pamphlets, and other sources written by other researchers that will help you understand the whole city and perhaps the whole society during the years in which you will be working. Try to understand something of the world in which the people lived who wrote those documents you will be studying. Second, try to locate a good, recent, scholarly study of a person, institution, event, or place similar to the one you hope to write about. If you want to write about the Irish in Baltimore in the nineteenth century, read Oscar Handlin's *Boston's Immigrants.* His book will raise many questions in your mind that you can "ask" when reading old documents or newspapers dealing with Baltimore's Irish immigrants. Third, try to talk with some other people who have been writing about those aspects of Baltimore's history that might relate to your own topic. The local libraries and archivists often know who has a good knowledge of various topics. Almost all of the colleges and universities in the Baltimore area have one or more persons who are experts on the history of Baltimore and on American urban history or who specialize in the history of ethnic groups, religious institutions, businesses and labor organizations, transportation, and a variety of other topics. They are always willing to help nonprofessional historians.

Oral history is one of the most valuable and interesting research techniques that has developed in recent years. With the availability of portable tape recorders, it has become possible to record the memories of people whose experiences and activities form the "grass–roots" of our history. Information gained from senior citizens and others document aspects of Baltimore's history that would be totally lost if no oral history record were available.

For some time the Maryland Historical Society has been conducting an Oral History Program under the direction of Mrs. Bettye Key. The society conducts seminars on oral history methods and maintains an archive of tapes and transcripts. It takes training and practice to conduct a good oral history interview so those who are interested are well advised to seek advice or formal training before plunging into a project.

Finally one can start to examine the raw data itself. This may lead you from one of the libraries or records centers mentioned here to some of the more highly specialized smaller historical archives in many of which you must rely totally on the librarian or archivist since the records are not regularly indexed or catalogued.

After you have collected all of your information, you begin to write the article, pamphlet, or book from the outline you have been preparing and revising as you gathered your data. After a first draft or two it is almost always wise to let one or two others read what you have written—especially those who have done work in the same broad area of the city's history. This will help focus your ideas and save you from many small errors. You are then ready to send off a good article to the *Maryland Historical Magazine* published by the Maryland Historical Society or to the forthcoming *Historic Baltimore Society Quarterly Journal* to be published by the H.B.S.

Remember, finally, that writing good history is a craft. It can be learned best from a professional historian, but many can learn how to do it themselves. It takes a great deal of time and effort to learn how to paint a fall landscape or write a good history of some part of the cityscape. People often spend several years gathering material for a 20–page article, and a book may take a decade to write. The extra thought, work, and time, however, usually result in a product that will stand the test of time. You will have the satisfaction of knowing that some important corner of the "dead past" is alive again. You can remember that your contribution to knowledge will serve this generation as well as those others who will be studying Baltimore's past 50 or 100 years from now.

Joseph Arnold

LANDMARKS: A Chronology of Baltimore Redevelopment

December, 1937—Housing Authority of Baltimore city established.

October, 1940—Poe Homes, first public housing, opens.

April, 1951—Waverly, first urban renewal area, gets underway.

December, 1956—Baltimore Urban Renewal and Housing Agency established, uniting renewal and public housing activities.

March, 1958—Committee for Downtown and Greater Baltimore Committee present city with concept for Charles Center.

May, 1958—City Council approves plan for extensive rehabilitation of Harlem Park area.

July, 1961—City Council approves Madison Park South renewal plan, providing for urban renewal of Bolton Hill area.

August, 1961—Ground broken for One Charles Center, first major building in Charles Center.

September, 1962—Jones Falls Expressway completed.

September, 1964—30-year program for redevelopment of Inner Harbor is unveiled.

September, 1964—Maryland Institute acquires Mount Royal Station, provides for first major recycling of a public building.

December, 1967—City Council adopts plan for renewal of Gay Street I area; first plan adopted with extensive community participation.

July, 1968—Department of Housing and Community Development established, bringing under one roof all of the principal housing and community development functions; first major city in country to do this.

September, 1968—Demolition starts at Inner Harbor.

October, 1969—First funding approved by U.S. for rehabilitation of houses under Vacant House Program.

January, 1970—Opening of Lakeview Tower, first development in a currently 3500–unit program to provide public housing designed exclusively for the elderly and disabled.

April, 1970—City Council approves plan for renewal of Oldtown area in East Baltimore.

May, 1970—City Council approves plan for renewal of Upton area in West Baltimore, providing for total redevelopment of Pennsylvania Avenue.

September, 1970—First City Fair.

July, 1971—Federal funding received from U. S. for renewal of Oliver area of East Baltimore and Orchard–Biddle area of West Baltimore; also for start of extensive modernization program in public housing.

January, 1972—City opens Home Ownership Development office.

April, 1972—City Council approves Washington Hill and Reservoir Hill renewal plans, establishing programs of major rehabilitation through urban renewal.

August, 1972—The Constellation moves to completed Constellation Dock on former Pier 1 of Inner Harbor.

November, 1972—Voters approve funding Rehabilitation Environmental Assistance Loan (REAL) loan program, enabling city to lend money to homeowners for rehabilitation.

December, 1972—Deaton Medical Center, first segment of Christ Lutheran Church complex for the elderly at the Inner Harbor, is dedicated.

January, 1973—City Council approves plan for Coldspring, community.

August, 1973—Plan for homesteading of Stirling Street is announced.

September, 1973—Board of Estimates authorized Urban Homesteading of tax–sale properties.

February, 1974—Houses awarded to first homesteaders.

April, 1974—Lexington Mall opens.

February, 1975—Work starts on Rash Field at Inner Harbor; renovation of City Hall begins.

March, 1975—City receives first Community Development Block Grant.

July, 1975—First houses in Otterbein area awarded to homesteaders by lottery.

June, 1976—Maryland Science Center opens; Old Town Mall completed and dedicated.

October, 1976—Hollander Ridge, 1000–unit public housing development, is opened.

July, 1977—Inspection activities consolidated as sanitary enforcement officers are transferred from the Health Department to HCD.

September, 1977—World Trade Center dedicated.

January, 1978—Construction starts on Charles Center Station of subway.

June, 1978—City reaches 500–homesteader mark.

August, 1978—Ground broken for Aquarium.

December, 1978—Pilot Block, 3700 block of Park Heights Avenue, is dedicated after total rehabilitation-homeownership experiment.

January, 1979—Ground broken for Walbrook Shopping Center; ground broken for Harborplace.

April, 1979—First Loft apartments completed.

May, 1979—Plan for construction—rehabilitation of Chessie property at Camden Station revealed.

June, 1979—Ground broken for Hyatt–Regency Hotel.

August, 1979—Baltimore Convention Center opens.

July, 1980—Harborplace opens.

October, 1980—City receives $9.1 million Urban Development Action Grant to permit $220 million expansion of General Motors plant on Broening Highway.

August, 1981—National Aquarium in Baltimore opens.

Index

Sources are available from the Historic Baltimore Society.
Note: Page numbers in roman refer to text. Page numbers in italic refer to photographs.

Cavalier Lounge, 265
Cavallieri, Grace, 214
CCB. *See* Community College of Baltimore
Celebrity Club, 265, 267
Centenary Biblical Institute (now Morgan State), 78
Center for Metropolitan Research and Planning for the Johns Hopkins University, 100
Center for the Study of Sudden Infant Death—University of Maryland, 54
Center for Urban Affairs, 78
Center Plaza, 14
Center Stage, 10, *35*, 158, 168–70, *168*, 173, 179, 186, 193, 207, 239, 285, 286
Center Stage Association, Inc., 168
Center Stage Hands, 169
Central Americans, 69
Central Savings Bank, 250
Central YWCA, 103
Century Theatre, 160
Chamber Music Society, 158, 177
Chamber of Commerce of Metropolitan Baltimore, 280
Chandler, Don, 271
Channel 2, 138, 139, 140, *141*, 141
Channel 11, 138, 140–41
Channel 13, 138, 139, 140
Channel 45, 138
Chanticleer, 265, 267
Chaplain's Office of the Johns Hopkins University, 175
Charcoal Club, 186, 193, 194
Charcoal Gallery, 193
Charcoal Hearth Restaurant, 167
Charles Center, 13, 14, *37*, 38, *38*, 39, 43–45, *43*, *44*, 46, 166, 167, 203, *203*, 204, 205, 207, 230, 246, 255, 256, 257–59, 280, 286
Charles Center–Inner Harbor Management Company (CCIHM), 45, 46, 228, 257–59, 280
Charles Center Management Office, 44, 257
Charles Center South, 45, 205
Charles Towers, 45
Charles Village, 6, 8, 11, 14, 15, 18, 286
Charles Village Civic Association, 8
Chart House, 268
Chaseman, Joel, 142
Check Mate, 266
Cheek, King (Dr.), 78

Cherbonnier, Alice, 127
Cherry Hill, 24, 28, 213
Cherry Valley Editions, 215
Chesapeake and Potomac Telephone Company, 280
Chesapeake and Potomac Telephone Company (Building), 49, 50, 205, *206*
Chesapeake Bay, 57, 153, 263, 279
Chesapeake Center, 10
Chesapeake Physicians, 53
Chesapeake Television, Inc., 138
Chesapeake United Presbyterian, 94
Chesapeake Weekly Review, 131, 132
Cheslock, Louis, 180
Chester, Paul L., 83
Chicanos, 69
Child Study Association. *See* Child Study Association of Baltimore
Child Study Association of Baltimore, 133, 265
Children's Experimental Theatre (CET), 170
Children's Hospital, 54, 55
Children's Museum. *See* Cloisters Children's Museum
Children's Theatre Association, 158, 170, *170*, 171
Chinese, 64, 67
Chizuk Amuno Congregation, 92, 96, *97*, 179
Christ Lutheran Church, 47, 291
Christian, Alan, 144
Christmas Festival of Lessons and Carols, 180
Christian Church, 87
Christ's Church, 214
Christ's Episcopal Church, 98
Church Home and Hospital (formerly Washington College Hospital), 151
Church of the Redeemer, 207
Cimino, Audrey, 165
Cimino, Joseph, 165
Cinemonde Internationale, 175
Citizens' National Bank, 233, 234
Citizens Planning and Housing Association, 25–30, 237, 280, 285–86
Citizens Temporary Committee on Educational Television, 134
CityArts, 214
City College and City College High School, 114, 164, 166, 233, 234, 236, 283, 285

City College (building), 119, 207
City Dweller (now *Baltimore Chronicle*), 127, 132
City Fair, 3, 4, 11, 12–16, *13*, 18, 29, 47, 70, 143, 232, 239, 286, 291
City Hall, 33, 34, 37, 39, 46, 147, 192, 195, 199, 205, 207, 234, 235, 243, 261, 274
City Hall Courtyard Galleries, 192
City Lights, 268
City Paper (formerly *City Squeeze*), 132
City Squeeze (now *City Paper*), 132
Civic Center, 39
Civic Design Commission, 194
Civil Service Commission of Baltimore City, 75
Claremont, 24
Clark, William, 32
Clarke, Mary Pat (Councilman), 106, 249
Classroom, the, 266
Claster, Bert, 141
Claster, Nancy (Miss Nancy), 141
Clayburn, Mary, 143
Clean Up Banking Compaign Committee, 75
Clement, Gabrielle, *197*
Clergy for Community Understanding (CCU), 93, 94
Clergymen's Interfaith Committee on Human Rights, 90, 93
Cleveland, 149
Clews, Vince, 174–75
Clifton, Lucille, 209–10, 217
Cloisters Children's Museum, 189, *198*, 199
Closet, the, 268
Club Casino, 76, 266
Club Charles, 265
Co–Accident and Pod Books, 215
Coburn, Donald, 213
Cochran, Alexander, 203, 208
Cochran, Stephenson and Donkervoet, Inc., 205, 207
Cockeysville, 18
"Cockpit in Court, The", 164
Codrescu, Andrei, 218
Cohen, Alexander, 167–68
Cohen, Ben, 138
Cohen, Herman, 138
Coldspring or Coldspring Newtown, 205, 208, 241, 256, *264*
Cole, Emory (Delegate), 81
Cole, Harry (Delegate), 81, 148

Davis Planetarium, 47, 57
Davis, Ray, 142, 144
Davis, Richard P., 4, 15
Davis, Tom, 143
Dead End Bar, 192
Dean, Larry, 143
Deane, Buddy, 139, 142
deFord, Sara, 213, 216
de Haven, Clarence, 164
Deltoff, John B. (Dr.), 109
D'Joint, 85
Delaware, 145
Delmarva Educational Television Project, 134
Denishawn Dance Company, 219
Denmark, Harvey, 161
Dennis, Claudia, 75
Dennis, Estelle, 219
Dennis, Olive, 103
Department of Education, 27, 28, 35
Department of Health, 26
Department of Housing and Community Development (formerly Baltimore Urban Renewal and Housing Association—BURHA), 12, 13, 14, 15, 19, 30, 31, 34, 44, 46, 72, 75, 110, 258, 281, 292
Department of Legislative Reference, 249
Department of Planning, 28
Department of Public Works, 239
Department of Public Welfare, 284
Department of Recreation and Parks, 8
Department of Recreation "Street Club Service," 185
Department of Public Works, 14, 127, 239
Department of Sanitation, 14
Department of Social Services, 110
Department of Transit and Traffic, 143
Department of Welfare, 284
Design Advisory Panel, 207
Detroit, 149
Dew Drop Inn, 267
Diamond, Danny, 222
Diamond Jim, 143
Diana Press, 216
Dick Ireland Memorial Dirty Limerick Contest, 218
Dickerson, Chris, 213
Dickinson, Hugh (the Reverend), 98
Dickeyville, 33
Didusch, Ann, 188

Dierken, Kitty, 141
Dietrich, Carl, 164
"Dimensional Dance Media," 220
Dimmock, Herb, 179
Diorio, Margaret, 215
DiPaula, Manuel, 265
Displaced Homemaker's Center, 105, 106
Distinguished Lecturer Series—Morgan State University, 287
Di Suvero, Mark, *46*
Dixon, Irma, 82
Dixon, Lucien, 215
Dobson, Harold, 94
Dobson, Tamara, 84
Dobson, Vernon (the Reverend), 80, 82, 94, 97
Dockery, Jim, 193
Doll, Harry Lee, (Bishop), 92, 94
Domres, Marty, 272
Donovan, Arthur, 269, 270
Dorchester (County), 218, 260
Dorchester County Courthouse, 217
Dorn, Wesley N. (Dr.), 133
Dorsey, Rhoda M. (Dr.), 117
Double Joints Women's Theatre Company, 165
Doughty, Glenn, 72
Douglas Memorial Church, 80
Douglass High School, 79
Douglass Homes, 24
Douglass, Lee, Jr., 18
Douglass, Frederick, 151
Douglass, Robert L., 18, 32, 76, 83
Dove, Ronnie, 265
Dowell, George, 164
Downtown, 36–50
Downtown Baltimore, *37, 38*
Drake, Carol, 220
Drucker, Arno, 179
Drucker, Ruth, 179
Druid Hill Park, 24, 259, 261–62
Druid Hill Park Zoo (Baltimore Zoo), 207, 231
Druid Lake, 14
DuMont Network (now WJZ–TV), *134*
Dryden, Lulu, 103
Dubel, Robert (Dr.), 134
Duff, Charles B., 184
Duffy, Kathleen, 163
Dumps, William (Father), 95
Dunbar Community Senior High School, 17, *17*, 113, 191
Duncan, Bruce, 165

Duncan, Ruth, 165
Duncan, Jeff, 221, *221*
Dundalk, 128
Dundalk Community College, 119, 188
Dunhill's, 267, 268
Dunn, James, 184
Dunn, Thomas B., 180
Dunn, William Kailer (the Right Reverend), 87
Dunnock, Mildred, 159
Dutch, 64, 152
Duvall, Jed, 143

East Baltimore, 5, 14, 18, 19, 66, 71, 73, 74, 125, 136, 149, 283
East Baltimore Community Development Corporation, 32, 73
East Baltimore Guide (formerly *Shoppers' Guide*), 125, 126, 127
East Baltimore Medical Center, 32, 73
East Baltimore Midway Development Association, 73
Eastern-Central Europeans, 263
Eastern College, 116, 118
Eastern High School, 114, 164
Eastern Opera Theatre, 184
Eastern Shore, 88, 162, 181, 209, 210, 260
Eastside Democratic Organization, 73
Eberhart, David, 218
Eberhart, Richard, 216
Echo House, 14
Eckman, Charlie, 143
Ecumenical Institute of Theology. *See also* St. Mary's Seminary and University, 100, 119–20
Edgar Allan Poe Homes, 24
Edgar Allan Poe Memorial Association, 215
Edgar Allan Poe Society, 214
Edmondson, Thomas (Dr.), 196
Edmondson Village, 18
Edmondson Village Shopping Center, 109
Edmunds and Hyde, Inc., 207
Ednor Gardens–Lakeside, 14
Educational Repertory Theatre, 161
Edwards, Martin, 142
Egan, Michael, 216, 218
Egeli, Peter, 199
Eglin's Garage, 45
Eichner, Maura (SSND), 212, 217

Biography

ADAMS, LISA—A graduate of Towson State University, Ms. Adams has worked as a writer and editor for several large corporations in the Baltimore area. Her freelance work has appeared in the *Baltimore Chronicle*.

ALEXANDER, HARVEY—Mr. Alexander has been teaching English and poetry at the Community College of Baltimore for over eight years. For the past 20 years, he has been writing poetry and is presently producing a poetry program for WBJC-FM radio. Mr. Alexander was one of the original producers of the Baltimore Film Festival and has written and produced several films. His credits also include coeditorship of a literary journal.

ALEXANDER, MARIANNE—Dr. Alexander is on the faculty of Goucher College in the field of Political Science. She specializes in Maryland history and government. With an interest in womens' studies, Dr. Alexander is a contributing author of the book, *Notable Maryland Women*. Presently, she serves as project director of an oral history project on Maryland women lawmakers.

APGAR, DOROTHEA—Mrs. Apgar was the fashion editor of the *News American* for 14 years and is now a general assignment journalist. She is a member of the Washington Press Club, the American Newswomen's Club, the Advertising Club of Baltimore, and the Baltimore Museum of Art. She has been a professional journalist for nearly a quarter century.

ARNETT, EARL—Mr. Arnett was a theater critic, reporter, and feature writer on the *Sunpapers* from 1966 to 1980. He is presently a critic on the TV program "Critic's Place." Mr. Arnett also teaches part-time at the Peabody Conservatory.

ARNOLD, JOSEPH L.—Dr. Arnold is a professor of history at the University of Maryland Baltimore County, specializing in the history of cities. He has published two books and has written numerous articles on the history of Baltimore. Dr. Arnold is a member of the board of editors of the Maryland Historical Magazine, and serves on the board of directors of the Baltimore Industrial Museum.

BARTTER, RIC—A *magna cum laude* graduate of Harvard University, Mr. Bartter wrote for two editions of *Let's Go*, a student travel guide. He has become a widely published freelance writer and photographer. His writings have appeared in the *Washington Post*, *Washington Review of the Arts*, *Washington Scene*, the *News American*, *Wine* magazine, *Food and Fine Living* magazine, the *Baltimore Chronicle*, and the *Courier*. Mr. Bartter has also had several local photographic exhibitions.

BONNELL, BARBARA—Since 1961, Ms. Bonnell has worked for the Inner Harbor-Charles Center Management as the director of information. Throughout the years she has been a guest speaker, bringing information about Baltimore's urban redevelopment locally and internationally. She is a coauthor of a textbook on American politics. Ms. Bonnell is a member of Phi Beta Kappa and a Fulbright Scholar and holds degrees from Wellesley College, University of Paris, and the Johns Hopkins University.

BRAIN, JOHN—Mr. Brain is the public relations director for the Baltimore Symphony Orchestra. Earlier in his career, he worked for a publishing company. He has published several articles.

BRAWNER, ALLISON—For the past two years, Ms. Brawner has been an employment counselor for the state of Maryland. While in college she worked on her school newspaper and studied writing. Upon graduation Ms. Brawner joined the staff of the *Baltimore Chronicle*.

BREADY, JAMES—Mr. Bready is a feature and editorial writer for the *Sunpapers*. Much of his writing deals with recently published local and regional books and the people behind them. He is an avid sports fan and is the author of a book about the Orioles.

BROWNE, GARY—Dr. Browne is an assistant professor of History at the University of Maryland Baltimore County. He is the editor of the *Maryland Historical Magazine*. Several of his articles on the history of Baltimore and Maryland have appeared in magazines. He has one book to his credit, *Baltimore in the Nation, 1789-1861*.

CEDRONE, LOU—Shortly after his graduation from the University of Maryland in 1951, Mr. Cedrone joined the *Evening Sun* as a police reporter. From that beat he became an entertainment editor and then television critic. He is now the movie and stage critic for this newspaper.

CHERBONNIER, ALICE—Ms. Cherbonnier was cofounder and editor of *Food and Fine Living* magazine. Currently, she is managing editor of the *Baltimore Chronicle* and coeditor of the *Courier* and *Monument Street News*. She was editor of the 1978 edition of CPHA's Baltimore guidebook, *Bawlamer*, and coeditor of the 1980 Mayor's Arts Ball Program book.

COCHRANE, ROBERT B.—Mr. Cochrane was operating the *Sunpapers'* Tokyo Bureau in 1946 when he was summoned home to become the first employee of WMAR-TV. From 1947 to 1975, he was responsible for supervising the station's programming. Mr. Cochrane has been published widely in newspapers and magazines, and his account of the surrender ceremony aboard the "Might Mo" battleship was republished in an anthology in 1963.

CORTADA, RAFAEL L.—Rafael L. Cortada, president of the Community College of Baltimore since 1977, earned his PhD. in history from Fordham University in 1967. His career as an educator and administrator includes positions as professor of history at several colleges and universities as well as dean and vice-president of City University of New York and president of Metropolitan Community College in Minneapolis. His book *Echoes of World Civilization* was published in 1963 and his articles and reviews have appeared in a variety of scholarly journals.

COX, RICHARD J.—Mr. Cox has been the archivist for the city of Baltimore since early 1978. Prior to this, he was curator of manuscripts at the Maryland Historical Society. He has authored over 50 articles and pamphlets, and is the book review editor for *Manuscripts*. He is Maryland membership chairman for the American Association for State and Local History; News Notes reporter for the *American Archivist*; and a member of the National Historical Publications and Records Commission, Maryland Advisory Board.

DAVIS, RICHARD P.—Since 1969, Mr. Davis has been director of public information for Baltimore's Department of Housing and Community Development. He came here in 1956 as a copy editor for the *Evening Sun*. In 1961, he joined the staff of the Newspaper Guild, and as its director, he visited many other countries. Mr. Davis was on the steering committee of the first City Fair in 1970, and has been associated with it ever since. In 1973 and 1974, he was president of Baltimore City Fair, Inc.

DRYDEN, CATHY—A graduate of the University of Maryland, Ms. Dryden has worked for several interest and environmental organizations. She was a media specialist with the Smithsonian Institution. Ms. Dryden's freelance writing has appeared in the *Baltimore Chronicle*.

DÜRR, WILLIAM THEODORE— Dr. Dürr is a professor of social studies at the University of Baltimore. He is also director of the Baltimore Region Institutional Studies Center. Since 1978, Dr. Dürr has directed the Baltimore Neighborhood Heritage Project. Presently, he is working on two books, one on social history and the other on information science. Dr. Dürr has had numerous articles published in professional publications, and prepared a 30-script program for public television.

EISENBERG, SANDY FRENKIL—Mrs. Eisenberg attended Johns Hopkins University and the University of Maryland, and taught English in Baltimore public schools.

She has served many community and cultural boards. Mrs. Eisenberg was vice president of the National Council of Jewish Women and the No. 9 Front Street Foundation, and has been Benefactor Chairman for the Mayor's Ball. She is a member of the Academy of American Poets and has assisted Gerson Eisenberg, her husband, with *Learning Vacations*, a historical travel guidebook.

FREEDLANDER, LEAH S.—Ms. Freedlander has been involved in education and political science for many years. She has taught at two local colleges, and has served on two educational commissions, including chairing the Committee on Instruction and Guidance. Other educational activities include serving as president and then board chairman of the Parent Teachers Association of Baltimore City; chairing the statewide adult education week; and serving on the Knapp Commission of School Libraries. In 1975, Ms. Freedlander was Mayor Schaefer's reelection campaign manager. She was also the state-wide coordinator of precincts for former Senator Joseph D. Tydings. Governor Tawes appointed her to the Constitutional Revision Commission, and, in 1967, Ms. Freedlander was elected to the Maryland State Constitutional Convention.

FROELICHER, FRANCES MORTON—Dr. Froelicher began her career as a history teacher and social worker. From 1940 on, she has been involved with many organizations, ranging from the Fair Rent Commission to becoming the executive director of the Citizens Planning and Housing Association. Dr. Froelicher organized the Baltimore Environmental Center in 1971 and the Better Air Coalition in 1976. She has won six awards, and is the author of three publications.

GALKIN, ELLIOTT W.—Dr. Galkin is director of the Peabody Institute. He is also a conductor and serves as musical director of the Baltimore Chamber Orchestra. He has been a visiting conductor of the Baltimore Symphony Orchestra. In Europe he was a guest conductor for two orchestras. He has received numerous awards in the music field. In addition, he was the music critic for the Baltimore *Sun* for 16 years. Dr. Galkin is presently writing a historical study of

musical performers and performances.

GARDNER, BETTYE J.—Dr. Gardner is an associate professor of history at Coppin State College. Her work has appeared in two historical publications, and she has presented a number of lectures and scholarly papers. Professor Gardner is a member of the Baltimore History Research Group, the Advisory Committee for the Maryland Commission on Black History, and the Advisory Committee for the Baltimore History Fair. She also served as a member of the Advisory Committee for the Baltimore Historical Sites Commission.

GORDON, STEPHEN J.—Mr. Gordon has authored 11 one-hour children's tapes and four novels. In addition, he has written numerous film and videotape programs for the Southern Education Association, South Carolina Educational Television, and the U.S. Department of Labor. Mr. Gordon is currently writing for the nationally televised series, "The Old House Works," for the Maryland Center for Public Broadcasting.

GRAU, RAWLEY—Mr. Grau received his B.A. degree from Johns Hopkins University, a master's degree in Slavic Studies from the University of Toronto, and is currently teaching there and working on his doctorate. He is a freelance writer and has published poetry in various journals, including *Arkenstone*.

GUNTS, EDWARD—Baltimore raised, Mr. Gunts studied architecture at Cornell University. He is the City Hall reporter for the *News American*, and writes about architecture and other subjects for this paper.

ISRAEL, RONALD—A dentist with a strong interest in Theatre, Dr. Israel wrote a theatre column in the *Baltimore Chronicle* for several years. Besides writing about theatre, he works with the Center Stage Hands, and has been the theatre arts chairman for the Jewish Community Center. Dr. Israel produced two cabaret revues and was the director of promotion for Girard's Discothèque.

JAY, PETER A.—Mr. Jay has been a columnist for the *Sun* since 1974. From 1980 to 1981 he took a leave of absence to run the *Record*, a Harford County weekly newspaper owned by him and his wife. He has resumed writing his thrice-weekly editorial page column. Before coming to Baltimore, Mr. Jay was on the staff of the *Washington Post*.

JOHNSON, GERALD W.—Along with H. L. Mencken, Mr. Johnson is acclaimed as Baltimore's most noted journalist. For many decades, Mr. Johnson was a columnist for the Baltimore *Sun*. He was a contributing editor for the *New Republic*, and frequently had his essays published in the *Atlantic*, the *American Scholar*, the *Virginia Quarterly Review*, *Harpers*, and other publications. Mr. Johnson was the author of numerous books. He died in 1981. Adlai Stevenson wrote of him:

> Every reader of Gerald Johnson is his debtor for a thousand rescues from boredom in an age when humor is suspect and conformity a virtue. When it comes to piercing stuffed shirts, when there are slobs to be speared and poisonous balloons to be burst, well, borrowing from Edmond de Goncourt, without Gerald Johnson there are but pygmies to bend the bow of Ulysses. He is the critic and conscience of our time.

KELLY, FREDERICK—Mr. Kelly has been writing for over 20 years for several newspapers in Connecticut, New York, and Maryland. He was the personal assistant to author Cornelius Ryan, who wrote *The Longest Day*, *The Last Battle*, and *A Bridge Too Far*. Mr. Kelly is a writer for the *Sun's Sunday Magazine*, a position he has held for over 10 years. He is noted for his wit and humor.

KELLY, JACQUES—Mr. Kelly, a native of Baltimore, is a columnist for the *News American* and a contributing editor to *Baltimore* magazine. In 1976, his *Peabody Heights to Charles Village*, a history of the development of his home neighborhood, was published.

KING, DIANNE—Ms. King has been a freelance writer for several years. Her work has appeared in the *Baltimore Chronicle* and *Metropolitan* magazine. She has also been a reporter for a local radio station.

KOBRE, SIDNEY—Dr. Kobre was a professor of journalism at Florida State University, The University of Maryland, and the Community College of Baltimore. Before his teaching career began, he worked on several newspapers, including holding the position of editor. He has written numerous freelance feature articles. His book, *Backgrounding the News*, was recently revised and reissued.

KRAIZER, AL—Mr. Kraizer, born in St. Louis, Missouri, had his first job as promoter at the Lorretta Hilton Theatre. In New York City he was one of the organizers of Tix to promote broadway theatre ticket sells. Mr. Kraizer came to Baltimore in 1976 and helped organize the new theatre festival. In 1981, he became Artistic Director for the International Theatre Festival. At present he is in Denver establishing the International Theatre Festival.

KRAUSE, LAURENCE—During the past decade, Mr. Krause was the founder and publisher of numerous local publications: the *Baltimore Chronicle*, the *Courier*, the *Monument Street News*, the *Old Town Times*, *Aura of the Arts*, and *Food and Fine Living* magazine. He serves as the editor of the first three of these publications, and was coeditor of the 1980 Mayor's Art Ball program book. Mr. Krause's poetry has appeared in six different poetry magazines, and he has been listed in the *International Who's Who of Poetry*.

LEHNERT, MARIE—Ms. Lehnert is a free-lance writer, director, and producer of theatre, film, and video productions. She has combined her interests in history and drama by writing and producing original scripts.

LEIBTAG, DEVORAH M.—Ms. Leibtag is a doctoral student in American literature at the University of Maryland College Park. She has been active as a freelance writer and editor.

LEVIN, GERALD—Gerald Levin earned his BA in history and his MA in U.S. history from UCLA. He taught U.S. and European history at Arkansas AM&N, then went to the Smithsonian's National Portrait Gallery where he created an exhibit on James Monroe and wrote the exhibit's catalog. From the Smithsonian he came to the Maryland Historical Society as registrar. With Eisenberg Educational Enterprises since 1979, he has assisted Eisenberg in writing *Learning Vacations*.

LIBBER, SHERIE BROOK—Ms. Libber holds a master's degree in Library Science, and a law degree from the University of Maryland. She is presently a health care lawyer and administrator for Chesapeake Physicians, P.A.

LIEBERMAN, ELLIOT—Mr. Lieberman is a freelance writer and a graduate student at the Johns Hopkins University. He served as public information officer and principal city planner with the Baltimore City Department of Planning before resuming doctoral studies at Hopkins.

LOTT, CLARINDA HARRISS—Ms. Lott is a Baltimore poet who teaches at Towson State University and is editor/president of the New Poets Series, Inc., a small press. She has published one collection of her poetry, *The Bone Tree*. With Sara de Ford, she coauthored *Forms of Verse: British and American*, and a verse translation of the book-length medieval poem, *The Pearl*. Her poems, as well as some fiction, have appeared in over a dozen publications.

MARBLE, LORI JACKSON—Ms. Marble is a member of the American Dance Guild, Sacred Dance Guild, and the Maryland Council for Dance. She began writing as the assistant fine arts editor of Towson State University's student newspaper. Ms. Marble has continued as a freelance writer for the *Towson Times* and the *Jeffersonian*.

MARQUA, LESLIE REHBEIN—Now a freelance promotion and public relations consultant, Ms. Marqua served as the assistant director of development for the Citizens Planning and Housing Association. She served as director of public information for the Baltimore City Fair, director of public information for Maryland Special Olympics, and editor of CPHA's book, *Beyond the White Marble Steps*. Ms. Marqua was also a columnist for *Computer Dealer* magazine.

MAUSNER, DAN—At present, Mr. Mauser works in the editorial department for the publishing company of Prentice Hall. His writing career began while working for the *Baltimore Chronicle* and the *Maryland Farmer*. He then took a job with the Baltimore Office of Promotion and Tourism, though continued writing on a free lance basis.

McCRORY, JANICE—Ms. McCrory has been a professional writer for over nine years. She is presently a marketing analyst for Stone and Associates. Ms. McCrory's work has appeared locally in *Food and Fine Living* magazine, *Metropolitan* magazine, and she is a regular contributor to the *Baltimore Chronicle*.

MILLER, MARK—Mr. Miller is the author of the recently published book, *Mt. Washington Baltimore Suburb*. He is a probation officer for the state of Maryland. Although his degree is in psychology from the University of Baltimore, Mr. Miller has a strong interest in local history, architecture, and preservation.

MONK, R. C.—In 1978, Dr. Monk received his Ph.D. in sociology from the University of Maryland. He taught sociology at area universities, and has been a freelance writer in Baltimore for over 10 years. Currently, he is an associate professor and program director of sociology at Northwest Missouri State University.

NARON, JACQUELINE NAST—Ms. Naron's interest in art has been expressed in many ways. She has a master's degree in medieval art; she has been an art historian, serving as a researcher and instructor; an art critic; an interior design consultant; and a practicing artist and musician. She has served as assistant to the registrar of the Maryland Historical Society.

NAST, LENORA HEILIG—Dr. Nast is a historian, lecturer, writer, editor, and artist. She holds a Ph.D. from the Ecumemial Institute of Theology, St. Mary's Seminary and University. She has lectured on public broadcasting; spoken to groups on parent education and the interfaith movement; and has presented oral book reviews. Her writings include local and state history, theology, parent education, children's stories, adult fiction, biographies, poetry, religion, and art. As a painter, Dr. Nast has worked in oils and acrylics.

NEALE, MERCER—In 1967, Mr. Neale came to Baltimore, where he began his teaching career at Gilman School. He is studying for a doctorate at the University of Maryland.

NEVERDON-MORTON, CYNTHIA—Dr. Morton is professor of history at Coppin State College where she serves as chairperson of the Department of History, Geography, and International Studies. She is a member of the Baltimore History Research Group, and is on the advisory committee for the Baltimore Neighborhood Heritage Project. Dr. Morton has published numerous articles, has presented scholarly lectures, and is currently conducting research through a fellowship for college teachers from the National Endowment for the Humanities.

OBRECHT, VICTORIA BONEY—Mrs. Obrecht is a graduate of Duke University where her writing career began with the Duke newspaper. Her first professional work was as sports writer for the *News American*. Later she covered sports for the *Times Herald* in Washington, D.C. where she wrote about horse shows, racing, and fights. Mrs. Obrecht has written on a variety of subjects for newspapers and magazines and has included her own photos. Her recent work has been on health care, with articles in the *Johns Hopkins University* magazine, *Baltimore* magazine, and *Life and Health*.

O'CONNOR, TOM—Mr. O'Connor worked in Baltimore radio for 40 years. Most of his career was spent at WBAL radio, where he was director of public service. He has also served as a visiting instructor in the mass communications department at Towson State University. During his career Mr. O'Connor served at various times as announcer, newsman, disc jockey, writer, sound effects man, actor, and program director. He was manager of WBAL-FM during the period when it was a classical music and all-news operation.

PENNER, BERNARD—Canadian born, Mr. Penner has been living in Baltimore for the past 16 years. He is working on a degree in law, and is a freelance writer. Mr. Penner's works have appeared in *Baltimore* magazine, the *City Paper*, and *Hard Crabs*.

PRATT, LAURLENE STRAUGHIN—Mrs. Pratt holds a master's degree in theatre and has devoted most of her life to that field. She is widely known as a drama teacher, she developed a three-year theatre curriculum in drama at Forest Park High School (Baltimore), where she taught from 1955 to 1969. Many of her graduates have gone on to professional theatrical careers. Ms. Pratt became the director of Theatre Hopkins in 1969.

PRICHETT, MORGAN HERBERT—Dr. Pritchett was graduated from the Johns Hopkins University in 1942, where he received degrees in German and history. He began teaching German at the college level. In 1964, he earned his Ph.D. then, in 1970, he earned a master's degree in library science. That same year, Dr. Pritchett became a librarian at Hopkins Milton A. Eisenhower Library. Four years later, he became the head of the Maryland Department of the Enoch Pratt Free Library.

PULA, CLAIRE I,—Ms. Pula received her B. A. in history in 1978. After graduation, she worked as a toymaker's apprentice, and then as a library assistant at the Maryland Historical Society. She acted as a consultant for a book on Maryland published by the Children's Press in Chicago.

SANDLER, GILBERT—Mr. Sandler is an advertising and publishing executive who directs his own agency. He is a frequent lecturer about Baltimore, and has been writing most of his life. As a freelance writer, Mr. Sandler has been published in the *Sun*, *Maryland* magazine, and *Baltimore* magazine. He was also a columnist for the *Evening Sun*.

SEIDEL, BETTY SAMUELS—Mrs. Seidel has been involved in many public service programs for which she has received numerous awards. She served as coordinator of the Eating Together in Baltimore program, and was field supervisor for the Girl Scouts of Central Maryland. Mrs. Seidel has also served as a consultant on retirement education.

SELLMAN, JANE—Ms. Sellman has been a college teacher for several years, teaching English composition, grammar, and reading. Ms. Sellman has been involved in research on women's history, religions and social movements, English literature, and film.

SLAGLE, JACOB, Jr.— Mr. Slagle, who operates Slagle and Slagle Homeowners Service, has been a freelance writer and photographer for over five years. His work has appeared in the *Sun*, *Bawlamer*, *Towson Times*, the *Messenger*, the *Bal-*

timore Chronicle, and *Food and Fine Living* magazine. Mr. Slagle also wrote an article about Baltimore for *Sky* magazine, a publication for Delta Airlines.

STEADMAN, JOHN—Mr. Steadman has been the long-time sports editor of the *News American*.

STOVER, LAREN E.—Ms. Stover, a graduate of the Maryland Institute College of Art, has been a staff member of the *Baltimore Chronicle*, and a freelance writer for the *Sun*. She has served as public relations director of the Art Center Without Walls in New Jersey, and is presently employed by a public relations firm in New York City. Ms. Stover's poetry has been published in *Gargoyle* magazine.

STRAUSBAUGH, JOHN—Mr. Strausbaugh is the associate director of Theatre Project. For two years he served as the arts editor of the *City Paper*. Mr. Strausbaugh's work has been published in *Analog, Prairie Schooner, Omega*, and the *San Francisco Chronicle*.

STROHECKER, CAROL—Ms. Strohecker served as the editor of the yearbook at the University of Maryland, College Park. As a student, she completed two internships with the National Geographic Society. She was an editor for the H.M. Rowe Company and is the present editor of publications for the Walters Art Gallery.

STROHECKER, DOROTHY PULA—Mrs. Strohecker is a teacher and writer. She is presently engaged in graduate studies in English at the University of Maryland College Park. She has taught at local high schools and colleges for the last 15 years. Her published works include teaching materials on fiction for Bantam Books; a Hampton Institute brochure called *Education for Life* published by Pridemark Press; and the most recent is *Applied English Essentials* for Rowe Publishers. She is currently completing a novel.

SUGAR, SANDRA—Ms. Sugar received her B.S. degree in English and education from Towson State University. She has served as a volunteer on various arts groups, including the Maryland Ballet, Center Stage, the Baltimore Museum of Art, a chairman of the Cultural Arts Institutions Exhibit for the Baltimore Arts Festival, and editor of the BMA's docent's newsletter. Ms. Sugar paints and has exhibited at City Hall. At present she is a docent at the BMA and teaches English at the Community College of Baltimore.

TAYLOR, BLAINE—Mr. Taylor was the managing editor for the Maryland State Medical Journal, from 1974 to 1981. He is now senior editor at Peterson, Howell and Heather. In the past 10 years, he has worked with many publications: assistant editor of *Baltimore* magazine; copy editor and special reporter for the Baltimore *Afro American*; and freelanced for the *Sun* papers, the Baltimore *News American*, Washington *Star*, the *Jewish Times*, the *Baltimore Chronicle*, the Stromberg's *Times* chain, *Performance*, and the *Paper*.

TRATTNER, BERNADETTE—Ms. Trattner, a day care teacher, has been a community liaison person for the Department of Social Services. She is a candidate for a master's degree in communications at American University. Her freelance work has been published in the *Baltimore Chronicle*.

VARGA, NICHOLAS—Mr. Varga is a professor of history at Loyola College (Baltimore), where he also serves as archivist. Presently, he is completing a history of that institution.

WATTS, PATTY—Ms. Watts graduated from Goucher College in 1981 with a B.A. degree in English. She is currently working in London for an arts publishing company. She writes fiction and non-fiction.

WEINER, WILLIAM—Mr. Weiner, an artist and art teacher, worked on the staff of the *Baltimore Chronicle* for over one year. He holds a Master's degree in fine arts, and has a special interest in the importance of art in the community. Mr. Weiner is presently studying at a yeshiva in New York city, where he is also continuing to paint. His art works have been exhibited in several Baltimore shows.

Photos by:
Anderson, Richard
Bartter, Ric
Bethlehem Steel
Bishop, Susan
Blow Up Studio
Catholic Center
Channel 2 Files
Corcoran, Janenne
Cotell, Barbara
Cultural Arts Program
Dixon, Maurice
Documentary Photographic Project
Doda, Dennis
Feinblatt, Eric
Fox, Peggy
Giza, Joe
Grice, Editha
Handakas, Peter
Housing and Community Development
Jerome, Jeff
Kelly, John
Kenneth M. Brooks Studios, Inc.
Klender, William
Kobre, Sidney
Kohl, Joe, Jr.
Krause, Laurence
Lawrence, Stephanie
Lightner, James Karmodt
Lockwood, William
Manekin, Theodore L.
Marble, Harry
Mayden, John Clark
Mayor's Office of Telecommunications
Oppenheimer, Morton
Payne, Frankie
Redifer, Betty
Rijmes, Joanne
Roszel, Elizabeth Merryman
Schamp, J. B.
Slagle, Jake, Jr.
Starr, Jan Sutherland
Strohecker, Carol
Sullivan, Joseph
Sussman Photography
Szczepanski, Philip
Troutner, Lee
Warren, Marion E.
Weiner, William
White, Jerry L.
Wojcik, Linda
Woods, Jerry
Yusaitis, John

Theatre Hopkins. Originally called *The Homewood Playshop*, its first home was a small building behind Homewood House until 1942 when the interior of the 1803 Barn was redesigned as a theatre for its use.

Alex Brown & Sons is America's oldest name in investment banking. Its 81-year old main office stands at 135 East Baltimore Street as an excellent example of the essence of Baltimore's renaissance: a respectful blending of the architecture of the past with the technology of the present. The balance is best seen in the simultaneous improvements made in June, 1982. While extensive upgrading was made in the office computer capacities, the magnificent stained-glass dome that is the focus of the building was meticulously restored, having been covered over during World War II. Photo courtesy of Barton-Gillet Company. Caption by: Jane Stoiko.

Baltimore ethnic diversity enriches the city's schools. City College students socialize. Photo courtesy of the Baltimore Public Schools.

After three successful years of serving as Baltimore's good-will ambassador, the *Pride of Baltimore* is once again under sail, this time to Bermuda, the West Indies, and Mexico. Since its launching in the spring of 1977, the *Pride* has logged a total of over 35,000 miles. The *Pride*, the idea of which was originated by Melbourne Smith, was initially a Bicentennial stationary display piece. But the arrival of the international tall ships under the auspices of Operation Sail inspired the *Pride*'s sponsors to convert it to a sea-going vessel. As such, the ship sails most of the year to various American and world ports to publicize and secure business for the city, most currently for Baltimore's new Convention Center. In port, the *Pride* is open for public tours and the staff gives receptions. The *Pride* sails under a crew of 12 persons (age range 18 to 28), most of whom stay for a period of 6 to 8 months. Dan Moreland is the current captain. Life on board the *Pride* is spartan and rigorous, with little break, which results in a fairly high turnover rate for ship personnel. Caption by Claire Pula. Photo by Editha Grice. (Written in 1980).